WE·THE PEOPLE

HOUGHTON MIFFLIN

Build Our Nation

WE·THE
PEOPLE

Build Our Nation

Sarah Bednarz
Catherine Clinton
Michael Hartoonian
Arthur Hernandez
Patricia L. Marshall
Pat Nickell

Washington, District of Columbia

HOUGHTON MIFFLIN · Boston
Atlanta · Dallas · Geneva, Illinois · Palo Alto · Princeton

AUTHORS

Sarah Bednarz
Assistant Professor
Texas A&M University
College Station, TX

Arthur Hernandez
Associate Professor
Division of Education
College of Social and
Behavioral Sciences
University of Texas at
San Antonio
San Antonio, TX

Catherine Clinton
W.E.B. Du Bois Institute
Fellow
Harvard University
Cambridge, MA

Patricia L. Marshall
Assistant Professor
Department of Curric-
ulum and Instruction
College of Education
and Psychology
North Carolina State
University
Raleigh, NC

Michael Hartoonian
Professor and Director
Carey Center
Hamline University
St. Paul, MN

Pat Nickell
Director
High School Curriculum
and Instruction
Fayette County Schools
Lexington, KY

Susan Buckley General Editor

Acknowledgments appear on page 703.

Printed in the U.S.A. ISBN: 0-395-76546-3   456789-VH-99 98

CONTENTS

UNIT 3   The American Colonies

THEME: NEW ENVIRONMENTS

UNIT 5   The Nation's Early Years
THEME: GOVERNING OURSELVES

UNIT 8 An Industrial Country
THEME: COPING WITH CHANGE

UNIT 9 The United States in the 20th Century
THEME: RESPONSIBILITY AND FREEDOM

FEATURES

Skills Workshop

LITERATURE

American Voices

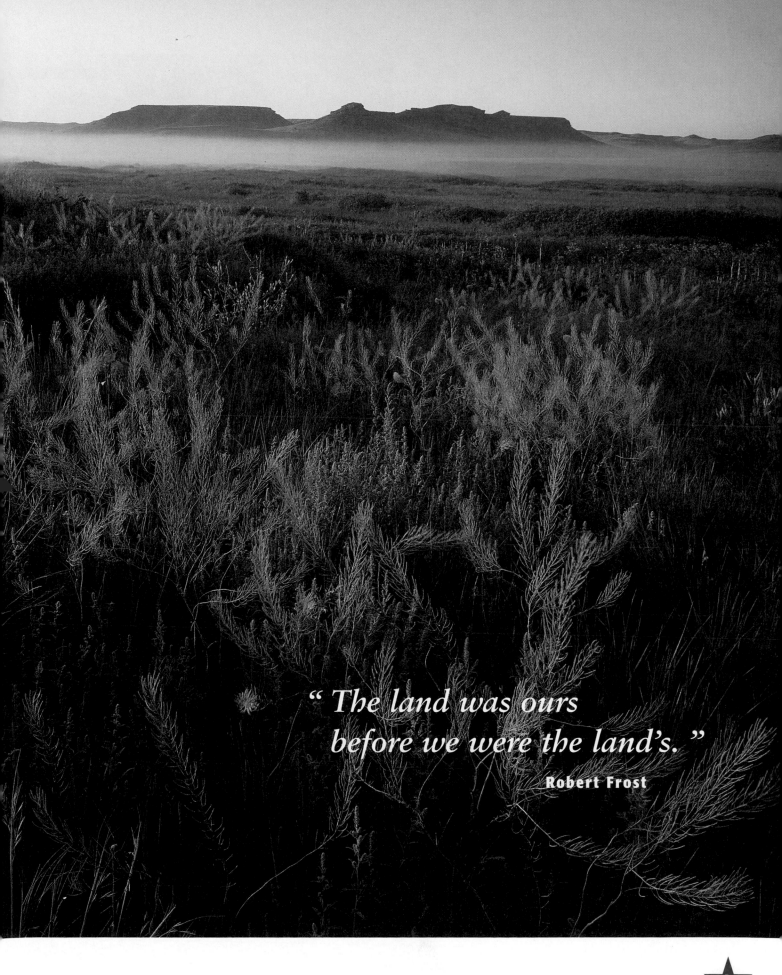

*" The land was ours
before we were the land's. "*

Robert Frost

> " *If you don't remember history accurately, how can you learn?* "
>
> **Maya Lin**

" . . . *life, liberty, and the pursuit of happiness* . . . "

Thomas Jefferson
Declaration of Independence

We are the

Spirit of America!

People of the Americas

"As long as the sun shines and the waters flow, this land will be here to give life to men and animals."

Blackfoot Chief

· THEME ·

Love of the Land

❝ *One resource that has affected my life a lot is the ocean. People can swim or play on the beach. We also get tasty seafood from the ocean.* ❞

Farwa Mohsin, Fifth Grade
Galveston, Texas

"**O**h beautiful, for spacious skies" — these words from "America the Beautiful" reflect most Americans' feelings about their country. Native Americans were the first of many people to depend on the land for their survival. America's varied landscape and plentiful resources have allowed people to live well for thousands of years.

Theme Project

Represent Your Group

You are a Native American living in 1500. You have been chosen to represent your community at a meeting of several Native American groups. Which Native American group do you belong to? Describe your home and your people:

- Create an illustrated map of your region.
- Write about how your group uses natural resources.
- Make gifts, such as tools or crafts, and present them to your audience. Explain their meaning.
- Describe an important tradition of your people.

RESEARCH: Look at Native American artifacts in library books or a museum. What do these tell about their culture?

◀ Oregon, River Gorge

WHEN & WHERE
ATLAS

The Americas were not an empty wilderness in 1500. As you can see from the map, many different Native American societies inhabited the land from northern Canada to South America. These native peoples shared a common heritage, but differed in important ways. The customs and ways of life they developed depended largely on the nature of the land on which they lived.

In this unit, you will learn about the geography of the Americas and the way people's environments can shape the way they live. You will read how the first people came to the Americas and developed civilizations. Finally, you will learn about the different Native American groups that inhabited what is now the United States.

Unit 1 Chapters

PACIFIC

OCEAN

km 0   300   600
mi 0   300   600

Legend

SIOUX Native Americans

■ Sites from earlier Native American cultures

● City or major settlement

—— Present-day boundaries

Unit Timeline

10,000 years ago

Grand Teton Mountain

You won't see mountains like these on the East Coast. Find out why.
Chapter 1, Lesson 1

Seattle Folklife Fair

All over the United States, people celebrate their varied heritage.
Chapter 1, Lesson 2

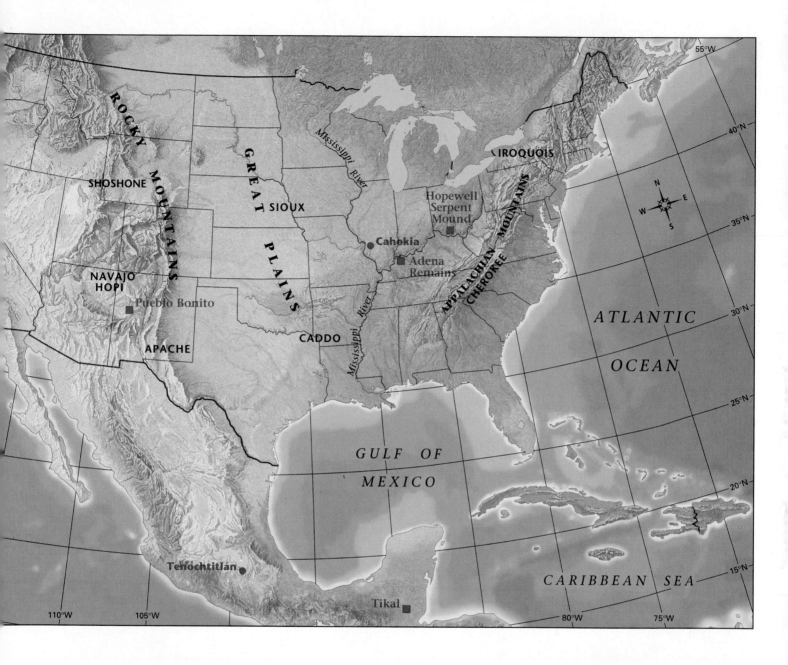

ROCKY MOUNTAINS

SHOSHONE

GREAT PLAINS

SIOUX

Mississippi River

IROQUOIS

NAVAJO
HOPI

Pueblo Bonito

APACHE

CADDO

Mississippi River

Cahokia

Adena
Remains

Hopewell
Serpent
Mound

APPALACHIAN MOUNTAINS

CHEROKEE

ATLANTIC

OCEAN

GULF OF

MEXICO

CARIBBEAN SEA

Tenochtitlán

Tikal

110°W   105°W   80°W   75°W

55°W   40°N   35°N   30°N   25°N   20°N   15°N

Today

Ruins of Tikal

No one knows why this city was abandoned, but there are some good guesses. *Chapter 2, Lesson 2*

Anasazi Jar

This jar could have been used to store something very precious — water. *Chapter 2, Lesson 2*

Kachina Dancer

What animal do you recognize in this dancer's headdress? *Chapter 2, Lesson 4*

The Land and the People

Chapter Preview: *People, Places, and Events*

10,000 years ago

Monument Valley

Do you know what a glacier and a plateau have in common? *Lesson 1, Page 15*

Coal Miner

How does this man's job affect you? You'll find out. *Lesson 1, Page 16*

Midwest Farm

One of the United States' most important resources is right under your feet. *Lesson 1, Page 18*

Features of the Land

Main Idea The United States is a large nation with many kinds of landforms and abundant natural resources.

Key Vocabulary
landform
plateau
basin
natural resource
mineral

From the jagged rocky coast of Maine to the deep red walls of the Grand Canyon, the United States offers a wide range of landscapes and geography. Yosemite National Park in California is just one of many places with amazing natural beauty. Its dramatic peaks and waterfalls have delighted visitors for decades. Carl Sharsmith was a park ranger at Yosemite for many years. He started working there in the 1930s and was still working when he was 91 years old. "Originally there was just a two-rut wagon road up here," he said. But times have changed. Today Yosemite and other national parks are filled with visitors who want to enjoy the beauty of these parks and the landforms they contain.

◀ Yosemite Falls, Yosemite National Park

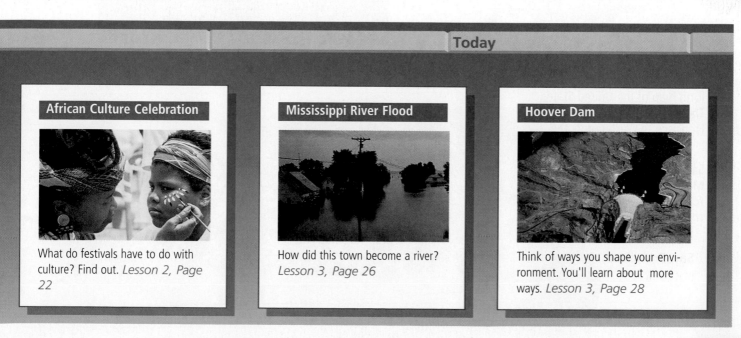

Today

African Culture Celebration

What do festivals have to do with culture? Find out. *Lesson 2, Page 22*

Mississippi River Flood

How did this town become a river? *Lesson 3, Page 26*

Hoover Dam

Think of ways you shape your environment. You'll learn about more ways. *Lesson 3, Page 28*

Landforms

Focus *What are the major landforms of the United States?*

Though the beauty of this country has shone for thousands of years, our national park system is less than a hundred years old. President Theodore Roosevelt loved the natural landscape of the United States so much that he asked Congress to set aside land simply to be enjoyed. He said:

> **"L**eave it as it is. You cannot improve on it; not a bit. The ages have been at work on it, and man can only mar it. **"**

The National Park Service was started in 1916 to protect the nation's natural treasures. Yosemite is one of more than 350 national parks and historic sites all over the United States.

Some of this country's most beautiful and unusual landforms

Landforms from Coast to Coast

Follow your way across the landform map of the United States. The map reaches from San Francisco to Washington, D.C.

San Francisco, California.
Map Skill: *Which landforms can be found on the west coast?*

San Francisco, California

Great Basin, Nevada

can be found in these parks. **Landforms** are physical features of the earth's surface. Hills, mountains, plains, volcanoes and prairies are all landforms. Other physical features include rivers, lakes, and glaciers.

National parks contain only some of the nation's landforms. The United States contains landforms on a large scale. All the land along the eastern and southern coast of the United States is a flat plain with some rolling hills. This region, called the Coastal Plain, reaches from New York to the Rio Grande in Texas. The Interior Plains are also flat and contain low, rolling hills. They have two parts, both full of rich soil: the Central Plains and, to the west, the dry, treeless plateau called the Great Plains. A **plateau** is an area of high, flat land rising above the nearby land on at least one side.

Two long mountain ranges cross the nation from north to south. (*See illustration below.*) In the East, the Appalachian Mountains stretch from Canada to Alabama. They divide the Coastal Plains from the Interior Plains. Rain and wind have worn down these once tall peaks over time. West of the Great Plains lie the Rocky Mountains. Like a huge bony spine, they stretch 3,000

Park rangers wear this patch on their coats. The white buffalo is a Native American symbol of harmony. **National Heritage:** *Can you think of other American symbols which reflect an appreciation of our land and the creatures living in it?*

Grand Teton Mountain, Wyoming

Prairies of the Great Plains, Badlands National Park, South Dakota

Hills in the Shenandoah Valley, Virginia

Washington, D.C. **Map Skill:** *Which landforms can be found on the east coast?*

Washington, D.C.

Curious Facts

Did you know that some people plug in their cars before driving them? Electric cars were invented to save gas and oil. They need to be plugged in to recharge — like a battery — when they run low.

Minerals are important natural resources.

Coal

Oil

Iron

miles from Alaska to New Mexico.

West of the Rocky Mountains is a dry, rainless area called the Great Basin and Range. A **basin** is a low-lying area surrounded by higher land. The Sierra Nevada border the Great Basin, and the Cascades hug the western coast. The farmland of California, some of the world's richest, lies between the two mountain ranges.

Natural Resources

Focus *What are the United States' important natural resources?*

The land of the United States is useful as well as beautiful because it is rich in natural resources. Resources are things that people use, so **natural resources** are useful things found in nature. Some resources, such as trees, can be renewed. But many resources are in a limited supply. Resources determine where and how people live.

Energy and Mineral Resources

When you wake up in the morning, you might first turn on a light. That uses electricity, which power plants make by burning fuel or using water power. Natural resources such as coal, natural gas, and oil are fuels. People burn fuels to make energy in the form of heat (for a home) or power (for an electric plant or a car). Coal is often used in electric power plants, so it was probably the energy resource used to turn on the light. Natural gas or oil may heat your house. Nuclear power plants use uranium, another natural resource.

The United States is incredibly rich in energy resources. Notice on the map on the next page that coal deposits are found all across the nation. Texas and Oklahoma contain oil and gas. Uranium is mined in the western states, such as New Mexico and Wyoming.

To make breakfast, you might cook eggs in an aluminum pan. This pan was made from minerals, a natural resource. **Minerals** are substances mined from the earth's surface. There are two kinds of minerals: metals and nonmetals. The aluminum in a pan is a metal mineral. The salt for your eggs is a nonmetal mineral. Energy resources like coal are nonmetal minerals.

We use minerals mainly for energy and manufacturing. Some mineral deposits are shrinking after years of mining. Still, the United States leads the world in producing many minerals such as aluminum, sulfur, and salt.

Energy Resources in the United States

The world relies on energy resources for industry and daily life. Oil, natural gas, and coal provide about 90 percent of the world's fuel. Look at the map to see which areas of the United States are particularly rich in resources. **Map Skill:** *Which energy resources can be found in Alaska?*

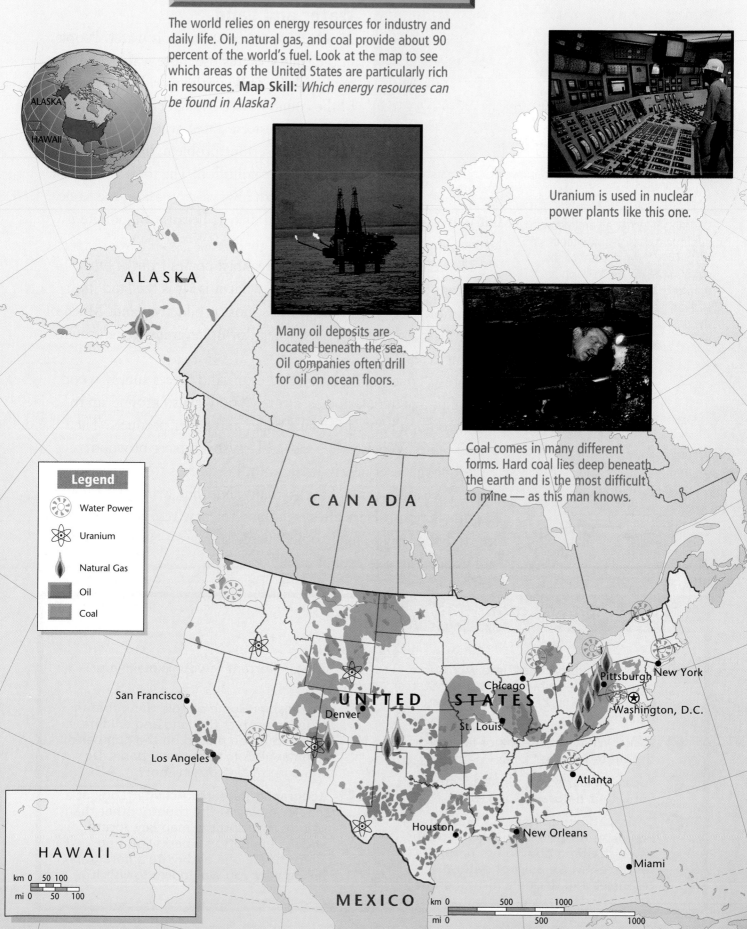

Uranium is used in nuclear power plants like this one.

Many oil deposits are located beneath the sea. Oil companies often drill for oil on ocean floors.

Coal comes in many different forms. Hard coal lies deep beneath the earth and is the most difficult to mine — as this man knows.

ALASKA

HAWAII

ALASKA

CANADA

UNITED STATES

MEXICO

Legend

- Water Power
- Uranium
- Natural Gas
- Oil
- Coal

San Francisco

Los Angeles

Denver

Chicago

St. Louis

Pittsburgh

New York

Washington, D.C.

Atlanta

Houston

New Orleans

Miami

HAWAII

km 0 50 100
mi 0 50 100

km 0 500 1000
mi 0 500 1000

We can see water all around us, but little of it is fresh (without salt in it). Only three percent of the earth's water is fresh. Much of that fresh water is locked into ice, such as glaciers or icebergs like the one above.

Water and Land

Another important resource is water. People in the United States use more water than many other people in the world. Most parts of the country have enough clean water, but in the dry western states, water shortages are common. A serious problem, like water shortages, is water pollution. The total amount of water on earth always stays about the same. But that water is getting dirtier and dirtier, because we pollute it faster than we can clean it.

The cereal you might eat for breakfast comes from another important resource. Can you guess what it is? It is the land itself. Our nation has some of the world's most productive land. Much of it is farmland, where the oats, wheat, or other grains were grown for your cereal.

Forests cover millions more acres of land. Trees supply wood for building materials and furniture. Wood is also ground up to make wood pulp, used to make paper and paper products. The United States is the world's second largest producer of wood.

All people everywhere need natural resources to survive. In this country we are lucky to have so many, but they won't last forever. For this reason, we are always looking for new resources. Scientists are studying how to make other energy sources — such as the sun and ocean waves — more usable.

Lesson Review: Geography

1. **Key Vocabulary:** Use these words in a paragraph describing the United States: landform, plateau, basin, natural resources, and mineral.

2. **Focus:** What are the major landforms of the United States?

3. **Focus:** What are the United States' important natural resources?

4. **Critical Thinking: Decision Making** People must think about many things when deciding how to use natural resources. Make a list of natural resources and decide which ones are most important to you. Explain your choices.

5. **Citizenship:** Some people think that in order to protect the land and wildlife, a limit should be placed on the number of summer visitors to national parks. Do you agree? Why or why not?

6. **Geography/Research Activity:** Look at a map of a part of the country other than your own. Using the map key, locate and list the national parks you find. Then choose one and write a paragraph telling why you would like to visit it.

Regions and People

Main Idea Geographers and historians divide the world into regions in order to study people and places.

Key Vocabulary

region
geographer
diverse
immigrant
culture

Think about traveling to another country. Everyone you meet asks what part of the United States you are from. What would you say? You would probably start by telling them the state you live in. But what if they don't know the states? What would you say then? If you're from Gary, Indiana, you might say you live in the Midwest. Or in the Great Lakes area. Or in the Breadbasket of America. All three answers would be correct!

How We Use Regions

Focus *What are some of the ways geographers divide land into regions?*

A term like "the Midwest" describes a region of our country. A **region** is an area that shares common characteristics. Geographers use regions as a tool to help make the complex geography of an area like the United States easier to understand. **Geographers** are people who study the earth and its features.

Some regions are defined by their location. The Midwest, for example, is a region made up of places that are located in the upper middle of the country. You probably know the locations of other regions in the United States such as the Northeast, South, and West.

Other regions, called physical regions, are defined by physical features they contain. The Great Lakes region is an example. This region, on the border between the United States and Canada, has a cluster of five lakes and its own particular climate and landscape.

The Breadbasket and the Rust Belt are examples of economic regions — regions defined by how the people in them make their

Regions in Indiana

Jasper, Indiana is located in several different regions. **Map Skill:** *In what region is Indianapolis located?*

living. Gary, Indiana, is an industrial city with factories and steel mills. It is part of a region called the Rust Belt because in the 1980s factories there shut down, leaving their machines to rust. Since that time, the jobs once found in those factories moved to other industrial areas. The Rust Belt is also part of a larger region called the Breadbasket, because it is the agricultural center of our nation. Indiana, with its many farms, is part of the Breadbasket.

The map at the bottom of the page shows one way of dividing the United States into regions. Each state belongs to one of these regions, which are defined by location. For example, you can see that the Northeast is in both the North and the East. But the states in each region share other characteristics. The region called the South includes states sharing a mostly warm and humid climate.

Regional and Cultural Differences

Focus *How do regions reflect the diversity of the people who live in the United States?*

Physical regions are just one way to study the United States. Another common way to study the nation is to divide it into human

This map shows four geographic regions of the United States. The United States census, which is taken every ten years and reports on the population, uses these regions in its reports.
Map Skill: *What region is your state in? What other states are in your region?*

Regions of the United States

WEST
Pacific
Mountain
MIDWEST
West North Central
East North Central
NORTHEAST
Middle Atlantic
New England
SOUTH
West South Central
East South Central
South Atlantic

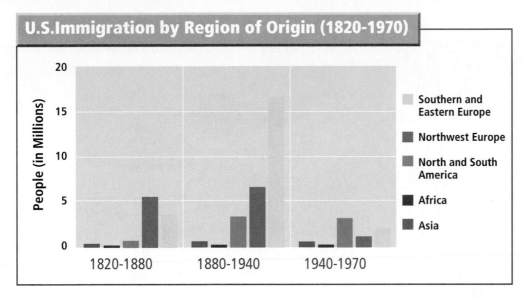

U.S. Immigration by Region of Origin (1820-1970)

People (in Millions)

20
15
10
5
0

1820-1880   1880-1940   1940-1970

- Southern and Eastern Europe
- Northwest Europe
- North and South America
- Africa
- Asia

This chart shows waves of immigration. Each colored bar matches an area on the globe. Pick a year, and look at the chart. The tallest colored bar shows where the most immigrants came from that year. **Chart Skill:** *From which area did most immigrants come in the 1920's?*

regions. Human regions are areas in which people share one or more common characteristics. In the United States there are many different human and cultural regions. That is because the American people are so **diverse,** meaning that they come from many different backgrounds.

A human region can be based on where the people living in it originally came from. An **immigrant** is a person who comes to a new place or country to live. Over the years, millions of immigrants from around the globe have come to the United States. Most African Americans were brought here against their will in the colonial period. Today, their descendants play an important role in every part of American life. Native Americans, descendants of immigrants, and new immigrants all contribute to our national identity. If you saw a map which showed where the people of the United States originally came from, you could identify some regions where many people share a common ancestry. Other places have no clear pattern.

Because the population of the United States is made up of many diverse groups, the country has an incredible mix of cultures. Culture is another feature which can be used to see areas that are alike and different. **Culture** is the language, beliefs, customs, and tools of a group of people. The religion you practice is part of your culture. The clothes you wear and the foods you eat are also part of your culture. Areas of the country where the majority of people practice a certain religion form a kind of human region as well.

People who came to this country as immigrants brought their native cultures with them. That is why Americans today celebrate holidays as diverse as Hanukkah (HAH nuh kuh), a Jewish holiday,

Cinco de Mayo celebrates an important Mexican battle victory. Many people of Mexican descent celebrate this day, as the children above are doing.

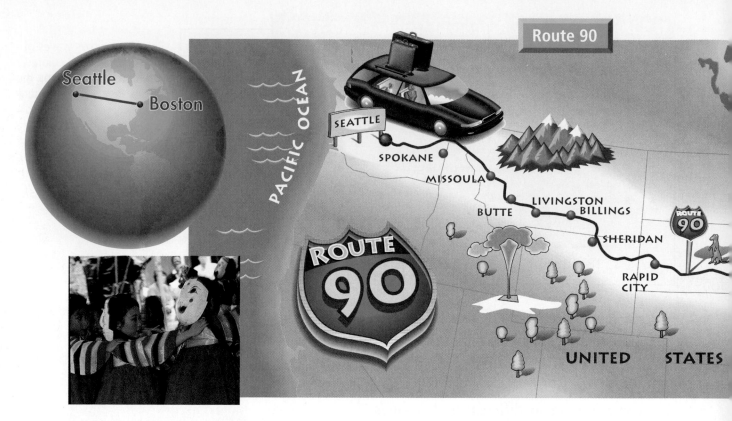

One way people learn about different regions is by traveling. Follow Route 90 along this page. You begin in Seattle, where you see girls dancing as part of the Folklife Festival. **Culture:** *What are some benefits of living in a country with many cultures?*

and Cinco de Mayo (SEEN koh deh MAH yoh), a Mexican American holiday.

The area peopled by a single culture is another kind of human region. In northern New Mexico and the northeastern part of Arizona, the Hopi (HOH pee) and Navajo (NAV uh hoh) speak their own languages as well as English. People in this region of the country celebrate festivals and maintain ways of life that have been passed down for hundreds of years.

A human region can be as small as a few city blocks. Take a walk along Mott Street in New York City. At the fruit and vegetable stands, people are speaking Chinese. The signs over the stores are written in Chinese characters. This neighborhood is a unique region of the city, largely peopled by Chinese Americans. Regions like this one are sometimes called "Chinatowns."

Most large American cities have neighborhoods where immigrants and their children have settled. In neighborhoods like these it is easy to see how people from different cultures live. Some human regions based on immigration can be very large, however. You can see from the map above both physical and human regions a family driving across the country might pass through.

People's attitudes toward the places they live in or visit affect how they view the world. For example, a tourist might see New York City as a vacation spot offering museums, plays, and

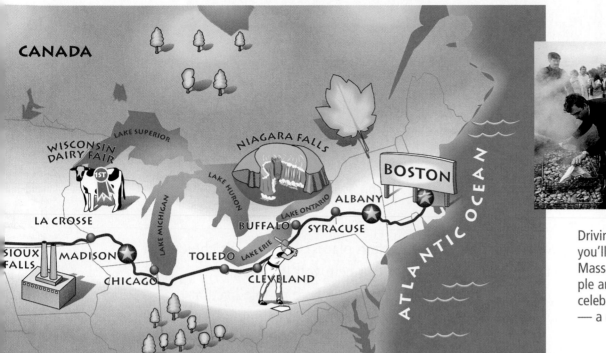

CANADA

WISCONSIN DAIRY FAIR

LAKE SUPERIOR

NIAGARA FALLS

BOSTON

ALBANY

LA CROSSE

LAKE HURON

LAKE MICHIGAN

LAKE ONTARIO

BUFFALO

SYRACUSE

SIOUX FALLS

MADISON

TOLEDO

LAKE ERIE

CLEVELAND

CHICAGO

ATLANTIC OCEAN

Driving along Route 90, you'll end up in eastern Massachusetts, where people are enjoying a popular celebration in that region — a clambake.

restaurants. A person who lives in the city, however, might think of the same place in terms of jobs or the cost of living.

As you have learned, regions can be defined by different features, such as culture and geography. They can also overlap. Regions help sort out the complexities of a large, varied land and the many people who live in it. To the geographer, regions are tools for understanding. You'll use those tools, too, as you study the history of the United States.

Lesson Review: Geography

1. **Key Vocabulary:** Write a paragraph about the lesson using the following: region, geographer, diverse, immigrant, culture

2. **Focus:** What are some of the ways geographers divide land into regions?

3. **Focus:** How do regions reflect the diversity of the people who live in the United States?

4. **Critical Thinking: Predict** Which type of region do you think is more likely to change over time, physical or human? Why?

5. **Theme: Love of the Land** Look at the land around you. What features does it have that make your region special?

6. **Geography/Art Activity:** Find out about the people who live in your town. Which cultural regions are you part of? Create a collage of pictures reflecting the cultures that live in your area. Try to show the things that bring them all together.

Skills Workshop

Comparing Population Maps

People Patterns

Why do people choose to live in certain places? Do people's choices change over time? **Population maps** can help you find out.

Comparing where people lived at different times can help you learn why those places might have attracted them.

You've seen population maps that use colored areas to show **population density,** or the number of people living in a square area. Dot maps show population density too, but in more detail.

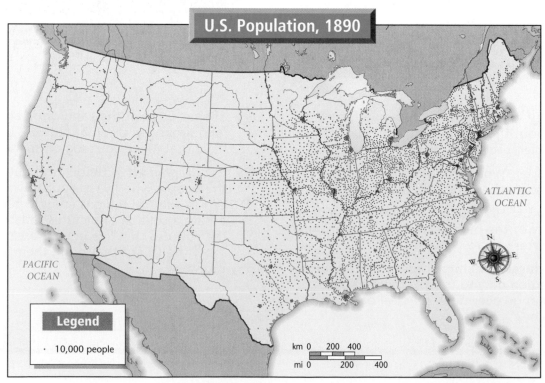

U.S. Population, 1890

ATLANTIC OCEAN

PACIFIC OCEAN

Legend

· 10,000 people

km 0   200 400
mi 0   200   400

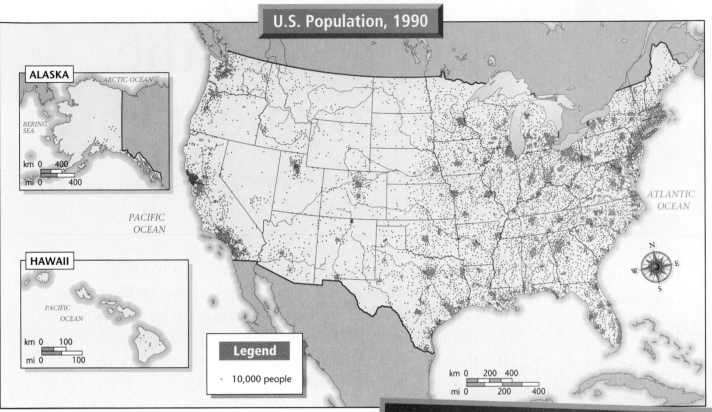

U.S. Population, 1990

ALASKA
ARCTIC OCEAN
BERING SEA
km 0 400
mi 0 400

PACIFIC OCEAN

HAWAII
PACIFIC OCEAN
km 0 100
mi 0 100

ATLANTIC OCEAN

Legend
· 10,000 people

km 0 200 400
mi 0 200 400

1 Here's How

These maps show population density in the United States in 1890 and 1990.

- Study the map legends carefully. What do the dots represent?

- On each map, look for clusters of dots. These are areas with dense populations — that is, many people living close together. In 1890, which regions had the most people? In which regions was the population sparse, with few people?

- Compare the two maps. Which regions have dense populations on both maps? Which regions show the greatest population growth over the century?

- On the earlier map, notice that people often settled along waterways — oceans, lakes, and rivers. How would you explain this pattern of settlement? Does settlement follow the same pattern on the recent map?

2 Think It Through

What kinds of things should you look at on a map to figure out why people settled in certain places?

The photograph above shows Denver, Colorado, today. The photograph on the opposite page shows Denver around 100 years ago.

3 Use It

1. Compare how population density changed from 1890 to 1990 in these regions:

   a) the Southwest

   b) the Central Plains

   c) the Southeast

2. What do you think attracted people to these areas? As you study the history and geography of the United States, see if your ideas are correct.

The Land and the People **25**

People and the Environment

Main Idea People shape the environment in which they live, just as the environment shapes them.

The rain pours down in East Dubuque (Duh BYOOK), Illinois. On the main street of town, dozens of men lift heavy bags of sand. They work quickly, piling the bags up to form a low wall. Rain drips off their faces as muddy water swirls around their knees. It is the summer of 1993, and these men are working desperately to hold back the flooding waters of the Mississippi River. If they fail — and it looks as though they will — their homes will soon be under water.

How the Environment Shapes Us

These two pictures show the same street in the town of McBride, Missouri. They were taken a day apart in 1993.

Focus *In what ways does the environment affect human life?*

Flooding used to be a way of life for people who lived along the Mississippi River. Every few years, heavy rains came, causing the river to surge over its banks and spread across farms and towns. People responded by building flood barriers called **levees** (LEHV ees). But in 1993, the level of the Mississippi rose to new heights. Many levees collapsed. Some places were under water for months.

Before and after the levee broke

In trying to hold back the river, people were trying to control their environment. **Environment** is a term used to refer to a person's surroundings. It includes such things as the physical conditions and the climate of a place. People have always tried to shape the environment to suit their needs. Throughout most of human history, they have often not had much success. More often, the environment shapes people.

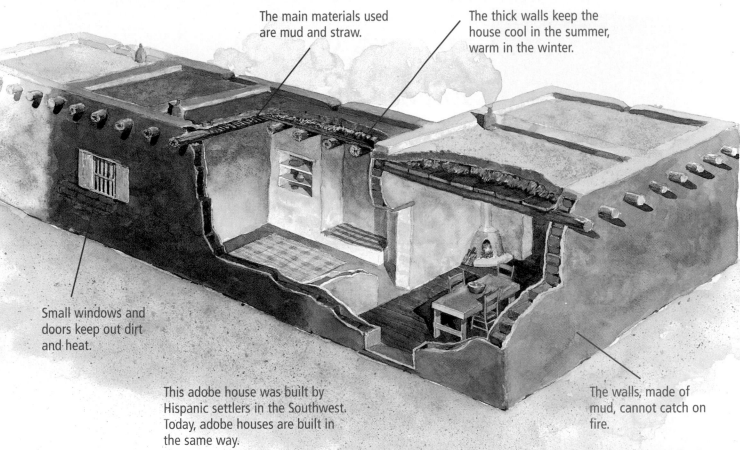

The main materials used are mud and straw.

The thick walls keep the house cool in the summer, warm in the winter.

Small windows and doors keep out dirt and heat.

This adobe house was built by Hispanic settlers in the Southwest. Today, adobe houses are built in the same way.

The walls, made of mud, cannot catch on fire.

Climate is an obvious example of this fact. If you lived in northern Michigan, you would not think twice about bundling up before going outside on a February day. In Florida, however, you might wear shorts and sandals to school every day of the year.

Climate influences the way we build our homes. In the North, a steep roof lets snow slide off in the winter. In the South, a porch keeps the rain off but lets breezes in. In the hot, dry Southwest, houses with thick adobe walls stay cool inside. (*See the picture above.*) Adobe is thick clay that is dried to make bricks and houses.

Lack of rain in the Southwest means that crops are mainly grown using **irrigation,** a method used to transport water to land. Because rain is so scarce, the people there have to be very careful not to waste water. The city of Tucson, Arizona, even has a "water cop" who gives tickets to people who water their lawns too much.

The environment shapes our lives in other less obvious ways. The availability of natural resources, such as water, timber, or minerals, often influences where cities are located. When towns and cities grow, they spread out according to the shape of the land. The shape of the land even affects the routes of highways and railroads.

Plants also adapt to their environment. The cactus stores water in its thick stems, which help it survive in the desert heat.
Science: *What are some of the ways that animals also adapt to their environments?*

How We Shape the Environment

Focus *What are some of the effects humans have on the environment?*

People throughout history have changed their surroundings. In this country, Native Americans and colonists affected their environment by clearing land and by cutting down trees. With advances in science, people are now able to change their environment on a gigantic scale. While change often benefits people enormously, it can sometimes damage the environment.

Benefits of the Dam

The Hoover Dam is a good example. It is located on the Colorado River, along the border between Arizona and Nevada. At 726 feet high, it is one of the largest concrete dams in the world. It was built in the 1930s. An entire town — Boulder City, Nevada — was created just to house the workers who built it.

This huge dam has changed the environment in some positive ways. Damming the river created Lake Mead, the largest reservoir (REHZ uhr vwahr) in the nation. A **reservoir** is a lake where water is stored for use. Lake Mead's water is used to irrigate over a million acres of land in southern California, Arizona, and Mexico. Lake Mead itself is the center of a national recreation area. People go there to fish, hike, swim, sail, and just enjoy nature.

The Hoover Dam supplies electric power to Arizona, Nevada, and southern California. It also helps control flooding on the Colorado River.

Affecting the Environment

But in spite of all the good that has come from the dam, it has created some environmental problems. The flow chart on the left shows how the Hoover Dam both helps people and hurts the environment — by changing the way the Colorado River flows. Because of the dam, the Colorado River is drier and shallower than it used to be, making it difficult for fish and wildlife to live there. One scientist describes the Colorado River as "almost dead."

Another example is the Columbia River, in the state of Washington. Damming it has changed the shape of the river and the way it flows. Salmon from the Pacific Ocean once swam up the

Hoover Dam

Lake Mead stores 2 years' worth of river water flow.

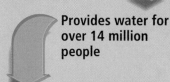

Provides energy for 500,000 homes in Arizona, Nevada and California

Provides water for over 14 million people

Irrigates more than a million acres of farms in US and Mexico

Much of the Colorado River is drier and more shallow as it runs its course to the ocean.

river to lay their eggs. Because the river's flow was halted by the dams, the salmon cannot get up the river. The people who work at the dam must now transport the salmon up river through the dams. The salmon lay their eggs and then return down the river to the Pacific Ocean. Some scientists think this kills more salmon than it saves.

Environmentalists believe that dams stop a river's flow of life. Reservoir water is often so deep and cold that there is not enough oxygen in it for fish and other animals to breathe. As a river flows into a reservoir and stops, the good soil carried by the river settles to the bottom. This means that beaches and wetlands at the river's mouth do not get the material they need to support life.

Today the United States government is planning more dams for rivers, to meet the demands of a growing population. But the government is also aware of the environmental risks. It is taking steps to protect the environment and the wildlife that depend on it. Its goal is not to keep people from using water, but to manage water resources wisely.

No matter what your background is or what region you live in, everyone benefits from our country's natural resources. If you ever visit a national park, take a look at the license plates on some of the cars in the parking lot. You will notice that cars are there from many states, some very far away. Even though a park may be in a different state, it belongs to you and to all residents of the United States. Part of loving the land is wanting to take care of it.

Lesson Review: Geography

1. **Key Vocabulary:** Write a short article about water use in the United States using the words **environment, reservoir,** and **irrigation**.

2. **Focus:** In what ways does the environment affect human life?

3. **Focus:** What are some of the effects humans have on the environment?

4. **Critical Thinking: Decision Making** People must use natural resources to live. Create some guidelines which would allow us to both use and protect these resources.

5. **Geography:** How has the environment shaped the growth of your town? How has your town changed the surrounding environment?

6. **Citizenship/Writing Activity:** You are going to advertise the job of environmental cop in the newspaper. Write the advertisement, making sure to include a description of the job and the qualifications that applicants must have.

Environment and Society

How Have People Changed the Everglades?

A hundred years ago, the Everglades was a slow-moving river, covered by tall grass. Fifty miles wide, and often less than six inches deep, it flowed from Lake Okeechobee to the Gulf of Mexico. Today, people think of the Everglades as a swamp. Geographers study the Everglades to learn how the use of an area by people can change the environment.

For centuries many people stayed away from the Everglades because of the humidity, mosquitoes, and alligator-filled waters. Eventually, people found more ways to use the area. They dug canals and dams to drain much of the northern Everglades in the early 1900s, creating rich farmland. This has reduced the amount of water in the part that is left. Some plants and animals may not survive this change. The Everglades became a national park in 1947, but human activity still threatens its existence.

Science Connection

The use of a wilderness area by human beings changes the environment. Cutting down too many trees, for example, can deprive animals of their homes or cause erosion of the soil. Are there wilderness areas near your home where human activity has affected the environment?

In the past the flow of fresh water kept the Everglades clean. Pollution has begun to build up now that the ancient flow pattern has been changed.

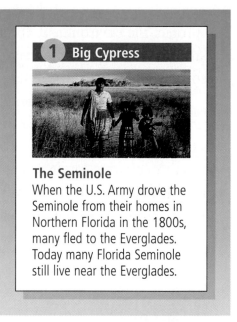

1 Big Cypress

The Seminole
When the U.S. Army drove the Seminole from their homes in Northern Florida in the 1800s, many fled to the Everglades. Today many Florida Seminole still live near the Everglades.

A River of Grass

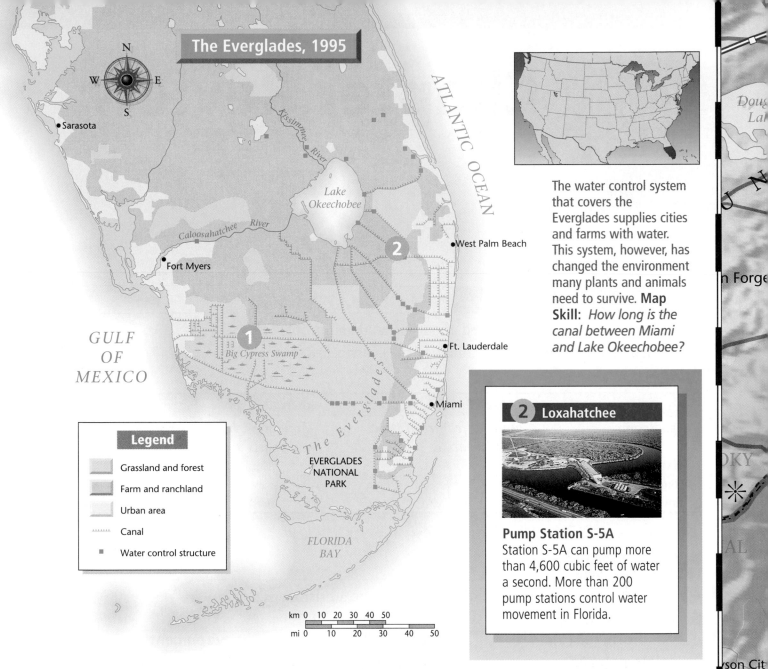

The Everglades, 1995

N W E S

• Sarasota

ATLANTIC OCEAN

Kissimmee River

Lake Okeechobee

Caloosahatchee River

• Fort Myers

2 • West Palm Beach

GULF OF MEXICO

1

Big Cypress Swamp

• Ft. Lauderdale

The Everglades

• Miami

EVERGLADES NATIONAL PARK

Legend

Grassland and forest

Farm and ranchland

Urban area

Canal

Water control structure

FLORIDA BAY

km 0 10 20 30 40 50

mi 0 10 20 30 40 50

The water control system that covers the Everglades supplies cities and farms with water. This system, however, has changed the environment many plants and animals need to survive. **Map Skill:** *How long is the canal between Miami and Lake Okeechobee?*

2 Loxahatchee

Pump Station S-5A
Station S-5A can pump more than 4,600 cubic feet of water a second. More than 200 pump stations control water movement in Florida.

Research Activity

The changes in the Everglades have affected most of the wildlife there.

1 Research one animal or bird that makes its home in the Everglades.

2 Write a brief report on how human activity has affected the animal or bird.

An average of 900 people move to Florida *every day!* This rapid population increase has raised the demand for water. **Chart Skill:** *How much was total water use in 1960?*

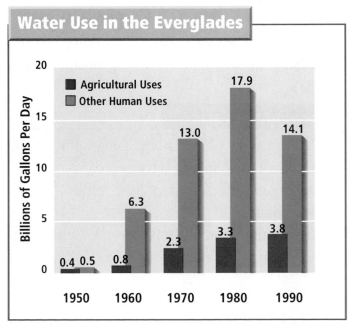

Water Use in the Everglades

Billions of Gallons Per Day

■ Agricultural Uses
■ Other Human Uses

Year	Agricultural Uses	Other Human Uses
1950	0.4	0.5
1960	0.8	6.3
1970	2.3	13.0
1980	3.3	17.9
1990	3.8	14.1

Chapter Review

Summarizing the Main Idea

1 Indicate what you have learned about the land and people of the United States by copying and filling in the chart below.

	What is it?	Interesting Fact
Landform	*A physical feature of the earth's surface*	*Mountains, hills, deserts, plains, rivers, and coasts are landforms.*
Natural Resource		
Region		
Environment		

Vocabulary

2 Using at least nine of the following terms, write a brief magazine article describing a trip across the United States.

landform (p. 15)	region (p. 19)	environment (p. 26)
plateau (p. 15)	geographer (p. 19)	irrigation (p. 27)
basin (p. 16)	diverse (p. 21)	levee (p. 26)
natural resource (p. 16)	immigrant (p. 21)	reservoir (p. 28)
mineral (p. 16)	culture (p. 21)	

Reviewing the Facts

3 What are some of the special geographic features of the United States?

4 How are natural resources used in the United States?

5 What do immigrants coming to the United States bring with them?

6 How does climate change the way people live? How can it make their lives harder?

7 How might a dam be helpful to the environment?

8 What environmental problems might a dam create?

9 Look at the population maps on pages 24–25. In what region did the population grow the most during the time period shown?

10 Compare the two maps on pages 24–25. Can you find a heavily populated city on the second map which did not exist on the first map?

Geography Skills

11 Look at the map on page 17. What kinds of natural resources might one region share with another?

12 Choose a place in the United States you would like to visit. Plan a trip there from your hometown. Write a schedule that includes places to visit and people to see.

Critical Thinking

13 **Cause and Effect** How might a region influence the day-to-day activities of people who live there?

14 **Predicting Outcomes** Think about the ways in which people use the land today.

What might happen in the future if we continue to use the land in these ways?

15 **Decision Making** If you could live anywhere in the United States, where would you live? Why did you choose this place?

Writing: Citizenship and Culture

16 **Citizenship** If you were mayor of a small town, how would you persuade people to do more to care for the land around them? Write a speech. Include a plan of action.

17 **Culture** Make a poster that celebrates the cultural diversity of the people in your class, town, or state.

Activities

History/Research Activity
Select a region and research how the environment, natural resources, and people have changed it over time. Think about other things that might have affected the region.

Geography/Art Activity
Choose two or more of the characteristics you read about in the chapter: landforms, natural resources, regions, people, environment. Draw a symbol to represent each. Use your symbols to Illustrate a map of the United States.

Internet Option

Check the **Internet Social Studies Center** for ideas on how to extend your theme project beyond your classroom.

THEME PROJECT CHECK-IN

Before you choose a Native American group to represent, use the information in this chapter to explain how geography affects the people who live in a region.
• What different regions are located in the Americas?
• What are some landforms and natural resources located in these regions?
• How would geography have been important to the groups who lived in each region?

The First Americans

Chapter Preview: *People, Places, and Events*

12,000 years ago

Glacier Today

What do glaciers have to do with the first Americans? *Lesson 1, Page 36*

Ancient Duck Decoy

Learn more about the ancient people who made these. *Lesson 1, Page 38*

Teotihuacán

This city was so beautiful that the Aztecs called it "place of the gods." *Lesson 2, Page 42*

The First Peoples

Main Idea The first Americans arrived here thousands of years ago as hunters and gatherers. Some of them gradually learned to farm.

Ages ago, as the Tsimshian (TSIHM shee uhn) people of the Northwest tell it, there were no tides. The oceans neither rose nor fell. People went hungry because good food — such as seaweed and clams — was far out of reach below the surface of the water.

The spirit Raven, wrapped in his black feathers, flew off to find out why. Soon Raven spied an old woman holding the "tide-line" tight in her hands. No wonder the oceans were so still! Cleverly, he tricked her into dropping the line by blinding her with dust. The tides rushed out. Food was plentiful and everyone ate and ate. Later, the old woman asked Raven to heal her eyes. "Only if you promise to let go of the tide-line twice a day," he told her, "so that people may gather food from the beaches." She promised, and Raven washed out her eyes. According to the Tsimshian, this explains why the oceans' tides go in and out twice each day.

Key Vocabulary

archaeologist

migrate

glacier

agriculture

Key Events

10,000 years ago
Ice Age ends

5,000 years ago
Corn cultivation
begins

◀ Taos Pueblo, New Mexico

Today

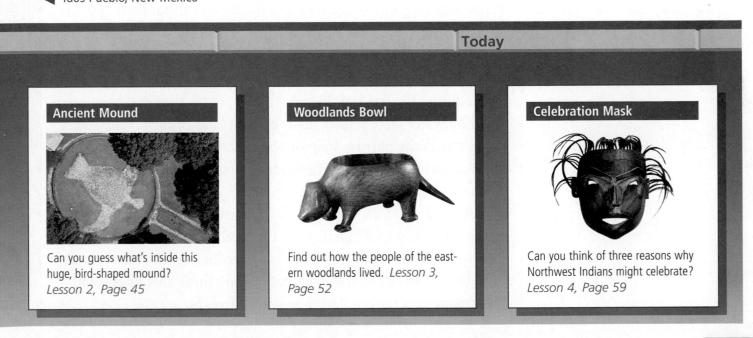

Ancient Mound

Can you guess what's inside this huge, bird-shaped mound?
Lesson 2, Page 45

Woodlands Bowl

Find out how the people of the eastern woodlands lived. *Lesson 3, Page 52*

Celebration Mask

Can you think of three reasons why Northwest Indians might celebrate? *Lesson 4, Page 59*

Journey to a New Home

Focus *How might the first people have migrated to the Americas from Asia?*

Stories like the one you just read played an important role in the lives of ancient peoples. Native Americans told stories to explain nature's mysteries, such as the tides, birth, death, and the sun. They also told stories to better understand themselves — where they came from and the journeys they took. Sometimes they told stories just for fun. Today, a good way to learn about the lives of early peoples is through their stories.

The work of archaeologists also helps us learn about ancient peoples. **Archaeologists** study bones, tools, pottery, and other artifacts to learn how ancient people lived. They find artifacts buried underground, in caves, in river beds, and on the ocean floor. They also make guesses based on what they know.

Archaeologists are like detectives, searching for and studying the clues that they have found all over the Americas. (See the map on page 37.) Although many Native American cultures have their own beliefs about their origins, most archaeologists believe that the first Native Americans journeyed to this continent on foot, many thousands of years ago, from another place — Asia.

No one can say for sure how these people got to North America. It is possible that some were sailors who came in small boats to settle and fish along the Pacific coast. Most were probably migrating hunters. (To **migrate** means to move.) They followed herds of large game — such as woolly mammoths and giant bison — across the frozen landscape of the last Ice Age. The Ice Age was a time when much of the world's water was frozen. So much water was locked in ice that land that had been underwater became visible again during the Ice Age. In some places, lands that had been separated by water were joined again by new land bridges. One such place was in the narrow strip of water between what is now Russia and Alaska. When the Ice Age ended, this land was flooded again. Today it is called the Bering Strait.

Glaciers are thick sheets of slowly moving ice. As the glaciers began to melt, a trail emerged on the land. Some archaeologists believe that when the early hunters arrived in North America, they used these trails to migrate south. Scholars think this migration took many generations and thousands of years.

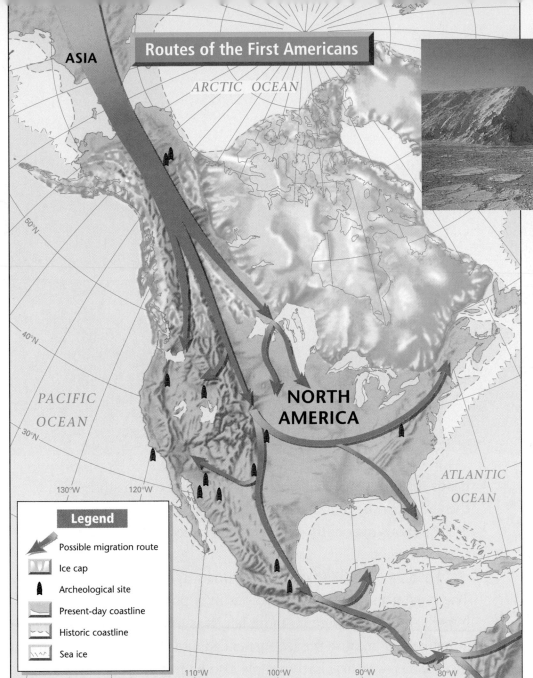

Routes of the First Americans

ASIA

ARCTIC OCEAN

NORTH AMERICA

PACIFIC OCEAN

ATLANTIC OCEAN

50°N

40°N

30°N

130°W   120°W   110°W   100°W   90°W   80°W

Legend

Possible migration route

Ice cap

Archeological site

Present-day coastline

Historic coastline

Sea ice

On the Diomede Islands between Russia and the United States, part of the original land bridge can still be seen.

Early peoples crossed the Bering land bridge to settle all over the Americas, on these routes and far beyond. **Map Skill:** *Why do you think they kept moving south?*

A Changing Way of Life

Focus *In what ways did the changing environment affect the lives of early peoples?*

Life for the first settlers in the Americas was a struggle for survival. Mostly they lived in caves or huts, wearing animal skins to protect themselves from the bitter cold. Game was plentiful — woolly mammoths, beavers as large as bears, and moose with antlers eight feet across. One woolly mammoth could feed and clothe 20 people for an entire winter. How did people hunt such huge animals? Often they used spears with spear-

Spears like this one were made by attaching wooden handles to sharpened stone points.

In this drawing, hunters chase bison off a cliff. This hunting technique was used by early hunters and continued to be practiced by Native Americans as late as the 1800s.

Graveyards of ancient bison bones are often found below cliffs. In ancient times, bison were larger and had longer horns than today's buffalo.

heads made of flint. Some used clubs or ropes with stones tied to the ends. One common way to hunt bison was to stampede the huge animals over cliffs. Hunters then collected the meat at the bottom of the cliff.

Then, about 10,000 years ago, this way of life began to change. The large mammals slowly died out. It is possible that they were hunted until there were no more left. It is more likely that the large animals died because the Ice Age ended and they could not adapt to the warmer weather. Early people also had to adapt to the change in weather. They needed different weapons and new ways to hunt the smaller animals. Bows and arrows replaced spears and heavy clubs.

As the ice melted, water filled the oceans and they began to rise. Early peoples — many moving around by boat — fished in lakes, streams, and the rising seas. They dug for clams and oysters. They studied their environment and learned which roots, seeds, nuts, and berries were good to eat. To carry these plants to their homes, they taught themselves how to weave baskets from tree bark or reeds.

Early peoples needed new tools for their changing way of life. They learned to make such tools out of stone and bone, using them to grind wild grain and seeds. They also began to try to grow the seeds and plants they found. Slowly, they became farmers.

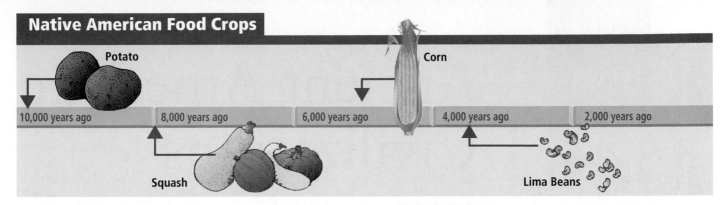

Native American Food Crops

Potato

Corn

10,000 years ago — 8,000 years ago — 6,000 years ago — 4,000 years ago — 2,000 years ago

Squash

Lima Beans

Native Americans discovered a plant about 5,000 years ago that came to have a huge influence on people all over the world. Can you guess what it was? It began as a wild plant, with small, brownish, one-inch-long cobs on it. This strange-looking plant was the ancestor of our corn. It can still be found in Mexico where it is called *madre de maíz* (MAH dreh deh mah EES), or mother of corn.

Early peoples learned how to grow corn and how to make it larger and tastier. Soon they were growing squash and beans as well. **Agriculture,** or the process of growing crops and farming, gradually changed the lives of most early peoples. It meant that people could grow extra food, and store it in their baskets or pottery dishes to use in the cold winter months. Because they could grow crops, they no longer needed to move around in search of food. Now they could live in more permanent villages. They had more time for other activities, such as weaving baskets or making pots in which to store food. A new way of life had arrived.

The timeline shows foods native to America and when they were first grown. These became important basic foods for the whole world. **Cultures:** *Many non-American cultures today depend on foods that originally came from America. Can you think of a country that depends on one of the foods above?*

Lesson Review

10,000 years ago — 5,000 years ago

10,000 years ago
Ice Age ends

5,000 years ago
Corn cultivation begins

1. **Key Vocabulary:** Write a paragraph about the Ice Age using **archaeologist, migrate,** and **glacier.**

2. **Focus:** How might the first people have migrated to the Americas from Asia?

3. **Focus:** In what ways did the changing environment affect the lives of early peoples?

4. **Critical Thinking: Generalize** Give reasons supporting this statement:

Agriculture is the most important discovery the world has ever known.

5. **Geography:** Which foods native to the Americas are used by people all over the world?

6. **Citizenship/Writing Activity:** Think of some objects that you could bury in the ground. An archaeologist 1,000 years later finds these artifacts. Write two paragraphs explaining what these objects might say about your society.

Ancient American Civilizations

Main Idea Agriculture was important in allowing many cultures in the Americas to become civilizations.

Some items for sale in markets in Guatemala today are like those once sold in Mayan markets.

A rooster's crow signals the start of another day. All over Mexico and Central America people, young and old, hurry to the marketplace to buy and sell goods in the open-air village plazas and on the nearby streets. Tomatoes, herbs, clothing, animals, and much more can be bought at the many stands. Busy market days are necessary for many people who depend on a good day's trade to make their living. It is a way of life that began in this part of the world thousands of years ago, and continues today.

The Growth of Civilization

Focus *What are some of the conditions that allowed civilizations to grow?*

Marketplaces like the one you just read about came into being as part of a changing way of life. Agriculture was an important part of this change. Farmers growing corn (maize), beans, squash and other foods gradually grew enough for a **surplus,** or extra amount, to store for use against hard times or for trade.

Farming was the usual way to get food surpluses, but there were other ways. Some people traded goods, and others fished. No matter how a society got its surplus, the result was the same: fewer people needed to farm the land. Those not needed for farming could learn special skills, such as weaving or making pottery. People skilled in fighting became warriors, while other people became leaders or priests.

Food surpluses also allowed populations to increase. Villages became towns, and towns became cities with temples and marketplaces. Such a

Early American Civilizations

NORTH AMERICA

ATLANTIC OCEAN

N

Gulf of Mexico

PACIFIC OCEAN

Anasazi
Mound Builders
Aztec
Maya

mi 0   400
km 0   400

Yucatán

CENTRAL AMERICA

Ancient civilizations of the Americas can be seen on this map. Tikal, pictured above, was an important Mayan city. **Map Skill:** *What is the difference between the geography of the Mayan settlements and that of the mound-building settlements?*

culture with cities, a government, and many different jobs for people is known as a **civilization**.

Mesoamerican Civilizations

Focus *What were the major features of the Maya and the Aztec cultures?*

Over thousands of years, many civilizations rose and fell in the regions of Mesoamerica and North America *(see map above)*. **Mesoamerica** lies in the southern part of North America. One of the earliest of these civilizations built an important city called Teotihuacán (teh oh tee hwah KAHN). Teotihuacán was one of the largest cities in Mesoamerica in the year 600. On the next page you can see its planned streets and some of the art from its temples, which influenced other cultures including the Maya and the Aztecs.

Ax heads like these were traded in marketplaces for feathers, gold, and animal skins.

The Maya

The Maya lived in what is now Guatemala and southern Mexico. Though this part of the world is thick with rain forests, the Maya managed to build a network of stone cities without using the wheel or work animals. Tikal (tee KAHL), one of the largest cities, was a busy center of 40,000 people. Tikal contained a central plaza surrounded by temple-topped pyramids. Bridges, palaces, and fancy stairways decorated Tikal. Priests and leaders lived in this center and were supported by the Mayan farmers, who lived outside Tikal.

The Mayan priests and leaders were powerful because of their knowledge. They knew how to make accurate calendars that helped people know when to plant and harvest. They invented a picture language and used it to write in books that may have been made of bark or pottery. Mayan builders planned cities based on what they learned from Teotihuacán.

Around the year 900 the Mayan civilization began to disappear. Tikal and other Mayan cities emptied out. Archaeologists who have studied the Maya still do not know why. Were they wiped out by disease? The most likely explanation is that the population had grown too large for the land to support, and their food ran out.

The Aztecs

Around the year 1170 in the Valley of Mexico to the north, another culture developed. The Aztecs were warriors who conquered

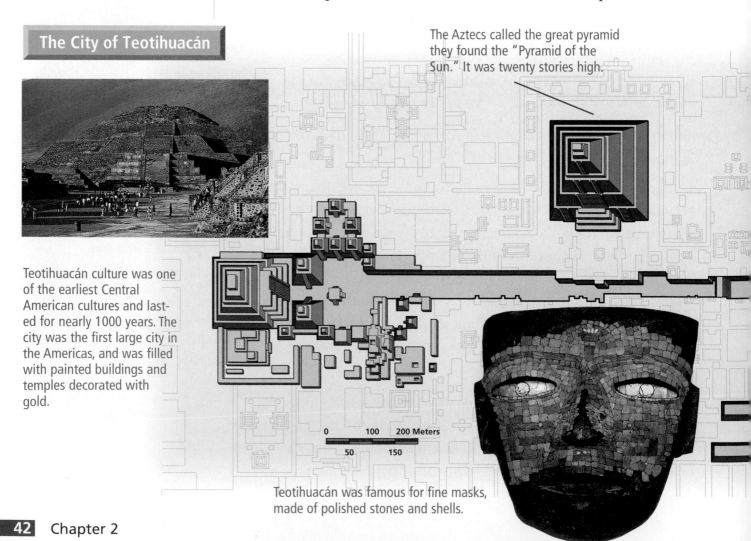

The City of Teotihuacán

Teotihuacán culture was one of the earliest Central American cultures and lasted for nearly 1000 years. The city was the first large city in the Americas, and was filled with painted buildings and temples decorated with gold.

The Aztecs called the great pyramid they found the "Pyramid of the Sun." It was twenty stories high.

0   100   200 Meters
   50   150

Teotihuacán was famous for fine masks, made of polished stones and shells.

farming peoples. By forcing the people they conquered to pay them money and goods, the Aztecs built a huge empire that lasted nearly 100 years. An **empire** is made up of land and people controlled by one ruler or government. Their capital city, which the Aztecs built on a small island, was called Tenochtitlán (teh nawch tee TLAN).

Religion was an important part of life for the Aztecs. They made Teotihuacán a religious center. In the Aztec language they called it the "place of the gods." War was also part of the Aztec religion. The Aztecs believed that bravery in battle would please their gods. Human sacrifice — offering a human life to the gods — was also part of their religious beliefs. Aztecs believed that sacrifices helped them succeed in war and farming.

All Aztec children went to school. Girls learned cooking, weaving, and other homemaking skills. Boys trained hard to become good warriors. These warriors helped the Aztecs conquer and control new lands. By the year 1500, the Aztec Empire, under several powerful rulers, had grown to include about one-third of Mexico.

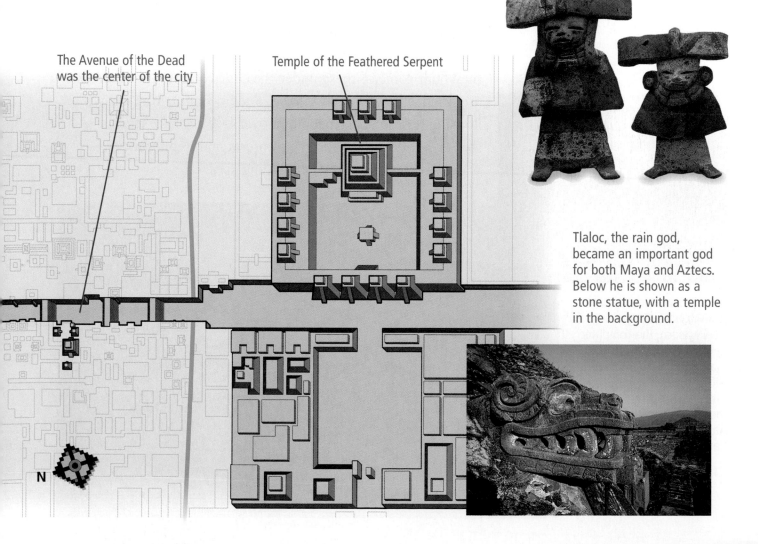

The Avenue of the Dead was the center of the city

Temple of the Feathered Serpent

N

Tlaloc, the rain god, became an important god for both Maya and Aztecs. Below he is shown as a stone statue, with a temple in the background.

North American Civilizations

Focus *How were the Anasazi and mound-building cultures affected by their environments?*

The Anasazi (Ahn uh SAH zee) were resourceful people. They had to be, living as they did among rock canyons on the Colorado Plateau of the Southwest. Water was scarce but the Anasazi still managed to farm. They irrigated the land by digging ditches from their land's few rivers, and by building reservoirs to catch rain.

Before the year 500, the Anasazi gathered food and roamed the land in search of animals to hunt. Farming changed that, as it did all over the world. Growing corn and beans needed time and care. The Anasazi — like many other cultures — settled down to a life of agriculture. They built permanent houses near their fields.

At first the Anasazi built pit houses: underground rooms with earth floors and walls of stone slabs. Then the Anasazi began building above ground, and the pit houses became ceremonial centers called *kivas* (KEE vahs) where people met on special occasions.

By the year 1100 the Anasazi no longer lived underground but in **pueblos** (PWEH blohs), a Spanish word for "towns." Because they built some of these under the edges of cliffs, the Anasazi are often called "cliff dwellers." Pueblo Bonito was a town housing thousands of people in over 800 rooms. All of it — stones, adobe, and wood from forests many miles away — was carried by hand to the building spot.

CHACO CANYON

LOOKING SOUTHEAST

This computer-made map shows Chaco Canyon in New Mexico. The computer helped archaeologists find roads leading to Anasazi cliff settlements. Archaeologists got much of their knowledge of the Anasazi from Chaco Canyon, shown on the right.

Crafts of the Anasazi

Black and white designs were the favorite style of Anasazi potters.

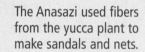

Lack of rain might have forced the Anasazi to leave their villages, leaving nothing behind but their crafts. Craftmaking was an important part of Anasazi daily life. Archaeologists often refer to the Anasazi as "basket makers" because of their beautiful woven baskets. They also made fine pottery, often black and white or with bold patterns.

Fine baskets were woven to carry and store goods.

The Anasazi used fibers from the yucca plant to make sandals and nets.

The Mound Builders

Cultures also developed on the other side of North America, in the woodlands of the East. These people are known as the Mound Builders — the Adena, Hopewell, and the Mississippians who lived in North America for over 2,000 years. The Adena and Hopewell gathered food, but the Mississippians practiced farming and settled in the rich land along rivers, near good food sources.

The Mound Builders got their name from the way they buried their dead. When a leader died, Adena people buried the body in a pit or a log tomb. Then they covered the grave with dirt to make a small mound. After a period of about 100 years, new pits were dug in these small mounds and covered with more dirt. In time, the mounds grew higher and higher and sometimes joined together.

The Hopewell continued this tradition. They often put pearls and other valuable items, such as scraps of copper and pottery, on their dead leaders before covering them with dirt.

As the Hopewell died out, a new mound-building culture developed around the year 900. It is called the Mississippian, because it was influenced by cultures located along the Mississippi River. The Mississippians also built mounds, though not all of them were graves. They used some as platforms for temples or for leaders' palaces. People also stayed on top of the mounds during floods.

You can see many layers of buried objects in this painting, which shows a cross-section of a Mississippian mound.

This stone statue was found in a mound in northern Georgia.
Economics: *How might burying valuable goods in graves affect the economy of a society?*

The largest Mississippian town was called Cahokia (Kah HOE kee uh), built near what is now the city of St. Louis, Missouri. Located near the meeting of two rivers, it was a perfect place for farming, trading, and fishing. Nearly six miles of burial mounds, 120 mounds in all, were found in the center of Cahokia. One of these, called Monks Mound, was at the time one of the tallest structures in North America.

By 1650, much of the Mississippian culture had begun to die out. But some of the Mississippian culture and ways of life would live on in the Native American groups of the eastern woodlands.

Lesson Review

500	1000	1500	

600
Teotihuacán flourishes

900
Mayan cities begin to empty

1170
Aztecs arrive in the Valley of Mexico

1. **Key Vocabulary:** Write a paragraph about the Americas using **surplus**, **civilization**, **Mesoamerica**, **empire**, and **pueblo**.

2. **Focus:** What are some of the conditions that allowed civilizations to grow?

3. **Focus:** What were the major features of the Maya and Aztec cultures?

4. **Focus:** How were the Anasazi and mound-building cultures affected by their environments?

5. **Critical Thinking: Classify** Divide the cultures you studied in this lesson into two groups, depending on how each lived.

6. **Citizenship:** What was the role of education in Aztec society?

7. **Geography/Science Activity:** Refer to the map on page 41 to see where the four civilizations you studied about lived. Make a chart showing the land features of each group and how each group adapted to their environment.

Using B.C., A.D., and Centuries

Keeping Track of Time

All around the world, people have come up with ways of counting years. How did they decide when to start counting? One system of counting used in the United States and many other countries, was created almost 1,500 years ago. It is based on the year that Jesus was born. Many think that was about 2,000 years ago. Dates before the birth of Jesus are B.C., or "before Christ." Dates after the birth of Jesus are A.D., which means "anno Domini" or "in the year of our Lord" in Latin. In both B.C. and A.D., every hundred years is called a **century**. How can a timeline tell you whether dates are B.C. or A.D.? How do you know in which century a year belongs?

Events in History

3000 B.C.	2000 B.C.	1000 B.C.	A.D. 1	A.D. 1000

3000 B.C.
Corn cultivation

400 B.C.
Maya begin
building pyramids

A.D. 700
Cahokia mounds begun

1000 B.C.
Adena culture
begins building mounds

150 B.C.
Teotihuacán
established

A.D. 1100
Anasazi build
cliff dwellings

1 Here's How

- Study the timeline. Notice which part of the timeline shows B.C. and which part shows A.D. Find the point at which B.C. ends and A.D. begins.

- Look at the dates on each side of the timeline. Notice that as you travel back through time, B.C. dates get larger. In B.C., you count backwards.

- Counting centuries is tricky. The 1900s are actually in the 20th century. How can that be? The first hundred years after Jesus' birth were the first century. So year 101 began the second century, and so on.

2 Think It Through

Why might it be helpful to have history divided into two periods, B.C. and A.D.?

3 Use It

1. Name one B.C. and one A.D. event on the timeline.

2. In which century was Cahokia built?

3. In which century are you living now?

THE SAD NIGHT

by Sally Schofer Mathews

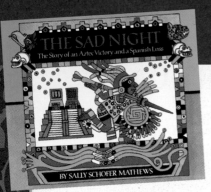

Historical Literature

The Americas were not really new — they only seemed new to the Europeans who journeyed there. Long before the first European explorers ever sailed west across the Atlantic Ocean, people had lived and raised families in North America. They had farmed and hunted. They had created art and music and poetry. In Mexico, some ancient peoples did even more. They studied astronomy and mathematics, and built amazing cities with temples and palaces and pyramids. Some of these cities died out before Europeans reached the Americas. Other great cities were destroyed not long after the Spanish came to Mexico. This first part of the story tells about the beginning of one of these civilizations — the Aztec empire — and its beautiful capital city. It also introduces the great Aztec emperor Montezuma (also called Moctezuma).

The Aztecs and other peoples of Mexico wrote with pictures on bark pages that were connected together in one long accordion-folded piece. We call these "books" codices.

Five hundred years ago, when Spanish soldiers conquered Mexico, they collected and destroyed almost all the codices. The artwork of this true story is based on the fewer than twenty codices and codex fragments that remain.

Long ago in Mexico, when volcanoes sent lava rivers steaming into the jungles and jaguars hissed messages to man, a wandering people listened to their leaders.

"We must move again," the priests said. "Put on your sandals and your robes and take your children by the hand, and walk and keep on walking until you see an eagle on a cactus with a rattlesnake in its beak. In that place, we will build an empire."

Every day they walked. To sleep, they curled up in their robes. To eat, they chopped up cactus and roasted rattlesnake meat. And one day, one very good day, they looked across a lake and saw an eagle on an island. It was perched on a cactus, with a rattlesnake twisting around in its beak. They named the island Tenochtitlán, which means "the place of the cactus stone."

"We must make boats," the leaders said, "to get from here to the island, and when we live there, we'll travel on streets of water. And we must make our buildings tall enough to meet the sun, for the sun will light the way for us to become a noble people."

The people worked hard. They built huge stone pyramids and put temples on top. They constructed palaces of stone with hundreds of rooms. They built causeways across the lake with bridges they could take away. They were safe. They were strong. They were the Aztecs.

They began to want their neighbors' land. Ferocious Aztec warriors, the Jaguar Knights and the Eagle Knights, took over territory that belonged to other Indians and forced them to pay again and again to stay alive.

causeway
a raised road built across a body of water to connect two pieces of land

ferocious
strong and able to terrify others

The Aztecs had built an empire in less than two hundred years. Everyone was afraid of them, and their king, Moctezuma, was the most powerful man in Mexico.

Meet the Author

Sally Schofer Mathews teaches art in an elementary school in Florida. This is her first children's book. She got the idea for The Sad Night while studying in the town of San Miguel de Allende in Mexico. She goes back there to visit whenever she can.

Additional Books to Read

City of the Gods Mexico's Ancient City of Teotihuacán by Caroline Arnold Learn about Mexico City's ancient pyramids.

The Ancient Cliff Dwellers of Mesa Verde by Caroline Arnold A fascinating look at archaeology in today's Colorado.

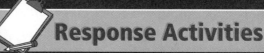

Response Activities

1. **Identify Main Idea** According to the author's story, what seems to be the main characteristic of the Aztecs?

2. **Expressive: Write a Story** Suppose you were one of the people mentioned at the end of the story who were conquered by the Aztecs. How might your story be different from that of the Aztecs? Write a story from your point of view.

3. **National Heritage: Make a Collage** Stories like The Sad Night help explain the origins of the Aztecs. Make a collage which reflects some of the origins of a Native American group in North America.

Life in the Eastern Woodlands

Main Idea Hunting, gathering, and the use of fire were important to the many Native American groups who lived along the eastern coast.

Lorraine Canoe

Many Woodlands groups grew and gathered foods like the persimmons, nuts and berries shown here.

Lorraine Canoe is one of around 35,000 Native Americans living in New York City. "It's not easy trying to find someone I can talk Mohawk with," she says. She has lived there for 35 years, but she plans to move back to her Mohawk community located between Canada and New York. There she can use her Mohawk name and speak her own language. She can also once again take part in the Mohawk ceremonies that connect her to her people.

Using the Land

Focus *How were the lives of Woodlands Indians related to their environments?*

The Mohawk today live in many different parts of the country. In 1500, they were one of many Native American groups that lived in the eastern half of North America. (See the map on the next page.) Because this area was largely forested in those years, it is called the eastern **woodlands**. Woodlands Indians spoke different languages and had different customs. They had a lot in common, too. They lived in dense, green forests filled with animals, rivers, and lakes. They shaped their lives by adapting to this environment.

The way they built their houses depended on climate and available resources. Wood was plentiful nearly everywhere in the East, so wood and bark were common building materials. Native Americans living along the coast often built homes with tall plants and stalks they found near the water. Northern groups built their houses with thick sides to keep out cold, while in the South people often left the sides open to keep cool. Many Native Americans in the Northeast lived in long houses like the one on the map, with many families all together.

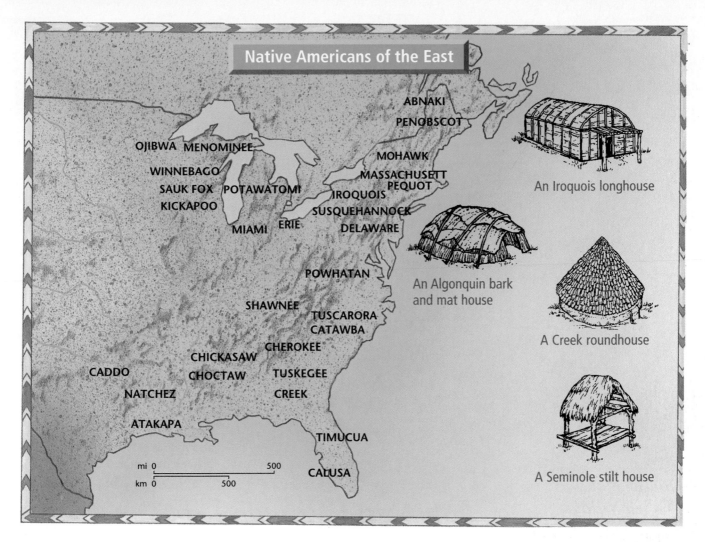

Native Americans of the East

ABNAKI
PENOBSCOT
OJIBWA MENOMINEE
WINNEBAGO
MOHAWK
SAUK FOX POTAWATOMI
MASSACHUSETT
PEQUOT
IROQUOIS
KICKAPOO
SUSQUEHANNOCK
MIAMI ERIE
DELAWARE
POWHATAN
SHAWNEE
TUSCARORA
CATAWBA
CHEROKEE
CHICKASAW
CADDO CHOCTAW TUSKEGEE
NATCHEZ CREEK
ATAKAPA
TIMUCUA
mi 0   500
km 0   500
CALUSA

An Iroquois longhouse

An Algonquin bark
and mat house

A Creek roundhouse

A Seminole stilt house

Woodlands Indians of the East used the materials around them for their housing. **Map Skill:** *What clues do the different houses give about the climate they were built in?*

The environment also shaped how and what people ate. A few Native American groups, like the Calusas (Kuh LOO suhs) of Florida, took much of their food from the sea. Woodlands groups got food in many ways including farming, hunting, and gathering. Some of the foods they grew and gathered are shown on page 52.

The thick woods were full of animals, and Native Americans developed many methods of hunting. Iroquois (IHR uh kwoy) hunters built V-shaped enclosures out of wood. In hunting season, they drove the deer into the V, where they shot the deer with arrows. Other hunters used a different method. They cleared an area of the forest with fire. The deer's favorite grass would grow in the cleared area. When the deer came to eat, the hunters caught them. Deer and other animals provided food and clothing.

These burned-out grassy areas where Native Americans trapped deer sometimes became fighting grounds, when men from different groups came across each other while hunting. Different groups tried to establish **boundaries,** or lines to separate their territory from other peoples' territories.

This round house provided shelter for old and sick people. The Creek also used it in winter for ceremonies, dances, and meetings.

A Creek Village

The Creek cleared forest land for their villages and crops.
Cultures: *What does the layout of this village tell you about the importance of the central plaza?*

Town and Village Life

Focus *How did the Creek plan their towns and villages?*

Woodlands groups built their villages among the forests, usually on hilltops near rivers. Here they could hunt, fish, and travel by birch-bark canoe. One such group was the Creek, people who lived along rivers in Alabama and Georgia and spoke languages that were similar to one another.

Like many Woodlands groups, the Creek planned their villages around a central plaza. Creek religious ceremonies and dances took place in this plaza. Buildings made of mud and poles surrounded the plaza. Some of these buildings were used for council meetings and storage. The Creek also built their houses near the plaza, and beyond the houses they cleared fields for farming.

Each town chose a leader who met with townspeople in the round house to plan festivals, decide when to plant crops, and discuss war. Every town was part of the Creek Confederacy. A **confederacy** is a large group made up of many smaller groups. The Creek Confederacy decided which towns would be "red" or "white." Red towns supplied the Creek with leaders of war, while white towns

The village was arranged in clusters of four houses. An extended family lived in each cluster, which included a winter house, a summer house, and two storehouses.

Then & Now

Woodland Indians enjoyed many games, especially a stick and ball game which French travelers called lacrosse. The game of lacrosse that we play today comes from the Iroquois.

provided leaders for the government and leaders skilled in medicine.

Religion was an important part of Creek life. The Creek marked times of the year with religious festivals such as the Green Corn Ceremony. The Creek celebrated the new corn harvest by feasting and taking part in a special dance called the Green Corn Dance.

The Creek planted their fields with corn, beans, and squash. Women tended the fields, made clothing, and wove baskets. Men hunted and made weapons and canoes. Hunting trips could last many months, and women often went along to help clean the skins and dry the meat that the men caught.

The Creek were one of many Woodlands groups who adapted to their environment, using it for food and shelter. In the West, other Native American groups were doing the same.

Lesson Review

1. **Key Vocabulary:** Write a paragraph about the Creek using woodlands, boundary, and confederacy.

2. **Focus:** How were the lives of Woodlands Indians related to their environments?

3. **Focus:** How did the Creek plan their towns and villages?

4. **Critical Thinking: Interpret** Based on their festivals and ceremonies, what kind of attitude do you think Native Americans had toward the land?

5. **Citizenship:** How did the organization of Creek towns benefit all the towns-people?

6. **Geography/Research Activity:** Woodlands Indians may have used hunting grounds as boundaries between groups. What kinds of things have other people used to make boundaries? Choose a country and research this question. Write two paragraphs on what you learn.

★ CITIZENSHIP ★

Making Decisions

Why Join Together Instead of Acting on Your Own?

Did you ever try to change something in your school or community all by yourself? How might other people have helped you? When people work together toward a common goal, change may happen faster and be more effective. That's what the Iroquois discovered many years ago.

Case Study

The Iroquois Great Peace

During the late 1500s, five related Iroquois Nations came together to form what is known as "The Iroquois League." The Five Nations were the Cayuga, the Mohawk, the Oneida, the Onondaga, and the Seneca. They lived in the woods and hills of New York State. The Iroquois called this union "The Great Peace." They did not want any more wars among themselves. They wanted to keep peace.

The Iroquois joined together for their common good. They created a council made up of leaders from each of the five Nations. Iroquois women picked the leaders, and they picked them for life. They chose leaders for their patience, good will, generosity, and ability to act in the best interests of all.

Because of their unity and peace-seeking, the Iroquois prospered for a long time. Their representative form of government also later inspired the American colonists.

The notched staff of the Iroquois Great Council.

Take Action

Now is your chance to form a league and accomplish something that can help many people. Can you, in the process, keep the peace? Here's what you need to do:

1 Make a list of some projects that you think would improve your school or community. Ask yourself: Will these projects be good for many people?

2 Form leagues. Share your list with league members. Vote on the three best ideas. List the pros and cons for each one. Use this list to decide which project you think could work best.

3 Write a formal plan describing the project you want and giving your reasons. Include your ideas for making this project happen.

4 Share your plan with the other leagues. Vote on the best plan. What makes it the best plan? Present the plan to the principal.

5 Discuss the difficulties your group had in deciding on a project and making a plan. Did you keep the peace? Why or why not?

Tips for Making Decisions

- Pick goals that you think can really happen.
- Describe what you want and give reasons.
- When you can't decide, list the pros and cons and use them to help figure out which is the best outcome.
- Pick several solutions to a problem so you have some choices.
- Try to include everyone's ideas.

Research Activity

The Iroquois had no written language. They used wampum belts to express their peace plans. Find out more about wampum belts. What were they made of? What did the colors and shapes mean? Create your own wampum belt design. Write a description of what it means. Hang up the design and description for your classmates to see.

Life in the West

Main Idea Native American groups of the West developed different cultures and patterns of life, according to their resources and environments.

I t is an early spring dawn in the Pacific Northwest around 1500, and the Makah (MAH kah) Indians are ready. A lookout has spotted gray whales a few miles offshore. Quietly, in redwood canoes over 30 feet long, the men paddle out into the ocean and near their prey. The head whaler lets fly a wooden spear with a razor-sharp blade made from a shell. Following his signal, the other whalers throw their spears. One man leaps onto the back of the whale and stabs it. Another man sews the whale's mouth closed with a rope. The hunt is a success! Special songs are sung in celebration. Back on shore, the villagers prepare a feast with the whale meat they caught. In the feast and ceremony that follow, the villagers express their hope that future hunts will be as successful as this one.

The whale was important to Northwest Indians, as you can see from their cave drawings. On their whale hunts they might have used redwood canoes and worn hats like the one below.

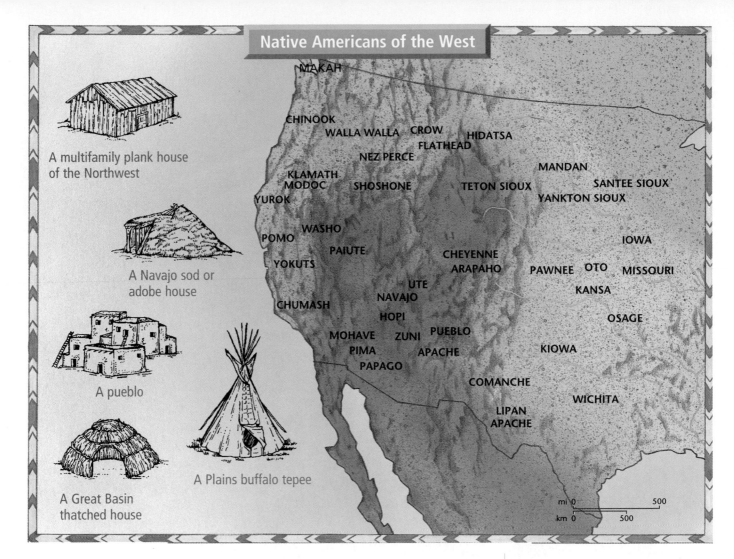

Native Americans of the West

MAKAH

CHINOOK
WALLA WALLA · CROW
FLATHEAD · HIDATSA
NEZ PERCE
KLAMATH · MANDAN
MODOC · SHOSHONE · TETON SIOUX · SANTEE SIOUX
YUROK · YANKTON SIOUX
WASHO
POMO · IOWA
PAIUTE · CHEYENNE
YOKUTS · ARAPAHO · PAWNEE · OTO · MISSOURI
UTE · KANSA
CHUMASH · NAVAJO
HOPI · OSAGE
MOHAVE · ZUNI · PUEBLO
PIMA · APACHE · KIOWA
PAPAGO
COMANCHE · WICHITA
LIPAN APACHE

A multifamily plank house of the Northwest

A Navajo sod or adobe house

A pueblo

A Plains buffalo tepee

A Great Basin thatched house

mi 0 — 500
km 0 — 500

Hunters and Gatherers

Focus *How did the environment shape the lives of Western Indians?*

Around the 1500s, the Makah Indians prospered because the ocean was full of whales they could hunt. Other Native American groups west of the Mississippi River relied on natural resources too. *(See the map above.)* Along the Pacific coast, from southern California to Alaska, natural resources were so plentiful that Native Americans did not need to farm. Why farm when the ocean was full of whales, and the forests were filled with animals, nuts, and berries?

Northwest Indians were very wealthy. In fact, they were so wealthy that they were able to make gift-giving an important part of their lives. They had a celebration for almost any occasion: the building of a house, the birth of a baby, or the naming of a new leader. They called the celebration a *potlatch.*

South and east of the northwest coast is the area known as the Great Basin and Range, which includes today's Nevada. Native

This map shows the location of western Native American groups, and the kind of houses they lived in. **Map Skill:** *How and why do western houses differ from those you saw in Lesson 3?*

What is a potlatch?

It is nighttime. As a daughter of one of the village's chiefs, you are being honored for weaving your first basket. The large, windowless room where you live is crowded and noisy. Everything smells of wood and smoke. You and your brothers and sisters stand off to one side while your parents, wearing colorful robes, give gifts to your neighbors: blankets, shell jewelry, copper ornaments, and more. The more and better gifts given, the more generous the community knows your family to be. A special song is sung to you, perhaps by your mother. Others join in. Afterward there is a feast — canoes full of clams, smoked salmon dipped in oil, whale skin, dried berries — plenty for all. The good spirits are thanked, and the potlatch is over. There will be another one soon.

Native Americans of the Northwest made special masks and feast bowls for the potlatch. This picture shows a Chilkat potlatch celebration of the 1800s.

Americans who lived here spent all their time trying to survive in a land where food was scarce and droughts were common. A **drought** is a long period of time, sometimes several years, with almost no rain. Summers were boiling hot, winters bitter cold. Because the land could not be farmed, people had to move about in search of food such as rabbits, snakes, seeds, and roots.

The Plains Indians living on the grasslands between the Mississippi River and the Rocky Mountains had somewhat easier lives. They followed the trails of animals, carrying little with them: bows and arrows, clothes, and animal-skin tepees, or strong tents. Horses had not yet been introduced into this part of the world, so they had to brave all sorts of weather on foot in search of buffalo.

Farmers of the Southwest

Focus *In what ways did religion affect the everyday lives of Southwest Indians?*

To the Southwest, Native Americans were leading very different lives. Instead of traveling around in search of food, farmers of the Southwest grew corn, beans, and squash. They lived in adobe pueblos much like their ancestors, the Anasazi. For this reason they are called the Pueblo Indians.

Pueblo Indians were deeply religious. Like most Native Americans, the Hopi, one group of the Pueblo, believed that everything — humans, animals, plants, even clouds — had a spirit. They respected the natural world and tried to live in harmony with it. They valued kindness and generosity. They believed that only a wrongful act would make a person sick. To stay well one needed to have a "good heart," which was shown by one's thoughts and actions.

The Hopi year was divided in half. For half of the year the friendly kachina (kuh CHEE nuh) spirits were among the villagers. Then, for the other half, the kachinas returned to their "World Below." Hopi religion centered around ceremonies giving praise and thanks to the kachinas.

In such ceremonies the Hopi asked the kachinas to carry messages and prayers to the gods. Masked and costumed Hopi men followed a "road" of sacred cornmeal sprinkled by priests, and danced to the sound of rattles and drums for rain and other blessings. Clothed kachina dolls — carved and painted — were given to children. These dolls were not toys, but were kept in special places inside homes to treasure as small parts of the spirits themselves.

Just as their ancestors the Anasazi had before them, the Pueblo used kivas as the center of religious activities. They reached the round, underground kivas by a ladder hanging from the wooden roof. Men used the kiva as a meeting place to discuss government

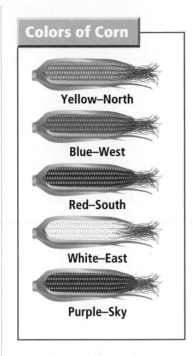

Colors of Corn

Yellow–North

Blue–West

Red–South

White–East

Purple–Sky

The Hopi ate corn at most meals. They grew corn of five different colors, and each color had a special meaning for them.

An eagle kachina dances at a Hopi celebration, which is practiced today just as it has been for hundreds of years. **National Heritage:** *Can you think of other celebrations that people have practiced for years?*

Pueblo men met inside the kiva to make community decisions and for religious ceremonies.

Pueblo potters decorated their pieces with paint that they made from local plants.

and other important matters. People gathered in the kiva for special religious ceremonies.

The Navajo (NAHV uh hoh) and Apache (uh PACH ee) also lived in the Southwest around 1500. These two groups also had many religious traditions. The Navajo and Apache depended on the spirits to help them in the events of everyday life — hunting or the birth of a child.

Navajo and Apache believed that both good and evil lay within each person, and that after death, evil became a dangerous ghost you had to watch out for. The Navajo believed that if the community sang a "healing song," they could cure a sick person. The Apache made paintings out of sand which they thought could help cure illness, because of a connection they felt with the earth.

Throughout history, people have had to adapt to their environment and, in some cases, shape it to their own ends. What all these

While men met inside the kiva, women ground up corn, baked bread, and made pottery.

Spanish explorers encountered adobe villages like this one when they arrived in the Americas around 1500.

Native American groups shared was an everlasting bond with nature and the world. As a Navajo sacred song tells us:

> **"Y**ou see, I stand in good relation to the earth. You see, I stand in good relation to the gods. You see, I stand in good relation to all that is beautiful. **"**

Lesson Review

1 Key Vocabulary: Write a sentence about the Southwest using drought.

2 Focus: How did the environment shape the lives of Western Indians?

3 Focus: In what ways did religion affect the everyday lives of Southwest Indians?

4 Critical Thinking: Sequence What economic conditions allowed Northwest Indians to have celebrations such as the potlatch?

5 Geography: Why do you think wood-carving became an important craft in the Northwest but not in the Southwest?

6 Citizenship/Research Activity: Look at the maps of Native American groups on pages 53 and 59. Choose a Native American group that lives in your area. Where and how do they live? What festivals do they celebrate? Write two paragraphs on what you learn.

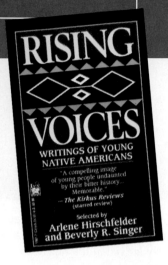

RISING VOICES

Writings of Young Native Americans
Selected by Arlene Hirschfelder and Beverly R. Singer

Native Americans have always had a strong relationship with nature. The land that early colonists found harsh and dangerous had been the home of Native Americans for countless years. They understood that if it is respected, the land will always renew itself.

The two poems below were written recently by teenagers. They express respect for nature and pride in the writers' Native American identity.

This Chippewa beaded bandolier *(above)* has pockets and was worn across the chest.

We Are the Many

We are the people of long ago.
We are the blue-green water
    that runs swiftly in the creek.
We are the flowers which blossom
    in the spring.
We are the rain that comes pouring
    down in the canyon.
We are the lightning
    that streaks in the sky.
We are the cottonwood trees
    that loom high into the air.
We are the gentle breeze of the many winds.
We are the blood of the mighty warriors.
We are the ancestors of the Havasupai children.

Ingrid Putesoy
Havasupai tribe

The rock painting above is on the Tobacopa Trail on the Havasupai Reservation.

loom

to appear as a massive or distinct image

The photograph on the left shows a winter scene in Minnesota, the home of the Chippewa.

As I Walk This Road

As I walk this road I hear
the laughter of the new season
coming forth.

I see the green as it makes its way
through the white snowy blanket
as it greets the morning sun.

The sun is gone now
and soon will appear again
to see the new colors of a new season
when the sap will flow.

As the last of the rice is put away,
and as we give thanks for a good harvest
it is time to cover our mother
with a white blanket
so she may rest.

Ricardo Rojas
Chippewa tribe

Response Activities

1. **Interpret** In the last stanza of the poem by Ricardo Rojas, who is "our mother?" How does this stanza explain the author's feelings about nature?

2. **Expressive: Write a Poem** How do you feel about the natural world around you? What do different seasons make you think of? What is special about the area where you live? Write a poem that expresses your feelings about nature.

3. **Cultures: Research Native Americans** Divide into small groups and research a Native American nation in your region. Use dance, poetry, art, or song to present your research.

Chapter Review

Chapter Review Timeline

900
Mayan cities begin to empty

| 400 | 600 | 800 | 1000 | 1200 |

600
Teotihuacán
flourishes

1170
Aztecs arrive in the
Valley of Mexico

Summarizing the Main Idea

1 Copy the chart below and fill it in for each of the cultures you have studied.

Who	How They Provided for Themselves	Achievement
Anasazi	*grew crops by using irrigation*	*Built cliff dwellings*

Vocabulary

2 Using four or more of the words below, write a journal entry describing a day in the life of one of the cultures you have studied.

archaeology (p. 36)
glacier (p. 36)
migrate (p. 36)
agriculture (p. 39)
surplus (p. 40)

civilization (p. 41)
Mesoamerica (p. 41)
empire (p. 43)
pueblo (p. 44)
woodlands (p. 52)

boundary (p. 53)
confederacy (p. 54)
drought (p. 60)

Reviewing the Facts

3 How did early peoples adapt to their changing environments?

4 What were some of the key achievements of the Maya and the Aztecs?

5 How did the Aztecs feel about war?

6 How were the lives of the Native American groups along the east coast different from those of the Pacific Northwest?

7 How did the Creek use their surroundings for food and shelter?

8 How were the Pueblo, Navajo, and Apache similar?

Skill Review: Using B.C., A.D., and Centuries

9 In what century did the Anasazi begin settling in cliff dwellings?

10 How many years ago did corn cultivation begin?

Geography Skills

11 Think about the different ways the lives of the first peoples were affected by the environment in which they lived. Which culture do you think had the easiest time working with its environment? Which culture had the most difficult time? Explain your answers.

12 Prepare a postcard about one of the civilizations you have studied. Show the type of environment the people lived in.

Critical Thinking

13 **Comparing Then and Now** Select an ancient civilization. Compare how people provided their basic needs (food, shelter) to how they are provided for you today.

14 **Drawing Conclusions** What are some of the reasons that an ancient city might have been abandoned?

Writing: Citizenship and Economics

15 **Citizenship** Do you think archaeologists have the right to remove the artifacts they find? What kind of guidelines should be set up to control the kinds of objects archaeologists take and what they do with them?

16 **Economics** Think about the natural resources the land provided for many of the ancient civilizations. Make a chart that shows how these resources were used.

Activities

Culture/Research Activity
Find out more about one of the civilizations you have studied. Write a list of objects to include in a time capsule to help others learn about the civilization. Explain why you chose these items.

History/Math Activity
Illustrate a timeline that reflects what you have learned about different ancient civilizations.

Internet Option

Check the **Internet Social Studies Center** for ideas on how to extend your theme project beyond your classroom.

THEME PROJECT CHECK-IN

Now you have learned more about the cultures of the first Americans. What important things would you like to tell other Native Americans about your culture?
- In what ways is your group unique?
- What special traditions do you have? Why do you have them?
- What is your region like? What are some of its landforms and natural resources?
- What things does your group value? Do you make objects from the things you value?

2 Different Worlds Meet

"Along this track of pathless ocean it is my intention to steer."

Christopher Columbus

· THEME ·

Exploration and Encounter

" The early explorers must have been really scared and uneasy as they traveled the vast sea. What brave and courageous people they were!"

Leigh Ammon, Fifth Grade
Norwell, MA

If you take a risk to learn something new, you can never be sure what you'll find. European explorers in the 1500s and 1600s learned this lesson well. While searching for trade routes to Asia — and the riches that would follow — they stumbled across the Americas. Here, they found civilizations they never knew existed. The meetings between Europeans and Native Americans changed the lives of both. These encounters would also change the world forever.

 Theme Project

Follow an Explorer

Follow in the footsteps of an explorer. Choose one of the routes taken by an explorer in this unit. What would you see if you traveled that route?

- Draw a map showing your route.
- Design clothes you will need for the climate.
- Write a story about the people who live on the route.
- Make a collage of the kinds of transportation you need.

RESEARCH: Look up facts about the people and the climate along the route you are traveling.

◀ A replica of Columbus's ship *Niña,* off the African coast

2

WHEN & WHERE
ATLAS

Long before Columbus, the people of Europe, Africa, and Asia traded with each other. As you can see, centers of population and trade existed throughout the world in the 1400s. A few bold adventurers set sail into uncharted seas to find a quicker, safer trade route to Asia. Instead, they landed in the Americas and changed the course of history.

In this unit, you will read about the continents of Africa, Asia, and Europe, and the growing connections among them. You will also learn about the first explorers to the Americas, and their encounters with native peoples there. Finally, you will learn about the European settlement of North America.

Unit 2 Chapters

150°W

HUDSON BAY

NORTH AMERICA

HURONS
IROQUOIS
Jamestown ●

PUEBLO

30°N

Tropic of Cancer

AZTEC
Tenochtitlán ●

TAINOS
CUBA
HISPANIOLA

PACIFIC

0°

OCEAN

SOUTH AMERICA

30°S

N
W ✥ E
S

60°S

150°W   120°W   90°W

Unit Timeline

700	900	1100

Viking Carving

People feared the sight of a Viking ship. Find out why. *Chapter 3, Lesson 1*

Montezuma and Cortés 1521

The arrival of one of these men meant the end of the Aztec Empire. *Chapter 4, Lesson 2*

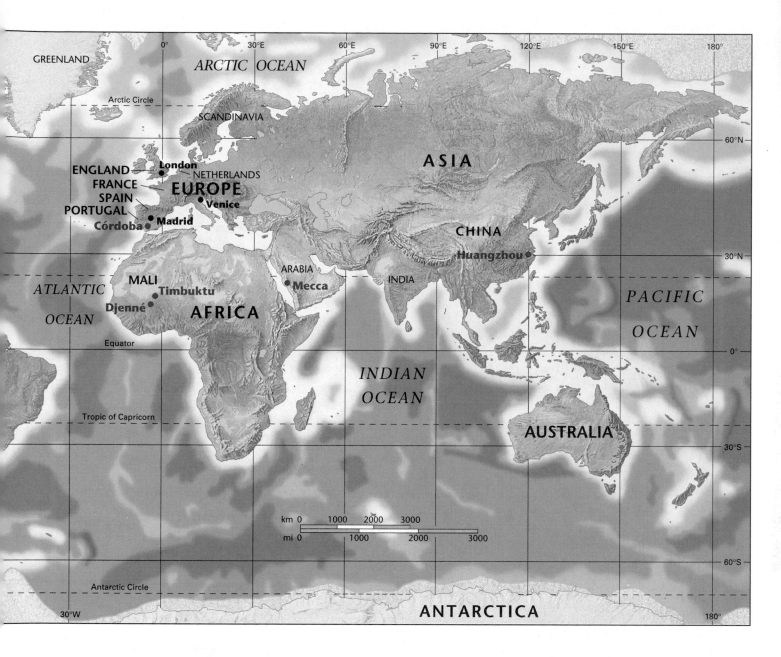

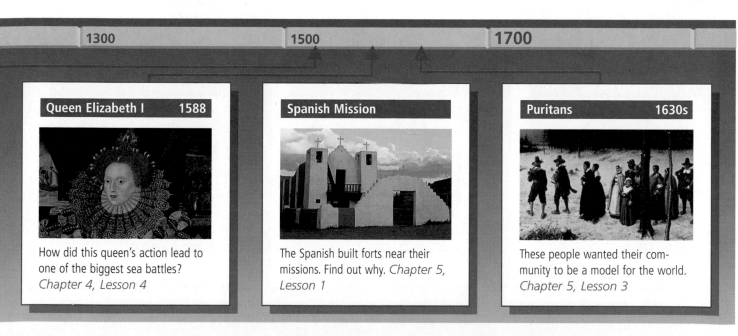

1300		1500		1700

Queen Elizabeth I   1588

How did this queen's action lead to one of the biggest sea battles? *Chapter 4, Lesson 4*

Spanish Mission

The Spanish built forts near their missions. Find out why. *Chapter 5, Lesson 1*

Puritans   1630s

These people wanted their community to be a model for the world. *Chapter 5, Lesson 3*

CHAPTER 3
The World of Africa, Asia, & Europe

Chapter Preview: *People, Places, and Events*

900	1000	1100

Viking Carved Head   900s

When did the Vikings come to North America? *Lesson 1, Page 75*

Djenné

Would you trade gold for salt? Read about people who did. *Lesson 1, Page 77*

Mansa Musa

How did the cities in West Africa become rich in trade? *Lesson 1, Page 78*

Trading Across Oceans and Continents

Main Idea Growing trade in Africa, Asia, and Europe improved people's lives and brought them into contact with new ideas.

In terrible weather, across hot deserts, and through dangerous lands, people traveled thousands of miles to exchange goods. Why did they do that?

Long before Europeans arrived in North and South America, the many peoples of Africa, Asia, and Europe were interested in trade and contact. They wanted to create a better life for themselves and gain new wealth. These travelers were also curious about other people, their possessions, and their way of life. This contact and exchange among the people of Africa, Asia, and Europe led to changing ideas about the world and fueled the desire to learn even more about it.

Key Vocabulary
- saga
- Islam
- pilgrimage
- mosque

Key Events
- **about 1000** Leif Ericson sails to North America
- **1324** Mansa Musa travels to Mecca

◀ Arab sailors traveling in a dhow, a type of ship that still exists today.

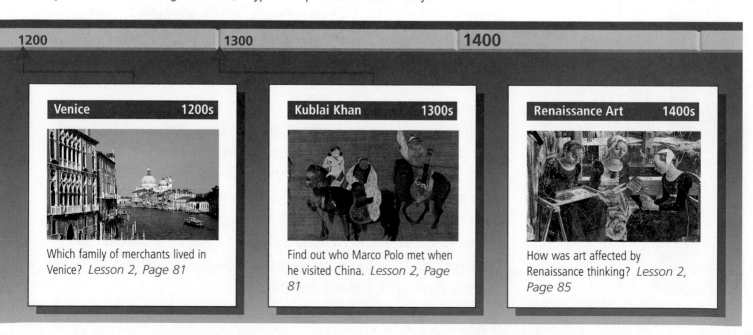

| 1200 | 1300 | 1400 |

Venice 1200s

Which family of merchants lived in Venice? *Lesson 2, Page 81*

Kublai Khan 1300s

Find out who Marco Polo met when he visited China. *Lesson 2, Page 81*

Renaissance Art 1400s

How was art affected by Renaissance thinking? *Lesson 2, Page 85*

Vikings traded and raided throughout Europe, the Middle East, and modern-day Russia. They even made their way across the Atlantic Ocean to North America. **Map Skill:** *How did landing on Iceland and Greenland help make it possible for the Vikings to sail to North America?*

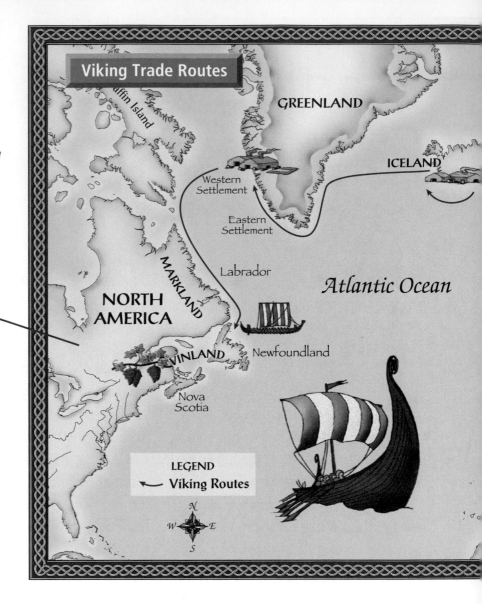

Viking Trade Routes

GREENLAND

Baffin Island

ICELAND

Western Settlement

Eastern Settlement

Labrador

Atlantic Ocean

MARKLAND

NORTH AMERICA

VINLAND

Newfoundland

Nova Scotia

LEGEND
← Viking Routes

N W E S

North America

A Viking settlement was unearthed in Newfoundland, Canada, in 1961. This discovery was important because until that time, no one knew for certain whether Vikings had traveled to North America.

This carved lion's head was found on a post in a burial mound in the city of Oseberg, Norway. The Vikings were skilled wood-carvers and decorated many ordinary objects.

Vikings Cross the Atlantic

| Focus | *How did the Vikings come to North America?*

The Vikings were a seafaring people from northern Europe who traded and conquered throughout Europe, the Middle East, and even across the Atlantic Ocean to Canada in North America. *(See the map above.)*

How did Vikings end up in Canada? The answer can be found in the ancient stories of Iceland, called **sagas.** Iceland is an island nation located in the North Atlantic, midway between Greenland and Europe. The sagas describe how Vikings came to Iceland about A.D. 870. One hundred years later, the sagas say, Vikings sailed farther west to Greenland to hunt walrus. Walrus were valued for their ivory tusks. Vikings built small towns in Greenland and set up an ivory trade with Iceland and Europe.

Europe

Vikings were originally from Scandinavia, which includes the European countries of Norway, Sweden, and Denmark. People throughout Europe and beyond feared the Viking warriors.

The Middle East

Vikings traded items throughout the Middle East, exchanging goods with Arab traders along the way. Although there is no evidence that Vikings traveled as far as China, they did trade for Chinese goods through the Arab people that they met.

From Greenland, a group of Vikings led by Leif Ericson sailed even farther west, landing on the coast of Canada. The Vikings later decided to start a settlement there. According to one saga,

> "There was no lack of salmon there in river or lake. . . . The nature of the land was so choice, it seemed to them that none of the cattle would require fodder [food] for the winter. . . ."

At first, the Vikings did not see any other people there. But one summer a group of Native Americans visited them. Soon afterward, a Viking and a Native American got into a fight, and war broke out between the two peoples. The Vikings left several months later in their ships and went back to Greenland.

For many years historians argued over whether Vikings really reached North America as the sagas say. But in 1961, archaeologists discovered ruins in L'Anse aux Meadows (lans oh meh DOHZ), or Meadows Cove, Newfoundland. They unearthed some pieces of iron and part of a Viking-style spinning wheel. Finally they had real proof that the Vikings had been in North America. Some historians believe that this was the first meeting between Native Americans and Europeans.

The Fabulous City of Timbuktu

Focus *How did trade lead to the rise of Timbuktu?*

While the Vikings were making history in the North Atlantic, other people were doing the same in West Africa. West Africans traded across vast stretches of sand, not water.

West Africans live on the edge of the earth's largest desert — the Sahara. It measures up to 1,200 miles from north to south and about 3,000 miles from east to west. As early as A.D. 900, regular trade developed across the Sahara. The city of Timbuktu (TIHM buhk TOO), located in Mali, was at the center of this trade.

West Africa was rich in gold, but it lacked salt. North Africa had plenty of salt, which came from salt mines in the desert. Salt was so important for preserving food that West Africans gladly traded gold for North African salt.

Timbuktu became a great center of trade and learning under Mansa Musa. The city had two mosques and a large central market. By the 1500s, the population reached about 50,000.
Economics: *Which parts of the city were important to traders?*

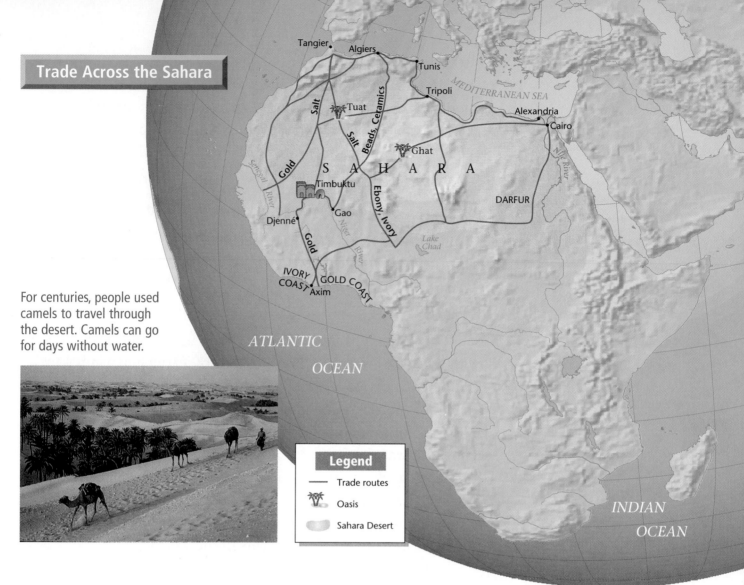

Trade Across the Sahara

Legend
— Trade routes
🌴 Oasis
▮ Sahara Desert

For centuries, people used camels to travel through the desert. Camels can go for days without water.

During the 700s, North Africa was conquered by the Muslims of the Middle East. Muslims practice a religion called **Islam,** a belief in one God based on the teachings of the prophet Muhammad. When Muslim traders brought their religion to West Africa, many people there became followers of Islam. One of these people was the West African leader Mansa Musa (MAHN sah MOO sah), who ruled the kingdom of Mali beginning in the year 1307.

As Timbuktu grew in size and importance, the number of trade routes increased as well. To get to Timbuktu, travelers had to cross the vast Sahara from the Middle East and North Africa. It was a very difficult journey, but one people were willing to make for the variety of trade items that could be exchanged in Timbuktu. **Map Skill:** *What cities might a trader pass through to get from Timbuktu to Tunis?*

The World of Africa, Asia, & Europe **77**

In 1324 Mansa Musa made a long journey to the Muslims' holy city of Mecca in Arabia. A journey to a sacred place is called a **pilgrimage**. Mansa Musa traveled with as many as 60,000 people and 100 camels loaded with bags of gold dust to pay for his travel expenses. One Egyptian wrote of Mansa Musa's visit to Cairo,

> " . . . Mansa Musa spread upon Cairo the flood of his generosity: there was no person, officer of the court, or holder of any office . . . who did not receive a sum of gold from him. "

When Mansa Musa returned to Mali, he brought Arab scholars with him. They took part in the centers of learning in Timbuktu and other cities like Djenné (jen AY). The Arab scholars participated in an important trade in books. They also built large, beautiful **mosques**, Muslim houses of worship. For the next 200 years, Timbuktu was rich in gold, learning, and the arts.

As people began to exchange goods, they also exchanged knowledge and ideas. In years to come, these exchanges would push people to travel even farther, eventually linking together knowledge and ideas from all of the continents of the world.

Lesson Review

1000	1150	1300	

about 1000
Leif Ericson sails to North America

1324
Mansa Musa travels to Mecca

1 Key Vocabulary: Write a sentence using saga, Islam, mosque.

2 Focus: How did the Vikings come to North America?

3 Focus: How did trade lead to the rise of Timbuktu?

4 Critical Thinking: Compare and Contrast What did Leif Ericson and Mansa Musa have in common?

5 Theme: Exploration and Encounter How is trade between different groups important to the growth of cities?

6 Geography/History Activity: Using the map on p. 74, determine which cities a Viking trader might pass through to get from Constantinople to Newfoundland.

Gathering Information in the Media

Stay Informed

In Mansa Musa's time, trade was an important way for people to learn what was happening in other parts of the world. Today, we have many different types of media to provide information. These include television, radio, newspapers, and even computer on-line services. If you know how to use the media to gather information wisely, you may find yourself not just watching the news, but getting involved in issues that matter to you.

1 Here's How

- Use the media to find out about events happening in the United States or in other countries. Pick an event or subject that interests you. Follow your subject in at least two kinds of media, for example, radio and television.

- Make a note of important facts, ideas, and opinions about your subject. Keep copies of newspaper and magazine articles to use later.

- Question what you hear, read, and see. Identify facts and opinions and develop informed opinions about issues.

- Gather more information. Look for other sources, such as articles that were published earlier, to learn more about news topics.

2 Think It Through

How can you use the information you gather from the media to become an informed citizen?

3 Use It

1. Choose an article about a world event in today's newspaper. Read it carefully, grouping information into who, what, when, and where categories.

2. Write a paragraph summarizing what you've learned.

VOLUME 248 • NUMBER 145

80 pages
50 cents

The Bost

WEDNESDAY, NO

Bosnia factions

Trade Brings New Ideas

Main Idea Trade and learning flourished in China and southern Europe in the 1300s and 1400s.

Key Vocabulary

merchant
emperor
astrolabe
Arabic numerals
Renaissance

Key Events

1200s Europeans learn about Aristotle from the Muslims

1295 The Polos return from China

early 1300s The Renaissance begins

Legend has it that Niccolò, Maffeo, and Marco Polo held a banquet to celebrate their return to the Italian city of Venice. After all the guests had gathered, the three men held up the coats they had traveled in. Suddenly they slashed the linings of their coats with knives, and out spilled a stream of jewels across the table.

When the three men had knocked on the door of their family home in 1295, no one believed that they were the Polos. They had been told that those men were dead. The Polos had left on a journey to China 24 years before and had not been seen since. Eventually, Niccolò, Maffeo, and Marco did persuade their family that they were the missing relatives. But not until the family saw the jewels that night at dinner did anyone believe that the three men really had been to China.

Marco Polo leaves Venice on a journey to China with his father and uncle.

Venice grew rich from trade. **Economics:** *What evidence of Venice's wealth can be seen in this picture?*

People in the 1200s traveled in Venice by boat on canals. You can still travel this way through Venice today.

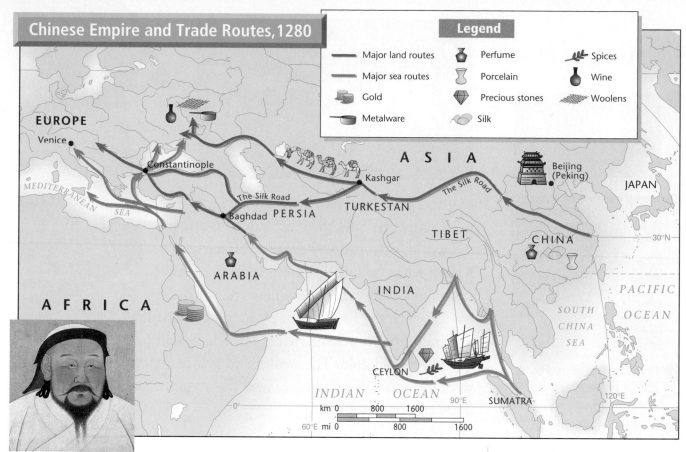

Legend

—— Major land routes	Perfume	Spices
—— Major sea routes	Porcelain	Wine
Gold	Precious stones	Woolens
Metalware	Silk	

The Wonders of China

Focus *What did Marco Polo see while he lived in China?*

Marco Polo was born in Venice in 1254. Venice was a lively trading city that grew more and more powerful as trade increased and people became wealthier. Marco's father Niccolò and his uncle Maffeo were **merchants,** people who make their living by buying and selling goods. When Marco was six years old, Niccolò and Maffeo left on a trading journey to Asia. Eventually, they reached China and met the great Kublai Khan (KOO bly KAHN), the emperor of China. An **emperor** is the ruler of an empire.

When Marco Polo was 17 years old, his father and his uncle made their second trip to China. Marco may have been trained as a merchant, possibly learning how to judge the quality of goods and how to load cargo onto a ship. Marco's father and uncle probably thought he could help them, because they took him with them on their long journey back to China.

When the Polos arrived in China again, they were welcomed into the emperor's court. There they learned a great deal about China. In many ways China was the most advanced society in the world. The Chinese used water power

The map above shows trade routes to and from the Chinese empire in the mid-1200s. On the left is a picture of Kublai Khan, ruler of the Chinese empire at that time. **Map Skill:** *Why was it so difficult to reach China by land from Europe?*

Chinese spices

81

Silk Making in China

1. The silkworm spins a cocoon from a single strand of silky protein.
2. Workers unwind the silk cocoons by soaking them in water.
3. Chinese women inspect a piece of woven silk.
4. Silk is still considered one of the finest fabrics today.

to grind grain, and had invented a way to print on paper. Silk, the most valued fabric in the world, was made by expert craftspeople. Kublai Khan had mail stations built to ease communication in the many lands he ruled. New trade, which the Khan encouraged, developed along the empire's great system of roads. The Khan built palaces of marble, silver, and gold. The wealth and prosperity of China, along with its industry and science, won the admiration of the world and drew travelers to China.

Marco Polo Takes a New Job

Kublai Khan brought men from different parts of the world into his service. He was very impressed by Marco Polo and offered the young man a job. Marco was to travel to distant parts of China and report on what was happening there. That job gave Marco Polo a chance to learn more about China than any European had before.

One thing that surprised Marco Polo was the size of China's

Achievements in China and Europe

Moveable Type
The earliest moveable type for printing was invented in China between AD 1041 and AD 1048. Each Character was made on a block of clay. In the 1200s, the clay blocks were replaced by wooden ones.

700	800	900	1000

Viking necklace
Many of the items on this necklace were gained through trade. Vikings traveled throughout Europe and beyond. There are items on this necklace from England and Russia.

Towers
Starting in about AD 1000, Europeans built slender towers that were up to 100 feet tall. They built them to hide church treasures during Viking attacks. The only entrance was up high and had a ladder that could be pulled inside.

cities. By the time of Marco Polo's visit, China's capital, Hangzhou (HONG JOH), had a population of about one million, about 10 times the number of people living in Venice at that time. Even more surprising were the discoveries and inventions the Chinese people had made. There was a black stone that burned like wood but produced far more heat. It was the first time a European had seen coal. There were printed slips of paper used in trade — paper money. Most amazing of all was an exploding dust — gunpowder. Chinese rulers spent money to develop new inventions, which eventually benefited many of China's people.

When he returned to Venice, Marco Polo wrote a book about his travels called *The Description of the World*. In the book he described much of what he saw in China. But people in Europe found it difficult to believe that the stories he told were true. As other travelers visited China, however, Europeans came to recognize the wonders of that distant land. Interest in China grew, and Europeans soon began to use many Chinese inventions.

Europe's Center of Learning

Focus *How did new ideas affect life in Europe in the 1300s?*

As you have read, Muslim armies swept over North Africa in the 700s. Muslim armies also conquered southern Spain. Spain's new rulers set up their capital in Córdoba (KAWR doh buh). For the

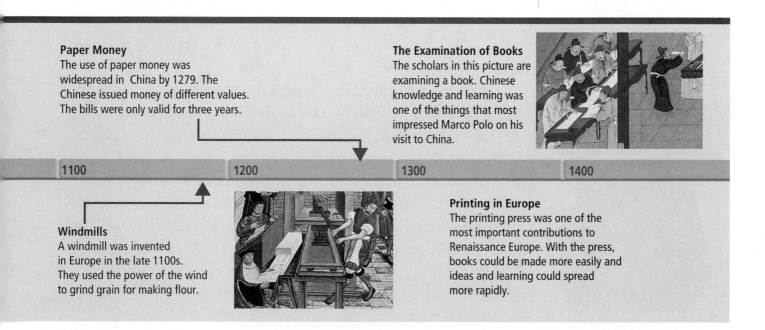

Paper Money
The use of paper money was widespread in China by 1279. The Chinese issued money of different values. The bills were only valid for three years.

The Examination of Books
The scholars in this picture are examining a book. Chinese knowledge and learning was one of the things that most impressed Marco Polo on his visit to China.

1100   1200   1300   1400

Windmills
A windmill was invented in Europe in the late 1100s. They used the power of the wind to grind grain for making flour.

Printing in Europe
The printing press was one of the most important contributions to Renaissance Europe. With the press, books could be made more easily and ideas and learning could spread more rapidly.

Renaissance Europe was divided into kingdoms and powerful cities. **Map Skill:** *Why was it easy for Renaissance ideas to spread quickly through Europe?*

A view of Córdoba today.

Legend

— Political boundary

This instrument was made in 1511 in Verona, Italy. It is a *lira da braccio*, a popular instrument during the Renaissance.

next 500 years, Córdoba's trade with the Islamic world made it Europe's largest city and its greatest center of learning. At a time when libraries elsewhere in Europe had only a few hundred books, Córdoba's library had about 400,000 volumes. Córdoba contained one of Islam's largest mosques, and unlike other European cities of its time, its streets were paved. The homes in Córdoba were graced with gardens and fountains.

The Muslims studied the writings of ancient Greece, Persia, and Arabia and then built on that foundation of knowledge. For example, they rediscovered the **astrolabe,** a device invented by the Greeks to measure the altitude of the sun and stars.

Muslims also made important discoveries of their own. They developed the system of algebra that is the basis for modern mathematics. Muslim doctors made great progress in early medicine. The Muslims also introduced **Arabic numerals,** the way of writing numbers that is still used in Western countries today. Their poetry, which they considered their most important art form, drew on traditions that were thousands of years old.

A Rebirth of Art and Learning

Muslim scholars based many of their ideas on the writings of Aristotle (AR ih staht l). Aristotle was a Greek thinker who believed that the world could be understood through logical thought. When Christian scholars brought Aristotle's books to the University of Paris, the church's officials forbade them. The officials said that knowledge could come only through religious faith.

In the late 1200s, a Christian monk named Thomas Aquinas (uh KWY nuhs) defended Aristotle. He said there was no conflict between Aristotle's ideas and Christian beliefs. Instead, Aquinas said, reason and faith should work together. To many people of the time, this was a new idea.

Europe's rediscovery of Aristotle and other Greek and Roman writers produced a great rebirth of learning and creativity that came to be called the **Renaissance** (rehn ih SAHNS). Poets, architects, and painters all looked to ancient Greece and Rome for inspiration. They produced literature, buildings, and works of art that are still treasured today.

Europeans also began putting ancient science and Muslim inventions to work. They used the astrolabe for navigation, which led to a great era of exploration. Trade with China had shown Europeans that there was a whole other world beyond their own. Europeans now had a way to explore it.

Michelangelo

Michelangelo di Lodovico Buonarroti Simoni is considered the greatest artist of his time. He could paint, sculpt, draw, and even write poetry. Michelangelo's most famous work is the statue *David*, which he made for the cathedral in the city of Florence, Italy. He carved *David* from a large block of marble. It took him over three years to complete this work!

Lesson Review

1200	1250	1300

1200s
Europeans learn about Aristotle from the Muslims

1295
The Polos return from China

early 1300s
The Renaissance begins

① **Key Vocabulary:** Write about Europe in the 1300s using **merchant** and **Renaissance**.

② **Focus:** What did Marco Polo see while he lived in China?

③ **Focus:** How did new ideas affect life in Europe in the 1300s?

④ **Critical Thinking: Interpret** Why might people in Venice have had trouble believing Marco Polo's descriptions of China?

⑤ **Geography:** Look at the maps of China and of Europe in this lesson. Could the Polos have made their trip from Venice to China all on land? What countries would they have traveled through?

⑥ **Citizenship/Art Activity:** During the Renaissance, people took pride in making their cities beautiful. Make a poster calling for ways to make your community more beautiful.

Chapter Review

Chapter Review Timeline

1295
The Polos return from China

1000	1100	1200	1300

About 1000
Leif Erickson sails
to North America

1200s
Europeans learn about
Aristotle from the Muslims

Early 1300s
The Renaissance
begins

1324
Mansa Musa
travels to Mecca

Summarizing the Main Idea

1 Copy and complete the chart below, indicating reasons for the growth of each trade center.

Trade Center	Africa	Asia	Europe
Reasons for Growth			

Vocabulary

2 Using at least three of the following terms, write a paragraph describing what you might see in one of the trade centers of Africa, Asia, or Europe.

saga (p. 74)   mosque (p. 78)   Renaissance (p. 84)
Islam (p. 77)   merchant (p. 81)

Reviewing the Facts

3 Who were the Vikings?

4 What did Mansa Musa accomplish?

5 Why did the Polo family travel to China?

6 How did living in China change Marco Polo's life?

7 What did the Muslims accomplish in Europe?

8 How did the Renaissance begin?

9 Select an article from your local newspaper. What event does it describe? Explain how it answers these other questions: Who? When? Where? Why?

10 Write a short script for a television show describing a recent newsworthy event in your community.

Geography Skills

11 Locate your state on a world map. Using the map scale, find out how far it is from your state to Timbuktu, China, or Córdoba. Use the most direct route.

12 Choose one of the great trade centers. Design a travel brochure that tells about the different adventures a person could have while traveling there.

Critical Thinking

13 **Cause and Effect** Why did trade centers also become centers of learning?

14 **Interpret** What advantages might the Renaissance have held for the people who experienced it?

Writing: Citizenship and Culture

15 **Citizenship** Research goods that are unique to your region. Then find out about items that your community cannot make for itself. Write a proposal for trade between your region and another.

16 **Culture** You are Marco Polo experiencing the wonders of China. Write a brief description of what you might see.

Activities

Cultures/Research Activity
Learn about a poet, architect, or artist who worked during the Renaissance. Locate copies or illustrations of their art and write a paragraph describing what you think about it.

History/Arts Activity
Illustrate a street scene of a flourishing trade center. What are people doing? Write captions describing the activities you have drawn.

Internet Option

Check the **Internet Social Studies Center** for ideas on how to extend your theme project beyond your classroom.

THEME PROJECT CHECK-IN

Use what you have read about African, Asian, and European travelers to begin your theme project. Start by asking the following questions about explorers:
• Why did people want to explore the world?
• How did they travel? What kinds of transportation did they use?
• What kinds of things did explorers bring with them?
• How did their travels change themselves and others?

Explorers Come to the Americas

Chapter Preview: *People, Places, and Events*

1400	1450	1500

Christopher Columbus 1492

How did Columbus find himself in the Americas? *Lesson 1, Page 93*

Bartolomé de las Casas 1511

Las Casas was upset with the Spanish settlers in the Americas. Find out why. *Lesson 2, Page 105*

Montezuma

What empire did Montezuma rule over? *Lesson 2, Page 102*

Searching for Trade Routes

Main Idea During the 1400s, Europeans came to the Americas in search of trade and land.

Did a beast with claws really rise out of the ocean only to disappear slowly back into the dark water? A sailor in the 1400s might truly have believed that he saw such a sea monster. To him, the dangerous seas were full of monsters, mermaids, and storms. This same water, though, was a route to trade and riches.

It was trade that pushed European sailors to travel farther and farther from home. There was a great deal of the world that they knew nothing about. They did not know that the Americas existed or that people lived there. The huge distance of the Atlantic Ocean kept these separate "worlds" apart. In the 1490s, the people of Europe and the Americas met. It happened by accident, really. But once it happened, the world would never be the same.

◀ Spanish conquistadors came to the Americas looking for riches and new land.

Key Vocabulary

navigation

enslaved

slavery

circumnavigate

Key Events

1434 Prince Henry's first explorer sails beyond Cape Bojador

1492 Columbus lands at San Salvador

1522 Magellan's expedition completes circling the world

1550	1600	1650	

Cutting Sugar Cane

Find out why Africans were enslaved and brought to the Americas. *Lesson 3, Page 106*

The Columbian Exchange

Why were pigs shipped across the Atlantic Ocean? *Lesson 3, Page 109*

Huron Box 1631

Who did French explorers meet when they arrived in North America? *Lesson 4, Page 114*

Explorers from Portugal

Focus *How did Portuguese sailors reach Asia?*

In 1415 Prince Henry of Portugal was in Africa. There, he saw gold and silver from southern Africa and other items like silk that came from Asia. Prince Henry wanted those riches for Portugal.

Prince Henry believed the best way to reach southern Africa was by sea. When he returned home, he set up a school of **navigation,** the science of plotting and controlling the course of a ship. He invited experts from Europe, Africa, and the Middle East to work there.

Several inventions made navigation safer and more accurate than before. One invention was the compass, which helped sailors find their way when out of sight of land. A compass is a magnet that always points north. By showing where north is, a compass helps sailors keep their ship going in the right direction. Using these new compasses, Portuguese ships set off to explore the coast of Africa. Their voyages were the start of what we now call the Age of Exploration. *(Find out more about navigational instruments below.)*

Starting in 1419, Henry sent 15 voyages south. Each one hoped to get past Cape Bojador (boh huh DOHR) on the west coast of Africa. All 15 failed to achieve this goal. They turned back in fear.

· Tell Me More ·

Using Navigational Instruments

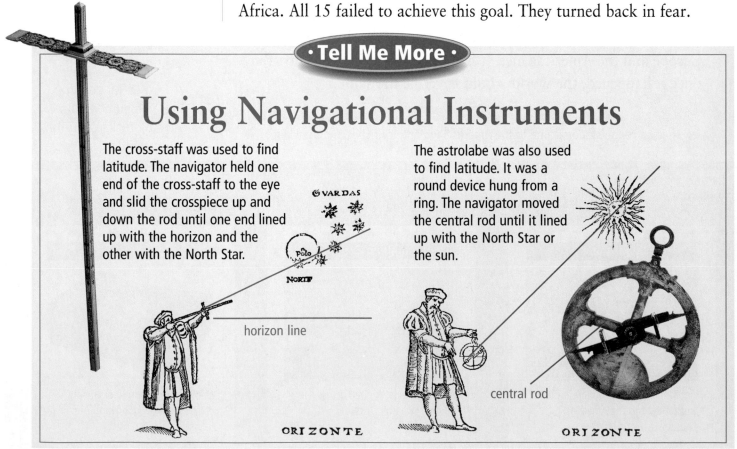

The cross-staff was used to find latitude. The navigator held one end of the cross-staff to the eye and slid the crosspiece up and down the rod until one end lined up with the horizon and the other with the North Star.

The astrolabe was also used to find latitude. It was a round device hung from a ring. The navigator moved the central rod until it lined up with the North Star or the sun.

horizon line

central rod

ORIZONTE

ORIZONTE

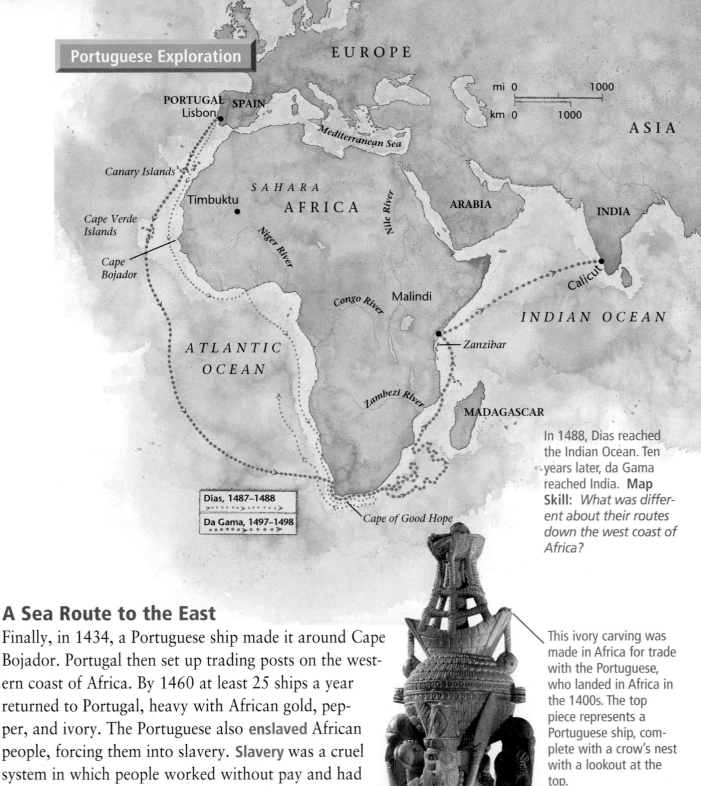

Portuguese Exploration

EUROPE

PORTUGAL SPAIN
Lisbon

Mediterranean Sea

ASIA

mi 0   1000
km 0   1000

Canary Islands

SAHARA
Timbuktu   AFRICA   ARABIA   INDIA

Niger River   *Nile River*

Cape Verde
Islands

Cape
Bojador   Calicut

Congo River   Malindi   INDIAN OCEAN

ATLANTIC
OCEAN   Zanzibar

Zambezi River

MADAGASCAR

Dias, 1487–1488
Da Gama, 1497–1498

Cape of Good Hope

In 1488, Dias reached the Indian Ocean. Ten years later, da Gama reached India. **Map Skill:** *What was different about their routes down the west coast of Africa?*

A Sea Route to the East

Finally, in 1434, a Portuguese ship made it around Cape Bojador. Portugal then set up trading posts on the western coast of Africa. By 1460 at least 25 ships a year returned to Portugal, heavy with African gold, pepper, and ivory. The Portuguese also **enslaved** African people, forcing them into slavery. **Slavery** was a cruel system in which people worked without pay and had no freedom.

In 1488 Bartholomeu Dias became the first European to sail around southern Africa. Ten years later, Portuguese captain, Vasco da Gama, reached India *(see the map above)*. Europeans had found a sea route to Asia, the land of spices and other rare items. These goods would bring a high price in Europe making traders and merchants very wealthy.

This ivory carving was made in Africa for trade with the Portuguese, who landed in Africa in the 1400s. The top piece represents a Portuguese ship, complete with a crow's nest with a lookout at the top.

This bottom part opens and was used to store salt. **Economics:** *Why might African traders have made such a fancy carving in which to store salt?*

Explorers from Spain

Focus *What was Columbus looking for, and what did he find?*

While Portuguese sailors were trying to reach Asia by sailing around Africa, an Italian sailor named Christopher Columbus had another idea. He believed he could get there by sailing west instead of east. By Columbus's calculations, Asia was just 3,000 miles straight west of Spain. (The real distance is about 10,000 miles.) He never thought that another continent might be in the way.

Christopher Columbus

The Santa María

Columbus sailed with three ships on his expedition. The Spanish king paid for two, and Columbus had to pay for the third. The *Santa María* was the largest of the three ships. It was a *nao,* a large, slow vessel that was probably about 80 feet long. No plans of the *Santa María* survive, so no one knows exactly what it looked like. This illustration is based on knowledge of ships in the time of Columbus.

Sleeping Quarters

As captain of the *Santa María*, Columbus had his own cabin. The rest of the crew were not as fortunate. The officers probably shared sleeping quarters, and the ordinary sailors had to sleep wherever they could find an open space.

Columbus had first asked the king of Portugal to pay for his voyage across the Atlantic. When that king refused, Columbus took his plan to Spain. The Spanish queen, Isabella, thought Columbus might be right. She and her husband, King Ferdinand, were also eager to expand Spanish power and to spread their Catholic religion to people in other lands. Isabella believed that finding a new route to the East would accomplish both of these goals. So they agreed to pay for part of the voyage. On August 3, 1492, Columbus set sail with a fleet of 3 ships, the *Niña*, the *Pinta*, and the *Santa María*, and a crew of 90 sailors.

With winds blowing steadily from the east, the ships made good progress. But after a month, the sailors became worried. On October 10, the crew agreed to sail on for three more days. If they sighted no land, they would go home. On the morning of October 12, Columbus and his crew spotted one of the Bahama Islands off the coast of Florida. The Tainos, who lived there, after growing used to the crew, swam out to greet them. Interested in befriending their visitors, the Tainos brought the sailors fresh food and water.

A devout Catholic, Columbus named the island *San Salvador* or "Holy Savior." Believing he had reached India, he called the Taino people "Indians." Columbus believed that he had found a new route to India by sailing due west from Spain.

After visiting other Taino communities in Cuba and Hispaniola (where Haiti and the Dominican Republic are today), Columbus hurried home, bringing gold and several enslaved Taino people with

Queen Isabella of Spain

The Route of Columbus

Columbus believed that he could reach the Indies by sailing west from Europe. **Map Skill:** *What did Columbus not yet know about the world?*

Ballast

Ballast was placed in the hold (bottom) of a ship to keep the ship upright. It usually consisted of loose stones or iron blocks.

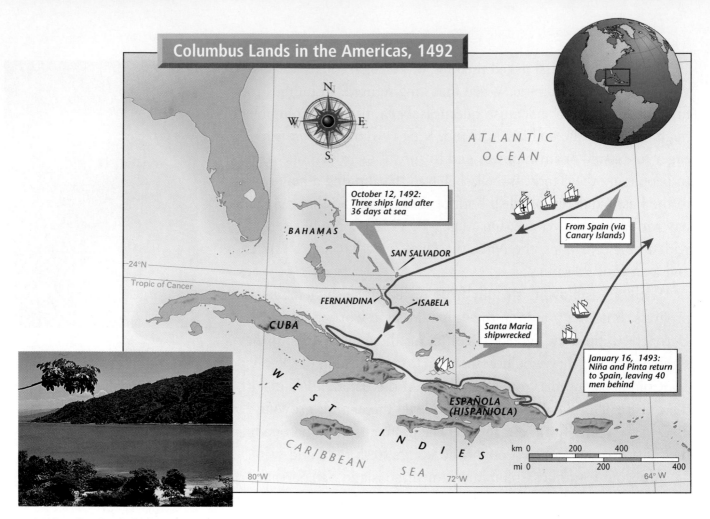

Columbus Lands in the Americas, 1492

ATLANTIC OCEAN

October 12, 1492: Three ships land after 36 days at sea

From Spain (via Canary Islands)

BAHAMAS

SAN SALVADOR

24°N

Tropic of Cancer

FERNANDINA

ISABELA

Santa Maria shipwrecked

CUBA

January 16, 1493: Niña and Pinta return to Spain, leaving 40 men behind

ESPAÑOLA (HISPANIOLA)

W E S T   I N D I E S

CARIBBEAN   SEA

80°W   72°W   64°W

km 0   200   400
mi 0   200   400

Columbus first landed on San Salvador *(above)*. He continued on, landing on the islands of Cuba and Hispaniola. **Map Skill:** *Look at Columbus's route. Who did Columbus name two of the other islands after? Why do you think he did this?*

him. Columbus made three more trips to the west. Each voyage brought more Spanish people to the Caribbean. Their arrival forever changed the islands and the lives of the people who were living there.

A Voyage Around the World

In 1519 a Portuguese ship captain named Ferdinand Magellan wanted to find out what lay to the west of the Americas. He heard that a Spanish soldier, Vasco Núñez de Balboa, had crossed Panama (in modern-day Central America) on foot in 1513. On the west side of Panama, Balboa had seen another ocean.

Magellan crossed the Atlantic Ocean, and then headed south to sail around the Americas to reach this other ocean (*see map on the right*). His ships did not hit any storms while crossing this new ocean. Magellan named it *Pacific*, which means "calm."

Near the end of the voyage, while in the Philippine Islands off of the mainland of Asia, Magellan was killed. Only one of his five ships, the *Victoria*, made it back to Spain in 1522. Juan Sebastián Del Cano was the captain. Of the approximately 250 men who had

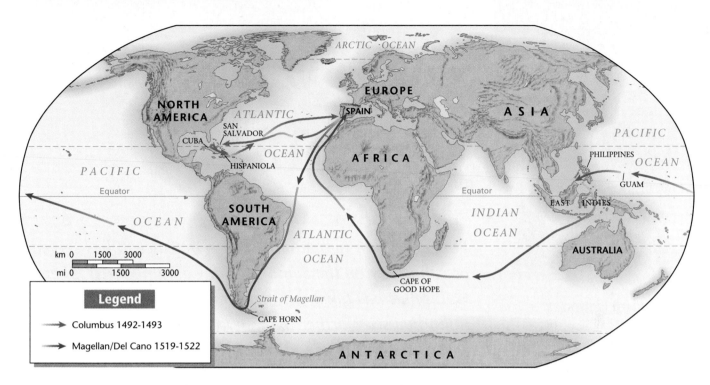

left Spain, fewer than 22 returned. The *Victoria* became the first ship to **circumnavigate,** or sail around, the world.

Spanish explorers would return to the Philippines years later. Like much of the Americas, these islands too, would eventually come under Spanish rule.

Magellan and Columbus each believed they could reach the Indies by sailing west. **Map Skill:** *Which continents did neither Columbus nor Magellan land on?*

Lesson Review

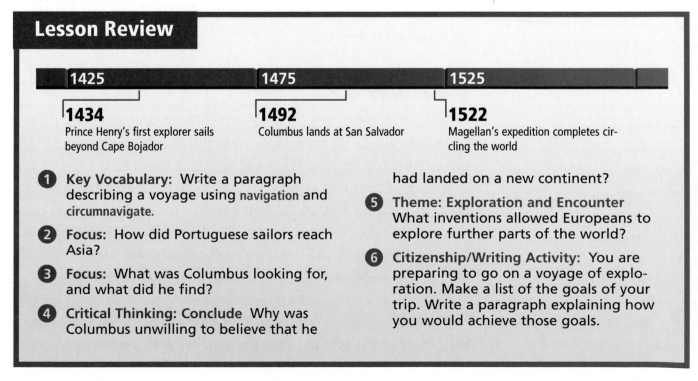

1425	1475	1525

1434
Prince Henry's first explorer sails beyond Cape Bojador

1492
Columbus lands at San Salvador

1522
Magellan's expedition completes circling the world

1. **Key Vocabulary:** Write a paragraph describing a voyage using navigation and circumnavigate.

2. **Focus:** How did Portuguese sailors reach Asia?

3. **Focus:** What was Columbus looking for, and what did he find?

4. **Critical Thinking: Conclude** Why was Columbus unwilling to believe that he

had landed on a new continent?

5. **Theme: Exploration and Encounter** What inventions allowed Europeans to explore further parts of the world?

6. **Citizenship/Writing Activity:** You are preparing to go on a voyage of exploration. Make a list of the goals of your trip. Write a paragraph explaining how you would achieve those goals.

Historical Fiction

fathom
The depth of water is measured in fathoms. One fathom equals six feet.

Pedro's Journal

by Pam Conrad

For more than two months Pedro de Salcedo has served as cabin boy on the Santa María. Captain Christopher Columbus has taken his men and ships westward into the unknown seas farther than anyone else has ever gone. The sailors have been afraid ever since they lost sight of the coast of Spain so long ago. They have begged to turn back, but the Captain has kept them going by reminding them that the first man to see land will be given 10,000 maravedis, coins worth a small fortune. Then, just when his men refuse to sail west for even one more day, Columbus himself sees land on the night of October 11, 1492. The next morning is a day of discovery, and Pedro tells us what he sees.

October 12

A lush green island was there in the morning, and our three ships approached it carefully, maneuvering through breakers and a threatening barrier reef. We could see clear down to the reef in the sparkling blue waters as we sailed through. And, ah, it is truly land, truly earth, here so far from Spain. The *Santa María* led the way into the sheltered bay of the island and got a mark of only five fathoms' depth. We anchored there and barely paused to admire the breathtaking beauty. Small boats were prepared, armed, and lowered, and in these some of us went ashore. Out of respect, all waited while Christopher Columbus leaped out of the boat, his feet the first to touch this new land. (I wondered what my mother would say if she knew her son had lost the 10,000 maravedis to the Captain, who claimed it for himself.)

The Captain carried the royal banner of our king and queen, and as everyone else scrambled out of the boats and secured them in the white sand, he thrust the banner into the earth and then sank down to his knees and said a prayer of thanksgiving for our safe arrival in India. Others dropped to their knees around him. Diego was beside me, and he clapped his hand on my shoulder. I knew he was happy to be on land again. I was, too, although I have been so long at sea that even on land the ground seems to buckle and sway beneath my feet.

The Captain made a solemn ceremony and formally took possession of the land for the king and queen, naming it San Salvador. We all witnessed this, and then little by little we noticed something else — there were people stepping out from the trees, beautiful, strong, naked people, with tanned skin and straight black hair. My mother would have lowered her eyes or looked away, as I have seen her do in our home when someone dresses, but I could not take my eyes off them. Some had boldly painted their bodies or their faces, some only their eyes, some their noses. They were so beautiful and gentle. They walked towards us slowly but without fear, smiling and reaching out their hands.

The Caribbean Islands where Columbus first landed are tropical islands with a warm climate and clear blue waters.

This image shows the first meeting between Columbus and his crew and the Taino people.

The sailors watched them in wonder, and when these people came near, the crew gave them coins, little red caps, whatever they had in their pockets. Columbus himself showed one native his sword, and the native, never having seen such an instrument before, slid his fingers along the sharp edge and looked startled at his fingers that dripped blood into the sand.

Everyone was smiling and so friendly. Close up, we could see how clear and gentle their eyes were, how broad and unusual their foreheads. The Captain especially noted and said to one of his men, "See the gold in that one's nose? See how docile they are? They will be easy. We will take six back with us to Spain."

I think at this, too, my mother would have lowered her eyes.

October 16

So much has happened. There is so much to remember and record, and so much I do not think I want to tell my mother. Perhaps I will keep these letters to myself after all. The natives think that we are angels from God. They swim out to us, wave, throw themselves in the sand, hold their hands and faces to the sky, and sing and call to us. The crew loves it, and no one loves it better than Columbus. He lifts his open palms to them like a priest at mass. I sometimes wonder if he doesn't believe these natives himself just a little bit.

They come right out to the ship in swift dugouts that sit forty men, and sometimes as they approach us the dugout tips, but in minutes they right it and begin bailing it out with hollow gourds. All day long the Indians row out to see us, bringing gifts of cotton thread, shell-tipped spears, and even brightly colored parrots that sit on our shoulders and cry out in human voices. For their trouble we give them more worthless beads, bells, and tastes of honey, which they marvel at.

The six native men Columbus has taken aboard are not very happy. One by one they are escaping, which I cannot help but say I am happy for. One jumped overboard and swam away, and another jumped overboard when a dugout came up alongside us in the darkness. Some of the crew seized another man coming alongside in a dugout and forced him on board. Columbus tried to convince him of our good intentions through sign language and broken words and more gifts of glass beads and junk, and the man rowed back to some people on the shore. They stood talking to each other and pointing at our ship. Columbus smiled and was convinced they know we are from God. Me, I am not so sure they will believe it for much longer.

Meet the Author

Pam Conrad has written more than 16 books for young people, many of them exploring the past. Readers of her books have lived with ship-wrecked sailors, hunted for dinosaur fossils, and even met up with 100-year-old ghosts.

Additional Books to Read

Morning Girl
by Michael Dorris
Describes life among
the Taino people.

I, Columbus
edited by Peter and
Connie Roop
Tells the voyage of
Columbus in his own
words.

Response Activities

1. **Predict** Do you think Pedro would have joined Columbus's crew if he had the opportunity? Why or why not?

2. **Narrative: Write a Journal Entry** How do you think a Taino child might have felt about the arrival of Columbus and his crew? Write a journal entry describing this child's reaction to the Spanish and his or her feelings toward them.

3. **Cultures: Make a Point of View Chart** Make a list of Spanish and Taino responses to the Spanish arrival in the West Indies. Create a chart to compare the two points of view. Do they ever agree?

Spain Builds an Empire

Main Idea During the 1500s, Spain conquered much of the Americas.

The Aztec people of Mexico believed the god Quetzalcoatl (ket sahl ko AHT ehl) had built their empire and then gone off to heaven. One day he would return and reclaim it. When the Aztec people heard that new visitors had arrived on the Mexican coast, they believed that Quetzalcoatl had returned.

In 1519, a strange-looking army landed on Mexico's coast. These soldiers had steel swords, which the Aztec people had never seen before. Some rode horses, which were unknown in the Americas. The first Aztec people who saw them thought horse and rider were a single creature. Messengers raced to the emperor to tell him that Quetzalcoatl had arrived.

In this modern painting, the Emperor Montezuma greets Cortés, Malinche, and an army of Spanish riders and foot soldiers.

The Conquest of Mexico

Focus *How did Cortés defeat the Aztec Empire?*

The army that looked so strange to the Aztec people was a force of 600 Spanish soldiers. Its commander was Hernán Cortés (kohr TEHZ). Cortés came from the Spanish colony on Cuba. He heard that there was a wealthy city full of gold and treasure in Mexico, and he came to conquer it. He was known as a conquistador (kohn kees tah DOHR). In Spanish, **conquistador** means "conqueror."

Cortés and his army marched toward the Aztec capital, Tenochtitlán (teh nawch tee TLAHN). On their way, the army fought Native Americans. Malinche (mah LEEN cheh), an Aztec woman who was sold into slavery to the Mayans as a child, joined Cortés and his army. She spoke several Mesoamerican languages and acted as an interpreter and guide for the Spanish conquistadors.

When the Spanish were within sight of Tenochtitlán in central Mexico, they could hardly believe their eyes. It was a city far larger than any in Spain, with about 350,000 people living in it. It was built on an island in a lake. Canals cut through the island so that people could get around by canoe. There were graceful buildings and lush gardens.

Ask Yourself

The search for gold and riches led many Spanish explorers to set out on lengthy, dangerous, and expensive journeys. What would your goals be for a journey to a faraway place, such as another planet?

? ? ? ? ? ? ? ? ? ? ? ? ? ? ?

Spanish Armor

Spanish conquistadors arrived for battle wearing a full suit of armor. Their helmets and swords *(below)* were often beautifully decorated. **Technology:** *What advantages did this armor give to the conquistadors? Can you think of any disadvantages?*

How did the Aztecs record their history?

Quetzalcoatl

When the Aztec emperor Montezuma heard reports of the arrival of strange new people, he ordered that Aztec paintings be examined. He wanted to know if anyone had ever recorded seeing these people before.

Paintings were used by the Aztec people to record information about their history. Through the use of pictographs, or picture writing, they kept a detailed record of people and events. These pictographs were put together as stories on a long scroll called a codex.

When the Spanish invaded Tenochtitlán, they destroyed many of the paintings that they found there. The ones that survive give us an exciting look into Aztec culture and society.

Battle between the Spanish and Aztecs

Cortés in power in Tenochtitlán

Montezuma and Cortés

Cortés approached the city of Tenochtitlán peacefully. The Aztec emperor, Montezuma, gave Cortés a palace to live in, and the Aztec people brought fresh food and gifts to the Spanish army.

Cortés betrayed Montezuma's good will. He lured the emperor to the house Montezuma had given him and took him prisoner. Montezuma continued to rule, but Cortés told him what to do. After six months, the Aztec people **rebelled,** or resisted the authority of the Spanish. During that time, Montezuma was killed.

A year later, Cortés returned with about twice as many soldiers. His army was joined by thousands of native people who were part of the Aztec Empire but who resented Aztec rule.

The Spanish sealed off the city, cutting off supplies. Weakened by war, starvation, and disease, the Aztecs were overrun. Tenochtitlán was destroyed. The citizens who survived were forced to mine gold for the Spanish. Within six months, Cortés conquered most of central Mexico. The Spanish would rule there for 300 years.

Searching for Cities of Gold

Focus *What were the Seven Cities of Gold, and where did the Spanish hope to find them?*

There was an ancient **legend,** a story handed down from earlier times, about seven leaders of the Church who left Europe to build the Seven Cities of Gold. At one time, Europeans thought the Seven Cities were in Africa. As reports reached Europe about the gold found in the Americas, many people began to believe that the Seven Cities were there. Some people actually went to look for them.

Exploring Florida

In 1528, Pánfilo de Narváez (nahr VAH ehs) went to Florida looking for the Seven Cities. He left Cuba with an army of about 600 men.

Native Americans in Florida defended themselves. They **ambushed,** or attacked by surprise, the army as it crossed a lake. In the end, only four people escaped. These men lived with the Yakui (yah KEE) Indians and other groups for years before they were able to return to Mexico.

Exploring the Southwest

Two of the survivors of the Narváez group were Esteban Dorantes (door AHN tehs), known as Estevanico, and Álvar Núñez Cabeza de Vaca (kah BEH sah deh VAH kah). Estevanico shared stories he had heard of large cities in what is now the southwest part of the United States. Could these be the Seven Cities?

In 1540, the Spanish sent an expedition of 300 soldiers and over 1,000 Native Americans to find them. They were commanded by Francisco Vázquez de Coronado. After months of travel, Coronado and his expedition reached one of the cities the Yakui had spoken of. But instead of glittering towers, the Spanish found a pueblo. They called the Native Americans they encountered there Pueblo Indians.

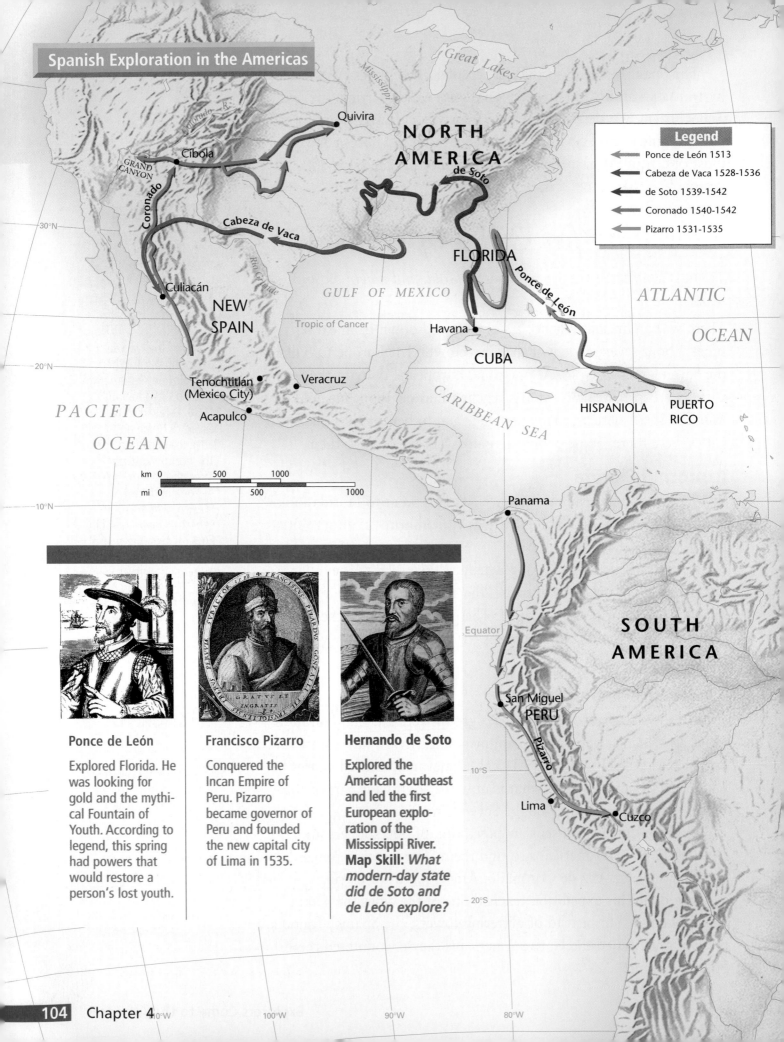

Spanish Exploration in the Americas

Legend
← Ponce de León 1513
← Cabeza de Vaca 1528–1536
← de Soto 1539–1542
← Coronado 1540–1542
← Pizarro 1531–1535

Great Lakes

Mississippi R.

NORTH AMERICA

Quivira

Cíbola

GRAND CANYON

Colorado R.

Coronado

Cabeza de Vaca

de Soto

FLORIDA

Ponce de León

30°N

20°N

Culiacán

NEW SPAIN

Rio Grande

GULF OF MEXICO

Tropic of Cancer

Havana

CUBA

ATLANTIC OCEAN

Tenochtitlán (Mexico City)

Veracruz

Acapulco

PACIFIC OCEAN

CARIBBEAN SEA

HISPANIOLA

PUERTO RICO

km 0   500   1000
mi 0   500   1000

10°N

Panama

SOUTH AMERICA

Equator

San Miguel
PERU

Pizarro

10°S

Lima

Cuzco

20°S

Ponce de León

Explored Florida. He was looking for gold and the mythical Fountain of Youth. According to legend, this spring had powers that would restore a person's lost youth.

Francisco Pizarro

Conquered the Incan Empire of Peru. Pizarro became governor of Peru and founded the new capital city of Lima in 1535.

Hernando de Soto

Explored the American Southeast and led the first European exploration of the Mississippi River.
Map Skill: *What modern-day state did de Soto and de León explore?*

110°W   100°W   90°W   80°W

Even then, Coronado was not ready to give up. He marched north in search of Quivira (kee VEER ah). Coronado expected to find a golden city, but instead found the villages of the Wichita Indians. Then he headed south. As the expedition traveled, Coronado and his men often treated Native Americans cruelly, trying to force them to tell where the golden cities were. Coronado and his men finally returned to Mexico, two years after they started. It had been a long, disappointing, and brutal journey.

Bartolomé de las Casas

Most Spanish leaders defended the conquest of the Americas. They argued that Spain brought progress to the Native Americans. Not everyone agreed. A famous critic of Spanish actions was the priest Bartolomé (bahr TOHL oh MEH) de las Casas. He had seen Spanish soldiers mistreat enslaved Native Americans working for the Spanish in silver mines. Las Casas spoke against these cruelties:

> **"M**ankind is one, and all men are alike in that which concerns their creation."

The Spanish king listened to las Casas' plea over a period of many months and even passed laws to protect the Native Americans. These laws were difficult to enforce from across the ocean, and the conquest continued.

People continue to explore unknown parts of the world. In the picture above, modern explorers attempt to learn more about one of the deepest caves in the Western Hemisphere, the Huautla (wah OOT lah) Cave system in southern Mexico.

Lesson Review

1520	1530	1540

1521
Cortés defeats the Aztec Empire

1528
Narváez lands in Florida

1540
Coronado begins to explore the Southwest

1. **Key Vocabulary:** Write a paragraph about the Spanish in the Southwest, using **conquistador**, **rebel**, **legend**, and **ambush**.

2. **Focus:** How did Cortés defeat the Aztec Empire?

3. **Focus:** What were the Seven Cities of Gold, and where did the Spanish hope to find them?

4. **Critical Thinking: Interpret** Based on what you know of Spanish explorers, do you think las Casas' criticisms were fair?

5. **Geography:** What modern American states did the conquistadors travel through?

6. **Citizenship/Arts Activity:** Create a series of pictographs that tell a story about a news event. Share your work in class.

The Columbian Exchange

Key Vocabulary

Columbian Exchange

plantation

immunity

epidemic

Key Events

1501 First enslaved Africans brought to the Americas

1519 Cortés reintroduces horses to the Americas

Main Idea Columbus's voyages led to an exchange of peoples, plants, and animals among continents.

A Navajo boy tends his family's sheep herd in northern Arizona. A farmer in China harvests his crop of sweet potatoes. A girl in Paris drinks a chocolate milk shake.

These people may never meet, but they are all sharing in something called the **Columbian Exchange.** That is the name used to describe the peoples, plants, and animals that crossed the Atlantic Ocean after Columbus's first trip to the Americas. The ships that traveled between Europe and the Americas carried people and goods in both directions. Some items were carried across the ocean on purpose, some by accident. Some people crossed the ocean against their will. All of these exchanges changed life on our planet in ways that still affect people throughout the world today.

Enslaved Africans were forced to work all day in the hot Caribbean sun. They cut and cleaned sugar cane stalks, preparing them for the milling process.

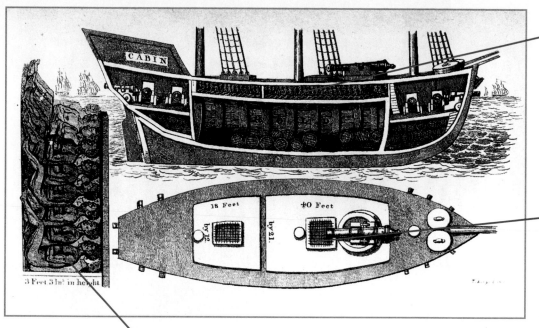

This print shows a slave ship of the 1820s. Look closely at the middle deck above the hold. People were imprisoned tightly together for transport.

The view from the top shows the hatches that would have been the only access from between decks to the fresh air and sunlight.

The image to the left is a close-up look at the way enslaved people were jammed together between decks. This inhumane method of transport developed as more people and more money became involved in the slave trade.

Sugar Cane and Slavery

Focus *How did the African slave trade begin in the 1500s?*

Sugar cane was one of the goods that was brought to the Americas on purpose. The Spanish found that sugar cane from Europe grew well in the warm climate of the Caribbean Islands. Sugar was replacing honey as the favorite sweetener in Europe. To meet the growing demand for more sugar, the Spanish built large farms called **plantations**.

At first the Spanish enslaved Native Americans to work on the plantations. The hard labor killed many of them. Some of the enslaved workers resisted their mistreatment or ran away. Many others died from a destructive force the Spanish had brought with them unknowingly. The Spanish carried with them diseases that did not exist in the Americas, such as smallpox and measles. Native Americans had no natural **immunity,** or resistance, to these diseases. Epidemics soon swept through the Caribbean and Mexico. An **epidemic** is the spread of disease among many people.

To find new workers for their mines and plantations, Europeans turned to Africa. By the 1460s the Portuguese were buying African people to enslave. They sold these people to the Spanish, who brought them to the Americas, possibly as early as 1506.

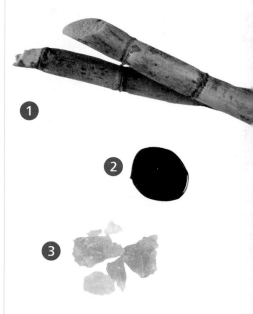

Sugar Production

1 Sugar cane was brought to the Americas from Europe.

2 After cutting, sugar cane was pressed and the sweet liquid was separated from the stalk.

3 The liquid was boiled and evaporated, creating thick molasses and raw sugar crystals.

The fruits, vegetables and beans shown below and on the opposite page are all items you might see every day, and they were all part of the Columbian Exchange.

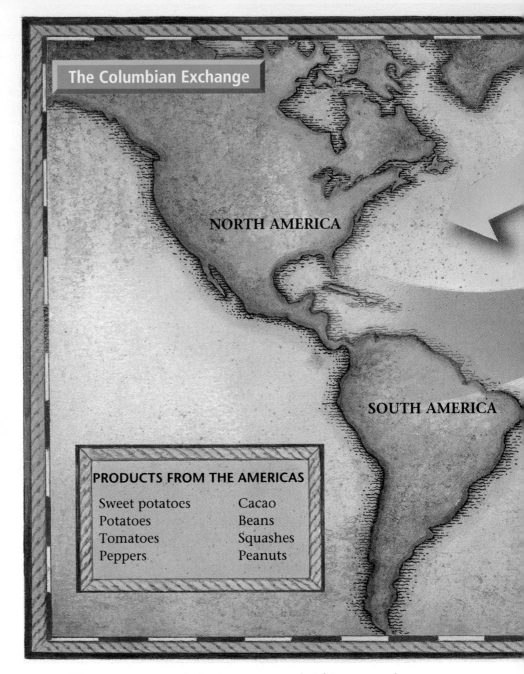

The Columbian Exchange

NORTH AMERICA

SOUTH AMERICA

PRODUCTS FROM THE AMERICAS

Sweet potatoes	Cacao
Potatoes	Beans
Tomatoes	Squashes
Peppers	Peanuts

Soon Europeans were bringing captured Africans to the Caribbean by the thousands. They packed men, women, and children together on the ships, leaving barely enough room to move. The journey was so dangerous that many people died, either from shipwreck or disease. By 1574, about 12,000 Africans lived on the island of Hispaniola alone. There, Africans did backbreaking work for no pay and with little chance of escape.

The Spanish found that enslaving Africans was no easier than enslaving Native Americans. Only the constant threat of violence could force people to work against their will. Sometimes there were organized revolts. But even when things seemed peaceful, there were small acts of rebellion. Throughout the 350 years of slavery in the Americas, Africans resisted their captivity.

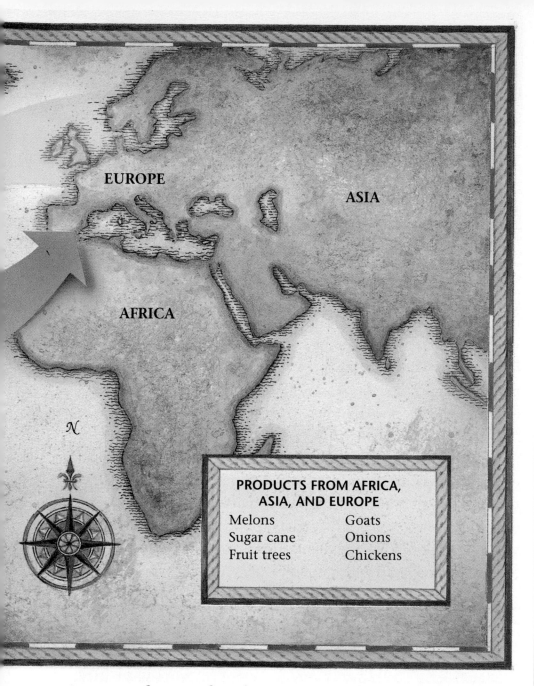

EUROPE

ASIA

AFRICA

𝒩

PRODUCTS FROM AFRICA, ASIA, AND EUROPE

Melons   Goats
Sugar cane   Onions
Fruit trees   Chickens

The Columbian Exchange led to the transfer of plants and animals between the Americas, Africa, and Europe. **Map Skill:** *What products traveled from Africa, Asia, and Europe to the Americas? Why would people traveling to the Americas have brought plants and animals with them?*

Transfer of Plants and Animals

[Focus] *What effect did the transfer of plants and animals have on the people of Europe, Africa, and the Americas?*

When regular trade started between Europe and the Americas, plants and animals traveled in both directions.

From Europe the Spanish brought wheat, onions, oranges, and, of course, sugar cane. Ships going back to Spain carried items such as corn, peppers, beans, pumpkins, and tomatoes. Each of these was unknown on the other side of the ocean, and all became major crops in their new homes. The American potato, in particular, became a basic part of the European diet from Ireland to Russia.

Curious Facts

It was difficult to transport horses across the ocean in the early 1500s. Without support, horses were in danger of falling and breaking their legs. The Spanish developed a system of slings to suspend horses in the air and keep their feet from touching the deck of the ship.

As time went on, American plants spread beyond Europe. Corn became an important food in Africa, and sweet potatoes were grown as far away as China. Today, American plants such as cocoa, peanuts, and avocadoes grow in many lands.

Animals made the journey across the ocean, too. Most important was the horse, which the Spanish brought to the Americas. Thousands of years ago, horses roamed the Americas, but they all died out. Before the 1500s, Native Americans had no beasts of burden except the llama. Cortés brought horses to Mexico in 1519 to conquer the Aztecs, and the animals thrived in the Americas.

Eventually, the horse came to play an extremely important role in the lives of Native Americans living on the Plains. After the horse was introduced to their culture, they were able to hunt buffalo on horseback, making hunting more efficient. In addition to the horse, livestock that is thought of as typically American — cows, pigs, chickens, and sheep — all came to the Americas from Europe.

Think of the exchange of plants and animals the next time you go to the grocery store. As you walk up and down the aisles, look closely at the items that are for sale. The oranges and orange juice, the milk and all of the many products that have milk in them, and even the dozens of cereals that contain wheat, are all available to you as a result of the great changes that began when the people of the eastern and western hemispheres met.

Lesson Review

1500	1525	

1501
First enslaved Africans brought to the Americas

1519
Cortés reintroduces horses to the Americas

1 **Key Vocabulary:** Write a paragraph about the lesson, using: **Columbian Exchange, immunity, epidemic,** and **plantation.**

2 **Focus:** How did the African slave trade begin in the 1500s?

3 **Focus:** What effect did the transfer of plants and animals have on the people of Europe, Africa, and the Americas?

4 **Critical Thinking: Cause and Effect** How has the transfer of plants and animals shaped the way people live in the Americas today?

5 **Citizenship:** You are a Spanish person living in Spain in the 1500s. How would you argue against the use of slavery in the Americas?

6 **Geography/Writing Activity:** You are traveling to the Americas in the 1500s and can take only three types of plants with you. Write a paragraph telling what you would take and why.

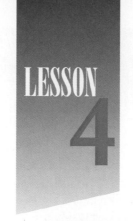

Challenges to Spain

Main Idea England, France, and Holland competed with Spain for power in the Americas.

The Spanish hated him. Queen Elizabeth I of England made him a knight. The sea captain Francis Drake was a hero in England, but to Spain he was nothing but a thief.

Francis Drake raided Spanish ships that were returning from the Americas heavy with gold and riches. Drake would lie in wait for the large, slow-moving Spanish vessels, and catch them easily with his smaller and faster ships.

When Drake returned to England, Queen Elizabeth made him a **privateer,** or the captain of an armed, privately owned ship, hired by a government to attack enemy ships. Soon Drake became the most dreaded captain on the high seas. The knighting of Drake was the final blow to the Spanish. If the Queen of England would not control Drake, they would do something about him themselves.

Key Vocabulary

privateer
invasion
armada
Northwest Passage
settlement

Key Events

1588 The Spanish Armada is defeated

1609 Champlain starts a settlement in North America

1609 Hudson claims the Hudson River Valley for Holland

Queen Elizabeth I of England wanted to compete with Spain for the riches and jewels of the Americas.
Citizenship: *Why did she reward Francis Drake for his raids on Spanish ships by making him a knight?*

The treasure below is made up of gold coins and raw emeralds.

This painting, by an unknown artist, is titled *Launch of Fireships Against the Armada.*

Chart Skill: *If the Spanish started with 130 ships and the British started with 197 ships, how many ships did both Spain and England have remaining at the end of the battle?*

The Battle of the Spanish Armada

Spanish losses	British losses
Ships **63**	Ships **1**
Sailors **15,000**	Sailors **under 100**

The Armada

Focus *What were the causes of the Battle of the Spanish Armada?*

During the 1500s, the gold and silver found in the Americas helped make Spain the world's richest nation. Because of this wealth, Spain grew very powerful and ruled over many lands, including Portugal and Holland. By the 1580s, Spain's King Philip planned to conquer England as well. Drake's attacks had angered the king, but he had other reasons, too. England was a mostly Protestant nation. Spain was a Catholic one. A Spanish victory over the English would be a victory for the Catholic Church.

In 1586, Spain began building the largest navy in the world. Drake led raids on this fleet and sank many vessels, but it was not enough to stop a Spanish invasion. An **invasion** is the use of force to conquer. In May of 1588, 130 Spanish ships filled with soldiers sailed for England. These were the best soldiers in Europe, armed with the finest muskets. King Philip called the fleet "the Invincible Armada." **Armada** means "fleet" in Spanish. Invincible means "unable to be defeated."

Drake had an idea. He set fire to several of his own ships and sent them floating straight into the Armada. One Spanish ship after another caught fire. As the others tried to escape, about 60 English ships drove the Spanish into the North Sea, where the wind did the rest. It scattered the proud Armada along the rocky coast of Ireland.

The year 1588 was a turning point in history. Before then, no nation in Europe could compete with Spain. After that year, both England and France began to challenge Spanish power.

The Northwest Passage

Focus *What were the results of England, France, and Holland's search for the Northwest Passage?*

England, France, and Holland started to explore the Americas soon after Columbus arrived there. Like Spain, these countries hoped to find a sea route to the riches of Asia. When England's John Cabot reached Newfoundland in 1497, he thought he was near China.

The Search for a Northwest Passage

Explorers hoped to find a water route from the Atlantic to the Pacific through North America.
Map Skill: *What would have been the advantages in finding another water route to Asia?*

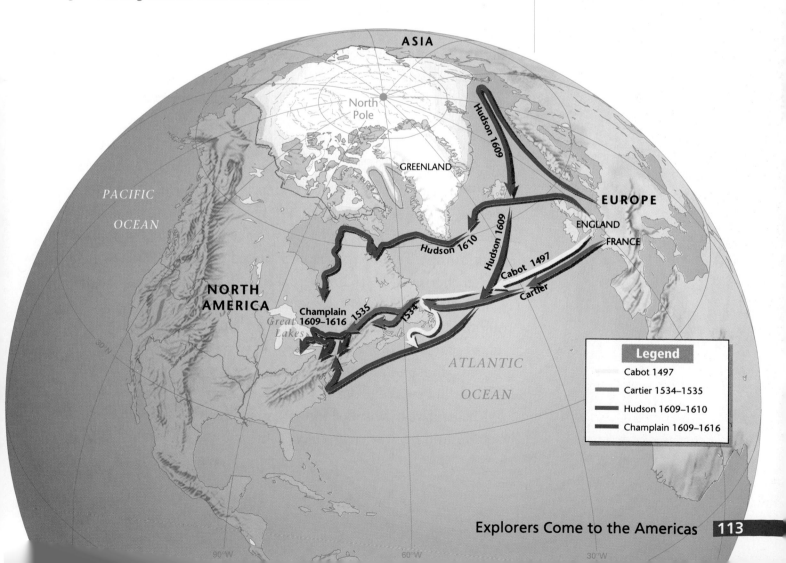

Legend

Cabot 1497

Cartier 1534–1535

Hudson 1609–1610

Champlain 1609–1616

The beaver pelt *(above)*, knife blade, fish hook, and scissors *(below)*, are some of the items that would have been exchanged between Native Americans and traders.

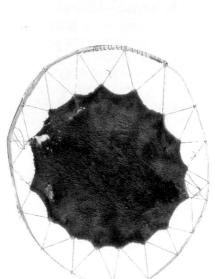

This led England and France to believe there was a waterway in that area that would lead to the East. They even had a name for it. They called it the **Northwest Passage**.

In 1534 the French captain Jacques Cartier (kahr TYAY) sailed up the river that is known today as the St. Lawrence, hoping it would take him to Asia. Instead, he met the Iroquois people and befriended them. The Iroquois leader even let two of his sons travel with Cartier back to France. Cartier returned in 1535 and again in 1541, but he never found a Northwest Passage.

Beginning in 1603, Samuel de Champlain (sham PLAYN) made several trips up the St. Lawrence River, looking for a route to Asia. In 1609 he gave up and started a French settlement in North America. A **settlement** is a community of people in a new region. The French traded with the Hurons for beaver furs, which were valued in Europe. Few French people wanted to endure Canada's cold weather, however. In 1625, there were still only 60 settlers there.

People in Holland also dreamed of finding a passage east. In 1609 the Dutch government sent Henry Hudson, an English captain, to search for it. He sailed up the river that is now named for him, the Hudson River. Hudson claimed the land that he saw for Holland. But he decided to look for a passage somewhere else.

The next year he sailed into a bay in northern Canada. Before he could find his way out, winter came and his crew rebelled. They

This detail from a map of the northeastern coast of North America was made around 1547. Maps of this period were often illustrated. This map shows an encounter between a group of French explorers and Native Americans. **Geography:** *Why would mapmakers of this period add so many details about people, animals, and plants to their maps?*

put him, his son, and a few men into a boat and set them adrift in the bay. The crew sailed back to England. No sign of Hudson's party was ever found. Today, that bay is called Hudson Bay.

None of these explorers ever found a Northwest Passage. Their search for it was important, however. Their expeditions brought Europeans from many countries to North America and led to the creation of early European settlements there.

Lesson Review

1590	1600	1610	

1588
The Spanish Armada is defeated

1609
Champlain starts a settlement in North America

1609
Hudson claims the Hudson River valley for Holland

1 **Key Vocabulary:** Write a sentence for each of the following words: **privateer, invasion, armada, Northwest Passage,** and **settlement.**

2 **Focus:** What were the causes of the Battle of the Spanish Armada?

3 **Focus:** What were the results of England, France, and Holland's search for the Northwest Passage?

4 **Critical Thinking: Cause and Effect** The Spanish and French settlements in the Americas grew at very different rates. What does this tell you about the effect of climate and available resources on rates of settlement?

5 **Theme: Exploration and Encounter** How was Cartier's way of dealing with the Iroquois helpful to future French exploration and settlement in Canada?

6 **Geography/Art Activity:** Make an illustrated map, like the one above, of the route you take from home to school.

Using Degrees and Minutes

Voyage Through a Continent

In 1673, Father Jacques Marquette and Louis Joliet explored the land south and west of the Great Lakes. They were searching for a passage to the Pacific Ocean. They paddled down the Mississippi River but did not find a route west, so they decided to turn back.

You can see Marquette and Joliet's route on the top map on the right. You know how to pinpoint a place on this map using latitude and longitude lines. What if the place falls between the lines? Mapmakers have divided every degree into 60 **minutes** so you can locate places more precisely.

Degrees and Minutes

Think of the earth as a big ball, or sphere. We can divide a sphere into 360 equal parts called **degrees.** When we divide the earth up this way, we create lines of latitude and longitude. (The equator and the prime meridian are 0°.) Each degree of latitude or longitude can be divided again into 60 equal parts. We call these **minutes**, written ('). Using degrees and minutes, we can accurately locate any place on the earth.

A Mile a Minute

We can use minutes of latitude to guess approximate distances. Sound impossible? Each degree of latitude is about 69 miles. So each minute of latitude is a little more than one mile! This only works for latitude, not longitude.

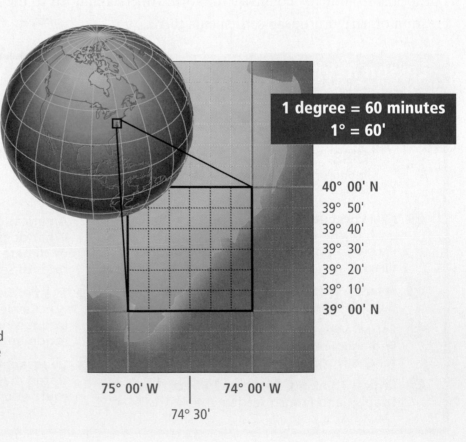

1 degree = 60 minutes
1° = 60'

40° 00' N
39° 50'
39° 40'
39° 30'
39° 20'
39° 10'
39° 00' N

75° 00' W   74° 00' W
74° 30'

1 Here's How

- Look at the map on the right. Study the latitude lines. This map covers the area between 30°N and 50°N. The *interval*, or space, between latitude lines here is 5°. What area do the longitude lines cover? What is the interval between longitude lines?

- Now study the map below. Note that it is a blowup, or inset, of a small area on the first map. It shows part of the return route.

- Notice that the interval between longitude and latitude lines on the inset map is one degree.

- Now find the minutes. These are the numbers between the latitude and longitude numbers. Count the 60 minutes that are between each latitude and longitude line.

- To name a place in degrees and minutes, first find the place on the map. For example, find the junction of the Illinois and Vermillion rivers.

- Find the nearest degree of latitude. It is 41°N. Now find the nearest minute. It is 20'. So the latitude is 41°20'N.

- Now find the nearest degree of longitude. It is 89°W. The nearest minute is 5', so the longitude is 89°5'W.

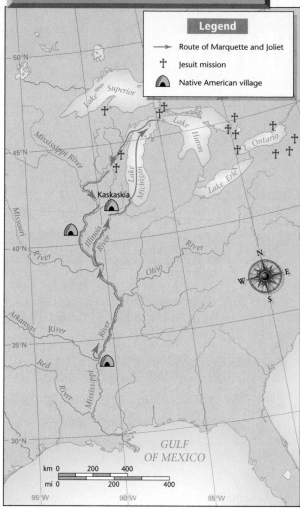

Voyage of Marquette and Joliet

Legend
→ Route of Marquette and Joliet
✝ Jesuit mission
🛖 Native American village

Marquette and Joliet's Return Voyage

→ Route of Marquette and Joliet
•••• Portage (place where canoe must be carried)
🌿 Marsh
🛖 Native American village

2 Think It Through

Why can you locate a place more exactly when you use degrees and minutes than when you use only degrees?

3 Use It

1. Find Kaskaskia on both maps. Using the map above, write down its location using only degrees. Using the map to the left, write down its location, using degrees and minutes. Which tells the most exact location?

2. Using the map on the left, name the place that is located at 87°45'W, 41°50'N. Can you find this exact location on the top map? Why or why not?

Chapter Review

Chapter Review Timeline

1522
Magellan's expedition circles the world

| 1450 | 1500 | 1550 | 1600 | 1650 |

1492
Columbus lands at San Salvador

1521
Cortés defeats the Aztec Empire

1540
Coronado begins to explore the Southwest

1609
Champlain starts a settlement in North America

Summarizing the Main Idea

1 Copy and complete the chart below, indicating the key people and accomplishments of each lesson.

	Key People	Accomplishments
Lesson 1		
Lesson 2		
Lesson 3		
Lesson 4		

Vocabulary

2 Using at least six of the following terms, write a brief biography of an imaginary explorer.

navigation (p. 90)
circumnavigate (p. 95)
conquistador (p. 101)

Columbian Exchange (p. 106)
plantation (p. 107)
immunity (p. 107)

epidemic (p. 107)
armada (p. 112)
Northwest Passage (p. 114)

Reviewing the Facts

3 What inventions made travel by sea easier?

4 What pattern did Columbus's later voyages set for Europeans in the Americas?

5 What did Magellan accomplish?

6 Why did Cortés come to Mexico in 1519?

7 Why did las Casas object to the Spanish conquest of the Americas?

8 What kinds of work were done by enslaved Africans in the Americas?

9 How did the defeat of the Spanish Armada change the balance of power in Europe?

10 What did Cabot, Cartier, Champlain, and Hudson have in common?

11 Look at the maps on pages 116 and 117. What is the latitude and longitude of the junction of the Illinois and Vermillion rivers in degrees and minutes?

12 Use an atlas of the United States to determine the latitude and longitude of your community. The distance between each degree of latitude is 69 miles.

Geography Skills

13 Look at the map on page 95. In which direction did Magellan choose to sail around the world? Why did he choose to travel in this direction?

14 Create a chart of all the explorers mentioned in the chapter. Include the year of their travels, the nations they served, and the places they explored.

Critical Thinking

15 Conclude What if the Spanish had not conquered and killed Native Americans? Would this have prevented the great decline in the Native American population in Central America during the 1500s?

16 Cause and Effect What effect did the conquest of the Americas have on the peoples of Africa?

17 Comparing Then and Now What nations built the first European settlements in Mexico and Canada? Is this still reflected in the cultures of these countries? How?

Writing: Citizenship and Geography

18 Citizenship In 1994 President Clinton met with leaders of the nearly 550 Native American peoples. Write a paragraph about the native people in your part of the United States. How many live there today?

19 Geography Think about the plants and animals that Spanish explorers discovered in the Americas. Then put yourself in their position. Write a letter to a friend in Spain describing your exciting new experiences.

Activities

Culture/Arts Activity
An Aztec poet wrote this in 1521: "There is nothing but grief and suffering . . . where once we saw beauty and valor." What events do you think the poet is describing? Write your own short poem or story about those events.

History/Research Activity
Soon after Cortés conquered Mexico, another conquistador, Francisco Pizarro, invaded the Inca Empire in South America. Find out how the Incas compared with the Aztecs. How were they similar? How were they different?

Internet Option

Check the **Internet Social Studies Center** for ideas on how to extend your theme project beyond your classroom.

THEME PROJECT CHECK-IN

As you continue to work on your project, pick an explorer discussed in this unit and answer the following questions:
- What is one area he explored? Whom did he meet? What did he encounter?
- How did the explorer treat the Native Americans who lived there?
- Was he able to adapt to the environment he explored?

The Founding of European Colonies

Chapter Preview: *People, Places, and Events*

1600	1610	1620

John Smith   1607

This man saved a colony — from itself. What did he do? *Lesson 2, Page 130*

Pilgrims   1620

These people gave us a national holiday. Find out how. *Lesson 3, Page 138*

Dutch Plate

The people who made this settled a now world famous place. Where? *Lesson 4, Page 144*

The Growth of New Spain

Main Idea Spain set up a colonial system that changed both the Native American and Spanish ways of life.

When she was eight years old, Juana de Asbaje (ahs BAH heh) begged her mother to dress her as a boy. Only boys could study at the university. She wanted to study at the university too.

The year was 1659, and the place was Mexico City. Along with the university, there were churches, elegant brick and stone houses, and a palace. Merchants sold goods in the great central square. Nearby were silversmiths, ironworkers, and silk merchants. Native Americans lived around the city's edge.

Although Juana never attended the university, she spent her life studying and writing. She became a nun. Under the name Sor (Spanish for "Sister") Juana Inés de la Cruz, she became a well-known poet and lived her life in prosperous Mexico City.

◄ The picture to the left is of Plimoth Plantation in Plymouth, Massachusetts.

Key Vocabulary

colony

viceroy

mestizo

hacienda

mission

presidio

Key Events

1598 Spanish settlers move into New Mexico

1680 Pueblo Revolt

1692 Spain regains New Mexico

1630   1640   1650

Peter Stuyvesant   1647

Why did this man attack Fort Christina? *Lesson 4, Page 147*

Juana Inés de la Cruz

This woman did something few women in her time did. What was it? *Lesson 1, Page 121*

Spanish Mission

This gateway led to a new world for two different peoples. Who were they? *Lesson 1, Page 124*

The colony of New Spain included parts of what is now the American Southwest.

Haciendas

Many people were needed to run a hacienda. There were field workers, cowhands, blacksmiths, carpenters, butchers, cooks, weavers, teachers, tailors, priests, and sometimes a doctor.

Spain's Colonies

Focus *Why did Spain want to establish colonies in the Americas?*

Mexico City was the capital of the colony of New Spain. A **colony** is a settlement ruled by a distant country, called the "mother country." Spain claimed land and people in the Americas as colonies, one of which was New Spain. Spain established the colony to add to its own wealth and power and to convert the local peoples to Christianity.

New Spain had valuable resources. There were gold and silver deposits deep in its mountains, tall tropical trees for lumber, and fertile soil to raise sugar cane. These riches were sent back to Spain.

There were not enough European settlers, however, to do all this work. Many of these settlers refused to work with their own hands. Since Spain claimed control over the people as well as the land, they made Native Americans do the hardest work for them.

New Spain was a society made up of many classes. At the top was the **viceroy,** a person sent by the king to rule in his place. Surrounding the viceroy was his court — his family and a few rich and powerful people who helped him govern.

The middle class was made up of skilled workers, craftspeople, miners, ranchers, shopkeepers, nuns and priests, doctors, and lawyers. At the bottom was the largest group. These were poor people who had few skills but did most of the hard work.

Most Spanish settlers, rich or poor, became permanent residents. Some Spanish people married Native Americans. Their children were called **mestizos,** (mehs TEE zohs). The majority of people in Mexico and Guatemala today are mestizos.

Haciendas

In the 1600s, most people in New Spain worked on large farming and ranching estates called haciendas (ah see YEHN dahs). **Haciendas** were huge land areas owned by the Spanish colonists.

Some haciendas were as big as several million acres and included towns and villages. A typical hacienda might have a cattle ranch, a farm, a mine, a lumber mill, a village, a large house for the owner, and a chapel.

Many Native Americans lived and worked on haciendas. Although their labor produced New Spain's wealth, this group was very poor. They usually owed money to the hacienda owner for food, clothing, or rent, and weren't allowed to leave until their debt was paid. Since they did not earn enough to pay such debts, they worked on the hacienda all their lives.

Surrounding the haciendas were smaller Spanish farms and Native American villages. The Native Americans living in these villages worked on the hacienda when the hacienda owners needed extra labor.

The artist has painted a mestizo family sharing a happy moment together. **Art:** *How does he show their closeness and love for one another?*

Spanish missions blended the Spanish building style with the Pueblo adobe-brick building style. The result was well suited to the region's blazing hot climate. It was later adopted for other buildings in the Southwest.

The Spanish Move North

Focus *Why did the Spanish establish missions in New Spain?*

In 1598, Don Juan de Oñate (oh NYAH teh), a wealthy Spaniard, went out to settle new lands. He marched north from Central Mexico with a band of colonists, armed troops, and friars. The friars were members of a religious order who wanted to convert Native Americans to Christianity.

De Oñate paused at the Rio Grande, near today's El Paso, Texas. Before him lay the vast lands of what is now the southwestern United States. He claimed possession of:

> **"L**ands, pueblos, cities, villas, of whatsoever nature now founded in the kingdom of . . . New Mexico . . . and all its native Indians.**"**

Over 16,000 Pueblo Indians lived in the area de Oñate claimed. Their settlements perched high on the mesas and dotted the plains. Like a sprawling apartment house, each settlement, or pueblo, was made of individual rooms joined together and several stories high.

The Pueblo were agricultural people with strong religious beliefs. The Spanish, however, believed the greatest kindness they could do for the Pueblo was to convert them to Christianity. To do this, the friars built **missions,** or church settlements, all over New Mexico. To protect the friars and their converts from the Apache and the Navajo, the Spanish built **presidios,** or forts. By 1680 a thin chain of missions and presidios stretched across the Southwest.

Many Pueblo continued to practice their religion in secret. When they were discovered, Spanish officials punished them. One of those punished was a spiritual leader named Popé (poh PEH). He believed the Spanish attempt to convert the Pueblo was harmful. Popé planned a revolt against the Spanish and got others to join him.

On August 10, 1680, Popé's followers rose up, burning churches and attacking haciendas. The Spanish fled south to El Paso. The Pueblo had driven the Spanish out of their land at least for a short time.

Popé ruled the Pueblo with an iron hand. He ordered every trace of the Spanish wiped out. He stopped the practice of Christianity and even the use of Spanish tools. The Pueblo people grew more and more unhappy with his rule.

Popé's death brought some relief, but the Pueblo still suffered a long drought and fierce Apache attacks. When Spanish troops marched from El Paso, the Pueblo were too weak to resist. In 1692 the Spanish commander offered the suffering people peace, and they agreed. New Mexico was once more Spanish land.

Lesson Review

1600	1650	1700

1598
Spanish settlers move into New Mexico

1680
Pueblo Revolt

1692
Spain regains New Mexico

1 **Key Vocabulary:** Write a paragraph about New Mexico, using the words colony, viceroy, mestizos, hacienda, mission, and presidio.

2 **Focus:** Why did Spain want to establish colonies in the Americas?

3 **Focus:** Why did the Spanish establish missions in New Spain?

4 **Critical Thinking: Conclude** What advantages did adopting the Spanish way of life offer the Pueblo? What disadvantages?

5 **Theme: Exploration and Encounter** What evidence do you see today of the influence of New Spain?

6 **Geography/Art Activity:** Make an illustrated map of a hacienda. Label the buildings and identify the activities that go on in each.

Places and Regions

What Do Southwestern Place Names Tell Us?

What's in a name? "More than you think," a geographer might answer. A name like Two Rivers tells about the physical geography of a place. A Spanish name like San José tells about the people who settled there in the past.

Some place names even give clues about several peoples who lived there at different times. The Arizona city of Tucson is a good example. Tucson's original Native American name was Chuk Shon, a Tohono O'Odham word meaning "village of the dark spring at the foot of the mountain." Spanish missionaries first came to Chuk Shon in 1692. They spelled its name Tuquison, which became Tucson. Today Tucson's name recalls both the original Tohono O'Odham residents and the Spanish who came afterward.

The Spanish at Chuk Shon added "San José" to its name, making it San José de Tuquison. Later it was shortened to just Tucson.

1 El Paso

A River Crossing
El Paso was originally called El Paso del Norte. That meant "the crossing of the northern river," in Spanish. El Paso was an important crossing of the Rio Grande. Do you know of any places named for roads, bridges, or rivers?

Art Connection

The Spanish borrowed from the building style of the Native American pueblos to build communities in the southwest. Southwestern artists today also combine Spanish and Native American influences in their art. Do you know of any other examples of two artistic styles blending together?

2 Taos

Taos Pueblo
Taos, in New Mexico, is the Spanish spelling of a Tewa Pueblo town. It may come from either the word tuota, meaning "red willow place" or tuatah, "at the village."

Place Names in the Southwest

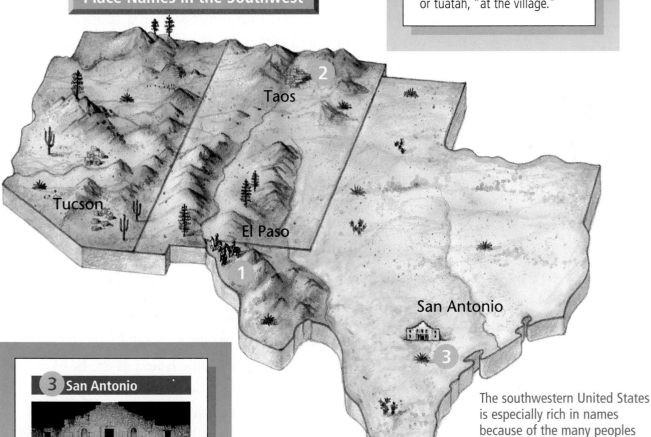

Taos

Tucson

El Paso

San Antonio

The southwestern United States is especially rich in names because of the many peoples who have lived there. Do you know of any other places whose names tell about their history?

3 San Antonio

San Antonio Mission
In 1691, Spanish explorers came to a river in Texas. Settlers named it San Antonio because it was the day of St. Anthony. Later, they built a town and mission named San Antonio. The town is still called San Antonio, but today the mission is known as the Alamo.

Research Activity

Almost every name has a meaning, even if people today have forgotten it.

1 Choose the name of a town or city in your state. Find out its meaning.

2 Explain the origin and meaning of the name to the class in an oral presentation.

The First English Settlements

Main Idea Private English companies established colonies in North America and traded with Native Americans.

Key Vocabulary

charter

invest

stock

indentured servant

Key Events

1587 Roanoke Island Colony started

1607 Jamestown Colony started

1619 First Africans arrive in Jamestown

How would you record your impression of a strange new place very few people had ever seen? Would you bring a camera or a tape recorder?

When Englishmen John White and Thomas Hariot were sent to a strange new land, they brought their sketchbooks and journals. The strange new land was Roanoke Island, off the coast of what is now North Carolina. The year was 1585.

Together, the artist White and the scientist Hariot recorded the daily life of the Algonquin Indians — their homes, plants, and tools. Thanks to their work, we have some information about the way of life of Native Americans in the late 1500s.

Roanoke Island Colony

Focus What is the mystery of the Roanoke Island Colony?

In 1587, John White returned to Roanoke Island as the head of a new colony of settlers. The Croatoans (kroh ah TOH uhns), the native people of the island, welcomed them with a feast. A few weeks later, the colony welcomed John White's granddaughter, Virginia Dare. She was the first English baby to be born in North America.

In 1588, John White returned to England for badly needed supplies. He had planned to return to Roanoke within a year, but England went to war with Spain. Most ships were needed for the fight, so he could not get back to Roanoke right away.

After almost three years, White made it back to the colony. To his surprise, it was deserted. The buildings were still standing, White's belongings had been carefully buried, and the colonists had disappeared. The only clues to this mystery were the word

This drawing by John White shows Algonquin fishing.
Science: *What are the different ways they use to catch fish?*

CROATOAN carved on a post and CRO carved on a tree.

White thought the colonists had gone to a Croatoan settlement on a nearby island. He tried to follow, but two storms in a row damaged the ships. The crew of the ships insisted that they return to England while the ships could still sail.

White could not make another trip to find the Roanoke settlers, and he never saw them again. A later colonist, however, reported seeing a Native American boy whose hair was "a perfect yellow." Was he one of the Roanoke settlers? No one knows.

The Homes

John White drew these views of a large Algonquin village in 1585. The houses were made of poles covered with reed matting. They sit along a wide main street.

The Fields

White drew corn fields in three stages of growth. Some are ready to harvest, some are ripening, and some are newly sprouted.

The Dance

Here, some Algonquin are dancing. Others are sitting for a meal next to baskets of food.

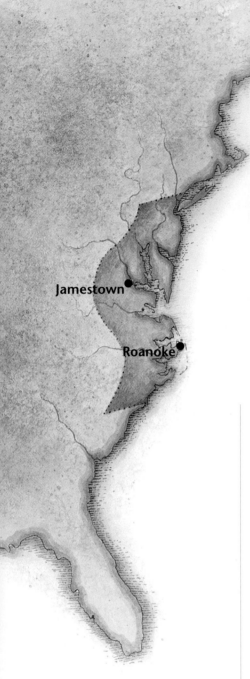

Jamestown

Look at the drawing of Jamestown, above right. John Smith was responsible for the three-sided wall around the settlement. **Math:** *Why are three sides easier to defend than four?*

Focus *What was life like during the first 10 years of the Jamestown settlement?*

Although the Roanoke Island Colony had failed, the English still hoped to start a colony in Virginia. A group of London merchants formed the Virginia Company. King James I of England granted them a **charter**, an official document that gave the company the right to settle in North America. Each merchant **invested** in, or gave money to, the company. They received **stock**, or part of the company, in return. Merchants hoped the colonists would find valuable resources and the merchants would make a profit.

At first, the colonists who landed in Jamestown, Virginia, in 1607 found few ways to make a profit. In fact, they had a hard time even feeding themselves. Most of the colonists were gentlemen, servants, and craftsmen — not farmers. They were not very successful at farming and hunting.

John Smith became a leader of the colony. He had no use for people who would not work. He organized the settlers into work groups and announced that "he that will not work, shall not eat." Under his leadership, life in Jamestown began to improve.

Smith often explored the Virginia countryside. He liked to tell the story of his capture by the Algonquins. Their chief, Powhatan, was going to kill him, Smith reported. Then the chief's 12-year-old daughter, Pocahontas, begged her father to spare Smith's life. No one is sure if this story is true. But Pocahontas was a real person. When she grew up, she married colonist John Rolfe.

Around 1611, before he married Pocahontas, John Rolfe planted some tobacco seeds from the Caribbean. The seeds grew extremely well. Since smoking tobacco was becoming popular in England, the colonists had finally found a crop that would make them rich. Now they needed enough people to grow the tobacco.

Much of the work of the colony was done by indentured servants. **Indentured servants** were people who worked for a certain number of years in return for the trip to America, and food, clothing, and shelter once they arrived. There were not enough indentured servants to meet the tobacco farmers' growing desire for more workers. The colonists began looking for another source of labor to grow their crops. They found it in African people who had newly arrived in Jamestown.

These first Africans arrived in the Virginia colony in 1619. More followed. Many served a term of indenture and then became free. As time went by, the English began lengthening the number of years Africans had to work. Within 42 years of the arrival of the first Africans in Jamestown, indentured servitude had given way to enslavement.

Pocahontas

After Pocahontas married John Rolfe, she traveled to England with him. There, she was treated like a princess. This painting of her was done in England and shows her wearing English clothing. She also adopted the English name of Rebecca. She died in England in 1617, while getting ready to return home.

Lesson Review

1580		1600		1620	

1587
Roanoke Island Colony

1607
Jamestown Colony started

1619
First Africans arrive in Jamestown

1. **Key Vocabulary:** Define these terms: charter, invest, stock, indentured servant.

2. **Focus:** What is the mystery of the Roanoke Island Colony?

3. **Focus:** What was life like during the first 10 years of the Jamestown settlement?

4. **Critical Thinking: Problem Solving** The first colonists went to Jamestown hoping to find gold and other valuables. Was this an advantage or disadvantage?

5. **Geography:** How did the distance from England affect John White's ability to help the Roanoke colonists?

6. **Citizenship/Writing Activity:** Your class is the first Jamestown Colony. What qualities do you want for a leader of the settlement? Work with the rest of the class to make a list.

Comparing Primary and Secondary Sources

Different Views

If you want to learn about indentured servants, where would you look? Richard Frethorne's letter (on the next page) from 1623 can help you understand what one man experienced as an indentured servant. The letter is a **primary source**. Primary sources give a first-hand account of a historical event. You can also look in **secondary sources** such as history books. Secondary sources are written by someone who did not witness an event. Secondary sources can give you a broader view of what happened.

*ned their indentur...
n, a shipload at a ti...
ncluding transporta...
person, was seldo...
olonies the agent c...
r each servant "set...
sly avoided when it...
owner bought a se...
ght a slave.)
ial profits to be ma...
usly deceitful, as w...
nt. Agents came t...
tations for having no qu...
getting him so drunk that he would p...
piece of paper shoved in front of him. If lies and...
n't work, a whack on the head usually would.
men and women were forced to the ship and...
d into the hold not to see daylight again until the...
s of England were out of sight.
blic outrage over such forced migration, particu-...
y when it involved children, spurred Parliament to...
ct laws that protected the citizen from the spirits...
d, at the same time, protected the honest agent from...
ise accusations of kidnapping by a servant with sec-*

*JUST ARRIVED, in the Ship JOHN, Capt. ROACH,
from DUBLIN,*
**A Number of HEALTHY, INDENTED
MEN and WOMEN SERVANTS:**
AMONG THE FORMER ARE,
*A Variety of TRADESMEN, with fome good FAR-
MERS, and ftout LABOURERS: Their Indentures will be diſpoſed
of, on reafonable Terms, for CASH, by
GEORGE SALMON.*

*Many Europeans could afford to come to America only by of-
fering themselves as indentured servants or redemptioners.
...r advertisements like the one above regularly an-
...of indentured servants.*

"*A ship docked at a Virginia harbor in 1635, and from its decks emerged nearly two-hundred newcomers from England, among them twenty-five-year-old Thomas Carter. For some the voyage had cost over £5 sterling. For others, the price was higher still: several years of their lives. Carter, like thousands of other penniless Europeans, had sold himself into bondage as an indentured servant to pay his passage to the colonies.*"

On these pages are part of a letter from Richard Frethorne to his parents and part of a magazine article titled "Colonists in Bondage: Indentured Servants in America."

- Read through each source. Clue words such as *I* and *me* tell you Frethorne is talking about his own experience and that the letter is a primary source. The author of "Colonists in Bondage" does not include any personal experiences, which is a clue that the article is a secondary source.

- Study each source further and think about what kind of source it is — a diary, a letter, part of a history book? You can guess that Frethorne's words come from a letter, and the article comes from a history book or magazine.

- Look for facts and opinions in each source, such as the fact that indentured servants paid for their trip on the ship with a period of servitude. Think about how facts and opinion can offer useful information.

② **Think It Through**

In what way is reading about history in a primary source different from reading about an event in a secondary source?

③ **Use It**

1. Find your own example of a primary source, such as a journal or an autobiography.

2. List the facts and opinions in your source.

3. Find a secondary source about the same subject. Compare the two sources and explain their similarities and differences.

" . . . since I came out of the ship, I never ate anything but peas, and loblollie (that is, water gruel). As for deer or venison, I never saw any since I came into this land; there is indeed some fowl, but we are not allowed to go and get it, but must work hard both early and late for a mess of water gruel, and a mouthful of bread and beef. A mouthful of bread . . . must serve four men, which is most pitiful . . ."

New England Settlements

Main Idea Pilgrims and Puritans began a new life by starting colonies in North America.

I t had been a long and stormy voyage. The ship may have been blown off course, and when the passengers finally arrived, they were tired and sick. Reaching a beach on Cape Cod, the small group of English settlers thanked God. Today we know these people successfully started a new life. On that day in 1620, they only knew they were beginning an uncertain adventure. Settler William Bradford later wrote that all the settlers could see was:

"**D**esolate wilderness, full of wild beasts . . . the whole country, full of woods and thickets, represented a wild and savage hue [color]."

The artist shows the Pilgrims encountering a snowy landscape at their Cape Cod landing.

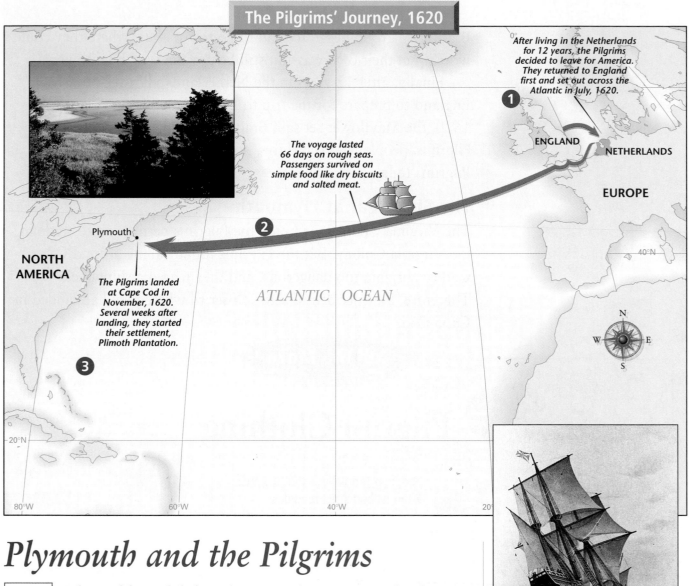

1 After living in the Netherlands for 12 years, the Pilgrims decided to leave for America. They returned to England first and set out across the Atlantic in July, 1620.

The voyage lasted 66 days on rough seas. Passengers survived on simple food like dry biscuits and salted meat.

2

The Pilgrims landed at Cape Cod in November, 1620. Several weeks after landing, they started their settlement, Plimoth Plantation.

3

Plymouth

NORTH AMERICA

ATLANTIC OCEAN

ENGLAND

NETHERLANDS

EUROPE

40°N

20°N

80°W   60°W   40°W   20

N
W   E
S

Plymouth and the Pilgrims

Focus *Why and how did the Pilgrims settle in New England?*

In the 1500s, the King of England left the Roman Catholic Church and created a new church — the Church of England. After a while, some people began to criticize the Church of England. These people were known as **Puritans,** because they wanted to "purify" the Church.

Some of the Puritans were called **Separatists.** They wanted to separate from the Church of England and start their own church. William Bradford and some other passengers aboard the *Mayflower* were Separatists.

By law, everyone in England had to belong to the Church of England. Because they refused to, the Separatists were treated badly. William Bradford's group fled from England to the Netherlands so they could practice their religion in peace. In the Netherlands, however, jobs were few and wages were low.

The *Mayflower* was a small ship. With over 102 people on board — passengers and crew — space was very tight during the two-and-a-half month trip. **Map Skill:** *When the Pilgrims were at latitude 42°N and longitude 40°W, about how much of their trip had they completed?*

The Founding of European Colonies   **135**

Bradford's group began to plan to go to America, where they could worship in their own way but still be governed by English laws.

Finally, after 12 years in the Netherlands, they returned to England to prepare for the trip to North America. In August of 1620, the Mayflower set sail. Bradford called the passengers **Pilgrims**, people who travel to a holy place. We still call them Pilgrims today.

The First Year at Plymouth

The Virginia Company granted the Pilgrims permission to settle in the Virginia Colony. But the Pilgrims found sailing around Cape Cod to Virginia too dangerous, and they feared a shipwreck. Therefore, they decided to settle closer to where they had landed in Cape Cod.

•Tell Me More •

Pilgrim Clothing

People often believe that because Pilgrims had strict religious beliefs, every part of their lives was strict and dull. This is not true. Pilgrim clothing, for example, was not dull in color. Pilgrims wore red, brown, yellow, orange, blue, and black. Pilgrims did, however, dress practically to make clothes last and to keep warm in the long, cold winters.

Collars were separate from shirts so that they could be washed separately.

This padded jacket was called a doublet. It was worn over a shirt.

The lower leg was covered with tight, knitted hose.

Men wore short pants, tied at the knee, called breeches. They were sometimes padded.

Pilgrim men and women wore hats whenever they went outdoors.

The waistcoat was worn over a long shift which was like the man's shirt, but longer.

Women also wore a long petticoat, or skirt.

This is one artist's idea of what the first Thanksgiving looked like. **Art:** *How does he show the idea of thankfulness?*

Since they were outside the Virginia Company territory, there were no rules in place to govern the Separatists and the other English settlers who sailed on the *Mayflower* with them. So the leaders wrote an agreement called the Mayflower Compact. Everyone on the ship agreed to a government and set of laws for their new community. Then, the entire group settled together in a place they called Plimoth Plantation. Today, the town is still called Plymouth.

It was late December when the Pilgrims landed at Plymouth. They began at once to build homes, storehouses, and a common house which was used for meetings and prayer. Building in winter was a difficult task, and many settlers were already weak from the journey. They did not have enough of the kinds of foods that would have kept them healthy. By spring, about half of the original 102 colonists had died.

During the winter, the colonists met a Pawtuxet (pah TUHKS iht) Indian named Squanto (SKWAHN toh). He was able to speak English with them because he had been captured seven years earlier by an English explorer. Squanto had been sold into slavery in Spain. After a time, he escaped and returned home.

With Squanto as interpreter, the Pilgrims made friends with the Wampanoag (wahm puh NOH ahg) Indians and their leader Massasoit (mass ah SOYT). The Wampanoag and the settlers made a treaty, promising peace between the two groups.

This cradle was used by a Pilgrim family. There were many young children aboard the *Mayflower*.

In good weather and in bad, Puritans went to church every Sunday. The sermons ran several hours in the unheated meetinghouse.

In the spring, the colonists planted the seeds they had brought with them. Soon, however, the colonists found that these seeds grew poorly in the New England climate. Squanto was able to help again. He introduced them to corn, teaching them to plant the seeds in small hills and to use fish as fertilizer to help the corn grow.

In the fall of their first year, the Pilgrims harvested their crop and celebrated with a festival. Massasoit and other Wampanoags came and contributed deer meat to the feast. Today we celebrate a version of their festival — Thanksgiving.

Puritans and the Massachusetts Bay Colony

Bibles were one of the most valued items Puritans owned. Some were passed down from parent to child for many generations.

Focus *What were the goals of the Puritans who settled in Massachusetts Bay?*

Back in England, life was growing difficult for the Puritans. In 1629, King Charles I threw many Puritan leaders into prison. Because of this, a group of Puritans decided to move to New England.

The Puritans wanted to create a model community, an example to the Church of England and the rest of the world. John Winthrop, their leader, said

> **"W**e must Consider that we shall be as a City upon a Hill, the eyes of all people are upon us."

The Puritans were educated people of learning and wealth — landowners, lawyers, and merchants. They had the time, money, and knowledge to prepare well. Winthrop studied reports from previous colonists to learn what they needed. For months he gathered ships, settlers, supplies, and equipment.

In April of 1630, the Puritan fleet set sail. Seven ships held some 700 passengers. Other ships were loaded with livestock and supplies. The Puritans were the first settlers to come to the Americas so well equipped.

In June, the fleet arrived at Massachusetts Bay, a large, sheltered harbor on the coast of New England. On its southern shore lay Plymouth, where the Pilgrims had settled. The Puritans chose for their settlement a small neck of land extending into the bay, north of Plymouth. They named it Boston.

During the next 10 years, about 15,000 Puritans arrived. As their numbers grew, they formed other towns outside of Boston. After a time, they surrounded the Pilgrim community at Plymouth. John Winthrop's "city on a hill" was on its way to becoming a roaring success. English settlers were in New England to stay.

Biography

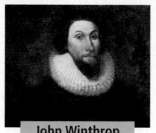

John Winthrop

John Winthrop was the first governor of the Massachusetts Bay Colony. Throughout his time as governor, he kept a diary of important events and experiences. That diary is now a book, *The History of New England.* It is one of the most valuable records we have of that time. Winthrop governed the colony for 19 years, until his death in 1649.

Lesson Review

1620	1630

1620
Pilgrims settle Plymouth

1630
Puritans settle Boston

1 **Key Vocabulary:** Write a paragraph about the colonists, using the words **Puritan, Separatist,** and **Pilgrim.**

2 **Focus:** Why and how did the Pilgrims settle in New England?

3 **Focus:** What were the goals of the Puritans who settled in Massachusetts Bay?

4 **Critical Thinking: Conclude** Why was the Mayflower Compact so important?

5 **Geography:** Why did both the Pilgrims and the Puritans settle near the coast?

6 **Citizenship/Writing Activity:** The Puritans wanted to create a model community. Write your plan for a model community. Compare your ideas with those of other students, then work together to create one plan.

Resolving Conflicts

Why Do We Have Rules?

What would it be like if people could drive cars wherever they wanted, even on the sidewalk? What freedom! But if you were walking somewhere, or riding your bike, you would have problems. Having no rules might sound great, but rules help guide us. The settlers aboard the *Mayflower* discovered that people needed rules to help themselves and one another.

Case Study

The Mayflower Compact

Two groups of people came on the *Mayflower*, and they didn't get along. Of the 102 passengers, about one third were Pilgrims. They wanted a place to worship freely. The others came hoping to find wealth in the new land. They expected to grow rich in Virginia, where they had been given rights to land and self-government. The *Mayflower* arrived in New England, instead. These people were not pleased. They threatened to go off on their own.

On board the *Mayflower*, the leaders drew up an agreement. Forty-one male passengers signed the Mayflower Compact. They  agreed to choose leaders together, to draw up "just and equal Laws," and to make decisions "for the general good of the Colony."

Take Action

Now is your chance to design a compact. The governor of your state has sent you a letter asking you to set up "an ideal classroom." "Please set up rules so children can learn their lessons well and be creative," the letter says. "Decide on rules that will work for everyone — including your principal and teacher!"

1 Sometimes, thinking about the other side of an issue can make your position clearer. In groups, describe a classroom where it would be hard for students to learn. What would happen there?

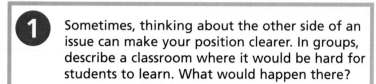

2 Now describe an ideal classroom. What would happen there?

3 List rules for how people should treat each other in this ideal classroom. Take turns coming up with rules. Write a reason for each rule you pick.

4 Decide which rules you can all agree on (including the adults). Add other rules if needed. Agree on a final list.

5 Write up a formal compact for the governor in which you list rules and reasons. Read your compact to the class. Does it sound like everyone else's? Why or why not?

Resolving Conflicts

- Focus on the goal you wish to achieve and try to be flexible about the ways to get there.
- Give reasons for what you want.

Research Activity

Peace agreements are also compacts. Find out about the peace agreements the United States helped create either in the Middle East in 1993 or somewhere else. What did each side want? What did each side get in the agreement? How did each side give up something?

French and Dutch Colonies

Main Idea The French and Dutch started colonies in North America to compete with other European countries.

Key Vocabulary

missionary

pelt

patroon

religious
  persecution

Key Events

1608 New France
established

1624 New
Netherland
established

Father Paul Le Jeune (luh ZHOON) spent 17 years living, eating, and traveling with Native Americans in the Quebec area. He wrote detailed reports about these experiences. Here he describes the women cutting trees to make their winter houses:

> "Now, *when we arrived . . . where we were to camp, the women, armed with axes, went here and there in the great forests, cutting the framework . . .*"

French Missions and Settlement

Jesuit Missions in New France

The Jesuit missions were the center of the Jesuits' work. Some Jesuits, like Father Le Jeune, lived with the Native Americans. Others traveled with French explorers.
Geography: *What natural feature did the missionaries and explorers use to travel throughout New France?*

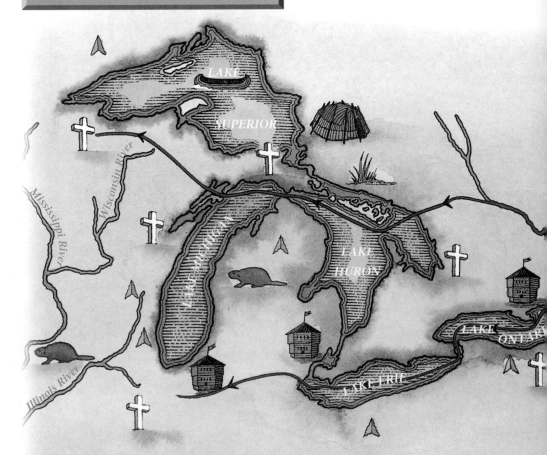

LAKE
SUPERIOR

Mississippi River

Wisconsin River

LAKE MICHIGAN

LAKE HURON

LAKE ONTARIO

LAKE ERIE

Illinois River

France Starts a Colony

Focus **Why did France establish a colony in North America?**

Father Le Jeune was one of a group of French people living in the colony of New France. This was a large area of North America claimed by France in 1608 after Champlain's explorations.

Champlain also explored and claimed the Great Lakes for France. From there, other explorers traveled down the Mississippi River. They claimed for France territory all the way down to what is now New Orleans.

Father Le Jeune was a missionary. A **missionary** is someone who travels to do religious work. Le Jeune was a Jesuit, a Roman Catholic priest. Like other Jesuits, he worked to convert the Native Americans to Roman Catholicism. The Jesuits built missions throughout New France. Look at the map below to see where these missions were located.

Other French colonists were explorers and fur traders. There were many more traders and explorers than there were farmers. The cold climate and short growing season in New France made farming difficult. Since animal furs — especially beaver — were very popular in Europe, fur trapping and trading made settlers more money than they could get by farming.

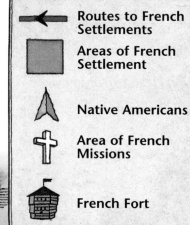

←	Routes to French Settlements
■	Areas of French Settlement
▲	Native Americans
✝	Area of French Missions
🏯	French Fort

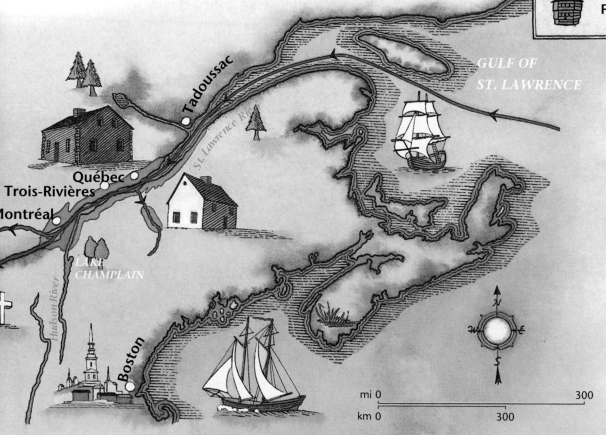

Tadoussac

GULF OF ST. LAWRENCE

St. Lawrence River

Québec

Trois-Rivières

Montréal

LAKE CHAMPLAIN

Hudson River

Boston

mi 0   300

km 0   300

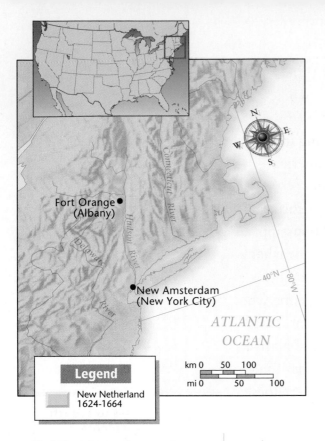

Find New Amsterdam on the map above. **Map Skill:** *What natural feature helped make it a successful port?*

From the first, the French enjoyed a lively trade with the Native Americans of the region, especially the Hurons (HYUR uhns.) The Hurons eagerly traded beaver pelts and other furs for French metal tools and weapons. A **pelt** is an animal skin with hair or fur still on it. The Hurons also taught French trappers how to find the animals, and how to build and use canoes and snowshoes.

Remember Quebec, the fur-trading post Champlain had founded on the Saint Lawrence River? That settlement grew very slowly. By 1625, only 60 settlers lived there. In 1665, France sent a new governor with 1,100 soldiers. Some of these soldiers were given land, and became permanent residents. But even with these new people, the number of French people in New France remained small.

The Dutch in New Netherland

Focus *Who were some of the different peoples of New Netherland, and why did they settle there?*

In 1624, the Dutch also claimed territory in North America. Their colony ran from the Delaware River to Manhattan Island and up along the Hudson River to Albany. They called it New Netherland.

This is an early picture of the settlement, made not long after it was founded. You can see how busy the town — filled with homes and other buildings — already was.

To encourage settlement, the Dutch West India Company granted large land areas to patroons. **Patroons** were wealthy men who could afford to bring people and supplies to settle the land. In return for these huge grants of land, each patroon agreed to send fifty colonists to settle on the new land.

Eager for the colony to grow, the Dutch welcomed people of other nationalities and religions. German, Norwegian, Swedish, French, Danish, and English people came to the colony. Some came to escape **religious persecution** in their homelands. That meant they could not practice their religion as they wanted to. As the Pilgrims had, they went first to the Netherlands, then to New Netherland.

New Amsterdam was the largest settlement in New Netherland. It was founded in 1626 when a settler named Peter Minuit (MIHN yoo iht) purchased Manhattan Island from the Manates (MAN nuh tees). He paid for it with trade goods.

New Amsterdam grew very quickly. A visitor in 1643 was amazed by both the size of the town and the variety of the people — about 500 people, speaking as many as 18 languages.

New Amsterdam was a disorderly settlement, however. In 1647, the Dutch West India Company sent Peter Stuyvesant (STY vih suhnt) to take control. This new director-general set and enforced strict rules.

He was intolerant of other religions. He persecuted settlers of many religions who did not want to follow

The painting of this young Dutch woman reveals her wealth. Notice the lace clothing, the coral necklace, and the Chinese fan — all expensive items. **Economics:** *What do the woman's ornaments tell you about trade in New Amsterdam?*

NORTH

AMERICA

ROCKY MOUNTAINS

GREAT
PLAINS

APPALACHIAN
MOUNTAINS

Missouri River

Arkansas River

Ohio River

Mississippi River

Rio Grande

Lake Superior

Lake Michigan

Lake Huron

Lake Erie

Lake Ontario

BAY

Québec
1608

Montréal 1642

Fort Orange
(Albany)
1624

Salem 1626

Boston 1630

Providence 1636

New Amsterdam
(New York)
1626

New Haven
1638

Roanoke Island 1585

Santa Fe 1609

ATLANTIC
OCEAN

St. Augustine 1565

PACIFIC
OCEAN

Monterrey 1579

GULF OF MEXICO

Havana 1519

Santo Domingo
1496

Mexico City
(Tenochtitlán until 1521)

Granada 1523

Legend

🚩	British
🚩	Dutch
🚩	French
🚩	Spanish

km 0   250   500

mi 0   250   500

50°N
40°N
30°N
20°N

100°W   90°W   80°W

This map shows Spanish, British, French, and Dutch land claims in North America. **Map Skill:** *Which country claimed the most land in the north? Which country claimed the most land in the interior?*

the religious laws of the Dutch Reformed Church. He tried to force new Jewish settlers to leave, but the Dutch West India Company refused to let him. These Jewish settlers had moved from Brazil. Originally from Spain and Portugal, they had fled to Brazil to escape persecution. When the Portuguese captured Brazil, they had to flee again.

Africans, enslaved and free, were also early residents of New Amsterdam. The Dutch West India Company sometimes granted enslaved people "half-freedom." They were free to travel, own property, and marry, but still had to work for the Company at certain times and pay the Company a set amount of money each year.

By 1638, Sweden had established fur-trading posts, or forts, in the Delaware River Valley. In 1655, Peter Stuyvesant expanded the Dutch holdings by attacking — and conquering — the nearby colony of New Sweden. He surrounded Fort Christina, an important Swedish fort. After 10 days, the fort surrendered. Sweden then gave up its holdings to the Dutch.

The Colonies in North America

By the mid-1600s, small European colonies dotted the continent of North America. The map on the opposite page shows where the colonies were located. Each colony included people who had come from different countries. These people had different goals, religions, languages, and ways of treating the Native Americans they encountered.

The Spanish and the French tried to convert the Native Americans to Catholicism. The Spanish used the labor of Native Americans to work the land, sending the wealth they made back to Spain. The French and the Dutch, however, mainly traded furs which were highly valued in Europe.

The English who settled in New England were looking for religious freedom. The English people who settled Virginia went there to acquire wealth. Some English settlements fought their Native American neighbors, while others befriended them.

For the next 150 years or so, each colony worked to survive and succeed. The Native Americans had a harder task. They had to deal with these strangers who had suddenly come to their shores.

Ask Yourself

Which colony — New France, New Mexico, Massachusetts Bay, New Netherland, or Virginia — would you move to if you lived in the 1600s? Why?

? ? ? ? ? ? ? ? ? ? ? ? ? ?

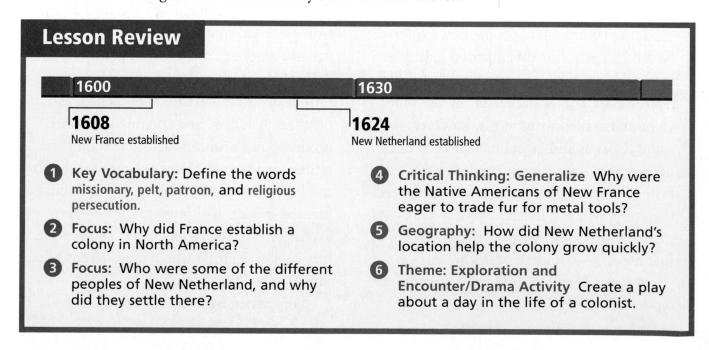

Lesson Review

1600		1630	

1608
New France established

1624
New Netherland established

1. **Key Vocabulary:** Define the words missionary, pelt, patroon, and religious persecution.

2. **Focus:** Why did France establish a colony in North America?

3. **Focus:** Who were some of the different peoples of New Netherland, and why did they settle there?

4. **Critical Thinking: Generalize** Why were the Native Americans of New France eager to trade fur for metal tools?

5. **Geography:** How did New Netherland's location help the colony grow quickly?

6. **Theme: Exploration and Encounter/Drama Activity** Create a play about a day in the life of a colonist.

FROM THE PAGES OF

Cobblestone **magazine**

the history magazine for young people

COBBLESTONE

June 1982

The North American Beaver Trade

The Fur Trade

by Jack Rudolph

The fur trade started as a simple system of barter between Native Americans and traders, but it quickly grew into one of the most important industries in North America.

The fur trade — especially the beaver trade — holds a special place in the history of North America. For nearly three hundred years it was almost the only business conducted on the frontier. It was the push behind most American exploration, including the Lewis and Clark expedition in 1804. The fur trade was also the rich prize over which the French and English fought in the French and Indian Wars from 1689 to 1763.

Long before white people first explored North America, fur was a prized luxury in European countries. Most of the furs came from Russia and Scandinavia. By the time Columbus sailed to America, however, the usual Russian and Scandinavian sources could not keep up with a growing demand for the fashionable furs. Fur traders were delighted, therefore, to learn that the new land across the Atlantic Ocean was the richest source of fine furs the world had ever known.

What was the fur trade and how did it work?

Before 1820, in the fur trading regions east of the Rocky Mountains, the fur trade was an exchange between white people and Indians in which the cured skins of trapped wild animals were swapped for manufactured articles needed and wanted in the wilderness. Beginning as a simple system of barter — a knife for a skin, etc. — it later became a complicated arrangement based on credit and involving several groups.

The fur trade might be described as a two-way road running from European factories to the forests of North America and then back to the clothes closets of wealthy Europeans. Manufactured goods such as blankets, hatchets, and cooking pots were produced in European factories. White fur traders and trappers then brought the goods to North America to trade them for animal furs the Indians had prepared. After the exchange, the European traders shipped the furs back to Europe where they were made into fashionable clothing.

Furs varied from coarse bearskins and

buffalo hides to soft mink and fox, but the backbone of the fur trading business was the pelt of the beaver. Beaver fur was in great demand for fur coats, but even more so for the felt from which men's hats were made. Hats made from beaver felt were popular for generations before beaver felt was replaced by wool felt and silk.

In North America, the beaver were plentiful. Millions of the busy brown animals built their dams and lodges all over the continent. So many beaver were taken by the trappers that the beaver pelt became a unit of exchange. Just as the dollar is used in the supermarket today to buy groceries, the beaver skin was the "money" of the beaver industry. In 1703, for example, one beaver skin could buy one shirt, six knives, or ten pounds of pork.

Trading between the Indians and the white people began as a swap in which neither side had much respect for the good sense of the other. The white strangers exchanged goods that they thought were trifles for valuable pelts. The Indians disposed of plentiful and generally useless skins for what, in their culture, were previously undreamed-of luxuries. Each gave to the other something valued lightly for something valued highly, and everybody was happy.

The simple approach didn't last long, however. It was soon replaced by a keen sense of bargaining on both sides. Through experience, the Indians learned the difference between junk and articles that were useful, between poor and good quality. They also learned to take advantage of the competition between white traders, and they learned to barter, getting the most they could for the beaver pelts.

At first, exchanges between Indians and white traders were direct and usually carried out in a single meeting. A trader arrived in an Indian village with a load of trade goods, swapped them for furs, and went away. As the frontier moved deeper into the wilderness, however, it became necessary to build permanent trading stations in the forests. These stations made larger exchanges of furs and better bargaining possible.

The best trapping season was late fall and winter when pelts were sleek and heavy. Travel, however, was difficult during those months. The trappers needed supplies to carry them through the winter, so goods were brought in during the fall and issued to them on credit.

In the spring the Indians and white trappers brought their winter catch to the trading posts. Here the pelts were shown one at a time. After much haggling a price was agreed upon. In this way, a trapper paid for the winter supplies he had received on credit. After the supplies were paid for, the trapper used his remaining beaver skins to purchase the goods he wanted for the summer. At the end of the summer the trapper received more winter supplies on credit and

the process began again. Money seldom changed hands.

Trading posts were much alike. They were usually clusters of crude buildings built around a boat landing. Nearly all trading posts were built near the water. Typically, there was a store, a warehouse, and living quarters for the manager and the crew. Large posts, or those that needed protection from unfriendly Indians were built as small forts surrounded by log walls.

Traders obtained their furs from three sources — the Indians in the East and Middle-west, hired white trappers whose catch belonged to the trading companies that hired them, and free white trappers in the Rocky Mountains who worked alone and shopped around for the best bargains.

A detail from North American Beaver, artist unknown. Courtesy of the Amon Carter Museum, Fort Worth, Texas.

The principal suppliers, however, were the Indians in the eastern and mid-western regions of our country.

Settlers eventually followed the trails blazed by the fur traders. Towns were built where the trading posts had been, and the beaver's natural habitats were destroyed, pushing the trappers and traders deeper and deeper into the wilderness. The beaver were hunted until they became nearly extinct, and probably would have become extinct if fashion had not changed in Europe. Silk hats became more popular than beaver hats, and the great demand for the beaver pelts disappeared. Before this change, however, the beaver trade had helped to open a vast continent for settlement.

Response Activities

1. **Interpret** According to the article, how did the fur trade "open a vast continent for settlement?"

2. **Descriptive: Write a Journal Entry** You are a fur trader in New France. Describe your plans for the upcoming trapping season, and your interaction with Native American traders.

3. **Economics: Trading Goods** Take turns choosing three items in your classroom. Decide which of your items you would trade for items belonging to other groups.

CHAPTER 5 Chapter Review

Chapter Review Timeline

1590 · 1600 · 1610 · 1620 · 1630

- **1598** Spanish settlers move into New Mexico
- **1607** Jamestown colony started
- **1608** New France established
- **1620** Pilgrims settle Plymouth
- **1624** New Netherland established

Summarizing the Main Idea

1. Copy and complete the following chart, indicating the people who settled the land, the location which they settled, and a noteworthy achievement.

Settlers	Spanish	Pilgrims	Puritans	French	Dutch
Location	*Mexico City*				
Achievement	*Built haciendas*				

Vocabulary

2. Using at least ten of the following terms, write a letter from a colonist to a relative who remained in Europe.

colony (p.122)
viceroy (p.122)
mestizos (p.123)
hacienda (p.123)
mission (p.125)
charter (p.130)
invest (p.130)
stock (p.130)
indentured servant (p.131)
Puritans (p.135)
Separatists (p.135)
Pilgrims (p.136)
missionary (p.143)
patroons (p.145)

Reviewing the Facts

3. How did Spain achieve its goal of increasing wealth and power with its colony?
4. What were haciendas?
5. Describe the conflict between Popé and the Spanish.
6. What do John White's sketches show us?
7. Why did the Jamestown settlement succeed?
8. What was the Mayflower Compact?
9. How was the Puritan settlement different from other settlements?
10. What were the major differences between New France and New Netherland?

⓫ Read each of the following sources from Chapter 5. Which one is a primary source and which is a secondary source? What information does each source provide?

"Although Juana never attended the university, she spent her life studying and writing."

"Now, when we arrived . . . where we were to camp, the women, armed with axes, went here and there in the great forests . . ."

Geography Skills

⓬ Indicate on an outline map of the United States the different colonies and the territories in which the colonists settled.

⓭ How did the location of each colony influence the ways in which the colonists provided for themselves?

Critical Thinking

⓮ **Cause and Effect** What effect did the growing colonies have on the lives of Native Americans?

⓯ **Conclude** What do you think might have happened to the settlement in Roanoke?

⓰ **Identifying Main Idea** Although each colony was settled by different people for different reasons, similarities existed among them. Write a short paragraph describing some of the similarities.

Writing: Citizenship and Economics

⓱ **Citizenship** It is your job to welcome the children of settlers who have just arrived in your colony. Write a brochure that might help these children feel at home.

⓲ **Economics** You are leading a group of settlers to America. Write a speech explaining where you would have the best chance of starting a successful colony and why.

Activities

History/Art
Work in a group to create a pictorial timeline that reflects the settling of the European colonies. Divide time periods among group members and have each person draw one or two pictures that highlight the important events. Include captions for the pictures.

Internet Option

Check the **Internet Social Studies Center** for ideas on how to extend your theme project beyond your classroom.

THEME PROJECT CHECK-IN

Use the information in this chapter to complete your project. Ask these questions:
• How were the native groups of the Americas affected by the European settlers?
• What new objects, customs, technology did the Europeans bring with them? How did this change America?
• What ideas did Europeans bring? What ideas did they adopt from Native Americans?

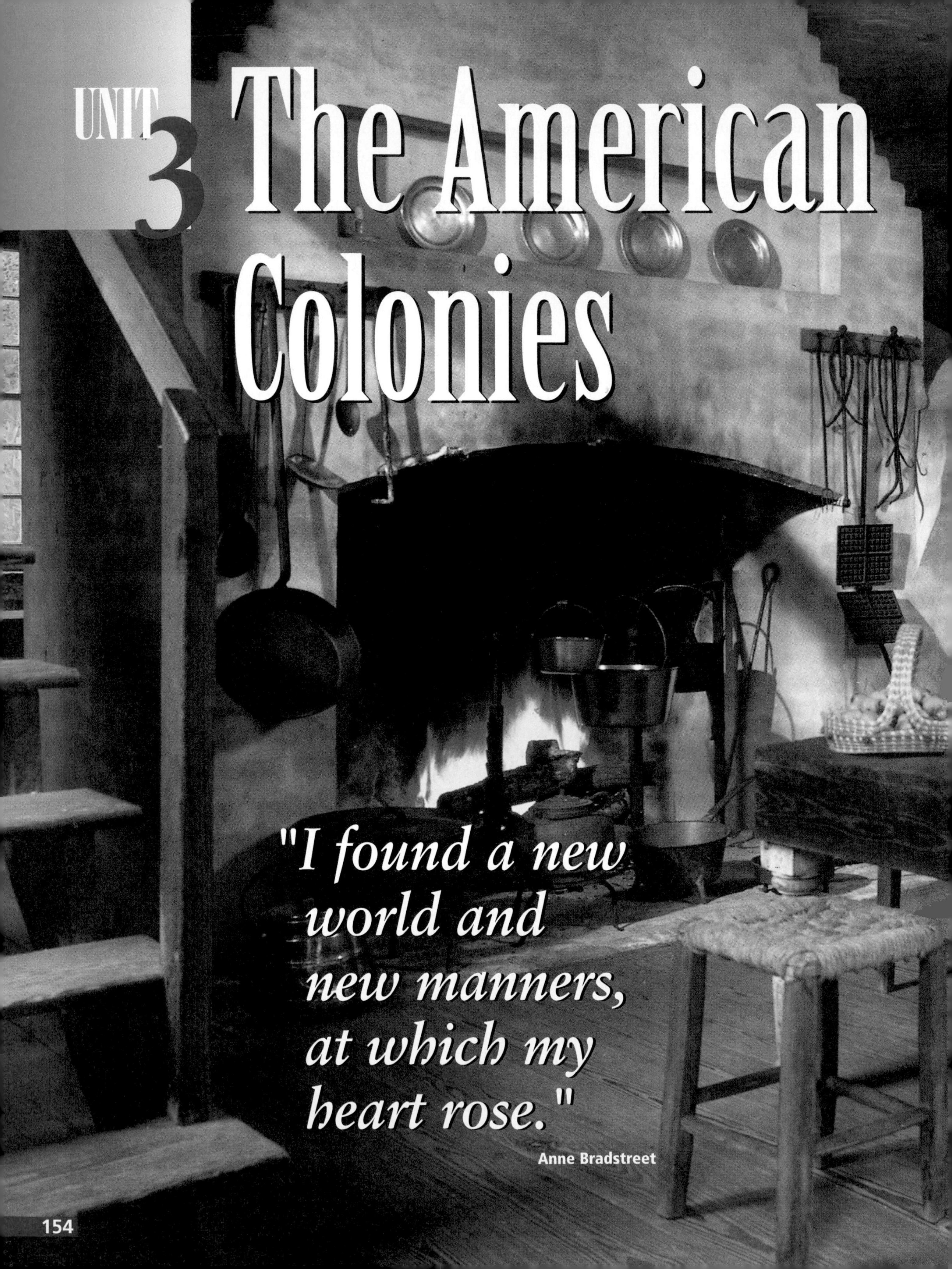

UNIT 3 The American Colonies

"I found a new world and new manners, at which my heart rose."

Anne Bradstreet

· THEME ·

New Environments

"It must have been hard for the colonists to move to America. Once they got there, they found new kinds of food."

Morgan Heatwole, Fifth Grade
Santa Rosa, CA

Have you ever moved to a new place? When people move, they bring ideas and hopes with them. They also have to adjust to their new home. When the European colonists began to settle the east coast of the United States in the 1600s, they met new peoples and new landscapes. As you read these chapters, you will see how people in New England, the Middle Colonies, and the South adjusted their thinking to fit their new environments.

Theme Project

Come to America!
Create a brochure that would attract settlers to the east coast of North America in the late 1600s or early 1700s.
- Draw a map showing what the land is like.
- Describe the Native Americans who live there.
- Explain the benefits of specific colonies, such as religious freedom or good soil for certain crops.
- Draw pictures of homes, clothing, and other everyday objects.

RESEARCH: Find out about the different kinds of homes colonists built, the food they ate, and what they did for fun.

◀ Heyward-Washington House in Charleston, SC

UNIT 3

WHEN & WHERE ATLAS

For many Europeans in the 1700s, the American colonies seemed like the promised land. Wild, unspoiled, and filled with resources, the colonies offered the hope of a new life for people who were struggling in Europe. As you can see on the map, the British claimed land all along the eastern seaboard of North America. For some Native Americans and Africans, this would mean an uprooting from their traditions.

In this unit, you will read how Europeans adjusted to life in the American colonies. You will learn what their arrival meant for Native Americans and Africans. You will also learn how the different geographic characteristics affected the lives of the people.

Unit 3 Chapters

Chapter 6 New England Colonies
Chapter 7 Middle Colonies
Chapter 8 Southern Colonies

PACIFIC OCEAN

Legend

CREEK   Native Americans

———   Indefinite boundaries

45°N
40°N
35°N
125°W
30°N
25°N
120°W   115°W   110°W

Unit Timeline

1600	1630	1660

Colonial Household

What chores would you have done if you had lived in this house? *Chapter 6, Lesson 3*

New York Woodlands

What attracted immigrants to this land? *Chapter 7, Lesson 1*

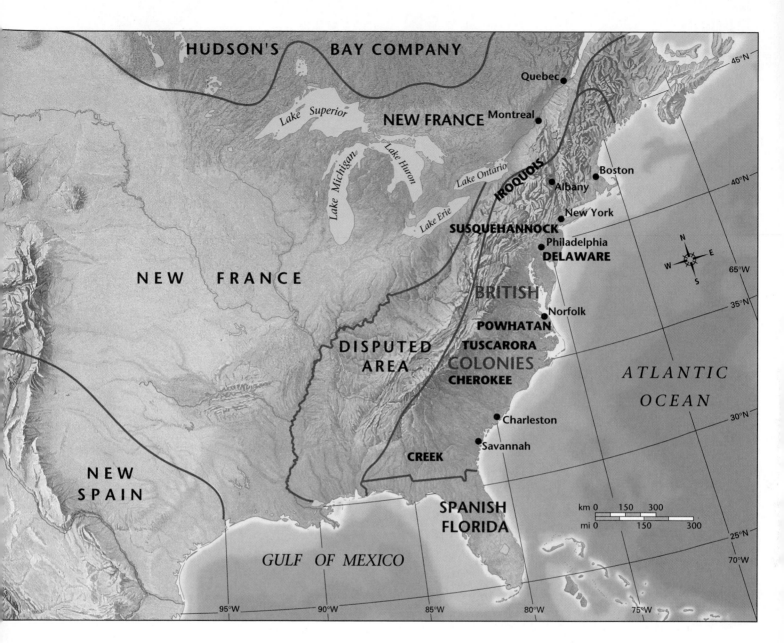

HUDSON'S BAY COMPANY

NEW FRANCE

Lake Superior

Lake Michigan

Lake Huron

Lake Ontario

Lake Erie

Quebec

Montreal

IROQUOIS

Albany

Boston

New York

SUSQUEHANNOCK

Philadelphia

DELAWARE

NEW FRANCE

BRITISH

Norfolk

POWHATAN

DISPUTED AREA

TUSCARORA

COLONIES

CHEROKEE

ATLANTIC OCEAN

Charleston

Savannah

NEW SPAIN

CREEK

SPANISH FLORIDA

km 0   150   300
mi 0   150   300

GULF OF MEXICO

95°W   90°W   85°W   80°W   75°W

45°N
65°W
40°N
35°N
30°N
25°N
70°W

N E
W S

1690   1720   1750

William Penn 1682

A state was named after this man. Do you know which one? *Chapter 7, Lesson 2*

Fort at Savannah 1732

Who did the people of Georgia want to protect themselves from? *Chapter 8, Lesson 2*

Charleston Harbor

New England wasn't the only region with thriving harbors. *Chapter 8, Lesson 2*

CHAPTER 6 New England Colonies

Chapter Preview: *People, Places, and Events*

1630	1650	1670

New England's Rocky Coast

Why is New England so rocky and its waters full of fish? *Lesson 1, Page 160*

Hingham Meetinghouse

Can you guess which building was the most important to Puritan life? *Lesson 1, Page 162*

Thomas Hooker   1636

Which colony did Thomas Hooker found? *Lesson 2, Page 169*

Colonists on the Land

Main Idea The geography and resources of New England shaped the lives of the people who lived there.

The first thing English settlers saw upon reaching the shores of New England was trees. Dark and unbroken, the forests rose from the shore and stretched as far as the eye could see. People said that the forests were so dense, a squirrel could travel from Maine to Florida without touching the ground.

English settlers were astonished by the forests. Back in England, most of the trees had already been cut down. Here, there were more than enough trees to provide shelter as well as fuel for cooking and for heating their homes in winter. They could also harvest the trees. "Wood grows so fast at every man's door, that after it has been cut down it will in seven years' time grow up again from seed to . . . firewood," said one settler.

Key Vocabulary
wilderness
meetinghouse
self-sufficient

Key Events
1636 Harvard College founded

1642 Passage of law for universal education

◀ A painting of a colonial merchant.

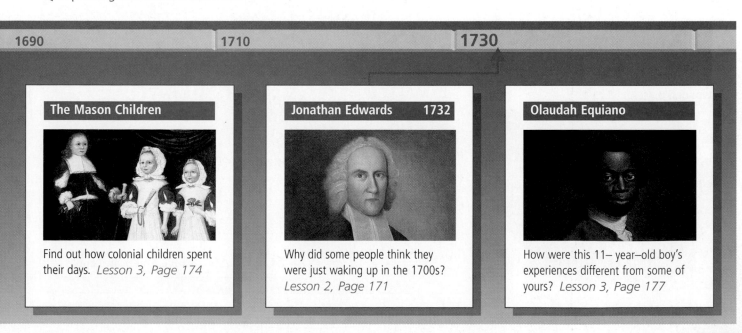

1690	1710	1730

The Mason Children

Find out how colonial children spent their days. *Lesson 3, Page 174*

Jonathan Edwards   1732

Why did some people think they were just waking up in the 1700s? *Lesson 2, Page 171*

Olaudah Equiano

How were this 11– year–old boy's experiences different from some of yours? *Lesson 3, Page 177*

Features of the Land

Focus *What kind of landscape did settlers find in New England?*

The dense forests of New England grew in rocky soil. Remember the glaciers of the Ice Age, which you read about in Chapter 2? The glaciers that had covered New England thousands of years earlier had swept the earth like bulldozers, taking away rich soil and leaving a thin, rocky layer of dirt.

The glaciers had worn high mountains into rolling hills. Along the seacoast, the moving glaciers carried dirt and rocks and dumped them near the water, creating rocky shorelines. Ocean waves

The map shows the geography and Native American groups who lived in colonial New England. **Map Skill:** *Why do you think Boston became the largest city of the region and the center of trade and shipbuilding?*

This Nipmuck feast bowl, carved around 1650, is one of the oldest surviving Native American wooden pieces.

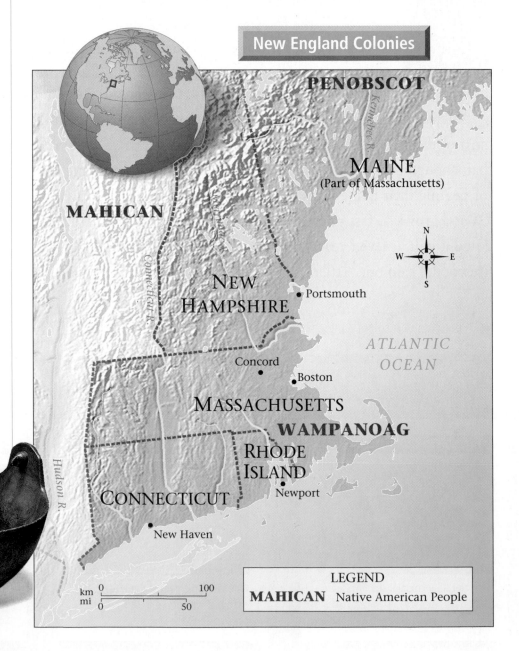

New England Colonies

PENOBSCOT

MAINE
(Part of Massachusetts)

MAHICAN

NEW HAMPSHIRE

Portsmouth

Concord

ATLANTIC OCEAN

Boston

MASSACHUSETTS

WAMPANOAG

RHODE ISLAND

Newport

CONNECTICUT

New Haven

Kennebec R.

Connecticut R.

Hudson R.

N
W E
S

km 0   100
mi 0   50

LEGEND
MAHICAN Native American People

chipped away at the land, forming hundreds of harbors. In the water away from the shore were banks, or mounds of dirt, that the glaciers had pushed underwater. Plants grew in the dirt, and millions of fish came there to feed. New England's soil was not ideal for farming. But with its harbors, numerous kinds of fish, and dense forests, New England was rich in natural resources.

Wood became the first product that the colonists sold for money. The many networks of rivers and streams running through the forests were perfect for transporting the wood that the colonists harvested. Tall white pines were used for shipbuilding. Cedars became shingles for houses. Willow branches went into barrel making. Settlers tapped maple trees with spouts to draw off sap, turning it into sugar and syrup as the Native Americans had taught them.

When they first arrived, the settlers thought the new land was a **wilderness**, a wild and unsettled land. The colonists soon learned that much of New England was not a wilderness at all. The Wampanoag (Wahm puh NOH ag), the Massachusetts, and the Pequot (PEE kwaht) Indians had cleared many areas for farming. They burned forests and created meadows for hunting game.

The Native Americans had abandoned much of this cleared land. Before the first colonists arrived in 1607, European fishermen and explorers brought diseases like smallpox to New England. Many Native Americans had already died from these diseases by the time the first settlers arrived.

Colonists called New England an untouched land, but it was actually a land whose original inhabitants were now mostly gone. New settlers found cleared lands and sometimes even empty dwellings where the Native Americans had lived.

Planning the Towns

Focus *How did Puritan communities arrange their towns?*

The Puritans came to New England with a mission. They wanted to do more than create new towns. They wanted to create new communities where people would serve both God and each other.

Puritan leaders believed that such a community could only be brought about through strict planning. Each family was given a plot of land for a house and farm. The size of the plot depended on the size of the family. It also depended on the family's importance in

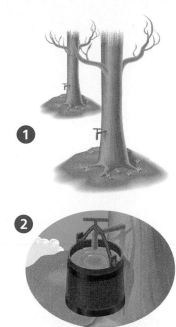

Making Maple Syrup

1 Colonists drilled holes into the lower part of the tree trunk. They put wooden spouts into the holes.

2 Colonists hung wooden buckets on the spouts. Sap slowly collected in the buckets.

3 Colonists poured the sap into a huge iron kettle. They boiled the sap for hours. Children collected wood to feed the fire under the pot. When the sap turned deep golden brown and was gooey enough, it was maple syrup!

the community. A blacksmith might get a larger share than most families, and the minister might get the largest plot of all.

At the crossroads of each Puritan village stood the most important building: the **meetinghouse**. Puritans made the meetinghouse the center of their religion and government. On Sundays, the whole community gathered there to worship. In some towns people also used the meetinghouse as the school.

•Tell Me More•

Inside a Meetinghouse

The meetinghouse was used for all kinds of community activities, from school to church. It was often not heated, even on cold winter days when a sermon might last several hours.

Unpolished wood was used for the hard benches, which had no cushions.

These joints held the building posts together. They were numbered so they could be properly matched at the building site.

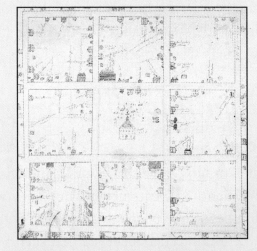

Men and women sat apart from each other on different sides of the church. Church leaders got the best seats.

Culture: *What does the design of the meetinghouse tell you about Puritans and their religion?*

This Puritan community in New Haven, Connecticut, centered around the meetinghouse. Plots of land for farming bordered the village.

New Englanders gathered in the meetinghouse for town meetings, where town leaders made decisions about government and town life. People decided many things in town meetings, from making town boundaries to choosing new ministers. Though town leaders made the decisions, all households had to agree. Fathers headed each household, and only the men shared in making decisions.

Because Puritans believed the Bible taught people the best way to live, they wanted everyone to be able to read it. Puritans used the Bible as the backbone of education in the many schools they built.

In 1636 they founded the first college in the colonies, Harvard College, to educate ministers. Six years later, the General Court of Massachusetts passed a law for universal education. That meant all parents and all masters of indentured servants in the colony had to teach children "to read and understand the principles of religion."

Puritans planned their towns so that the community could live together and serve God, without depending on anyone else. They wanted to be **self-sufficient**, to provide for all of their own needs. Puritans succeeded in this, and soon their settlements became thriving towns and villages.

Some people thought success had come at a price. Puritan leaders who had come to New England for the freedom to practice their religion did not always extend that freedom to others. Some colonists disagreed with Puritan leaders, and began to speak out.

Curious Facts

In the early years of Harvard College, students sometimes paid for their schooling with cows and sheep.

Lesson Review

1635	1640	1645

1636
Harvard College founded

1642
Passage of law for universal education.

1. **Key Vocabulary:** Define early New England using **wilderness, meetinghouse,** and **self-sufficient.**

2. **Focus:** What kind of landscape did settlers find in New England?

3. **Focus:** How did Puritan communities arrange their towns?

4. **Critical Thinking: Conclude** William Bradford described early New England as a "wilderness," but Native Americans probably didn't see it that way. What might explain the differences in views?

5. **Geography:** New England settlers found Native Americans already living there. How might settlers' lives have been different if they had been the first?

6. **Citizenship: Map Activity** Plan a town on a new, unknown continent. Make a map of your town, and label things in it. Be able to explain your plan and why you used the land in the way you did.

We Turn Sap to Syrup

by Peter Martin,
as told to Carolyn Duckworth

Snow's on the ground, but spring's in the air. Soon it'll be time for my family to make fresh maple syrup, perfect for pancakes.

How would you like to eat pancakes smothered in maple syrup? I'm talking *real* maple syrup, not that stuff with maple flavoring in it. If you lived in New England, you might eat maple syrup a lot. You might even make your own syrup just as my family does.

We live in Vermont, where there are lots of hills and mountains covered with trees. Many of those trees are *sugar maples*. The sap of a sugar maple has more sugar in it than sap of other trees.

Indians taught European settlers how to make syrup and sugar from the sap. These were the only sweeteners, other than honey, that many settlers used.

sap
water full of sugar and minerals a tree needs to grow

Vermonters still make a lot of maple syrup — over 500,000 gallons (2 million liters) each year! All of that syrup is made in a few weeks each spring called sugaring time.

Where we live, *sugaring time* is a sure sign that spring is on its way. The days start warming up, but the nights are still freezing cold. Those warm days and cold nights are like magic: They start the sap flowing in the sugar maple trees. (During the cold days and nights of winter, sap doesn't flow.)

Some years we have to wait until late March for sugar weather to arrive. Other years we can start sugaring when February's deep snow still covers the ground.

When the weather is just right, my brother Jim and I take our tapping tools to our *sugar bush*. (That's what syrup makers call a group of maple trees.) It's time to *tap* the trees.

To tap a sugar maple, I drill a hole into a tree with a tool called a *brace*. Then I hammer a *spile*, or spout, into the hole. Almost right away sap starts dripping out of the spile. As fast as I can, I attach plastic tubing. The tubing will carry the sap into a bucket. Sometimes a drop or two of sap will leak from the spile before the tube is on. That's just an extra treat for me. Maple sap is sweet straight from the tree.

Freezing nights and warm days of early spring mean the start of "sugaring time." That's when we begin collecting the sugar maple sap and get ready to make lots of sweet maple syrup.

We keep the fire going all day and sometimes all night, waiting for sap to turn into syrup.

I'm not the only one who likes sweet maple sap. Ants will find the spiles before long, and every day they'll drink their fill. Mice would love to climb into a bucket to sip some sap too. So I always put a lid on each bucket to keep them out.

Each spring we put in about 30 taps. Small trees get just one tap; larger trees get three. These 30 taps will keep us plenty busy collecting buckets and carrying them up to the barn each day.

I used to worry that tapping would harm the trees, but then I found out that some of the trees in our sugar bush are almost 200 years old, and that people have been tapping them most of that time. The sugar maples are still healthy and strong, so tapping must not hurt them very much!

Even though maple sap is

In this photograph Martin is tending the hot sap. He has to watch it very carefully to make certain that it doesn't overcook.

very sugary, it's still mostly water. To make syrup, we have to thicken the sap by boiling away most of the water. We call this *boiling down*.

Boiling down is the most important part of sugaring, but it can be the most boring too. We have to keep the stove's fire going until the sap turns into syrup. And that can mean a *very* long night!

While the sap is boiling in the bottom pan, we have to check its temperature every few minutes. When the sap reaches the right temperature, it'll be perfect maple syrup. But past that point, the perfect maple syrup turns into gooey, gluey gunk. If that happens, all we can do is throw it away and start all over again. Nobody wants to waste all that sap and work, so we're super-careful.

When the syrup is done, we drain it into jars. As the syrup runs out of the pan, we strain it to get rid of "sugar sand." That's what we call the minerals that boil out of the sap. Then we seal and label the jars.

When the sap is flowing steadily, we make all the syrup we need in just a week. All that bucket-hauling and fire-building is hard work. But my brother and I have grown up eating pure maple syrup on our pancakes. We know it's worth the trouble!

After all of his hard work is done, Martin ends up with jars of delicious maple syrup.

Response Activities

1. **Compare Then and Now** Compare the way the children in this article make maple syrup with the description on page 161. How do you think the process is different today from what it was 200 years ago? How is it the same?

2. **Informative: Write a Summary** What activities do you and your family or friends do together as a group? Write a summary of what you do. How do you think this kind of activity has changed through the years?

3 **Geography: Draw a Chart** Make a chart of natural products in your region and tell how they are used.

New England Grows

Main Idea Puritan settlement spread to other parts of the region.

A statue of Anne Hutchinson is in Boston, Massachusetts.

A tired man trudged through the snow. Roger Williams was leaving Massachusetts and making his way toward the unsettled area to the south. Why was this gentle minister leaving his warm fire in the bitter cold of winter? He disagreed with the way Puritan leaders were running the community. To these leaders Williams was a troublemaker. In 1635 the church leaders **banished** him from, or forced him to leave, Massachusetts. He founded the colony of Rhode Island in 1636.

A Changing Community

Focus *How did religious disagreements affect colonial New England?*

Puritan settlements depended on people believing the same religion and laws. Leaders watched the community to make sure they did. Ministers led the church, and **magistrates** led the government. The magistrates made laws dealing with town affairs and people's relations with one another. Often magistrates, influenced by the ministers, passed laws dealing with religion. Roger Williams strongly objected to that. He believed that the church and its ministers should be completely separate from the government and its magistrates.

Puritan leaders wanted to control people's religious lives, but Williams believed in what he called "soul liberty." That meant people should be free to find God by following the inner guidance God gave each person. The ministers said soul liberty would lead to chaos, but Williams thought people's "soul conscience" would keep them on the right path.

Williams was banished for expressing these views.

Anne Hutchinson was another Puritan from Boston who disagreed with the church. She was the wife of a merchant, the mother of many children, and a spiritual advisor. Her weekly prayer meetings drew many women to her home.

Hutchinson's teachings got her in trouble because they criticized the way that church leaders taught religion. The magistrates and ministers put her on trial, accusing her of teaching false ideas. The fact that she was a woman did not help her case. Women, the ministers believed, should obey men on spiritual matters. In 1637 Hutchinson was found guilty and, like Williams, banished from Massachusetts Bay Colony.

Williams and Hutchinson were both **dissenters**, people who disagreed with the views of their leaders. Thomas Hooker was another dissenter. He was not banished, but he and his followers, disagreeing with Puritan leaders, decided to leave Massachusetts. They founded their own settlement in Connecticut in 1636.

Fact File:

Colony	Date Settled	Reasons Founded
New Hampshire	1623	Farming, trade
Massachusetts	1620	Religious freedom
Connecticut	1634	Religious freedom, farming
Rhode Island	1636	Religious freedom

In this 19th century painting, Thomas Hooker leads his followers into Connecticut, where he founded the town of Hartford. **Geography:** *How does the painting show the richness of the land?*

This chart shows to what age adults in Andover, Massachusetts, lived in colonial times. **Chart Skill:** *How many women lived to their eighties?*

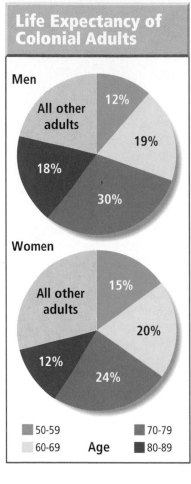

Life Expectancy of Colonial Adults

Men

All other adults
12%
19%
18%
30%

Women

All other adults
15%
20%
12%
24%

50-59 70-79
60-69 **Age** 80-89

Dissenters founded these new colonies so that they and their followers could practice their religion the way they wanted. Rhode Island became the first colony with true religious freedom. People in Rhode Island were not forced to go to one particular church. They were free to practice their own faith and "rule themselves" in religious matters. Soon other dissenters — Quakers from England and Jews from South America and the Caribbean — also moved there.

The Salem Witch Trials

Banishing dissenters like Roger Williams and Anne Hutchinson did not end the problem of dissent in the community. The ministers still wanted to control the colonists, but people did not like being told what to believe. Over the next hundred years, new people, especially young people, began to leave the church.

With the Puritan hold on religion weakening and new people arriving in the colonies, people began to distrust one another. Neighbors were not as close as they once were. This new atmosphere was partly responsible for a wave of excitement in which people began accusing each other of being witches.

In the 1600s many people around the world believed in witches.

Trials to decide whether or not a person was a witch had occurred in New England and Europe before. But in 1692 they became a central part of life in Salem, Massachusetts.

The excitement began when some young girls started acting strangely. A doctor thought they were victims of witchcraft. Soon, neighbors began accusing each other of being witches. Hundreds of people were put on trial and 20 were killed. The witch trials lasted only about a year, but they shocked the Puritan community.

The Great Awakening

In the 1730s, young ministers such as Jonathan Edwards and George Whitefield began preaching fiery sermons all over New England. These ministers and their followers were called the New Lights. (The traditional Puritan ministers and their communities were called the Old Lights.) People flocked to their sermons.

Children of many Puritans felt less connected to the church than their parents had. Therefore, the ministers asked people to renew their faith. Because of this, the movement was known as the Great Awakening, or a waking up to new faith.

The Great Awakening spread to people all over New England and the other colonies. The words and actions of people like Williams, Hutchinson, Edwards, and Whitefield changed the faith of many New Englanders. Though they still believed in religion, most people could no longer accept the strict ways of the Puritan church. The community had changed. They had come to a new land with one religion . . . and had ended up with many.

George Whitefield was one of the most popular Great Awakening ministers. People often cried with emotion at his sermons. **Culture:** *How might the Great Awakening have affected the government as well as the religion of New England?*

Puritans led simple lives, but one place they liked decoration was on gravestones like this one. Feathers carved on the stones symbolized the flight to Heaven.

Conflicts Over Land

Focus *What problems arose between the Puritans and Native Americans?*

Relations between settlers and Native Americans were changing as well. Peaceful relations had seemed possible when the Pilgrims were the only settlers in New England. Native Americans had much to offer them. They taught the Pilgrims how to grow corn and other crops. As you have read, they saved the Pilgrims' lives during those first difficult years.

The Pilgrims had much to offer Native Americans as well. Their guns were better than arrows or spears for hunting game. Their finished wool cloth saved countless hours of tanning animal hides. A brisk trade quickly developed between the two groups, using the Native American form of money called wampum. **Wampum** was made from polished shells that were put onto strings.

The Puritan settlers who arrived in 1630, however, were different from the Pilgrims. While the Pilgrims were few in number, there were many Puritans. And they wanted more land than the Pilgrims had wanted. By 1675, there were about 50,000 colonists and fewer than 20,000 Native Americans in New England.

Roger Williams was one of very few Englishmen to try and learn Native American languages and customs. When he was still living in Massachusetts, he claimed that Puritan leaders had no rights to the land they took. He believed that Puritans should buy the land with the agreement of Native Americans. Most Puritans, however, did not agree with him.

Puritans and Native Americans used the land and resources in different ways. The Puritans chopped down many trees and let their animals roam in the forests. These animals often ended up trampling Native American crops. One Narragansett (Nair uh GAN set) chief expressed his views on this subject:

Paul Revere made this engraving of King Philip in 1772. **Art:** *Artists often use their drawings and paintings to express how they feel about a subject. What does this picture tell us about how the artist viewed King Philip?*

The Wampanoags carved and decorated beautiful clubs to use in battle. This one belonged to King Philip.

> **"B**ut these English having gotten our land, they with scythes cut down the grass, and with axes fell the trees; their cows and horse eat the grass, and their hogs spoil our clam banks, and we shall be starved."

Small conflicts over land soon gave way to large battles. In 1637, the Puritans attacked and burned the Pequot fort on the Pequot River. Other attacks by the colonists followed.

A Wampanoag chief named Metacomet (MEHT uh com eht), called King Philip by the English, decided that his people had to fight back. In 1675 he began attacking Puritan villages. Other Native American groups had wanted to stay out of the conflict at first. But when they saw Metacomet's success, groups such as the Pequot, Nipmuck, and Narragansett joined Metacomet.

Metacomet and the other Native Americans attacked colonial settlements all across New England, in what is called King Philip's War. Taking the Puritans by surprise, they captured and killed hundreds of colonists. With more soldiers and better weapons, the Puritans were still able to defeat the Native Americans. The Wampanoag and their friends were forced to give up their land.

Ned Jalbert was not looking for anything special at the yard sale he went to in 1995. But when he saw the old wooden club, he knew he had found something valuable. After he bought the club, he learned that it had belonged to Metacomet and was probably used by him in King Philip's War.

Lesson Review

1630	1680	1730

1636
Rhode Island founded

1675
King Philip's War

1 Key Vocabulary: Write a story about New England using the words **banish, magistrate, dissenter, and wampum.**

2 Focus: How did religious disagreements affect colonial New England?

3 Focus: What problems arose between the Puritans and Native Americans?

4 Critical Thinking: Interpret The Great Awakening did not directly challenge the Puritan religion, so why did Puritan leaders feel threatened by it?

5 Theme: New Environments How did the arrival of the Puritans create a "new environment" for the Native Americans?

6 Citizenship/Drama Activity: Act out the trial of Anne Hutchinson, with half of the class siding with Hutchinson and half with the Puritan ministers. After the trial, vote on whether Anne should be banished or allowed to remain in the community.

Making a Living

Main Idea People in New England made a living from the land and the sea.

Key Vocabulary

import
triangular trade
Middle Passage
industry
shipyard

Key Events

1712 Whaling
Industry begins

Colonial children did not have much time for playing, as you can see from this description of a boy's life on a Connecticut farm. The boy:

> "**M**ust rise early and make himself useful before he went to school, must be diligent there in study, and promptly home to do 'chores' at evening. His whole time out of school must be filled up with some service, such as bringing in fuel for the day, cutting potatoes for the sheep, feeding the swine, watering the horses, picking the berries, gathering the vegetables. He was expected never to be reluctant and not often tired. **"**

Can you imagine not being tired after such a day?

Work at Home and on the Farm

Focus *What was everyday life like in colonial New England?*

As you can see, children participated in the work of home and farm as soon as they were able. At home, they helped make food and household items. In the fields, they helped grow the crops.

The Home

Colonial homes were different from many homes today. They were dark and cramped. Glass was expensive, so they had few windows. Homes were not just places to live. They were also small workshops, especially during cold weather. Other than a few English goods — like metal pots and pans — almost everything was made at home. Women, girls, and sometimes boys wove the cloth for the family's clothes. They preserved fruits and vegetables for the winter.

Can you find all of these objects in the painting below?

The living room was often the bedroom too.

New England's thick forests provided wood for dishes and for furniture.

Women used wooden churns to make butter. **Economics:** *Why might colonial homes be called small workshops?*

They also cooked food. The center of every colonial home was the enormous fireplace, like the one in the painting on page 175. Women hung all kinds of pots and pans on hooks over the fire.

During daytime, houses buzzed with activity. Most had only one large room, called the "hall." At mealtime, a long table was pulled out. Parents sat on chairs, but children often stood to eat. At night, tick mattresses were laid on the floor. Tick was a mix of cloth scraps and straw. Wealthy families might have houses with lofts, and children climbed ladders to sleep on mattresses above.

Puritan families were large, usually numbering between four

and eight people. Also, some households included enslaved or indentured servants who lived with the family.

Farms and Towns

People's lives followed the seasons. From spring to fall, the men and boys walked to the fields at dawn and worked till sundown. They planted crops in the spring and harvested them in the fall. Women joined in the fieldwork, especially in busy times of planting and harvest. Young children helped by bringing lunches of cheese, bread, and apple cider. During the winter, men worked at home.

Colonial New Englanders had many skills. They made candles and soap from animal fat, and cloth from wool. They dried beef and made maple syrup. The family used most of what they made. They traded some items with neighbors, and sold the rest in nearby towns on market days.

There were a few things families could not produce themselves. They needed cash to pay for these imports. **Imports** are items bought from distant places. New Englanders imported coffee, tea, sugar, and ready-made goods like ribbons and guns. Merchants brought these items on big ships from many countries in Europe and the Caribbean.

Trading, Fishing, and Shipbuilding

Focus *Why were trading and fishing important to colonial New England?*

A great deal of shipping went on between Africa, Europe, and North America. It was called the **triangular trade**, because the merchant ships involved in the trade route took paths which formed a triangle.

The Triangular Trade

The triangular trade routes connected ports on the east coast of North America (such as Boston and New York) to Africa, Europe, and the Caribbean. On this route, ships carried and traded rum, iron, other manufactured goods, and enslaved Africans. Look at the map on page 177. In one side of the triangle, American ships carried rice and other agri-

Ask Yourself

How were the lives of colonial children similar to and different from your life?

? ? ? ? ? ? ? ? ? ? ? ? ?

Trade ships skimming the waters of New England brought all kinds of imports, including silk ribbons like these.

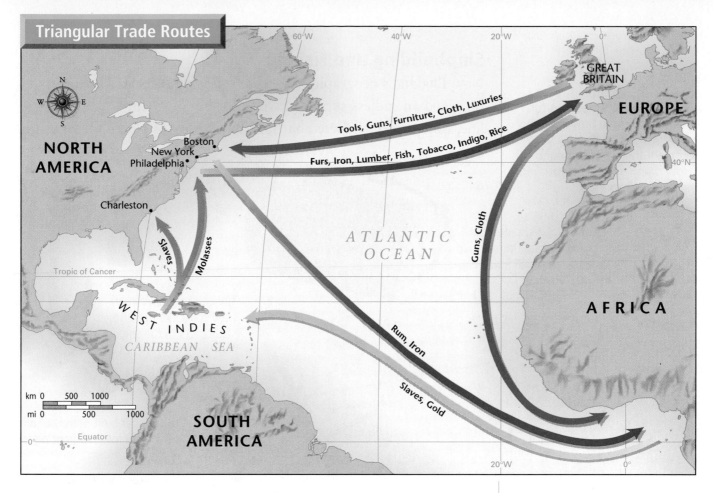

Triangular Trade Routes

Tools, Guns, Furniture, Cloth, Luxuries

Furs, Iron, Lumber, Fish, Tobacco, Indigo, Rice

Guns, Cloth

Rum, Iron

Slaves, Gold

Slaves

Molasses

GREAT BRITAIN

EUROPE

NORTH AMERICA

Boston
New York
Philadelphia

Charleston

Tropic of Cancer

WEST INDIES

CARIBBEAN SEA

ATLANTIC OCEAN

AFRICA

SOUTH AMERICA

Equator

km 0   500 1000
mi 0   500   1000

cultural products to England to trade for furniture and finished goods. What things were traded in other sides of the triangle?

The triangular trade made New England merchants very wealthy. Much of that wealth was built on the suffering of enslaved Africans. Their trip across the Atlantic Ocean was called the **Middle Passage**. To make the most money, ship captains tightly packed Africans into ships, almost on top of each other. Traders had to be on guard against revolts by Africans eager to regain their freedom.

The Africans who survived the voyage often wound up in one of the colonies. Olaudah Equiano (OL uh dah eh kwee AH noh) was taken from his West African village as a boy and sold into slavery. Many years later he bought his freedom and wrote a book describing the terrible Middle Passage. The conditions of the boat in the Middle Passage, he wrote,

> **"B**rought on a sickness among the slaves, of which many died. . . The shrieks of the women and the groans of the dying rendered the whole a scene of horror almost inconceivable [unthinkable]. **"**

This map shows the routes and products of the triangular trade. **Map Skill:** *Trace the movement of one product, for example, iron. Where did it come from? Where did most of it end up?*

Olaudah Equiano was only eleven years old when slave traders captured him.

Shipbuilding and Fishing

New England's geography was ideal for using the sea. The forests provided an endless supply of wood for building ships. The coastline, dotted with sheltered harbors, had plenty of places for ships to

Shipbuilding provided jobs for many people. The finished ship contained the work of at least 20 different trades. **Economics:** *How many trades can you find in the illustration?*

Sailmakers turned out dozens of different sails using all kinds of materials.

The caulker (KAW kuhr) used tools like these to seal cracks in the ship.

The cooper built barrels of all sizes to fit into different parts of the ship.

Rope was made out of plant fibers that were tightly twisted together.

dock. From their seaside villages, New Englanders quickly made the sea the center of their lives. Shipbuilding became the largest **industry**, or business to make and sell a product or service, in colonial New England.

By 1700, New England's **shipyards**, places where ships are built and repaired, were turning out 150 ships a year. Colonists sold some ships in Europe, but most were used in New England's other two industries: fishing and trade.

The fishermen of New England had a name for the fish that filled their nets. They called it "the mighty cod." Dried and smoked, colonists shipped cod by the ton to Europe and the Caribbean. By 1700 Boston was a center of fishing and trade, and was one of the wealthiest cities in the colonies.

Another important industry was whaling, or catching whales for the products that could be made from them. At first, colonists used whales that washed up on beaches, boiling their blubber, or fat, into oil for lamps. In 1712, the first whalers began hunting at sea. Colonists built whale-watching towers to spot the huge creatures.

New Englanders adapted to their new environment by becoming skilled fishermen and shipbuilders. People elsewhere were also adapting to their environments. As New England towns became busy seaports, people in the Middle Colonies turned to the rich land to make their living.

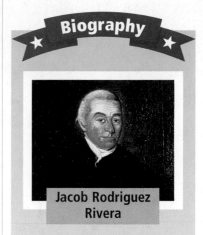

Biography

Jacob Rodriguez Rivera

The Rivera family fled Spain when Jews there were told to convert to Catholicism. They went to the Dutch West Indies, where Jacob Rodriguez Rivera learned the whaling industry. Hearing of Rhode Island's religious freedom, he moved there in 1748. He taught people how to use whale blubber for oil and candles.

Lesson Review

1710	1730	1750

1712
Whaling industry begins

1. **Key Vocabulary:** Describe New England life using import, triangular trade, Middle Passage, industry, and shipyard.

2. **Focus:** What was everyday life like in colonial New England?

3. **Focus:** Why were trading and fishing important to colonial New England?

4. **Critical Thinking: Interpret** Puritan children wore long robes until they were about eight years old. Then they began wearing clothes that looked exactly like those of their parents. What does this tell you about Puritan society?

5. **Geography:** Settlers in New England lived close together in small villages. Why do you think they did that?

6. **Citizenship/Research Activity:** Find out about the daily lives of one of the Native American groups of the colonial period. Write down activities that were part of a typical day for that group.

Analyzing Change with Maps

Mapping Time

What was Boston like in 1722? Horses, buggies, and hand-pushed carts were everywhere. A few streets had cobblestone paving, but most were covered with mud. Boston Common was a wide stretch of green park in the middle of the city.

What is modern Boston like? From Boston Common you can see the golden dome of the State House. Cars, taxis, and buses rush down busy streets. Skyscrapers tower over the business district.

Comparing historical maps to modern maps can show you changes over time more clearly than words can describe them.

A view of modern-day Boston. Is it easier or harder to see Boston Common in the photograph than on the maps? Why do you think this is so?

Boston Common

Charles River

① Here's How

- Study the two maps on the next page. Find the date of each one.

- Look for features that appear on both maps. Find Boston Common and the Charles River. Do both maps show the same view of the city? If not, how do they differ?

- Compare Boston Common on the two maps. Has it become larger, smaller, or stayed the same size?

- Find the Mill Pond on the earlier map. What appears in this location in the 1995 map? What might have caused this change?

- Think about how life has changed in Boston since 1722. Can you see any of these changes in the maps? What parts of old Boston remain?

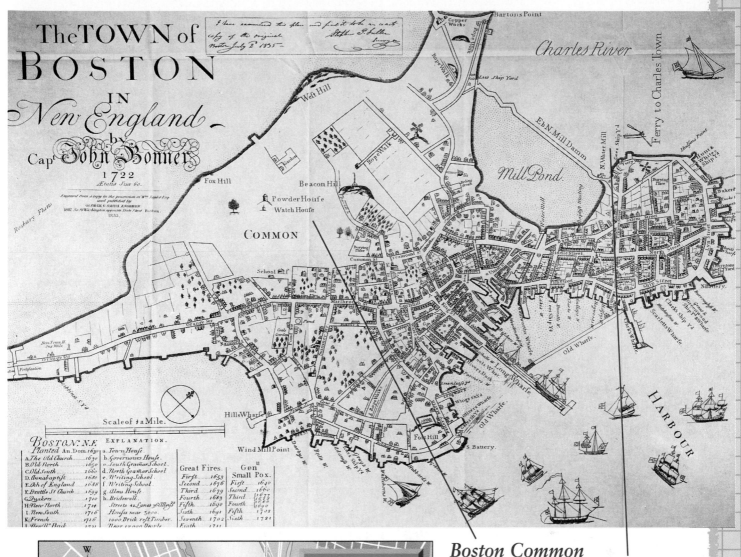

The TOWN of BOSTON IN New England by Capt John Bonner 1722

Boston Common

Charles River

Boston, 1993

Legend

— Original shoreline

Land prior to 1775

Land filled from 1775 to 1830

Land filled from 1830 to present

Parks

km 0   1/5   2/5
mi 0   1/5   2/5

2 Think It Through

What can you tell about the history of a place by comparing an older map to a new one?

3 Use It

1. Examine the two maps again. Make a list of all the differences you find between them.

2. Now list the similarities between the maps.

3. Why do you think these features changed or stayed the same over time? Write down your ideas beside each item on your lists.

Chapter Review

Chapter Review Timeline

| 1630 | 1650 | 1670 | 1690 | 1710 | 1730 |

1675
King Philip's War

1642
Passage of law for universal education

1712
Whaling industry begins

1636
Rhode Island founded

Summarizing the Main Idea

❶ Copy the chart below and fill in the missing information to create a summary of information about the New England colonies.

New England Colonies	
Features of the land	*Dense forests, abundant wildlife, rocky soil, many rivers and streams*
Features of the towns	
Religious beliefs	
Ways of earning a living	

Vocabulary

❷ Complete the word puzzle below using eight key vocabulary words.

A. A place where ships are built and repaired (p. 179) — _ _ _ P _ _ _ _

B. Native American form of money (p. 172) — _ _ _ _ U _

C. A person who led the government (p. 168) — _ _ _ _ _ _ R _ _ _

D. To force someone to leave (p. 168) — _ _ I _ _

E. The building that was the center of Puritan life (p. 162) — _ T _ _ _ _ _ _ _ _ _

F. The name for the path of shipping that went on between Afric, Europe, and North America (p. 176) — _ _ _ _ _ _ _ _ A _ _ _ _ _ _

G. People who disagreed with established views (p. 169) — _ _ _ _ _ N _ _ _

Reviewing the Facts

3 Why did Puritan leaders believe that their communities needed strict planning?

4 What was the meetinghouse used for?

5 Which colonies were founded so that people could practice freedom of religion?

6 What was the Great Awakening?

7 What caused war to break out between the colonists and Native Americans?

8 What kinds of activities went on inside the homes of New Englanders?

9 Why did the sea become the center of New Englanders' lives?

Skill Review: Finding Change in Historical Maps

10 The map on page 162 shows New Haven, Connecticut, in the 1600s. Describe the town and the way people used the land.

11 Today New Haven is a city of more than 130,000 people. What changes would you expect to see in a map of the city today?

Geography Skills

12 Look at the map on page 177. What kind of goods did the colonies send to England? What goods did England send to them?

13 You are a settler in New England. Write a letter to your family in England describing the land and resources of your new home.

Critical Thinking

14 **Validity** Can the New England of the Puritans be described as democratic?

15 **Cause and Effect** How did the triangular trade affect New England's economy?

Writing: Citizenship and Economics

16 **Citizenship** Write a letter to Native Americans and Puritans suggesting things they could have done to prevent war.

17 **Economics** Write an ad for an indentured servant, explaining what work the servant must do on your New England farm.

Activities

Economics/Research Activity
Colonists made almost everything they used, from food to candles. Research the steps used in one of these economic activities, such as making soap or churning butter. Make a poster that explains the process in words and pictures.

Cultures/Writing
Describe in a poem the clash of cultures that occurred when English settlers began arriving in larger and larger numbers. Write your poem from the point of view of a Native American. Share your poem with your classmates.

Internet Option

Check the **Internet Social Studies Center** for ideas on how to extend your theme project beyond your classroom.

THEME PROJECT CHECK-IN

The information about the New England colonies will help you to begin your brochure.
• What New England geographic features and resources are important to show on your map?
• What groups of Native Americans live there? What can you tell people about them?
• How can colonists make their living in the New England Colonies?

Middle Colonies

Chapter Preview: *People, Places, and Events*

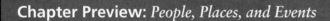

1630	1650	1670

Pennsylvania Waterfall

What does a waterfall have to do with making bread? *Lesson 1, Page 188*

Quaker Meetinghouse

What brought these people to the Middle Colonies? *Lesson 2, Page 190*

Pennsylvania Founded 1682

This man affected the lives of many people in the Middle Colonies. Find out how. *Lesson 2, Page 190*

People Living on the Land

Main Idea The Middle Colonies had rich land for farming and many large rivers for transportation.

Everyone arrived at the Pennsylvania farm before dawn. One of the German farmers was building a new barn, and all his neighbors had come to help.

While the men worked on the barn, the women prepared plate after plate of food and set them out on long tables. After the barn was "raised," or the main part finished, everyone ate. Then they enjoyed a dance on the new barn's floor.

In the early 1700s, the Germans were just one of many groups who joined the Dutch in the Middle Colonies. These immigrants worked hard to make their farms a success. They often combined work with community celebration, making even the clearing of fields into a sort of festival. Settlers quickly took advantage of the geography and rich resources that they encountered in the Middle Colonies.

◀ This young Dutch girl was one of many immigrants to the Middle Colonies.

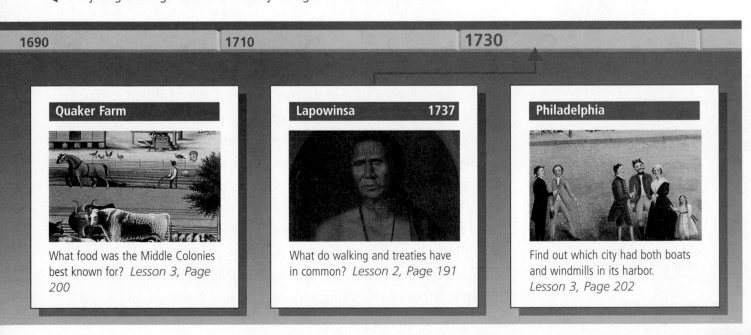

| 1690 | 1710 | 1730 |

Quaker Farm

What food was the Middle Colonies best known for? *Lesson 3, Page 200*

Lapowinsa 1737

What do walking and treaties have in common? *Lesson 2, Page 191*

Philadelphia

Find out which city had both boats and windmills in its harbor. *Lesson 3, Page 202*

This map shows the geography and Native American groups who lived in the four Middle Colonies. **Map Skill:** *What geographical feature influenced where large cities were located?*

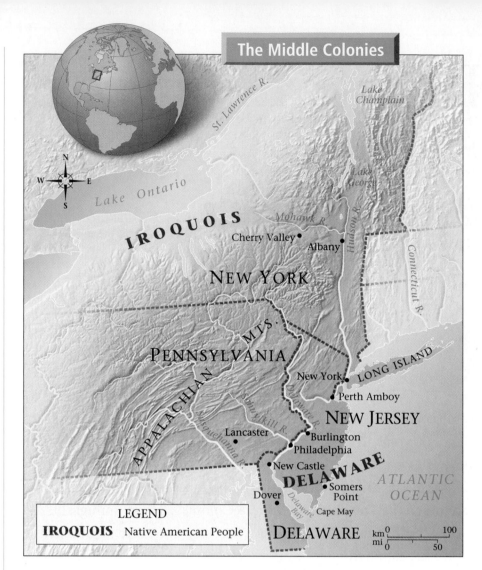

The Middle Colonies

IROQUOIS

NEW YORK

Cherry Valley
Albany

PENNSYLVANIA

APPALACHIAN MTS.

LONG ISLAND

New York
Perth Amboy

NEW JERSEY

Lancaster
Burlington
Philadelphia
New Castle

DELAWARE

Dover
Somers Point

Cape May

DELAWARE

ATLANTIC OCEAN

Lake Ontario

St. Lawrence R.

Lake Champlain

Lake George

Mohawk R.

Hudson R.

Connecticut R.

Schuylkill R.

Susquehanna R.

Delaware R.

Delaware Bay

LEGEND
IROQUOIS Native American People

km 0 — 100
mi 0 — 50

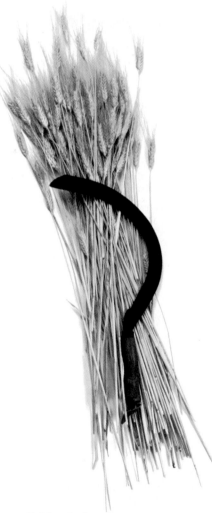

Fields of wheat were a common sight in the Middle Colonies.

Features of the Land

| Focus | *Why did the geography of the Middle Colonies make it a good farming region?*

Long before the first European settlers arrived, Ice Age glaciers had moved south, scraping the topsoil of New England and Canada. The glaciers stopped in the Middle Colonies, dropping thick, fertile soil on the rolling hills and valleys. Because the Middle Colonies were south of New England, the growing season was longer, with more sunny days. This warmer weather and good soil made the Middle Colonies perfect for farming and raising livestock.

Forests and deep, wide rivers also enriched the region's land *(see map above)*. Otter, raccoon, fox, and bear lived in the huge hardwood forests. Hunters trapped and traded the fur of these animals, particularly the valuable beaver. As early as 1620, the Dutch had established a trade in beaver pelts. This trade was the region's first industry. Most of the immigrants who came between 1630 and

1750, however, cleared the land for farming. Both fur traders and farmers depended on the wide rivers, like the Delaware, for water and transportation *(see illustration below).*

Life Along the Delaware River

The Delaware River flowed along the Pennsylvania and New Jersey border, all the way down to the busy fresh-water port of Philadelphia.
Geography: *How did settling along rivers make life easier for colonists?*

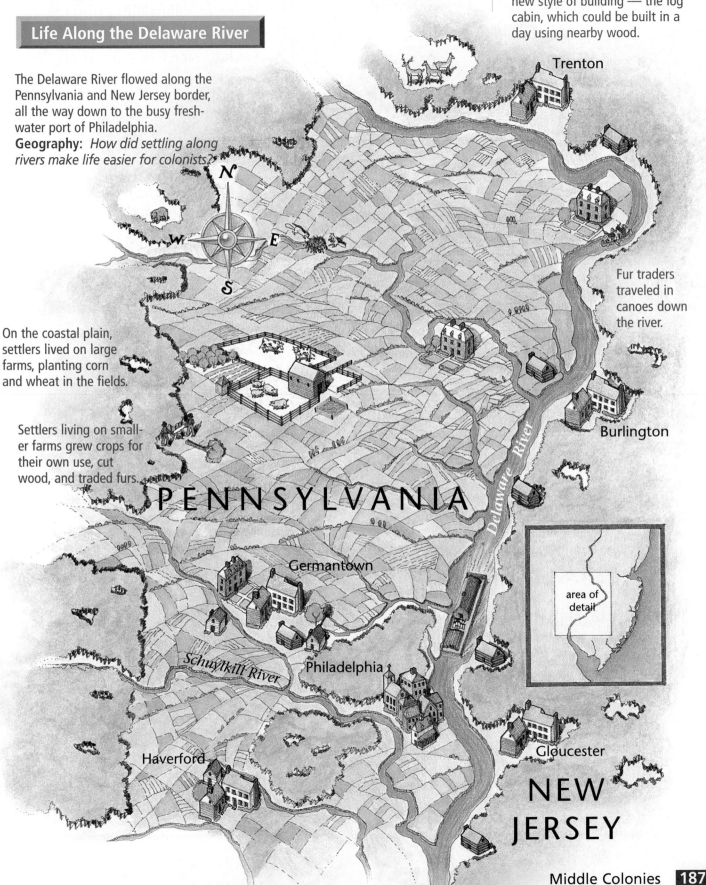

Swedish settlers introduced a new style of building — the log cabin, which could be built in a day using nearby wood.

Fur traders traveled in canoes down the river.

On the coastal plain, settlers lived on large farms, planting corn and wheat in the fields.

Settlers living on smaller farms grew crops for their own use, cut wood, and traded furs.

Trenton

Burlington

Gloucester

Germantown

Philadelphia

Schuylkill River

Haverford

PENNSYLVANIA

Delaware River

NEW JERSEY

area of detail

The fast-moving rivers of the Middle Colonies run from the Appalachian Mountains through a region of rolling hills called the **Piedmont**.

From the Piedmont, rivers flowing to the ocean fall from the height of the hills to the coastal plain below. This line of waterfalls is called the **fall line**, and it exists up and down the East Coast *(see the map on left)*.

The rapidly moving water and waterfalls at the fall line kept boats from continuing up the rivers. Colonists still managed to use this water in another way. Waterfalls powered sawmills and gristmills throughout the colonies. The sawmills cut trees into lumber, and the gristmills ground corn and wheat into flour.

The fall line also separated settlement regions. Free and indentured Scots-Irish settlers moved to the Piedmont, where the land was cheaper. English and Germans settled the coastal plain.

Whether in the Piedmont or on the plains, the Middle Colonies offered settlers plenty of resources. From 1700 on, immigrants poured in from all over Europe to make new lives for themselves on the farms and along the rivers of the Middle Colonies.

The fall line halted boats, but its waterfalls offered settlers other opportunities. **Economics:** *How did the fall line affect the economy of the Middle Colonies?*

Lesson Review: Geography

1. **Key Vocabulary:** Describe the geography of the Middle Colonies using **Piedmont** and **fall line**.

2. **Focus:** Why did the geography of the Middle Colonies make it a good farming region?

3. **Critical Thinking: Cause and Effect** How does geography influence how people in an area make their living?

4. **Theme: New Environments** Why might a region with many good resources lead to a society with many different cultures?

5. **Geography/Art Activity:** The Delaware River was very important to settlers in the Middle Colonies. What do you think is the most important part of your city or town? Make a sketch like the one on the previous page to show activities in that area.

A Mixture of Many Cultures

Main Idea Many different people came to the Middle Colonies making this region a mixture of many cultures.

Key Vocabulary

proprietor

religious toleration

"holy experiment"

Key Events

1664 New Netherland becomes New York and New Jersey

1682 Pennsylvania founded

William Beekman was a Dutch man who arrived in New Amsterdam in 1647. By 1658 he was a wealthy land and flour mill owner and a member of the Dutch government there. Twenty years later Beekman was still a member of the government, but the government was now the English government of New York. How did he do that without moving?

New York and New Jersey

Focus *How did New York and New Jersey become colonies?*

In 1664, the Duke of York, the King of England's brother, sent war ships into New Amsterdam Harbor. The Dutch surrendered without firing a shot. The English had wanted and got all the land that had been New Netherland.

This was an enormous amount of land — what is today New York, New Jersey, Pennsylvania, and Delaware. Because the Duke of York was the single owner of all this land, he was called the **proprietor** of the entire colony. He renamed it New York. It was a peaceful turnover, and Dutch citizens like William Beekman kept their land and jobs.

The Duke gave part of this vast amount of land to two friends, who named their colony New Jersey. Because New York and New Jersey belonged to proprietors they were called proprietary colonies.

These proprietors wanted to make money from the colonies by renting land to the colonists. The land was very fertile and good for farming. To encourage settlers, the proprietors also offered all Christians **religious toleration**, or the freedom of

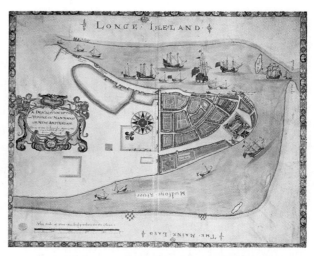

This map, called the "Duke's Plan," shows New York and New Jersey. It was drawn in 1664 after the British took control of New Amsterdam.

The meeting between Penn and the Lenni Lenape shown here did not actually happen. **Arts:** *What was the painter, Edward Hicks, trying to express with his view of the treatymaking?*

everyone to practice their religions as they wanted to. This guarantee of religious toleration attracted many settlers to New York and New Jersey.

Penn's "Holy Experiment"

Focus *How did Quaker beliefs affect life in Pennsylvania?*

When William Penn was a 12-year-old boy living on his father's farm in Ireland, he heard a man preach. This man was a member of the Society of Friends, known as Quakers. The Quaker's words were so moving that Penn never forgot them. When he grew up, he decided to join the Quakers.

Quakers tried to live according to the truth within their hearts. Ministers did not lead their church services. Instead, men and women spoke in the service whenever they felt called to do so. Quakers opposed war and believed in religious toleration.

In the 1600s, those were dangerous beliefs. Quakers were sometimes jailed and even hanged. William Penn went to jail several times before his luck changed. His father had loaned King Charles II money, and the king was ready to pay it back. Penn asked for land in America instead. In 1682, Penn's proprietary colony was founded and named Pennsylvania,

Fact File:

Colony	Date Founded as English Colony	Reasons Founded
New York	1664	Trade, farming
New Jersey	1664	Trade, farming
Pennsylvania	1682	Religious freedom, farming
Delaware	1682	Trade, farming

which means "Penn's Woods." Part of Penn's Woods was called the land of Delaware.

Like the Puritans, the Quakers now had a colony where they could practice their religion freely. But while the Puritans allowed only their own religion to be practiced, Penn said that Pennsylvania would be a "free colony for all mankind."

Penn called his colony a **"holy experiment."** It was holy because it was governed according to Quaker beliefs; it was an experiment because it might not work. In his experiment Penn hoped to create a new kind of society in which all people, including the Lenni Lenape (LEN ee LEN uh pee), known as the Delaware, had a voice.

Penn showed his friendship to the Lenni Lenape by learning some of their language. He also tried to work out treaties that everyone could agree on. Native Americans from other areas even moved to Pennsylvania because of Penn's reputation for fairness. Unfortunately, as you will read below, his sons were not as fair.

• Tell Me More •

The Walking Purchase

When William Penn met with the Lenni Lenape to buy land, they offered him a "walking" treaty. This meant he could have the amount of land a man could walk in a day and a half. Out of friendship, Penn bought the amount of land the Lenni Lenape understood to be a day and a half's walk, without actually making the walk. Penn returned to England, and in 1737 his sons tried to get more land. They told the Lenni Lenape chief Lapowinsa, pictured above, that they wanted to actually walk out the treaty. Then they hired three men to walk as fast as they could for a day and a half. By the end, the settlers had claimed twice the amount of land Penn had originally bought from the Lenni Lenape. The Lenni Lenape were forced to move west.

Penn recorded the treaty in the usual European way, by writing it down. The Lenni Lenape made a wampum belt which shows two people with hands clasped in friendship.

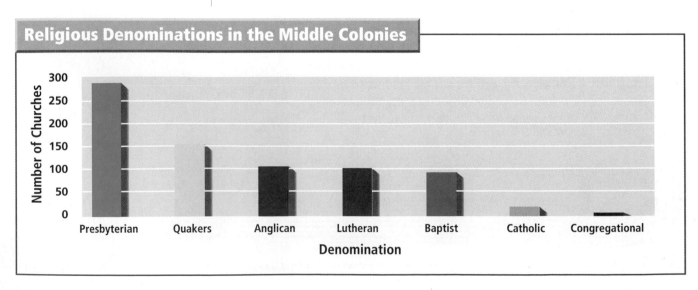

Susannah Wright

This was the home of Susannah Wright, a Quaker woman in Pennsylvania. She was a doctor, and some of her patients were Native Americans. She wrote poetry and exchanged letters with Ben Franklin. After the Conestoga Indians were attacked by colonists, she wrote a widely read pamphlet defending the Conestoga.

This chart shows religious diversity in the Middle colonies around 1776 **Chart Skill:** *How many Lutheran churches could be found in the Middle Colonies?*

Growing Diversity

Focus *Who immigrated to the Middle Colonies?*

William Penn's sons used the walking treaty to gain more land for themselves and other colonists in Pennsylvania.

Penn had advertised the colony of Pennsylvania in newspapers all over Europe. Attracted by Penn's description of rich farmland and religious toleration, Germans, Scots-Irish, and even settlers from other colonies swarmed into Pennsylvania. These ads also drew settlers to New York.

Michel Guillaume Jean de Crèvecoeur (krehv KUR) immigrated from France to settle a New York farm in 1765. Crèvecoeur was curious about his new home and admired its people. He wrote:

> **"I** *could point out to you a family whose grandfather was an Englishman, whose wife was Dutch, whose son married a French woman, and whose present four sons have now four wives of different nations.* **"**

Dutch, Swedish, and Finnish people were already living in New Netherland when it became New York and New Jersey. Soon the English and other European settlers joined them. Many Europeans wanted to leave areas in their home countries that had been damaged by war. While many settlers bought land, some worked as indentured servants, hoping to one day buy their own land.

Religious Denominations in the Middle Colonies

Number of Churches (y-axis: 0, 50, 100, 150, 200, 250, 300)

Denominations (x-axis): Presbyterian, Quakers, Anglican, Lutheran, Baptist, Catholic, Congregational

Denomination

How many languages can you find in the names of these foods?

The word *pail* probably comes from the French.

The words *maize*, *squash*, *succotash*, and *persimmon* come from Native American languages.

Cookie, coleslaw, and *waffle* all come from the Dutch.

Chowder comes from the French word *chaudière* (Show dee AIR).

Sauerkraut (SOW uhr krowt) is German. **National Heritage:** *Can you think of holidays that first came to us with immigrant groups?*

Some immigrants came to the Middle Colonies because of the promise of religious toleration *(see the chart on the left.)*

Enslaved Africans came to the Middle Colonies against their will. By 1740, enslaved people made up about ten percent of the population. Many in Philadelphia and New York worked as house servants or in shipyards. Slavery was not common in the countryside, except on large farms. In the Middle Colonies these enslaved peoples, along with immigrants and indentured servants, enriched the nation's languages, customs, and foods.

Lesson Review

1650		1700	

1664
New Netherland becomes New York and New Jersey

1682
Pennsylvania founded

1 **Key Vocabulary:** Write a paragraph about the Quakers, using **proprietor, religious toleration,** and "**holy experiment.**"

2 **Focus:** How did New York and New Jersey become colonies?

3 **Focus:** How did Quaker beliefs affect life in Pennsylvania?

4 **Focus:** Who immigrated to the Middle Colonies?

5 **Critical Thinking: Predict** How would the arrival of thousands of settlers affect the Native Americans?

6 **Theme: New Environments** Penn advertised Pennsylvania to attract settlers. How might he have described it?

7 **Citizenship/Language Arts Activity:** Read Crèvecoeur's quote on page 192. Then look up the Middle Colonies in an encyclopedia. How do the primary source and the secondary source differ?

Human Systems

What Did Colonial Americans Share?

A new culture began to take shape in the colonies during the 1700s. Different groups of immigrants brought their own traditions to America. As they started new lives, they observed and learned from each other and from Native Americans. The new ideas and customs they adopted included tools, music, styles of architecture, types of food, and even words.

Gradually, these ideas spread through the colonies and blended together. Geographers refer to this kind of blending as cultural diffusion. Modern American culture is the result of over 200 years of cultural diffusion.

Music Connection

All over the world today, people listen to jazz, rock and roll, country, and other musical styles from the United States. Most American popular music grew from the blending of African and European musical styles. Have you ever heard a singer or band from another country that played an American musical style?

① Virginia

Pumpkins
Early English settlers survived because Native Americans taught them to grow new foods. Settlers all over the continent learned to grow Native American crops like maize (corn) and pumpkins.

The Native Americans who lived in Virginia called this animal *arakun* (ah-rah-KOON), which means "he scratches with his hands." How do English-speaking people in America pronounce its name today?

The People of the 13 Colonies, about 1750

Great Lakes

St. Lawrence River

MAINE
(Part of Mass.)

Portsmouth
NEW HAMPSHIRE

Albany

MASSACHUSETTS

Boston

NEW YORK

Newport

Hartford

RHODE ISLAND

New Haven

CONNECTICUT

New York

Perth Amboy

PENNSYLVANIA

NEW JERSEY

Philadelphia

Burlington

New Castle

Annapolis

DELAWARE

MARYLAND

VIRGINIA

Williamsburg

NORTH CAROLINA

New Bern

ATLANTIC OCEAN

SOUTH CAROLINA

Charleston

GEORGIA

Savannah

MOUNTAINS

APPALACHIAN

FLORIDA
(Spanish)

km 0   100   200
mi 0   100   200

Legend

- English
- German and Swiss
- Scots-Irish
- Scotch Highlanders
- African
- Dutch
- ▲ Swedish
- ■ Welsh
- ★ Provincial capital (British)

The map shows where people who came from different parts of the world lived. But the map shows only which group was the majority in an area. Other groups also lived in these areas. **Map Skill:** *Where did most of the Scots-Irish settle?*

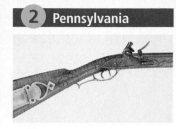

2 Pennsylvania

An Accurate Rifle
German immigrants brought many ideas to America. One was for an accurate hunting rifle, based on older German rifles. Most of the new rifles came from Pennsylvania. Even so, they became known as "Kentucky Rifles" after some were brought to Kentucky.

3 Delaware

Swedish Log Cabin
Some immigrants had lived in cabins made of logs in Sweden. They built log cabins in North America as well. Soon other colonists began to build log cabins. Logs for cabins were easy to find in the timber-covered wilderness of the Appalachian Mountains.

Research Activity

Many other American words have been contributed by different ethnic groups.

1 Find five words that came from the same ethnic group.

2 Make a chart explaining those words.

BENJAMIN FRANKLIN

Ingri & Edgar Parin d'Aulaire

History

thrifty
spending money wisely

Throughout most of the colonial period, printing presses were imported from Europe. The first colonial press was built in 1750.

Benjamin Franklin

by Ingri and Edgar Parin d'Aulaire

Many of America's early leaders were landowners or farmers, people at home in the woods and the fields — people who didn't like having neighbors living too close. Not Benjamin Franklin. Born in Boston in 1706, Benjamin Franklin was a city dweller all his life. When he was 60 years old, he moved to London for 10 years, and as an even older man he lived in Paris for nine years. For most of his life, the bustling colonial city of Philadelphia was his home. In Philadelphia a young Benjamin Franklin learned to be a fine printer, a clever writer and inventor, a great thinker, and a good citizen.

He was merry and happy and, though he was a master printer now, he did not hold himself too grand for any work. His fellow townsmen saw him pushing his paper through the streets on a wheelbarrow. "He will go far," one neighbor said to the other. "We see him at work when we get up. He is still working when we go to bed."

He saved every penny he made and in this way he could not help but prosper. He got more and more printing to do and soon he had a house of his own and helpers and apprentices working for him. He began to look for a thrifty and hard-working wife. And whom should he marry in the end but the girl who had stood in the doorway and laughed when he first came to town! Her name was Deborah Read. She did not care much about reading or writing, but she admired her Benjamin above all and she made him a good wife.

She ran his house. She helped him in the shop. She wasted no money on finery, idle servants, or costly food. They lived well and happily together and soon they had a son and daughter of their own. There was much laughter and gaiety in Benjamin's house, for he was a great one for making jokes and witty puns. It was Benjamin Franklin's wit and common sense that first made him famous up and down the coast of America.

He printed books. He printed pamphlets. He printed a newspaper of his own. When he was twenty-six years old, he also began to print his own calendar. He called it *Poor Richard's Almanack*. He pretended it was written by a poor stargazer whose name was Richard Saunders. Poor Richard had a shrew of a wife who was always scolding him for watching the stars, predicting weather and wind, instead of making a livelihood. To satisfy her, he put his observations into a calendar, hoping that many people would buy it. And the spaces between the dates were filled with puns and funny sayings.

While the whole town slept, Benjamin sat at his desk and chuckled to himself as he wrote Poor Richard's proverbs. And from Rhode Island to North Carolina people chuckled with him. Soon there was hardly a house where his calendar did not hang on the wall. Poor Richard made Benjamin Franklin prosperous.

Still, he and his family lived as simply as ever. Great was his surprise when he came to breakfast one morning to see a silver spoon and a china dish at his place. He thought an earthen dish

finery
fine or fancy clothes and ornaments a person carries or wears

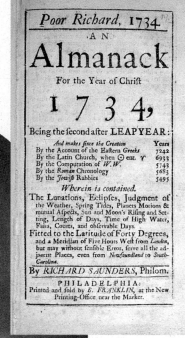

Benjamin Franklin, drawn here in 1783, used his press to print out newspapers and almanacs like the one above.

proverb
a short, common saying that demonstrates a truth

Pennsylvania Hospital was the first hospital built in the colonies. Franklin asked for money from wealthy people in Philadelphia to make the project a success.

welfare

well-being; health, happiness, and other things which bring about well-being

and pewter spoon were good enough for him. But his wife said that if her neighbors' husbands could have china and silver, so could her husband, who was a greater man than any of them!

Benjamin Franklin was a good citizen. Though he was busy, he always had time to help others. Soon it came to pass that, if anything was to be done for the welfare of the town, people came to ask his advice. He started a library so that everybody who wanted to read could have books. He started a fine school, for he said that he who teaches himself often has a fool for a master. That school became the University of Pennsylvania. He started a night watch for the protection of honest people. He begged money for a hospital for the poor. He organized a fire department so that the whole town would not burn down. That was the first Volunteer Fire Department in the American colonies and Philadelphia became the safest town. As one of the city fathers, Franklin helped to govern the town. He became postmaster of Philadelphia, and he was so able that he was made postmaster of all the American colonies. He had become well-to-do and respected.

Benjamin Franklin never cared for money for money's sake, but for the leisure it gave him. He bought himself a larger house where he had room for his books and a quiet study and workroom for himself. While his faithful helpers kept his presses running, he spent long hours in his study. There he used his clear head and skilled fingers to work out many small inventions that would make life easier and simpler for him and his fellow citizens.

Benjamin hated waste. One day, looking at his fireplace, he thought how it ate all the wood he fed it and gave back very little heat. He pitied the women who did much of their work at the fireside. The heat shriveled their faces, and the drafts in the cool room behind them made their backs stiff. So he built a little iron stove with an open front that fitted into the fireplace. The stove drew in the cold drafts, heated the air, and sent the warm air into all the corners of the room. The women blessed him. The fame of the Franklin stove spread even to Europe, but his work on electricity was to mean even more to the world.

leisure
free time to spend as one pleases

Meet the Author

Ingri d'Aulaire and her husband Edgar worked as a team for more than 40 years making children's books. Among the 25 books they made together, seven were biographies. Neither of the d'Aulaires are living now, but their books are still popular and very much alive. You may also enjoy their award-winning book *Abraham Lincoln.*

Additional Books to Read

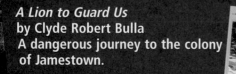

A Lion to Guard Us
by Clyde Robert Bulla
A dangerous journey to the colony of Jamestown.

The Sign of the Beaver
by Elizabeth George Speare
A wilderness story of survival and friendship.

Response Activities

1. Comparing Literature and History
How do you think William Penn would have felt about Benjamin Franklin's contributions to Philadelphia? Would Penn have agreed with Franklin's ideas?

2. Informative: Write a Newsletter
Benjamin Franklin wrote and printed his own newspapers. In his papers he shared the news with Philadelphia's citizens and also told them things he thought were important. Create a one-page newsletter to give to your class, which shares important information.

3. Citizenship: Create an Invention
Benjamin Franklin got many of his ideas for inventions from noticing problems people around him were having. What kind of invention could you develop that would help people around you do their work better?

Farm and City Life

Main Idea The Middle Colonies were characterized by productive farms and diverse centers of commerce.

Key Vocabulary

yeoman

backcountry

subsistence

apprentice

Key Events

1682 Philadelphia founded

1723 Benjamin Franklin comes to Philadelphia

Benjamin Franklin was a self-made man and proud of it. He said when he arrived in Philadelphia in 1723 that his "whole stock of cash consisted of a Dutch dollar . . ." By the time he died 67 years later, he was a well-respected writer and publisher famous for sayings like the ones below.

> "**E**arly to bed, and early to rise, makes a man healthy, wealthy and wise."
>
> "**L**aziness travels so slowly that poverty soon overtakes it."

He wrote these and other sayings in *Poor Richard's Almanac,* a popular series of books offering practical advice to colonial farmers.

Farm Life

Focus *How were backcountry farms different from farms in settled areas?*

Franklin's advice — and his life — were models for many in the Middle Colonies. Nearly all of the population there lived on farms of various sizes. In New York, English landlords and Dutch patroons, large landowners, owned up to a million acres. Small farmers rented land from these large owners. In Pennsylvania and other places, self-sufficient farmers called **yeomen** owned their land. In all places, the poorest people worked on other people's farms.

The fields of the Middle Colonies were devoted to growing grains like wheat, corn, and barley. Farmers in this region grew so much wheat that the Middle Colonies became known as the Breadbasket Colonies. Farmers took the grain they grew

Benjamin Franklin was 40 years old when this portrait was painted in 1746.

to mills to have it turned into flour. Some mills were built along the fall line and powered by river water. The wind provided the power for other mills. The illustration below shows how a windmill works.

Colonial Windmill

Colonial farms turned wheat into flour using wind and water. **Technology:** *Which kind of mill do you think was more reliable, one powered by wind or water?*

The huge sails, made out of canvas, caught the wind and powered the mill.

The wind-powered sails turned this enormous wheel, which turned the stones and kept the wheat flowing.

Men poured the wheat into a tub. It then flowed through three stones, called millstones, that crushed the wheat between them.

When the wheat was ground up, the hard outer part, or germ, separated from the flour. A chute carried the germ away. People often used the germ to feed animals.

Colonists often swapped stories and advice while their flour was loaded onto wagons waiting below the mill.

Did you know that in some parts of the world, stores don't have price tags? Shoppers talk over the price with storekeepers to decide what they will pay. The Quakers did not believe in this system, so they used only fixed prices.

Some colonists — especially the Scots-Irish — moved to the **backcountry**. The backcountry was the unsettled, or wilderness part of each colony, usually beyond the fall line. The land there was cheaper to buy because it was farther away from the cities.

Backcountry farms were rough. People lived in log cabins and planted their crops among the trees in the woods. In more settled areas, people lived in houses and farmed land in open fields.

The difference was most obvious at harvest time. In the backcountry, farmers raised just enough wheat or corn to feed themselves. This was called **subsistence** farming. In more settled areas, farmers grew enough grain to feed themselves, as well as surpluses to export. These farms provided flour for American towns, Caribbean plantations, and English and American cities.

Centers of Commerce

Focus | *Why did New York and Philadelphia become large and wealthy cities?*

Much of that flour flowed into the two largest cities in the Middle Colonies — Philadelphia and New York. Both cities were much smaller than a city of today. You could walk across them in minutes. Both were busy and diverse places. Merchants, artisans, and laborers of many backgrounds filled their buildings and streets.

Philadelphia

Philadelphia was an important port city and center of trade for Pennsylvania, Delaware, and western New Jersey. The excellent location was no accident. William Penn had carefully chosen a site

You can see boats, ships, and windmills in this 1752 painting of Philadelphia. **Economics:** *How did Philadelphia's harbor help it grow into a busy city?*

where the Delaware River flowed into a wide harbor, convenient for both seagoing ships and riverboats.

These boats brought sugar and molasses from the Caribbean, wine from Europe, and cloth and metal goods from England. Settlers from the backcountry paddled down the Delaware River to trade their beaver pelts and other furs in Philadelphia.

Trade of pelts and other goods made up only a part of the city's economy. Furniture makers designed pieces as fashionable as those manufactured in Europe. Also, Philadelphia became a center for newspaper and book printing. Benjamin Franklin was one of many printers.

Unlike most cities of the time, Philadelphia was built with a plan. William Penn designed the city on a grid pattern (see picture above.) Philadelphia became one of the first colonial cities to pave its streets — an idea of Franklin's. Trees lined the hundred-foot-wide streets. Though many colonial cities had walls to protect them, Penn planned Philadelphia without them. He expected colonists and Native Americans to live in peace.

Soon merchants and artisans replaced wooden buildings with fancier brick ones. Philadelphia lived up to William Penn's claim. It was "a greene country towne, which will never be burnt and all-ways be wholesome."

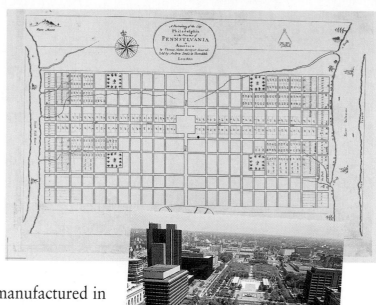

Penn chose a site between the Delaware and Schuylkill rivers. Thomas Holme drew this plan of Philadelphia in 1683. You can still see the careful grid planning in Philadelphia's streets today.

Apprentices like the one above helped build cabinets and other fine pieces of furniture, using tools like this one.

New York

New York also sat on a harbor, where the Hudson River flowed into the ocean. Unlike Philadelphia, it was not a planned city. The streets of New York were crooked, narrow, and busy.

A wealth of grain, fur, and cheese came down the Hudson River from the farms and trading posts of the backcountry and into New York. Merchants also imported items from Europe, Africa, and the Caribbean. Their papers record imports of everything from elephant tusks to lime juice.

Trades flourished as well, and young apprentices filled the workshops of the city. An **apprentice** is a person who works with an older, experienced person to learn a skill. Apprentices learned to make all sorts of items — shoes, clothing, furniture, books, and many other things. Benjamin Franklin got his start as an apprentice to a printer.

From the beginning, New York was a diverse city. A person visiting New York in 1643 would have heard as many as eighteen different languages spoken on its streets. Africans made up 12 percent of New York's population. Many worked as artisans and ship laborers.

The diversity of the Middle Colonies, like its rich soil and easily traveled rivers, was an important resource of this growing region.

Lesson Review

1650	1700	

1682
Philadelphia founded

1723
Ben Franklin comes to Philadelphia

1. **Key Vocabulary:** Write a paragraph on farming in the Middle Colonies using patroon, yeoman, backcountry, and subsistence.

2. **Focus:** How were backcountry farms different from farms in settled areas?

3. **Focus:** Why did Philadelphia and New York become large and wealthy cities?

4. **Critical Thinking: Interpret** In what ways was life on the many kinds of farms different from life in the cities?

5. **Geography:** Based on what you have learned about colonial cities, how does geography affect the planning of a city?

6. **Citizenship/Writing Activity:** The year is 1700, and you are moving to America. Decide what is important to you, and choose a colony based on this. Then write an advertisement for your colony.

Skills Workshop

Reading for Cause and Effect

Getting Results

"Early to bed and early to rise makes a man healthy, wealthy, and wise." This saying, made famous by Ben Franklin, shows a **cause-and-effect** relationship. If you get up early, then you will be successful in life. Historical events often have cause-and-effect connections. This means that one event causes another. Finding causes and effects helps you understand how and why events occurred.

❶ Here's How

Read "Creation of a Fire Department," at right.

- Identify the event or problem that's being described.

- Identify the possible causes. Why did this happen?

- Identify the effects. What happened as a result?

- Look for clue words. *Because, since, for, if,* and *in order to* alert you to a cause; *so, therefore, then,* and *as a result* show an effect.

❷ Think It Through

Can you think of other signals, besides clue words, that tell you events are related?

❸ Use It

Make a flow chart like the one to the right. Show all the cause-and-effect relationships you find in "Creation of a Fire Department." Be careful — there may not always be signal words to give you clues.

Creation of a Fire Department

Benjamin Franklin realized that fire was the worst enemy of people living in cities. Therefore, Franklin did something to get people involved in the management of fires. He wrote a letter in the newspaper encouraging people to be careful in their homes with candles and fireplaces. People in Philadelphia read this letter . . . [and] decided to form a volunteer fire department. Since so many people volunteered for the department, they made several different departments all over the city. Because of these volunteer fire departments, Philadelphia was one of the safest cities in the world at this time.

Cause:
Fires were a problem

Effect:
Franklin wrote a letter to a newspaper

★ CITIZENSHIP ★

Making Decisions

Should You Speak Out?

Has there ever been a time when you wanted to speak your mind about something, but didn't? As people of the United States, we have the right to express our opinions, whatever they are. At the same time, we need to think about the effect our words may have. In the case study below, one man published some newspaper articles, even though he knew they might get him in trouble.

Case Study

The Zenger Trial

In 1733, the royal governor of New York was the greedy, bad-tempered William Cosby. Cosby fired people whenever they disagreed with him. John Peter Zenger ran a newspaper, The *New-York Weekly Journal*. For nearly two years, Zenger published articles criticizing the governor. In 1734, Cosby had Zenger thrown in jail.

Zenger was charged with libel. Back then, any criticism of the royal governor was called libel. Zenger's lawyer argued that criticism of the government should be allowed. He said, "There is no libel if the truth is told," and he argued that Zenger's statements were true. The jury agreed, finding Zenger not guilty.

Take Action

The Zenger trial established an important principle: the freedom of the press to publish the truth. This freedom, like freedom of speech, is a basic right of the people of the United States. But how do you decide when to use that right? Join one of three groups to decide how to handle this issue.

1 Music producers: A popular group wants to record song lyrics that some people won't like. You think the lyrics are bad, too. Do you make the record?

2 News editors: Your top reporter has discovered that a person working for the government has broken the law. Do you publish the story?

3 Private citizens: A big political town meeting is happening next week. You are strongly against the views being presented. Do you express how you feel? If so, how?

4 When you're done, take turns presenting your decisions. How did you arrive at them? Compare your processes.

Tips for Making Decisions

- Decide what you plan to say or publish.
- Think about who will be affected and how.
- Think about your reasons for speaking out. Will some good come from it?
- List the reasons for your decision. Are they good reasons?
- Compare the possible good and bad effects. Is it worth it?

Research Activity

The First Amendment to the Constitution guarantees people the freedom of speech. Many times, this freedom has come under question. Find out about an important law case in the last 10 years that dealt with First Amendment rights. What are the facts of the case? What did the judges decide? Do you agree with their decision?

Chapter Review

1723
Ben Franklin comes
to Philadelphia

| 1650 | 1670 | 1690 | 1710 | 1730 | 1750 |

1682
Pennsylvania founded

1664
New Netherland becomes
New York and New Jersey

Summarizing the Main Idea

1 Create a web such as the following, using terms and words to describe the Middle Colonies.

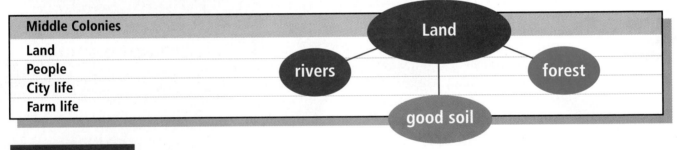

Middle Colonies
Land
People
City life
Farm life

Land — rivers, forest, good soil

Vocabulary

2 Using at least five of the following terms, describe a typical day of a settler in one of the Middle Colonies.

Piedmont (p. 188)   **religious toleration (p. 189**   **backcountry (p. 202)**

fall line (p. 188)   **"holy experiment"(p. 191)**   **subsistence (p. 202)**

proprietor (p. 189)   **yeoman (p. 200)**   **apprentice (p. 204)**

Reviewing the Facts

3 Why did farming become the main activity of the Middle Colonies?

4 How did settlers use natural resources?

5 What were the differences between the Piedmont and the coastal plain?

6 Who moved to the Middle Colonies? Why?

7 What was Penn's "holy experiment"?

8 What was the difference between large landowners, yeomen, and backcountry farmers?

9 Why was Philadelphia a successful center of trade?

10 How were Philadelphia and New York similar? How were they different?

11 Read pages 190 and 191 again. What caused William Penn to receive land in the colonies?

12 On the same pages, what were some of the effects of Penn's treaty making?

Geography Skills

13 Find a modern map of Philadelphia. Compare it to the map on page 203. What differences do you see between the two maps? What are the similarities? Is Philadelphia still a port city?

14 Illustrate a map of the Middle Colonies that shows the natural resources that were available to the settlers. How did they use each of these resources? Which ones were necessary for their survival? Which ones could they have lived without?

Critical Thinking

15 Interpret Why did William Penn make a treaty with the Lenni Lenape? How did his actions show that he believed in fairness?

16 Identifying Main Idea How would you describe the Middle Colonies? Write three or four sentences that include the most important facts about them.

17 Conclude Why did Philadelphia and New York grow so quickly? Explain what drew people to these bustling cities.

Writing: Citizenship and Culture

18 Citizenship Make your own collection of sayings for a modern day almanac. What advice might you offer your classmates? Combine your sayings with those of another student and bind them to make a book.

19 Culture Write a diary entry as a Quaker child who has just moved to Philadelphia. How have you adapted to your new life? How has your life changed? Include examples of how you spend your time.

Activities

History/Drama Activity
You read about ways that the Quakers and the Lenni Lenape made treaties. Act out a play which shows the meeting between these two groups of people.

Culture/Writing Activity
Crèvecoeur wrote about the people who he encountered in the Middle Colonies. Suppose you were a traveler visiting your town or city. Describe the people you encounter in a few paragraphs.

Internet Option

Check the **Internet Social Studies Center** for ideas on how to extend your theme project beyond your classroom.

THEME PROJECT CHECK-IN

As you continue working on your theme project, use the information about the Middle Colonies. The following questions will help you:
- What geographic features and resources from the Middle Colonies are important to show on your map?
- How do people make their living in the Middle Colonies?
- Why would the diversity of the Middle Colonies attract people there?

CHAPTER 8

Southern Colonies

Chapter Preview: *People, Places, and Events*

Tidewater Land

What is so special about this hot, swampy land? *Lesson 1, Page 212*

Rice Cultivation

When is a house also a small village and a rice farm? *Lesson 1, Page 213*

Maryland Founded   1632

Maryland began as a piece of paper and became a home for immigrants. *Lesson 2, Page 216*

Geography of the South

Main Idea The Southern Colonies became wealthy by raising valuable crops and selling them to Europe and to other colonies.

When stories about Spanish exploration in the Americas first reached England in the 1500s, most people had no idea how the new land looked. People used their imaginations to picture it.

One London play about the first colonists in Virginia claimed, "For rubies and diamonds, they go forth . . . and gather 'em by the seashore to hang on their children's coats."

To their great disappointment, the English settlers found little gold and no jewels in Virginia. They did, however, find a different kind of wealth: a land and climate perfect for raising crops that they could not grow in England.

Key Vocabulary

tidewater

cash crop

export

Key Events

1744 First successful crop of indigo grown in South Carolina

◀ The Governor's Palace in Williamsburg, Virginia

1690	1710	1730

Backcountry Cabin

What kind of house do you build when you live in the forest? *Lesson 2, Page 218*

The Post Road   1750

Colonists in the South sometimes went to the tavern to pick up their newspapers. *Lesson 3, Page 223*

Slave Cabins

Nobody wants to sleep on a cold dirt floor. But some people were forced to. *Lesson 3, Page 227*

The tidewater of Virginia, with its rich soil and plenty of moisture, was perfect for growing tobacco.

The map shows geography and Native American groups who lived in the five Southern Colonies. **Map Skill:** *Near which geographic feature did most colonists settle?*

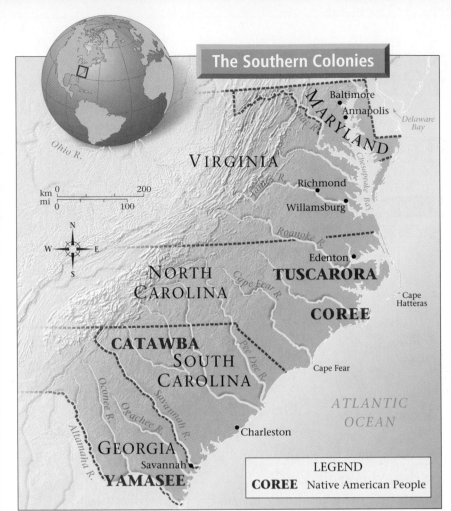

The Southern Colonies

MARYLAND
Baltimore
Annapolis
Delaware Bay
Ohio R.
VIRGINIA
Richmond
Willamsburg
Roanoke R.
Edenton
TUSCARORA
Cape Hatteras
NORTH CAROLINA
Cape Fear R.
COREE
CATAWBA
SOUTH CAROLINA
Pee Dee R.
Cape Fear
ATLANTIC OCEAN
Oconee R.
Ogachee R.
Savannah R.
Charleston
GEORGIA
Savannah
Altamaha R.
YAMASEE

km 0 — 200
mi 0 — 100

N W E S

LEGEND	
COREE	Native American People

Geography and Agriculture

Focus *Why did farmers in the Southern Colonies concentrate on growing cash crops?*

The geography of the Southern Colonies differed from that of most of England. The southern coast, with its many rivers, bays, and swamps, was a watery world. The coastal area was called the **tidewater** because it had rivers that were affected by ocean tides. About 150 miles inland, the tidewater ended at the fall line. The fall line divided the tidewater from the Piedmont's rolling hills.

At first, most colonists settled in the tidewater region, with its easy access to the ocean. They quickly discovered that this region was perfect for growing crops. The growing season in the warm South lasted seven or eight months. Plentiful rainfall fed the rich soil.

The Powhatans had taught Virginia's first settlers how to grow corn. Corn continued to be an important crop during the colonial period, especially for backcountry settlers. Colonists grew corn in all parts of the South, to feed both themselves and their farm animals. They grew many other vegetables as well.

Along with food for themselves, colonists grew **cash crops,** crops grown just to be sold. Unlike Northern colonists, many tidewater settlers grew mainly cash crops. Half of all southern crops were **exports,** or goods shipped to other countries to be sold. These crops were often grown on plantations like the one below, large farms where most of the labor was done by enslaved Africans.

Remember the tobacco that John Rolfe planted in Virginia? Tobacco was the first cash crop in the Southern Colonies, followed by rice. The weather and wet coastline of South Carolina were better

Making baskets with a coil pattern is one of the oldest African crafts in the United States. This basket was used to clean rice.

A Southern Plantation

The layout of the plantation was similar to that of a small, self-sufficient village.

Buildings like these were used as kitchens, workshops, and storehouses.

The plantation was located next to a river, which made shipping easier.

As it needed much water, rice was grown and harvested as close to the river as possible.

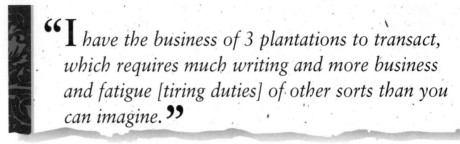

Making Indigo Dye

1 Workers harvest the indigo plants grown in the fields.

2 The indigo leaves are thrown into big tubs of water where they are soaked three times. Workers stir the indigo constantly.

3 The soaked indigo leaves are pressed into cone-shaped containers and hung on poles to dry. Now the cones of indigo are ready to be used as a blue dye.

suited for rice than tobacco. Soon the English colonists who began growing rice learned that many Africans, who had grown rice in Africa, were more skilled than they were. Colonists learned from Africans the best ways to plant, harvest, and polish the rice.

South Carolina grew other important cash crops, one of them made profitable by the efforts of a girl named Eliza Lucas. In addition to her studies, she ran the house and plantation. She wrote,

> **"I** *have the business of 3 plantations to transact, which requires much writing and more business and fatigue [tiring duties] of other sorts than you can imagine.* **"**

When she was 16, Lucas began to experiment with many plants on her father's plantation. In 1744, she produced her first successful crop of indigo plants. Indigo grew in places where rice did not, and per pound had 100 times the value of rice. Indigo plants were used to make a blue dye which produced a color like that in blue jeans.

Lucas and other planters shipped and traded products on riverbanks near their homes. The region's many rivers meant that ocean-going ships could go far inland. With the South's ideal geography and the forced work of enslaved Africans, tobacco, rice, and indigo became three of colonial America's most valuable exports.

Lesson Review

1650		1700		1750	

1744
First successful crop of indigo grown in South Carolina

1 **Key Vocabulary:** Write a sentence about the South using **tidewater**, **cash crop**, and **export**.

2 **Focus:** Why did farmers in the Southern Colonies concentrate on growing cash crops?

3 **Critical Thinking: Conclude** Why would a state or a country use most of its land to produce only one or two crops?

4 **Geography:** Why did plantations become common in the South, but not in New England?

5 **Theme: New Environments/Art Activity** Some colonists' decisions to come to a new country were based on what they heard about it. Make a poster showing things in your state that would attract people to it.

Expansion of the Colonies

Main Idea The Southern Colonies expanded because of increased immigration and the colonists' desire for more farm land.

Key Vocabulary

House of Burgesses
representative
debtor
trustee

Back in 1619, the colony of Virginia had performed a bold act. They had created the **House of Burgesses** to make laws for the colony. A burgess was a **representative**, or a person who speaks for other people. All free men in Virginia could vote to elect the burgesses. By creating the House of Burgesses, Virginia created the first representative government in the colonies, giving Virginians a clear voice in their government. Why, then, less than 60 years later, would Virginia be the scene of a rebellion against its leaders?

Key Events

1632 Maryland founded

1663 Carolina given second charter

1676 Bacon's Rebellion

1732 Georgia founded

Virginia and Maryland

Focus *How did the growing of cash crops affect the societies of Virginia and Maryland?*

Tobacco plants wore out the soil quickly, often in three to seven years. Planters wanted more land to keep growing tobacco, and to get it they soon began invading the territory of the Powhatans.

In 1622 and again in 1644, the Powhatans fought to take back their land, killing many backcountry settlers in these conflicts. The governor of Virginia, William Berkeley, thought the only way settlers and Native Americans could get along was to be separated. In 1646, he set up boundary lines around Native American land that colonists were not allowed to cross.

In 1651 England passed a new law, the first Navigation Act. This law gave backcountry settlers another reason to feel mistreated by their government. By limiting colonial trade, the law meant that England gained most of the profit from tobacco. Rich planters got what little profit was left. The House of Burgesses, controlled by such wealthy planters, passed laws that favored the owners of large plantations.

Tobacco shaped the economy of the South.

This stained glass window of Nathaniel Bacon once hung in a church in Williamsburg, Virginia. Bacon was often called "the Rebel."

Colonists were also angry because Berkeley recognized that Native Americans, like the nearby Pamunkeys, had rights to their land. Soon conflicts between settlers and Native Americans erupted.

Bacon's Rebellion

Nathaniel Bacon was a wealthy farmer whose farm had been attacked by Native Americans and was annoyed by the way Berkeley dealt with conflicts. Bacon wanted the power to deal with Native American conflicts in his own way. Gaining the support of some settlers, he attacked the peaceful Pamunkey Indians in the spring of 1676.

The actions of Bacon and his followers became known as Bacon's Rebellion. In September, Bacon's men burned Jamestown to the ground. The rebellion ended in October when Bacon died from an illness, and Governor Berkeley hanged 23 of Bacon's followers.

Berkeley's action shocked the king of England, who pressured Berkeley to resign. The rebellion made it clear that it was very difficult to have laws satisfying both settlers and Native Americans. From around 1675 on, the House of Burgesses allowed settlers to live wherever they chose. Native Americans were given smaller and smaller pieces of land on which to live.

The Founding of Maryland

As the Puritans and Quakers had before them, English Catholics looked to the Americas for religious freedom. Lord Baltimore, a Catholic landowner in England, wanted to create a colony for Catholics. In 1632, King Charles I gave him a charter for a large piece of land on Chesapeake Bay. The king named the colony Maryland after his Catholic wife, Henrietta Maria.

Lord Baltimore's son carried out his father's plans. This second Lord Baltimore knew there were not enough Catholic immigrants to settle Maryland. He therefore invited English people of all religions, promising religious toleration.

Maryland's climate and geography were similar to Virginia's. The new colony also grew tobacco, using indentured servants and enslaved Africans to grow it. Shipping and trade went on in the port of Baltimore. As they did in Virginia, plantation owners settled the tidewater and ran the government. Farmers settled the backcountry.

Fact File:

Colony	Date Founded	Reasons Founded
Virginia	1607	Trade, farming
Maryland	1632	Religious freedom, farming
North Carolina	1663	Trade, farming
South Carolina	1663	Trade, farming
Georgia	1732	Home for debtors

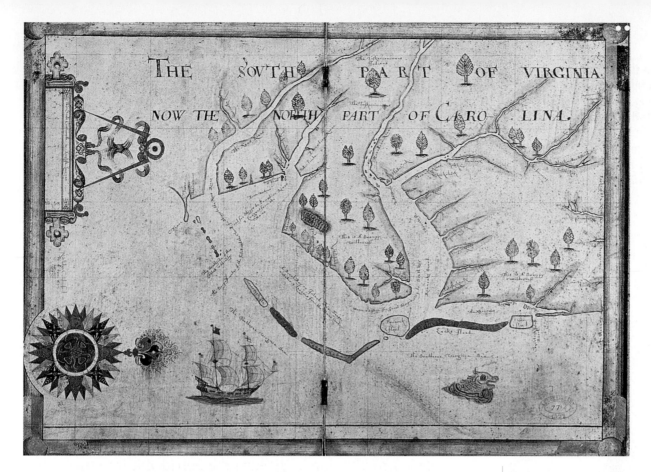

The Carolinas and Georgia

Focus *Why were the Carolinas and Georgia founded?*

For the first half of the 1600s, Europeans heard rumors that the land south of Virginia was "fruitful and pleasant." In the 1650s, a few people decided to settle along Albemarle (AL buh mahrl) Sound, in what is now North Carolina. *(See the map above.)*

The Carolinas

North and South Carolina began as one colony. Charles I had founded the colony in 1629, naming it after himself (*Carolus* is Latin for Charles). There were no settlers, however. In 1663 Charles II, the new king of England, granted eight men a proprietary charter for the same lands between Virginia and Florida.

Early efforts to settle these lands failed. Only one settlement founded before 1700 — Charleston, in southern Carolina — survived. With its excellent harbor and rich land nearby, Charleston grew quickly. As in Maryland, the settlement's religious freedom drew people from all over, including Europe and the Caribbean.

Charleston became a wealthy city. Planters built second homes in the city, beautiful brick houses that faced the bay. Planters stayed in these homes in the summer to escape the heat of their tidewater

°This map of 1657 shows southern Virginia, which later became North Carolina. The settlement shown was the first permanent settlement in the Carolinas. **Map Skill:** *What geographic features might have helped settlers in this area?*

Settlers in the backcountry cleared land among thick forests to build log cabins and grow crops. **Math:** *Count the stumps in the picture. If a man cut down three trees a day, how long did it take him to clear this land?*

Backcountry settlers made bags like the one above from the skins of the animals they hunted.

plantations. They enjoyed fancy parties and imported fine goods — silver, china, and silk fabrics — that arrived on European ships.

In 1729, England bought Carolina from its proprietors and made it a royal colony. The king then divided it into two colonies: North and South Carolina. South Carolina's geography and economy resembled Virginia's. Large plantations, producing rice and indigo, lined the wide rivers of the tidewater.

North Carolina could not produce all the valuable crops that made South Carolina so rich. Its vast forests, however, provided colonists with wood, tar, and pitch. The English navy used tar and pitch to seal and waterproof their ships. By 1753 the colony was selling tens of thousands of barrels of such products to England.

The forests also provided animal furs and skins to be made into leather. Both fur and leather became important industries for North Carolina. Settlers and Native Americans in the backcountry developed a valuable trade in deerskins. One settler wrote:

> "There is such infinite Herds, that the whole Country seems but one continued [deer] Park."

Of course, people also farmed in the Carolinas. Like poorer immigrants in the Middle Colonies who settled in the backcountry, poorer immigrants in the South moved to Carolina's backcountry. Many lived in cabins like the one above. They traded forest products and grew crops for their own use.

Georgia

The last of the 13 colonies England settled in North America was also perhaps the most unusual. Georgia was settled by poor people who were **debtors,** or people who owed money.

England created Georgia in 1732 in order to have safe territory between Carolina and Spanish Florida. James Oglethorpe, a member of Parliament, had the idea of sending debtors to settle Georgia. They could start a new life and help protect the British empire.

In 1732, King George II granted Oglethorpe a royal charter for land for the "poor persons of London." In November of that year, Oglethorpe and about 35 debtors' families set sail for Georgia.

Once there Oglethorpe quickly established friendly relations with the Creek Indians, who gave the settlers tidewater land. Oglethorpe knew that in colonies to the north, relations between colonists and Native Americans had often turned rocky when the fur trade grew. For that reason he carefully controlled the fur trade between settlers and the Creek.

Georgia was the only colony to ban alcohol and slavery. But settlers moving from South Carolina to Georgia in search of more land asked the colony's **trustees,** or managers, to change these laws. In 1742, the trustees of Georgia lifted the ban on liquor. Eight years later, they allowed slavery. Within 25 years, the number of enslaved Africans in Georgia was nearly equal to the number of Europeans.

Biography

James Oglethorpe

Though his family was wealthy, James Oglethorpe was always interested in improving the lives of poor and imprisoned people. In 1728 he led a group that studied problems with the English prison system. His research caused the government to pass new laws correcting the worst problems.

Lesson Review

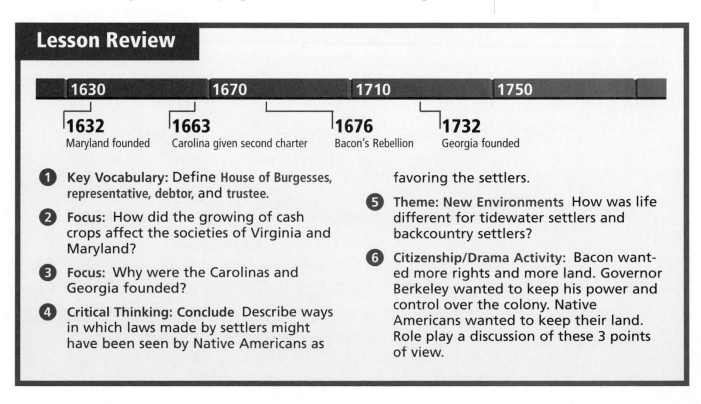

1630	1670	1710	1750

1632
Maryland founded

1663
Carolina given second charter

1676
Bacon's Rebellion

1732
Georgia founded

1. **Key Vocabulary: Define** House of Burgesses, representative, debtor, and trustee.

2. **Focus:** How did the growing of cash crops affect the societies of Virginia and Maryland?

3. **Focus:** Why were the Carolinas and Georgia founded?

4. **Critical Thinking: Conclude** Describe ways in which laws made by settlers might have been seen by Native Americans as favoring the settlers.

5. **Theme: New Environments** How was life different for tidewater settlers and backcountry settlers?

6. **Citizenship/Drama Activity:** Bacon wanted more rights and more land. Governor Berkeley wanted to keep his power and control over the colony. Native Americans wanted to keep their land. Role play a discussion of these 3 points of view.

Skills
Workshop

Interpreting Flow Lines on Maps

Go with the Flow

In the 1700's, where did colonial merchants ship their different crops? Which crops did Europeans want most? You can answer these questions using a map with flow lines. **Flow lines** show where something came from and where it went. Flow lines can show how much went from one place to the other. Study the map to learn more about colonial trade.

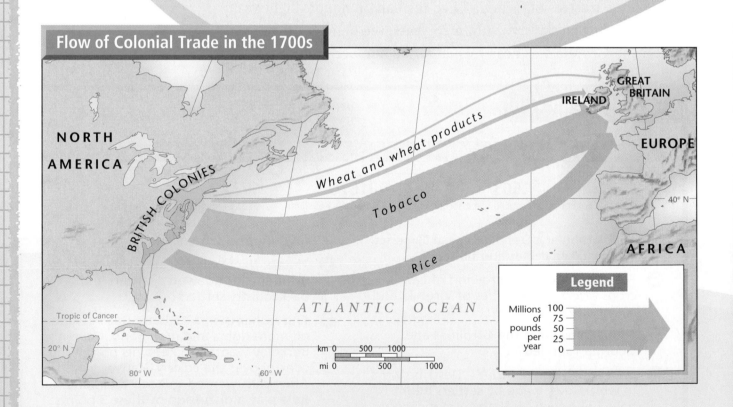

Flow of Colonial Trade in the 1700s

NORTH AMERICA

BRITISH COLONIES

Wheat and wheat products

Tobacco

Rice

ATLANTIC OCEAN

Tropic of Cancer

20° N

80° W   60° W

GREAT BRITAIN

IRELAND

EUROPE

40° N

AFRICA

km 0   500   1000
mi 0   500   1000

Legend

Millions of pounds per year
100
75
50
25
0

The items on the blue arrow are products shipped from England to the colonies. The items on the green arrow are products shipped from the colonies to England.

① Here's How.

- Study the map. Look carefully at the flow lines. To what direction do the arrows point? Notice that different colors represent different trade products.

- Now study the map legend. To use the legend, first measure the thickness of each flow line. Then see how it measures up to the legend.

- Compare the flow lines. Which lines are thickest and thinnest? What does this tell you about the amount of each product traded?

② Think It Through

Suppose the flow lines had no arrowheads. How would that change the information you could get from the map? What if the flow lines were all the same thickness? What other kinds of information could flow lines on a map help you to show?

③ Use It

1. List the products that the colonies sent to England in order of the amounts traded.

2. Use this list to write a paragraph explaining how colonial trade helped both England and the colonies.

Agriculture and Society

Key Vocabulary

post road

profit

Key Events

1732 Post road first extended to the South

Main Idea The Southern Colonies' dependence on agriculture shaped the way people lived.

Getting around the South was not easy. A visit to church, the mill, or the blacksmith often required a 10 mile journey. Rough roads made these trips long and uncomfortable. There were few towns, and people lived far apart from each other. Southerners came to depend on visitors for news and entertainment.

One traveler wrote that southerners' way

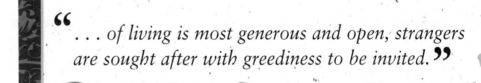

> *" . . . of living is most generous and open, strangers are sought after with greediness to be invited."*

Southern innkeepers even complained that they could not find paying guests, as most travelers chose to stay at people's homes.

Travel in the South

Focus *Why was the post road so important in the South?*

A traveler in the South had two choices, and both were slow. Most people preferred to travel by water, in either ocean-going ships or river canoes. The other option was to travel overland by horse and wagon. There were not many good roads in the South in the early colonial period. Most roads were bumpy and full of holes. When it rained they became streams of mud.

In the late 1600s a post road was first built in the Northeast. A **post road** is a route used by the postal service to deliver mail. In time this post road reached all the way from Maine to Georgia. More and more, travelers chose to go overland by the post road, which offered the traveler the company of the mail carriers. Look at the map on the right to learn about sights along the post road.

Traveling along the post road was bumpy and tiring, but sometimes offered travelers beautiful views.

Williamsburg

Construction of the post road began slowly, and was limited to the Northeast. The southern part of the road was only begun in 1732, and was harder to build because it covered greater distances. In 1753, Benjamin Franklin became postmaster and planned many additions to the road. By 1776, mail on the post road went from Boston to Philadelphia in six days. But sometimes it was still faster to send mail from Charleston to New York by way of England!

The post road ran along the coast, and still exists as part of highway U.S. 1 today.

Appalachian Mountains

Traveling wagons might have passed signs like this one. Inn and tavern owners hoped their signs would attract people to stay or eat with them.

Charleston

Travelers often stayed overnight at plantation houses like this one. There they could eat, rest, and exchange news.

Crossroads and Ports

Inns, often found at crossroads, were the center of local life. They served as meetinghouses, taverns, and post offices. Travelers brought news and local residents gave directions. Letters and newspapers were laid out on tables until people came in to claim them.

There were a few southern towns with colonial governments. Only one city, Charleston, was as large as northern cities. Rice and indigo planters brought their crops to Charleston, a center of culture and trade. Charleston soon became a busy port with a diverse population that included Jews, Scots-Irish, French, and Africans.

Tradespeople, such as metalsmiths, cabinet makers, and carriage makers, prospered by working for Charleston's rich planters. Many of these craftsmen were free Africans, whose iron fences and balconies can still be enjoyed today as symbols of their creativity.

Plantations and Farms

Focus *How did life in the South center around the farm?*

Plantations were large farms like those in the Middle Colonies. They produced surplus crops to sell for a profit. A **profit** is extra

• Tell Me More •

Comparing Lives

Plantation Life

Plantation families could afford luxuries — such as having their portraits painted.

Silver coffeepots were imported and brought on ships to Charleston harbor.

Carter's Grove plantation was one of the largest plantations in Virginia.

Fine furniture like this chair could have been imported from Europe or from Philadelphia.

money available after all expenses have been paid. Still, there were many differences between plantations and farms. Plantations were like small villages, with bakeries, blacksmiths, and craft workshops. Plantation owners imported only a few items such as metal pots and fine luxury goods from Europe. Live-in teachers taught the planters' children. The most striking difference was that workers on plantations were enslaved. They were not paid, and they could not quit.

Some plantations were huge. When Virginia's Robert Carter died in 1732, he left 300,000 acres and over 700 enslaved Africans as his personal property. Most plantations were smaller, with 20 to 100 enslaved workers.

Both men and women ran plantations. Husbands directed the fieldwork and wives the household work. Enslaved Africans, however, did almost all the hard work. Most worked the fields. Some worked as servants in the house. A few were artisans who made the tools, wheels, horseshoes, and other things plantations needed.

Most Southerners did not live on plantations. They were yeoman farmers who did not own enslaved people. They worked farms in the backcountry of the Piedmont. They grew their own crops, and used the plantation owner's docks for shipping. Women often helped in the fields, where yeomen planted food and cash crops.

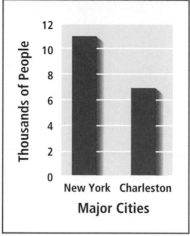

Population of Colonial Cities, 1743

This chart compares the population of New York to that of Charleston. **Chart Skill:** *How many people did Charleston have in 1743?*

Yeoman Farm Life

Yeomen lived in log cabins or small houses which they built themselves.

Yeoman farmers might have traded furs they caught for metal goods like this pot.

Yeoman farmers made their own furniture in their spare time, using local wood.

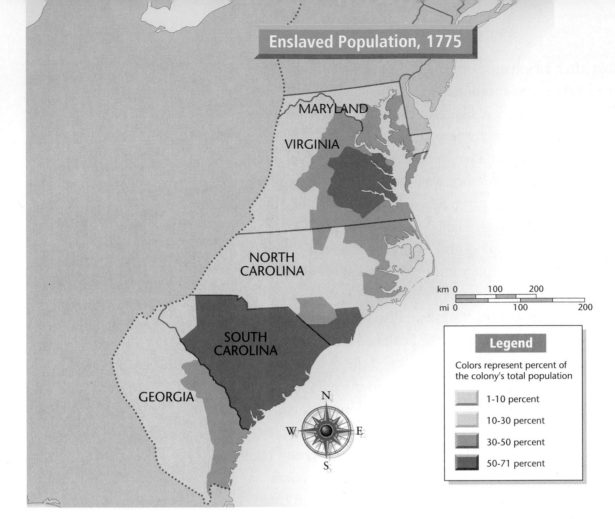

MARYLAND

VIRGINIA

NORTH
CAROLINA

SOUTH
CAROLINA

GEORGIA

km 0   100   200
mi 0   100   200

Legend

Colors represent percent of
the colony's total population

1-10 percent

10-30 percent

30-50 percent

50-71 percent

N
W   E
S

This map shows the number of enslaved Africans in the South around 1775. **Map Skill:** *Which colony had the most enslaved Africans?*

Life Under Slavery

Focus *What was life like for enslaved Africans in the South?*

A small number of free Africans farmed land in the backcountry, like the yeomen, or came to the colonies as indentured servants. Others worked as laborers, craftsmen, and sailors in southern towns. Some enslaved Africans were set free, or gained their freedom by risking great danger to escape from the plantations.

Most Africans in the South were not free, however. As you read in Chapter 6, most Africans were first brought to ports in the Caribbean. From there they were sent to the Southern Colonies. Most Africans who were brought to the plantations came from different cultures but had one thing in common — they were enslaved. In parts of Virginia and South Carolina, enslaved Africans soon outnumbered whites. *(See the map above.)*

Enslaved Africans did backbreaking work from dawn to dusk. They lived in small, crowded cabins, and they had to rely on their owners for food and clothes. Plantation owners often outlawed African customs in an attempt to wipe out African culture.

You can see a southern plantation house with its rows of slave cabins. **Cultures:** *How do you think living apart from the main house helped Africans maintain their own cultures?*

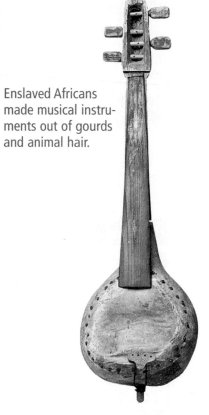

Enslaved Africans made musical instruments out of gourds and animal hair.

Despite these hardships, Africans were able to hold onto many of their own cultures and religions. Because they came from many different cultures and spoke many different languages, Africans had to learn a common language to speak with each other. Usually this was English, but in the Sea Islands of South Carolina and Georgia they developed a new language called Gullah.

Enslaved Africans began to develop a common culture as well. In the plantation cabins, they told stories from their homelands and played traditional music. Over time, these and other African traditions enriched the nation's culture.

Lesson Review

1650	1700	1750

1732
Post road first extended to the South

1. **Key Vocabulary:** Write a paragraph about plantations using **post road** and **profit**.

2. **Focus:** Why was the post road so important in the South?

3. **Focus:** How did life in the South center around the farm?

4. **Focus:** What was life like for enslaved Africans in the South?

5. **Critical Thinking: Interpret** Why do you think plantation owners did not want enslaved Africans to practice their own customs?

6. **Geography:** Why were ports so important to the economy of the South?

7. **Theme: New Environments/Research Activity** For enslaved Africans, the colonial South was a new environment. Use the encyclopedia to find out more about the environments and cultures that many Africans came from.

Chapter Review

Chapter Review Timeline

| 1600 | 1630 | 1660 | 1690 | 1720 | 1750 |

1663 Carolina given second charter

1744 First successful crop of indigo grown in South Carolina

1632 Maryland founded

1676 Bacon's Rebellion

1732 Georgia founded

Summarizing the Main Idea

1 Copy and complete the chart below, indicating the influence geography and agriculture had on the colony.

Colony	Geography/Agriculture
Virginia	*Tobacco plants thrived but used up the soil.*
Maryland	
Carolina	*Nathaniel Bacon protested in an attack known as Bacon's Rebellion.*
Georgia	

Vocabulary

2 Using as many of the following terms as possible, write about a day in one of the Southern Colonies.

tidewater (p. 212)   representative (p. 215)   post road (p. 222)

cash crop (p. 213)   debtor (p. 219)   profit (p. 224)

export (p. 213)   trustee (p. 219)

Reviewing the Facts

3 Why was water such an important natural resource for farmers in the South?

4 People other than the colonists were responsible for their success. Who were these people and what did they do?

5 What kind of problems did the tobacco farmers in Virginia have?

6 What was Bacon's Rebellion?

7 What were the differences between North and South Carolina?

8 How was Georgia different from the other colonies?

9 What kinds of activities occurred on plantations?

10 How did enslaved Africans keep their own culture?

Interpreting Flow Lines on Maps

11 Refer back to the map on page 220. Which products were most valuable in the trade that went on between England and her colonies?

12 Look at the map on page 177. What kind of flow lines does it have? Given what you know about New England, which lines do you think would be thickest?

Geography Skills

13 Put yourself in the position of an Englishman settling in one of the Southern colonies. Write a letter describing your new home. Include details about the land and how you are benefiting from it.

14 Compare what you know about the colonies in New England with the colonies in the South. How are they different? How did the geography of the land influence their growth and development?

Critical Thinking

15 **Predict** As a result of Bacon's Rebellion, a new governor of Virginia was appointed by the King of England. Do you think it was necessary for England to intercede at this point? What might have happened had the colonists been left alone to resolve the problem?

16 **Conclude** Why do you think it was important for enslaved Africans to practice their own customs?

Writing: Citizenship and Economics

17 **Citizenship** The growth of the southern colonies affected people who lived in the South in different ways. Compare how life changed for colonists, Native Americans, and Africans as the South prospered.

18 **Economics** You are about to introduce a new plant that will grow successfully in the South. How would you go about sharing your ideas? What kind of effect might this have on your colony?

Activities

Geography/Arts Activity
You are sent by the King of England to the Southern colonies to document life in the South. Use both pictures and words to capture what you see.

Economics/Research Activity
Pick one or two southern states and find out what crops they grow today. Are the crops exported to other states or countries, or are they used by local people?

Internet Option

Check the **Internet Social Studies Center** for ideas on how to extend your theme project beyond your classroom.

THEME PROJECT CHECK-IN

Use the information about African, Asian, and European travelers to begin your theme project. Begin by asking the following questions about explorers:
• Why did people want to explore the world?
• How did they travel? What kinds of transportation did they use?
• How did their travels change them and others?
• What things did explorers bring with them? What did they trade them for?

The American Revolution

"Nothing short of independence, it appears to me, can possibly do."

George Washington

· THEME ·

Becoming Independent

"Patriots . . . fought for freedom and independence. Thanks to their sacrifices we have equal rights today in our society."

Frances Valle, Fifth Grade
Chicago, IL

For nations as well as people, becoming independent is a process that takes time. That is what it was like for American colonists in the 1760s and 1770s. As relations with Britain grew worse, colonists faced a painful choice. Should they stay loyal to Britain or should they declare independence? Their decision led to the American Revolution and the creation of a new nation: the United States of America.

Theme Project

Patriot or Loyalist?

The year is 1774. You live in the English colonies. You must decide whether to become a Patriot or remain a Loyalist. How can you decide?

- Write two short newspaper articles. Describe colonial events from your character's point of view.
- In a small group, role-play reactions to different events.
- Write a letter to a friend explaining why you became a Patriot or a Loyalist.

RESEARCH: Find out more about a person who lived in the colonies. How did he or she make this decision?

◀ Old North Bridge, Concord, Massachusetts

231

WHEN & WHERE
ATLAS

Few American colonists in 1750 dreamed of starting a new country. Most were happy to be part of Great Britain. Twenty-five years later, the American colonies had declared their independence and were waging a war with Britain. The map shows the locations of British and American troops and forts in 1778.

In this unit, you will learn how relations between the American colonies and Great Britain grew steadily worse following the French and Indian War until tensions exploded into war in 1775. You will also learn more about the course of the war and the American victory that resulted in the creation of a new nation.

Unit 4 Chapters

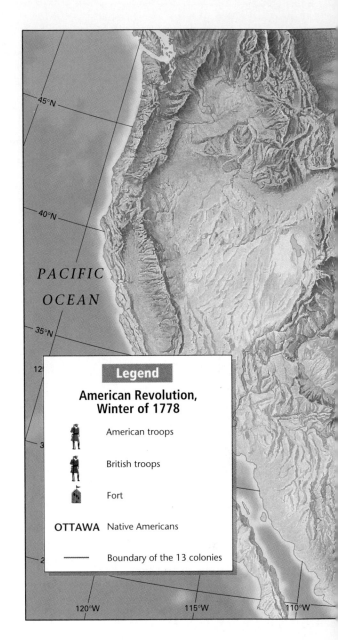

Legend

American Revolution, Winter of 1778

American troops

British troops

Fort

OTTAWA   Native Americans

———   Boundary of the 13 colonies

PACIFIC OCEAN

Unit Timeline

1750   1760   1770

Mercy Otis Warren

This woman supported the Patriot cause with her pen. *Chapter 9, Lesson 2*

Boston Massacre   1770

Why did the Patriots call this a massacre? *Chapter 10, Lesson 1*

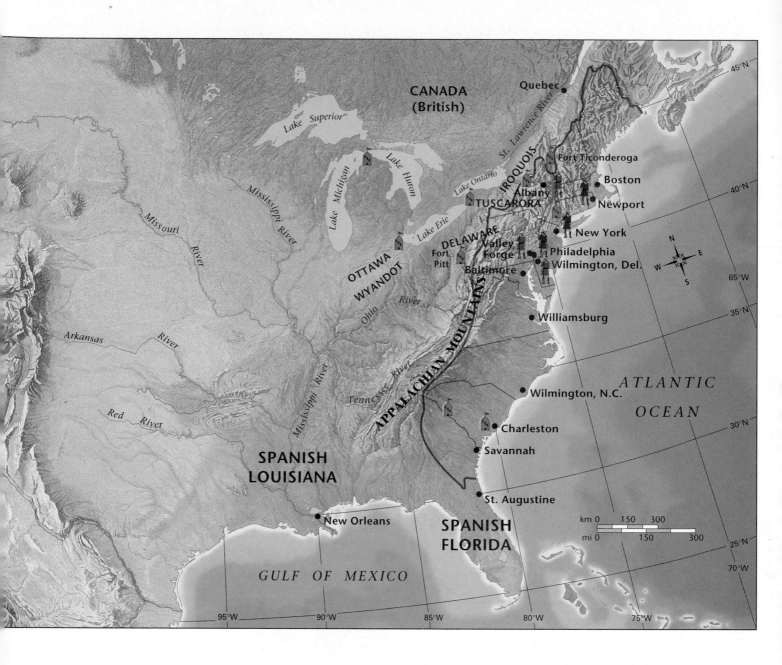

CANADA
(British)

Lake Superior

Lake Michigan

Lake Huron

Quebec

St. Lawrence River

Fort Ticonderoga

Boston

Lake Ontario

IROQUOIS

Albany

Newport

Lake Erie

TUSCARORA

Mississippi River

Missouri River

OTTAWA
WYANDOT

DELAWARE

Valley
Forge

New York

Fort
Pitt

Philadelphia

Baltimore

Wilmington, Del.

Ohio River

APPALACHIAN MOUNTAINS

Williamsburg

Arkansas River

Tennessee River

Red River

Wilmington, N.C.

ATLANTIC
OCEAN

SPANISH
LOUISIANA

Charleston

Savannah

St. Augustine

New Orleans

SPANISH
FLORIDA

GULF OF MEXICO

95°W 90°W 85°W 80°W 75°W

45°N
40°N
35°N
30°N
25°N

65°W
70°W

km 0   150   300
mi 0   150   300

1780   1790   1800

Salem Poor

Contributors To The Cause...
Salem Poor *Gallant Soldier*

Salem Poor was a hero of the Battle of Bunker Hill. *Chapter 10, Lesson 2*

Joseph Brant

On which side did the Iroquois fight during the war? *Chapter 11, Lesson 2*

Treaty of Paris 1783

Find out who is missing in this painting. *Chapter 11, Lesson 3*

Background to the Revolution

Chapter Preview: *People, Places, and Events*

1750   1755   1760

George Washington

What did fighting the French teach George Washington? *Lesson 1, Page 237*

"Join or Die" Cartoon 1754

JOIN, or DIE.

Benjamin Franklin's cartoon urged the colonies to unite. Did they? *Lesson 1, Page 237*

Fort Carillon 1759

This military marvel will play a key role in the French and Indian War. *Lesson 1, Page 237*

The French and Indian War

Main Idea The French and Indian War changed Britain's role in North America.

In 1753, a young man set out to deliver an important letter. There were few roads where he was going. The weather was awful — it rained or snowed many days. Once, someone shot at him. Going home he fell into a freezing river. "I can't say," he wrote later, "that ever in my life I suffered so much anxiety. . . ."

The young man was George Washington. The letter was from the governor of Virginia to the French military leader in the Ohio River Valley. Virginia claimed this area. The governor was ordering the French to give up their land holdings in the valley.

Washington delivered his letter, and received the answer. Wet, cold, and tired, he arrived back in Virginia with bad news. The French would not leave the region without a fight.

◄ Charles Willson Peale painted this portrait of George Washington in 1776.

Key Vocabulary

congress

ally

proclamation

Key Events

1754 Albany Plan of Union

1756 French and Indian War declared

1759 Battle of Quebec

1763 Treaty of Paris

1763 Proclamation of 1763

1765   1700   1775

Stamp Act 1765	Patrick Henry	Daughter of Liberty

This item changed America forever. Find out how. *Lesson 2, Page 242*	Patrick Henry argued with a king. Why? *Lesson 2, Page 243*	These women challenged the British government — and won. *Lesson 2, Page 245*

Mounting Tensions

Focus *Why did tensions increase between the French, Native Americans, and British?*

Snow around forts could be quite deep in the winter. Soldiers had to wear snowshoes to walk outside.

Long before George Washington's trip, the Iroquois fought with other Native American groups for control of the Ohio River valley. When British fur traders entered the area in the 1740s, a similar struggle arose between the French and British. The Iroquois remained neutral in this struggle and traded with both sides. The French feared, however, that the Iroquois would eventually unite with the British against them. To protect their fur trade, and their claims on the land, the French built a line of sturdy forts. Fort Carillon (kar uh LAHN) protected their claims in the north *(see illustration below)*, while Fort Duquesne (doo KAYN) guarded the place where the Ohio and Allegheny (al ih GAY nee) rivers met *(see map below)*.

This action worried the British and their colonists. These forts kept them from trading furs and farming the land. Who would control this fertile river valley?

In 1754, the governor of Virginia again sent George

Fort Carillon

Forts were important battlegrounds in the French and Indian War. **Map Skill:** *On what natural feature is the fort located?*

Washington to challenge the French. This time, Washington had 150 men with him. They built a simple fort for protection near the French Fort Duquesne and called it Fort Necessity.

Within weeks, French forces attacked Fort Necessity. They had twice as many troops. Washington and his men held out for nine hours in a pouring rain, but finally had to surrender. The French let them go home. Although Washington lost the battle, he gained valuable experience as a military leader.

Albany Plan of Union

During this time, the colonies also gained valuable experience — not in fighting, but in bringing people together. In 1754, seven colonies sent representatives to a **congress,** or meeting of representatives, in Albany, New York. There, they met with the Iroquois chiefs. They tried to persuade the Iroquois to join with the British and their colonists. But the Iroquois would not take sides.

Some representatives thought the colonies needed to help each other. Benjamin Franklin, who attended the congress, made a proposal called the Albany Plan of Union. He wanted the colonies to join together to fight the French. The colonies rejected Franklin's plan. They were not yet ready to work together for a common goal.

The French often built forts in a star-shape design. (See illustration below.)

❶ Bake ovens, a blacksmith shop, and a hospital were built outside of the fort walls.

❷ The men slept and kept their clothes and other belongings in the barracks, or living quarters. This fort could hold 400 men.

❸ Gun powder — the material that made the shot or bullets fly — was stored within the walls of the fort where soldiers could easily get it.

❹ This was a storage area which could also be used as a dungeon to hold prisoners.

War and British Victory

Focus *What were the effects of Britain's victory?*

A British ship built to fight in the French and Indian War sank in Lake George over 200 years ago. Preserved by very cold water, it was found in 1990 by divers using sonar. Today the spot is marked so that other divers can visit the ship.

Pontiac was a skilled leader. He brought Native American nations together to stop the British.

In 1755, British General Braddock arrived in the colonies with an army of 1,000 men. His orders were to drive the French out of the Ohio River Valley. But Braddock never reached his target. His army was attacked by a smaller force of Native Americans and French. Braddock was killed, and his troops suffered heavy losses. Washington, who was there, said the British soldiers "ran as sheep pursued by dogs."

With Braddock's defeat many Native Americans joined the French. They became allies (AL lys). **Allies** are people who join together for a specific purpose. These Native Americans hoped a French victory would keep British colonists from taking the land.

Britain declared war on France in 1756, officially beginning what we call the French and Indian War. This war was a contest for control over North America. Britain also fought the French in Europe and as far away as India. Because it went on for seven years, this larger struggle is often called the Seven Years' War.

For two years the war in North America went badly for Britain. Then, in 1758, Britain sent more men and money to the fight. They began to win. The next year the British captured Fort Carillon and renamed it Fort Ticonderoga (TY kon duh ROH ga).

The turning point in the war came in 1759, when Britain captured Québec, the capital of New France. Within a year, the French surrendered to the British. *(See the map, next page).*

Pontiac's Rebellion

With the defeat of the French, British colonists began moving west to the area the French had claimed. An Ottawa chief from the Great Lakes region united several Native American nations to stop them. His name was Pontiac. He led a series of very successful attacks on British forts. By the spring of 1763, he and his allies had captured 8 forts.

In response, the British government issued the Proclamation of 1763. A **proclamation** is an official announcement. This proclamation helped Native Americans living west of the Appalachian Mountains. It forbade settlers from moving there. But the colonists, wanting new land, ignored the Proclamation. They kept moving west.

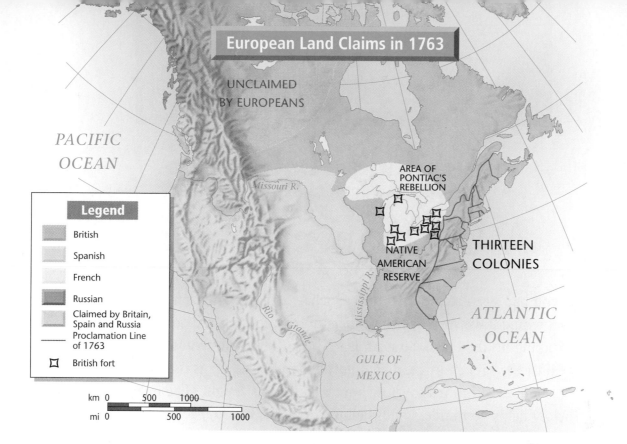

European Land Claims in 1763

UNCLAIMED BY EUROPEANS

PACIFIC OCEAN

Missouri R.

AREA OF PONTIAC'S REBELLION

NATIVE AMERICAN RESERVE

THIRTEEN COLONIES

Mississippi R.

Rio Grande

ATLANTIC OCEAN

GULF OF MEXICO

Legend
- British
- Spanish
- French
- Russian
- Claimed by Britain, Spain and Russia
- Proclamation Line of 1763
- ⛉ British fort

km 0 500 1000
mi 0 500 1000

Treaty of Paris

In 1763, the Treaty of Paris ended the war and changed boundaries dramatically. France lost almost all land claims in North America. Britain gained a huge amount of land to use — and to protect. The cost of this protection would cause trouble between Britain and its colonists.

This map shows the division of North America after the French and Indian War. **Map Skill:** *What land did France still claim in North America?*

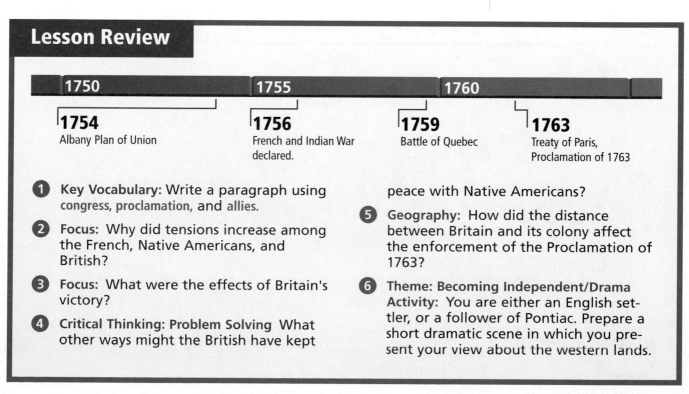

Lesson Review

1750	1755	1760	
1754 Albany Plan of Union	**1756** French and Indian War declared.	**1759** Battle of Quebec	**1763** Treaty of Paris, Proclamation of 1763

1. **Key Vocabulary:** Write a paragraph using congress, proclamation, and allies.

2. **Focus:** Why did tensions increase among the French, Native Americans, and British?

3. **Focus:** What were the effects of Britain's victory?

4. **Critical Thinking: Problem Solving** What other ways might the British have kept peace with Native Americans?

5. **Geography:** How did the distance between Britain and its colony affect the enforcement of the Proclamation of 1763?

6. **Theme: Becoming Independent/Drama Activity:** You are either an English settler, or a follower of Pontiac. Prepare a short dramatic scene in which you present your view about the western lands.

Interpreting a Battle Map

A Cliffhanger Battle

If you had been at the cliffs near Québec on a dark night in 1759, you would have seen British soldiers dressed in their red coats, sneaking up the cliffs. You can learn how the British won this battle against the French by reading a **battle map**. Battle maps use symbols and descriptions to show how a battle was fought. The map below helps you understand the historic Battle of Québec.

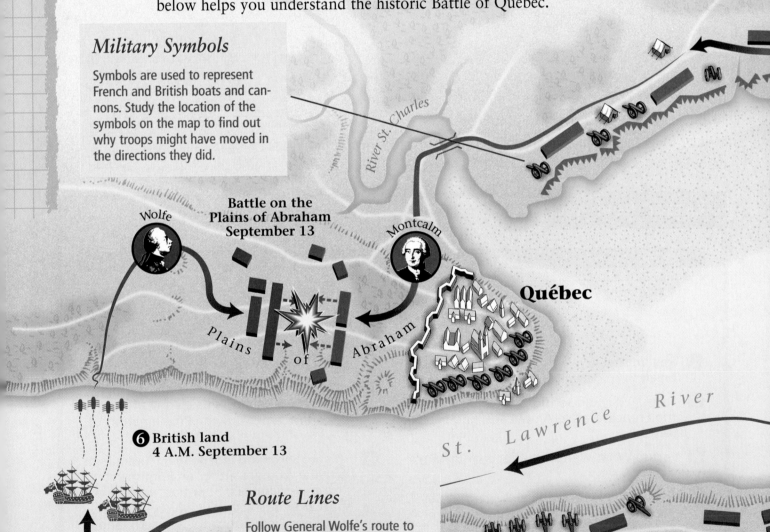

Military Symbols

Symbols are used to represent French and British boats and cannons. Study the location of the symbols on the map to find out why troops might have moved in the directions they did.

Wolfe

Battle on the Plains of Abraham September 13

Montcalm

Québec

Plains of Abraham

6 British land 4 A.M. September 13

St. Lawrence River

River St. Charles

Route Lines

Follow General Wolfe's route to Québec. He had control of the water and used it to land his troops secretly at night.

① Here's How

This map shows the Battle of Québec in 1759. Use the map to get information about how this battle was fought.

- Use the legend to identify which symbols represent the boats, the troops, and the route of British General Wolfe.

- Find these symbols on the map.

- Find the French camps and the location of their cannons and guns. Then find the British camps.

- Follow the route the British took from their camp to the cliffs below the Plains of Abraham.

② Think It Through

What can you learn about this battle, just from looking at the map? How is seeing the conflict on a map different from reading about it?

Military Forces

The French flag is used here to show the location of the French army headquarters. Notice how the French troops, led by the Marquis de Montcalm, defended a wide area.

③ Use It

1. Write a description of General Wolfe's route. Include the dates he stopped at each camp.

2. Why do you think the British troops had to sneak into battle position at night?

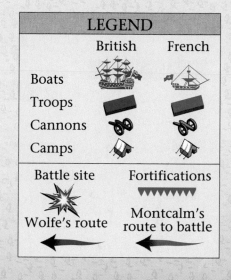

LEGEND

	British	French
Boats		
Troops		
Cannons		
Camps		

Battle site — Fortifications

Wolfe's route — Montcalm's route to battle

Montcalm's Headquarters

Beauport

Floating gun platform

Wolfe's Headquarters & Main British Camp July 9 to September 3

Unsuccessful British attack July 31

④

The Bason

Leave September 3 ⑤

Land July 9 ③

Point Levis Camp

Isle of Orleans Camp

Land June 29 ②

June 26 ①

km
mi

0   1

0   .5

Key Vocabulary

tax

Parliament

repeal

duty

boycott

Growing Conflict with Britain

Main Idea Anger at British decisions caused the colonists to resist.

When George III became king of Great Britain in 1760, the American colonies celebrated. Newspapers printed proclamations declaring that the colonists would ". . . show ourselves Dutiful, Loyal, and Faithful Subjects." But those loyal feelings would soon change from praise to protest.

The Stamp Act and Its Effects

Focus *Why did Britain tax the colonies, and what was their response?*

Because of the French and Indian War, Great Britain was deeply in debt. Added to that debt was the cost of sending troops to protect the western lands. The British government decided to turn to the colonists to help pay for these troops. This was only fair, they reasoned, since the troops were there for the colonists' protection.

To raise money from the colonies, the British used a tax. A **tax** is money people pay to their government. In 1765, **Parliament**, Britain's lawmaking body, passed the Stamp Act. It required almost everything printed on paper in the American colonies to have an official stamp before it could be bought, sold, or used. The money paid to purchase the stamp was the tax.

The British government had used stamps to raise money in Britain. Yet British citizens could be taxed only by their elected representatives in Parliament. Not even the king could tax the people.

The colonists were British citizens, too. Surely this meant they had the same right to be taxed only by their representatives. But the

This is King George III. His crown is shown at the top of the page.

The fake coffin represents the death of the Stamp Act.

The straw man rides high on a pole through the streets so the whole crowd can see him.

This angry colonist picks up a stone from the street to throw at the figure.

colonists did not have any representatives in Parliament. The Virginia House of Burgesses, the colony's lawmaking body, was the first to point this out in May 1765. With a young lawyer named Patrick Henry as spokesman, Virginia issued a statement about the new tax. The statement said that only the House of Burgesses had the "right and power" to tax Virginians.

Other colonial assemblies agreed and issued similar statements. Newspapers printed angry letters and drawings. You can see one of these drawings above.

Nine colonies sent representatives to a Stamp Act Congress in October 1765. They asked Parliament to **repeal**, or cancel, the Stamp Act, and to let the colonists tax themselves.

While some used words to protest the Stamp Act, others chose action. In Boston, Massachusetts, a group of men calling themselves the Sons of Liberty encouraged colonists to defy the Stamp Act. Other cities soon organized their own Sons of Liberty. They burned the stamps and threatened the stamp sellers. Some stamp agents were covered with tar or molasses, then coated in feathers. Soon no one was willing to sell the stamps.

Back in England, Parliament debated what to do. Some

Colonists held public demonstrations to show their anger at the stamp tax. This drawing shows one of those protests. Here, they have made a straw man to represent the stamp agent.

The maker of this teapot shows his feelings about the Stamp Act very clearly. **History:** *Who was buying and using these teapots?*

British	Colonists
1765 Stamp Act requires colonists to buy a stamp for almost all printed paper. Affects newspapers, playing cards, and official notices.	Colonists refuse to buy stamps. Sons of Liberty organize protests. Nine colonies meet in Stamp Act Congress.
1766-1767 British government repeals Stamp Act, but tries new taxes - the Townshend Acts.	Colonists boycott all British-sold goods. Daughters of Liberty make own tea and cloth. Colonists cry "No taxation without representation."
1768 Alarmed and angered by the protests, Parliament sends British troops to Boston.	

members of Parliament angrily defended the Stamp Act, while others said the colonists were right. The group agreeing with the colonists won, and the Stamp Act was repealed in 1766.

The Townshend Acts

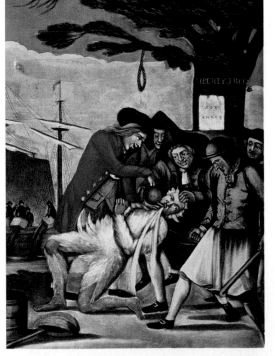

This cartoon shows a British official, covered with tar and feathers, and forced to drink tea.

| Focus | *How did the colonists resist the Townshend Acts?*

Britain still needed to raise money. A British official named Charles Townshend was determined to raise money from the colonies. Townshend placed a new set of taxes on products the colonists imported from England. A tax on imported goods is called a **duty**. This new set of taxes was called the Townshend Acts. With these, Townshend believed he had found a way to raise money which the colonists would obey.

Resistance Builds

Townshend was wrong. Protests against the Townshend Acts — which taxed paint, paper, glass, lead and tea — were very strong. The colonists wanted to be taxed only by their own lawmakers. They began to say:

"No *taxation without representation!"*

Up and down the colonies, women calling themselves the Daughters of Liberty started a boycott of British-made goods. A **boycott** is a refusal to buy a product or service, or to deal with a business, or nation. It is used as a means of protest.

Instead of buying British tea and cloth, the Daughters of Liberty made their own tea from herbs and wove their own cloth. To pressure the British even more, the colonists boycotted both taxed and untaxed items alike.

The Sons of Liberty became active again. They organized resistance throughout the colonies. Boston was especially active in the protests. Samuel Adams made fiery speeches and James Otis wrote pamphlets on the rights of colonists. James's sister, Mercy, wrote patriotic plays and poems. Alarmed by this activity in an important port city, the British sent troops to Boston in 1768.

British merchants lost a great deal of money because of the boycott. They asked Parliament to repeal the Townshend duties, and in 1770, Parliament did — all except the duty on tea.

The colonists had won — for now. They believed their boycott had worked. But conflicts remained. Britain still needed money. Tea was still taxed. The colonists were still angry about being taxed without being represented. Boston was tense about the troops stationed there. There was trouble ahead.

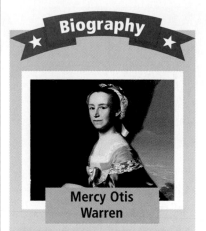

Biography

Mercy Otis Warren

Mercy Otis Warren was born in 1728 into a wealthy and well-known Massachusetts family. She was an active supporter of the American Revolution. She also wrote letters exchanging ideas with Samuel Adams, General Henry Knox, and Thomas Jefferson. In 1805, she published a three-volume history of the American Revolution. She died at age 86 in 1814.

Lesson Review

1764	1767	1770
1765 Stamp Act	**1767** Townshend Acts	**1770** Townshend Acts repealed

1 **Key Vocabulary:** Write a paragraph about the lesson using the following tax, repeal, duty, and boycott.

2 **Focus:** Why did Britain tax the colonies, and what was their reaction?

3 **Focus:** How did the colonists resist the Townshend Acts?

4 **Critical Thinking: Predict** What will the colonists do if Britain continues to place taxes on them?

5 **Geography:** Why would port cities be especially angered by the Stamp Act and the Townshend Acts?

6 **Citizenship/Writing Activity:** You are a colonist and your best friend is a stamp agent. Write a letter to him or her explaining why you, even though you think of yourself as a British citizen, will refuse to buy stamps.

Chapter Review

Chapter Review Timeline

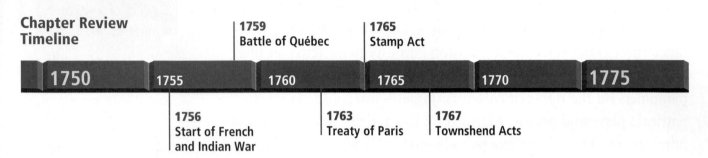

1750	1755	1760	1765	1770	**1775**

1759 Battle of Québec

1765 Stamp Act

1756 Start of French and Indian War

1763 Treaty of Paris

1767 Townshend Acts

Summarizing the Main Idea

1 Copy the chart below and fill in the missing information to identify the cause of each of the following events:

CAUSE	EVENT
France and Great Britain each wanted control of the Ohio River Valley.	French and Indian War
	Pontiac's Rebellion
	Proclamation of 1763
	Stamp Act passed

Vocabulary

2 Using at least five of the following terms, write a speech that Samuel Adams might have given to protest the Townshend Acts.

congress (p. 237) tax (p. 242) duty (p. 244)

ally (p. 238) Parliament (p. 242) boycott (p. 245)

proclamation (p. 238) repeal (p. 243)

Reviewing the Facts

3 Why did Benjamin Franklin suggest the Albany Plan of Union?

4 What conflicts happened in the Ohio River Valley before the French and Indian War?

5 How did the French and Indian War change Britain's role in North America?

6 What kinds of items needed an official stamp after the Stamp Act became law?

7 Why did colonists object to the Stamp Act?

8 How did the Stamp Act and the Townshend Acts tax the colonies differently? How were these taxes similar?

9 Why did the British send troops to Boston in 1768?

10 Look at the map on pages 240–241. Study the geography of Québec. Why was it better for the British to fight on the plains rather than storming the city directly?

11 How did ships help the British win the Battle of Québec? Why was it so important that General Wolfe controlled the water?

Geography Skills

12 Look at the map on page 239. Why do you think the Proclamation of 1763 drew the boundary along the Appalachian Mountains?

13 Why were rivers so important in colonial America? Make a map of the major rivers in the Ohio River Valley. Show how someone could have used them to reach the sea.

Critical Thinking

14 **Predict** What would have happened if colonists had agreed to the Albany Plan of Union in 1754? Would the Revolution have started earlier than it did?

15 **Conclude** In the growing conflict between the colonies and Britain, which side do you think Native Americans supported? Why?

16 **Problem Solving** How might Britain have avoided conflict with colonists over taxes?

Writing: Citizenship and Economics

17 **Citizenship** What rights was Pontiac trying to defend against the British? Which side would you have supported? Write a letter to the editor of a colonial newspaper explaining your opinion of the conflict.

18 **Economics** Why is a boycott an effective means of protest? Write a pamphlet as if you were James Otis. Explain to the colonists why they should take part in the boycott of British goods.

Activities

Citizenship/Writing Activity
Write a letter to the Fort Ticonderoga museum requesting information about the history of the fort and the exhibits they have on display. The address is: Fort Ticonderoga, P.O. Box 390, Ticonderoga, NY 12883.

Economics/Research Activity
During the 1760s, colonists started businesses that made paint, paper, glass, lead, and other products. Find out how one of these products was made during colonial times. Make an illustrated flow chart that shows the steps involved.

Internet Option

Check the **Internet Social Studies Center** for ideas on how to extend your theme project beyond your classroom.

THEME PROJECT CHECK-IN

To help you decide whether you are a Patriot or Loyalist, use the information you have read about the beginning of the Revolution. Try answering these questions:
• What reasons might you have for supporting British rule?
• What reasons might you have for opposing British rule?
• How do others in your community feel about British rule?

The Road to Independence

Chapter Preview: *People, Places, and Events*

1770	1772	1774

Boston Massacre   1770

Find out how snowballs started the Boston Massacre. *Lesson 1, Page 250*

The Boston Tea Party   1773

Why were people fighting over tea? *Lesson 1, Page 252*

Paul Revere's Ride   1775

Whom was Paul Revere trying to warn? *Lesson 2, Page 263*

Crisis in Boston

Main Idea Boston's resistance to British control led Parliament to pass a harsh new set of laws.

In 1770, Crispus Attucks was in Boston. Born into slavery, Attucks had run away to sea as a young man. On the streets of Boston, Attucks would have seen some of the hundreds of British soldiers who were in the city.

Because they were poorly paid for their military service, many soldiers hired themselves out as workers on the docks. The colonists feared that the soldiers would take their jobs. They called them "redcoats," referring to the bright red coats of the British army, and yelled insults at them. "Lobster backs for sale!" youths called to the soldiers.

"Yankees!" the soldiers jeered back, using the term to make fun of the colonists. Fistfights often broke out between the soldiers and the colonists. Each day, tension grew between the two groups. Attucks may have realized that Boston was ready to explode.

Key Vocabulary
- massacre
- propaganda
- Patriot
- Loyalist
- committee of correspondence

Key Events
- **1770** Boston Massacre
- **1773** Boston Tea Party
- **1774** Intolerable Acts

◀ The image to the left depicts the Battle of Bunker Hill.

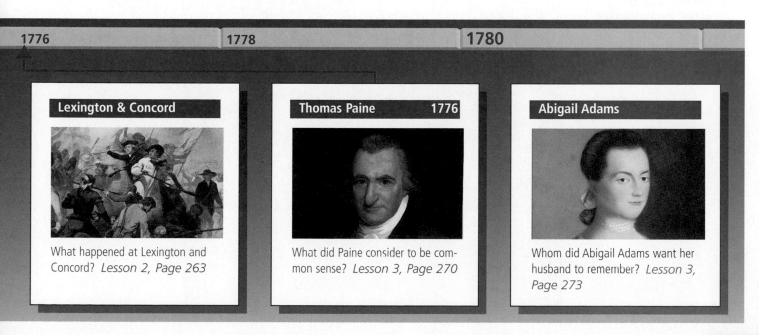

1776   1778   **1780**

Lexington & Concord

What happened at Lexington and Concord? *Lesson 2, Page 263*

Thomas Paine   **1776**

What did Paine consider to be common sense? *Lesson 3, Page 270*

Abigail Adams

Whom did Abigail Adams want her husband to remember? *Lesson 3, Page 273*

The Boston Massacre

Focus *What were the causes and results of the Boston Massacre?*

On March 5, 1770, Boston did explode. A group of colonists had gathered at the Boston Custom House. The group, led by Crispus Attucks and others, began to throw snowballs at a British soldier on duty. Soon eight other British soldiers arrived. "Come on, you rascals," the mob yelled. "You lobster scoundrels. Fire if you dare." For a while, the soldiers did nothing.

The group grew larger and larger. Fearing for their safety, the soldiers began to panic. Suddenly, in the confusion, a soldier fired. Then the other soldiers fired. When the smoke cleared, Attucks and two other men lay dead. Two more would die later from their wounds.

Colonial leaders called the event the Boston Massacre. A **massacre** is the killing of a number of defenseless people. Colonists used the shooting as **propaganda**, information used to win support for a cause. By calling the incident a massacre, the colonists suggested that having British troops in the colonies was dangerous.

Paul Revere, a colonial silversmith, made this etching of the Boston Massacre. Colonial leaders used the etching to tell their version of what happened. **Arts:** *Why might a picture be a powerful tool for creating propaganda?*

The words *Bloody Massacre* appear in the title of the etching.

Revere used words like *fierce barbarians* to describe the British soldiers.

The soldiers are shown firing at a peaceful, defenseless group of colonists.

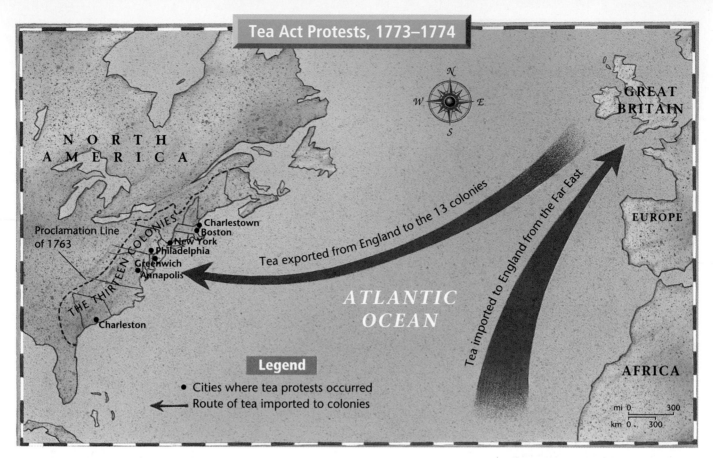

Tea Act Protests, 1773–1774

NORTH AMERICA

Proclamation Line of 1763

Charlestown
Boston
New York
Philadelphia
Greenwich
Annapolis

THE THIRTEEN COLONIES

Charleston

ATLANTIC OCEAN

Tea exported from England to the 13 colonies

Tea imported to England from the Far East

GREAT BRITAIN

EUROPE

AFRICA

Legend
● Cities where tea protests occurred
← Route of tea imported to colonies

mi 0   300
km 0   300

Tea was purchased in China and brought to England. From England it was shipped to the colonies.
Map Skill: *In which colonies did protests against the Tea Act take place?*

The Tea Act

Focus *How did the Tea Act increase tensions between Britain and the colonies?*

After the Boston Massacre, the colonies stayed calm for a few years. Britain repealed the Townshend Acts. The colonial boycott had hurt their trade and they wanted colonial business. They kept a tax on one product — tea — to show the colonists that Britain still had the right to tax them.

Then Britain faced a new problem. The East India Company, one of the largest companies in England, was losing money. To help it recover, Parliament passed the Tea Act in 1773. This Act allowed the Company to send its tea to the colonies without paying a tax to the British government. With no taxes to pay, the Company could lower the price of tea and sell more. The colonists, however, still had to pay a tax on tea. The Tea Act also let the Company decide which American merchants would be allowed to sell the tea.

Colonists were angry that Parliament would give any one company total control of an item of trade. Shopkeepers were mad because only agents appointed by the government could sell the tea. Tea was still being taxed without their consent. As far as the

Ask Yourself

Few people throughout the colonies drank tea after the Tea Act was passed. For example, Penelope Barker *(above)* and 50 other women in Edenton, North Carolina, organized a boycott of tea and other British goods as a protest. Would you give up a favorite food or drink for a cause you believed in?

? ? ? ? ? ? ? ? ? ? ? ? ?

This picture of the Boston Tea Party in 1773 was etched by an artist years after the event. Many colonists disguised themselves by dressing up to look like Mohawks. It took about 3 hours for the colonists to dump some 45 tons of tea into the harbor. **History:** *Why would the people at the Boston Tea Party want to disguise themselves?*

colonists were concerned, the Tea Act was a sneaky way of getting them to buy taxed tea.

Trouble started in Boston when the first East India Company ships arrived in the harbor. The Sons of Liberty posted a guard to make sure the tea was not unloaded. Governor Hutchinson ordered the ships to unload. The Sons of Liberty had a "Meeting of the People" to see if they could make Hutchinson send the ships back to England. Hutchinson refused. So the Sons of Liberty put into motion a carefully thought-out and secret plan.

The Boston Tea Party

On a December evening in 1773, the Sons of Liberty held what would soon become the most famous "tea party" in history. The group headed down to the docks. They had dressed up as Mohawk Indians and blackened their faces with soot so they would not be recognized. The group leaders demanded lights and keys from the ships' crews and went to work. They hauled 342 chests of tea on deck and dumped them overboard.

When they were finished, the colonists swept the decks and

repaired a padlock they had broken. They wanted it understood that they had no love of lawlessness, but that they would resist any law that they thought was unjust.

News of the event spread, and other colonists began to follow Boston's example. On Christmas Day, when a ship with 697 chests of tea tried to dock in Delaware, 8,000 people turned it back. The next spring, in New York, mobs boarded a tea ship and destroyed the tea. Throughout the colonies, people rebelled against the British. *(See the map on page 251.)*

The Intolerable Acts

The Boston Tea Party hit its mark in England. Parliament, the British public, and especially King George III were outraged by it.

Instead of backing down as it had with the Stamp Act and the Townshend Acts, Parliament struck back. For weeks it debated how to punish the colonists. Finally, in the spring of 1774, it passed what the English called the Coercive Acts. (To coerce means to force.) On the other

This bottle contains tea that was thrown into Boston Harbor during the Boston Tea Party.

TEA THROWN INTO BOSTON HARBOR DEC 16. 1773.

The tea chest below was used to ship some of the tea that was dumped overboard during the Boston Tea Party.

Fact File:

Intolerable Acts

1. Boston port was closed to trade until the tea was paid for.
2. The colonial government would no longer be elected. Instead, it would be appointed by the king.
3. Colonists were required to quarter, or provide housing to, British troops, who would soon arrive to enforce the new laws.
4. Town meetings were tightly controlled. The governor had to approve the agenda.

The crest of King George III of England.

side of the Atlantic, some colonists called them the Intolerable Acts. (Something is intolerable when it cannot be withstood.) The Fact File to the left lists some of the Intolerable Acts and the new rules that they imposed on the colonies.

The Intolerable Acts helped split the colonies in two. Some people were enraged by Britain's new laws. Other people supported what the king was doing in the colonies. The **Patriots** were the people who opposed the British government. The colonists who supported the British were called **Loyalists** because they were loyal to Great Britain.

Patriots throughout the colonies were stunned by the Intolerable Acts. The punishment was even worse than they had feared. Boston depended on shipping for its livelihood. With the port closed, people would starve. And no more elections? It was too much for a free people to bear.

The picture at right shows a Patriot barber forcing a British captain out of his barber shop. Patriots did everything they could to make life difficult for the British while they were in the colonies.

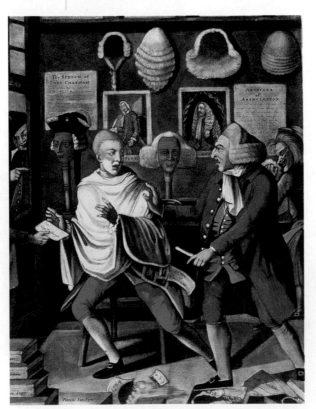

The Colonies Respond

In other colonies, news of the Intolerable Acts was greeted by a storm of protest. Food and supplies poured into Boston in support of the colonists there. From South Carolina came rice; from Philadelphia, flour. Connecticut and New York sent flocks of sheep.

Virginia also thought that representatives from each colony should meet to discuss the events in Boston. Its Assembly proposed the idea of a Continental

Congress. A congress is a meeting of representatives. The plan was circulated among the colonies through a network called the **committees of correspondence**. The committees wrote to each other, sharing information about what the British were up to and what the colonies were doing about it. Samuel Adams started the first committee of correspondence in Boston, and the idea quickly spread.

The First Continental Congress met in Philadelphia in September 1774. For more than seven weeks its members discussed how to support the Massachusetts Patriots. They voted to put a stop to all trade with Britain until the Intolerable Acts were repealed. They also advised each colony to begin training soldiers.

This meeting of the Continental Congress was one of the first times colonial leaders banded together to resist the British. Most representatives did not yet want to fight for independence; they were looking for a peaceful solution. Still, they took their rights seriously and continued to meet, even though they knew they were breaking British law.

When the meeting ended, the representatives agreed to meet again the following spring if conditions had not improved. By that time it would be too late. Fighting between the colonies and Britain would have already begun.

Patriot Samuel Adams started the first committee of correspondence in Boston.

Lesson Review

1770	1772	1775

1770
Boston Massacre

1773
Boston Tea Party

1774
Intolerable Acts

1 Key Vocabulary: Describe Boston in the 1770s using massacre, propaganda, Patriot, Loyalist, and committee of correspondence.

2 Focus: What were the causes and results of the Boston Massacre?

3 Focus: How did the Tea Act increase tensions between Britain and the colonies?

4 Critical Thinking: Interpret Since the colonists were not fighting for independence at first, what would have been the ideal outcome of their protests?

5 Geography: Look at the map of the tea trade. Would it have been faster to sail tea directly from China to the colonies? Why wouldn't the British have done that?

6 Citizenship/Arts Activity: Re-enact the Boston Tea Party. Assign roles and write lines for each group member. Stage your re-enactment.

★ CITIZENSHIP ★

Participating

How Can Your Opinions Make a Difference?

Sometimes you want to let people know what you think about things. One way to do this is to write letters. You can write letters to people you know, to editors of newspapers and magazines, or to organizations and people in government. Read below to learn how the colonists wrote letters to express and act on their concerns.

Case Study

The Committees of Correspondence

In 1772, the Patriot Samuel Adams encouraged colonists in Boston to take up their pens and write letters to other colonists. Adams urged them to form Committees of Correspondence.

At first, the colonists wrote to spread the news about England's decision to pay the salaries of the governor and judges in Massachusetts. People were upset that this would tie these officials to the British king and government rather than to the colonists. The people wrote letters about this and other concerns to express their views and to gain support. Soon, more than 80 Committees of Correspondence existed in Massachusetts. It wasn't long before more Committees formed throughout the colonies.

Take Action

As a student, you might have special concerns or causes that other people — younger or older — might not know about or totally understand. Here's a chance to let your cause be known and to gain others' support.

1 In small groups, list issues that concern you. Your issues could relate to your family, school, community, or the world. Choose one issue that you wish to tackle.

2 Find and contact a person who could respond to your letter. This could be a representative in government, a school administrator, a person from another class, a friend, or a family member.

3 Write a letter to that person expressing your concern. Propose ways that you wish the person would respond to your issue. Keep up the correspondence until the issue has been settled.

Tips for Participating

- Be open-minded about presenting and listening to ideas.
- Use the phone book to help you find resources.
- Express your concerns in ways that show you are not just bossing other people around.

Research Activity

Who are your representatives and senators in Washington, D.C.? Find out the issues they have been working on. Write one of them a letter expressing your opinion about one of those issues. You can also write or e-mail the President at this address: President@WhiteHouse.GOV

4 Report your results to the class. Did any action result from your letters? Why were some letters more successful than others? Explain.

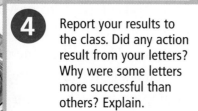

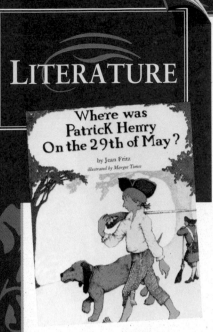

History

orator

a person who is skilled in public speaking

provision

a section of a document that demands a certain condition

Where Was Patrick Henry on the 29th of May?

by Jean Fritz

Patrick Henry loved freedom. When the king of England began to try to make Henry and his fellow Virginians pay unfair taxes and obey bad laws, he spoke out boldly. He was a man with a gift for speaking, and he used his powers to advance the cause of American freedom and independence. Even before the war began, there were sacrifices to be made for liberty. He was at the Continental Congress with his friend and neighbor George Washington when his wife Sarah died. Still, he kept working.

It was a good thing for America, as it turned out, that Patrick Henry became an orator at the same time that England was unfolding her new plan. Taxation was England's next step. Although Americans had always managed their own money, suddenly in 1765 the English government, without any kind of by-your-leave from America, slapped down a stamp tax on the colonies. It had provisions for taxing 55 separate items and Patrick Henry was ready to fight every one of them.

On May 29th, 1765, Patrick became twenty-nine years old. He and Sarah had four children now and were living in a four-room house on top of a hill in Louisa County. And on the 29th of May, what was he doing?

Well, he was bawling out the king again. He had become a member of the House of Burgesses, Virginia's governing body, only nine days before and now he was standing up in his buckskin breeches before the finest men of Virginia, using such bold language that at one point there was a cry of "Treason!" But Patrick went right on reeling off resolutions. Later these resolutions were printed and sent out through the colonies, giving other Americans courage to oppose the taxation. Indeed, there was so much opposition to the Stamp Tax that after a year the king repealed it.

But England did not give up the idea of taxation nor did Patrick give up talking. In 1773, when England decided to enforce a tax on tea, Patrick went right to the floor of the House. He was so spellbinding that in the middle of one speech the spectators rushed from the gallery to the cupola of the capitol to pull down the English flag. The members of the House, noticing the commotion, thought there was a fire and ran for safety.

Patrick and Sarah had six children now and were back in Hanover County in an eighteen-room house set on a thousand acres. Patrick was a public figure. When he went out, he wore a black suit or perhaps his peach-blossom-colored one, silver buckled shoes, and a tie wig which he was said to twirl around his head when he was excited.

On March 23rd, 1775, just a few weeks after Sarah's death, Patrick delivered his most famous speech at St. John's Church in Richmond, Virginia. By this time everyone knew who Mr. Henry was; they had all heard of his passion for liberty and of the extraordinary quality of his voice. There were those who swore that Patrick Henry could not even announce that it was a cold evening without inspiring awe. So of course on March 23rd St. John's Church was filled to overflowing—people standing in the aisles, in doorways, sitting on window ledges.

Patrick Henry wore spectacles like these when he wrote and gave his speeches.

Patrick Henry was angry not only at the king who was disregarding America's petitions, insisting on taxation, and preparing for war, but he was also angry at those people in America who still wanted to be friendly to the king and keep peace. Patrick stood up and pushed his glasses back on his head which was what he did when he was ready to use his fighting words.

"Gentlemen may cry peace, peace," he thundered, "but there is no peace . . . Is life so dear or peace so sweet, as to be purchased at the price of chains and slavery?" Patrick bowed his body and locked his hands together as if he, himself, were in chains. Then suddenly he raised his chained hands over his head.

"Forbid it, Almighty God!" he cried. "I know not what course others may take but as for me — "Patrick dropped his arms, threw back his body and strained against his imaginary chains until the tendons of his neck stood out like whipcords and the chains seemed to break. Then he raised his right hand in which he held an ivory letter opener. "As for me," he cried, "give me liberty or give me death!" And he plunged the letter opener in such a way it looked as if he were plunging it into his heart.

The crowd went wild with excitement. One man, leaning over the balcony, was so aroused that he forgot where he was and spit tobacco juice into the audience below. Another man jumped down from the window ledge and declared that when he died, he wanted to be buried on the very spot that Patrick Henry had delivered those words. (And so he was, 25 years later.)

The next year war came, and Virginia volunteers marched off to battle with Liberty or Death embroidered on their shirtfronts.

embroider
to work a design into cloth using a needle and thread

Meet the Author

Jean Fritz has always been fascinated by famous historical characters, and her writing makes them come to life. She tells true stories with a good sense of humor. You can choose from more than a dozen of her other biographies. One you might especially enjoy is *And Then What Happened, Paul Revere?*

Additional Books to Read

Why Don't You Get a Horse, Sam Adams?
by Jean Fritz
Take a fun look at American history.

Paul Revere's Ride
by Henry Wadsworth Longfellow
This poem describes a dangerous ride to warn the Patriots.

Response Activities

1. **Conclude** How did Patrick Henry's words and actions affect American history? Would events have been different without the speaking skills of Patrick Henry?

2. **Narrative: Write a Speech** Think about a subject which is important to you. Write a speech about this subject. Try to use as many powerful and colorful words as you can to describe your ideas.

3. **History: Give a Speech** Go to the library to learn about other great speakers who affected historical events. Choose a speech that you find exciting, and read it to the class.

The Fighting Begins

Main Idea Tensions in the colonies led to the first battles between British troops and the colonists.

Key Vocabulary

militia
Minutemen
delegate
casualty
peninsula
fortify

Key Events

April 1775 Battles of Lexington and Concord

May 1775 Second Continental Congress

June 1775 Battle of Bunker Hill

Signs of war were everywhere in Boston that spring of 1775. A new British governor, General Gage, had arrived the previous year, bringing with him 4,000 soldiers. The clump-clump-clump of the soldiers' boots echoed through the streets. The port was closed, and the docks were empty of boats and people. In Britain, some members of Parliament sided with the colonists. They argued that the Intolerable Acts were too harsh. One member warned,

> **"N**o people can ever be made to submit to a form of government they say they will not receive.**"**

He was right, but no one would listen.

Lexington and Concord

Focus How did the battles of Lexington and Concord begin?

The colonists' earlier boycotts had led to the repeal of the Stamp Act and the Townshend Acts. Colonists thought that refusing to trade with Britain would force Parliament to repeal the Intolerable Acts, too. This time, however, Parliament would not budge.

Some of the colonists responded by preparing to fight. In Massachusetts, John Hancock became the head of a Committee of Safety. This committee collected weapons, set up a spy system, and organized a militia. A **militia** is an army made up of ordinary citizens instead of professional soldiers. The militia needed to be ready to fight at a minute's notice, so they called themselves **Minutemen**.

In the spring of 1775, British spies sent word to General Gage

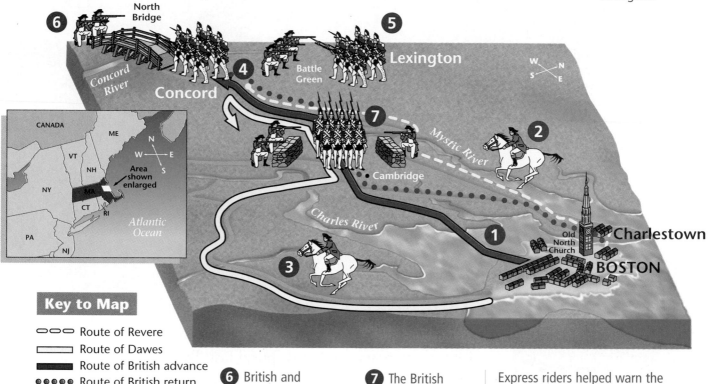

The Battles of Lexington and Concord

1. British troops ferry across the Charles River.
2. Revere gallops off to warn the countryside.
3. Dawes sets off for Lexington.
4. British troops stop Revere. Dawes escapes.
5. British and Minutemen fight at Lexington.

North Bridge

Concord River

Concord

Lexington

Battle Green

Mystic River

Cambridge

Charles River

Old North Church

Charlestown

BOSTON

Key to Map

- ○○○ Route of Revere
- ▭▭▭ Route of Dawes
- ■■■ Route of British advance
- ●●●● Route of British return

6. British and Minutemen battle at Concord.
7. The British retreat.

Express riders helped warn the Minutemen that the British were approaching Concord. Nearly 4,000 Minutemen answered the call. **Map Skill:** *In which town did the British retreat end?*

that the Minutemen were collecting weapons and storing them in Concord, a town about 17 miles northwest of Boston. On April 18, Gage prepared to send about 800 soldiers there to seize the weapons. Patriot spies learned of Gage's plans. That night, two men, Paul Revere and William Dawes, snuck out of Boston on horseback to warn the surrounding towns that the British were coming. By midnight, every Minuteman for miles around knew of the British advance. (Follow their routes on the map above.)

At dawn, the crisp beat of a drum cut through the air on Lexington Green. The battle that followed was hardly a battle at all. Sixty Minutemen faced about 250 of the best-trained soldiers in the world. No one knows who fired first, but when the firing had stopped, eight colonists lay dead.

After a victory cheer, the British marched on to Concord. Some soldiers were sent to secure the bridges; others set out to destroy the supply of weapons. They never found it. Instead, they ran into about 500 Minutemen. The two sides fought, and three

Paul Revere had three friends signal the British advance to the Patriots. If the British came by land, they would put one lantern in the Old North Church. If they came by sea, two lanterns would burn.

The picture to the right by Amos Doolittle is based on sketches that were made by Minuteman and artist Ralph Earl, who fought at the Battle of Lexington. The picture shows British soldiers firing at fleeing American Minutemen in Lexington. **History:** *Why might Earl have chosen to draw this scene?*

The drum above was used by 16-year-old William Diamond to sound the alarm at the Battle of Lexington. The roll on this drum was the first call to battle of the Revolutionary War.

British soldiers and two Minutemen were killed.

While the British were deciding what to do next — retreat or wait for more men — word spread fast. Bells rang, alarm guns were fired, and riders thundered along country roads, spreading the word. Thousands of Patriots headed toward Concord.

The British finally decided to march back to Boston. For most of the 17-mile march, Minutemen shot at them from behind trees and stone walls. By the time the British troops staggered into Charlestown, they were beaten, bloody, and exhausted.

Moving Closer to Independence

Focus *How did the Battle of Bunker Hill bring the colonies closer to independence?*

Less than a month later, in May 1775, delegates met in Philadelphia for the Second Continental Congress. **Delegates** are people chosen to represent a group of people. From Massachusetts came John Hancock, John Adams, and his cousin, Samuel Adams. Benjamin Franklin was Pennsylvania's delegate, and Virginia sent George Washington, Richard Henry Lee, and Patrick Henry.

Everyone was talking about Lexington and Concord — the first battles of what was to be called the Revolutionary War. The British had suffered 273 **casualties,** people killed, wounded, and missing.

The colonists had fewer than a hundred casualties. The Patriots also had managed to surround Boston, trapping the British inside.

The Congress agreed to support the Patriots and voted to send 10 companies of riflemen to join the militia outside Boston. It renamed the militia the Army of the United Colonies. For its leader they appointed the "generous and brave" George Washington.

The Battle of Bunker Hill

On June 23, 1775, Washington headed to Boston to take command of his new army. On the way north, he learned that the Battle of Bunker Hill had just been fought.

Two hills — Bunker Hill and Breed's Hill — were located on a peninsula in Charlestown, near Boston. A **peninsula** is a piece of land that juts out into a body of water and is connected to a larger piece of land. The Patriots had surrounded Boston on every side except Charlestown, so they decided to **fortify,** or strengthen, this peninsula.

On the night of June 16, one thousand Minutemen marched in the dark to Bunker Hill. Their commander, Colonel William Prescott, decided at the last minute to fortify nearby Breed's Hill instead, because it was closer to Boston.

The next morning the British saw what the colonists were up to on Breed's Hill. They ordered their warships to begin bombarding the hill with cannon. At the same time, they ferried thousands of soldiers across the river to form battle ranks at the base of the hill.

While they watched and waited, the Americans tried to control their fear. They kept repeating to themselves the order Colonel Prescott had given them:

 "Don't one of you fire until you see the whites of their eyes. **"**

When the order finally came to shoot, the Patriots' fire sent the line of British soldiers reeling. One British soldier who survived the battle later wrote that "such a slaughter was, perhaps, never made before upon British troops."

The British, with many soldiers killed or wounded, were forced to retreat. Within minutes they launched a

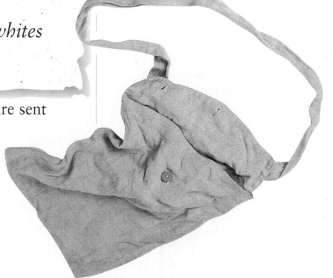

Haversacks like the one below were used by Minutemen to carry their possessions.

The Battle of Bunker Hill was a British victory. However, the Patriots fought so well that one British officer described his losses as "greater than we can bear." **Chart Skill:** *Which side had more troops, the British or the American? About how many more? Which side had more casualties? About how many more casualties?*

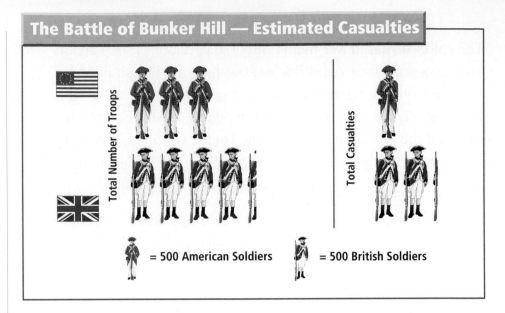

The Battle of Bunker Hill — Estimated Casualties

= 500 American Soldiers = 500 British Soldiers

second attack against the hill. The Patriots beat them back again. The British general sent his men up the hill a third time. Once again, the Patriots pushed back the British front line. But the British soldiers kept moving forward until the Patriots finally ran out of ammunition. That's when the British charged with their bayonets, forcing the Patriots to give up the hill and flee to safer ground. By the end of the day, the British had taken over the Charlestown peninsula.

Most of the fighting took place on Breed's Hill, but this battle became known as the Battle of Bunker Hill. Though it was a victory of sorts for the British, it cost them. As the chart above shows, British casualties were much higher than Patriot casualties.

Although they lost Breed's Hill and Bunker Hill, the Americans were joyful. They had stood up to the greatest army in the world.

Salem Poor   Gallant Soldier

This stamp was created in 1976 to honor Salem Poor, a hero of the Battle of Bunker Hill. Fourteen officers petitioned the Massachusetts legislature to reward Poor for his bravery.

A Call for Freedom

The battles at Lexington, Concord, and Bunker Hill tested Patriot will and courage. The Patriots passed these tests with flying colors. At that time, not all Americans were fighting for independence. Most people still believed they were British citizens. They just wanted their king to stop acting like a tyrant.

For one group of Americans, the battles had a very different meaning. African Americans, some of them enslaved, fought at all three battles. Peter Salem, who had been born into slavery, was granted freedom so he could join the militia.

Early in the war, the Continental Congress decided to no longer allow enslaved or free African Americans to join the Continental Army. They feared that African American soldiers might want to be freed in exchange for fighting. The British governor of Virginia offered in November 1775 to free all African Americans who were enslaved by Patriots if they joined the British forces. The Patriots then decided to allow African Americans to join their army again.

The Patriot call for liberty had deep meaning for African Americans. Many gave their lives for the cause. In turn, enslaved African Americans in Massachusetts petitioned for their freedom. One petition stated,

> **"W**e have in common with all other men a . . . right to our freedoms . . . as we are a freeborn People. **"**

Patriots were not, however, moved to act on these petitions. They were focused on fighting and were unwilling to give up the labor of enslaved people.

Patriots had mixed thoughts about the results of the battles of Lexington, Concord, and Bunker Hill. They had fought to repeal the Intolerable Acts. As they joined together as Americans, however, many felt a growing desire to separate themselves from Britain.

Lesson Review

1775

April
Battles of Lexington and Concord

May
Second Continental Congress

June
Battle of Bunker Hill

1. **Key Vocabulary:** Describe the Patriots first battles against the British using militia, Minutemen, casualties, and fortify.

2. **Focus:** How did the battles of Lexington and Concord begin?

3. **Focus:** How did the Battle of Bunker Hill bring the colonists closer to independence?

4. **Critical Thinking: Generalize** Look up the word *escalate.* How does this term describe what happened in the battles of Lexington, Concord, and Bunker Hill?

5. **Theme: Becoming Independent** What was the colonists' response to the battles of Lexington, Concord, and Bunker Hill?

6. **Citizenship/Writing Activity:** You are a British survivor of the Battle of Bunker Hill. Write a letter to your family telling them about the hardships you have faced.

Environment and Society

How Did Land and Water Affect a Battle?

Have you ever played "King of the Hill"? If you have, then you know that in order to win, you try to keep the other players from reaching the top. "King of the Hill" is just a game. Many real battles are fought to control important geographic features like hills or waterways.

The Battle of Bunker Hill is a good example of a struggle affected by geographic features. In the summer of 1775, an army of Patriots had the British army trapped in Boston. The American leaders decided to have troops occupy the high ground in Charlestown, across the Charles River from Boston. They hoped that from there, Patriot cannons would be able to fire at British soldiers in Boston, and British ships in Boston Harbor.

Science Connection

The hills of Charlestown were made by glaciers thousands of years ago. These hills, called drumlins, are usually long and oval-shaped. They have steep sides and gently rounded tops. Why would these hills be easy to defend, but hard to attack?

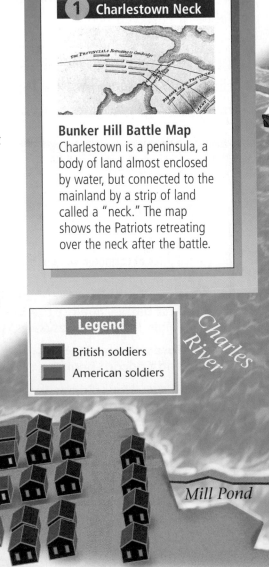

1 Charlestown Neck

Bunker Hill Battle Map
Charlestown is a peninsula, a body of land almost enclosed by water, but connected to the mainland by a strip of land called a "neck." The map shows the Patriots retreating over the neck after the battle.

Legend
British soldiers
American soldiers

Charles River

Mill Pond

The Americans built simple fortifications on top of Breed's Hill. This made the hill even harder to attack. Why do you think the British lost so many soldiers?

Research Activity

Take a walk around your neighborhood or town.

1 Take notes on whether it is hilly or flat. Identify geographic features and human structures, like roads and buildings, that affect your daily life.

2 Make a map of your observations to share with the class.

3 Breed's Hill

The British Troops Attack
Twice the British soldiers attacked the front and sides of Breed's Hill. Twice they were pushed back by the Patriot forces. On the third try, the British took the hill but lost almost half of their soldiers.

On the afternoon of June 17, 1775, British troops rowed across the Charles River. British cannons set fire to Charlestown with red hot cannonballs after Patriots fired at them from inside the town. At 3:00 P.M. the British launched the first attack on Breed's Hill.

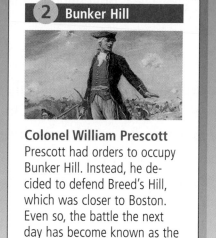

2 Bunker Hill

Colonel William Prescott
Prescott had orders to occupy Bunker Hill. Instead, he decided to defend Breed's Hill, which was closer to Boston. Even so, the battle the next day has become known as the Battle of Bunker Hill.

Charlestown

Boston

Battle of Bunker Hill, June 17, 1775

Bunker Hill

Mystic River

Breed's Hill

School Hill

Patriots' fort

Morton's Hill

Charlestown

Boston Harbor

Boston

W N S E

Declaring Independence

Main Idea After a year of fighting, the colonists declared independence.

Key Vocabulary

petition

declaration

treason

Key Events

1775 Olive Branch Petition

1776 *Common Sense* published

1776 Declaration of Independence signed

Soon after the Battle of Bunker Hill, Congress tried again to patch things up with King George III. On July 5, 1775, they voted to send him a petition. A **petition** is a written request signed by many people. This one was called the Olive Branch Petition. (The olive branch is a symbol of peace.) In it they begged King George III to bring about a "happy and permanent reconciliation." The king refused, calling the colonists rebels.

Support for Independence

Focus *How did Common Sense contribute to the movement for independence?*

In January 1776, a few months after the Olive Branch Petition was sent, a pamphlet titled *Common Sense* was published. Its author was Thomas Paine, an Englishman who had recently arrived in the colonies. Paine wrote that independence from Britain was the only way to prevent Britain from abusing the colonists' rights.

Common Sense sold over 100,000 copies in three months, an astonishing number in those days. By the spring, Paine's arguments had convinced many people that the time for independence had come. On June 7, Richard Henry Lee of Virginia asked Congress to vote for independence. Before voting, however, Congress decided to draft a **declaration,** or statement, telling why the colonies wanted to be free of British rule. Congress appointed a committee to write it. The committee members were John Adams, Benjamin Franklin, and Robert Livingston from New York, Roger Sherman from Connecticut, and Thomas Jefferson from Virginia.

The committee asked Thomas Jefferson, a young, red-haired lawyer, to write the first draft. Jefferson suggested that John Adams

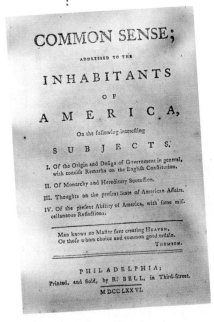

The pamphlet *Common Sense* helped to convince colonists to seek independence.

do it. Adams was older and had worked for independence longer, but he refused Jefferson's offer. He later recalled their conversation.

"What can be your reasons?" Jefferson asked.

"Reason first — You are a Virginian, and a Virginian ought to appear at the head of this business. Reason second — I am obnoxious, suspected, and unpopular. You are very much otherwise. Reason third — You can write ten times better than I can."

"Well, if you are decided, I will do as well as I can."

The Declaration of Independence

Focus *Why is the Declaration of Independence important to Americans?*

Jefferson spent about two weeks writing and rewriting the Declaration of Independence. The first part of the document explains why the colonies had the right to separate from Britain.

> **"W**e hold these truths to be self-evident, that all men are created equal, that they are endowed by their Creator with certain unalienable Rights, that among these are Life, Liberty and the pursuit of Happiness....**"**

Thomas Jefferson wrote the Declaration of Independence in only a few weeks. He designed the desk below, which he used to write sections of the Declaration of Independence. **Technology:** *What tools would someone writing a declaration use today?*

In the painting above, members of Congress are given the Declaration of Independence to sign. Some of the signers are identified in the numbered sketch above.

1 John Adams

2 Roger Sherman

3 Philip Livingston

4 Thomas Jefferson

5 Benjamin Franklin

Jefferson meant that everyone had certain rights and that no government should take those rights away.

In addition, the Declaration includes a list of acts that Britain committed against America. It also states that the colonists had no choice but to break free from Britain. In this section, Jefferson wrote, "We therefore declare. . . that these United Colonies are, and of right ought to be, FREE AND INDEPENDENT STATES. . . ." *(You can read the entire Declaration starting on page 654.)*

The Signing

On July 4, 1776, Congress officially approved the Declaration of Independence. Two months later, on August 2, the document signers gathered in silence. They knew they were committing **treason** — revolt against the government — and that the penalty for this crime was death by hanging. Legend has it that John Hancock signed his name with a flourish and warned that they all needed to sign the Declaration. "There must be no pulling different ways. We must all hang together."

Franklin is said to have then replied to Hancock, "Yes, we must indeed all hang together, or most assuredly we shall all hang separately."

Equality for All?

Jefferson wrote the words "all men are created equal" in a time very different from ours. In 1776, not all people had the same rights. Only white men who owned property could vote. As the years passed, however, the ideas in the Declaration spurred people into action. African Americans asked Congress and the states to end slavery and grant them equal rights. Women, too, looked to the Declaration. In 1776, Abigail Adams wrote to her husband,

> **"** . . . in the new Code of Laws which I suppose it will be necessary for you to make . . . Remember the Ladies . . . [We] will not hold ourselves bound by any Laws in which we have no voice, or Representation. **"**

John Adams treated his wife's request as nothing more than a joke, but time would prove him to be wrong. It took many years, but women have gained equality under the law. So have African Americans, Native Americans, and other groups. The American belief in liberty and equality can be found in Thomas Jefferson's famous words. As the Declaration of Independence says, "We hold these truths to be self-evident, that all men are created equal. . . ."

Then & Now

People can still look at the Declaration of Independence today. It is on display in the National Archives in Washington, D.C. During the peak visiting hours of the summer, hundreds of people come every day to read its powerful words.

Lesson Review

1774	1775	1776	

1775
Olive Branch Petition

1776
Common Sense published
Declaration of Independence signed

1. **Key vocabulary:** Write a paragraph about the signing of the Declaration using petition, declaration, and treason.

2. **Focus:** How did *Common Sense* contribute to the movement for independence?

3. **Focus:** Why is the Declaration of Independence important to Americans?

4. **Critical Thinking: Interpret** If today your state declared independence from the rest of the nation, what do you think might happen? Explain.

5. **Geography:** Do you think that the great distance between England and the colonies was a factor in becoming independent? Why or why not?

6. **Citizenship/Art Activity:** Answer the question What do the words "Life, Liberty and the pursuit of Happiness" mean to you? by creating a collage.

Interpreting Historical Documents

Investigating the Past

Every historical document has a story to tell. Why was it written? Whose lives did it affect? What did it change? The Declaration of Independence is one of America's most important historical documents. Thomas Jefferson wrote the Declaration to publicly list the colonists' complaints against King George III.

Reading a document written long ago can be difficult. You may not know all the words. The meaning of some words may have changed over time. The steps below can help you **interpret** — or understand for yourself — the words of the Declaration of Independence, or any other historical document.

① Here's How

The words quoted on the right are from the section of the Declaration of Independence that lists colonists' complaints against George III.

- Read the sentence carefully. You'll probably need to read it more than once.

He has plundered our seas, ravaged our Coasts, burnt our towns, and destroyed the lives of our people.

- Use a dictionary to look up meanings of words you don't know, such as "plundered" and "ravaged." Remember, the meanings of some words have changed over time.

- Think about the main idea.

- Rewrite or say the passage aloud in your own words. For example, "He has plundered our seas" might become "He robbed us on the ocean. . . ."

- After you've found the meaning of the words, ask yourself what story or ideas the words are telling.

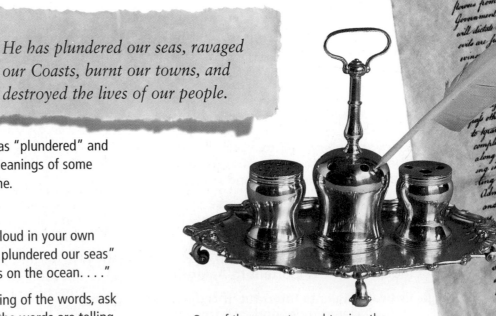

One of the pen sets used to sign the Declaration of Independence.

② Think It Through

What's different about the way historical documents were written and the way we write now? How is a dictionary helpful when you read a historical document?

We hold these truths to be self-evident, that all men are created equal, that they are endowed by their Creator with certain unalienable Rights, that among these are Life, Liberty, and the Pursuit of Happiness.

③ Use It

1. Write a list of rules to use when reading a historical document. What else could you apply these rules to?

2. Now read the excerpt from the Declaration of Independence on this page.

3. Use the rules you have just listed to come up with your own interpretation of the excerpt.

4. Write a paragraph to answer the question "What story is being told here?"

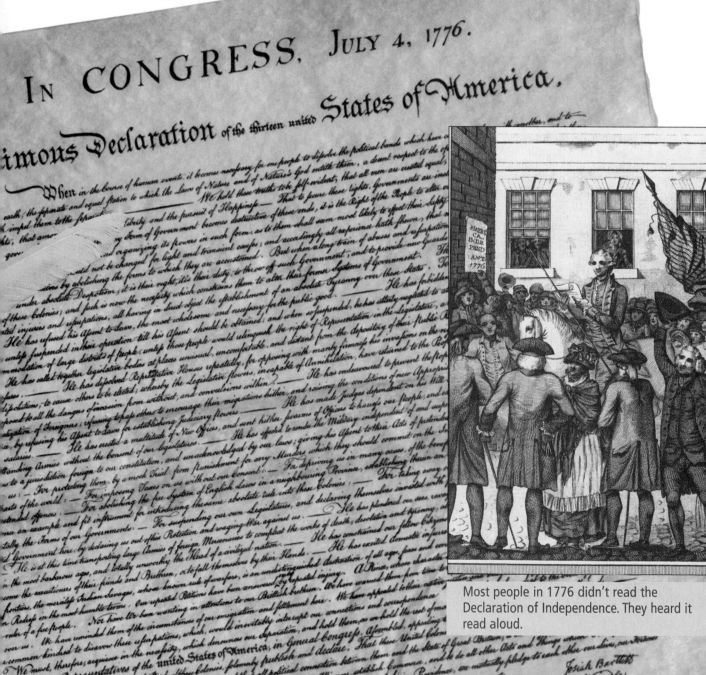

Most people in 1776 didn't read the Declaration of Independence. They heard it read aloud.

Chapter Review

Chapter Review Timeline

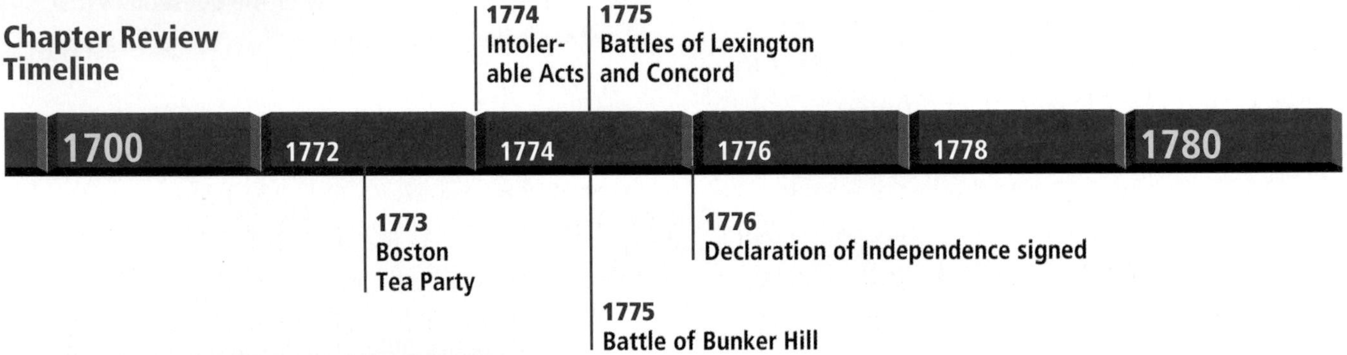

| 1700 | 1772 | 1774 | 1776 | 1778 | 1780 |

1774 Intolerable Acts

1775 Battles of Lexington and Concord

1773 Boston Tea Party

1776 Declaration of Independence signed

1775 Battle of Bunker Hill

Summarizing the Main Idea

1 Copy the chart below and fill in the missing information to show British actions and colonial reactions.

BRITISH ACTION	COLONIAL REACTION
Boston Massacre leaves 5 dead	*Opposition to British troops in the colonies mounts*
Tea Act is passed	
Intolerable Acts are passed	
Soldiers seize weapons at Concord	
Olive Branch Petition is rejected	

Vocabulary

2 Using at least six of the following terms, write a paragraph about whether the colonies should break away from Great Britain.

propaganda (p. 250)
Patriot (p. 254)
Loyalist (p. 254)
committee of correspondence (p. 255)

militia (p. 262)
Minutemen (p. 262)
delegates (p. 264)
casualties (p. 264)
peninsula (p. 265)

fortify (p. 265)
petition (p. 270)
declaration (p. 270)
treason (p. 272)

Reviewing the Facts

3 What message did the Boston Tea Party send the British?

4 What effect did *Common Sense* have on the colonists?

5 What did the words "all men are created equal" mean to people in 1776?

6 Why was the signing of the Declaration of Independence such a serious occasion?

Skill Review: Interpreting a Historical Document

Read the excerpt from *Common Sense* at the right and answer these questions.

7 What do the words "asserted," "flourished," and "fallacious" mean?

8 According to Paine, what argument do some people give for remaining a colony of Great Britain?

9 Why does Paine disagree with these arguments?

"I have heard it asserted by some, that as America has flourished under her former connection with Great Britain, the same connection is necessary towards her future happiness, and will always have the same effect. Nothing can be more fallacious than this kind of argument. We may as well assert that because a child has thrived upon milk, that it is never to have meat...."

Geography Skills

10 Look at the map on page 263. Why were the British "beaten, bloody, and exhausted" when they returned to Charlestown?

11 Prepare a travel guide called "Road to Independence." List places for people to visit and learn more about this part of history.

Critical Thinking

12 **Decision Making** If you were an enslaved African American in 1775, would you join the British or the colonial army? Why?

13 **Identify the Main Idea** What is the main idea of the Declaration of Independence?

Writing: Citizenship and Economics

14 **Citizenship** Which event in this chapter would have convinced you that it was time to declare independence? Explain your answer in the form of a journal entry.

15 **Economics** You are a merchant living in Boston. Write a letter to a friend in England explaining the effect that British taxation is having on your business.

Activities

History/Arts Activity
With other classmates, prepare a play of the Boston Massacre. After you have presented it, discuss with members of the audience whether they think the term "massacre" accurately describes the events they witnessed.

Cultures/Literature Activity
Read these lines from the gravestone of an African American: "Here lies the body of JOHN JACK . . . Tho' born in a land of slavery, / He was born free; / Tho' he lived in a land of liberty, / He lived a slave...." What do these lines tell about life for enslaved people in the colonies?

Internet Option

Check the **Internet Social Studies Center** for ideas on how to extend your theme project beyond your classroom.

THEME PROJECT CHECK-IN

How do the important events in this chapter affect your decision to be a Patriot or a Loyalist? Think about the information you have read and ask yourself these questions:
• Which side do you think will win? The Patriots or the Loyalists?
• Why is it important that you choose a side?
• What are your reactions to some of the events? How have others reacted?

The War for Independence

Chapter Preview: *People, Places, and Events*

1770	1774	1778

British Uniform

These bright red coats looked nice, but made the British easy targets. *Lesson 1, Page 280*

Fort Ticonderoga — 1775

Which Patriot hero captured British forts? The answer may surprise you. *Lesson 1, Page 282*

Valley Forge — 1778

These men were so hungry that they ate leaves and dirt. *Lesson 2, Page 286*

Fighting the Revolution

Main Idea Colonists faced difficulties but received enough support to continue fighting.

News of the signing of the Declaration of Independence spread through the colonies like wildfire. People had to decide. Were they Patriots or Loyalists? Which cause were they ready to fight for?

Ten-year-old Israel Trask of Massachusetts was a young Patriot ready to fight. He joined the Continental Army as a cook and messenger. When he was 12 years old, he sailed aboard a **privateer**, a privately owned, armed ship used by the colonies to attack British ships. Five years and many adventures later, Israel escaped from a prison ship and returned to Massachusetts. When the war ended in 1783, he was just 17. Though younger than most, Israel was typical of the farmers and artisans who left homes, fields, and shops to fight for the Patriot cause.

Key Vocabulary

privateer

mercenary

revolution

strategy

Key Events

Dec. 1776 Battle of Trenton

Oct. 1777 Battle of Saratoga

◀ Molly Pitcher takes the cannon in place of her fallen husband.

1782   1786   1790

Nathanael Greene

Some people thought this Patriot was more talented than Washington. *Lesson 2, Page 288*

Treaty of Paris   1783

How did this piece of paper affect many nations and two continents? *Lesson 3, Page 295*

African American Churches

African Americans like this man fought for freedom in every way they could. *Lesson 3, Page 297*

The Uniforms of Two Soldiers

How uncomfortable were the British soldiers' red uniforms? Made of heavy wool, they were hot in the summer and itchy in the winter. The red uniforms made bright targets for the Minutemen to fire at.

Soldiers on both sides had to carry heavy packs and equipment. Sometimes their packs, loaded with equipment, utensils, and clothing, weighed over 100 pounds. While British soldiers were given all their equipment, Minutemen had to bring theirs. They often even had to make their own musket balls!

Goatskin pack

Brush for musket

Breeches

Stockings

British Soldier

Homemade shirt

Box for ammunition

Trousers

Bayonet

Musket

Continental Soldier

Different Armies, Different Ideals

Focus *What were the main strengths and weaknesses of the Patriot and British forces?*

The British called Trask and other Patriots "Yankee Doodles." They laughed at the Americans' swords. Some looked as if they had been made out of farm tools. Even their most experienced officer, George Washington, had never commanded an entire army before.

How could these beginners hope to beat the well-trained professional army and navy of wealthy Britain? King George scoffed, "Once these rebels have felt a smart blow, they will submit . . . ."

The king discovered that sending supplies across 3,000 miles of ocean was expensive. Also, British fighting methods did not work well on the American landscape. Some British people were in no hurry to fight their colonial cousins. The king had to hire paid soldiers, or **mercenaries,** just to get enough men to fight.

King George also overlooked the Patriots' greatest strength — their enthusiasm. They were fighting a **revolution,** which is an attempt to overthrow one government and replace it with another. They were fighting for the right to govern and tax themselves.

Some Patriots fought for other ideals. When Rhode Island promised freedom and the same wages as those paid to white soldiers, some African Americans joined the Patriots. The First Rhode Island Regiment was the first unit made up of mainly African Americans. However, most African Americans remained enslaved.

Women also fought for the Patriots. Margaret Corbin took her turn at the cannon when gunners were shot down. Some women disguised themselves as men and fought as soldiers or acted as spies. Most women did their part by running farms, homes, and hospitals.

A Nation Divided

While two-fifths of the colonists were Patriots, about one-fifth were Loyalists. Colonists were after all still British citizens, and some found it hard to break ties with Britain. Native Americans also fought for the British, who supplied them with trade goods. They saw no reason to help the colonists, who had invaded their lands. Only a few, such as the Oneida (oh NY duh) and the Tuscarora (tuhs kuh RAWR uh), fought for the Patriots. About two-fifths of the colonists chose not to join the war. As people chose sides, or whether to pick a side at all, families and communities split apart.

British and Continental Armies

British Army
Strengths:
- well-trained men, good equipment, wealthy country
- the world's best and largest navy
- support of most Native American groups

Weaknesses:
- had to fight on unfamiliar land
- expensive to ship supplies all the way to the colonies

Continental Army
Strengths:
- fighting on their own familiar land
- more support from colonists than British had
- fighting for a cause

Weaknesses:
- poorly trained, ill-equipped troops
- little money and few leaders

Both British and Patriot forces had many strengths and weaknesses. Chart Skill: How did geography contribute to the strengths and weaknesses of both armies?

Washington Crossing the Delaware was painted years after the event took place. The artist used a flag that was not adopted until 1777. One of Washington's oarsmen was Prince Whipple, an African American soldier who later petitioned New Hampshire for his freedom.

Benedict Arnold became an early Patriot hero after storming Fort Ticonderoga and capturing it from the British in 1775. In 1780, he shocked Patriots by switching over to the British side. For this reason he has been called a traitor.

War in the North

Focus *What were each side's goals in the early part of the war?*

The British **strategy**, or plan of action, was to stop the rebellion quickly before the colonists could get France and Spain to join. Forced out of Boston in March of 1776, the British sailed to Canada to prepare for more fighting. Sailing on to New York, the British almost ended the war right then and there by capturing Washington's troops. Only Washington's speed in escaping with his men across the East River kept the Patriot cause alive.

The British soon followed, capturing New York City. During this time, the British caught Captain Nathan Hale, a Patriot spy. Just before he was hanged, Hale said,

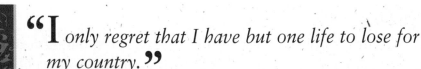

❝I *only regret that I have but one life to lose for my country.***❞**

Washington's strategy was to fight where he had to and then retreat, saving strength for the next battle. He tried to do this at Fort Washington, in New York. The fighting at Fort Washington was terrible, with nearly 3,000 Patriot prisoners captured. After the battle the rest of Washington's army fled across the Hudson River to New Jersey, with the British hot on their heels.

Mar. 17, 1776
British flee Boston

Dec. 25, 1776
Washington crosses
the Delaware

Dec. 26, 1776
American victory
at Trenton

March Apr. May Jun. Jul. Aug. Sept. Oct. Nov. Dec.

Aug. 27, 1776
British take Long Island

Sept. 15, 1776
British occupy New York City

Nov. 16, 1776
British win at Fort Washington

Victories at Trenton and Saratoga

The Patriots fled down New Jersey and across the Delaware River
into Pennsylvania. By now it was December. The spirits of the
Patriots were very low. Washington had 3,000 men with him, and
half would soon go home. The enemy, he believed, had over
10,000.

Some British mercenaries were back in New Jersey, celebrating a
snowy Christmas Day. That night, Washington and his men crossed
the ice-choked Delaware River and marched through the bitter cold
to Trenton. They captured about 900 sleeping mercenaries in this
battle and around 200 more in a second victory at Princeton.

The turning point came in October of 1777 in Saratoga, New
York. British General John Burgoyne lost the Battle of Saratoga,
surrendering about 5,700 men. Across the Atlantic Ocean, the
French were joyful. Maybe France's old enemy would lose after all.

Lesson Review

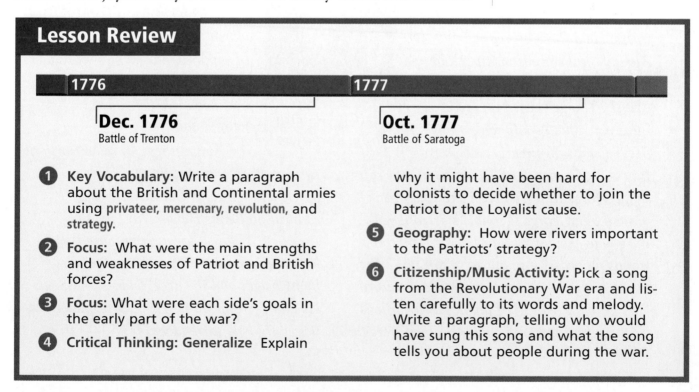

1776 1777

Dec. 1776
Battle of Trenton

Oct. 1777
Battle of Saratoga

1 **Key Vocabulary:** Write a paragraph
about the British and Continental armies
using **privateer, mercenary, revolution,** and
strategy.

2 **Focus:** What were the main strengths
and weaknesses of Patriot and British
forces?

3 **Focus:** What were each side's goals in
the early part of the war?

4 **Critical Thinking: Generalize** Explain

why it might have been hard for
colonists to decide whether to join the
Patriot or the Loyalist cause.

5 **Geography:** How were rivers important
to the Patriots' strategy?

6 **Citizenship/Music Activity:** Pick a song
from the Revolutionary War era and listen carefully to its words and melody.
Write a paragraph, telling who would
have sung this song and what the song
tells you about people during the war.

Maps from Written Descriptions

Map It Yourself

The British had a good plan. Three British officers coming from different directions would meet in Albany, New York. They would crush the American Revolution by cutting off New England from the rest of the colonies. The plan failed, however, partly because of British General John Burgoyne. Find out why General Burgoyne never got to Albany. You can use the written description on this page to make your own map of his route.

The Battle of Saratoga

The battle plan called for General Burgoyne to move his troops south out of Canada, following lakes and rivers. He'd force his way to Albany on the Hudson River and take the Hudson Valley for the British. Things started off well. Burgoyne sailed south with a huge fleet of ships on June 17, 1777. By July 6, he'd taken Fort Ticonderoga, the star-shaped fort located where Lake Champlain meets Lake George. Trouble started when Burgoyne decided to travel across land. The troops moved at a snail's pace through thick forest, rugged hills, and steep valleys toward Fort Edward. Ahead of them, Patriot troops destroyed bridges and chopped down trees to

British General John Burgoyne

block the British path. Burgoyne's army took 24 days to travel from Fort Ticonderoga to Fort Edward, which they captured. Now short of supplies, Burgoyne sent soldiers east in search of cattle and horses, but they were defeated at Bennington.

At Saratoga, 40 miles north of Albany, Burgoyne met the Patriot army led by General Horatio Gates. Gates was camped on Bemis Heights, just south of Saratoga, a perfect location because it overlooked the Hudson River. It was protected by its height and the deep ravines and thickets that surrounded it. There, after fierce battles, Burgoyne surrendered his 5,700 troops.

This officer's star-shaped lantern, which dates back to the mid 1700s, was made of metal and glass and used with a candle or small oil lamp.

1 Here's How

- Look back at the description of the Battle of Saratoga. Notice the direction the British traveled, the places they passed, the events they experienced, and the landscape along the way.

- To make your own map, you can trace this one onto your own paper. Be sure to add a title.

- Design symbols for your map key. Use a line to show Burgoyne's route. Create symbols for features such as boats, forts, forests, and battles.

- Decide where to place the symbols on your map, matching directions and distances from the description.

- Now draw General Burgoyne's route.

- Are there other features, place names, or information from the description that you could add to your map? Be sure you've added the compass directions and map scale.

2 Think It Through

How does drawing a map help you when you read written descriptions of how to get from one place to another?

3 Use It

1. Follow the steps in Here's How to make your map.

2. Now look at your map and find some of the natural features that worked against the British. How does the map tell the story of Burgoyne's route?

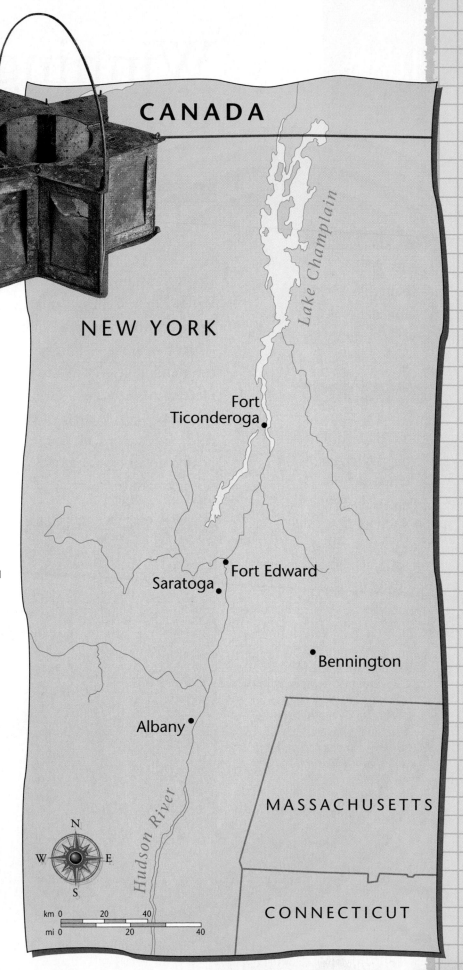

CANADA

NEW YORK

Lake Champlain

Fort Ticonderoga

Fort Edward

Saratoga

Bennington

Albany

MASSACHUSETTS

Hudson River

CONNECTICUT

N
W   E
S

km 0   20   40
mi 0   20   40

Winning the Revolution

Main Idea With the support of other countries, the colonists overcame obstacles to win the war.

Key Vocabulary

intervention
neutral
surrender

Key Events

Dec. 1777–June
1778 Valley Forge

Feb. 1778 France
enters the war

Feb.–May 1780
Battle of Charleston

Oct. 1781
Surrender at
Yorktown

W ashington's army spent the long, hard winter of 1778 at Valley Forge, Pennsylvania. A surgeon in the colonial army described the experience in his journal. "Poor food — hard lodging — cold weather — fatigue — nasty clothes — nasty cooking . . . I can't endure it — why are we sent here to starve and freeze . . . Here comes a bowl of beef soup — full of burnt leaves and dirt."

Nearly one-quarter of the soldiers at Valley Forge died from cold, disease, or lack of food. Many others were so horrified and beaten down by the terrible conditions that they left the army without permission.

In this engraving, the Marquis de Lafayette talks with George Washington at Valley Forge. Below are some utensils the soldiers might have used.
Arts: *How can you tell from the picture that life was hard for soldiers at Valley Forge?*

Help from Europe

Focus *How did European nations help the Continental Army?*

Since May 1776, France had been sending supplies to the Patriots. As the winter at Valley Forge would show, the colonists needed more. In December of 1776, Benjamin Franklin, wearing spectacles and a beaver fur cap, went to Paris to ask France to formally recognize the Patriot fight for independence. In a city where many wore fancy clothes and powdered wigs, his simple ways won French hearts. Fondness for Franklin, however, was not enough to convince the French to step in. They were willing to fight their old enemy, the British, but they wanted to be sure they were on the winning side.

News of the October, 1777 victory at Saratoga finally convinced the French. In February, 1778, France formally entered the war. In June, able French officers, well-trained troops, and the French navy began to aid the Patriots. French intervention changed the war. **Intervention** is when one nation enters the affairs of another nation.

Now Britain had two battles to fight, one against the colonists and one against the French. Britain sent thousands of troops to attack French colonies in the Caribbean. This meant that the British had fewer troops available for fighting the colonial forces.

New Military Leaders

In the following years, Washington gained the assistance of many skilled European soldiers. Freedom lovers like the French Marquis de Lafayette (mahr KEE duh lah fay ETT) came over from Europe in the summer of 1777. With Lafayette came the Baron de Kalb, a professional soldier. In the winter of 1778, a soldier from Prussia (which is now part of Germany), calling himself Baron von Steuben (SHTOY ben), came to volunteer his services. Washington quickly put him to work training the inexperienced Patriot troops.

The men enjoyed the peppery baron and learned many needed skills from him. The baron learned something too of the independent Patriot spirit. In a letter to a European friend, he said, "You say to your soldier, 'Do this,' and he doeth it, but I am obliged to say, 'This is the reason why you ought to do that,' and he does it."

Muskets of the Revolutionary War weighed around 14 pounds and were nearly as tall as a man. This one belonged to a Minuteman.

Curious Facts

Did you know that shoes supplied by the Continental Army were not made for right and left feet? Soldiers were told to switch their shoes often, so they would not take the shape of their feet. If a soldier died, his shoes could be given to another soldier to wear.

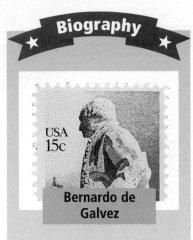
The War Moves West and South

Focus *How did events in the West and South end the war?*

In the beginning the war was fought mainly in the Northeast. Then it began to spread — to the West, to the Spanish territories in the Southwest, and to the South. In each place, heroes sprang up to fight for the Patriot cause. *(See the map on the next page.)*

One of those heroes was George Rogers Clark. He and a small band of riflemen set out to take the Ohio River Valley away from the British and their Native American allies. With fewer than 200 men, Clark captured three forts in the summer of 1778. During the winter, Clark captured Fort Vincennes on the Wabash River. He had only about 150 men left. Cold and hungry, they marched 180 miles through flooded lands to reach the fort. Taking the British troops by surprise, Clark forced them to surrender.

On June 21, 1779, Spain formally declared war on Great Britain. Bernardo de Galvez, governor of the Spanish territory of Louisiana, gathered in New Orleans an army of militia, Native Americans, African Americans, and other volunteers. They successfully attacked the British at Pensacola, Natchez, and Baton Rouge.

Battles of the South

The battles deciding the outcome of the war took place in Georgia and the Carolinas. The British wanted to move the war to the South, thinking this region was full of Loyalists ready to battle for the British. They were wrong. Most southern Loyalists were too afraid of their Patriot neighbors to fight. Also, because some British soldiers robbed and terrorized civilians, many people who had been **neutral,** or who chose to stay out of the war, joined the Patriots.

Still, the British seemed to be winning. Moving north from Georgia through the Carolinas, the British won important battles at Savannah, Charleston, and Camden. In the defeat at Charleston, the Patriots lost over 5,400 troops, as well as ships and supplies.

Though the British won in the cities, they lost in the countryside because of Patriot fighters like Francis Marion. Marion, called the "Swamp Fox," knew his way around the South Carolina low country and was as quick and clever as a fox. He and his small band of poorly-equipped men attacked the British with hit-and-run raids.

General Nathanael Greene was in charge of the Continental Army in the South. He decided to adopt Marion's tactics. He

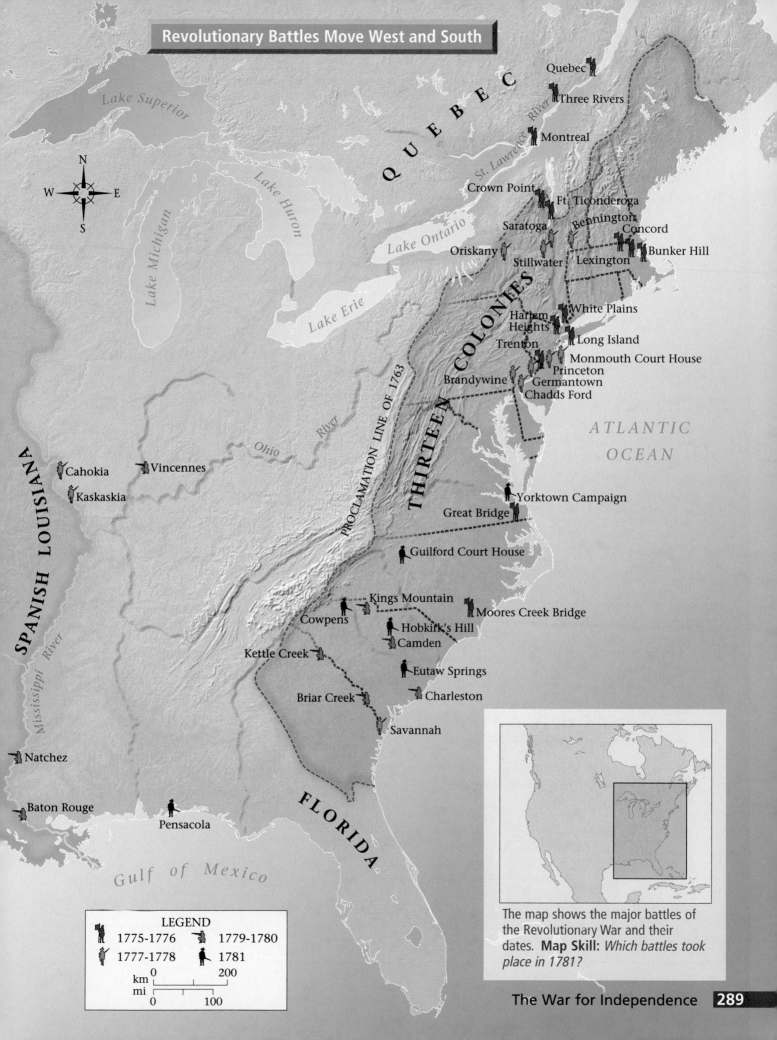

QUEBEC

Quebec

Three Rivers

Montreal

St. Lawrence River

Lake Superior

Lake Huron

Lake Michigan

Lake Ontario

Lake Erie

Crown Point
Ft. Ticonderoga
Saratoga
Bennington
Concord
Oriskany
Stillwater
Lexington
Bunker Hill
White Plains
Harlem Heights
Long Island
Trenton
Monmouth Court House
Brandywine
Princeton
Germantown
Chadds Ford

N
W   E
S

SPANISH LOUISIANA

Mississippi River

Ohio River

PROCLAMATION LINE OF 1763

THIRTEEN COLONIES

ATLANTIC OCEAN

Cahokia
Vincennes
Kaskaskia

Yorktown Campaign
Great Bridge

Guilford Court House

Kings Mountain
Cowpens
Moores Creek Bridge
Hobkirk's Hill
Camden
Kettle Creek
Eutaw Springs
Briar Creek
Charleston
Savannah

Natchez

Baton Rouge
Pensacola

FLORIDA

Gulf of Mexico

The map shows the major battles of the Revolutionary War and their dates. **Map Skill:** *Which battles took place in 1781?*

LEGEND

1775–1776	1779–1780
1777–1778	1781

km 0 — 200
mi 0 — 100

Rebecca Motte

Rebecca Motte was a true Patriot , willing to destroy her own home for the cause. She obeyed the Patriots' request to burn her home to drive out the British who were inside.

Charles Cornwallis

British General Charles Cornwallis was a brilliant leader, but even he could not stop the Patriots. Forced to surrender, he couldn't bring himself to hand over his sword. He had his next-in-command hand it over.

moved his troops swiftly in small groups, attacking the British now here, now there. Of his battles in the Carolinas, he wrote,

> "**W**e fight, get beat, rise, and fight again."

The British liked to fight traditional battles in which two armies stood still, faced each other, and shot. The Patriot methods left them at a loss. How could they fight properly if the enemy wouldn't stand still and be shot? Battles like those in the Carolinas showed that the most powerful army in the world was no longer winning.

Surrender at Yorktown

British General Cornwallis retreated to Yorktown, Virginia, where he thought his troops would be safe. Washington marched south from New York, with thousands of French soldiers and Patriots. The French navy sailed north from the Caribbean to meet him. Cornwallis, his troops outnumbered two to one, was caught in between. After brief fighting, he was forced on October 19, 1781, to **surrender**. He gave up and admitted that he was defeated.

One Patriot soldier was guarding prisoners when he heard news of the victory. He said the Patriot soldiers threw their hats into the air and yelled, "America is ours!"

Prices of basic foods went up in hard times of the Revolutionary War, as this chart shows. **Chart Skill:** *How did the price of sugar change from the beginning of the war to the end of the war?*

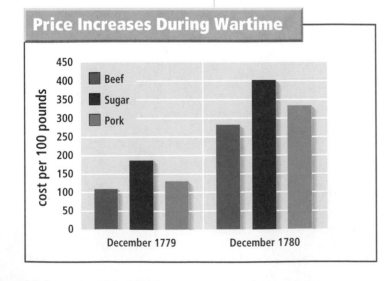

Price Increases During Wartime

cost per 100 pounds

- Beef
- Sugar
- Pork

December 1779   December 1780

Nathanael Greene

Patriot Nathanael Greene was well-known for his courage and cleverness. When Washington put him in charge of army supplies, he devoted all his energy to searching the countryside for food and clothing for his men.

Joseph Brant

Joseph Brant split the Iroqouis League by leading his Mohawks into battle on the British side. When the British lost, he persuaded Britain to give his people money to buy land in what is now Canada.

They knew, as did the British, that the war was as good as over.

Years later, a Patriot cook and laundress named Sarah Osborn could still recall the vivid scene of the surrender. She was standing by the side of the road as the British army rode up. The British officers came first, followed by the foot soldiers. She remembered the sad tune the men played as they marched, their drums covered with black handkerchiefs, and black ribbons tied around the fifes. She also remembered a portly British general riding at the head of the army. As he rode by, she saw tears rolling down his cheeks.

Lesson Review

1777	1778	1780	1781

Dec. 1777–June 1778
Valley Forge

Feb. 1778
France enters the war

Feb.–May 1780
Battle of Charleston

Oct. 1781
Surrender at Yorktown

1. **Key Vocabulary:** Write a paragraph about the Revolution using **intervention, neutral,** and **surrender.**

2. **Focus:** How did European nations help the Continental Army?

3. **Focus:** How did events in the West and South end the war?

4. **Critical Thinking: Conclude** Why did France and Spain help the Patriot cause?

5. **Geography:** What advantages did the Patriots have by fighting on their own soil?

6. **Theme: Becoming Independent/Writing Activity:** You are a British citizen who has American relatives. Write a letter to them expressing your feelings about the outcome of the war.

Resurrecting Patriots, and Their Park

During the Revolutionary War over 11,000 men lost their lives, not in battle, but in prison. These men refused to switch sides and support the British cause. They were held prisoner on ships in New York Harbor. Today, over 200 years later, those men are recognized as patriots and heroes.

Shrine to Revolution's Martyrs Is Part of Fort Greene Renewal

crypt
an underground vault or chamber, especially one that is used as a tomb beneath a church

allegiance
loyalty or devotion to one's country, to a king, or to a cause

by Douglas Martin

Richie Williamson, a blacksmith, helped force open the bronze door of the crypt at Fort Greene Park in Brooklyn. In the dim light, on the nearest shelf, he could see a human jawbone, more than 200 years old, covered with blackened cobwebs.

He made the sign of the cross over his heart and prayed for the souls of 11,500 American heroes, men who died on prison ships in New York Harbor during the Revolutionary War. Some were within sight of their homes and farms in Brooklyn and Manhattan, but they refused to switch their allegiance to the King of England in exchange for their freedom.

"This is a holy place," whispered Mr. Williamson. "Where would we be without these guys?"

The image above shows the prison ship *Jersey*. American captives were kept on 11 prison ships in Wallabout Bay for seven years.

Early this week, for the first time since the Bicentennial in 1976, Mr. Williamson and other workers opened the crypt tucked inside the Prison Ship Martyrs' Monument. They found 20 heavy slate boxes, each two feet by seven feet, containing thousands of bone fragments.

Inside the crypt, the 20 boxes of shattered bones are unlabeled, though historians have indentified some 8,000 who perished on British prison ships in Wallabout Bay, which was later filled in to make the Brooklyn Navy Yard. Because the prisons were brimming, the captives were kept on 11 ships from 1776 to 1783.

Mr. Spinner of the Old Brooklynites notes that the eternal flame intended for the eight-ton urn at the top of the monument has never been lighted. Plans to light it about a decade ago collapsed when sponsors learned the cost would approach $10 an hour. Environmental regulators also warned that a flame would emit too much carbon dioxide.

Mr. Spinner's solution was to build and donate a fiberglass structure in the shape of a flame, then coat if with gold in the manner of the restored torch on the Statue of Liberty.

A marine in World War II, Mr. Spinner says he is driven by an awe of the courage of the long-ago prisoners of war, who could have saved themselves in an instant by claiming to switch sides.

slate
a fine-grained rock that splits into thin layers with smooth surfaces

Response Activities

1. **Interpret** Divide a piece of paper into two columns. List all the facts in this article in one column and all the opinions in the other. How can you tell if a piece of information is fact or opinion?

2. **Descriptive: Write a Story** Write your own story about the capture of an American soldier kept aboard a British prison ship. Describe his life as a soldier and his reasons for remaining a prisoner instead of siding with the British.

3. **National Heritage: Create a Monument** Make a drawing of your own monument to the Revolutionary War soldiers. What words would you put on the monument?

The Impact of the Revolution

Main Idea The Revolution dramatically changed the lives of Americans.

Key Vocabulary

diplomat

negotiate

Key Event

Sept. 1783

Treaty of Paris

H ours after the last British troops sailed from New York, George Washington told his officers good-bye. The war had begun eight years before, and he was now a gray-haired 51-year-old hero. Washington could hardly trust his voice when he began speaking to the officers.

> **"W**ith a heart full of love and gratitude, I now take leave of you. I most devoutly wish that your later days may be as prosperous and happy as your former ones have been glorious and honorable.**"**

His eyes filling with tears, he threw his arms around one of his officers. Then each officer, in turn, walked up to Washington and embraced him. These officers, who had started the war as colonial dependents, were now citizens of a new country with new borders.

The British recognized American independence when the Treaty of Paris was signed. **Map Skill:** *How does this map, which shows the territory that the United States gained, hint that additional conflict with other countries might lie ahead?*

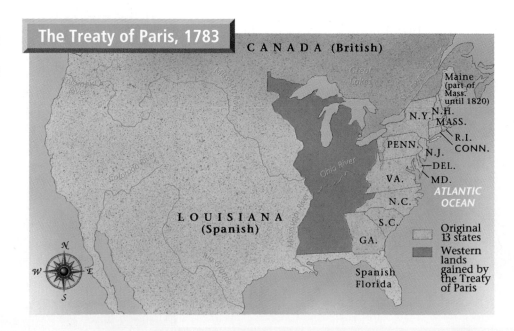

The Treaty of Paris, 1783

CANADA (British)

Maine (part of Mass. until 1820)

N.Y. N.H. MASS.

R.I. CONN.

PENN. N.J.

DEL.

VA. MD.

ATLANTIC OCEAN

N.C.

LOUISIANA (Spanish)

S.C.

GA.

Spanish Florida

Original 13 states

Western lands gained by the Treaty of Paris

The Treaty of Paris

Focus *How did the Treaty of Paris change the map of North America?*

General Cornwallis' surrender at Yorktown ended the war. The British and Americans still needed to end it officially. In September of 1782, Britain agreed to meet with diplomats from the United States. A **diplomat** is a government's representative who deals with other nations. By agreeing to meet, Britain made possible the first part of the Treaty of Paris. This first part stated that the United States was an independent country.

By October, diplomats John Adams, John Jay, and Benjamin Franklin had gathered in Paris to negotiate for the United States. To **negotiate** means to talk over issues and try to reach an agreement. The American diplomats did not fully trust their French allies. Therefore, for two months they only negotiated with Britain, establishing the Treaty of Paris in 1783. Spain, France, and the Netherlands later joined in to negotiate their own separate peace treaties with Britain.

In addition to recognizing the independence of the United States, the Treaty of Paris set boundaries for the new nation. The United States now reached west to the Mississippi River, north to Canada, and south to Spanish Florida. *(See map on the left.)*

Benjamin West painted this version of the Treaty of Paris, shown above in its written form. The painting was left unfinished, because the British diplomats standing next to the Americans refused to pose.

Some Loyalists who lost their homes after the Revolutionary War had to leave their familiar surroundings and go to places where they did not know anyone.

What would you have done if your family had been Loyalists? Would you have been willing to move far from friends, just because of an ideal?

?????????????

Coins made after the end of the war expressed the ideals of the new nation. **National Heritage:** *Besides liberty, what are some other American ideals?*

The War Changes America

Focus *How did the Revolution affect the lives of Americans?*

By the end of the war, 80,000 Loyalists had fled to Canada, England, or the British Caribbean. Among them were ex-soldiers, Native American allies, and thousands of African Americans. Some African American Loyalists returned to Africa, to the new British colony of Sierra Leone. There they settled in the community of Freetown.

The war's end was not an easy victory for all Patriots. Many of the men who signed the Declaration of Independence suffered during the war. Some were captured by the British. Others had their homes and property destroyed by the British.

For Native Americans on both sides, the Revolution was a disaster. No one had invited them to the Paris peace talks, even though the western lands discussed in these peace talks actually belonged to them. Settlers, eager to move westward, wanted that land. Native American councils made many appeals to the new United States government. In the words of one 1793 appeal:

> **"W**e want peace. Restore to us our country, and we shall be enemies no longer.**"**

It did not seem to matter which side Native Americans fought on. The Oneida, also members of the Iroquois League, had fought for the Patriots, without reward. In the years following the war, the government took millions of acres of their land.

A Different Fighting Continues

The Revolution was fought for liberty and equality. Now that it was over, how could liberty, equality, and slavery exist together? Many enslaved African Americans brought "freedom suits" to the new nation's courts, in which they argued for their American rights.

Elizabeth Freeman was an enslaved African whose husband had fought and died for the Patriots. She brought a freedom suit to the court of Massachusetts, claiming that slavery was not legal. She won her suit in 1781. In the years during and after the war, many other northern colonies began restoring freedom to enslaved people.

Some enslaved Africans in the South who fought for the Patriots also gained freedom. The number of free African Americans in Virginia, for example, went from about 3,000 to almost 13,000 in the eight years after the war. Still, most southern states felt slavery was too important to their wealth and way of life to ban it completely.

In the years after the Revolution, free and enslaved African Americans began standing up for their rights in every way they could. One way they did so was by creating their own churches. One historian writes that this church movement brought a new "organized independence and self-expression" to African Americans in the new nation.

A New Nation

After the Revolution, the United States faced a new challenge. The Americans had gained their independence. What did that really mean? They were no longer British citizens. They had to understand how that fact would affect their future.

Fighting for a representative government was a revolutionary idea. The rest of the world watched as the changes began to take place. In the words of writer Mercy Otis Warren, America was "as a child just learning to walk." In the next few years, the new country would take many first steps to try to live up to its ideals.

This stained glass window shows the Reverend Andrew Bryan, who was born into slavery and founded the First African Baptist Church in Savannah, Georgia. **Culture:** How might forming churches contribute to the freedom and independence of a people?

Lesson Review

1781	1783

1783
Treaty of Paris

1. **Key Vocabulary:** Write a sentence about the Treaty of Paris using **diplomat** and **negotiate**.

2. **Focus:** How did the Treaty of Paris change the map of North America?

3. **Focus:** How did the Revolution affect the lives of Americans?

4. **Critical Thinking: Interpret** Do the winners of revolutions always benefit from it? What do the outcomes of the American Revolution suggest about the advantages and disadvantages of revolution?

5. **Theme: Becoming Independent** What did independence mean for different Americans?

6. **Geography/Research Activity:** Look at the map of European Land Claims on page 239 and the map of the Treaty of Paris on page 294. Find one area that remained under British control. Then research the history of that area.

CHAPTER 11

Chapter Review

Chapter Review Timeline

| 1775 | 1777 | 1779 | 1781 | 1783 | 1785 |

1776 Battle of Trenton

1777 Battle of Saratoga

1778 France enters the War

1781 Surrender at Yorktown

1783 Treaty of Paris

Summarizing the Main Idea

1 Copy and complete the chart below, sequencing the events that led America to independence.

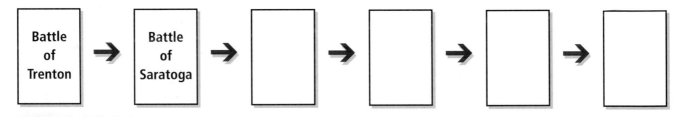

Battle of Trenton → Battle of Saratoga → ☐ → ☐ → ☐ → ☐

Vocabulary

2 Use each of the words below in a sentence describing the difficulties the colonists faced in their battle for freedom.

privateer (p. 279) strategy (p. 282) surrender (p. 290)

mercenary (p. 281) intervention (p. 287) diplomat (p. 295)

revolution (p. 281) neutral (p. 288) negotiate (p. 295)

Reviewing the Facts

3 What made fighting difficult for King George and the British army?

4 What was the main difference between the Patriots and the Loyalists?

5 What were the results of the war in the North?

6 How did the Europeans help the Patriots?

7 What did George Rogers Clark do?

8 Discuss how the British and Patriots fought differently.

9 How did the Patriots react to the surrender at Yorktown? How did the British react?

10 Why was the Treaty of Paris important?

11 What did African Americans hope to accomplish with their freedom suits?

Making Maps from Written Descriptions

12 Look at the description of the beginning of the war in the North on page 282. Draw a map of the North showing the area in which the battles took place.

13 Put symbols on your map that show the numbers of troops on each side. Also make arrows showing the routes the British and Patriots took.

Geography Skills

14 How did location, environment, and climate affect the War of Independence?

15 You are a British Redcoat. Write a journal entry describing your thoughts about America. Why do you think the Patriots are fighting for independence?

Critical Thinking

16 **Predict** Patriots fought for their own freedom, but hardly recognized the importance of independence for people other than themselves. What can you predict about future conflict in the United States based on their treatment of Native Americans, enslaved Africans, and women?

17 **Interpret** Explain why the Patriots continued to fight the British even when it seemed at times that they could not win.

Writing: Citizenship and History

18 **Citizenship** Considering that the Patriots were in America to stay, propose a plan for ways in which the Patriots and the Native Americans could share the land.

19 **History** You are one of the Patriot leaders. Write a short speech to deliver before an important battle. What words would you use to increase your troops enthusiasm?

Activities

History/Arts Activity
Benjamin West is known for his famous paintings of the Revolutionary War. Visit the library to find one of his paintings. Write a brief description of the painting and tell whether you think it captures the spirit of the American Revolution.

Economics/Research Activity
Several European countries decided to help the Patriots by sending them equipment, funds, and soldiers. Why might helping the Patriots fight the Revolution benefit their own futures? Discuss your ideas with your classmates.

Internet Option

Check the **Internet Social Studies Center** for ideas on how to extend your theme project beyond your classroom.

THEME PROJECT CHECK-IN

Now that you have decided which side to take, think about the information in this chapter and ask the following questions:
• How do the results of the battles affect your decision?
• What is it like to live in a community where colonists are taking different sides?
• What is your reaction to the changes the Revolution is causing? How do others react?

The Nation's Early Years

"I viewed the Constitution as a Promise, . . . of freedom, and equality, and justice to all of us."

Roger Wilkins

· THEME ·

Governing Ourselves

"It is important to make rules that are good for everyone and that everyone can live by so that people can be safe."

Woldegergis Afeworki, Fifth Grade
Kansas City, MO

Setting up rules is not easy, especially if you know you will have to follow them for a long time. But setting up rules is just what Americans did in 1787 when they created a new government for their country. It took weeks of debate and many compromises to get it right. The nation's leaders created a constitution that is still the basis for our government today. Our country's early struggles helped establish the character of the United States.

Theme Project

Constitutional Expert

Become an expert on the Constitution. How was it created? What effects has it had?

- Create a chart showing how the Constitution set up the federal government in three branches.
- Make drawings of important people and events.
- Act out a debate between Constitutional delegates.
- Write a newspaper editorial as if it were the 1780s. Tell readers why the Constitution should be ratified.

RESEARCH: Find out about a Supreme Court case involving the Bill of Rights. Report on what you learned.

◀ Statue of George Washington beneath the Capitol dome

WHEN & WHERE ATLAS

Winning the War for Independence was difficult. Governing the new nation was just as hard. The greatest challenge was creating a government strong enough to solve the nation's problems while protecting the rights of citizens. When the first attempt failed, America's leaders created a new system of government. As the map shows, their efforts succeeded. By the early 1800s, the United States was strong and growing.

In this unit, you will learn how weaknesses in the Articles of Confederation led to the creation of a new constitution. You will read about the creation of a new government based on this constitution. Finally, you will learn how the young United States gained territory and defended itself against Britain.

Unit 5 Chapters

Chapter 12 The Constitution
Chapter 13 The Early Republic

PACIFIC OCEAN

45°N
40°N
35°N
125°W

CHINOOK
BLACKFOOT
DISPUTED TERRITORY
FLATHEAD
NEZ PERCE
KLAMATH MODOC
SHOSHONE
POMO
SPANISH POSSESSIONS
PAIUTE
CHUMASH
Colorado R.
NAVAJO
HOPI

Legend

America during Jefferson's Presidency

OTO   Native Americans

Frontier town

Louisiana Purchase boundary

States in 1803

120°W   115°W   110°W

Unit Timeline

1780	1790	1800

Signing the Constitution 1787

Guess how many people signed the Constitution. *Chapter 12, Lesson 2*

Thomas Jefferson

Some people called Jefferson the most talented American President. *Chapter 13, Lesson 1*

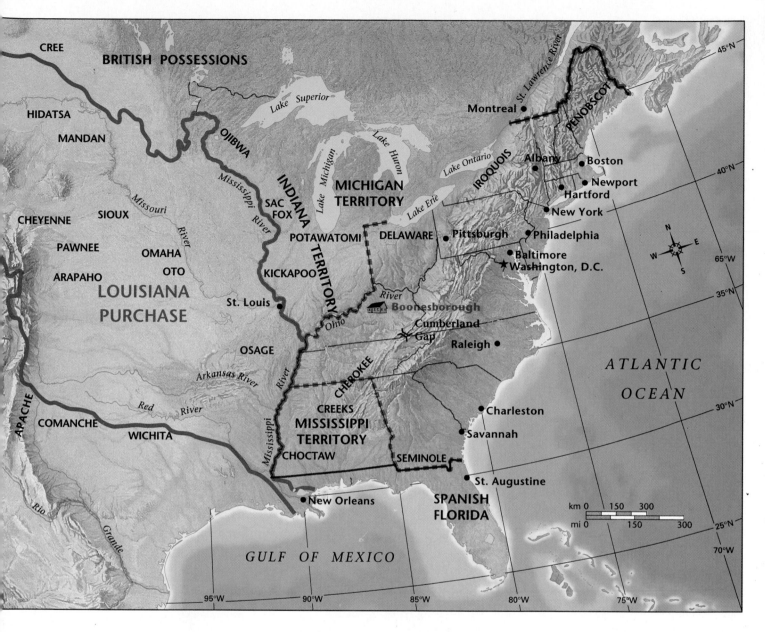

CREE

BRITISH POSSESSIONS

HIDATSA

MANDAN

OJIBWA

Lake Superior

Montreal

St. Lawrence River

PENOBSCOT

45°N

CHEYENNE

SIOUX

Missouri River

Mississippi River

SAC FOX

POTAWATOMI

INDIANA TERRITORY

MICHIGAN TERRITORY

Lake Michigan

Lake Huron

Lake Ontario

Lake Erie

IROQUOIS

Albany

Boston

Newport

Hartford

New York

40°N

PAWNEE

OMAHA

OTO

KICKAPOO

DELAWARE

Pittsburgh

Philadelphia

Baltimore

Washington, D.C.

65°W

ARAPAHO

LOUISIANA PURCHASE

St. Louis

River

Boonesborough

Cumberland Gap

Raleigh

35°N

OSAGE

Ohio

Arkansas River

River

CHEROKEE

ATLANTIC OCEAN

APACHE

Red River

Mississippi

CREEKS

MISSISSIPPI TERRITORY

CHOCTAW

SEMINOLE

Charleston

Savannah

30°N

COMANCHE

WICHITA

St. Augustine

New Orleans

SPANISH FLORIDA

km 0   150   300

mi 0   150   300

Rio Grande

GULF OF MEXICO

95°W   90°W   85°W   80°W   75°W

25°N

70°W

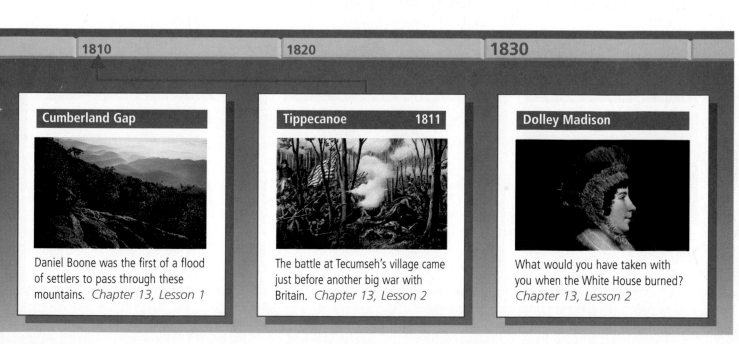

1810	1820	1830

Cumberland Gap

Daniel Boone was the first of a flood of settlers to pass through these mountains. *Chapter 13, Lesson 1*

Tippecanoe   1811

The battle at Tecumseh's village came just before another big war with Britain. *Chapter 13, Lesson 2*

Dolley Madison

What would you have taken with you when the White House burned? *Chapter 13, Lesson 2*

CHAPTER 12 The Constitution

Chapter Preview: *People, Places, and Events*

| 1786 | 1787 | 1788 |

Northwest Ordinance 1787

The Northwest Ordinance created a plan for settling new territories. *Lesson 1, Page 307*

James Madison

Why is James Madison called the "Father of the Constitution"? *Lesson 2, Page 311*

The Signing 1787

This quill pen was used in the signing of the new Constitution of the United States. *Lesson 2, Page 315*

The Government in Trouble

Main Idea With the Revolution over, the former colonies faced difficult problems.

Imagine a school with 13 classrooms — each with its own rules and no principal. No class will share its part of the hallway with the others. To make money, classes tax each other when they use each other's computers and books. Even worse, each class has its own kind of money. Money used by one class isn't always accepted in others. What a mess!

Now imagine that the school is a country — your country after winning the Revolution. The 13 classrooms are the 13 states, and they have similar problems. They fight over land and money, over boundaries, rivers, and trade. The spirit that kept them together during the war is fast disappearing. What are they going to do?

Key Vocabulary

constitution
territory
convention

Key Events

1781 Articles of Confederation approved
1786 Shays' Rebellion
1787 Northwest Ordinance

◀ Independence Hall, Philadelphia

1789	1790	1791

Celebrating the Constitution

Why did people celebrate the Constitution 200 years after it was written? *Lesson 3, Page 321*

The New President   1789

People wondered how to treat the new President of the United States. *Lesson 4, Page 323*

Benjamin Banneker

Benjamin Banneker helped plan Washington, D.C., the new American capital. *Lesson 4, Page 325*

Do you think your classroom has a government? If so, what kind does it have?

? ? ? ? ? ? ? ? ? ? ? ? ? ?

States issued paper money in different amounts. The bill *(below)* from Pennsylvania was worth just 12 shillings. The bill from Virginia was worth $1,200 dollars. **Economics:** *Why did differences in money make buying and selling between states difficult?*

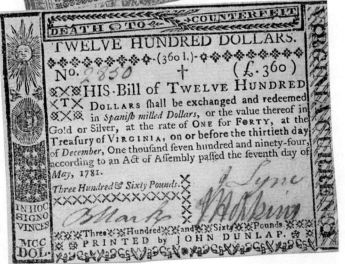

Thirteen Nations or One?

Focus *What happened to the 13 states after the Revolution?*

Before the Revolution, the colonists had been British subjects. Who were they afterwards? We now speak of them as Americans, but back then people in the 13 former colonies didn't think of themselves that way. They thought of themselves as Virginians or New Yorkers first, and Americans second.

In fact, the former colonists had never had a real national government. During the war, people knew they had to work together to defeat Britain. However, Congress had limited powers. It didn't even have the power to tax. It could only ask the states for money, but the states could refuse. Remember the hard winter Washington and his army spent at Valley Forge? Part of the reason for the ragged uniforms and empty stomachs was that the Continental Congress couldn't raise enough money to support the army.

After the war, the former colonies saw even less need to give Congress much power. They were afraid Congress might meddle in their affairs as Parliament had. Each state had its own **constitution,** a written plan of how its government worked. In 1781 the states finally approved the Articles of Confederation, a national constitution that Congress had passed in 1777. However, the Articles gave most powers to the states.

Most of the states had their own navies. At the end of the war, some of those navies were larger than the Continental navy. Even the nation's money had little value. In fact, when people wanted to say something was worthless, they said it was "not worth a Continental" — referring to the paper money the Continental Congress issued. In its place, people used gold or silver coins from other countries.

Without a strong national government, the states began to act like 13 different countries. Maryland and Virginia both claimed the right to control the Potomac River. New Jersey placed a tax on goods brought into it from New York. And New York taxed goods from New Jersey. When John Adams went to London in 1785 as an ambassador, the British made fun of him. Do you represent one nation, they asked, or 13?

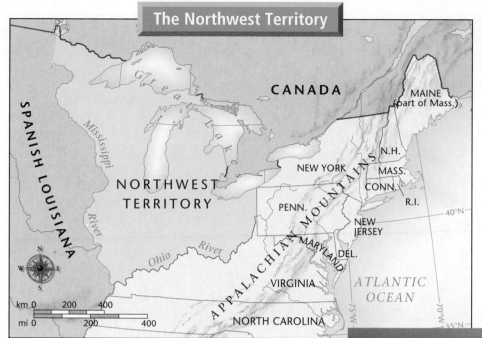

The Northwest Territory

Congress made clear rules about how to divide and sell land in the Northwest Territory. **Map Skill:** *What bodies of water played a role in the rapid settlement of the Northwest Territory?*

One Problem Solved

Focus *How did Congress settle the disputes over the Northwest Territory?*

By the early 1780s, people by the tens of thousands were moving west across the Appalachian Mountains and starting new communities. Here was another headache for Congress. Some of this land was claimed by more than one state. Native Americans insisted the land was theirs. Who would control it?

The division of land into square plots in the Northwest Territory created fields that look like a patchwork quilt.

Although it took time, states without claims were able to persuade other states that Congress should control the western lands, which were called the Northwest Territory. (*See map above.*) Congress also signed a peace treaty with the Native Americans to allow settlers to live there. Then it drew up rules by which the lands north of the Ohio River could become new states. Five states were eventually carved out of the Northwest Territory.

One important rule was a ban on slavery. At the time, no one realized just how important this would turn out to be. The rules became law under the Northwest Ordinance of 1787, which became the model for settling all future territories. A **territory** is an area of land under the rule of government. The Ordinance was one accomplishment of which Congress could be proud.

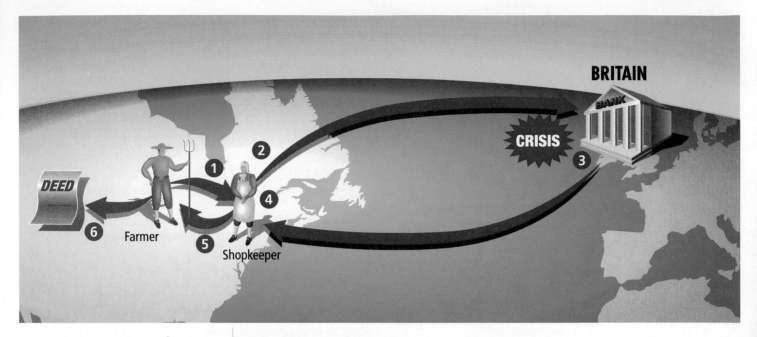

Chain of Debt

A chain of borrowing linked farmers in Massachusetts to bankers in London.

1 Farmers buy goods on credit from shopkeepers.

2 Shopkeepers borrow money from American merchants.

3 Merchants (not shown on diagram) borrow money from British banks. When the banks face a crisis, they demand money from merchants.

4 Merchants (not shown) demand money from shopkeepers.

5 Shopkeepers demand money from farmers.

6 Farmers have to sell their land. With less land they can not pay their debts.

Chart Skill: *Why did a financial crisis in Great Britain result in Massachusetts farmers having to sell land to pay their debts?*

A Second Revolution?

Focus *What was the cause of Shays' Rebellion and what were its effects?*

The national government was still weak, as a threatened rebellion revealed. Like the rebellion that had led to the Revolution, the fight began over taxes. Fighting the world's largest empire had been expensive. The states had borrowed large amounts of money to pay for the war. To pay back that money, the states raised taxes. Many farmers were unable to pay these new taxes.

The problem was especially bad for farmers in western Massachusetts. Like most farmers, they had to borrow money between harvests. Higher taxes made it harder to pay back their loans. When they failed to repay, the state took away their farms.

By 1786, farmers in western Massachusetts were furious. Under the leadership of Daniel Shays, a hero of the Battle of Bunker Hill, they asked the state for time to pay their debts. The state ignored them and continued to seize farms.

The farmers made plans to defend themselves. One farmer said: "The great men are going to get all we have, and I think it is time for us to rise and put a stop to it, and have no more courts, nor sheriffs, nor collectors, nor lawyers."

Some of the farmers marched on several courthouses where farms were to be sold. They closed the courthouses, stopping the sales. The states sent soldiers — paid for by wealthy merchants —

to confront the farmers. The farmers, however, would not be scared off. They did not believe that soldiers who had fought beside them in the Revolution would shoot them. They were wrong. The troops fired, leaving four farmers dead.

Shays' Rebellion, as it came to be called, was soon over. It sent shock waves through the country. To George Washington, it looked as though the long war to establish a new nation had been fought for nothing. He asked:

This plaque in Springfield, Massachusetts, marks the spot where Shays' Rebellion came to an end in early 1787.

> **"A**re we to have the goodly fabric, that eight years were spent in raising, pulled over our heads? What is the cause of all these commotions [these troubles]? When and how will they end?**"**

With unrest spreading now, Congress asked each state to send delegates to a **convention** in Philadelphia in May of 1787. A convention is a meeting of people who share a common purpose. The purpose of this convention would be to revise the Articles of Confederation and make them stronger.

Lesson Review

1780	1785	1790

1781
Articles of Confederation approved

1786
Shays' Rebellion

1787
Northwest Ordinance

1. **Key Vocabulary:** Write a paragraph about the response to Shays' Rebellion using **constitution** and **convention**.

2. **Focus:** What happened to the 13 states after the Revolution?

3. **Focus:** How did Congress settle the disputes over the Northwest Territory?

4. **Focus:** What was the cause of Shays' Rebellion and what were its effects?

5. **Critical Thinking: Problem Solving** The

Massachusetts farmers want more time to pay back their loans, but the state refuses. What compromise can you suggest?

6. **Geography:** In 1787 the Northwest Territory was considered the far west. What is this region called today?

7. **Citizenship/Writing Activity:** Form a group of four or five. Write rules for the school described at the start of this lesson.

Something New Under the Sun

Main Idea The Constitutional Convention drew up a plan for a new kind of national government.

Key Vocabulary
democracy
republic
compromise
ratify
federal system

Key Events

1787 Constitutional Convention

1788 Constitution ratified

Like many Americans, George Washington felt an urgent need to create a new, stronger national government. He feared that independent states fighting each other and their national government would lead only to destruction. As he wrote to his friend James Madison, a member of Virginia's state assembly, in early 1787:

> **"T**hirteen sovereignties pulling against each other and all tugging at the federal head, will soon bring ruin on the whole.**"**

Madison favored a strong national government. But he wanted to make sure it would be the best government it could be.

Delegates

James Madison

Member of Congress
Madison was the first convention delegate to arrive. He worked out a plan for a new government. He also kept notes on the convention. He's known as the Father of the Constitution.

Roger Sherman

Lawyer
He was called "An old Puritan, honest as an angel" by John Adams. A former farmer and shoemaker, Sherman taught himself the law. His Great Compromise helped the delegates resolve their differences.

Madison's Plan

FOCUS *How did James Madison come up with a plan for a strong national government?*

In the fall of 1786, Madison wrote to Thomas Jefferson in France, asking for books about the history of democracies. A **democracy** is a government in which people make political decisions by voting, and the majority rules. The books arrived by the trunkload, and Madison pored over them. He made long lists of the strengths and weaknesses of earlier democratic governments in ancient Greece, in Switzerland, in the Netherlands, and Germany.

Many Americans were afraid a strong national government could become as overbearing as Great Britain's had been. Patrick Henry, for example, refused to be a delegate to the 1787 convention. When he was asked why, the famous speaker answered simply, "I smelt a rat."

Madison understood these fears. He drew a plan for the new republic very carefully. A **republic** is a government in which citizens elect leaders to represent them. In Madison's plan, the new government would consist of different branches, or parts. Each branch would have some power but wouldn't be able to make full use of it unless other branches agreed. Madison believed that with several branches competing for power, none would be able to get too much.

Benjamin Franklin

Scientist, Politician
A great debater and the oldest delegate, Franklin brought his skills to the Convention. With his sense of humor, he made the delegates laugh when tensions rose too high. Franklin had to be carried to the Convention because he was ill.

Edmund Randolph

Governor of Virginia
A popular man, Randolph had the honor of presenting Madison's idea for a new Constitution to the delegates. He was one of a few who did not sign the Constitution. He felt it gave too much power to the national government.

The Convention Begins

After preparing so carefully, Madison must have been discouraged by the way the convention started. Of 13 states, delegates from only seven were present when the convention began on May 25, 1787. Many of the others were delayed by spring rains that had turned roads to mud. Rhode Island refused to send any delegates.

Yet the delegates gathered in the Pennsylvania State House included some of the nation's best leaders. Many had fought in the Revolution and served in Congress. General Washington was there. So were Edmund Randolph, the popular governor of Virginia; Alexander Hamilton, an intelligent young man from New York;

Philadelphia during the Constitutional Convention

The map below shows the layout of Philadelphia in the late 1700s. The Second Continental Congress was held in the Pennsylvania State House, not Carpenters' Hall. **Map Skill:** *Were these two buildings located in the same or in different parts of the city?*

Congress Hall became the meeting place of the United States Congress from 1790 to 1800. The Senate Chamber is shown here.

Built between 1732 and 1757 as the Pennsylvania State House, Independence Hall was the site of the adoption of The Declaration of Independence and the drafting of the United States Constitution.

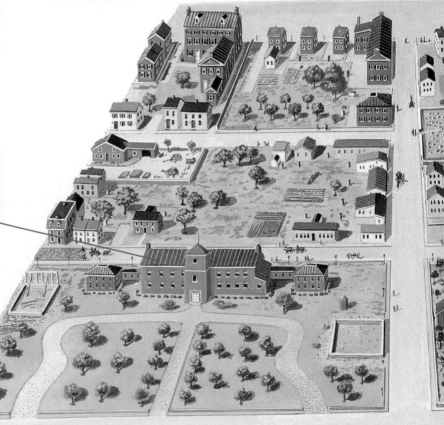

and Pennsylvania's Gouverneur Morris, a wonderful speaker. Benjamin Franklin, now 81, stayed home that first day because of the pouring rain, but he too would join the convention.

No one at the convention represented the nation's nearly two million women, 700,000 African Americans, or tens of thousands of Native Americans. No one represented the nation's small farmers either, yet the farmers were heard. As the delegates settled down to work, messengers brought word that a group of angry farmers in Virginia had set fire to a courthouse and burned it to the ground. As they worked, the delegates kept uprisings like that one in mind. They knew they needed to find a way to stop them.

The chessmen in Ben Franklin's traveling chess set are carved from ivory and the squares on the board are made of leather.
Culture: *Why might Franklin have wanted a chess game with him when he traveled?*

Carpenters' Hall was built in 1770 by the Carpenters' Guild of Philadelphia. The delegates to the First Continental Congress met here in September 1774.

After months of debate, the delegates stepped forward to sign the completed Constitution.

Problems and Compromises

Focus *How did the delegates to the Constitutional Convention settle their differences?*

Quickly the delegates chose Washington to head the convention. That was easy. They also posted guards to keep people from hearing what was said inside. They didn't want the country arguing about their ideas until they'd agreed to them. Despite the heat, for the next four months the convention went on behind closed doors.

By now most delegates realized they needed to do more than just strengthen the Articles of Confederation. Randolph presented Madison's well-thought-out plan for a new constitution. It called for a national government divided into three branches. Most delegates were already used to three-branch governments in their own states. Madison also suggested they divide one branch, Congress, into two different parts, or houses.

Up to this time each state had had an equal voice in Congress. Under Madison's plan, a state's number of representatives in each house would depend on population. Large states would have far more power than before. Delegates from the smaller states were outraged. They said they would never accept this plan.

The delegates argued throughout June and the first half of July. It was the hottest summer in almost 40 years. Temperatures soared and tempers frayed. All that kept the convention together was the knowledge that if it failed, America might fail, too.

Finally, Roger Sherman offered a solution that has become known as the Great Compromise. A **compromise** is an agreement in which each side of an argument gives up something it wants in order to end a dispute. The delegates compromised by agreeing that each state would have an equal vote in one house of Congress, the Senate. In the other house, the House of Representatives, votes would be based on a state's population.

That raised another problem. In counting the people in each state, should enslaved people be counted? Southern delegates said yes. Northern delegates said no, because enslaved people were not allowed to vote. The delegates reached a second compromise. Only three-fifths of a state's enslaved people would be counted in determining how many representatives that state had in Congress. The three-fifths compromise was a painful reminder that enslaved African Americans did not receive equal treatment under the new Constitution.

On September 17, 1787, after weeks of work, 39 delegates finally signed the Constitution. Their plan could take effect only if nine of the states **ratified,** or approved, it. And that, every one of them knew, would be a long, uphill battle.

The Great Compromise

Large states said:
In both houses of Congress, states with more people should have more votes.

Small states said:
In both houses of Congress, all states should have the same number of votes.

Great Compromise:
Senate: Equal number of votes for each state.
House of Representatives: States with more people have more votes.

Chart Skill: *How did this compromise affect the balance of power between large and small states?*

The People Speak

Focus *How was the Constitution approved by the states?*

Soon the debate that had raged in Philadelphia all summer spread across the nation. Those who supported the Constitution called themselves Federalists. They were for a **federal system** of government, one in which power is shared between a nation and its smaller parts, the states. Federalist leaders argued their side in *The Federalist Papers. (See Historical Documents section on page 654.)* Their opponents,

All during the convention Franklin had wondered whether the half sun on the back of Washington's chair was rising or setting. When the Constitution was finally complete, he said he realized it was a rising sun. **History:** *What do you think he meant?*

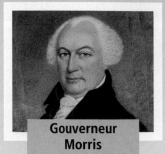
who wanted the states to have more power, were called Antifederalists.

The Antifederalists pointed out that the delegates had only been asked to revise the Articles of Confederation. Why had they come up with a plan for a whole new government? The Antifederalists also objected that the Constitution had no bill of rights, as most state constitutions did. As writer Mercy Otis Warren put it,

> "The rights of individuals should be the primary object of all governments."

Writing from Paris, Thomas Jefferson agreed. The Constitution seemed destined for defeat. Then the Federalists promised to add a bill of rights. With this promise, New Hampshire became the ninth state to ratify on June 21, 1788. Virginia and New York soon followed. Eventually all 13 states ratified the Constitution.

On July 4, 1788, Philadelphians held a huge parade to celebrate ratification. Benjamin Rush, the Philadelphia doctor who had signed the Declaration of Independence, described how people walked the streets in "solemn silence." They seemed too moved for cheering. "'Tis done," Rush wrote. "We have become a nation."

Lesson Review

1786	1788	1790

1787
Constitutional Convention

1788
Constitution ratified

1. **Key Vocabulary:** Describe the Constitutional Convention using the words democracy, republic, compromise, ratify, and federal system.

2. **Focus:** How did James Madison come up with a plan for a strong national government?

3. **Focus:** How did the delegates to the Constitutional Convention settle their differences?

4. **Focus:** How was the Constitution approved by the states?

5. **Critical Thinking: Interpret** List the benefits of keeping the Constitutional Convention debate secret.

6. **Theme: Governing Ourselves** Why did the Antifederalists want states to have more power than the federal government?

7. **Citizenship/Art Activity:** Act out the debate over representation. Take on the roles of delegates from large and small states. Then act out the moment when Sherman offers his compromise.

Using Organizational Charts

Who's in Charge?

Who has power? How should it be used? Delegates at the Constitutional Convention answered these questions. They set up our government's organization. The President heads one branch of government. How can you easily show the structure of this branch of government, or any other organization? An **organizational chart** uses words and arrows to show who's in charge.

① Here's How

Read the chart's title. Then study the chart.

- Look at the boxes. Notice the placement of each one. This placement can give you information about the flow of power. For example, if boxes are stacked one on top of the other, the box above has power over the box below.

- Look at the arrows. What do they connect? In which direction do they point? This chart, for example, shows that the President has authority over the executive branch.

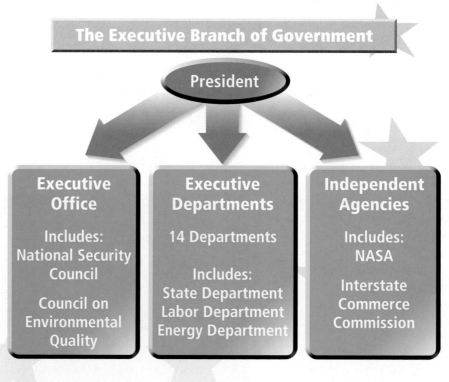

The Executive Branch of Government

President

Executive Office	Executive Departments	Independent Agencies
Includes: National Security Council Council on Environmental Quality	14 Departments Includes: State Department Labor Department Energy Department	Includes: NASA Interstate Commerce Commission

② Think It Through

What else might an organizational chart be useful for? What more can an organizational chart show you than the flow of power?

③ Use It

1. Write a sentence or two about the chart. Explain what it shows you about the organization of this branch of government.

2. Make a chart that shows the organization of your school.

Our Federal Government

Key Vocabulary

legislative branch
executive branch
judicial branch
checks and balances
amendment

Key Events

1791 The states
approve the Bill of
Rights

Main Idea The Constitution divided government power in a way that had never been tried before.

> **"I**f men were angels, no government would be necessary. If angels were to govern men, [no] controls on government would be necessary. **"**

James Madison wrote these famous words. He knew, as well as anyone, that governments need to be controlled. This was the reason he suggested having a government with three branches. Each branch, he hoped, would keep the others from becoming too powerful. That is also why today the national government and the states divide power between them.

How does a divided government work? And what happens when the people aren't happy with the way it's working?

Once a year the President delivers a speech to Congress on the state of the nation.

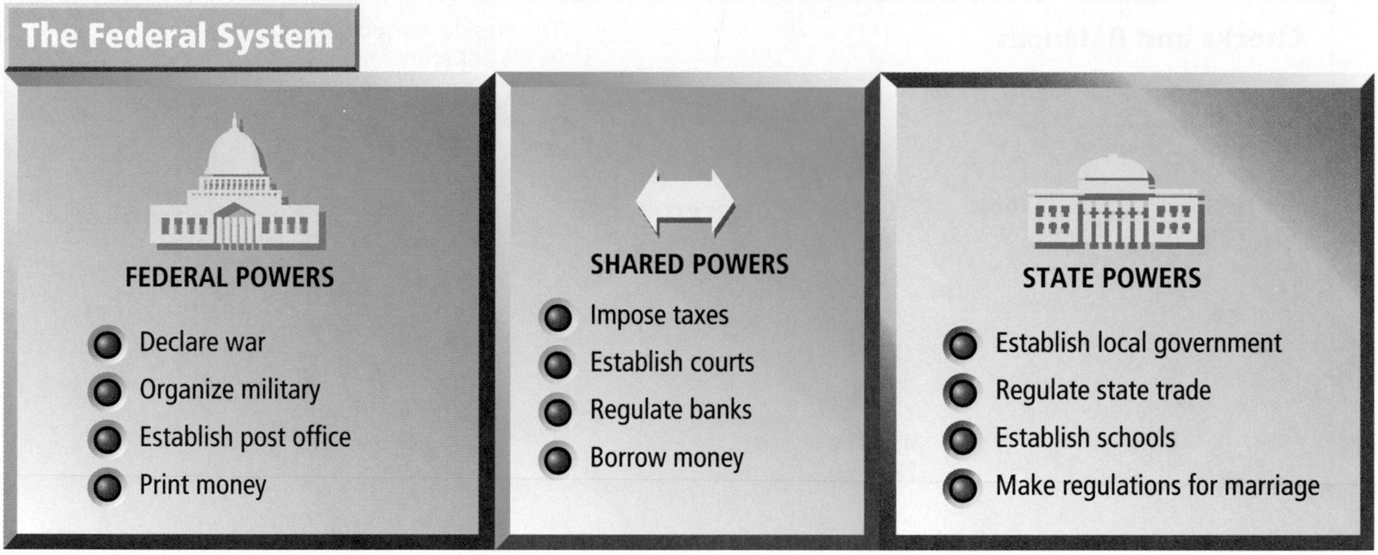

The Federal System

FEDERAL POWERS
- Declare war
- Organize military
- Establish post office
- Print money

SHARED POWERS
- Impose taxes
- Establish courts
- Regulate banks
- Borrow money

STATE POWERS
- Establish local government
- Regulate state trade
- Establish schools
- Make regulations for marriage

Chart Skills: *Identify one power the states have that the national government does not.*

Sharing Power

Focus *How does the Constitution divide power between the states and the federal government?*

The problem with the government under the Articles of Confederation was that it was too weak. Under the Constitution the national government is much stronger. For example, it can raise taxes to get the money it needs and regulate trade between states, two things the old government could not do. States still have some power, though. The U.S. government is called a federal government because it shares power with the states.

The Constitution says which powers belong to the national government and which ones belong to the states. The framers of the Constitution believed local voters should decide local issues. So state governments control such important areas as education, welfare, and health. *(See the chart above.)* Not all democratic nations are ruled this way. In countries like Britain and France, the national government tells local governments what they can and cannot do.

A System of Checks and Balances

Focus *How does the Constitution separate powers within the federal government?*

The Constitutional Convention decided upon a government of three branches. Each branch has its own job. The **legislative branch,** or Congress, makes the laws. As Madison wanted, Congress is divided into two houses — the Senate and the House of Representatives.

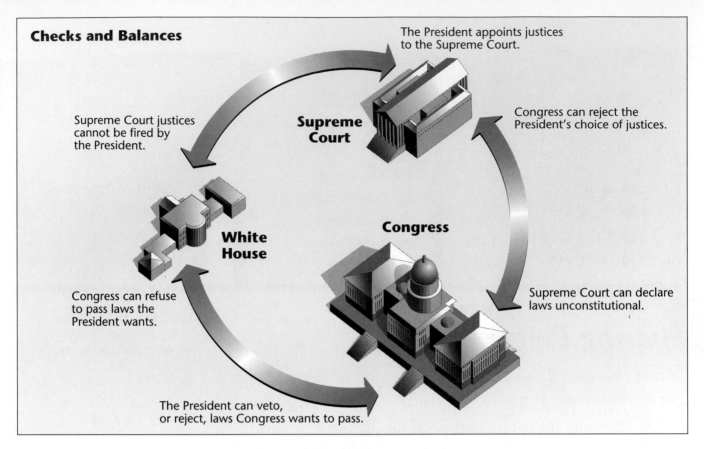

Checks and Balances

The President appoints justices to the Supreme Court.

Supreme Court

Supreme Court justices cannot be fired by the President.

Congress can reject the President's choice of justices.

White House

Congress

Congress can refuse to pass laws the President wants.

Supreme Court can declare laws unconstitutional.

The President can veto, or reject, laws Congress wants to pass.

The three branches of the government check and balance each other. **Chart Skill:** *How does Congress check the President? How does the President check the Supreme Court? How does the Supreme Court check Congress?*

The President, who heads the **executive branch,** carries out the laws. The President also conducts relations with other countries and heads the armed forces. The Supreme Court heads the **judicial branch**. If an argument arises about the meaning of a law or the Constitution, the Supreme Court settles the dispute. *(See chart above.)*

Each government branch can do some things on its own but also depends on the other branches. For example, the President is commander-in-chief of the armed forces, but only Congress can declare war. This system of separating government powers is called **checks and balances**. Each branch has the power to check, or halt, the power of the others.

Changing the Constitution

Focus *How does the Constitution provide for change?*

> **"I**n framing a system which we wish to last for ages, we should not lose sight of the changes which ages will produce.**"**

James Madison, who wrote these words, knew that as times changed, the Constitution would have to change too. So he and the other delegates created a way for the people to make any changes, or **amendments,** that were needed. Three-quarters of the states must approve an amendment for it to take effect.

In all, Americans have passed 27 amendments since 1789. As promised, the first 10 amendments — the Bill of Rights — were passed in 1791, three years after the Constitution went into effect. As you remember, democracy means the majority rules. What if the majority passed a law that hurt others? The Bill of Rights protects individual rights. It lists rights that cannot be taken away. *(See the Historical Documents section at the back of the book and the Bill of Rights feature on page 330.)*

Many amendments following the Bill of Rights broadened these rights. Although the Constitution begins "We, the people," as first written, it left some people out. Since then it has been amended to outlaw slavery, give all citizens the right to vote, and change some of the government's basic rules. Americans have struggled to make sure that "We, the people," the opening words of the Constitution, truly means all the people, and that is why we chose We the People as the title for your social studies program.

Then & Now

In May 1987 people celebrated the bicentennial, or 200th birthday, of the United States Constitution. They held parades, gave speeches, and released balloons to honor this very important document and the role it plays in the government of the United States.

Lesson Review

```
1790          1791          1792
```
1791
States approve Bill of Rights

1. **Key Vocabulary:** Use three other key terms to describe checks and balances.

2. **Focus:** How does the Constitution divide power between the states and the federal government?

3. **Focus:** How does the Constitution separate powers within the federal government?

4. **Focus:** How does the Constitution provide for change?

5. **Critical Thinking: Decision Making** Should amending the Constitution be easy or difficult? Give reasons for your answer.

6. **Theme: Governing Ourselves** How do checks and balances protect democracy?

7. **Citizenship/Research Activity:** Find out how a bill becomes law and describe the process in chart form.

A New Beginning

Main Idea George Washington led the new government.

Key Vocabulary

inauguration
precedent
cabinet
political party

Key Events

1789 George Washington becomes the first President

1791 Washington, D.C., planned

Americans unanimously elected George Washington as the first President in February 1789. Although he wanted to stay at Mount Vernon, his Virginia plantation, he felt a sense of duty to the American people. That April he left Virginia and traveled to New York City to be sworn in. Crowds cheered all along the way.

On April 30, a bright spring afternoon, Washington had his **inauguration** — his swearing in as President. He stood on the platform outside New York's Federal Hall. People packed the streets, windows, and rooftops. After a simple ceremony, the new President slowly and nervously delivered a short speech. "This great man," a senator later wrote, was more disturbed "than ever he was by . . . cannon. He trembled, and several times could [hardly] read."

Washington Takes Office

Focus *What important precedents did Washington set?*

Washington had good reason to be nervous. He was now the head of a new kind of government — one that had never been tried before. To make matters worse, Washington knew that everything he did would become a **precedent,** or model, for future presidents. Every choice he made, from what he was called to the way he dealt with foreign nations, would have long-lasting effects.

Washington began by appointing four advisors to help him make decisions. They are shown in the painting on the right. Three of these advisors headed departments responsible for different tasks. They came to be called the President's **cabinet,** or group of advisors. Every President since has had one.

This pitcher was made in honor of George Washington's inauguration as President in 1789.

Washington's Cabinet

George Washington realized he would need help to make difficult and complicated decisions for the nation. At its first session in 1789, Congress established four executive posts: Secretary of State, Secretary of the Treasury, Secretary of War, and Attorney General. Washington chose the best people he could find to fill these posts. Soon he was consulting them regularly for their opinions and advice. Today, the 14 leaders of the executive departments are known as the cabinet.

The people in the painting are *(from left to right)*:

Henry Knox, Secretary of War, was in charge of military activities.

Thomas Jefferson was Secretary of State. He took care of relations with foreign countries, coining money, and patents.

Edmund Randolph was Attorney General. He represented the government in legal matters.

Alexander Hamilton was Secretary of the Treasury. He was in charge of financial matters.

George Washington headed the executive branch.

Congress had to figure out how to address the president. John Adams suggested "His Most Benign Highness," but that was too undemocratic. Yet "Mr. Washington" seemed too informal. Congress finally settled on the simple but dignified "Mr. President."

Two Views of the Future

Focus *What were the opposing views of the nation's future in the 1790s?*

Two men in Washington's cabinet, Jefferson and Hamilton, took opposing sides on almost all issues facing Congress. Should the new government repay the money the old government had borrowed to fight the Revolution? Hamilton said yes. Jefferson said no. Should the United States help its old allies, the French, who were fighting

Thomas Jefferson was the first leader of the Republican party, which later became today's Democratic party. The modern Republican party was not founded until 1854.

Alexander Hamilton founded the Federalist party. Although the name was the same, this party was different from the group of people, known as the Federalists, who supported the ratification of the Constitution.

their own revolution? Jefferson said yes. Hamilton said no. Hamilton wanted to establish a national bank. Jefferson didn't.

Hamilton and Jefferson had different ideas about government, too. Hamilton thought most people needed to be ruled by the rich and powerful. A strong national government, he believed, was needed to keep order. Jefferson worried that a government that was too strong could take away people's freedom. He trusted most ordinary people to rule themselves. He said:

> **"I** *have no fear but that the result of our experiment will be that men may be trusted to govern themselves without a master.* **"**

Hamilton, of course, disagreed. He said:

> **"I**t *has been observed that a pure democracy, if it were practicable, would be the most perfect government. Experience has proved that no position is more false than this.* **"**

They also had different pictures of the kind of country the United States should be. Hamilton pictured a nation of cities and large businesses. Jefferson pictured a nation of family farms.

By the time Washington left office in 1797, many Americans had chosen sides in this dispute. Hamilton and his supporters formed a political party called the Federalist party. A **political party** is a group of people with similar goals who work together to gain power in government. Jefferson, Madison, and others formed the Republican party.

After two terms as President, Washington was ready to retire. Once again, he was setting a precedent. For over 140 years, no President would seek a third term. George Washington had always disliked political parties. In his farewell address, he warned against the bad effects of "the spirit of party," which causes "jealousies and false alarms." Americans chose to ignore this advice. He also said that America's policy should be "to steer clear of permanent alliances, with any portion of the foreign world." Americans followed this advice for another 100 years.

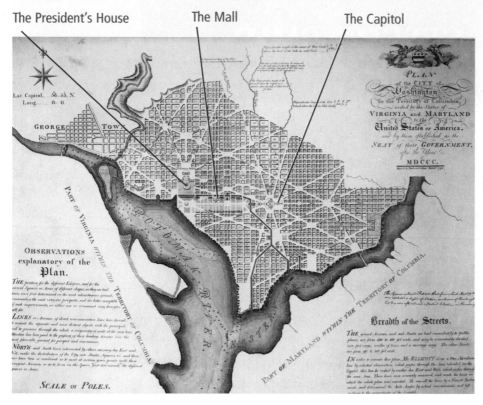

The President's House   The Mall   The Capitol

PLAN of the CITY of Washington in the Territory of Columbia, ceded by the States of VIRGINIA and MARYLAND to the United States of America, and by them established as the SEAT of their GOVERNMENT, after the Year MDCCC.

Washington is located in the District of Columbia between Maryland and Virginia.

Biography

Benjamin Banneker

Banneker, who taught himself astronomy, made calculations and predictions for a yearly almanac. George Washington appointed him to the commission that laid out Washington, D.C.

Washington served his two terms in New York and Philadelphia. In 1791 he chose the spot for a new capital along the Potomac River. French engineer Pierre L'Enfant (lahn FAHN) planned the city. American surveyors Andrew Ellicott and Benjamin Banneker helped. It would be called Washington, D.C., in honor of the nation's first President.

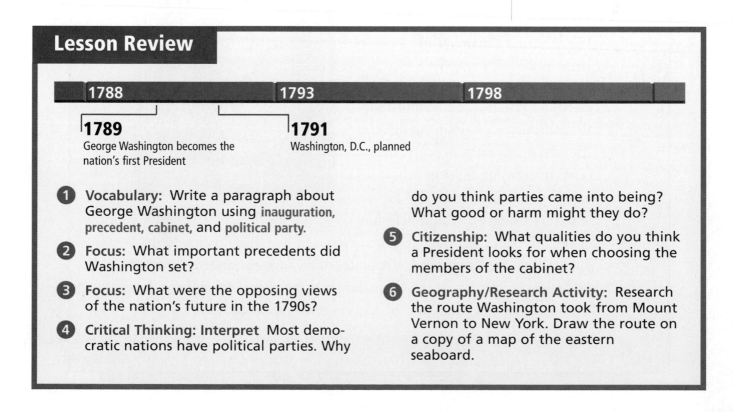

Lesson Review

1788   1793   1798

1789
George Washington becomes the nation's first President

1791
Washington, D.C., planned

1. **Vocabulary:** Write a paragraph about George Washington using **inauguration**, **precedent**, **cabinet**, and **political party**.

2. **Focus:** What important precedents did Washington set?

3. **Focus:** What were the opposing views of the nation's future in the 1790s?

4. **Critical Thinking: Interpret** Most democratic nations have political parties. Why do you think parties came into being? What good or harm might they do?

5. **Citizenship:** What qualities do you think a President looks for when choosing the members of the cabinet?

6. **Geography/Research Activity:** Research the route Washington took from Mount Vernon to New York. Draw the route on a copy of a map of the eastern seaboard.

Making Decisions

Who Judges the Laws?

Suppose you have a job in your home, and you don't do it. Or you forget to call home when you get to a friend's house. Who decides what happens to you? In most homes, parents do. Sometimes you can talk with them to change their rules. But most often, they have the final say. In the United States, the Supreme Court has the final say. The case study below shows how this came to be.

Case Study

Marbury v. Madison

In 1803, the Supreme Court decided the case of William Marbury. Marbury was named a judge by President Adams. But when President Jefferson took over, Marbury's papers hadn't been processed. So Jefferson denied him the job. Marbury took John Madison, Jefferson's Secretary of State, to court for refusing him the job. Marbury argued that a 1789 law passed by Congress would help him

Chief Justice John Marshall

get the job back. But the Supreme Court, led by Chief Justice John Marshall, decided that the law violated the Constitution. Marbury lost his case. Ever since, the Court has had the power to strike down any Act of Congress it believes is unconstitutional.

Take Action

The Supreme Court's power to decide whether a law is constitutional is called judicial review. Suppose you were a judge. On what would you base your judgments? Are there rules for judging rules? Try this:

1 You are on the Supreme Court. A teacher comes before you and says: "The rule in my classroom is no talking without raising your hand and being called on! These children broke that rule:

Wilma for asking Fred for a piece of paper.
Fred for telling her to 'ask someone else.'
George for telling Martha he dislikes cherries.
Martha for laughing loudly.
Juliet for saying 'God Bless you' when Romeo sneezed. (He's allergic to chalk dust.)
Al for telling Sue, 'stop it.' (Sue took his chair.)"

2 The teacher wants everyone except Sue and Romeo to stay after school. Decide: did all these children break the law? Do they all deserve to be punished? What about Romeo and Sue? Vote on a final judgment for each student. Be able to state your reasons.

3 How did you decide that someone had broken the rule? Write a set of rules for judging rules.

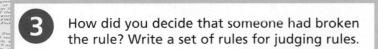

4 Share your vote and rules with the class. Did you all agree?

Tips for Making Decisions

- Think through your position and the reasons for it.
- Write down your thoughts. Use language that is simple and direct.
- Weigh each of the consequences before you make a final decision.

Research Activity

Marbury v. Madison was one of the earliest decisions in the long career of Chief Justice John Marshall. Marshall has been called the Great Chief Justice. Do research to find out why. Write up your findings in the form of a biography.

Chapter Review

Chapter Review Timeline

| 1786 | 1787 | 1788 | 1789 | 1790 | 1791 |

1787
Constitutional Convention

1789
George Washington becomes the first President

1786
Shays' Rebellion

1788
Constitution ratified

1791
The states approve the Bill of Rights

Summarizing the Main Idea

1 Copy the chart below and fill in the missing information.

Topic	Problem	Solution
Northwest Territory	*Land was claimed by more than one state.*	
Shays' Rebellion		
Constitutional Convention		

Vocabulary

2 Using at least 10 of the following terms, write a newspaper article describing the newly formed American government in 1787.

constitution (p. 306)
territory (p. 307)
convention (p. 309)
democracy (p. 311)
republic (p. 311)
compromise (p. 315)

ratify (p. 315)
federal system (p. 315)
legislative branch (p. 319)
executive branch (p. 320)
judicial branch (p. 320)

checks and balances (p. 320)
amendment (p. 321)
inauguration (p. 322)
precedent (p. 322)
cabinet (p. 322)

Reviewing the Facts

3 Why were the former colonies afraid to give Congress much power?

4 How did Congress shape the future of the Northwest Territory?

5 What was the result of Shays' Rebellion?

6 What did the Great Compromise do?

7 What are the responsibilities of the three branches of government?

8 Why is the system of checks and balances necessary?

9 What were the differences between Federalists and Republicans?

10 Create an organizational chart that shows how your school or class government is organized.

11 Look at the diagram on page 320. How is the information here similar to the information you would find in an organizational chart of the federal government?

Geography Skills

12 Compare the map on page 307 with the political map of the United States on pages 636–637. What five states were carved out of the Northwest Territory?

13 Look at the political map of the United States on pages 636–637. Do you think Washington, D.C., is still an appropriate place for the government to be located?

Critical Thinking

14 **Sequence** Create a timeline showing the events that shaped the nation's government from the end of the Revolutionary War to Washington's inauguration.

15 **Decision Making** Imagine you were helping to organize a school government. What kind of government would you suggest?

Writing: Citizenship and History

16 **Citizenship** What qualities do you think are necessary in a President of the United States?

17 **History** Read Jefferson's and Hamilton's statements on page 324. Write a response agreeing or disagreeing with one statement.

Activities

National Heritage/Research Activity
Find out more about the Constitution. Where is the original copy of it stored? What steps have been taken to keep this copy from decaying?

History/Writing Activity
Put yourself in the position of an African American, a Native American, or a woman when the Constitution was ratified. Then write a journal entry explaining how you feel about the Constitution.

Internet Option

Check the **Internet Social Studies Center** for ideas on how to extend your theme project beyond your classroom.

THEME PROJECT CHECK-IN

Use the information about the creation of the Constitution to begin your theme project. Think about these questions:
• Who were some of the people who created the Constitution? What did they do?
• What issues did these people want to address in the Constitution?
• In what ways was the creation of the Constitution an important event?

The Bill of Rights

Sweet Land of Liberty

People in the United States talk a lot about liberty and freedom. In the Pledge of Allegiance, we say, "liberty and justice for all." In the Declaration of Independence, we read about "life, liberty, and the pursuit of happiness." In patriotic songs like the National Anthem and "America," we sing about "the land of the free" and "sweet land of liberty." If anyone tries to stop us from doing something we have the right to do, we may say, "You can't stop me. It's a free country."

The United States *is* a free country. The most important freedoms we have are named in the Bill of Rights. They are the first ten amendments to the Constitution.

Here is an explanation of what each one says. (You can read their exact words in the historical documents starting on page 654.)

In 1987, Americans celebrated the 200th anniversary of The Constitution of the United States. The American flag in this picture was made out of balloons.

First Amendment

The government may not favor one religion over another or stop people from practicing their religion in peace. People have the right to say, write, and publish their opinions. They also have the right to gather together and to ask the government to correct wrongs.

Second Amendment

Because people may need to fight to protect their state, they are allowed to own weapons.

Third Amendment

People don't have to let soldiers stay in their homes unless special laws are passed during a time of war.

Fourth Amendment

The police cannot search people or their homes without a good reason.

Fifth Amendment

People accused of a crime have the right to a fair trial. They can't be tried twice for the same crime. They don't have to speak against themselves at a trial.

Sixth Amendment

People accused of a crime have the right to a speedy, public trial by a jury. They also have the right to a lawyer, to be told what crime they are accused of, and to question witnesses.

Seventh Amendment

People who have a disagreement with each other about more than $20 have a right to a jury trial.

Eighth Amendment

Normally, people accused of a crime can stay out of jail if they put up bail, a sum of money they will lose if they don't show up for their trial. Courts cannot ask for bail that is too high, or fines that are too large, or punish anyone in cruel or unusual ways.

Ninth Amendment

People have other rights besides those mentioned in the Constitution.

Tenth Amendment

Any powers the Constitution does not give to the federal government belong to the states or the people.

The First Amendment guarantees freedom of religion.

Freedom of speech is one of the rights given in the First Amendment.

The Sixth Amendment guarantees the right to a speedy, public trial.

The Seventh Amendment allows people to have a jury trial if they have a disagreement over more than $20.

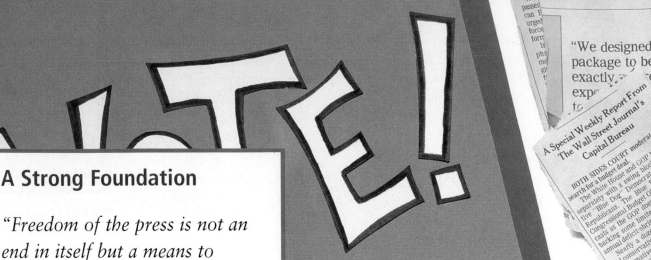

A Strong Foundation

"Freedom of the press is not an end in itself but a means to . . . a free society."

Supreme Court Justice
Felix Frankfurter, 1954

The First Amendment gives us rights to freedom of speech and freedom of the press. These rights allow us to speak our minds and hear other points of view. By allowing for a free exchange of ideas, First Amendment rights make other rights, like voting, possible.

Take Action Find out how freedom of speech affects voting.

• Divide into three groups to put on a TV broadcast. In two of the groups, choose someone to be a candidate for class president. In these groups, write the candidate's campaign speech. Make election posters. The third group must try to keep one of the candidates from being heard.

• When the show is over, discuss what happened. How did interfering with free speech affect a person's right to vote?

No Rights Without Responsibilities

"Freedom of speech does not include freedom to cry 'Fire' in a crowded theatre."

William Rusher,
American television commentator, 1979

The quote above suggests that rights also have responsibilities tied to them. Your right to speak your mind, for example, includes a responsibility not to create a danger to public safety.

Take Action Chart your rights and responsibilities.

• Make a chart. List the right in each Bill of Rights amendment. Next to it list the responsibility that you think is connected to each right.

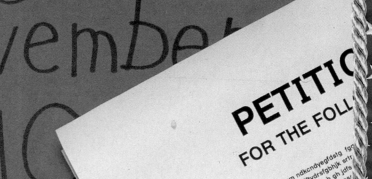

Agreeing to Disagree

". . . we must be prepared to extend [freedom] to everyone, whether they are rich or poor, whether they agree with us or not, no matter what their race or the color of their skin."

Republican Party presidential nominee
Wendell Wilkie, 1943

Rights are not just for people and ideas we agree with. Even unpopular ideas have a right to be heard.

Take Action Listen to opposing views.

- In pairs, choose an issue to debate. Here are some possibilities: school uniforms, year-round school, animal rights. Decide which side to take.

- As your partner presents his or her argument, listen carefully. Write down the points that he or she makes.

- Read them back. Does your partner agree that you listened carefully enough to really hear what was said?

Keeping Liberty Alive

"Liberty lies in the hearts of men and women; when it dies there, no constitution, no law, no court can save it."

Judge Learned Hand, 1944

You can keep the spirit of liberty alive by knowing and caring about the rights and responsibilities of freedom.

Take Action Share what you've learned about the First Amendment.

- Create a bulletin board. Display on it a poster of the Bill of Rights and other items that show the importance of the First Amendment. Here are some ideas: a rights and responsibilities chart or cartoon strip; a newspaper with sections inked out to show the importance of the First Amendment; a collage of photographs of people speaking in public.

CHAPTER 13

The Early Republic

Chapter Preview: *People, Places, and Events*

1770	1780	1790

Daniel Boone   1775

Daniel Boone traveled the Wilderness Trail. Where did the trail lead? *Lesson 1, Page 336*

Lewis and Clark

Find out why Lewis and Clark were exploring west of the Mississippi. *Lesson 1, Page 338*

Patriotic Symbols

Why did Americans create patriotic symbols? *Lesson 3, Page 355*

The Age of Jefferson

Main Idea The nation expanded rapidly westward during Thomas Jefferson's presidency.

He designed buildings, trained horses, played the violin, and studied the stars. He experimented with growing different kinds of plants. He collected one of the first libraries in the United States. He wrote the Declaration of Independence, and in 1801, he became the third President of the United States — Thomas Jefferson.

One of Jefferson's fondest dreams was to explore the land west of the Mississippi River. He wrote,

> **"I**t is impossible not to look forward to distant times, when our rapid multiplication will... cover the whole northern ... continent. **"**

Key Vocabulary

pioneer

frontier

expedition

corps

Key Events

1801 Jefferson becomes President

1803 The Louisiana Purchase

1804 The Lewis and Clark expedition begins

◀ This painting is called *Snap the Whip* and it was painted by Winslow Homer.

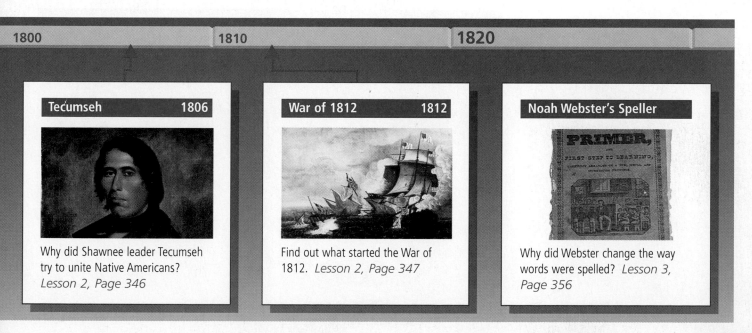

1800   **1810**   **1820**

Tecumseh 1806	War of 1812 1812	Noah Webster's Speller
Why did Shawnee leader Tecumseh try to unite Native Americans? *Lesson 2, Page 346*	Find out what started the War of 1812. *Lesson 2, Page 347*	Why did Webster change the way words were spelled? *Lesson 3, Page 356*

The linen rifleman's shirt *(below)* is a reproduction of the typical shirt of the last quarter of the 1700s. These shirts developed on the frontier.

Westward Movement

Focus *What early events set the stage for westward settlement?*

Even before Jefferson became President in 1801, settlers were pushing west. They moved across the Appalachian Mountains into the wilderness of what is now Kentucky, Tennessee, and Ohio.

Some people went for adventure. Some people went to hunt and trap. Others moved with their families in search of new land to farm. These settlers are known as pioneers. A **pioneer** is someone who ventures into an unknown or unclaimed territory. In reality, however, Native Americans had been living in the land west of the Appalachian Mountains for thousands of years.

Daniel Boone and the Wilderness Trail

Because the land west of the Appalachians was unknown to the pioneers, they called it the frontier. A **frontier** is a region just beyond, or at the edge of, a settled area. Those who explored this area and established roads for settlers to follow were called frontiersmen.

Daniel Boone was one of these frontiersmen. In 1775, Boone and others cut a trail from eastern Virginia to the Kentucky River, in present-day Kentucky. The 300-mile path ran through the Cumberland Gap, a space between the Appalachian Mountains. This "Wilderness Trail" opened the west for thousands of settlers.

Boone helped build a settlement in Kentucky which came to be named after him — Boonesborough. Similar settlements soon appeared all over the frontier.

This painting by George Caleb Bingham, which is set on the background of the Cumberland Gap area, shows Daniel Boone leading pioneers on the Wilderness Trail.

The Louisiana Purchase

Along with trails and roads, rivers provided an important means of transportation. Traders and farmers used the Mississippi and Ohio rivers to send goods to the southern port city of New Orleans. From there the goods were sent to Europe and Asia.

In the late 1700s, Spain controlled the land that the Mississippi flowed through (*see the map on the right*). France had turned this land over to Spain when they lost the French and Indian War. In 1800, Spain made an agreement with Napoleon, the emperor of France, to return the Louisiana Territory to France.

This alarmed President Jefferson. Would Napoleon close off the Mississippi River? Would frontiersmen and farmers still be able to sail their goods out of New Orleans?

Jefferson sent a special representative, James Monroe, to France. He arrived in April, 1803. Monroe's instructions were to buy New Orleans and the Floridas from France. To his surprise, however, Napoleon offered the entire Louisiana Territory, 828,000 square miles. Napoleon knew he was going to war with Great Britain and needed money to pay for it. President Jefferson considered the offer for some months, and then said yes. For a total of $27,267,622 — little more than five cents an acre — the United States doubled its size.

The Louisiana Purchase, 1803

This map shows the area of the Louisiana Purchase. **Map Skill:** *How does that area compare in size to that of the United States?*

The painting above shows Lewis and Clark with Sacagawea and York standing at the Great Falls of the Missouri River in 1805.

The Lewis and Clark Expedition

Focus *How did the Lewis and Clark expedition increase Americans' knowledge of the western territories?*

At the beginning of the 1800s, the land between the Mississippi River and the Rocky Mountains was a blank space on American maps. President Jefferson had long been curious about this vast, uncharted western land. Like others, he wondered if a river crossed the continent that would offer ships a shortcut to the Pacific Ocean.

Even before the Louisiana Purchase, Jefferson asked Congress to fund an expedition up the Missouri River. An **expedition** is a journey taken by a group for a definite purpose. Jefferson chose his private secretary, a young army captain named Meriwether Lewis, to lead what Jefferson called the "Corps of Discovery." A **corps** (kor) is an organized group of people. Lewis asked his old friend William Clark to serve as co-captain of the expedition.

Lewis and Clark set out from the frontier outpost of St. Louis in May 1804. About 40 men went with them, including an enslaved African American named York. In addition to trying to find a water route across the continent, their goal was to learn more about the land, plants, animals, and people of the West. *(See Think Like a Geographer on pages 340–341.)*

During the summer and fall of 1804, the expedition moved up the Missouri River. The explorers were struck by the huge herds of

This was William Clark's compass. Clark was responsible for mapping the territory.

Lewis and Clark's notes and maps were highly valuable to later explorers. **Science:** *Why do geographers keep journals?*

buffalo and the wide expanse of prairie grass. In November they built a fort near a Mandan (MAN dan) village in what is now North Dakota. A French trader and his Shoshone (shoh SHOH nee) wife, Sacagawea (sak uh juh WEE uh), joined them as interpreters.

The Corps set out again in April 1805. At the Rocky Mountains, they ran into a group of Shoshone. The Shoshone guided the explorers across the mountains to the Clearwater River.

After following the Clearwater to the Snake and Columbia rivers, the weary Corps reached the Pacific Ocean in November 1805. There they spent the winter at Fort Clatsop, before heading home in March 1806. They were back in St. Louis by September.

Although they did not find a Northwest Passage, Lewis and Clark brought back information about the lands west of the Mississippi and paved the way for further western expansion.

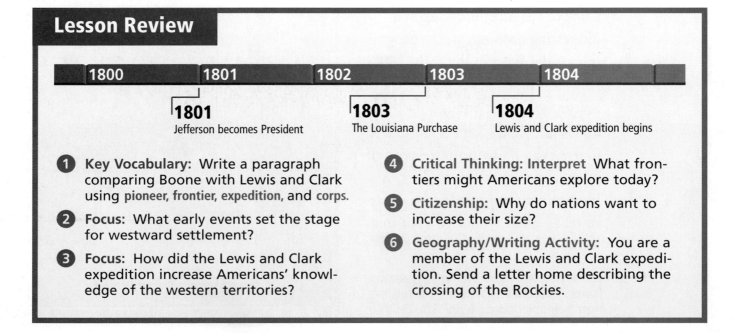

Lesson Review

1800	1801	1802	1803	1804

1801
Jefferson becomes President

1803
The Louisiana Purchase

1804
Lewis and Clark expedition begins

1 **Key Vocabulary:** Write a paragraph comparing Boone with Lewis and Clark using **pioneer**, **frontier**, **expedition**, and **corps**.

2 **Focus:** What early events set the stage for westward settlement?

3 **Focus:** How did the Lewis and Clark expedition increase Americans' knowledge of the western territories?

4 **Critical Thinking: Interpret** What frontiers might Americans explore today?

5 **Citizenship:** Why do nations want to increase their size?

6 **Geography/Writing Activity:** You are a member of the Lewis and Clark expedition. Send a letter home describing the crossing of the Rockies.

Places and Regions

How Did Lewis and Clark Learn About the West?

Thomas Jefferson's instructions to Lewis and Clark were clear. The purpose of their journey was to gather scientific and geographic information. President Jefferson wanted to find out about the territory west of the Mississippi: its rivers and mountains, its plants and wildlife, its climate and peoples. He told Lewis and Clark to take careful notes about everything they saw: "Your observations are to be taken with great pains and accuracy," he said.

Lewis and Clark kept detailed records of the land, plants, and wildlife they saw during their travels. They also learned by talking to the Native American peoples they met along the way. Their descriptions of the land they saw are some of the most accurate and interesting accounts of the geography of the West in the early 1800s.

Language Arts Connection

Lewis and Clark kept a journal. A journal is a daily written record of what someone thinks or does. A journal may be intended for others to read. What would you put in a journal about where you live?

Lewis and Clark called their winter camps "forts," because they were more permanent than their other camps. **Map Skill:** *How far was it from St. Louis to Mandan Fort?*

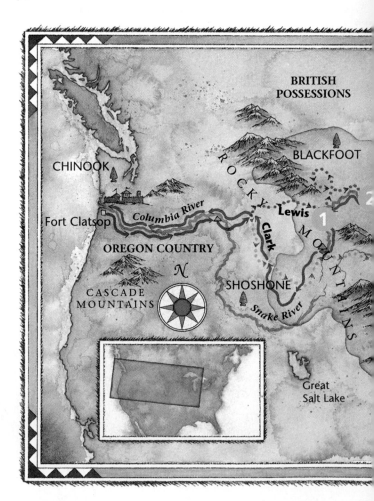

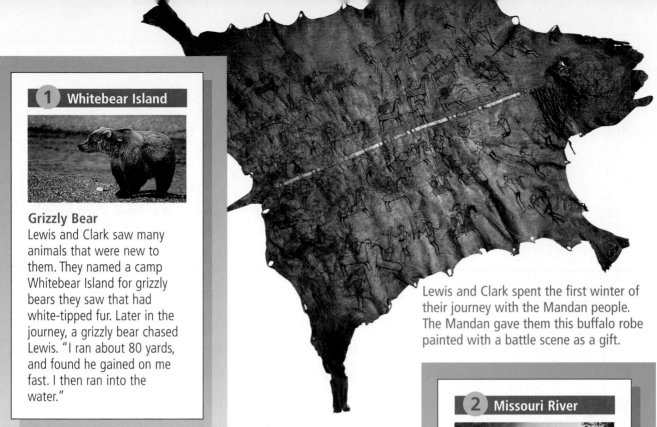

1 Whitebear Island

Grizzly Bear

Lewis and Clark saw many animals that were new to them. They named a camp Whitebear Island for grizzly bears they saw that had white-tipped fur. Later in the journey, a grizzly bear chased Lewis. "I ran about 80 yards, and found he gained on me fast. I then ran into the water."

Lewis and Clark spent the first winter of their journey with the Mandan people. The Mandan gave them this buffalo robe painted with a battle scene as a gift.

2 Missouri River

The Great Falls

Lewis heard the Great Falls of the Missouri River before he saw them. He wrote, "I saw the spray rise above the plain like a column of smoke." When he arrived at the falls, he saw "a smooth even sheet of water falling over a [cliff] of at least 80 feet; the remaining part...forms the grandest sight I ever beheld."

The Lewis and Clark Expedition, 1804-1806

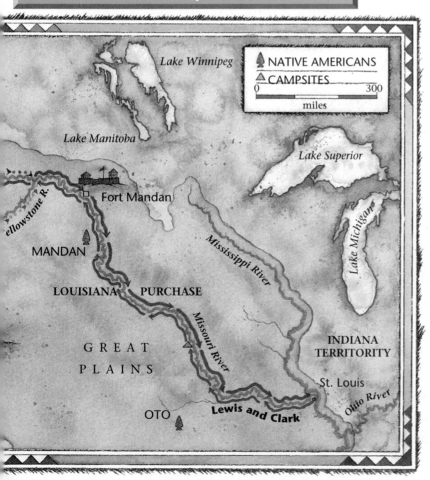

NATIVE AMERICANS
CAMPSITES
0   300
miles

Lake Winnipeg

Lake Manitoba

Lake Superior

Yellowstone R.

Fort Mandan

MANDAN

Mississippi River

Lake Michigan

LOUISIANA   PURCHASE

Missouri River

G R E A T
P L A I N S

INDIANA
TERRITORY

St. Louis

Ohio River

OTO   Lewis and Clark

Research Activity

Choose a park near you to explore with an adult.

1 Make a field trip to find out about its landforms, waterways, plants, and wildlife.

2 Write the results of your research in a journal.

3 Share it with the class.

THE STORY OF
SACAJAWEA,
Guide to Lewis and Clark
BY DELLA ROWLAND

ILLUSTRATED BY RICHARD LEONARD

Biography

SACAJAWEA, Guide to Lewis and Clark

by Della Rowland

One of the Lewis and Clark expedition guides, a French trapper named Charbonneau (SHAR bun noh), had married a young Indian woman named Sacagawea (also spelled Sacajawea). Captured years earlier by a tribe called the Minnetarees, Sacajawea's people were the Shoshone, also known as the Shoshoni, the very tribe from whom the expedition would need to buy horses to carry them through the Rocky Mountains. On the day they finally came to a Shoshoni camp, 15-year-old Sacajawea proved just how important she was to the success of the expedition.

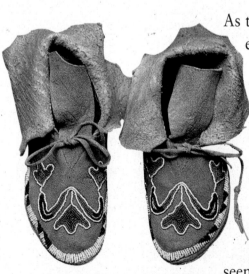

The Shoshoni liked using beads to decorate their clothes and moccasins.

As the expedition entered the Shoshoni camp, the Indians gathered around them. Suddenly, a young woman pushed through the crowd toward Sacajawea. It was her childhood friend who had also been captured by the Minnetarees. Sacajawea couldn't believe her eyes! They held each other tightly, crying softly.

Years ago, the two friends had shared their hardships and sadness when they were prisoners in the Minnetaree camp. After her friend had run away, Sacajawea never knew if she was alive or dead. It was such a long way back to the Shoshoni village from the Minnetaree camp. It didn't seem possible to Sacajawea that her friend could have made it. Sacajawea's friend never thought she would see her companion again, either. But there she was, standing right in front of her with a beautiful baby son! The friends from days gone by had a million questions to ask each other.

In the meantime, other women crowded around Sacajawea, hugging and talking excitedly. She went from one to another, searching for familiar faces. Once again, she was speaking the language of her childhood! Many things were familiar—the way her people walked and dressed and the way their camp smelled. Her family! Were they here? It was too late to ask. Someone had just sent for her; she was needed at council.

The leaders had gathered in a nearby tent. After everyone took off their moccasins, they smoked the peace pipe. Captain Clark was presented to Cameahwait. He seated Clark on a white robe and tied six small shells in the captain's red hair. These sea shells were very valuable to the Shoshoni. Giving them to Clark was a great sign of friendship.

In a solemn ceremony, Cameahwait gave his own name to Captain Clark. This was an honor because names were very important to the Shoshoni. The men of the tribe had several names— only one of which was used in war. This was because they believed that they would lose their strength if an enemy heard their real name. Giving Clark his real name was a sign of Cameahwait's sincerity and respect. From then on, the captain was called Cameahwait by the Shoshoni.

Sacajawea entered the tepee and sat down. As an interpreter, she was an important person at the council. But it must have felt strange to her to be there. Women were allowed to watch council, but never to talk. She *must* speak now, though. The expedition depended on her to help them get horses and guides for the trip west.

When Cameahwait began to speak, Sacajawea stared at him for a moment. Suddenly, she jumped up and threw her blanket over his shoulder. Cameahwait was her brother! He was alive! Sacajawea couldn't hold back her tears.

After many travels, Sacajawea and her husband eventually settled at Fort Manuel on the Missouri River.

peace pipe
a long-stemmed pipe used by Native Americans for ceremonial purposes

interpreter
someone who translates from one language into another

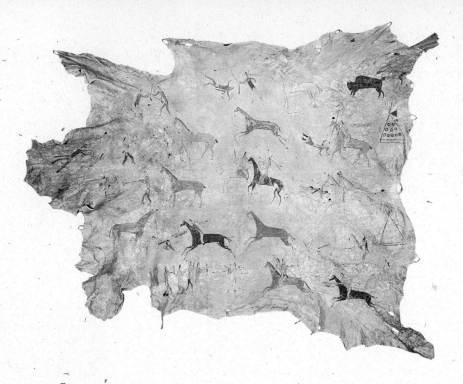

The Shoshoni used animal skins to make clothes, tepees, and artwork.

At first, Cameahwait was bewildered. He didn't know who she was. Then he realized it was his younger sister, Little Bird, whom he had thought was captured and lost forever! He did his best not to weep, too—especially in front of the white men. But the council could tell how moved he was.

Everyone waited while Sacajawea and Cameahwait spoke quietly with each other for a few minutes. Sacajawea sat down again to interpret, but she was too overcome with happiness and kept bursting into tears. The captains understood what this day meant to her, and they let her take her time at council. Lewis now realized how wrong he had been to think that Sacajawea didn't care about finding her people.

Lewis and Clark gave gifts to all those present. Several other Indian leaders were given medals with President Jefferson's face stamped on them. One of them received a uniform coat and a pair of red pants. Lewis passed out red paint, moccasins, tobacco, and looking glasses. The Indians were especially fond of beads, and they were very happy to get metal knives.

Then the discussions began. The translation went through four languages. First the captains spoke to Drewyer in English, then he repeated what they said to Charbonneau in French, then Charbonneau conversed with Sacajawea in Minnetaree. From Minnetaree, Sacajawea translated into Shoshoni.

Through Sacajawea, the captains told the Indians that the United States now owned this land. Their Great White Father, President Jefferson, wanted to trade with them for furs. In turn, the Shoshoni could get many useful things from the United States, including food. In order to set up this trade, the Great Father's messengers needed the Shoshoni's help. They needed horses to get across the mountains.

Cameahwait said he didn't have any horses to spare, but he would send someone to his people's village over the mountains and ask them to bring horses. Even though Cameahwait was an important Shoshoni leader, he couldn't order his people to sell their horses. A Shoshoni leader could only advise his people or suggest that they do something.

After the council, Cameahwait told Sacajawea what had happened to her family. It was sad news. All but Cameahwait, her older brother, and her sister's small son had been killed on that fateful day when they had been ambushed by the Minnetarees.

ambush
to attack suddenly from a hidden position

Meet the Author

Della Rowland has written a number of other books for young people. One of them is another biography, entitled *Martin Luther King, Jr.: The Dream of Peaceful Revolution.*

Additional Books to Read

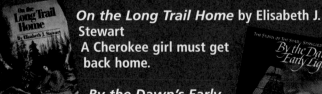

On the Long Trail Home by Elisabeth J. Stewart
A Cherokee girl must get back home.

By the Dawn's Early Light by Stephen Kroll
Read the story of our National Anthem and the War of 1812.

Response Activities

1. **Predict** What do you think would have happened to the Lewis and Clark expedition if Sacajawea had not been with them. Why?

2. **Narrative: Write a Dialogue** What kind of conversation do you imagine Lewis having with Cameahwait when they first met? Write a dialogue that you think could have taken place.

3. **Cultures: Make a List** What did you learn about Shoshoni culture from this reading? Make a list of every example of Shoshoni customs, beliefs, and daily life that you read about.

The War of 1812

Main Idea Tensions between the United States and Britain led to the War of 1812.

Remember Washington's farewell advice to the young republic? He said the country should

> **"S**teer clear of permanent alliances, with any portion of the foreign world. **"**

Washington meant that the United States should stay out of foreign conflicts and remain neutral.

In 1803, about seven years after Washington gave that advice, the French ruler Napoleon was at war with Britain. The battles took place all over Europe and on the sea as well. The United States needed to trade with both sides. Would the United States be able to follow Washington's advice and not enter the war?

Conflict Begins

Focus *Why did the United States go to war with Britain?*

Since the United States was neutral, American merchants traded with both Britain and France. Both Britain and France, however, attacked U.S. ships trading with their enemy and took their cargoes for themselves. Britain went a step further. The British captured American sailors and impressed them into the British navy. **Impressment** means to force people into military service.

Battle of Tippecanoe

There were other problems brewing as well. Tensions between settlers and Native Americans were growing in the Northwest Territory. In 1806 Tecumseh (tih KUHM suh), the chief of the Shawnee (shaw NEE), began to work to unite all midwestern Native American nations. He believed Native Americans could turn the settlers back by fighting together. Tecumseh's brother, known as

This painting shows the battle of Tippecanoe, with Americans fighting both the British and Native Americans. **Arts:** *Why might an artist want to paint a picture of a battle scene?*

"the Prophet," was a spiritual leader. Together they gathered an army in a Shawnee village by the Tippecanoe River in Indiana.

One night in 1811, when Tecumseh was away, Indiana Territory Governor William Henry Harrison attacked the village with a 1,000-man army. The Shawnee, using weapons from the British, fought fiercely. After many losses on both sides, Harrison's force finally won. This serious defeat for the Shawnee ended Tecumseh's dreams of a Native American union.

Because the British had sided with the Shawnee, many settlers blamed Britain for stirring up trouble. This group started calling for war with Great Britain. In Congress, men like Henry Clay of Virginia and John C. Calhoun from South Carolina led a group known as the War Hawks, because they were eager to fight. They wanted to end British support of Native American uprisings and the impressment of American sailors.

War Breaks Out

Focus *How was the war fought?*

President Madison finally agreed with the War Hawks. In June 1812, Congress declared war on Britain. The War of 1812, as it was called, was fought along the Atlantic coastline, in the western territories, and on both sides of the border between the United States and the British colony of Canada.

Biography

Tecumseh

Tecumseh's name means "Shooting Star." He was named this because a meteor was seen the night he was born. He learned English and read the Bible, history books, and Shakespeare. He died two years after the Battle of Tippecanoe, fighting on the side of the British in another battle.

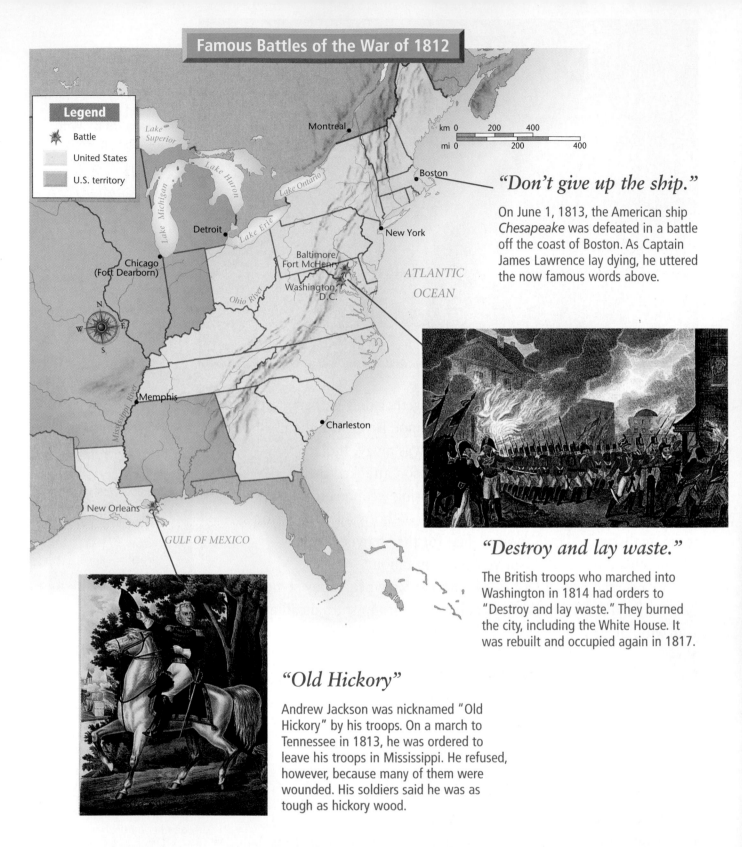

Famous Battles of the War of 1812

Legend

⭐ Battle

☐ United States

☐ U.S. territory

Lake Superior

Lake Huron

Lake Michigan

Montreal

Lake Ontario

Boston

Lake Erie

Detroit

New York

Chicago (Fort Dearborn)

Baltimore/ Fort McHenry

Washington, D.C.

Ohio River

ATLANTIC OCEAN

Mississippi River

Memphis

Charleston

New Orleans

GULF OF MEXICO

km 0   200   400
mi 0   200   400

"Don't give up the ship."

On June 1, 1813, the American ship *Chesapeake* was defeated in a battle off the coast of Boston. As Captain James Lawrence lay dying, he uttered the now famous words above.

"Destroy and lay waste."

The British troops who marched into Washington in 1814 had orders to "Destroy and lay waste." They burned the city, including the White House. It was rebuilt and occupied again in 1817.

"Old Hickory"

Andrew Jackson was nicknamed "Old Hickory" by his troops. On a march to Tennessee in 1813, he was ordered to leave his troops in Mississippi. He refused, however, because many of them were wounded. His soldiers said he was as tough as hickory wood.

Map Skill: *In what states does the map show that battles took place during the War of 1812?*

For the first two years, neither side was winning. Then, in 1814, Britain ended its war with France and immediately sent more soldiers to fight in the United States. This larger British force attacked Washington, D.C. British troops burned down the Capitol, the White House, the national treasury, and the national library.

Next, the British army and navy went to Baltimore. There, the outcome was different. U.S. troops, led by Major General Samuel Smith, were ready for the British attack. Fort McHenry, with its huge United States flag in full view, survived a two-day attack from the sea. Eventually, the British turned back. The United States had won a crucial battle in the war.

In 1815, the British and Americans fought at the city of New Orleans. The British sent 7,500 well-trained troops to fight against an American army of white militiamen, Native Americans, African Americans, and pirates. General Andrew Jackson was the commander in charge of the American troops.

The British lost more than 2,000 men, while the Americans lost only 21. The Battle of New Orleans was an overwhelming victory for the United States. It also made a hero of Andrew Jackson because of his strong leadership.

What neither side knew during the Battle of New Orleans was that a peace treaty had been signed between Britain and the United States two weeks earlier. Because news took a long time to travel, this information did not reach New Orleans in time to prevent the battle.

In the end, neither side won the War of 1812. Still, Americans were proud to have met Britain's challenge. American unity was on the rise.

Biography

Dolley Madison

When British troops marched into Washington, word reached First Lady Dolley Madison at the White House. She packed valuable items — including a famous portrait of George Washington — into a wagon. Her action saved these treasures from burning when the troops set the White House on fire. News of Dolley Madison's heroic action spread quickly.

Lesson Review

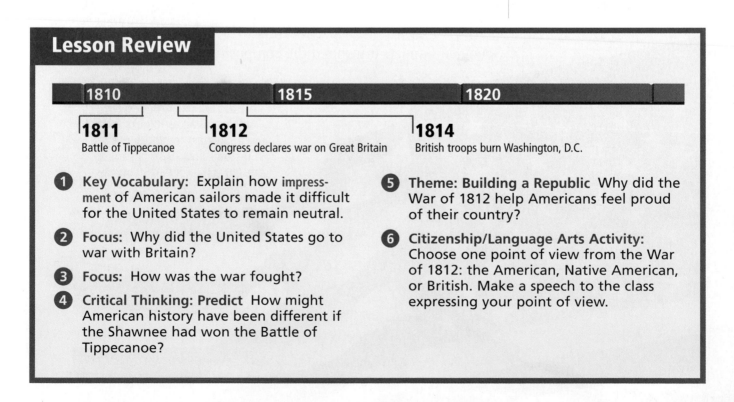

1810	1815	1820

1811
Battle of Tippecanoe

1812
Congress declares war on Great Britain

1814
British troops burn Washington, D.C.

1. **Key Vocabulary:** Explain how impressment of American sailors made it difficult for the United States to remain neutral.

2. **Focus:** Why did the United States go to war with Britain?

3. **Focus:** How was the war fought?

4. **Critical Thinking: Predict** How might American history have been different if the Shawnee had won the Battle of Tippecanoe?

5. **Theme: Building a Republic** Why did the War of 1812 help Americans feel proud of their country?

6. **Citizenship/Language Arts Activity:** Choose one point of view from the War of 1812: the American, Native American, or British. Make a speech to the class expressing your point of view.

THE STORY OF THE

'Star-Spangled Banner'

by Lester David

Our national anthem was born during a long, violent September night in 1814.

After weeks of working almost night and day, it was finished at last. Mary Pickersgill, her elderly mother and 14-year-old daughter looked proudly on their handiwork, an immense American flag.

The flag had 15 stars and 15 stripes, representing states in the union that year, 1813.

On the very day the flag was completed, it was hoisted atop the staff at Fort McHenry, at the entrance to Baltimore Harbor on the east coast of the United States. There it snapped in the breeze day after day.

This magnificent flag would go down in history as the Star-Spangled Banner. It inspired the composition of our national anthem.

hoist
to lift up

The picture below shows the American flag as it looks today, with 50 stars to represent the 50 states and 13 stripes to represent the original 13 colonies.

Guns Blast in the Dawn's Early Light

In the early morning hours of Sept. 14, 1814, a gray haze outlined the grim battlements of mighty Fort McHenry in Maryland.

Dawn was still several hours away when a fleet of 16 British warships outside the harbor fired a fusillade of shells toward the Americans inside the fort. Hour after hour the big guns pounded away.

Why the Nations Fought

Fighting had broken out because Americans were angry about British interference with U.S. ships.

Cargo vessels, vital to our trade, were being halted by the British while the ships were approaching French ports and other ports under their control. The Britons would force Americans to pay fees before being allowed to transport goods.

And worse: The British navy, always in need of seamen, was claiming that many of its men had deserted to the Americans. They stopped U.S. ships on the high seas, boarded them and forced the deserters back into British service. Although there were indeed deserters, many Americans too were being taken away by the British.

For years the United States tried to right these wrongs by talks and persuasion, but all efforts failed. Finally there was no choice. War was declared on June 18, 1812.

The Peril to Baltimore

Fighting raged on sea and land.

In the first week of September, word flashed throughout the city: The British were about to attack. They would bombard the fort [Fort McHenry] until its defenders surrendered, then storm Baltimore with 6,000 troops.

Meanwhile, some 13,000 Americans, consisting of regular army soldiers, volunteers and militiamen, were braced inside Baltimore for the assault.

A Lawyer-Poet Enters the Scene

While the fort was enduring shot and shell, a young man, telescope to his eye, was watching the bombardment from a small sloop anchored in the harbor.

His name was Francis Scott Key.

Why was he there?

fusillade
the firing of many guns at the same time or in rapid succession

bombard
to attack with bombs or explosive shells

Francis Scott Key

Francis Scott Key watches the battle at Fort McHenry.

During the sacking of Washington, the British had captured William Beanes, a prominent elderly physician, and taken him prisoner. Key, flying a white flag of truce, had sailed out on a small sloop to seek the release of the doctor, who was one of his close friends.

Key was allowed to board the British warship *Tonnant*, where he pleaded with the British to free the doctor. The British relented and said Dr. Beanes could go free.

But there was a hitch.

The long-planned assault on Fort McHenry was about to begin. The British could not allow Key to return to Baltimore and warn the Americans.

Key and the doctor were told they would have to return to the small sloop and remain there, guarded by British marines, during the attack.

Seeing Proof Through the Night

Key stood on deck, waiting and watching as both sides fired on each other throughout that day and into the night.

Key strained to peer through the thick gunsmoke.

Was Mrs. Pickersgill's majestic flag still fluttering above the fort? The smoke cleared just enough to allow a glimpse. Yes, the flag was still there!

The explosions were deafening; the rockets turned night into day. And still, Key saw that the huge flag remained aloft.

The Flag Was Still There

All through that night, Key watched as the bombardment continued. The flag still flew. It was proof that the fort had not surrendered.

The bombardment continued for 25 hours. A drizzly rain began to fall. Key found it harder and harder to see the flag.

Suddenly, just before dawn, the horizon brightened. There was the flag, still high above the fort! The bombardment stopped at last. A breeze caught the great banner and snapped it out, defiant and glorious.

Fort McHenry had not fallen. Baltimore was safe.

Key dug into his jacket pocket and found an old envelope. He began to compose a poem that had formed in his head as he watched the shelling. It began: "Oh say can you see, by the dawn's early light . . . ."

Our Song, Our Pride

After the British withdrew, their effort to topple Fort McHenry a failure, they released Key and Dr. Beanes. In Baltimore, Key completed his poem, which he called "In Defense of Fort McHenry."

At that time, an old English song called "To Anacreon in Heaven" was popular in America. Key wrote his words to the melody and meter of that song.

On Sept. 21, 1814, Key's song was first published. Thereafter, it was played at parades, school functions, and even before sports events.

It was not until March 3, 1931, that Congress designated Key's poem as America's national anthem.

Wherever it is played and sung, "The Star-Spangled Banner" stands for the love, confidence and pride that every American has in "the land of the free and the home of the brave."

You can read The Star-Spangled Banner *in the Historical Documents section beginning on Page 654.*

Response Activities

1. **Interpret** Make a chart of facts about the battle at Fort McHenry and opinions on patriotism in the article.

2. **Expressive: Write a Poem or Song** Can you think of a current event that gives you pride in America? Record your impressions of the event in either a poem or a song.

3. **History: Impersonate a Character** Choose a character who lived in the early 1800s. You can be a Native American, a War Hawk, a British subject, Mary Pickersgill, or even the President of the United States. Do you think that the United States should fight in another war? Present your arguments either for or against the War of 1812 to your class.

Becoming American

Main Idea Growing national pride in the decades following the War of 1812 helped Americans feel a common bond.

Have you heard the story about George Washington and the cherry tree? The story says that when Washington was six years old, he cut down a cherry tree. When his father asked who had done it, Washington told his father, "I cannot tell a lie. I did it with my hatchet."

This has become a famous American story. The truth, however, is that it never happened. A man named Parson Weems made up this story, along with other stories about Washington. He included real and made-up events in a book he wrote about Washington. His stories helped make America's first President even more famous than he already was.

Patriotic Heroes and Symbols

Focus *What led to the increase of patriotic heroes and symbols following the War of 1812?*

By the early 1800s, Americans were proud of their young nation. America had successfully fought Britain — twice. Thirteen separate states had combined into one nation. The country was growing.

Men and women like George Washington, Daniel Boone, Andrew Jackson, and Dolley Madison were heroes because they were strong, courageous, or noble. A **hero** is a person who is known for a special achievement. These heroes had played important roles in America's brief history.

There were stories, paintings, sculptures, and poems showing these famous Americans as brave, honest, and wise. Celebrating their contributions helped Americans to feel good about their country. Americans used these heroes to teach their children the **virtues,** or values, that would make the country strong. These values

There are several patriotic symbols in this image. **Citizenship:** *Can you find three of them?*

included the right to private property and the freedom to make economic choices.

Patriotic symbols also began to appear on coins, pottery, quilts, weathervanes, and elsewhere. A **symbol** is something that stands for something else, such as a flag standing for a country. George Washington, Philadelphia's Liberty Bell, and Miss Liberty all became important symbols. *(See Miss Liberty on page 354.)*

The Liberty Bell has words from the Bible written inside it, which capture the American spirit of independence:

> **"P**roclaim liberty throughout all the land unto all inhabitants thereof. **"**

Another important patriotic symbol was — and still is — the United States flag. The Continental Congress first approved a national flag in 1777. Its design changed several times before 1818.

• Tell Me More •

Designing a National Symbol

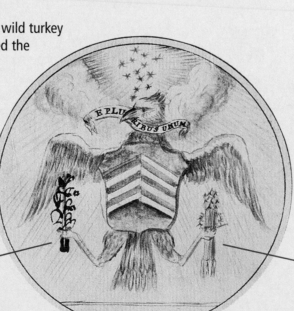

Benjamin Franklin wanted the wild turkey to be the national bird. He liked the turkey for two reasons: it was only found in North America and it had been an important source of food for the Pilgrims. If Congress had followed Franklin's advice, you would see the wild turkey on a quarter instead of the eagle!

The bald eagle was chosen by Congress as the national bird in 1782. Eagles have been symbols of power for hundreds of years.

In some images, the eagle holds an olive branch and arrows in each claw. The olive branch is a symbol of peace.

The arrows that the eagle is holding in this image are a symbol of war.

Then Congress chose the design we know today. The stripes represent the original 13 states, so there are 13 stripes. The stars represent all of the states, so a new star was added each time a new state was added. Today, there are 50 states, so the flag has 50 stars.

Language and Education

Focus *How did changes in language and education make Americans feel more connected to one another?*

The United States had its own flag, its own heroes, even its own holidays. However, Americans were still using British dictionaries and British spellings. Noah Webster, a schoolmaster, thought this needed changing.

His dictionary listed many words never before printed in a dictionary. Some of these words, such as *skunk*, came from Native

The "Blue-Backed Speller" got its name because its cover was blue.

American words. Others, like *presidency*, came from new American ideas.

Another Webster book, commonly known as the "Blue-Backed Speller," changed many British spellings. The British word *colour* became the American *color*. *Labour* became *labor*, *plough* became *plow*, *waggon* became *wagon*, *centre* became *center*. Webster's spelling books and readers grew popular in American schools.

Children who went to school in the early 1800s were taught reading, writing, math, and how to be good citizens. Schoolhouses outside of the large cities were often one-room buildings. One teacher taught students of all ages in that room. Older students sometimes helped teach, too. Students wrote with quill pens and

Schoolhouses in the country could be cold in the winter. **History:** *What helps keep this building warm? Do you see any items that you use in your school today?*

Students said their lessons aloud to show the teacher what they had learned.

ink, or slate boards and chalk. Birchbark was sometimes used in place of paper.

Not every child went to school. Some children worked to help support their families. Wealthy white boys attended private schools or had private teachers at home. White girls — wealthy or not — usually did not go to school. Free African American children could go if they could pay for private school. Enslaved African Americans were denied schooling.

American literature began to change at this time too. Early American writers copied the style of European writers. After the new spirit of democracy moved across the United States, American writers, like James Fenimore Cooper and Washington Irving, began to write stories that were truly American. Irving wrote about New York State, describing its Dutch-English heritage, and Cooper wrote about understanding and appreciating the American wilderness with a hero named Natty Bumppo.

American literature, education of the young, westward exploration, patriotic symbols, even an American dictionary — all helped the new nation create its own special identity.

Lesson Review

1775	1780	1785	

1777
First national flag approved

1782
Bald eagle is made national bird

① **Key Vocabulary:** Write a paragraph explaining how George Washington was both a hero and symbol.

② **Focus:** What led to an increase of patriotic heroes and symbols following the War of 1812?

③ **Focus:** How did changes in language and education make Americans feel more connected to one another?

④ **Critical Thinking/Predict** Would Americans feel differently about the country if we had no patriotic symbols? Why or why not?

⑤ **Citizenship:** Why is education believed to be such an important part of being a citizen?

⑥ **Theme: Building a Republic/Art Activity** Groups today create symbols to help to unify them. Create a symbol for your class, one that represents everyone's interests and unifies you as a class.

Skills Workshop

Organizing and Recording Information

Word for Word

What if you were doing research for a report about Lewis and Clark, and you found a quotation that fit your topic perfectly? If you give credit to the speaker or writer, you can include this **direct quotation**. You can also **paraphrase**, or restate it in your own words. Either way, you need to give credit to your sources.

1 Here's How

- As you read through books and articles, use note cards to record useful information.

- Be sure to note information you'll need to credit the source. Include author, title, publisher, publication date, and page number.

- For direct quotations, copy all spelling and punctuation exactly. Use quotation marks.

- If you paraphrase, don't worry about copying word for word. Jotting down important facts and key phrases should be enough.

2 Think It Through

Why might you decide to quote someone directly? Why might you want to paraphrase instead?

3 Use It

1. Paraphrase Thomas Jefferson's quotation on page 335.

2. Find a nonfiction book about the adventures of Lewis and Clark.

3. Find and copy a quotation. Find another quotation to paraphrase. Jot down the information you need to credit the source.

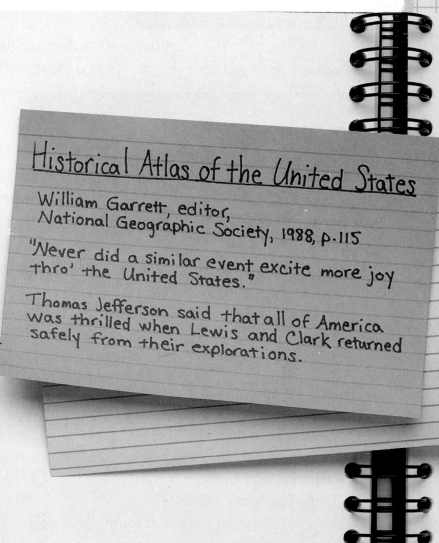

Historical Atlas of the United States

William Garrett, editor,
National Geographic Society, 1988, p.115

"Never did a similar event excite more joy thro' the United States."

Thomas Jefferson said that all of America was thrilled when Lewis and Clark returned safely from their explorations.

Chapter Review

Chapter Review Timeline

1800	1803	1806	1809	1812	**1815**

1801
Jefferson becomes President

1804
The Lewis and Clark expedition begins

1811
Battle of Tippecanoe

1812
Congress declares war on Great Britain

Summarizing the Main Idea

1 Copy and complete the chart below. Include events that show that the United States was growing and prospering in the early 1800s.

	Events
Lesson 1	
Lesson 2	
Lesson 3	

Vocabulary

2 Using at least five of the following terms, write an invitation to a fellow explorer asking him or her to join you on a journey westward.

pioneer (p. 336)   corps (p. 338)   symbol (p. 355)

frontier (p. 336)   impressment (p. 346)   virtues (p. 354)

expedition (p. 338)   hero (p. 354)

Reviewing the Facts

3 How did Daniel Boone help other explorers and settlers?

4 Why did President Jefferson want to purchase the Louisiana Territory?

5 Why were Lewis and Clark's accomplishments important?

6 What was Tecumseh's goal?

7 How did Americans feel about private property in the early 1800s?

8 What is the significance of the design on the American flag?

9 What symbols or objects helped Americans feel pride and share a common bond?

10 What do you need to do when you include a direct quotation in a report?

11 Work in a group. Select one of the heroes you studied in this chapter. Visit the library and gather one or two sources that provide information about your hero.

Prepare at least two notecards that give information about the hero. Share your notecards with the class and discuss how you might use them if you were to write a report.

Geography Skills

12 Why were rivers important to Lewis and Clark in their expedition through the West?

13 You want to join Lewis and Clark on their expedition. Write a letter convincing them that you should be allowed to join them.

Critical Thinking

14 **Decision Making** Would you rather have helped Daniel Boone cut the Wilderness Trail or joined Lewis and Clark on their expedition up the Missouri River? Explain.

15 **Cause and Effect** What events led to the War of 1812?

Writing: Citizenship and History

16 **Citizenship** Write a letter to a student in another country identifying one of our national symbols and explaining why it is important to Americans.

17 **History** Write a brief biography describing someone who you think is an American hero. Include background information, some of the person's achievements, and the reasons why you think he or she is a hero.

Activities

National Heritage/Research
Noah Webster changed many British spellings in his dictionary and spelling books. Do further research on this topic. Then make a list of at least 12 of the words Webster changed, including both their British and American spellings.

Cultures/Literature
Find and read one of Washington Irving's short stories. Prepare a brief oral report for the class explaining what this story shows about American culture in the early 1800s.

Internet Option

Check the **Internet Social Studies Center** for ideas on how to extend your theme project beyond your classroom.

THEME PROJECT CHECK-IN

To complete your theme project, use the information in this chapter. The questions below will help you:
• How did the Constitution help strengthen the United States?
• What challenges was the United States able to meet in the early 1800s that the states could not have met individually?

The Nation Expands

"In entering upon the great work before us . . . we shall make every effort within our power to secure our object."

Declaration of Sentiments, Elizabeth Cady Stanton

· THEME ·

Crossing Frontiers

"The people who crossed the frontier must have been courageous and strong, since it was such a dangerous trip."

Chris Haynes, Fifth Grade
Rumford, ME

A frontier is an unknown territory — unsettled land or unexplored ideas. During the first half of the 1800s, Americans were exploring a number of new frontiers. Some pushed westward into new regions. Others took part in an industrial revolution that led to the rise of factories and cities. Still a third group launched reform movements to make the nation a better place to live. The people who crossed these frontiers were all pioneers, and they would shape the United States well beyond the 19th century.

 Theme Project

Journey Across America

The year is 1835, and you are traveling across America to settle in new territory. Make a record of your trip.

- Create a map of a route that you might take. Include at least one city on your journey.
- How far will you travel? How long will it take?
- Draw pictures of the transportation you might use.
- Write letters describing the people you meet.

RESEARCH: Find out about diaries and letters from people who journeyed west. What were they like?

◀ *The Oregon Trail,* by Albert Bierstadt, 1869

WHEN & WHERE
ATLAS

In the early 1800s, few people could vote, most Americans lived on farms, and "the West" was the land just past the Appalachian Mountains. By 1850, all that had changed. Rapid industrial growth and political and social reforms shook American society. As the map shows, the United States gained much territory, and new industrial and cotton growing areas developed during these years.

In this unit, you will read how the revolution in American politics was accompanied by an industrial revolution. You will also learn about the reforming spirit in the nation and growing divisions between North and South. Finally, you will read how, by the mid-1800s, the United States stretched "from sea to shining sea."

Unit 6 Chapters

Chapter 14   People in a Growing
            Country
Chapter 15   Moving West

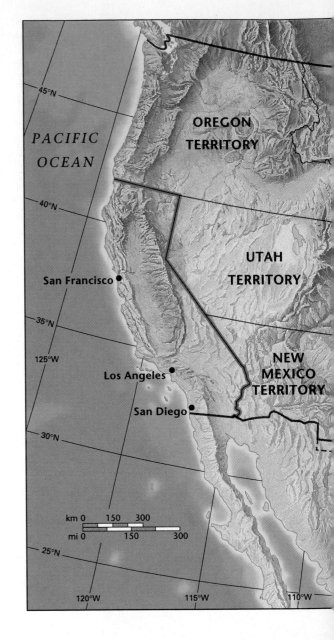

Unit Timeline

1790	1805	1820

Sequoya

Find out which alphabet this man invented. *Chapter 14, Lesson 1*

Mill Girls   1814

What are these girls making?
Chapter 14, Lesson 2

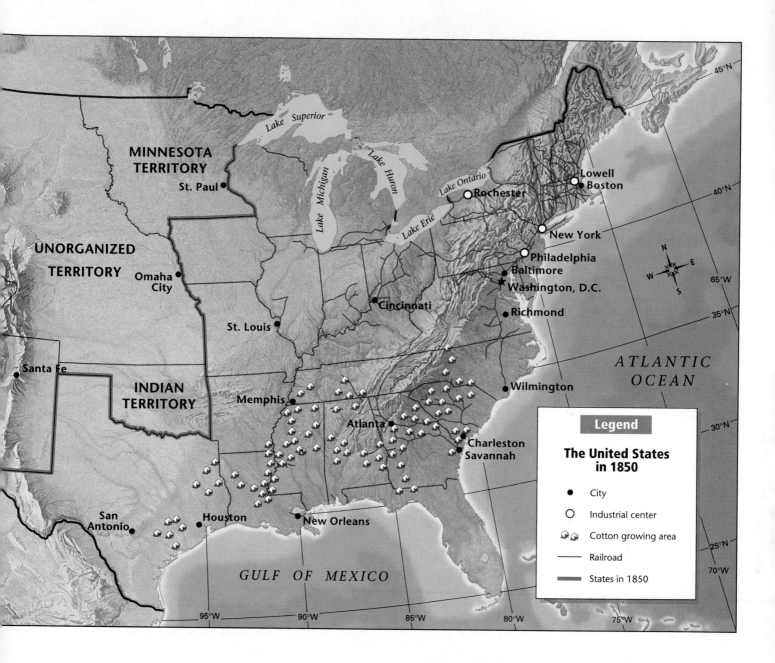

The United States in 1850

Legend

The United States in 1850

- ● City
- ○ Industrial center
- 🌿🌿 Cotton growing area
- —— Railroad
- ▬▬ States in 1850

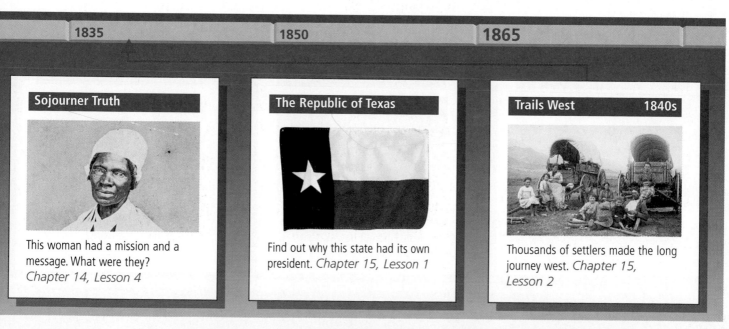

1835   1850   1865

Sojourner Truth

This woman had a mission and a message. What were they? *Chapter 14, Lesson 4*

The Republic of Texas

Find out why this state had its own president. *Chapter 15, Lesson 1*

Trails West   1840s

Thousands of settlers made the long journey west. *Chapter 15, Lesson 2*

CHAPTER 14 People in a Growing Country

Chapter Preview: *People, Places, and Events*

1790   1800   1810

Textile Mills

How would you like to work at this machine? *Lesson 2, Page 375*

The Cotton Gin   1793

Cotton that goes in this box comes out clean. Find out how. *Lesson 3, Page 377*

Slavery in the South

Enslaved people did the heavy labor on plantations. *Lesson 3, Page 378*

Jackson: A New Kind of Politics

Main Idea A frontier America elected Andrew Jackson as President. Westward movement forced Native Americans off their lands.

"One uninterrupted stream of mud and filth." That is how one Washington, D.C., member of Congress described the excited crowd pouring into the White House. It was March 4, 1829, and nearly 20,000 people had followed Andrew Jackson from the Capitol, where he had taken an oath to become their new President. Inside the White House, they spilled orange punch and broke china dishes. Rugged frontiersmen with muddy boots stood on expensive chairs, hoping to catch a glimpse of their hero. To save the White House from complete destruction, the crowd was moved outdoors on the front lawn. These rowdy people were supporters of a new democracy. Many of them had voted for the first time. Jackson was a new kind of President, and he would begin a new kind of politics.

Key Vocabulary

suffrage
candidate

Key Events

1828 Andrew Jackson is first elected

1830 Indian Removal Act is passed

1838 Trail of Tears

◀ This painting is called "Verdict of the People" by George Caleb Bingham.

1820   1830   1840

Andrew Jackson 1828

Barbecues, parties, and parades helped elect this man. *Lesson 1, Page 369*

The Trail of Tears   1838

Where are these Cherokee going? And why? *Lesson 1, Page 370*

Susan B. Anthony

Whose rights did this woman stand up for? *Lesson 4, Page 387*

This chart shows the increase in the number of people who could vote and the number of voters during two election years. **Chart Skill:** *How many more people voted in the 1828 presidential election than in the 1824 election? Why?*

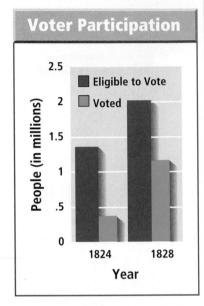

Voter Participation

People (in millions)

- ■ Eligible to Vote
- ▢ Voted

2.5
2
1.5
1
.5
0

1824   1828

Year

By 1822, another 11 states had joined the original 13 colonies. **Map Skill:** *How many of the new states were west of the original 13 colonies?*

The Growth of Democracy

Focus *How did the growth of democracy in the United States help Andrew Jackson?*

According to the United States Constitution, each state controls which of its citizens can vote. In the late 1700s, most states said that only those white men who owned private property and paid taxes could vote. African Americans, Native Americans, women, and the poor did not vote. Big changes were happening, however.

As Americans moved west, where land was cheap and plentiful, the number of states increased *(see map below)*. Frontier people wanted more democracy. They believed that they and their neighbors were equals and that rights should not be based on wealth. The new states wrote constitutions that fit that democratic spirit. They were the first to give suffrage to all white men. **Suffrage** is the right to vote. Gradually, the eastern states followed. The growth of democracy went only so far; most free African Americans, women, and Native Americans still could not vote.

Jackson — The Common Man's President

Now that poor farmers and workers could vote, they wanted a President who would represent them. To achieve that goal, people

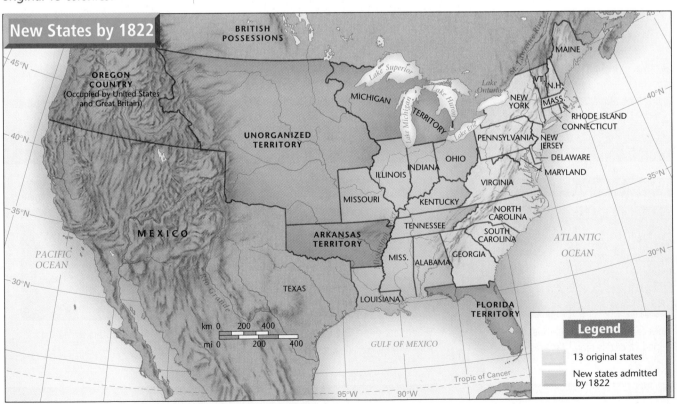

New States by 1822

BRITISH POSSESSIONS

OREGON COUNTRY (Occupied by United States and Great Britain)

MICHIGAN TERRITORY

MAINE

VT. N.H.

NEW YORK   MASS.

RHODE ISLAND CONNECTICUT

UNORGANIZED TERRITORY

PENNSYLVANIA   NEW JERSEY

DELAWARE

OHIO

INDIANA

ILLINOIS

MARYLAND

MISSOURI

VIRGINIA

KENTUCKY

MEXICO

NORTH CAROLINA

TENNESSEE

ARKANSAS TERRITORY

SOUTH CAROLINA

PACIFIC OCEAN

MISS.   ALABAMA   GEORGIA

ATLANTIC OCEAN

TEXAS

LOUISIANA

FLORIDA TERRITORY

km 0   200   400
mi 0   200   400

GULF OF MEXICO

Tropic of Cancer

Legend

▢ 13 original states

▢ New states admitted by 1822

George Caleb Bingham, an American painter and a politician, often painted scenes related to politics. In this painting, *Country Politician*, three men discuss politics. **Citizenship:** *How does this painting suggest an increase in political participation by the common man?*

joined the Democratic-Republican Party. The Democrats, as they were called, urged every man to vote. They held barbecues, parties, and parades to stir up support for their candidate, Andrew Jackson. A **candidate** is a person running for political office.

Like many westerners, Jackson was a "self-made man." Born on the frontier, he grew up poor and lost both of his parents by age 15. As you learned in Chapter 13, he became a hero in the War of 1812 as a general in the Battle of New Orleans.

Jackson won the 1828 election, largely because of his many thousands of supporters from America's western states. Not all Americans, however, looked forward to his presidency. Senator Daniel Webster of Massachusetts wrote:

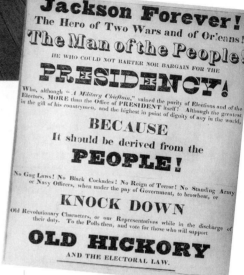

In the War of 1812, Jackson earned the nickname "Old Hickory," after one of the hardest kinds of wood. Democrats stuck hickory poles in the ground and hung posters like the one above to rally for Jackson. **Citizenship:** *How does this poster show what was important to voters in the election of 1828?*

> "**M**y opinion is that when he comes he will bring a breeze with him. Which way it will blow, I cannot tell. . . . My fear is stronger than my hope."

As President, Jackson worked to limit the power of wealthy men, who he believed controlled the country's government and economy. He closed the private Bank of the United States, believing that it helped the rich grow richer. He supported laws that helped farmers and working people. Jackson believed it was the President's duty to "protect the liberty and rights of the people." Sadly, while protecting the rights of some people, he trampled on others.

① October 1-November, 1838 About 15,000 Cherokees begin the journey to Indian Territory.

② The trails turn to mud during heavy rains. Farmers charge high prices for food.

③ Due to hunger and exposure, hundreds of Cherokees die each day.

④ The Mississippi clogs with loose ice, delaying some groups for up to a month. Winter storms cause many more deaths.

⑤ January 4-March 25, 1839 11,000 Cherokees arrive in Indian Territory.

MISSOURI

KENTUCKY

Neosho River

Gasconade River

ILLINOIS

④ ③

Springfield

Cumberland River

APPALACHIAN MTS.

SMOKY MTS.

INDIAN TERRITORY

② Nashville

Canadian River

Ft. Gibson

ARKANSAS

TENNESSEE

① New Echota

⑤

Ft. Coffee

Mississippi River

Memphis

Tennessee River

CHEROKEE HOMELAND

GEORGIA

ALABAMA

MISSISSIPPI

km 0   100

mi 0   100

The removal of the Cherokee was called the Trail of Tears. **Map Skill:** *Through which states did the Trail of Tears pass?*

Native American Removal

Focus *How were Native Americans removed from the Southeast?*

As American settlers crossed the Appalachians, they entered territory controlled by five Native American nations: the Cherokee, Chickasaw, Choctaw, Creek, and Seminole.

Settlers wanted this rich land and pressured Congress to pass the Indian Removal Act in 1830. It required Native Americans to sell their land to the United States government and move to a territory west of the Mississippi River, in present-day Oklahoma.

While some Native Americans left their homelands peacefully, many refused to go. The Seminoles, led by Chief Osceola, fought a seven-year war with the United States Army, from 1835 to 1842. In the end, Osceola was captured, and the Seminoles were forced to leave their homeland.

Native Americans who resisted removal were rounded up by the U.S. Army, and forced to march west. A Creek woman tells the story of a seven-year-old Creek girl on the long journey:

*"**H**er grandmother held her very close by the campfire and told her that they had come far far away from home and they would never see their homeland and advised her to be brave and never cry."*

When Georgia state officials tried to push the Cherokee out of their homes, the Cherokee took the state of Georgia to court. In 1832, the Supreme Court ruled that Georgia officials could not enter Cherokee lands. Although it was Jackson's job to enforce the Supreme Court ruling, he ignored it and did not stop the removal of the Cherokee from their lands.

For each of the Native American groups, the forced move west was a long and harsh journey. Around 15,000 Cherokee made the trip. As many as 4,000 of them died on the way. Because the removal of the Cherokee in 1838 caused so much suffering, the journey is known as the "Trail of Tears" *(see map at left).*

For many American settlers the West offered new opportunities. But for Native Americans, heading west meant the loss of their lands and change in their way of life.

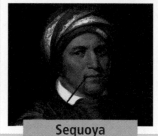

Sequoya

Before 1821, the Cherokee told stories and sang songs to pass on their history. They didn't have a written language. A Cherokee named Sequoya worked for 12 years to create the first Cherokee writing system. Soon, many Cherokee learned to read and write their language. In 1828, the tribe published their first newspaper called the *Cherokee Phoenix.*

Lesson Review

| 1820 | 1830 | 1840 | |

1828
Andrew Jackson is first elected

1830
Indian Removal Act is passed

1838
Trail of Tears

1 **Key Vocabulary:** Write a paragraph about Andrew Jackson's election using **suffrage** and **candidate**.

2 **Focus:** How did the growth of democracy in the United States help Andrew Jackson?

3 **Focus:** How were Native Americans removed from the Southeast?

4 **Critical Thinking: Generalize** Compare the experience of the settlers who moved west with the experience of

Native Americans after the Indian Removal Act.

5 **Theme: Crossing Frontiers** A frontier can be an unsettled place or a new area of knowledge. Are there any frontiers that exist today?

6 **Citizenship/Math Activity:** Find out how many people voted in the last election for President. How does that compare to the number of voters in Andrew Jackon's election in 1828?

The Industrial Revolution

Main Idea New inventions led to new kinds of transportation and the growth of factories.

Key Vocabulary

Industrial
Revolution

canal

interchangeable
parts

mass production

Key Events

1790 First spinning
mill

1807 Fulton builds
a steamboat

1825 Erie Canal
opens

One day in 1830, Peter Cooper stood in front of an odd-looking vehicle he called "Tom Thumb." It was a steam engine placed on a wooden platform with four wheels. The steam engine powered the platform forward.

Until then, horses were the fastest transportation over land. The first American railroads were horse-pulled wagons on wooden tracks. Soon, the horse was replaced by imported trains from England. America did not yet have its own steam-engine industry.

Tom Thumb was ready for its first trip. Starting slowly, it steadily gained speed, reaching an incredible 18 miles per hour! America's first public steam-engine railroad was under way. Who could have guessed that 30 years later, railroads would link most of the country's major cities? Tom Thumb was a sign that the Industrial Revolution had come to America.

The first trains burned wood for fuel and had tall, funnel-shaped smokestacks. Later, as coal replaced wood, the stacks became straight — as in this illustration of a mid-1800s steam-engine train.

The public railroad allowed people to travel long distances over land much more easily. As a result, more people moved west.

With railroads, goods and cattle could be transported. This greatly increased trade.

A Nation on the Move

Focus *What impact did steamboats, canals, and railroads have on the nation?*

The **Industrial Revolution** is the name given to the great changes that began in England with a series of inventions in the middle and late 1700s. As new machines led to the growth of factories, people started working in factories instead of in their homes or small shops. By the early 1800s, the Industrial Revolution was beginning to change America, too. It was helped by a revolution in transportation — the way people and goods moved across the country.

Steamboats, Canals, and Railroads

In the late 1700s, traveling by water was the quickest and cheapest way to carry people and goods over long distances. The problem with rivers, though, was that boats or barges had a hard time moving upstream against the current. American inventors solved that problem by creating steam engines to power boats.

A man named Robert Fulton was the first person to build a steamboat that was a financial success. On August 17, 1807, Fulton's boat made a 150-mile trip on the Hudson River in 30 hours, averaging five miles per hour. So effective was the steamboat that people wanted to use boats where rivers didn't exist.

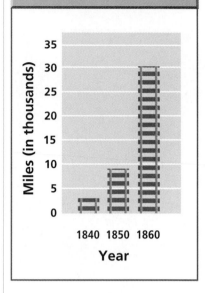

Growth of Railroads (1840-1860)

This graph shows the increase in miles of tracks in the United States during the 1800s.
Graph Skill: *Was the increase in railroad tracks greater between 1840 and 1850 or between 1850 and 1860?*

Coal is burned to heat water, turning it into steam, which powers the train. The tender, a small car behind the engine, holds the water and coal.

Smoke from the burning coal escapes through the smokestack.

They did — by building canals. A **canal** is a waterway that is made by people. Canals can link a river and a lake or make shortcuts on a winding river. The greatest canal of all, the Erie Canal, opened in 1825. It stretched 363 miles, from Albany to Buffalo, New York.

Farmers in Indiana could now load their crops onto canal boats and sell them in New York. With this greater movement of goods, the economy grew in the new western states.

Not everyone could transport their goods, or themselves, along rivers or canals. Many parts of the country didn't have waterways. In those places, people turned to the railroad.

New England and New York took the lead in building railroads. They were soon joined by the rest of the country. Rail transportation made it easier for settlers to move west and move their products back east. Railroads proved more dependable than canals and could be built anywhere. The railroads helped spread the Industrial Revolution across the United States.

The Growth of Factories

Focus *How did inventions lead to the growth of industry?*

In 1789, Samuel Slater left England for America. His pockets were empty, but in his head he carried something more valuable than money. He had memorized the plans for building cotton mills.

England's economy depended on the cotton industry. To prevent competition, England did not allow designs for mills out of the country. Slater had worked in mills since he was 14. He knew all about spinning machines. A year after he arrived in America, Slater used his knowledge to build a mill in Pawtucket, Rhode Island.

Spinning Mills

Before the Industrial Revolution, turning raw cotton into cotton yarn was a long, hard task usually done in the home. New machines made the process faster and easier. These spinning machines were put in large buildings, called mills.

Spinning machines needed a lot of water power to run. New England had many fast rivers with waterfalls — the perfect spot for mills. By 1815, nearly 165 mills dotted river banks in Rhode Island, Connecticut, and Massachusetts.

The above engraving, which was owned by Samuel Slater, shows young women operating machines in a mill.

A bobbin *(below)* held cotton yarn, and a shuttle *(bottom)* guided the yarn through looms that were used in spinning mills.

In 1814, Francis Cabot Lowell built a factory in Waltham, Massachusetts. His was the first mill to contain the entire process for turning raw cotton into printed cloth. He recruited young New England farm girls to work in the mill. Many girls already knew how to spin and weave, and he paid them less than he would have to pay men. Soon, "mill girls" became a common sight in cotton mills everywhere. Mary Paul, a worker at a cotton mill, described the daily routine in a letter to her family:

> "**A**t half past six (the bell) rings for the girls to get up and at seven they are called into the mill. At half past 12 we have dinner, are called back again at one and stay till half past seven."

Despite the hard conditions, the mills gave many young women their first taste of independence and money to send home.

· Tell Me More ·

The Life of a Mill Girl

As cotton mills sprung up across New England, ads like the one at right attracted young girls from their farms. Packing their belongings in trunks, they set out for the mills.

Mill girls faced long, hard days working in cotton mills. They worked side by side for hours, then lived together in boarding houses, sometimes with six girls in a room. Throughout the day, bells rang to tell the girls what to do. Inside the mills, the girls worked in steamy, noisy rooms filled with up to 1,200 machines. Tiny pieces of cotton filled the air — and the girls' lungs. Despite the hardships of mill life, young women continued to leave home.

This trunk held the personal belongings of a mill worker named Eliza Adams. In it are scissors, a pair of gloves, her journal, a book, and a framed silhouette — perhaps of someone she missed.

75 Young Women
From 15 to 35 Years of Age,
WANTED TO WORK IN THE
COTTON MILLS!
IN LOWELL AND CHICOPEE, MASS.

I am authorized by the Agents of said Mills to make the following proposition to persons suitable for their work, viz:—They will be paid $1.00 per week, and board, for the first month. If it is presumed they will then be able to go to work at job prices. They will be considered as engaged for one year, cases of sickness excepted. I will pay the expense of those who have not the means to pay for themselves, and the girls will pay it to the Company by their first labor. All that remain in the employ of the Company eighteen months will have the amount of their expenses to the Mills refunded to them. They will be properly cared for in sickness. It is hoped that none will go except those whose circumstances will admit of their staying at least one year. None but active and healthy girls will be engaged for this work as it would not be advisable for either the girls or the Company.

I shall be at the Howard Hotel, Burlington, on Monday, July 25th; at Farnham's, St. Albans, Tuesday forenoon, 26th, at Keye's, Swanton, in the afternoon; at the Massachusetts' House, Rouses Point, on Wednesday, the 27th, to engage girls,—such as would like a place in the Mills would do well to improve the present opportunity, as new hands will not be wanted late in the season. I shall start with my Company, for the Mills, on Friday morning, the 29th inst., from Rouses Point, at 6 o'clock. Such as do not have an opportunity to see me at the above places, can take the cars and go with me the same as though I had engaged them.

I will be responsible for the safety of all baggage that is marked in care of I. M. BOYNTON, and delivered to my charge.

I. M. BOYNTON,
Agent for Procuring Help for the Mills.

Mass Production

Mill owners like Samuel Slater and Francis Cabot Lowell developed a faster way of making goods. Another businessman and inventor, Eli Whitney, also helped create a modern manufacturing system.

In 1798, the United States government ordered 10,000 muskets from Whitney. He had never made a gun in his life, and 10,000 muskets was a huge number. Why was Whitney so sure he could make the guns? Because he had a new plan.

At his gun factory outside New Haven, Connecticut, Whitney built machines that could quickly stamp out identical parts of a gun. The parts were interchangeable, meaning a part from one gun could be used on another. Before Whitney's system, guns were made separately by hand. With **interchangeable parts**, fewer workers could make more guns. This is known as **mass production** — making large amounts of goods in a short time.

Whitney's system quickly caught on. Other American manufacturers used interchangeable parts and mass production to make items such as clocks, watches, and sewing machines. With mass production, workers with fewer skills could make more goods. At the same time, many crafts people who took pride in their work lost their jobs. Those who could find jobs now had to stand and work at a machine. The Industrial Revolution changed people's lives and began a new age of American manufacturing.

Above is a photograph of the first clock made with interchangeable parts. This meant that each part of this clock was mass-produced separately by a different machine.

Lesson Review

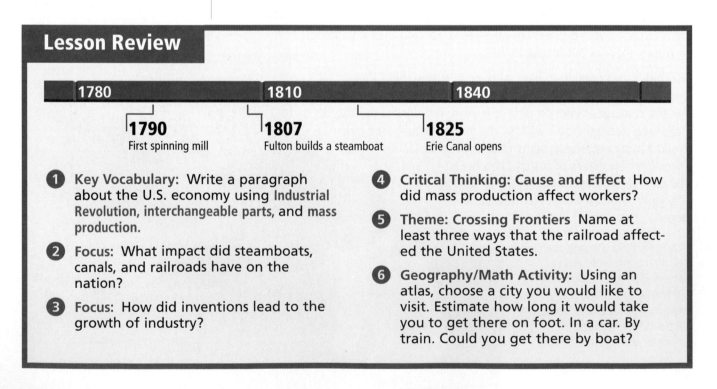

1780   1810   1840

1790
First spinning mill

1807
Fulton builds a steamboat

1825
Erie Canal opens

1. **Key Vocabulary:** Write a paragraph about the U.S. economy using **Industrial Revolution, interchangeable parts,** and **mass production.**

2. **Focus:** What impact did steamboats, canals, and railroads have on the nation?

3. **Focus:** How did inventions lead to the growth of industry?

4. **Critical Thinking: Cause and Effect** How did mass production affect workers?

5. **Theme: Crossing Frontiers** Name at least three ways that the railroad affected the United States.

6. **Geography/Math Activity:** Using an atlas, choose a city you would like to visit. Estimate how long it would take you to get there on foot. In a car. By train. Could you get there by boat?

North and South: Worlds Apart

Main Idea The North and South developed increasingly different economies and ways of life in the early 1800s.

America's Industrial Revolution changed both the North and South, but in very different ways. In 1793, five years before building his gun factory, New Englander Eli Whitney visited the Georgia plantation of Catherine Greene. Whitney learned of a dilemma in the South: While demand for the South's cotton crop was high, cleaning and producing cotton was a slow process. He wrote to his father,

> **"I***f a machine could be invented which would clean the cotton [easily] . . . it would be a great thing both to the country and the inventor.* **"**

Within ten days Whitney created that machine: the cotton gin.

Key Vocabulary
overseer

tenement

Key Events
1793 Invention of cotton gin

1808 Closing of Atlantic slave trade

1831 Nat Turner's rebellion

The soft fiber of the cotton boll must be separated from the sharp stem. Enslaved workers cut their hands while picking cotton.

To clean the cotton, the small seeds hidden inside must be removed. Before the cotton gin, it took one worker an entire day to clean one pound of cotton.

When the handle of this cotton gin is turned, wire teeth separate the seeds from the cotton.

The cotton is placed in here.

Cotton and Slavery

Focus *How did the rise of the cotton kingdom and the spread of slavery change the South?*

Only a few southern states grew cotton before the invention of the cotton gin. With Whitney's machine, however, planters could plant more cotton, clean it faster, and sell more. Soon cotton was grown throughout the South. Southerners still grew other crops, but as one southern senator said, "cotton is king."

Slavery

In 1808, the United States halted the entry of enslaved Africans into the country. As cotton farming boomed, the demand for enslaved workers increased. Most African Americans in the region were forced to work on plantations. Solomon Northrup, a free black from New York who was captured and sold into slavery, described the hard life he encountered:

> "The hands are required to be in the cotton field as soon as it is light in the morning, and with the exception of [lunch] they are not permitted to be a moment idle until it is too dark to see."

William Henry Brown created this work of art by drawing, cutting, and then assembling each figure in this scene of enslaved workers hauling cotton to the gin.

HAULING THE WHOLE WEEKS PICKING

Enslaved workers like Northrup worked under the watchful — and often cruel — eyes of overseers. An **overseer** managed the field workers for the plantation owner. Overseers often used whips to make sure enslaved African Americans did the work. While most African Americans in the South worked in the fields, a few worked in the plantation houses or learned skilled trades. A small number lived in cities, working as servants and in skilled jobs.

No matter where they lived or what they did, enslaved people always faced the fear of being separated from their family. If a slaveowner died or faced hard times, enslaved families were often separated and sold. An owner could decide at any time to sell his workers. At an auction, buyers inspected the human merchandise, probing muscles, feeling hands, and looking at their teeth. Even those family members who had the same owner or lived nearby might not see one another more than once or twice a year.

Many enslaved workers resisted their conditions daily. Occasionally rebellions broke out. The most famous of these rebellions was led by an enslaved man named Nat Turner. In 1831, Turner recruited about 60 or 70 enslaved people to help him attack plantation owners in the Virginia countryside. Most of Turner's followers and more than 50 whites died in the two days of fighting. Turner himself was captured and executed.

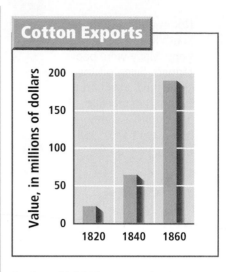

Cotton Exports

By the mid-1800s, cotton had become the most important crop in the South. **Graph Skill:** *How does this graph help explain the increase in slavery during the 1800s?*

If enslaved workers were captured after trying to escape, they were put in shackles like these to prevent them from escaping again.

Many enslaved workers tried to escape to freedom. Slave owners posted notices, like the one above, offering rewards for the return of a worker.

Not everyone in the South lived on plantations. Many were poor farmers, living off the crops they grew. John Bunyan Bristol called this painting of a southern home, *On the St. Johns River.*

Ask Yourself

In the 1800s, the South's economy depended on agriculture, whereas the North's economy focused on industry. Is the region where you live agricultural or industrial?

? ? ? ? ? ? ? ? ? ? ? ? ?

The Other South

Slavery and plantations played a major role in southern society during the 1800s. They did not, however, represent the whole South. By 1860, the South had about 350,000 slaveowners out of a white population of eight million. Typical white families lived off the food they could grow and the stock they tended. These farmers were much poorer than most plantation owners.

Farming was the main way of life for most southerners. But the South did have some cities and industry. The South built railroads, spun cotton in mills, and produced iron. Most of the cities were ports like New Orleans and Savannah. Within the cities, free blacks often found more freedom, working as carpenters, masons, blacksmiths, barbers, and seamstresses.

The Industrial North

Focus *How did the Industrial Revolution change the North?*

While the South's economy depended on agriculture, the North became increasingly industrial and urbanized. By 1860, about one out of three northerners lived in cities and large towns, more than twice as many as in 1830. Not everyone who flocked to the cities came from the countryside. Europeans came too, often looking for a better life in the United States.

The North was more industrial than the South and soon had many large, crowded cities. Thomas Horner painted this New York City scene, called *Broadway, New York,* in 1836. **Geography:** *What attracted people to cities like New York?*

Immigration

During the 1820s, nearly 143,000 Europeans left their homes, friends, and families to make the 3,000-mile journey to America. By the 1850s, the number of immigrants arriving in the United States had grown to 2.6 million.

Most immigrants came looking for work. When they arrived, many found factory jobs in the North's new industries. Few immigrants went south, where there were fewer factory jobs available.

In the mid-1800s, the largest number of immigrants to the United States came from Ireland and Germany. Between 1845 and 1847 a plant disease wiped out Ireland's potato crop. Thousands of people fled from starvation. Many German immigrants left their homeland to escape economic and political trouble.

The Irish headed mostly for New York, Boston, and other places in the Northeast. Germans, on the other hand, tended to settle on farms in the Midwest, or in Milwaukee, Chicago, and St. Louis. By 1860, more than half the people in New York and Chicago were immigrants or the children of immigrants.

City Life

Immigrants and farmers streamed into American cities looking for work. In 1830, St. Louis was a small frontier town of about 5,000 people; by 1860, it was a bustling city of 160,000. Chicago's population increased from about 3,000 in the 1830s to 100,000 by

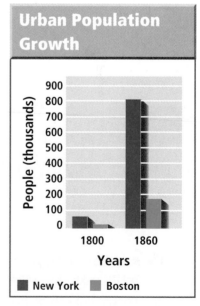

This graph shows the increase in population in two northern cities. **Graph Skill:** *Which city had more population growth between 1800 and 1860?*

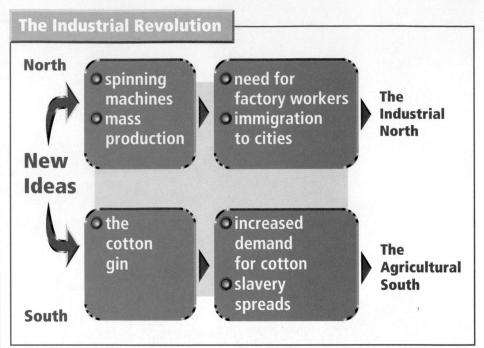

The Industrial Revolution

North

New Ideas →
- spinning machines
- mass production

→
- need for factory workers
- immigration to cities

→ **The Industrial North**

New Ideas →
- the cotton gin

→
- increased demand for cotton
- slavery spreads

→ **The Agricultural South**

South

1860. Originally called "Mudtown," for its dusty streets that turned to mud when it rained, Chicago soon became the railroad center of the Midwest.

Growing cities had growing problems. The cities' new citizens, poor and unskilled, jammed together in run-down apartment buildings called **tenements**. Some tenements had dirt floors and little or no heating and plumbing. Crowded conditions and the lack of sewers led to the spread of disease. As things got worse in the cities, some people tried to find solutions to new problems. A desire to make things better, to reform America, was sweeping the country.

Lesson Review

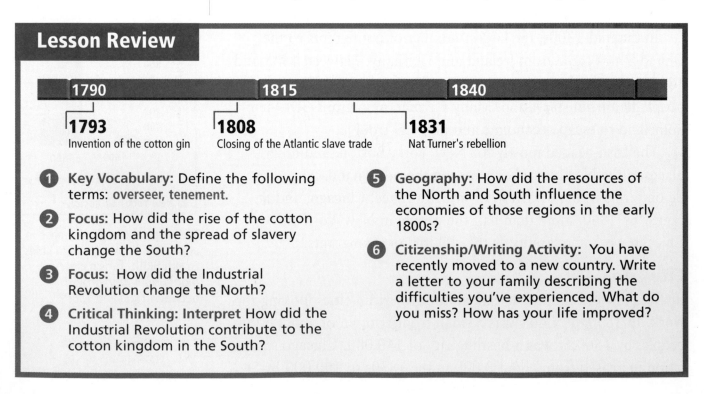

| 1790 | 1815 | 1840 | |

1793
Invention of the cotton gin

1808
Closing of the Atlantic slave trade

1831
Nat Turner's rebellion

1 **Key Vocabulary:** Define the following terms: **overseer, tenement.**

2 **Focus:** How did the rise of the cotton kingdom and the spread of slavery change the South?

3 **Focus:** How did the Industrial Revolution change the North?

4 **Critical Thinking: Interpret** How did the Industrial Revolution contribute to the cotton kingdom in the South?

5 **Geography:** How did the resources of the North and South influence the economies of those regions in the early 1800s?

6 **Citizenship/Writing Activity:** You have recently moved to a new country. Write a letter to your family describing the difficulties you've experienced. What do you miss? How has your life improved?

Comparing Line and Circle Graphs

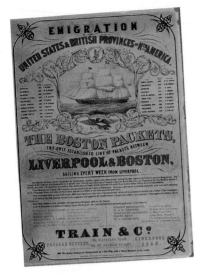

Booming Growth

In the 1800s, hundreds of thousands of immigrants came to the United States. Numbers tell only part of their story. A line graph helps you see changes over time, such as the growth in immigration. A circle graph lets you compare information, such as the number of immigrants from different countries. Together these graphs help you understand immigration more completely.

❶ Here's How

The graphs on this page show immigration patterns over 40 years.

- Read the title of each graph. How is the information related?

- Examine the circle graph. What does the whole graph stand for? What do the parts stand for?

- Study the line graph. What does the horizontal information show? What does the vertical information show?

- Compare the information in the two graphs. How is it the same or different?

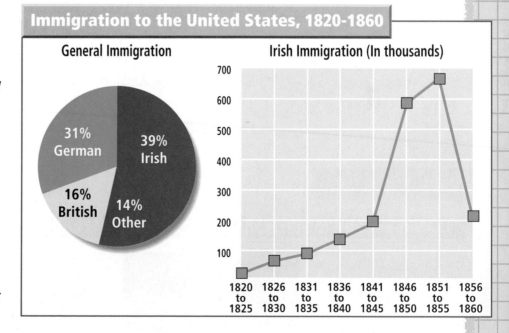

Immigration to the United States, 1820-1860

General Immigration

- 39% Irish
- 31% German
- 16% British
- 14% Other

Irish Immigration (In thousands)

(Line graph with vertical axis from 100 to 700; horizontal axis: 1820 to 1825, 1826 to 1830, 1831 to 1835, 1836 to 1840, 1841 to 1845, 1846 to 1850, 1851 to 1855, 1856 to 1860)

❷ Think It Through

If one of the graphs were not shown, how would this change your understanding of immigration during these years?

❸ Use It

1. In the circle graph, examine the information about Irish immigrants. Is it bigger, smaller, or the same size as the other parts?

2. Looking at the line graph, describe any trend or pattern you see in Irish immigration.

3. Use the information in both graphs to write a paragraph describing Irish immigration.

Spirit of Reform

Main Idea During the 1830s and 1840s, Americans joined many movements designed to make the nation a better place.

Across western New York, people gathered at huge outdoor revival meetings to hear the fiery words of minister Charles Finney. With piercing eyes and shaking fists, Finney boomed a simple message: work hard, go to church, don't drink alcohol, and help others live useful lives. Finney was part of a religious movement that swept the United States in the early 1800s. The Second Great Awakening, as it was called, inspired many Americans to join volunteer groups and get involved with social concerns.

The Antislavery Movement

Focus *How did people work against slavery?*

One of the most important reform movements during the time of the Second Great Awakening was the antislavery movement. Since the 1700s, free African Americans like Philadelphia businessman James Forten had worked hard to abolish, or end, slavery. People who fought against slavery came to be known as **abolitionists**.

Abolitionists

William Lloyd Garrison

On January 1, 1831, William Lloyd Garrison published the first issue of *The Liberator,* the most famous antislavery newspaper in America. In *The Liberator,* Garrison demanded that all enslaved people be freed immediately.

The Grimke Sisters

Two sisters, Sarah and Angelina Grimke, were pioneers in the fight against slavery. They made speeches opposing slavery, shocking many Americans who thought only men should speak in public. Their persistence and determination led them to become leaders in the women's rights movement as well.

In 1829, an African American named David Walker wrote four articles, known today as his *Appeal*. "Freedom is your natural right," he told enslaved people. During the 1830s, the antislavery movement grew. Leading the way was a white Massachusetts man named William Lloyd Garrison. In speeches and articles, Garrison spoke out harshly against slavery. In 1833, he and other leading abolitionists founded the American Anti-Slavery Society.

In 1841, Frederick Douglass heard Garrison speak. Douglass, who had only recently escaped from slavery, soon became an influential leader in the antislavery movement:

> "**M**y acquaintance with the movement increased my hope for the ultimate freedom of my race, and I united with it from a sense of delight, as well as duty. "

Other abolitionists, both black and white, helped African Americans to escape from slavery. They worked on a system called the Underground Railroad. The **Underground Railroad** didn't have a locomotive or tracks, and it didn't run underground. It was a secret network of men and women, called "conductors," who led enslaved workers to freedom. Men, women, and children were moved from one safe house, called a "station," to the next. *(See map on the next page.)*

Frederick Douglass

Frederick Douglass learned to read and write as an enslaved house servant. After escaping from slavery in 1838, Douglass soon began lecturing and writing books against slavery. In 1847, Douglass started an abolitionist newspaper called *The North Star.*

James Forten

James Forten was a respected leader in the African American community. As a wealthy Philadelphia sailmaker, he contributed money and moral support to the antislavery movement. His financial aid helped William Garrison start *The Liberator.*

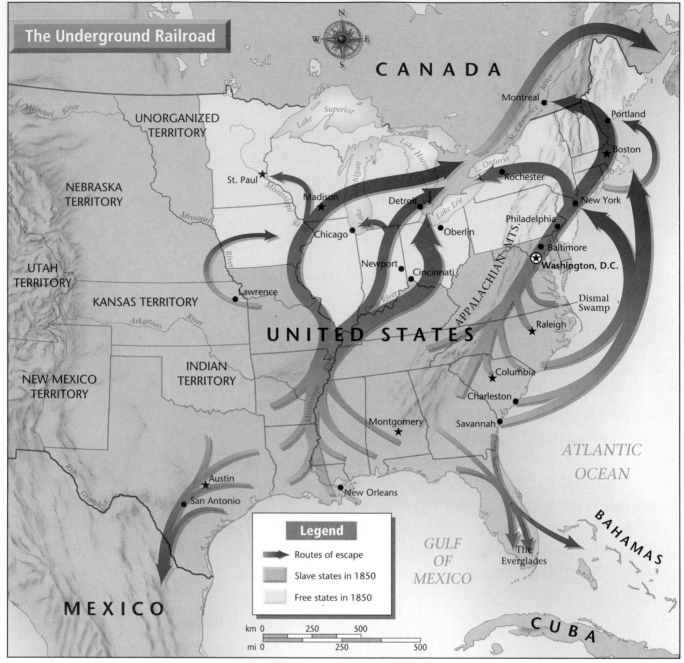

The Underground Railroad

Legend
- ➤ Routes of escape
- Slave states in 1850
- Free states in 1850

km 0   250   500
mi 0   250   500

The map above shows the various routes enslaved people followed to freedom. **Map Skill:** *What countries outside the United States were destinations on the Underground Railroad?*

A journey on the Underground Railroad was dangerous for everyone involved. Runaways were hidden in barns, under floorboards, or in secret rooms. The photo on the right shows a cabinet that was actually a hidden room where runaways could hide.

Harriet Tubman (holding pan) is shown in this photograph with some "railroad" passengers. Tubman was the most famous conductor on the Underground Railroad. Often in disguise, she risked her life guiding enslaved people to freedom. Slaveowners offered a $40,000 reward for her capture.

The Fight for Women's Rights

Focus *What led to the rise of the women's rights movement in the United States?*

Many women were involved in the antislavery movement. Lucretia Mott and Elizabeth Cady Stanton met in London in 1840 during the World Anti-Slavery Convention. They had to sit behind a curtain, away from the men, and were not allowed to speak or vote.

Mott and Stanton resented this treatment. They believed women were equal to men. Stanton wrote that women needed "a public meeting for protest and discussion" of their poor treatment by men. Working with Mott and three other women, Stanton organized the Seneca Falls Convention in 1848. Stanton wrote a plan called a "Declaration of Sentiments and Resolutions," demanding equality and the right to vote for women.

The Seneca Falls Convention launched America's first organized women's movement. Most men — and many women — were opposed to this movement. At another women's convention in Akron, Ohio, one clergyman spoke of the weakness and helplessness of women. A tall, strong woman named Sojourner Truth inspired the women in the audience with her reply:

Sojourner Truth was born into slavery with the name Isabella Baumfree. In 1843, at age 46, she was religiously inspired to change her name to Sojourner Truth and spread her message. For the next 40 years, Truth fought against slavery and for women's rights, influencing audiences everywhere she spoke.

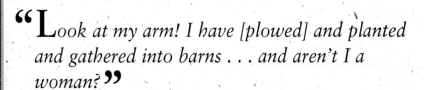

> "**L**ook at my arm! I have [plowed] and planted and gathered into barns . . . and aren't I a woman?"

In 1850, Elizabeth Stanton met Susan B. Anthony. For the next 40 years they worked together to fight for women's rights. In 1869, they headed the National Women's Suffrage Association. With their words and actions, leaders of the women's rights movement created new opportunities for women in education and public life. Women's struggle for the vote, however, would continue for many decades.

Fact File:

Date	Name	Achievement
1823	Catharine Beecher	Started formal schools to train women how to teach.
1837	Mary Lyon	Set up Mount Holyoke, one of the first colleges for women.
1848	Maria Mitchell	First woman astronomer elected to the American Academy of Arts and Sciences.
1849	Elizabeth Blackwell	First woman in the United States to receive a medical degree.
1852	Harriet Beecher Stowe	Published her best-selling book, Uncle Tom's Cabin.

This painting, by Winslow Homer, shows a typical classroom in the 1800s. **History:** *How does it look different from your classroom?*

The textbook *(above)* helped children learn to read. Good students often received an award like the one at top.

Other Reform Movements

Focus *What other reform movements had an impact on American life?*

American reformers tackled other tough issues during the 1830s and 1840s. They worked to improve education, fight the use and abuse of alcohol, and help the mentally ill.

Before 1820, about two children out of three did not attend school. Most children who did go to school came from wealthy families. Beginning in the 1820s, however, states began requiring that all white children go to school. One man took the lead in reforming public education in America: Horace Mann.

Starting in 1837, Mann worked for 12 years to improve Massachusetts schools. His efforts led to the first law requiring students to go to school for at least six months a year. Mann's efforts influenced school reforms in other states.

School reformers didn't do much for African American children. Those who went to school attended separate schools. Most of these schools didn't provide the same quality of education that white children received. The first schools to have both black and white children started in Boston in 1855.

Alcoholism was another widespread concern in the United States in the early 1800s. Reformers wanted **temperance** — for people to stop drinking altogether. They believed that alcohol led to crime, family violence, and mental illness.

The campaign against drinking alcohol — known as the temperance movement — was one of the largest and most popular reform movements of the period. Founded in 1826, the American Temperance Society soon had over 200,000 members. Within six years, more than 1.2 million Americans pledged to stop drinking alcohol. Local temperance groups held rallies to attack the evils of alcoholism.

In 1841, a school teacher named Dorothea Dix volunteered to teach Sunday school at a local prison. She was horrified to see mentally ill people locked up with criminals. Dix researched how the mentally ill were treated in Massachusetts and discovered they were kept "in cages, closets, cellars, stalls, pens" and "beaten with rods and lashed into obedience." Dix prepared a report for the Massachusetts legislature, and officials were horrified by what they discovered. The state improved conditions for the mentally ill. Dix was not finished. By 1845, she traveled 10,000 miles, calling for change. In return, 15 states set up special hospitals to treat the mentally ill.

Reformers like Dix saw problems in America and tried to change them. Change was everywhere in the early decades of the 1800s. Andrew Jackson and his supporters changed the political process, and the Industrial Revolution changed the way people lived and worked. The changes continued as the country kept growing.

★ **Biography** ★

Dorothea Dix

In 1841, Dorothea Dix, a schoolteacher and writer, led a one-woman crusade to improve the treatment of the mentally ill. Dix traveled the country to observe their treatment. Her demands for reform led to new hospitals.

Lesson Review

1820	1835	1850	

1829
David Walker's *Appeal*

1833
American Anti-Slavery Society founded

1848
Seneca Falls Convention

1. **Vocabulary:** Write a paragraph about reform using **abolitionist, temperance,** and **underground railroad.**

2. **Focus:** How did people work against slavery?

3. **Focus:** What led to the rise of the women's rights movement in the United States?

4. **Focus:** What other reform movements had an impact on American life?

5. **Critical Thinking: Interpret** Choose one of the reform movements. As a reformer in that movement, what would you say to convince someone to join your cause?

6. **Geography** Why did most of the routes on the Underground Railroad lead North?

7. **Citizenship/Research Activity:** Identify an issue or topic that you would like to see improved. Research and design a plan for your own reform movement.

Biography

Tubman was born into slavery in Maryland.

HARRIET TUBMAN

ANTISLAVERY ACTIVIST

by M.W. Taylor

Harriet Tubman is best known for leading around 350 enslaved Africans north to freedom during the years before the Civil War. For this untiring work she became known as Moses, after the ancient Hebrew leader who led his people to the Promised Land from their slavery in Egypt. Her story begins with her own escape from slavery. Her first attempt to escape failed because her two brothers were afraid and turned back to the plantation. She tried again — this time on her own.

Two days after the botched escape, a slave from a nearby plantation gave Tubman bad news: She had been sold and was scheduled to start south the next day. This time she knew she would have to run alone. Years later, she described her thoughts at that moment: "There was one of two things I had a *right* to, liberty or death; if I could not have one, I would have the other; for no man should take me alive; I should fight for my liberty as long as my strength lasted, and when the time came for me to go, the Lord would let them take me."

Tubman wanted someone in her family to know she was leaving on her own, that she was not on her

This 1850s painting shows fugitives arriving at a station of the Underground Railroad in Ohio.

way south. After her last experience, she would not tell her brothers. How could she relay the news safely? Legend has it that she made her way toward "the big house," where one of her sisters was working in the kitchen. Walking back and forth near the window, Tubman sang an old spiritual:

> I'll meet you in the morning,
> When I reach the Promised Land,
> On the other side of the Jordan.
> For I'm bound for the Promised Land.

That night, after her husband was asleep, Harriet Tubman wrapped up a little cornbread and salt herring, then tucked her favorite patchwork quilt under her arm. Did she kiss John Tubman good-bye as he slept? Did she

Enslaved African Americans had to wear tags showing the name of their owners.

regret leaving him? No one will ever know, for she never said. But perhaps she hinted at her feelings in her choice of a name: For the rest of her life, she identified herself as "Mrs. Tubman."

Tubman had heard of a local white woman who was said to help runaways, and she made her way through the woods to the woman's house. When she saw Tubman at her door, the woman seemed to know what her visitor wanted. She invited her in, then gave her two slips of paper, explaining that each contained the name of a family on the road north. When Tubman presented the slips, said the woman, these people would give her food and tell her how to get to the next house. The slips of paper were Tubman's first "tickets" on the Underground Railroad. In gratitude, Tubman gave the woman her precious quilt, then started on her way.

Reaching the first house just after dawn, Tubman presented her slip of paper. The woman of the house responded by giving her a broom and telling her to sweep the walk. Tubman was shocked. Was this a betrayal? Was she now this woman's slave? But she soon realized the move was for camouflage. A black woman with a broom would hardly be noticed, certainly not suspected as a runaway.

camouflage
a method of hiding something from an enemy

Tubman *(far left)* is shown here with some of the former enslaved African Americans she led to freedom.

As soon as night fell, the woman's husband put Tubman in the back of his farm wagon, covered her with vegetables, and drove her north to the next "station." In this way, sometimes helped by others, sometimes left to her own devices, Harriet Tubman made her way north, walking up the Eastern Shore peninsula toward Pennsylvania. She began to learn the route she was to use so often and so effectively in the future.

Traveling by night, hiding in the daylight, Tubman trudged through 90 miles of swamp and woodland. At last, many days after she started, she found herself across the magic line, on free soil. Years later, she said of that morning: "I looked at my hands to see if I was the same person now that I was free. There was such a glory over everything; the sun came like gold through the trees, and over the fields, and I felt like I was in heaven."

This stamp honored Tubman's courage and achievements.

Meet the Author

M. W. Taylor worked as an editor for the *New York Times* and *Los Angeles Times* newspaper syndicates. She was also an editor for *Life* magazine. This book about Harriet Tubman is the first biography she has written.

Additional Books to Read

Frontier Home
by Ramond Bial
This book gives a realistic look at pioneer days.

Sarah, Plain and Tall
by Patricia MacLachlan
Read about a family's life on the prairie.

Response Activities

1. Compare Literature and History How does reading about Harriet Tubman's life help you to understand why people were involved in the antislavery movement and in reform groups in general?

2. Descriptive: Describe a Scene Suppose you are Harriet Tubman. You have just arrived in the North and gained your freedom. Write a paragraph describing how it feels to be free.

3. Geography: Draw a Map Look at physical and political maps of the United States. Draw a map that shows the route an enslaved African American might have taken following escape from a plantation near Jackson, Mississippi.

Participating

Whose Vote Is It, Anyway?

Today, in most elections, only about half the people who are registered to vote actually vote. That's unusual when you think about how hard Americans have fought to gain the right to vote. Voting can be a powerful tool, but only if we do it. The case study below shows how one group of Americans first demanded that right.

Case Study

The Seneca Falls Convention

"We hold these truths to be self-evident: that all men and women are created equal. . . ." Wait a minute. Thomas Jefferson didn't write that, did he?

No. Elizabeth Cady Stanton, a housewife and mother from Seneca Falls, New York, did, in 1848. The scene was the first women's rights convention ever held. At the convention, Stanton read a list of rights that she and other women were demanding. Among those rights was the right to vote.

Nothing could have shocked the American public more. It took 72 years for the idea to win acceptance. At last, in 1920, the Nineteenth Amendment to the Constitution was ratified, giving women the vote.

Take Action

What is it like to be part of a democracy? Here's a chance to find out. Imagine that you and your classmates have founded several new colonies. One colony will govern the others. You need to elect some leaders.

1 Do two things: For each colony, nominate one member to run for president, and select another member to be on an election committee.

2 Candidates: Talk to your classmates and give a 30-second speech to the whole class telling why you should be president of the colonies.

3 Election Committee: Hold a class election by secret ballot. (Candidates and election committee members vote, too.) Count the votes and write the results on the board. The candidate with the most votes becomes president; the candidate with the second most votes becomes vice president.

4 Talk about what happened. Was it a fair election? Are most students satisfied with the process and the results? If not, what could be done differently? Come up with your own set of election rules.

Tips for Participating

- Find out who the candidates for each office are.
- Learn what the issues are and where the candidates stand on the issues.
- Discuss the candidates and issues with other people. Listen to other viewpoints.
- On election day, go out and vote!

Research Activity

Find out more about women's rights in the mid-19th century. You know they couldn't vote. What else couldn't they do? Make a chart comparing the rights of women then with the rights of women today.

Chapter Review

1831
Nat Turner's Rebellion

1848
Seneca Falls Convention

| 1790 | 1805 | 1820 | 1835 | 1850 |

1793
Invention of the Cotton Gin

1833
American Anti-Slavery Society founded

1830
Indian Removal Act is Passed

Summarizing the Main Idea

1 Copy and complete the chart, showing changes that took place in the United States and how they affected the people who lived there.

	Changes	Effects
Lesson 1		
Lesson 2		
Lesson 3		
Lesson 4		

Vocabulary

2 Using at least eight of the following terms, write a paragraph describing the impact new inventions had on the United States.

suffrage (p. 368)

candidate (p. 369)

Industrial Revolution (p. 373)

interchangeable parts (p. 376)

mass production (p. 376)

overseer (p. 379)

tenement (p. 382)

abolitionist (p. 384)

Underground Railroad (p. 385)

canal (p.374)

temperance (p. 388)

Reviewing the Facts

3 How did voting rights change in the early 1800s?

4 Who were the Democratic Republicans?

5 Why were Native Americans removed from the Southeast? How did they react?

6 What was the Industrial Revolution?

7 Why did the need for enslaved people increase in the South?

8 Who were the abolitionists?

9 What was the Underground Railroad?

Skill Review: Evaluating Point of View

10 What kind of information does a line graph illustrate? What kind of information does a circle graph illustrate?

11 If you wanted to show how the population of the nation was divided by region (North, East, South, and West), would you use a line graph or a circle graph? Explain.

Geography Skills

12 Find the Erie Canal on a map of the United States. What rivers or lakes did it connect? Which states benefited from it?

13 Imagine you are a Native American traveling along the Trail of Tears with your family. Write a dialogue you might have with one of your parents about your journey.

Critical Thinking

14 **Interpret** By providing young girls with work in cotton mills, mill owners gave them experience and money. Do you think these benefits outweighed the hazards of the harmful working conditions?

15 **Conclude** Many different reform movements started during the 1830s and 1840s. Why do you think there was no organized movement to support the rights of Native Americans?

Writing: Citizenship and Economics

16 **Citizenship** Write a letter to President Jackson explaining why Native Americans should be allowed to remain in the Southeast. Include a proposal for a peaceful resolution between settlers and the Native Americans.

17 **Economics** Compare and contrast the influence the Industrial Revolution had on the South and the North. Write a paragraph describing each region and the changes that were taking place.

Activities

National Heritage/Research Activity
Find out where Native Americans live today. Indicate your findings on an outline map of the United States. Use what you have learned about the treatment of Native Americans by early American settlers to draw your conclusions.

History/Science
Create a chart that includes the major technological advances that occurred in the late 1700s and early 1800s, the dates these occurred, and the impact they had on the nation.

Internet Option

Check the **Internet Social Studies Center** for ideas on how to extend your theme project beyond your classroom.

THEME PROJECT CHECK-IN

Include the information in this chapter in your description of traveling across the United States in 1835.
• What is happening in the newly created states?
• What effects have the Industrial Revolution had on your journey?
• Are you in the North or South? How does this affect what you see on your journey?

Chapter Preview: *People, Places, and Events*

| 1810 | 1820 | 1830 |

Mexican Texas   **1821**

Mexican cowhands tended herds of cattle on the plains of Texas.
Lesson 1, Page 400

Sam Houston   **1836**

This man helped Texas become an independent nation.
Lesson 1, Page 401

Migrating West

Where is this family going and how will they get there?
Lesson 2, Page 407

Texas and the Mexican War

Main Idea Texas became a republic in 1836 and joined the United States nine years later.

Key Vocabulary

annexation
Manifest Destiny
dispute

Key Events

1836 Texas wins independence
1845 Texas joins the United States
1846–1848 The Mexican War

Texas is the second largest state in the United States — an enormous 261,914 square miles in size. As many as 170 states the size of Rhode Island could easily fit inside its borders!

In 1800, when Texas was still part of the Spanish Empire, around 3,200 colonists from New Spain lived in all that wide-open space. Most lived in small southeastern towns and worked on ranches along the Rio Grande. Apache and Comanche Indians lived on the prairies above the coastal plains. Spain could not control this vast land without more people to settle it.

Moses Austin from Missouri was ready and willing to be one of those settlers. Spain granted land in Texas to Austin and 300 families that he would bring with him. Before he could carry out his plans, however, Austin died. That same year, in 1821, Texas became part of the newly independent nation of Mexico.

◄ A view across the plains.

1840	1850	1860

The Oregon Trail   1843

What equipment did families need for their trip west?
Lesson 2, Page 408

The Gold Rush   1849

Find out what these people are searching for.
Lesson 3, Page 415

Ghost Towns

What happened to Silver City, Poverty Hill, and Tombstone?
Lesson 3, Page 416

Settlement of Texas

Focus *How did Texas become an independent nation?*

Stephen Austin continued with his father's plans, taking over responsibility for the land grant. Starting in 1821, Austin sold land in Texas to 297 families of settlers.

The Mexican government encouraged settlement by giving land grants to people like Austin. The people holding the land grants then sold the land to settlers for the low price of 10¢ an acre. To many Anglo-Americans — as the English-speaking immigrants from the United States are called — this was a bargain, especially since land in the United States was selling for $1.25 an acre.

Soon the new settlers outnumbered the Mexicans. By 1827, there were 12,000 immigrants, about 5,000 more than the number of Mexicans in Texas. The growing number of immigrant settlers brought tensions to the surface. Anglo-Americans complained that they didn't have enough representation in their local government. The Mexican government complained that not all immigrants were obeying Mexican law. Mexico's greatest fear, however, was that the United States wanted Texas for itself.

"Remember the Alamo"

Mistrust grew on both sides. In 1830, Mexico passed a law stopping further settlement by Anglo-Americans. The law also said that Americans could no longer bring enslaved people to Texas. The

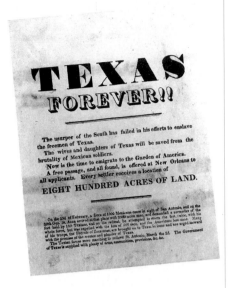

In the early 1820s, posters such as the one above encouraged American settlers to immigrate to Texas. This poster called Texas "the Garden of America" and promised, "Every settler receives a location of eight hundred acres of land." **Economics:** *Why would the promise of land draw American settlers to Texas?*

Texas Wins Independence

1820	1825	1830	1835

1821
Stephen Austin leads 297 families to Texas.

1830
Mexico passes a law ordering a halt to further settlement by Anglo-Americans.

1833
Mexico reopens its doors to Americans.

1836
On March 2, Texans declare their independence. Four days later, Texans suffer defeat at the Alamo. On April 21, they defeat the Mexican army and Texas wins its independence.

Stephen Austin

The Alamo

Mexican government's actions angered the Texas settlers. To quiet growing unrest, Mexico reopened its doors to Americans in 1833. However, two years later, Mexican president Antonio López de Santa Anna took all government power into his own hands. This pushed Texans further toward independence.

In 1835, Santa Anna led an army of over 5,000 men north into Texas. The Texans declared their independence from Mexico. They formed an army of their own, with Sam Houston at its head. Houston had distinguished himself in the War of 1812, fighting under Andrew Jackson.

In San Antonio, a small army of Texan men led by William B. Travis was occupying an abandoned Spanish mission known as the Alamo. Mexican forces surrounded the Alamo for 12 days. Then, early in the morning of March 6, 1836, the Mexican army charged the Alamo. Both the Texans and the Mexicans fought bravely for more than and hour and a half. In the end, almost all of the 187 men inside the Alamo were killed. Included among the dead were famous frontiersmen Davy Crockett and Jim Bowie. Losses on the Mexican side were also high.

Defeat at the Alamo united the Texans in their fight for independence. With cries of "Remember the Alamo!" echoing across the battlefield, Sam Houston's army attacked the Mexican forces at San Jacinto on April 21, 1836. *(See map on page 402.)* The Texans captured Mexican president Santa Anna and won their independence. Texas had become an independent nation.

Lorenzo de Zavala

Lorenzo de Zavala was a Mexican politician who helped the Texas revolution. A passionate supporter of democracy, Zavala moved to Texas in 1835 because he opposed Mexican president Santa Anna. In 1836, he signed the Texas Declaration of Independence and was soon elected vice-president of the new Republic of Texas.

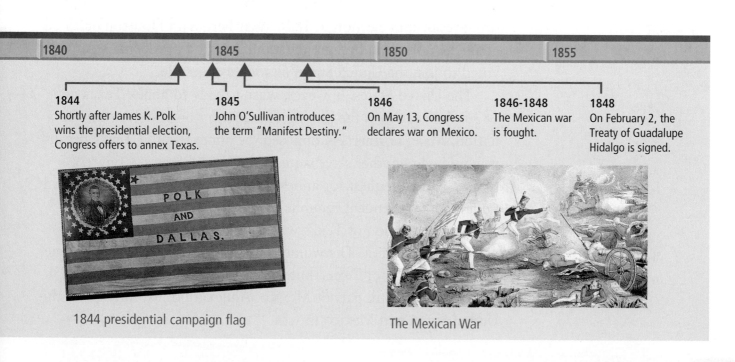

| 1840 | 1845 | 1850 | 1855 |

1844
Shortly after James K. Polk wins the presidential election, Congress offers to annex Texas.

1845
John O'Sullivan introduces the term "Manifest Destiny."

1846
On May 13, Congress declares war on Mexico.

1846-1848
The Mexican war is fought.

1848
On February 2, the Treaty of Guadalupe Hidalgo is signed.

1844 presidential campaign flag

The Mexican War

Texas won its independence with the Battle of San Jacinto. **Map Skill:** *Why do you think the majority of Anglo-American settlers in Texas came from the southern part of the United States?*

Texas, 1836-1845

UNITED STATES

DISPUTED AREA

REPUBLIC OF TEXAS

MEXICO

The Alamo

San Jacinto

Arkansas River

Rio Grande

Red River

Rio Grande

Legend

→ Santa Anna's route

✺ Battle

km 0   150   300
mi 0   150   300

The Lone Star flag *(above)* was adopted in 1839 to represent the Republic of Texas. When Texas joined the United States in 1845, the Lone Star flag became the state flag. It is flown today all across Texas.

The Lone Star Republic

The Texans modeled their new government on that of the United States. They drafted a constitution, establishing a president, a congress, and a judicial system. The government also allowed settlers to bring enslaved people to Texas. The new republic held its first presidential election in 1836. War hero Sam Houston defeated Stephen Austin and became the republic's first president. Texans voted to join the United States as soon as possible.

The United States, however, wasn't ready to annex Texas in 1836. **Annexation** is the joining of a country or other territory to a nation. Many northerners opposed the annexation of Texas because it would add another slave state to the United States. Congress refused Texas' request for annexation and as a result, Texas would remain an independent republic for nearly ten years.

The annexation of Texas was an important issue in the 1844 presidential election. The winner, James K. Polk, favored the immediate annexation of Texas, but the Mexican government insisted that Texas was still part of Mexico. Annexation just might lead the United States and Mexico to war.

War with Mexico

Focus *What was the impact of the Mexican War?*

By the 1840s, Americans were enthusiastic about annexation. Many believed that it was the destiny, or future, of the United States to expand across the continent. This belief became known as **Manifest Destiny** when John O'Sullivan, a magazine editor, wrote that it is ". . . our manifest destiny to overspread the continent . . . ."

In 1845, after Polk became president, Texas joined the Union. Mexico responded by breaking off friendly relations with the United States. The two sides **disputed,** or argued, bitterly over where the border between their countries lay. In January 1846, Polk ordered U.S. troops into the disputed area on the Rio Grande. *(See map at left.)* Fighting broke out in April, and on May 13, Congress declared war. Within two years, U.S. troops captured Mexico City.

The war ended with the signing of the Treaty of Guadalupe Hidalgo (gwah dah LOO peh ee DAHL goh) on February 2, 1848. Mexico not only surrendered its claim to Texas above the Rio Grande, but also gave up land that was to become Arizona, California, Nevada, Utah, and parts of many other western states. *(See map on page 405.)* Mexico had lost almost half its territory. The United States now stretched to the Pacific Ocean. Many Americans believed their nation had achieved its Manifest Destiny.

Then & Now

Texas was an independent nation for nearly 10 years, and Texans are proud of their history. Today, many students in Texas show their pride every morning by saying a pledge and salute to the Texas Flag:

"Honor the Texas Flag. I pledge allegiance to thee, Texas, one and indivisible."

Lesson Review

1830	1840	1850

1836
Texas wins independence

1845
Texas joins the United States

1846–1848
The Mexican War

1 **Key Vocabulary:** Use **annexation** and **Manifest Destiny** in a sentence about Texas.

2 **Focus:** How did Texas become an independent nation?

3 **Focus:** What was the impact of the Mexican War?

4 **Critical Thinking: Interpret** What advantages did Texas have as an independent nation? Did it gain any advantages by joining the United States?

5 **Theme: Crossing Frontiers** What were some of the reasons that American settlers flocked to the Mexican province of Texas?

6 **Citizenship: Writing Activity** You are a newspaper editor in May 1846 and you've just learned that Congress has declared war on Mexico. Write an editorial either supporting or criticizing the war.

Human Systems

How Did Countries Agree on Borders?

"Good fences make good neighbors," the old saying goes. The idea is that clear boundaries between neighbors can prevent disagreements. The same holds true for nations. Many wars have begun as a result of arguments over borders. Other wars have been prevented because both sides worked out their disagreements first. The current borders of the United States are the result of treaties, some of which followed wars.

Not all borders are the same. Some follow natural physical features such as rivers or mountain ranges. Others follow human-made lines like latitude or longitude. As a result, borders can appear very different, depending on how they were agreed upon. You can see this on the map at the right.

1 Oregon Country

United States and Britain
In the 1840s, many Americans wanted to fight against Britain over the Oregon Country. They believed that the boundary with Canada should be at latitude 54°40'N. An 1846 treaty set the border at 49°N.

In places where many people cross the Canada-U.S. border, each country has inspection stations. They keep track of people and goods entering and leaving each country.

This marker in the Rocky Mountains shows the border between Canada and the United States.

Math Connection

Land surveys determine the boundaries of an area. Surveying, a way of measuring the earth, is based on geometry. Angles and triangles play an important part. Surveyors use special measuring tape, sensitive instruments, and precise calculations to do their work. Measure the floor of your classroom to find its length and width. What is its area?

2 Spanish Lands

United States and Spain
The United States gained Florida from Spain in an 1819 treaty. In return, Americans agreed to respect Spanish claims to territory in the West.

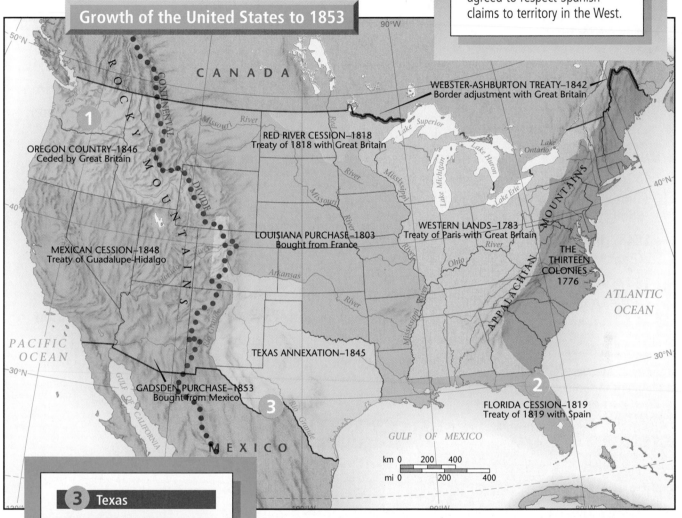

Growth of the United States to 1853

CANADA

WEBSTER-ASHBURTON TREATY–1842
Border adjustment with Great Britain

1

OREGON COUNTRY–1846
Ceded by Great Britain

RED RIVER CESSION–1818
Treaty of 1818 with Great Britain

ROCKY MOUNTAINS

CONTINENTAL DIVIDE

Missouri River

Lake Superior

Lake Michigan

Lake Huron

Lake Ontario

Lake Erie

MEXICAN CESSION–1848
Treaty of Guadalupe-Hidalgo

LOUISIANA PURCHASE–1803
Bought from France

WESTERN LANDS–1783
Treaty of Paris with Great Britain

Missouri River

Mississippi River

Ohio River

APPALACHIAN MOUNTAINS

THE THIRTEEN COLONIES – 1776

Arkansas River

Rio Grande

ATLANTIC OCEAN

PACIFIC OCEAN

TEXAS ANNEXATION–1845

GULF OF CALIFORNIA

GADSDEN PURCHASE–1853
Bought from Mexico

3

Rio Grande

FLORIDA CESSION–1819
Treaty of 1819 with Spain

2

MEXICO

GULF OF MEXICO

km 0   200   400
mi 0   200   400

3 Texas

BOUNDARY OF THE UNITED STATES OF AMERICA | LIMITE DE LOS ESTADOS UNIDOS MEXICANOS

INTERNATIONAL BOUNDARY AND WATER COMMISSION | COMISION INTERNACIONAL DE LIMITES Y AGUAS

United States and Mexico
In 1846, the United States claimed that Texas' border was the Rio Grande. Mexico claimed it was the Nueces River. The Rio Grande became the border after Mexico lost the Mexican-American War.

The Colorado River forms a border between California and Arizona. **Map Skill:** *What other rivers form state borders?*

Research Activity

Boundaries can be the result of treaties, trades, wars, old traditions, or even mistakes by geographers!

1 Research the boundaries of your state or one nearby.

2 Make a map of your state. Mark each boundary with an explanation of how it was agreed upon.

3 Share your map and findings with the class.

Across the Continent

> *Main Idea* The promise of land and a new life inspired thousands of Americans to move west across the continent.

J edediah Strong Smith's middle name said it all. Once, a grizzly bear grabbed him around the head and ripped off part of his scalp and ear. Smith stayed calm and somehow managed to escape. Later, a friend sewed his ear back on with a needle and thread.

Smith was one of many mountain men who roamed the American West in the early 1800s. Dressed in furs and fringed buckskins, they explored the mountainous region beyond the Great Plains, trapping beaver and trading furs. They also had frequent contact with Native Americans, who showed them the trails they had been using for thousands of years. It was from the Crow Indians, in fact, that Smith learned in 1824 of a **pass,** or opening, through the mountains. South Pass, in the Rocky Mountains, soon became a gateway for pioneers heading west on the Oregon Trail. Mountain men like Smith blazed the way for an expanding nation.

The Oregon Trail became a passageway to the west for thousands of American settlers. **Map Skill:** *What part of the trail went into Mexico?*

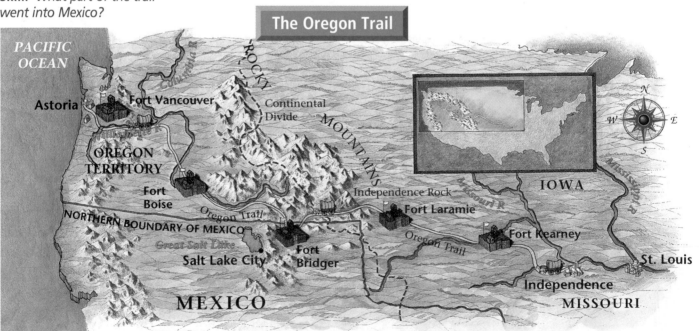

The Oregon Trail

PACIFIC OCEAN

Astoria — Fort Vancouver

OREGON TERRITORY

Fort Boise

NORTHERN BOUNDARY OF MEXICO

Great Salt Lake

Salt Lake City

Fort Bridger

Oregon Trail

ROCKY

Continental Divide

MOUNTAINS

Independence Rock

Fort Laramie

Oregon Trail

Fort Kearney

MISSISSIPPI R.

IOWA

St. Louis

Independence

MEXICO

MISSOURI

The Oregon Trail

Focus *What led American settlers to cross the Great Plains in large numbers during the 1840s?*

The first settlers to travel over South Pass were missionaries hoping to convert Native Americans to Christianity. In 1834, a minister named Jason Lee came to Oregon. Two years later, he was joined by a determined Presbyterian missionary named Marcus Whitman. Whitman traveled the Oregon Trail with his wife Narcissa.

The missionaries failed to convert many Native Americans to Christianity, but they did attract thousands of settlers to Oregon. Their letters to family and friends back East sparked an Oregon fever that swept the nation. Booklets and articles pictured a land blessed with a mild climate and fertile soil. One boy remembered hearing Oregon described as "a pioneer's paradise" where "the pigs are running about under the great acorn trees, round and fat, and already cooked, with knives and forks sticking in them so that you can cut off a slice whenever you are hungry."

The Long Journey

Oregon-bound travelers packed all their belongings into covered wagons. During the 2,000-mile-long journey they faced many hardships and dangers.

Women's responsibilities on the trail often included gathering fuel, preparing food, and caring for the children.

Wagons were packed full of furniture, clothing, cooking utensils, and supplies for the trip. Travelers carefully packed their flour in double sacks to keep out moisture.

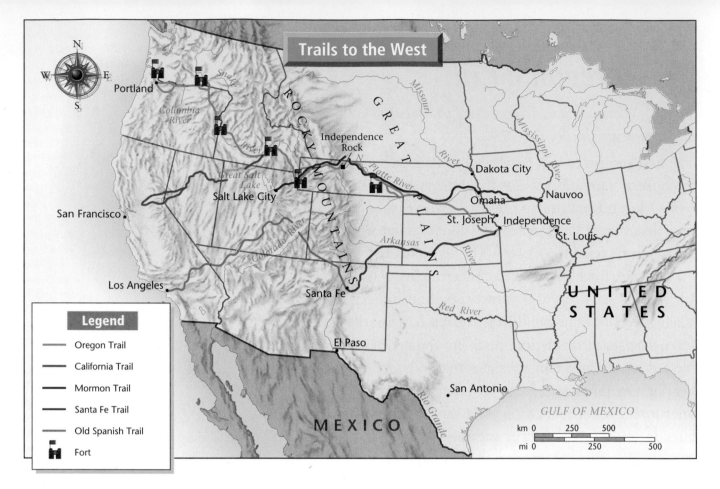

Trails to the West

Portland · Columbia River · Snake River · ROCKY MOUNTAINS · GREAT PLAINS · Missouri River · Mississippi River

Independence Rock · Platte River

Great Salt Lake · Salt Lake City · Dakota City

San Francisco · Colorado River · Omaha · Nauvoo

St. Joseph · Independence · St. Louis

Arkansas River

Los Angeles · Santa Fe · Red River

UNITED STATES

El Paso

San Antonio

Rio Grande · GULF OF MEXICO

MEXICO

km 0   250   500
mi 0   250   500

Legend
— Oregon Trail
— California Trail
— Mormon Trail
— Santa Fe Trail
— Old Spanish Trail
🏰 Fort

Pioneers heading west followed many different trails. **Map Skill:** *Identify the shortest route to California from St. Louis. Is it the easiest route to travel? What factors could add to the difficulty of a trail?*

Pioneer children might bring one toy to comfort them during the long journey.

The great migration over the Oregon Trail began in 1843. In early spring, pioneers gathered in Independence, Missouri, to load their wagons for the six-month journey. They eventually crossed the **Continental Divide**, which includes the crest of the Rocky Mountains. All rivers that run from this ridge flow either east, draining into the Atlantic Ocean, or west into the Pacific Ocean.

Pioneers faced many dangers. In her diary, Amelia Stewart Knight described how even foul weather could be a hardship:

❝ *Wednesday, June 1 — It has been raining all day long .... The men and boys are all soaking wet and look sad and comfortless .... all this for Oregon.* ❞

By 1845, more than 3,000 settlers had passed over the Oregon Trail. While some Native Americans traded with the travelers, most viewed the migration as a threat to their lands and way of life. Pawnee leader Curly Chief later recalled what one of his people had told the first settlers who came: "We do not want your presents, and we do not want you to come into our country."

Other Trails West

Focus *What other trails led to the settlement of the West?*

Ask Yourself

If your family were packing up to follow the Oregon Trail out west, what possessions would you choose to bring with you? What do you think would be most useful to have in a new place?

? ? ? ? ? ? ? ? ? ? ? ? ? ?

Not all of the pioneers headed to Oregon. Many Americans followed the California Trail. For that journey, pioneers faced the difficult task of crossing the Sierra Nevada before winter set in. Earlier, in the 1820s, pioneers and traders had followed the old Santa Fe Trail to New Mexico. They brought clothes, hardware, and textiles to trade for furs, gold, and silver.

Some Americans went west for religious reasons. Persecuted in the East, and then again in the Midwest, the members of the Church of Jesus Christ of Latter Day Saints, known as Mormons, moved west to find a new home. In 1847, their leader Brigham Young led the first group westward along what became known as the Mormon Trail. Arriving at the shores of the Great Salt Lake in Utah, they saw the land was dry and barren — "the paradise of the lizard, the cricket and the rattlesnake." Young quickly organized his people to begin work. They built irrigation canals that brought water from the mountains. Soon, their desert community flourished with produce and grain.

In search of land, money, and religious freedom, a steady stream of pioneers traveled across trails to the West. Soon, a new discovery would bring many, many more.

Lesson Review

1820	1835	1850

1824
Jedediah Smith learns of South Pass

1843
Oregon Trail Great Migration

1847
Mormons settle Utah

1 **Key Vocabulary:** Write a sentence about the Oregon Trail using pass and Continental Divide.

2 **Focus:** What led American settlers to cross the Great Plains in large numbers during the 1840s?

3 **Focus:** What other trails led to the settlement of the West?

4 **Critical Thinking: Cause and Effect** How did the environment influence migration routes west?

5 **Geography:** What were some of the difficulties posed by the environment that pioneers faced on the Oregon Trail?

6 **Citizenship: Drama Activity** Act out a scene between two families who are considering moving to Oregon. One family has decided to go; the other is still unsure. Write down what the members of each family might say.

Reading a Contour Map

Ups and Downs

The thousands of settlers who traveled on the Oregon Trail passed by Independence Rock in Wyoming, a popular stopping place along the trail. If you visited Wyoming today, you might like to hike around this historic area. If you did, what kind of map would be best to bring?

You could use elevation or relief maps to see the general height of the land. If you wanted to climb to the top of a hill, though, your best choice would be a **contour map**. Contour maps show the elevation of the land in great detail. They help you plan routes by showing the difference between cliffs and gentle slopes.

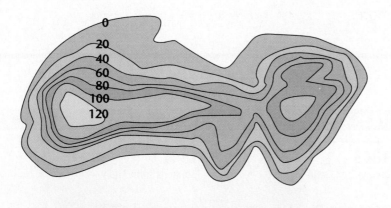

What are contour lines?

On a contour map, imaginary lines called **contours** show how the land rises and falls. Each contour line connects all the places at the same elevation. If you could walk along one line, you would always be at exactly the same height above sea level. Your path wouldn't rise or fall.

Contour map of a hill

The top diagram shows a hill from above, as though you were above the hill looking down. Imaginary lines connect points of the same elevation around the hill. The steeper an area is, the closer together the lines are. The bottom diagram shows the same hill from the side. The numbers show the elevation in feet of each line.

LEGEND: Measurements are in feet

❶ Here's How

Study the contour map on the right.

- Look for lines that are close together. This shows a steep slope.

- Find an area where the lines are farther apart. This shows a more gentle slope.

- Find an area with no contour lines. This land is almost flat.

- Look for a shape with no lines inside it. This is the top of a hill or mountain peak. Find the two peaks on Independence Rock.

- Read the **contour interval**, or space between each contour line.

- Figure out the elevation of a line without a number marked on it. First, find an elevation that is marked. Then count up or down.

- Find the elevation of the Oregon Trail where it crosses the river. Look for the closest contour line to the trail. Follow the line with your finger until you reach an elevation number. Here, the Oregon Trail is at 5,880 feet.

❷ Think It Through

When would it be better to use a contour map than an elevation map?

❸ Use It

1. What is the contour interval on this map?

2. Write the elevations of the three peaks on this map.

3. Write a description of the land you would hike through if you headed south from Independence Rock, crossing the river. Would you expect to hike up, down, or across flat land?

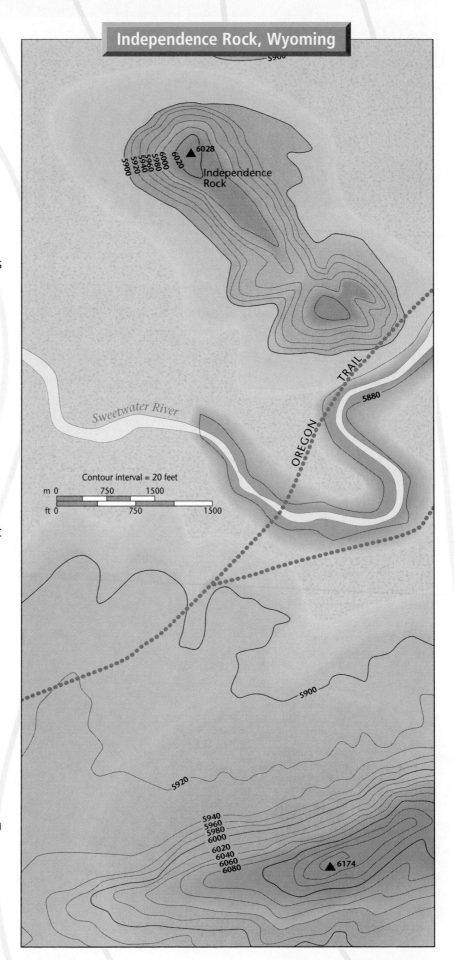

Independence Rock, Wyoming

Contour interval = 20 feet

Sweet Betsy from Pike

This song was popular among the cross-country pioneers. There are many more verses, some of which are very funny. Even though the song has a happy rhythm and a bouncy melody, it describes many of the hardships faced by the overland travelers.

This hide-covered trunk with clothes *(below)* was used by pioneers on the Oregon Trail. The bonnet *(above, right)* would have kept the sun off a woman's face while she was riding across the prairie.

The Shanghai ran off an' the oxen all died.
That morning the last piece of bacon was fried.
Poor Ike got discouraged an' Betsy got mad,
An' the dog wagged his tail and looked wondrously sad.
Sing too-ral-li-oo-ral-i -oo-ral-i-ay,
Sing too-ral-li-oo-ral-i -oo-ral-i-ay.

They swam the wide rivers and crossed the tall peaks,
And camped on the prairie for weeks upon weeks.
Starvation and cholera and hard work and slaughter,
They got 'cross the country, spite of heck and high water.
Sing too-ral-li-oo-ral-i -oo-ral-i-ay,
Sing too-ral-li-oo-ral-i -oo-ral-i-ay.

Pioneers had to carry all their own supplies with them on the trail. This cooking pot (above) would have gotten plenty of use on the long trip.

This picture entitled *Emigrants Crossing the Plains* was engraved by Darley and Hall in 1869.

Response Activities

1. **Interpret** After a hard day's journey, travelers relaxed by singing songs and telling stories. How do you think a song like "Sweet Betsy from Pike," would help to keep the travelers' spirits up?

2. **Expressive: Write a Diary Entry** If you were a cross-country pioneer, how would you describe your trip? Write a diary entry for a typical day on the Oregon Trail.

3. **Geography: Find and Trace a Map** Trace a map of the Rocky Mountains. Label the states the pioneers passed through. Could they have avoided crossing the mountains to get to Oregon?

Mining the West

Main Idea The discovery of gold and silver attracted many settlers to the West.

Key Vocabulary

forty-niner
boomtown

Key Events

1849 California
Gold Rush

1850 California
becomes a state

1859 Comstock
Lode

Sam Brannan's curiosity perked up one day in March of 1848. A couple of customers in his California general store paid for their purchases with gold. A little detective work satisfied his curiosity. He found out that workers at a sawmill on the nearby American River had discovered gold.

Brannan figured this could be good for business. He spent the next few weeks quietly filling the shelves of his store with supplies that miners might need. On May 12, he went to San Francisco to advertise. Walking through the streets, he held a bottle of gold dust in one hand and waved his hat in the other. Excitedly he shouted to the winds, "Gold! Gold! Gold from the American River!"

The news soon spread, and the Gold Rush was on. As one government official said,

> **"T**he blacksmith dropped his hammer, the carpenter his plane, the mason his trowel, the baker his loaf . . . . All were off for the mines . . . .**"**

Forty-niners flocked to California to search for gold nuggets like these.

The California Gold Rush

Focus *What impact did the discovery of gold in California have on that territory?*

The sawmill where gold was discovered belonged to a Swiss immigrant named Johann Sutter. James Marshall, a carpenter at the mill, found the first nugget of gold on the morning of January 24, 1848. Sutter and Marshall tried to keep the discovery a secret, but such exciting news traveled quickly. By 1849, a flood of people arrived in California in search of gold. These gold seekers who came from all over the country during the rush of 1849 were called **forty-niners.**

In this photograph, taken in 1852, gold miners search for gold in the ground. **Economics:** *How might the way of life and success of a gold miner differ from that of a store owner or a farmer?*

Once in California, forty-niners often failed to find gold. Louise Clappe, one of the very few women to live in a mining camp, tells the sad tale in a letter to her sister:

> "**G**old mining is nature's great lottery scheme. A man may work in a claim for many months, and be poorer at the end of the time than when he commenced [began]; or he may take out thousands in a few hours. It is a mere matter of chance."

In spite of the risks, California's population soared. San Francisco grew from less than 900 people in 1848 to about 25,000 in two years. The increase in population gained statehood for California in 1850.

As word about the Gold Rush continued to spread, people traveled from all over the world to strike it rich in California. Many of the most experienced miners came from Mexico and other Latin American countries. In addition, about 25,000 Chinese gold seekers had settled in California by 1852. They called their new home *Gum Shan*, which means "golden mountain."

California's Native American population declined rapidly during the Gold Rush, due mainly to disease and violence. Their population fell from about 150,000 in 1845 to about 30,000 in 1870.

Searching for Gold

1 Use your shovel to dig for gold, and your pick to break up rocks.

2 Use your sifter, called a cradle, to sift gold dust out of sand taken from the river.

3 Use your pan, like this forty-niner, as another way to sift gold nuggets or gold dust from dirt or sand.

Mining the Mountains

Focus *What role did mining play in the settlement of the West?*

Rumors of gold sent thousands of miners rushing to the West. In 1859, word spread of gold in Nevada. Miners who had failed in California made their way eastward over the Sierra Nevada. Some miners who found gold complained that it wasn't pure because it was mixed with a blue-colored rock. Someone decided to have this "blue stuff" examined. It was silver! This rich silver find, called the Comstock Lode, led to a silver rush in Nevada. The Comstock Lode produced $300 million worth of silver in the next 20 years.

Miners also searched the hills of Arizona, Colorado, Idaho, Montana, and Wyoming. As miners followed rumors of new discoveries, towns sprang up across the West — places like Tombstone, Deadwood, Cripple Creek, Poverty Hill, Poker Flat, and Silver City. They were known as **boomtowns** because they grew quickly in population and wealth.

Life in these rough-and-tumble mining communities was wild and often dangerous. Without a government to make and enforce laws, miners formed citizens' organizations to combat crime. When gold and silver ran out, many of the boomtowns turned into ghost towns. Other places, like San Francisco, grew steadily as miners turned into settlers.

Population (in thousands)

Year	
1847	
1850	

This chart shows the increase in the population of California after the Gold Rush of 1849. **Chart Skill:** *How could this chart help explain why California became a state in 1850?*

· Tell Me More ·

The First Blue Jeans

More successful than the gold miners were the merchants, who sold supplies to the miners. They realized that the best way to make a fortune was by "mining the miners," rather than mining for gold.

In the 1850s, a merchant from Bavaria named Levi Strauss brought a load of canvas to sell to the California miners for tents. He soon found a better use for his canvas: making clothes for the miners. These clothes included work pants much like the blue jeans you wear today.

This Montana boomtown, photographed in 1865, was called Last Chance Gulch. Many boomtowns turned to ghost towns when the gold ran out, but this town became the capital of Montana and changed its name. **Geography:** *What is the name of this town today?*

In the mid 1800s, the nation was growing by leaps and bounds. In 1821 there had been 24 stars on the United States flag, representing its 24 states. All but two of these states lay east of the Mississippi River. By 1850, seven new stars had been added to the flag. Now the country stretched from sea to sea. Drawn by land and gold, thousands of settlers had followed trails to the West. New ports in California welcomed settlers from abroad. And land that had been gained through war and negotiations added Mexican territory to the United States.

Lesson Review

1840	1850	1860

1849
California Gold Rush

1850
California becomes a state

1859
Comstock Lode

1. **Key Vocabulary:** Describe the Gold Rush using **forty-niner** and **boomtown**.

2. **Focus:** What impact did the discovery of gold in California have on that territory?

3. **Focus:** What role did mining play in the settlement of the West?

4. **Critical Thinking: Generalize** What skills and knowledge would a person need to be a gold miner?

5. **Theme: Crossing Frontiers** Write a paragraph explaining the following statement: "By 1850, the United States stretched from sea to sea."

6. **Geography: Art Activity** You have just discovered gold in Colorado. Soon, thousands of gold miners will be joining you. Draw the layout of a new mining town, labeling the stores and other buildings you'll need.

CHAPTER 15

Chapter Review

Chapter Review Timeline

1830 | 1835 | 1840 | 1845 | 1850

- **1836** Texas wins independence
- **1843** Oregon Trail Great Migration
- **1845** Texas joins the United States
- **1846–1848** Mexican War
- **1849** California Gold Rush

Summarizing the Main Idea

1 Copy and complete the chart below, indicating the territories that became part of the United States and why the U.S. gained control over them.

Territory	Reason U.S. gained control
Texas	
Oregon	
Utah	
California	
Nevada	

Vocabulary

2 Use each of the following terms in a sentence about westward expansion.

annexation (p. 402)
Manifest Destiny (p. 403)
dispute (p. 403)
pass (p. 406)
Continental Divide (p. 408)
forty-niner (p. 414)
boomtown (p. 416)

Reviewing the Facts

3 Why did so many Anglo-Americans move to Texas?

4 Who was Sam Houston?

5 What was the impact of the defeat at the Alamo?

6 What did the United States gain from the Mexican War?

7 What were some of the reasons that pioneers traveled to the West? What hardships did they face?

8 How did the Gold Rush change the population of people who lived in California?

9 Why did many boomtowns grow quickly and then become ghost towns?

Skill Review: Reading a Contour Map

10 Explain the difference between an elevation map and a contour map.

11 Imagine if the pioneers traveling west had been able to use elevation and contour maps. How might their journeys been different had they had these tools?

Geography Skills

12 Which of the rivers involved in the border dispute between the United States and Mexico is located further to the south: the Neuces River or the Rio Grande?

13 Look at a modern-day map of the United States. If you were to drive, what route might you take to get from your hometown to Oregon? Why did you choose it?

Critical Thinking

14 **Interpret** Why do you think the government of Mexico invited Anglo-Americans to live in Texas? How could Mexico have protected its land while still allowing people to settle there?

15 **Conclude** Thousands of people flocked to California to search for gold even though chances were slim that they would find it. Why were people willing to uproot themselves and leave their homes, friends, and families in search of gold?

Writing: Citizenship and History

16 **Citizenship** Many Americans in the 1840s believed in Manifest Destiny. Write an editorial in support of or against Manifest Destiny.

17 **History** Write a book promotion for a book about the Gold Rush. What historical information would you highlight as being included in your book?

Activities

Geography/Writing Activity
Pick one of the areas settled in the West (California, Arizona, Nevada, Utah, or Oregon). Create a travel guide for someone visiting that area today. What interesting things are there to see and do?

History/Art Activity
Create a boomtown. Illustrate a large map of the town showing the different kinds of buildings, the roads, and so on. Include a population chart. Add symbols and a legend.

Internet Option

Check the **Internet Social Studies Center** for ideas on how to extend your theme project beyond your classroom.

THEME PROJECT CHECK-IN

Use the information in this chapter to complete your project. As you work, think about these questions:
- How did you decide on the route you chose for your journey?
- What difficulties did you encounter on your journey that you might not have expected before starting?
- What made you and others during this period undertake such dangerous journeys?

The Civil War

"A house divided against itself cannot stand."

Abraham Lincoln

· THEME ·

Conflict and Resolution

"It would have been devastating to live through the Civil War because of all that shooting. It was important for the North and South to unite."

Edward Klueg, Fifth Grade
Evansville, IN

Differences do not have to lead to conflict. In the United States, during the mid-1800s, they did. The North and South differed greatly — in their economies, and in their views on government and slavery. Attempts to settle these differences peacefully failed, and a civil war broke out. It tore families and friends apart and killed many people. It also ended slavery. The nation reunited following the war, but the wounds did not heal for many years.

 Theme Project

Making History

The Civil War has ended. You have survived it. A historian asks you to tell how the war changed your life.

- Make a chart with the headings "before" and "after." Use it to describe your life before and after the war.
- Write an account of what you saw and did during this period. How has your region changed?
- Tape-record your thoughts about the war.

RESEARCH: Find out about a real person who lived through the Civil War. How did it affect him or her?

◀ Cemetery Ridge, Gettysburg, Pennsylvania

WHEN & WHERE
ATLAS

When tension between the North and South began to build in the first half of the 1800s, the two regions compromised, and resolved their differences. For a time, these compromises worked. As the debate over slavery and states' rights grew more bitter, conflict threatened to break out again. As the map illustrates, this conflict led to a civil war that threatened to divide the nation forever.

In this unit, you will read how western expansion raised the issue of slavery several times in the early 1800s and led to growing tension between North and South. You will also learn about the major events of the Civil War. Finally, you will read how efforts to reunite and rebuild the nation resulted in some successes and some failures.

Unit 7 Chapters

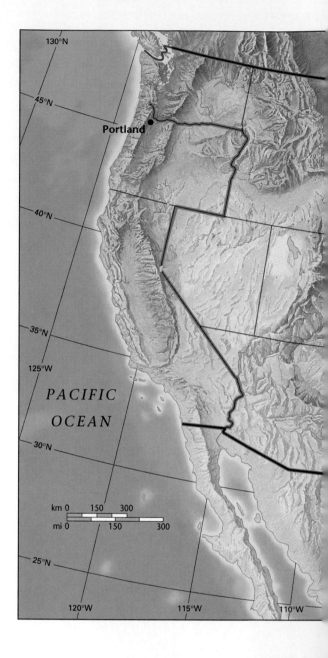

Unit Timeline

1820	1835	1850

Abraham Lincoln   **1860**

How did southern states react to Lincoln's election?
Chapter 16, Lesson 1

Civil War Cannon

Civil War weapons caused high casualties. Why was that so?
Chapter 16, Lesson 2

CANADA

Lake Superior

Lake Michigan

Lake Huron

Lake Ontario

Lake Erie

UNITED STATES OF AMERICA

Portland

Boston

Detroit

Chicago

Cleveland

New York

Pittsburgh

Philadelphia

Wilmington

Cincinnati

Washington, D.C.

Kansas City

St. Louis

Charleston

Richmond

ATLANTIC OCEAN

Chattanooga

Memphis

Atlanta

Charleston

Savannah

CONFEDERATE STATES OF AMERICA

Jacksonville

Mobile

New Orleans

Galveston

GULF OF MEXICO

MEXICO

45°N

40°N

65°W

35°N

30°N

95°W   90°W   85°W   80°W

N
W   E
S

Legend

The Union and the Confederacy

- ● City
- ★ Capital
- — United States and its territories
- — Confederate states
- ▨ West Virginia (admitted to Union, 1863)

1865   1880   1895

Appomatox   1865

General Lee said he would rather die a thousand deaths than do this.
Chapter 17, Lesson 1

Civil War Nurse

Learn about the many ways that women worked during the war.
Chapter 16, Lesson 4

The Freedmen's Bureau

Why was education important to people who were now free?
Chapter 17, Lesson 2

A House Divided

Chapter Preview: *People, Places, and Events*

1840   1845   1850

| Henry Clay 1850 | Uncle Tom's Cabin 1852 | Soldier's Shoulder Plate |

Henry Clay   **1850**

This man worked to keep peace between the North and South. *Lesson 1, Page 426*

Uncle Tom's Cabin   **1852**

The Queen of England wept when she read this book. Find out why. *Lesson 1, Page 428*

Soldier's Shoulder Plate

This shoulder plate stopped a bullet. How did new weapons change the fighting? *Lesson 2, Page 434*

Compromises and Conflicts

Main Idea The growing conflict between North and South over the issues of slavery eventually led the nation to war.

As a young woman, Harriet Beecher Stowe could not forget what she had once seen as a child. One day, standing on the banks of the Ohio River, she watched a boat go by. It was filled with African Americans, locked in chains, on their way to the South to be sold into slavery.

Growing up in the North, Stowe had only heard about slavery. What she saw that day made her sad and angry.

Many years later, those feelings led her to write *Uncle Tom's Cabin,* a novel that described the cruelties of slavery. Northerners who read Stowe's book were shocked. In the South, the book was banned. By 1852, when the book was published, there had already been years of conflict over the issue of slavery. Both the North and the South were running out of compromises.

◀ Union soldiers standing by a cannon.

Key Vocabulary

free state

slave state

Union

secede

Confederate

Key Events

1820 Missouri Compromise

1850 Compromise of 1850

1860 Lincoln elected President

1860 First southern state secedes

1855   1860   1865

African American Soldiers

These soldiers had waited a long time for the right to fight.
Lesson 3, Page 444

Life on the Home Front

With all the men away at war, who worked in the fields and factories?
Lesson 4, Page 448

Civil War Camp Life

What were some of the hardships that these children faced?
Lesson 4, Page 450

Debate over Slavery

Focus *How did new territory cause conflicts over slavery?*

Conflicts between the North and South over slavery began years before *Uncle Tom's Cabin.* In 1819, the United States was made up of 11 free states and 11 slave states. **Free states** did not allow slavery. **Slave states** permitted slavery. After the Mexican War, the United States gained territory that would become new states. North and South debated whether to permit slavery in these new states.

A word people used to describe the nation during this period was the **Union** — the states united under the Constitution. Each new state admitted to the Union would tip the political balance in Congress. Plantation owners in the South wanted more slave states, because representation in the Senate was by state. More slave states gave more voting power in the Senate to the South. The North, with its larger population, had more congressmen in the House of Representatives. More free states increased voting power for the North. Abolitionists fought to end slavery completely. Most northerners wanted at least to stop its spread into new states.

Compromises Between North and South

In 1819, Missouri asked to join the Union as a slave state. The Senate agreed, but the House of Representatives refused. A heated debate began. In 1820, the Speaker of the House, Henry Clay, proposed a solution — the Missouri Compromise. *(See map.)* Admit Missouri as a slave state, he said, but draw a line along its southern border. Territory north of that line could be admitted only as a free state. Maine would also join the Union, making the number of free and slave states equal again. For 30 years this compromise worked.

Ask Yourself

When the North and South argued over the spread of slavery, Congress made compromises to settle the dispute. Which of these compromises would you have voted for if you had been in Congress?

? ? ? ? ? ? ? ? ? ? ? ? ? ?

Throughout the first half of the 1800s, the spread of slavery into new territories caused conflict between the North and South. Congress fought to keep peace between the two sides by proposing compromises in 1820, 1850, and again in 1854. **Map Skill:** *How do these maps show that the Kansas-Nebraska Act broke the Missouri Compromise?*

The Compromises

MISSOURI COMPROMISE, 1820

UNORGANIZED TERRITORY

MISSOURI

Legend

Free state or territory

Slave state or territory

Territory open to slavery

Debate over the Compromise of 1850

John C. Calhoun, senator from South Carolina, called slavery a "positive good" and thought it should be allowed in new states.

Henry Clay, congressman from Kentucky and Speaker of the House, suggested strengthening the Fugitive Slave Law in return for California entering the Union as a free state.

Citizenship: *Why are speeches important in politics?*

Daniel Webster, a Massachusetts senator, argued for the compromise in order to save the Union.

Then, in 1850, California asked to join the Union as a free state. Because no other territory was joining as a slave state, the South wanted something in return. In the Compromise of 1850, Clay proposed strengthening the Fugitive Slave Law to satisfy the South. This law demanded that federal agents and ordinary citizens help capture escaped enslaved people and return them to slavery. Fearing a war between the North and the South, Senator Daniel Webster of Massachusetts urged Congress to vote for compromise:

> **"I** *wish to speak . . . not as a Massachusetts man, nor as a northern man, but as an American. . . . I speak today for the preservation of the Union.* **"**

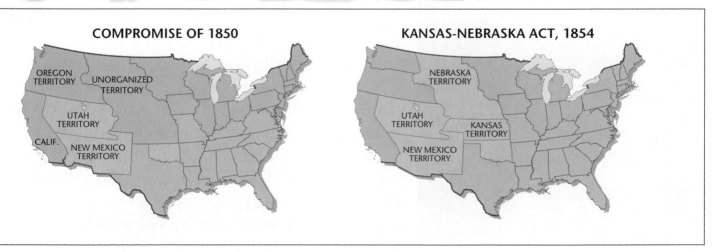

COMPROMISE OF 1850

OREGON TERRITORY
UNORGANIZED TERRITORY
UTAH TERRITORY
CALIF.
NEW MEXICO TERRITORY

KANSAS-NEBRASKA ACT, 1854

NEBRASKA TERRITORY
UTAH TERRITORY
KANSAS TERRITORY
NEW MEXICO TERRITORY

300,000 Americans bought Harriet Beecher Stowe's novel *Uncle Tom's Cabin*, the first year it was sold. Translated into many languages, it later sold millions of copies all over the world.

In this painting, John Brown is shown surrounded by armed southerners and kissing a baby. **Arts:** *Do you think a northerner or a southerner painted this image. Why?*

In 1854, peace was shattered when Congress passed a third compromise: the Kansas-Nebraska Act. This law stated that settlers in these territories could vote to determine whether they would be slave or free. Both Kansas and Nebraska were north of the Missouri Compromise line, and for this reason northerners and abolitionists believed they should have been free. Southerners disagreed. Settlers for and against slavery rushed into Kansas to seize control of the territory. For years, they fought violently with each other.

Growing Conflict

Focus *Why did compromises fail to stop the conflict between the North and South?*

Kansas was only one of many problems between the North and South. The Fugitive Slave Law had angered many northerners. It inspired Harriet Beecher Stowe to write *Uncle Tom's Cabin*. Soon, the North and South grew even further apart.

From Dred Scott to John Brown

In 1857 an important Supreme Court case heated up the slavery debate. Dred Scott, an enslaved African American, sued for his freedom because he had lived in free territory for four years. With the help of abolitionists, Scott brought his case to court, arguing that living in free territory made him a free man. The Supreme Court ruled against Scott, saying that enslaved people were not U.S. citizens. They were property, the Court said, and the right to property was protected by the Constitution. That meant that Congress could not prevent slaveowners from bringing property — in this case enslaved people — into a new territory. The Dred Scott decision made northerners furious because it erased the Missouri Compromise. Now slavery could exist anywhere.

In 1859, an abolitionist named John Brown led a small band of supporters into a weapons warehouse at Harpers Ferry, Virginia. He planned to start a slave revolt that would spread throughout the South. Captured before his revolution began, he was found guilty of treason and hanged. Many northerners applauded Brown, calling him a hero who died for a good cause. Southerners were horrified by northern praise of such a violent man.

The Election of Lincoln

Events of the 1850s divided the country, but the presidential election of 1860 created a final split. The Democrats nominated two candidates, one for the North and one for the South. The new Republican Party nominated just one — Abraham Lincoln.

Lincoln was born in a humble log cabin on the Kentucky frontier. The son of poor parents, he educated himself by reading every book he could borrow. At age 21, Lincoln moved to Illinois. He worked as a rail-splitter, surveyor, country storekeeper, and lawyer. He served in the state legislature and for one term in the U.S. House of Representatives. He ran for the Senate in 1855 and 1858. He lost both times but became well known for his speeches against slavery.

Lincoln was elected President of the United States in 1860. A Virginia newspaper called his election "the greatest evil that has ever befallen this country." In protest, South Carolina immediately **seceded,** or broke away from the rest of the country. By the time Lincoln was inaugurated in March, six more southern states had seceded: Mississippi, Florida, Alabama, Georgia, Louisiana, and Texas. They formed their own independent nation, the Confederate States of America. **Confederate** means part of a group united for a common purpose. The Confederacy elected Jefferson Davis as president. By June, Virginia, Arkansas, Tennessee, and North Carolina also joined, making a total of 11 Confederate states.

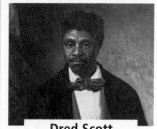

Dred Scott

As an enslaved child, Dred Scott dreamed of freedom. In his 30s, he was bought by an army doctor who traveled often. Scott traveled with him, living in free territory for four years but returning to Missouri, a slave state. When the doctor died, Scott sued in court for freedom. He filed his "freedom suit" in 1846. It was an important case for African Americans and the entire nation.

Lesson Review

1820	1840	1860

1820
Missouri Compromise

1850
Compromise of 1850

1860
Lincoln elected President
First southern states secede

1. **Key Vocabulary:** Describe the conflicts between the North and South using: **free state, slave state, secede, Confederate.**

2. **Focus:** How did new territory cause conflicts over slavery?

3. **Focus:** Why did compromises fail to stop the conflict between North and South?

4. **Critical Thinking: Cause and Effect** How did *Uncle Tom's Cabin* influence people's opinions about slavery?

5. **Theme: Conflict and Resolution** In each of the three compromises, what did both North and South have to give up?

6. **Geography/Math Activity:** In 1820, there were an equal number of free and slave states. Did the North and South have the same amount of land? Use the map on page 426 to make a chart.

Places and Regions

How Did Regions Vote in the 1860 Election?

Have you ever traveled to a different part of the country? If so, you may have noticed differences in the way people talked, in the way the landscape looked, or even in the architecture of the buildings. These are examples of regional differences.

Visitors to the United States in the 1850s could see regional differences between the North and the South. The South was a region of plantations and farms. Its way of life was supported by cotton and slavery. The North had many more large cities and factories, and opposed slavery.

These differences played a big role in the presidential election of 1860. Voters turned away from their usual political parties and voted according to regional interests. The election map on the next page shows how sharply divided the nation had become by 1860.

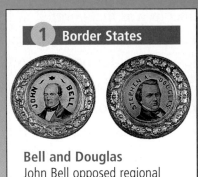

1 Border States

Bell and Douglas
John Bell opposed regional divisions. He won three slave states near the North that did not want to choose between North and South. Northern Democrat Stephen Douglas wanted a compromise on slavery. He won only in Missouri and part of New Jersey.

The painting above shows farmland in the South. At right is a northern factory. What were some of the South's main crops?

Songs showed differences between the North and the South. In 1859, Daniel Emmett wrote "Dixie," a song that praised the South. It became a marching song for the South during the Civil War. In 1861, Julia Ward Howe wrote "The Battle Hymn of the Republic," which became a marching song for the North. What songs represent regions or places today?

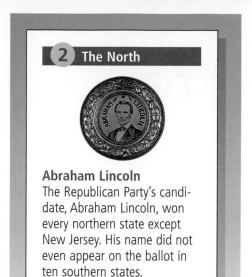

2 The North

Abraham Lincoln
The Republican Party's candidate, Abraham Lincoln, won every northern state except New Jersey. His name did not even appear on the ballot in ten southern states.

The Presidential Election of 1860

Legend

Lincoln – *Republican*

Douglas – *Democratic*

Breckinridge – *Democratic*

Bell – *Constitutional Union*

The split between North and South was not exact. Lincoln won California even though part of it was farther south than some states that Breckinridge won. **Map Skill:** *How many states did Lincoln win?*

3 The South

John Breckinridge
Regional differences split the Democratic Party in two. The Southern Democrats favored slavery. They nominated John Breckinridge as their candidate. He won nearly every southern state in the election.

Research Activity

1 Find out about a city or town the same size as your own but in another region. How are they different? How are they alike?

2 Chart your results. Share it with the class.

A House Divided **431**

Marching to Battle

Main Idea The North and South each had successes during the first two years of the Civil War, but the North gained the advantage in 1863.

Key Vocabulary

civil war

mobilize

volunteer

blockade

siege

Key Events

1861 First Battle of Bull Run

1862 Battles of Shiloh and Antietam

1863 Battle of Gettysburg

Just months after Lincoln's election, thousands of South Carolina men surrounded a Union fort in Charleston Harbor. Trapped inside Fort Sumter, Union soldiers were cut off from help and supplies. Lincoln, still hoping to reunite the country, delayed taking action. Then, southern representatives delivered a message to Fort Sumter. The Union commander must surrender or be fired upon. On April 12, 1861, the South Carolina men opened fire. The next day, the Union soldiers surrendered. The Civil War had begun.

The Fighting Begins

Focus *What advantages did each side have early in the war?*

A **civil war** is a war fought between regions of one nation. The U.S. Civil War, also called the War Between the States, forced many northern and southern friends to fight against each other, sometimes even father against son. One Indiana grandmother cried when

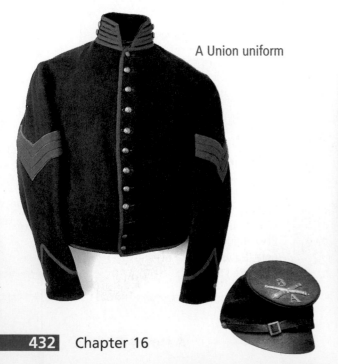
A Union uniform

A Union soldier and his family

she heard the news, "Oh, to think that I should have lived to see the day when Brother should rise against Brother."

Blue and Gray

As the North and South **mobilized,** or prepared for war, they each had certain advantages. In many ways, the North seemed stronger. It had a larger population, so it could have more **volunteers,** or people who chose to become soldiers. The North also had more industry, money, and railroads, so it could more easily supply, feed, and move its army. *(See chart at right.)* Most importantly, the North had their determined leader, Abraham Lincoln.

The 11 states of the Confederacy had far fewer people, and about one-third of the population was enslaved. Money, industry, and railroads were also more scarce in the South. Yet underdogs had won before. Many southern soldiers were hardy farm boys used to riding and shooting. Northern troops would have to conquer the South, while southerners would be defending their homes.

In addition, the Confederate army was led by some of the best generals in the country. Robert E. Lee, a Virginian and an officer in the United States Army, was one of many Americans with divided loyalties. He was a strong supporter of the Union, yet he declined President Lincoln's offer to lead the Union army. He took command of the Army of Virginia instead, writing to a northern friend:

> **"I** *cannot raise my hand against my birthplace, my home, my children.* **"**

Northern and Southern Resources

Railroad Mileage

71%

29%

Manufacturing Plants

86%

14%

■ North ■ South

This chart shows the large difference between the resources of the North and the South. **Chart Skill:** *How could these resources help the North win the Civil War?*

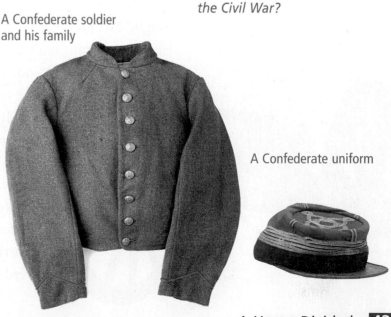

A Confederate soldier and his family

A Confederate uniform

This painting was done by Captain James Hope of the Second Vermont Volunteers, a survivor of the Battle of Antietam. It shows Union troops as they march across Antietam Creek facing constant fire from Confederate soldiers.

In early battles, soldiers fought at close range. They quickly realized that their weapons were not the same as in the past. Improved muskets made it possible to kill a person from half a mile away. Cannons were also more powerful and accurate than before.

Early Battles

On July 21, 1861, the First Battle of Bull Run was fought just south of Washington, D.C. This was the first real battle of the war. The North was confident of a quick victory. They planned to capture the nearby town of Manassas, Virginia, then march to the Confederate capital of Richmond. Hundreds of northerners, picnic baskets in hand, came to watch. One Connecticut soldier wrote, "We thought it wasn't a bad idea to have the great men from Washington come out to see us thrash the Rebs." Instead, it was the Rebels, as Confederate soldiers were called by the Union, who won. Union troops and frightened sightseers fled to Washington in a panic. Many southerners were convinced they had won the war.

The war would not be easily won by either side. After a hard-fought battle in April 1862, at Shiloh, Tennessee, Union General Ulysses S. Grant realized how true this was. He decided that it would not be possible to save the Union without completely conquering the South.

In September of 1862, Confederate General Robert E. Lee drove north, planning to conquer Pennsylvania. He fought Union troops to a draw at Antietam Creek, near Sharpsburg, Maryland. Because his army was too exhausted to continue, however, he had to retreat. The North claimed the victory. Over 50,000 men were killed or wounded at Shiloh and Antietam.

The Union Leads

Focus *How did the Union begin to gain the advantage in 1863?*

An anaconda is a snake that squeezes its prey to death. The North tried to squeeze the South into giving up, and it called this strategy the Anaconda Plan. *(See chart at right.)* The plan had three parts. First, the Union navy **blockaded** southern ports. *(See map below.)* This meant that northern ships stopped all traffic from entering or leaving the ports, so that the South couldn't ship its goods, or buy supplies from other countries.

The War at Sea

The Union rapidly built hundreds of wooden ships for the blockade of the southern coast. To defend its ports, the South developed a secret weapon — an ironclad ship. They raised a sunken northern ship called the *Merrimack* and covered it with iron plates. The *Virginia*, as this ship was renamed, could destroy wooden ships by running into them. Cannonballs would bounce off its sides. Hurriedly, the North built its own ironclad ship, the *Monitor*, to protect its fleet of wooden ships. On March 9, 1862, the two ships

The Anaconda Plan

Plan	Purpose
Part 1 Blockade Southern Ports	To prevent the South from selling cotton and buying military supplies
Part 2 Control Mississippi River	To limit shipping and divide the Confederacy
Part 3 Send Armies from the East and West	To squeeze Confederate troops into surrender

Chart Skill: *How did the plan squeeze the South's economy?*

Map Skill: *Which battle gave the Union control of the Mississippi?*

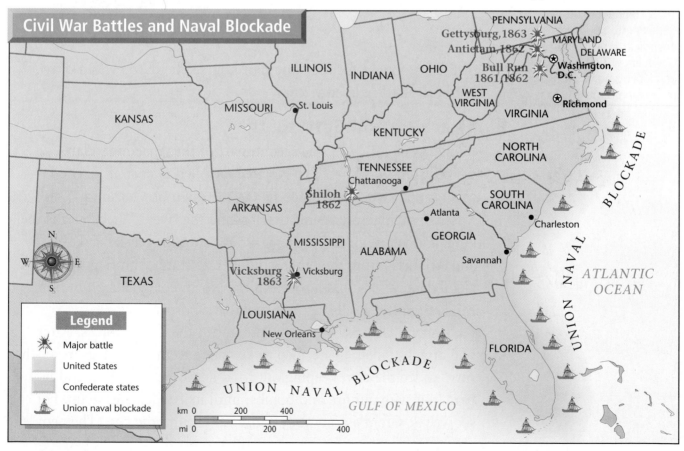

Civil War Battles and Naval Blockade

PENNSYLVANIA
Gettysburg, 1863
MARYLAND
Antietam, 1862
DELAWARE
Bull Run 1861, 1862
Washington, D.C.
ILLINOIS
INDIANA
OHIO
WEST VIRGINIA
Richmond
KANSAS
MISSOURI
St. Louis
VIRGINIA
KENTUCKY
NORTH CAROLINA
TENNESSEE
Chattanooga
Shiloh 1862
SOUTH CAROLINA
ARKANSAS
Atlanta
Charleston
GEORGIA
MISSISSIPPI
ALABAMA
Savannah
Vicksburg 1863
Vicksburg
TEXAS
ATLANTIC OCEAN
LOUISIANA
New Orleans
UNION NAVAL BLOCKADE
FLORIDA
GULF OF MEXICO

Legend
- Major battle
- United States
- Confederate states
- Union naval blockade

km 0 | 200 | 400
mi 0 | 200 | 400

A House Divided **435**

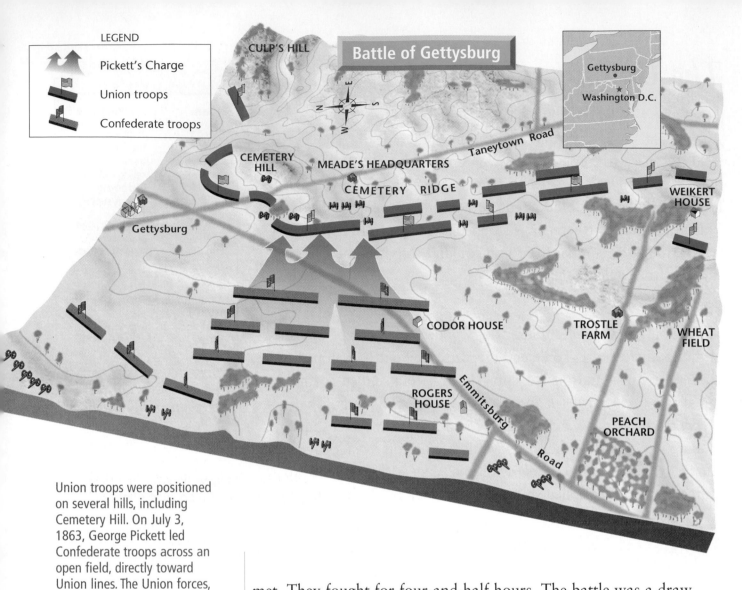

LEGEND

Pickett's Charge

Union troops

Confederate troops

CULP'S HILL

Gettysburg

Washington D.C.

CEMETERY HILL

MEADE'S HEADQUARTERS

Taneytown Road

CEMETERY RIDGE

WEIKERT HOUSE

Gettysburg

CODOR HOUSE

TROSTLE FARM

WHEAT FIELD

ROGERS HOUSE

Emmitsburg Road

PEACH ORCHARD

Union troops were positioned on several hills, including Cemetery Hill. On July 3, 1863, George Pickett led Confederate troops across an open field, directly toward Union lines. The Union forces, on higher ground, easily fired on the approaching troops.

met. They fought for four-and-half hours. The battle was a draw, but both sides claimed victory.

Vicksburg and Gettysburg

By the spring of 1863, the second part of the Anaconda Plan seemed to be working. The North controlled almost all of the Mississippi River. One holdout was the town of Vicksburg, Mississippi, high on a bluff overlooking the river. "Vicksburg is the key," Lincoln said. Capturing it would cut off Louisiana, Texas, and Arkansas from the other Confederate states, splitting up the Confederacy. It would also mean the North controlled all of the Mississippi River, closing more southern ports.

General Ulysses S. Grant commanded the Union forces. After two attacks failed, he decided to lay **siege** to the city. This means he surrounded the city, keeping out food and other supplies, and bombarded it with gunfire and bombs, until its residents gave up. For six weeks, Grant's army drew closer in around the city. The people of Vicksburg were trapped. They could not leave or get help. Finally, on July 4, Vicksburg surrendered. As General Grant later said, "The fate of the Confederacy was sealed when Vicksburg fell."

While Union forces were closing off the West, Confederate troops were invading the North. After General Robert E. Lee won two battles in Virginia — at Fredericksburg and Chancellorsville — he led his troops to the small town of Gettysburg, Pennsylvania.

On July 3, Lee ordered a direct attack on Union troops. *(See map at left.)* Under the command of General George Pickett, 15,000 men charged uphill and across open fields, under enemy fire. Union forces, positioned on Cemetery Ridge, picked off the advancing troops. Still, line after line of gray-uniformed soldiers kept on coming. As one Union soldier described Pickett's Charge, "Foot to foot, body to body, and man to man they struggled and pushed and strived and killed." The battle was a massacre. More southern soldiers were killed or wounded at Gettysburg than in any other battle of the war — almost one-third of those who fought.

The battles of Gettysburg and Vicksburg marked turning points in the war. Five days after Vicksburg, Union forces gained complete control of the Mississippi River, dividing the Confederacy. The Battle of Gettysburg showed both northerners and southerners that Robert E. Lee could be beaten.

Today, groups get together to re-enact battles from the Civil War. They dress in uniforms like the ones soldiers then wore, carry weapons that resemble theirs, and even ride horses like the men above. These groups often play the roles of the specific military units that were present at these battles.

Lesson Review

1861	1862	1863
1861 First Battle of Bull Run	**1862** Battles of Shiloh and Antietam	**1863** Battle of Gettysburg

1 **Key Vocabulary:** Discuss the Civil War using these words: civil war, mobilize, volunteer, blockade, siege.

2 **Focus:** What advantages did each side have early in the war?

3 **Focus:** How did the Union begin to gain the advantage in 1863?

4 **Critical Thinking: Interpret** Explain why Lincoln said, "Vicksburg is the key." Why was the Mississippi River so important?

5 **Theme: Conflict and Resolution** Explain how the Union blockade hurt the South's chances of winning the war. Do you think it also hurt civilians?

6 **Geography/Art Activity:** Use the map on the opposite page to build a model of the land at the Battle of Gettysburg. Show the high and low ground.

Comparing Historical Images

Two Views of History

To learn more about the Battle of Vicksburg, you might look at paintings of battle scenes. Or you might study photographs taken at the battlefield — photography was invented shortly before the war. What might a painting show you that a photograph might not? What can you learn from a photograph that you can't learn from a painting? How might pictures show how an artist or photographer felt about the event? How can you use these images to get the full picture of an event?

This painting shows the 8th Pennsylvania Cavalry charge near Chancellorsville.

1 Here's How

These pages show a painting and a photograph of Civil War battlefields.

- What do you notice when you look at these battlefield images? What do you think the artists were trying to show about their subjects?

- Look for details that are shown in the painting but not in the photograph, such as the moving horses. Photography in the 1860s could not capture movement. What details does the photograph show that are not in the painting? For example, how do the soldiers' gestures in the photograph look different from those in the painting?

- Which image do you think is more true to life? How can a painter change reality? How can a photographer "set up" a photograph?

- How might the artists' opinions about the Civil War affect each image?

2 Think It Through

Think about your own views and knowledge of the Civil War. What do the photograph and the painting tell you that you did not know before? Suppose you saw only one of the two images. How might your understanding of the Civil War change?

3 Use It

1. Draw a chart with two columns labeled Photograph and Painting.

2. Compare these details in each picture: a) number of people b) actions taking place c) facial expressions or physical gestures d) landscape.

3. Write about how an artist's choice of subject and details can influence our understanding of history.

George N. Barnard took this photograph of a Confederate fort in 1864.

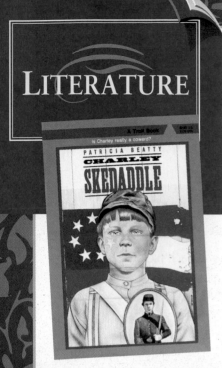

Historical Fiction

CHARLEY SKEDADDLE

By Patricia Beatty

When 12-year-old Charley Quinn hears his brother was killed at Gettysburg, he leaves New York City to become a drummer boy in the Union army. He sees a friend killed in a battle and, terrified, he "skedaddles" — runs away. He is captured by a Confederate soldier and brought into camp, where he witnesses another battle.

The boy was just settling himself onto the ground when he was forced to leap to his feet to keep from being run over by a host of men racing toward him. Rebels! Rebels retreating as fast as they could.

Then a great animal-like roar rose up from a thousand throats, and Charley saw other tattered Rebels racing forward through the ranks of their retreating comrades. A charge! As they ran, they screeched the famous Rebel yell, *"Ee ee-ee-ee-ee."*

Behind them came a tall, gray-bearded officer in a gray uniform under a black cloak, riding a dapple-gray horse with a black mane and tail. As the officer reached the charging men, a few of them, hearing the hoofbeats, slackened their speed. At once, a wild shouting rose up from these men: "Go back, General Lee. Go back!"

Lee? Robert E. Lee? Charley Quinn gaped in amazement, as did the other prisoners. Generals were seldom seen anywhere, and certainly not in infantry charges.

Charley watched, fascinated, as a sergeant of the charging Texas Brigade sprang forward to grab hold of the bridle of Lee's horse, stopping the famous Traveller from going into battle with his master.

Now many Texans halted their attack to turn and shout, "We won't go unless you go back!"

A Confederate officer rode up to Lee's side and began to argue with him. When Lee slowly shook his head, the sergeant let go of the rein to release it to his commander-in-chief. An enormous cheer crashed into the smoky air as Lee turned his horse around and began to ride toward some horsemen in a knoll to his right.

"Lee! Lee!" echoed soldiers' deep voices. While their comrades cheered, those men of the Texas Brigade who had forced Lee back to safety resumed their charge against the Yankees among the trees.

As for Charley Quinn, he sat down again at a bayonet's prod until a corporal came over, pointed to him, and then jerked him to his feet. Hustled along, he was taken to a tent where a sad-faced, balding Confederate officer sat at a little folding table. It was hot inside, and the front and rear tent flaps were open for ventilation.

Once the corporal had gone, the officer asked, "Who are you, lad?"

"Charley. Charley Skedaddle."

"I know that word. And I doubt that is your real last name."

Charley swallowed and said, "It's Quinn, sir."

"You are not a soldier, are you?"

"No, sir. I never signed any papers to enlist. I was only a drummer."

At this, the officer put down the pen he had in his hand. "A drummer boy. I thought as much. What is your age?"

"Twelve, sir."

"What is your regiment?"

Charley didn't answer. All soldiers had been warned that if they were ever captured, they were to tell only their name and rank. He had done that already, and now he said, "I can't tell you that, sir."

Yankee
the name southerners gave to Union soldiers

This charcoal drawing by Winslow Homer is of a Union drummer boy.

The Drummer Boy was painted by Edwin Forbes. Boys such as this one beat their drums during charges to tell soldiers how fast to march, when to fire, and when to reload.

regiment
a fighting unit of soldiers

minié ball
a rifle bullet used during the Civil War

The officer smiled slightly. "Have you ever gone to school?"

"Oh, yes, sir. I can read and write just dandy."

"I'm glad to hear it. I was a schoolmaster at one time." He sighed. "How did you get separated from your regiment? I think you can tell me *that*, you know."

Blushing, Charley lowered his gaze. He stuttered, "I — I got scared when I saw my drum hit by a minié ball and saw my friend Jem get killed, so I ran away." Mother Mary, no, he wouldn't dare say he'd picked up a musket and killed a Reb. That'd bring him more trouble, for sure.

"So you ran away? I thought you had. Well, you are only a child, after all. Have you ever heard of Andersonville Prison?"

"No, sir, I haven't."

The Confederate officer sighed again. "It's a prison camp for Yankee soldiers down in Georgia. It would be a very bad place to send a boy your age. You should be in a classroom. If any of the men from your regiment in Andersonville found out you were a deserter, it would be even worse for you. Well, then, I think I shall have to do something else with you. You will note that I have not written down one word about you. I'll have no record of you."

"What will you do with me, sir?"

"Have you any money with you?"

"A little bit."

"Good. Yankee money is worth quite a bit more here than our money. Do you see the open tent flap behind me?"

"Yes, sir, I do."

"Then be so good, Charley Skedaddle, as to skedaddle through it right now. As I see it, you are of no use to us. And I don't want it on my conscience that I sent a twelve-year-old boy to Andersonville."

Response Activities

1. **Interpret** Why were battle charges so dangerous? Did weapons change during the Civil War? How did these weapons make charges more dangerous?

2. **Narrative: Write an Autobiography** How might Charley Skedaddle describe the battles he saw to his grandchildren? Write a paragraph of Charley's memories.

3. **History: The Role of Generals** Why were the Confederate soldiers so determined to keep General Lee safe? Why are generals so important? What do generals do during a battle?

African Americans Join the Fight

Main Idea African Americans played a major role in both the Union war effort and the struggle to end slavery.

Key Vocabulary

contraband
emancipation
proclamation
injustice

Key Events

1862 First African American regiments organized

1863 Emancipation Proclamation takes effect

The 107th Colored Infantry, shown here at Fort Corcoran, helped defend Washington, D.C.

Many people, especially African Americans, believed that the Union was fighting the South to end slavery. Although President Lincoln opposed slavery, his sole purpose in fighting the Civil War was "to save the Union." At the beginning of the war, African Americans were not allowed to join the army. Yet they knew it was important that they join the fight. Abolitionist Frederick Douglass argued that the enlistment of African American troops would do more than help the Union win the war:

"**L**et him get an eagle on his button and a musket on his shoulder and bullets in his pocket, and there is no power on earth which can deny that he has earned the right to citizenship in the United States."

From Fighting to Freedom

Focus *What events led to the Emancipation Proclamation?*

Northern troops didn't plan to end slavery when they occupied southern territory. As soon as they set up camps, however, enslaved African Americans fled to them. Uncertain of what to do with the refugees, the Army declared them **contraband** — property taken from the enemy — and put them to work. The African Americans carried supplies, built barriers, and spied for the Union cause, but they weren't allowed to fight.

Winning the Right to Fight

African Americans wanted to fight. They were eager to go to battle to end slavery and defend the Union. Lincoln, however, hesitated to let them. Enlisting African American soldiers, he was afraid, might cause Missouri, Kentucky, Maryland, and Delaware to secede. These border states allowed slavery but had remained loyal to the Union, and Lincoln didn't want to lose them.

As the war wore on, northerners saw that it would not be won quickly or easily. They would need all the help they could get. So in July 1862, Congress voted to enlist African American troops.

Around the same time, Lincoln began to think about ending slavery. African Americans and antislavery forces in Congress had been asking him to do this for over a year. He had been reluctant, but the need for soldiers helped turn his thinking around. Enslaved African Americans, he realized, were being forced to help the South. If they were

A poster used to recruit African Americans to fight in the Union army.

This young boy, known only as Jackson, was born into slavery but became a drummer for the 78th Colored Troops.

Ask Yourself

Why do people fight wars against each other? Are there right and wrong reasons for fighting a war?

? ? ? ? ? ? ? ? ? ? ? ? ? ?

freed, they could help the North. Also, the South was trying to get help from England. Lincoln knew that England wouldn't support the Confederacy if the North took a stand against slavery. Finally, more northerners had become convinced that giving **emancipation,** or freedom, to African Americans was the right thing to do.

Emancipation Proclamation

Lincoln waited for a Union victory before proclaiming the end of slavery. After the Battle of Antietam in September 1862, he issued the Emancipation Proclamation. A **proclamation** is an official announcement. This proclamation stated that all enslaved people in Confederate states would be free on January 1, 1863:

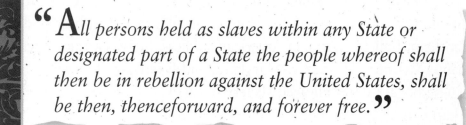

> **"A**ll *persons held as slaves within any State or designated part of a State the people whereof shall then be in rebellion against the United States, shall be then, thenceforward, and forever free.***"**

January 1, 1863, was a day of great joy among many African Americans in both North and South. "Slavery chain done broke at last," people sang. "No more auction blocks for me." One London newspaper declared, "The war in America has resolved [changed] itself into a war between freedom and slavery." The Union would now have to win the war to make Lincoln's promise come true.

In this painting, Lincoln reads the Emancipation Proclamation to his Cabinet. Later, he read it to the nation, and on January 1, 1863, all enslaved people in the Confederate states were officially free. **Citizenship:** Why would Lincoln read an important proclamation to his Cabinet first?

Among the Bravest of Soldiers

Focus *How did African Americans help the Union war effort?*

Regiments of freedmen, like the First South Carolina Volunteers, marched proudly through towns where they had once been enslaved. In the North, the two sons of Frederick Douglass were among the first to join the famed Massachusetts 54th regiment — a regiment made up of African American soldiers.

In the summer of 1863, Union troops marched forth to capture Fort Wagner in Charleston harbor. The men of the 54th volunteered for the honor, and danger, of leading the attack. In the face of massive gunfire, they fought bravely. Almost half of them were wounded, captured, or killed. Although the attack failed, the regiment's courage proved the dedication of black soldiers.

Despite their service and bravery, African American soldiers were paid less than whites. They protested this **injustice**, or unfairness, in a letter to President Lincoln. "We have done a Soldier's Duty," the letter said. "Why can't we have a Soldier's pay?" In June 1864, Congress corrected this wrong.

Close to one in ten African Americans served in the Union Army. Most came from Confederate states. Together, they made up 10 percent of the entire army and navy. Without the African American troops, the North might not have won the war.

Twenty-three African Americans won Congressional Medals of Honor during the Civil War.

Lesson Review

1860	1863

1862
First African American regiments organized

1863
Emancipation Proclamation takes effect

1. **Key Vocabulary:** Describe how African Americans gained their freedom using these words: **contraband, emancipation, proclamation, injustice.**

2. **Focus:** What events led to the Emancipation Proclamation?

3. **Focus:** How did African Americans help the Union war effort?

4. **Critical Thinking: Decision Making** Some people think African Americans should

celebrate January 1 as Freedom Day. Do you agree? Explain why or why not.

5. **Theme: Conflict and Resolution** Why did Lincoln hesitate to allow African Americans to fight? Was he right to do this?

6. **Citizenship/Research Activity:** Find out what a soldier does to be awarded a Congressional Medal of Honor.

Behind the Lines of Battle

Main Idea Northerners and southerners who were not soldiers also experienced hardships and contributed to the war effort.

Key Vocabulary

home front

civilian

inflation

draft

Key Events

1862 Confederate Congress introduces a draft law

1863 Draft riot in New York City

Young Carrie Berry turned 10 in Atlanta in 1864. Childhood during the war was not easy, and this birthday was not a happy one for Carrie:

> **"I** *did not have a cake. Times were too hard so I celebrated with ironing. I hope by my next birthday we will have peace in our land so that I can have a nice dinner.***"**

Everyone living in the United States during the Civil War had difficult times. Women, children, and men who could not fight, all made sacrifices. The effects of the war spread across the nation. Hunger, shortages of goods, and outbreaks of disease hurt many people. Thousands were forced to go without simple pleasures. Almost everyone made great changes in their daily lives.

Women and the War Effort

Focus *How did women in the North and South contribute to the war effort?*

Before the war, most women performed work that was related to the home. As more men left their families to go fight — and as many of them were killed or wounded in battle — there were more jobs that needed to be done. Women began taking these jobs over.

While driving past wheat fields in the Midwest, one government volunteer noticed how harvest time had changed during the war. "Women were in the fields everywhere, driving the reapers . . . and

Carrie Berry of Atlanta, Georgia

loading grain, until then an unusual sight." A young worker explained her situation:

> "**M**y three brothers went into the army, all my cousins, most of the young men about here, and the men we used to hire. So there's no help to be got but women. . . ."

Some women worked as teachers, saleswomen, or government clerks. Others made ammunition in factories or sewed uniforms. The actress Pauline Cushman was a spy. She gathered information for the Union army while performing in southern cities. Belle Boyd spied for the Confederacy. When she learned of a Union plan to blow up bridges in Virginia, she ran across open fields to warn General Jackson as "rifle balls flew thick and fast about me."

Nursing was a great contribution. Until the Civil War, most nurses were men. Once the fighting began, thousands of women poured into hospitals and onto battlefields. All were shocked by what they found. Hospitals were dirty, crowded, and poorly run. Besides tending soldiers, nurses had to fight to get desperately needed supplies. One nurse fought so hard a surgeon ordered her out of the hospital. "If you bar all the doors against me," she told him, "I'll come in the window, and the patients will help me in."

Nurse Anne Bell *(left)* cares for wounded soldiers in a Tennessee hospital. Poor conditions and limited medical supplies took many lives. At least twice as many soldiers died from diseases as from battle wounds. **Citizenship:** *Why did nurses work so hard to help wounded soldiers?*

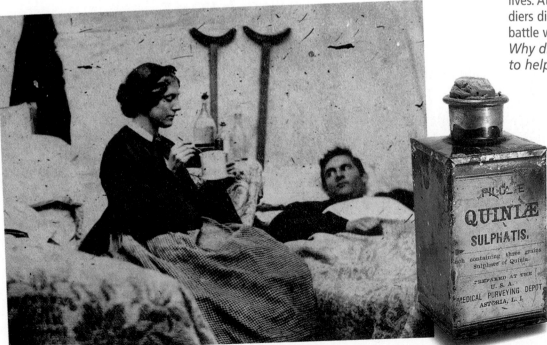

Quinine was used to relieve symptoms of malaria.

Camp Life

Some women cared for their families in military camps. This woman and her children *(right)* stayed with her husband, a member of the 31st Infantry. Soldiers carried their own mess tins *(above)* with them. These small tins could fit easily in their backpacks.

Life for people in military camps was also very difficult. Shelter was usually poor and food was scarce. Union troops ate a steady diet of hardtack or dry biscuit *(left)*, meat, beans, and coffee. Confederate troops had even less to eat. Sometimes they didn't have anything at all. "I came nearer to starving," one southern soldier remembered, "than I ever did before. . . ."

Life on the Home Front

Focus *What hardships faced people on the home front?*

Life on the home front could be almost as hard as life in the army camps. The **home front** describes the people who are not in the military but live in a country that is at war. These people are also called **civilians**. Their sacrifices often helped soldiers keep fighting.

Hardships in the South

Many Civil War battles took place in the upper South, where families lived on small farms. The Confederate army often took animals and crops from these farms to feed soldiers. This, along with the Union blockade, caused food shortages. In Richmond, Virginia, women protested the shortages by marching to the governor's mansion. When the protest turned into a riot, President Jefferson Davis threatened to order troops to fire. Similar riots sprang up in other southern cities. Even when food was available, poor people couldn't buy it because the war caused inflation. **Inflation** means that money is worth less and goods cost more. Something costing one Confederate dollar in 1861 cost 27 dollars three years later.

In April of 1862, the Confederate Congress passed a draft law. The **draft** is a system of choosing people and forcing them to join the army. However, any man who had twenty or more enslaved people didn't have to serve. Other rich men could pay someone else to take their place. Poor people had no way to avoid the draft. They called the war "a rich man's war and a poor man's fight."

Problems in the North

The North also ordered a draft. There, a man could avoid it by paying $300 — about as much as a working man could earn in a year. The draft law angered poor people, especially Irish immigrants who competed with free African Americans for jobs. They didn't want to fight a war to end slavery. In 1863, a riot broke out in New York City. For days, people opposed to the draft roamed the streets.

The Civil War created hardships across the country. Women took over the running of farms and businesses, and they cared for the sick and wounded. Poor people had a difficult time finding enough to eat, and landowners had to give crops away to feed soldiers. The Civil War touched the lives of all American people.

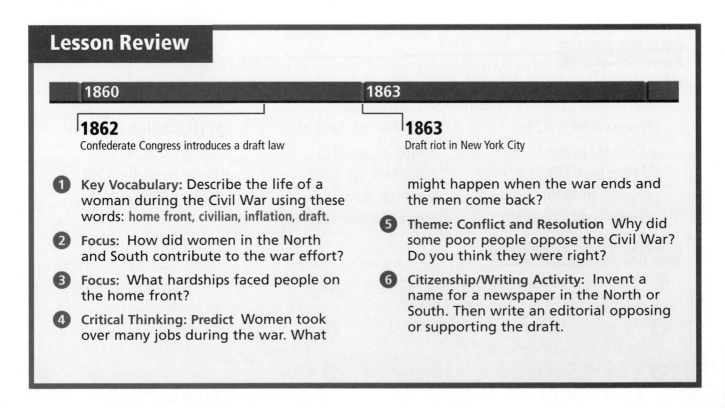

Lesson Review

| 1860 | | 1863 | |

1862
Confederate Congress introduces a draft law

1863
Draft riot in New York City

① **Key Vocabulary:** Describe the life of a woman during the Civil War using these words: **home front, civilian, inflation, draft.**

② **Focus:** How did women in the North and South contribute to the war effort?

③ **Focus:** What hardships faced people on the home front?

④ **Critical Thinking: Predict** Women took over many jobs during the war. What might happen when the war ends and the men come back?

⑤ **Theme: Conflict and Resolution** Why did some poor people oppose the Civil War? Do you think they were right?

⑥ **Citizenship/Writing Activity:** Invent a name for a newspaper in the North or South. Then write an editorial opposing or supporting the draft.

Chapter Review

Chapter Review Timeline

1820	1830	1840	1850	1860	1870

1820
Missouri Compromise

1850
Compromise of 1850

1863
Battle of Gettysburg

1863
Emancipation Proclamation takes effect

1861
First Battle of Bull Run

Summarizing the Main Idea

1 Slavery was a controversial issue both before and during the Civil War. Copy the chart below, and fill in the missing information.

Decision	What Was the Reason?
Missouri Compromise	*To keep the number of free and slave states equal*
Compromise of 1850	
Organizing African American regiments	
Emancipation Proclamation	

Vocabulary

2 Use at least seven of the following terms to write about life as a soldier in either the Union or the Confederate army.

free state (p. 426)
slave state (p. 426)
Union (p. 426)
secede (p. 429)
Confederate (p. 429)

Civil War (p. 432)
mobilize (p. 433)
volunteer (p. 433)
siege (p. 436)
emancipation (p. 446)

proclamation (p. 446)
injustice (p. 447)
home front (p. 450)
draft (p. 451)

Reviewing the Facts

3 What were some of the conflicts between the North and the South in 1820?

4 What was the Fugitive Slave Law and why was it strengthened?

5 When the war began, what strengths and weaknesses did each side have?

6 Why was Lincoln reluctant to end slavery? Why did he change his mind?

7 Did the Emancipation Proclamation change how people thought of the war?

8 What sacrifices did civilians in the North and South make during the war?

Skill Review: Comparing Historical Photographs and Paintings

9 Compare the painting on page 438 with the photograph on page 439. Why could paintings of the Civil War show more action than photographs?

10 Compare the photograph of a fort on page 439 with the painting of a battle on page 434. Which helps you better understand what soldiers in the war felt like?

Geography Skills

11 Use the map on page 426 to find the line established by the Missouri Compromise. Then compare this with the results of the 1860 election, shown on page 431. Could you have used the Missouri Compromise to predict that election?

12 You are a Union soldier from Pennsylvania fighting at Vicksburg in 1863. What states might you have traveled through? Choose a route and then write a letter to your family describing how you got there. Add details about what you saw.

Critical Thinking

13 **Identify Main Idea** Why did some northerners think that the Dred Scott decision erased the Missouri Compromise?

14 **Predict** Could ironclad ships have changed the outcome of the war?

15 **Interpret** Why did Lincoln end slavery only in Confederate states?

Writing: Citizenship and Economics

16 **Citizenship** What might an African American have said to convince the Union to allow him to fight in the army? Write a short persuasive speech.

17 **Economics** Write a journal entry a southern child might have made during the war. Describe a trip to the store. What can you afford to buy? What's too expensive?

Activities

National Heritage/Literature Activity
What kind of poetry did Americans write about the Civil War? Find one poem written about the war by a northerner and one by a southerner. How did these poets see the war differently?

History/Arts Activity
Draw two living rooms during the Civil War — one of a southern family and one of a northern family. Choose items to include that show the similarities and differences between these families.

Internet Option

Check the **Internet Social Studies Center** for ideas on how to extend your theme project beyond your classroom.

THEME PROJECT CHECK-IN

Use what you have read about the Civil War to begin your project. A historian might ask you questions like the ones below. Think about them as you work on your project.
• How did your life and region change once the Civil War began?
• How do you feel about the Civil War?
• What important Civil War events happened near your home?

CHAPTER 17 The Nation Reunited

Chapter Preview: *People, Places, and Events*

| 1860 | 1862 | 1864 |

Burning of Richmond   1865

What other southern cities burned during the Civil War? *Lesson 1, Page 457*

Lincoln's Family

President Lincoln led the nation through the Civil War. *Lesson 1, Page 459*

Learning to Read

Who went to the South to teach freed African Americans? *Lesson 2, Page 463*

A Union Preserved

Main Idea General Ulysses S. Grant used a new approach to war to lead the North to victory in 1865.

It is November 19, 1863, at Gettysburg, Pennsylvania. A terrible battle has been fought, and a memorial for those who died is in progress. President Lincoln steps on the stage. He knows his audience is discouraged. So many have died. So many are still suffering.

He speaks for only two minutes. "Four score and seven years ago our fathers brought forth on this continent, a new nation . . . dedicated to the proposition [idea] that all men are created equal." Then Lincoln talks of those who died in battle. Americans, he says, must make sure that these deaths do not lose their meaning. "It is rather for us to be here dedicated to the great task remaining before us . . . that government of the people, by the people, for the people, shall not perish from the earth."

◀ Monument at the battleground at Shiloh.

Key Vocabulary

address

total war

desertion

assassinate

Key Events

1863 Gettysburg Address

1864 Sherman's March to the Sea

1865 Lee surrenders

1865 Lincoln is assassinated

1866 1868 1870

Sharecropping Store

How did sharecropping affect poor southerners? *Lesson 2, Page 464*

Impeachment Ticket 1868

Why did Congress impeach President Johnson? *Lesson 3, Page 470*

Black Politicians

Did freed African Americans become U.S. congressmen? *Lesson 3, Page 471*

Grant Takes Charge

Robert E. Lee *(above)* was a famous soldier even before the Civil War. Ulysses S. Grant *(below)* was unknown. He soon gained a reputation, however, as an intelligent, powerful leader who could win battles.

Focus *Why were Grant's strategies against the South successful?*

When Lincoln delivered his **address**, or speech, at Gettysburg, the Civil War had been going on for more than two years. No end was in sight. By winning the Battle of Gettysburg, the North had ended the South's hopes of taking Washington. By early 1864, Lee's troops were suffering huge losses and had limited supplies. Even so, his army showed no signs of surrendering. It seemed the South might hold on longer than northerners were willing to fight.

Discontent with the war was increasing in the North. It peaked in the summer of 1864. "The people are wild for peace," a political leader said. Some northerners even wanted to restore slavery so the South would stop fighting. Lincoln, however, would not allow that.

Displeased northerners were beginning to blame their President, who would soon have to run for re-election. When the Democrats nominated popular General George McClellan as their candidate, Lincoln was worried. "I am going to be beaten," he said, "and unless some great change takes place, badly beaten."

A great change did take place. In March 1864, the President made Ulysses S. Grant head of the Union army. Grant, the commander at Vicksburg, was the leader Lincoln needed. Up until now, the North had been hurt by generals who were not strong fighters. Grant was different. He believed the best way to win a war was to get to the enemy as fast as possible, with as many soldiers as possible, then strike hard, strike often, and move on.

To destroy the Confederacy, General Grant knew that he had to destroy the farms, factories, and railroads that supported its soldiers. Without food, weapons, and transportation, the Confederate army would have to surrender. In May 1864, Grant sent General Philip Sheridan to Virginia's Shenandoah Valley. He ordered Sheridan to take or ruin everything in this fertile farming region.

"[T*urn*] *the Shenandoah Valley [into] a barren waste . . . so that crows flying over it for the balance of this season will have to carry their provender [food] with them.*"

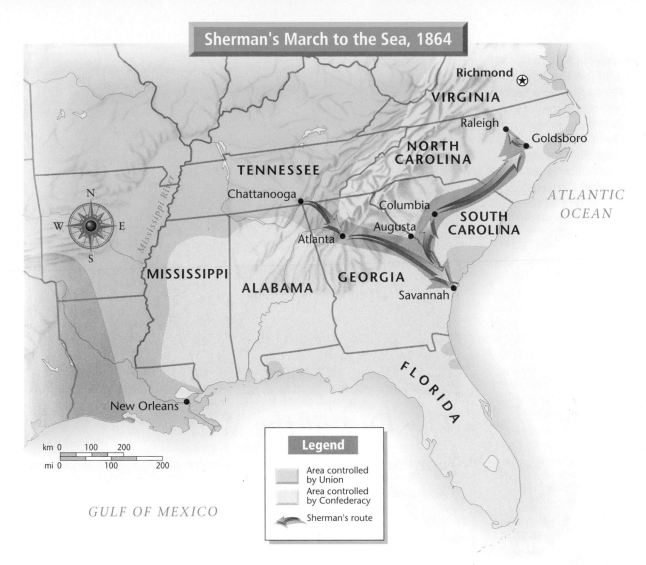

Sherman's March to the Sea, 1864

Richmond ✪

VIRGINIA

Raleigh
Goldsboro

NORTH
CAROLINA

TENNESSEE

Chattanooga

Columbia

*ATLANTIC
OCEAN*

SOUTH
CAROLINA

Atlanta
Augusta

Mississippi River

MISSISSIPPI

ALABAMA

GEORGIA

Savannah

FLORIDA

New Orleans

km 0   100   200
mi 0   100   200

Legend

Area controlled
by Union

Area controlled
by Confederacy

Sherman's route

GULF OF MEXICO

At the same time, Grant ordered General William Tecumseh Sherman to move southeast from Chattanooga, Tennessee. (*Find his route on the map above.*) Sherman captured Atlanta in September 1864. He burned it in November. He then set out for Savannah, on the Georgia coast. On the way, his troops ripped up railroad tracks, cut down telegraph wires, destroyed livestock, and uprooted crops. They burned bridges, houses, and factories. By the time his "march to the sea" was over, Sherman had left behind a path of destruction 300 miles long and 60 miles wide.

This was what Sherman called **total war.** "We have devoured the land . . ." he wrote at the end of his march. "To realize what war is one should follow in our tracks." His purpose was not only to destroy everything southern soldiers could use. He wanted to make southern civilians tired of the war. And southerners had suffered greatly. To them his army had seemed like a natural disaster — like a terrible flood. "The deep waters are closing over us," one woman wrote as he advanced.

Sherman reached Savannah, Georgia, just over a month after he left Atlanta. One of the many things he ordered his army to destroy was railroad tracks, so the Confederacy could not use them to move troops or supplies. **Map Skill:** *Which of the southern states were affected by Sherman's March to the Sea?*

This painting of Lee surrendering shows Grant *(on the left)* more neatly dressed than he actually was. People who were there remembered that Lee wore a full-dress uniform, with a gleaming sword. Grant wore a common soldier's shirt, unbuttoned at the neck. **National Heritage:** *Why was this one of the most important events in American history?*

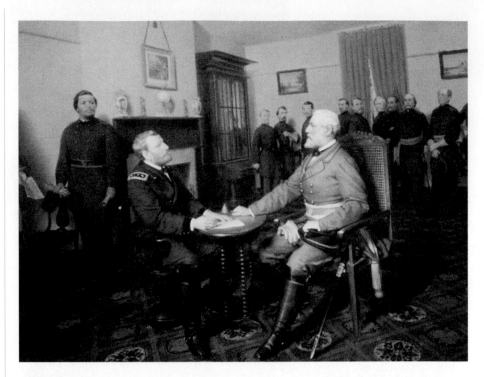

Curious Facts

In 1861, Wilmer McLean lived next to the Bull Run stream. In the first Battle of Bull Run, a Union cannonball landed in his dining room. To avoid the war, McLean moved to a tiny town called Appomattox Courthouse. Four years later, Lee surrendered to Grant in Wilmer McLean's parlor.

The End of the War

Focus *What events led to the surrender of the Confederate army?*

The success of Grant's plan brought the end of the war in sight. Northerners took heart. In November 1864, they elected Lincoln to a second term. Two months later, a victorious Republican Congress passed the 13th Amendment, which outlawed slavery.

While Sherman marched through Georgia, Grant launched his drive to take Richmond. Throughout the summer and fall of 1864, he fought a series of costly battles against Lee in Virginia. Although Union casualties were terrible (60,000 of Grant's soldiers were killed or wounded in a single month), the North had fresh reserves of both men and supplies. Meanwhile, the fighting spirit of Confederate troops was falling fast. More and more of them chose **desertion**, which means they simply ran away from their army.

By the spring of 1865, Union troops outnumbered Confederate forces by almost two to one. Grant trapped Lee and his army near the small Virginia town of Appomattox Courthouse. On April 7, Grant requested that he surrender. Lee realized his position was hopeless. "There is nothing left for me to do," he said, "but go and see General Grant. And I would rather die a thousand deaths."

On April 9, 1865, the two generals met in a private house in Appomattox. Grant's terms of surrender were generous. Lee and his officers could keep their dignity and their swords. The Confederate troops could keep their horses. No one would be put on trial for fighting against the North. As Lee rode away, joyful Union troops began to fire off their guns. Grant ordered them to be silent:

> **"T**he war is over. The rebels are our countrymen again.**"**

Lincoln Assassinated

With the war over, Lincoln turned his attention to the problem of putting the country back together. Like Grant, he hoped to bring a spirit of forgiveness to the reunion of North and South.

Some could not forgive. On April 14, 1865 — less than a week after the South surrendered — Lincoln went to see a play. A southerner and former actor named John Wilkes Booth slipped into the President's box and shot him in the head. Lincoln died the next day, the first President to be **assassinated**, or murdered.

Millions of Americans lined the railroad tracks between Washington and Springfield, Illinois, as a train carried Lincoln's body home. His firm leadership had brought the nation through a terrible civil war. The fighting was over. The Union was preserved. But with Lincoln dead, who would shape the peace to come?

Booth escaped after shooting Lincoln by riding off on a horse. The search, however, did not last long. Soldiers captured him two weeks later, hiding in a Virginia tobacco barn.

Lesson Review

1861	1863	1865	

1863
Gettysburg Address

1864
Sherman's March to the Sea

1865
Lee surrenders
Lincoln is assassinated

1. **Key Vocabulary:** Write a paragraph about the end of the Civil War using these words: **total war, desertion, assassinate.**

2. **Focus:** Why were Grant's strategies against the South successful?

3. **Focus:** What events led to the surrender of the Confederate army?

4. **Critical Thinking: Cause and Effect** Discuss in your own words how Grant helped Lincoln get re-elected.

5. **Theme: Conflict and Resolution** Why do you think Grant and Lincoln wanted to forgive their defeated enemy?

6. **Geography/Research Activity:** Research Sheridan's march through Virginia's Shenandoah Valley. Make a map showing where he went. Use the map of Sherman's march as a model.

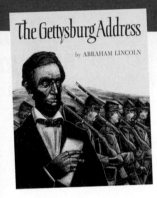

The Gettysburg Address
by ABRAHAM LINCOLN

The Gettysburg Address

by ABRAHAM LINCOLN

The Battle of Gettysburg lasted three long days, July 1, 2, and 3, in 1863. It is not known exactly how many soldiers died, but about 43,000 men were reported as killed, wounded, captured, or missing — more than 20,000 each from the northern and southern armies. Because all of those who died could not be taken home for burial, the government established the Gettysburg National Cemetery. Five months after the battle, Abraham Lincoln traveled there to dedicate it.

The Gettysburg Address

score

twenty years. four score and seven years is 87 years

Four score and seven years ago our fathers
brought forth on this continent, a new nation,
conceived in Liberty, and dedicated to the
proposition that all men are created equal.
Now we are engaged in a great civil war,
testing whether that nation, or any nation
so conceived and so dedicated, can long endure.
We are met on a great battle-field of that war.
We have come to dedicate a portion of that field,
as a final resting place for those who here
gave their lives that that nation might live.

It is altogether fitting and proper that we should do this. But, in a larger sense, we cannot dedicate — we cannot consecrate — we cannot hallow — this ground. The brave men, living and dead, who struggled here, have consecrated it, far above our poor power to add or detract.

The world will little note, nor long remember what we say here, but it can never forget what they did here. It is for us the living, rather, to be dedicated here to the unfinished work which they who fought here have thus far so nobly advanced.

It is rather for us to be here dedicated to the great task remaining before us — that from these honored dead we take increased devotion to that cause for which they gave the last full measure of devotion — that we here highly resolve that these dead shall not have died in vain — that this nation, under God, shall have a new birth of freedom — and that government of the people, by the people, for the people, shall not perish from the earth.

Gettysburg, Pennsylvania
November 19, 1863

consecrate
to dedicate to some worthy purpose

in vain
to no use or advantage to

from the book titled The Gettysburg Address *illustrated by Michael McCurdy*

Response Activities

1. **Interpret** In the "Gettysburg Address," Lincoln wrote that the "new nation" was ". . . dedicated to the proposition that all men are created equal." He was using words from *The Declaration of Independence.* Why do you think he repeated these words in his speech?

2. **Narrative: Write a Newspaper Article** Write an article based on an interview you might have had with President Lincoln if you had been a reporter covering the "Gettysburg Address."

3. **History: Make a Timeline** Put the major events of the Civil War between the time of the Gettysburg Address and Lincoln's assassination on a timeline.

Freedom's Challenge

Main Idea Emancipation brought difficult challenges for African Americans following the Civil War.

Key Vocabulary

freedmen
redistribute
sharecropping
credit

Key Events

1865 Freedmen's
Bureau created

Thirteen-year-old Mary Brodie sensed a change on the plantation where she was enslaved. "Missus and marster began to walk around and act queer," she later recalled. "The grown slaves were whisperin' to each other." Gunfire sounded in the distance, growing louder every day. Everyone seemed disturbed. No one did any work. She even heard the white owners crying.

Finally, Mary and the others were called to the great house. The master and mistress stood side by side on the front porch. One hundred and fifty African Americans faced them in silence. "You could hear a pin drop," Mary remembered. "Everything was so quiet." Finally, the master spoke. "Men, women, and children, you are free. You are no longer my slaves. The Yankees will soon be here."

The Promise of Freedom

Focus *What were the hopes of newly freed African Americans?*

After the war, African Americans who had once been enslaved were called **freedmen.** They numbered about four million, and they all had high hopes for liberty.

Many chose new names to replace the ones their former owners had given them. Together, they built their own churches, using them for religious, social, and political gatherings. Most southern states had made it illegal to educate enslaved people, so African Americans now grabbed at any chance to learn to read and write.

First of all, they had to earn a living. Freed people were eager to work, but many wanted to work only for themselves. In the North, some argued that the national government should "furnish them with homesteads from . . . rebel property." Throughout the South, freed families dreamed of owning their own farms.

Slavery separated African American families. Many freed people searched for lost family members, even advertising in newspapers.

In March 1865, Congress created the Freedmen's Bureau to help both African Americans and poor whites adjust to life after the war. The Bureau sent food and clothing south for people in need.

The Bureau also sent teachers. Educated northerners — men and women, African Americans and whites — flocked south to open schools. They were thrilled to see how eagerly they were greeted. When one group of freed people in Mississippi heard they were to have schools, "they fairly jumped and shouted in gladness."

In addition, Congress gave the Bureau power over land. Many southern landowners had lost their plantations during the war. Congress said the Bureau could **redistribute** this land — divide it up and sell it to African Americans. Rumors swept the South that the government would give them "40 acres and a mule." This phrase became a symbol of hope for many families. It seemed like a small repayment for hundreds of years of slavery.

Black Codes and Sharecropping

Focus *What laws and practices took away the rights of African Americans?*

African Americans, however, were not given this land. The plantations were returned to the people who owned them before the war. In May 1865, the federal government decided that redistributing land would take away the landowners' right to private property.

The Freedmen's Bureau set up schools such as this one throughout the South. The Bureau existed from 1865 to 1872. During this time, it spent more than $15 million helping newly freed people in many ways, including education. **Economics:** *Why was education a good way to spend the money of the Freedmen's Bureau?*

Late in 1865, Southern states began enacting Black Codes to restrict African Americans. These laws prevented freed people from voting, traveling, or doing certain kinds of work. If they couldn't prove they had a job, they could be forced to work on a plantation.

One problem faced both white and black people in the South. Few had any money. African Americans and some whites who wanted to farm could not rent or buy land. Landowners who needed people to work their plantations could not pay anyone to do it.

A system called **sharecropping** was developed to solve this problem. Landowners rented land to both white and African American farmers. In return, the farmers promised to give the landowners part of their crop once it was harvested. The owners often provided these families seeds, tools, food, and clothing on **credit,** which means they did not have to pay for them right away.

·Tell Me More·

The Economics of Sharecropping

Account for the Year 1870

Money Borrowed		Money Earned		Leftover Debt
Food	-$83.25	Cotton	+$90.45	
Clothing	-$64.75			
Farm Supplies	-$75.08			
Medicine	-$2.17			
TOTAL -$225.25		+$90.45		-$134.80

In the years following the Civil War, both whites and African Americans in the South became sharecroppers. Because sharecroppers usually had little money of their own, they bought almost everything — even food and clothing — with credit. Often, a good crop could not pay off all the money they had borrowed.

Many farmers had to borrow money again, right after selling their harvest. They had worked hard, but they still did not have what their families needed to make it through the winter. These farmers fell deeper into debt with every passing year. (See chart.)

This chart shows how much a sharecropper might have borrowed in a year and how little he earned.
Chart Skill: *How much more did this farmer need to earn to make a profit?*

As the practice of sharecropping grew after the Civil War, many landowners established stores on their plantations. These stores became a central part of the daily lives of many people in the South, both white and African American. They called the storekeepers "furnishing merchants," because they furnished or supplied goods on credit.

At first, sharecropping seemed to meet everyone's needs. Unfortunately, most landowners took advantage of the system. They often charged farmers too much for the goods they bought on credit, forcing the sharecroppers to remain dependent on them.

Events after the war disappointed many African Americans. One former slave named Millie Freeman described how freedom seemed to her. "Everything just kept on like it was. We heard that lots of slaves was getting land and some mules to set up for theirselves. I never knowed any what got land or mules nor nothing." Although they rejoiced that they could no longer be bought or sold, African Americans still faced many painful difficulties.

Lesson Review

1864	1865	1866

1865
Freedmen's Bureau created

1 **Key Vocabulary:** Describe the challenges African Americans faced after the war, using these words: **freedmen, sharecropping, credit.**

2 **Focus:** What were the hopes of newly freed African Americans?

3 **Focus:** What laws and practices took away the rights of African Americans?

4 **Critical Thinking: Conclude** Why were freed people so eager to learn? Why was education so important?

5 **Theme: Conflict and Resolution** Who should have gotten the old plantations, the freed people or the landowners? Can you think of a compromise?

6 **Citizenship/Math Activity:** Look at the chart on the opposite page. Make your own chart to show how the sharecropper's debt might increase over 10 years.

★ CITIZENSHIP ★

Resolving Conflicts

Can Enemies Forgive?

Have you ever had a serious disagreement with your best friend? What happens when it's over? When all the angry words have been said, then what? When the Civil War ended, Americans on both sides were searching for answers to these kinds of questions. The case study below shows President Lincoln's goals for the nation after the war.

Case Study

Lincoln's Second Inaugural Address

On March 4, 1865, Abraham Lincoln was sworn in as President for the second time. The war was nearly over. In his speech, Lincoln asked all Americans to take care of the people who had suffered in the war. Lincoln ended his speech with these words:

"With malice toward none, with charity for all, with firmness in the right as God gives us to see the right, let us strive on to finish the work we are in, to bind up the nation's wounds, to care for him who shall have borne the battle and for his widow and his orphan — to do all which may achieve and cherish a just and lasting peace. . . ."

Weeks later, Lincoln was dead. But his goals were clear: he wanted neither blame nor punishment, just forgiveness.

Take Action

Could Lincoln's aims for the Union be a model for resolving conflicts today? Try this to find out.

1 Choose a conflict that you wish you could resolve. For instance, have you had a disagreement with a friend? Have you argued about how to use your free time at school? Do you disagree with your family members about how long you may use the telephone? List the reasons for the disagreement. What does each person want?

2 Brainstorm ideas for resolving the conflict. Consider the rights and needs of everyone involved. Map out a strategy.

3 Share your strategies with the rest of the class.

4 Discuss: Were you able to find ways of resolving conflicts "with malice toward none, with charity for all"? If you think your strategy passes that test, send it to the person or people involved.

Tips for Resolving Conflicts

- Figure out who is involved in the conflict.
- Listen to all sides.
- Determine what each side wants and whether they have a right to those demands.
- Decide what is possible.

Research Activity

Many conflicts are resolved by arbitration. Find out what arbitration is. Research a conflict that was settled through arbitration. Who was involved? What happened?

Rebuilding the South

Main Idea After Lincoln's death, government leaders struggled over conflicting plans for rebuilding the South.

Key Vocabulary

Reconstruction
Radical Republican
impeach
scalawag
carpetbagger
segregation

Key Events

1867 Reconstruction Act

1868 President Johnson is impeached

1877 Reconstruction ends

Thaddeus Stevens wrote laws to protect the rights of African Americans, including the 14th Amendment.

The war was over. Lincoln had been assassinated and Andrew Johnson was President. The time had come to put the nation back together. Could the North and the South forgive and forget, so soon after so many people had died?

In 1865, a new war broke out in Washington. This was a political war — between people who disagreed about **Reconstruction,** or the rebuilding of the South. President Johnson, a southerner and a Democrat, stood on one side. Congressman Thaddeus Stevens, a northerner and a Republican, led the fight against him. Their weapons were speeches and votes.

Radical Republicans

Focus *What different ideas did people have about how to bring the South back into the Union?*

President Johnson and Congressman Stevens were fighting over a very important question: How involved should the national government be with what happens inside each state?

Stevens was an abolitionist who had fought to end slavery for many years before the war. The senators and congressmen who followed him were called **Radical Republicans.** They believed that the national government should do everything necessary to protect the rights of African Americans. Stevens made this point, saying:

> "The cause of the war was slavery. We have liberated the slaves. It is our duty to protect them. . . ."

Johnson announced his plan for Reconstruction in May 1865. The President believed that the Constitution left it to the states to decide how they should govern their citizens. His plan for Reconstruction allowed the southern states to pass Black Codes. It also allowed the former leaders of the Confederacy to gain power again.

Johnson's plan outraged the Radical Republicans. Early in 1866, Congress passed an act to stop the Black Codes. Later that same year, they passed the 14th Amendment, which forbids any state from denying rights to U.S. citizens. *(See the chart at right.)* Encouraged by President Johnson, almost all the southern states refused to ratify, or approve, this amendment.

Congress, however, refused to accept their decision. Radical Republicans passed the Reconstruction Act of 1867 and sent the U.S. Army marching back into the South. The states in the old Confederacy were now under military rule. Troops protected the rights of African Americans. Congress told the South that the soldiers would remain there until the states ratified the 14th Amendment. Later, in 1870, the 15th Amendment was passed, guaranteeing all male citizens the right to vote.

The Republicans' war with President Johnson had not ended. He continued to fight fiercely against them. In turn, they did something Congress had never before done to a President. In 1868, they impeached him. To **impeach** a President is to accuse him of being unfit to hold office.

Amendments

13th Amendment Date Passed: 1865

Slavery prohibited throughout the United States.

14th Amendment Date Passed: 1868

Equal protection of the law to all United States citizens.

15th Amendment Date Passed: 1870

Yes   No

No citizen shall be denied the right to vote because of race, color, or previous servitude.

This chart shows the three amendments to the Constitution that Congress passed, first to free African Americans from slavery and then to give them their full rights as United States citizens. **Chart Skill:** *Which amendments were ratified after Congress passed the Reconstruction Act?*

Andrew Johnson

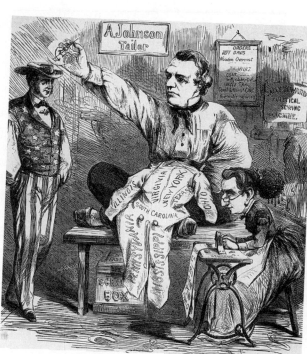

Before he became a politician, Andrew Johnson was a tailor. As President, Johnson believed his plan for Reconstruction would make the United States one country again. This newspaper cartoon pictures him doing his old job — sewing northern and southern states back together.

Carpetbags were a kind of suitcase. During Reconstruction, some northerners came to the South with only the belongings they could fit in luggage such as this.

After the war, riots broke out in some southern cities. This painting shows the army keeping order.

First, the House of Representatives had to vote to bring charges against the President. After two months of debate, they voted to impeach him. Then Johnson was put on trial in the Senate. If two-thirds of the senators found him guilty, he would no longer be President. Thousands of tickets were sold for admission to the trial. Newspapers screamed the details all over the country. At last, the day of judgment arrived. Everyone listened anxiously as each senator announced his vote. The President was saved, by a single vote.

Reconstruction

Focus *What impact did Reconstruction have on the South?*

Reconstruction removed all former Confederate army officers and government leaders from power. They were not even allowed to vote. As a result, three other groups began leading the South.

The first group, white southerners who had remained loyal to the Union, hoped to rebuild the South quickly. Many ex-rebels viewed these people as traitors. To insult them, they called them **scalawags,** a word meaning "old, useless horse."

Here a U.S. Army officer separates angry whites and African Americans.
Citizenship: *Did the army bring justice to the South?*

Many African Americans were determined to defend their newly won rights.

The second group included northerners who came south either to help freed people or to make money. Many southerners did not want them to be there. They called these northerners **carpetbaggers,** because they carried traveling bags made of the same heavy cloth used for carpets.

The third group consisted of newly freed African Americans. In 1867, about 700,000 blacks registered to vote in the South. With the U.S. Army protecting their right to vote, freedmen changed southern government.

African Americans did more than vote. They ran for public office and won elections. Men who had once been enslaved now served as mayors, sheriffs, and justices of the peace. More than 600 were elected to state legislatures. These new leaders set up public schools, built new hospitals, and repaired roads, bridges, railroads, and telegraph lines.

Sixteen African Americans served in the U.S. Congress. Two of these men, Hiram R. Revels and Blanche K. Bruce, were senators. After centuries of slavery, African Americans could finally help run the country in which they lived.

The End of Reconstruction

Political leadership for African Americans did not last. In 1877, President Rutherford B. Hayes pulled the army out of the South. With the troops gone, southern whites regained complete power.

States passed laws to keep African Americans out of politics. They imposed restrictions on voting, including a poll tax, which meant people had to pay money to vote. Most African Americans were too poor to do this. To frighten them away from voting, some whites formed the Ku Klux Klan. In robes and hoods to hide their faces, they beat or murdered African Americans and the whites who supported them.

Southern states also passed laws to keep the races apart. This is called **segregation.** It became illegal for African Americans to sit, ride, eat, or learn in the same places whites did. "It seemed like it took a long time for freedom to come," Millie Freeman said about life after slavery. Almost one hundred years would pass before African Americans reclaimed all their rights.

Events after the Civil War, however, hurt almost everyone in the South, both white and black. Sharecropping forced farmers to grow only cotton, and the South became dependent on this crop

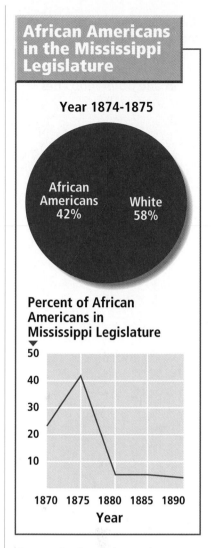

African Americans in the Mississippi Legislature

Year 1874-1875

African Americans 42%

White 58%

Percent of African Americans in Mississippi Legislature

The graph above shows the changing participation of African Americans in Mississippi state politics between 1870 and 1890. **Chart Skill:** *How quickly did the number of African American legislators increase? How quickly did it decrease?*

The South began building more factories at the end of the 19th century. **Economics:** *Why did the South need to develop factories and other industries after the Civil War?*

alone. Newspaper editorials called for a "new South" — one where people worked in factories and the economy was not based only on farming.

Textile mills were built in some southern cities. Birmingham, Alabama, became such an important center for manufacturing steel that it was often called the "Pittsburgh of the South." But wages for people who worked in factories were much lower than in the North. The economy of the South continued to suffer from the effects of the war until well into the 20th century.

Lesson Review

1865	1870	1875

1867
Reconstruction Act

1868
President Johnson is impeached

1877
Reconstruction ends

1. **Key Vocabulary:** Describe U.S. politics after the Civil War using these terms: **Reconstruction, Radical Republicans, impeach.**

2. **Focus:** What different ideas did people have about how to bring the South back into the Union?

3. **Focus:** What impact did Reconstruction have on the South?

4. **Critical Thinking: Decision Making** Why do you think Congress impeached the

President? What did this accomplish?

5. **Citizenship:** Were there any ways for Congress and the President to resolve their disagreements? What should they each have done to reach a compromise?

6. **Geography/Research Activity:** Why did Birmingham become a center for steel manufacturing? Were rivers important? Compare the geographic features of Birmingham with those of Pittsburgh.

Making Database Searches

Ask Your Computer

How can you see, hear, and learn about people and events of the 1800s without getting out of your chair? By plugging into the past with a computer database or a CD-ROM encyclopedia. Computer databases store huge amounts of information electronically. CD-ROM encyclopedias bring the sights and sounds of history to life in maps, time-lines, videos, and even real voices of famous people.

❶ Here's How

- Decide what topic you want to research. Identify a main subject your topic falls into, such as "United States history."

- Think of a question to focus your research. For example, "Who were the carpetbaggers?" Then think of a key word or phrase in your question, such as "carpetbaggers."

  - Follow the directions in your computer's encyclopedia database or in your CD-ROM encyclopedia to enter the main subject of your topic ("United States history") or the key word or phrase ("carpetbaggers").

    - You can print out copies of useful information to refer to later.

❷ Think It Through

What are some advantages and disadvantages of using a computer database or CD-ROM encyclopedia rather than an encyclopedia in book form?

❸ Use It

1. Review this chapter and find a topic you'd like to learn more about. Write down your topic and a main subject it falls into.

2. Write a question to focus your research. Then write a key word or phrase to describe your question.

3. If your school or public library has a computer database or CD-ROM encyclopedia, enter your main subject and key words to find information on the topic. Print out your findings.

Chapter Review

Chapter Review Timeline

1860		1865		1870		1875		1880

1865 Lee surrenders

1864 Sherman's March to the Sea

1865 Lincoln is assassinated

1867 Reconstruction Act

1877 Reconstruction Ends

Summarizing the Main Idea

1 People disagreed about how to treat the South after the Civil War.
Copy the chart below, and fill in the missing information

Leader	Decision
General Grant	*Promised that Confederate soldiers would not be tried for treason*
President Johnson	
Congressman Stevens	

Vocabulary

2 Use at least 7 of the following terms to write captions for a museum exhibit about life in the South immediately after the Civil War.

total war (p. 457)   sharecropping (p. 464)   scalawag (p. 470)

desertion (p. 458)   credit (p. 464)   carpetbagger (p. 471)

freedmen (p. 462)   Reconstruction (p. 468)   segregation (p. 471)

redistribute (p 463)   impeach (p. 469)

Reviewing the Facts

3 Explain why Sherman ordered his troops to destroy so much during his March to the Sea. What did he intend to accomplish?

4 What did "40 acres and a mule" mean to newly freed African Americans?

5 What were two things the Freedmen's Bureau did for African Americans?

6 How did Black Codes take away the rights of newly freed African Americans?

7 What was President Johnson's plan for Reconstruction? Why did it anger Radical Republicans?

8 How did African Americans gain political power during Reconstruction?

Finding Information Using a Computer

9 How can a computer help you learn about people that lived more than a 100 years ago? Explain the steps you might follow to use a CD-ROM encyclopedia.

10 Use a CD-ROM encyclopedia to find out what it was like to live on a farm in the South after the Civil War. You might try these key words: *sharecropping, agriculture, farming, plantation.*

Geography Skills

11 Look at the map of Sherman's March to the Sea on page 457. What states did he not go through? Why do you think he didn't march farther south?

12 What if Lee had marched through the North the way Sherman marched through the South? Would a march like this have made northern civilians tired of the war?

Critical Thinking

13 **Generalize** Was sharecropping a fair system? Why or why not?

14 **Interpret** Was the South punished after the Civil War? Is this why Congress passed the Reconstruction Act?

15 **Cause and Effect** Why did African Americans in the South need land? How would their lives have changed if they had been given land from old plantations?

Writing: Citizenship and History

16 **Citizenship** Write a letter to a newspaper about President Johnson's impeachment. Do you think he deserved to be impeached? Give reasons for your answer.

17 **History** The year is 1869. You are a newly freed African American running for Congress. Write a brief campaign speech describing what you hope to do in office.

Activities

National Heritage/Art Activity
Robert S. Duncanson was an African American artist who painted before and after the Civil War. Prepare an oral presentation about his life and art.

Economics/Math Activity
Choose three things you would buy if someone lent you the money. Find out how much they cost. How long would it take you to pay off your debt?

Internet Option

Check the **Internet Social Studies Center** for ideas on how to extend your theme project beyond your classroom.

THEME PROJECT CHECK-IN

Use the information you have read about the end of the Civil War and Reconstruction, and think about what you would tell the historian. The questions below will help you:
• How is your life and region different from before the Civil War?
• Now that the war has ended, how will the North and South resolve their differences?
• What do you think about Reconstruction?

An Industrial Country

QuakerOats
The food that tells

QUAKER OATS   QUAKER OATS   QUAKER OATS

"If there is no struggle, there is no progress."

Frederick Douglass

· THEME ·

Coping with Change

❝ *I think it would have been hard to move from a farm to a city. On a farm you are your own boss, but when you live in a city, someone else is your boss.* ❞

Phuong Pham
Fort Smith, AR

The years following the Civil War were a time of transformation in the United States. Advances in transportation and communication, the rise of great industries, a surge in immigration, and the growth of cities dramatically changed the nation. These rapid changes also brought new challenges. By facing these challenges during the late 1800s, Americans helped to create the United States you live in today.

 Theme Project

Changing Times

You are living during the late 1800s. You see big changes taking place around you: new inventions, ideas, people. Create a character from this period — perhaps a farmer or factory worker — who might be affected by these trends.

- Create a map showing where in the United States you live. If you moved, show your journey on the map.
- Write an editorial about the effects of a new invention.
- Create diagrams showing your life before and after.
- Make a timeline of important events during your life.

RESEARCH: Find out about an invention from the 1800s that is still in use today. How has it changed?

◀ Elevated railway in New York City, 1903

UNIT 8

WHEN & WHERE
ATLAS

 New technologies caused many of the changes that swept the United States after the Civil War. Inventions brought the growth of huge new industries. These industries then attracted Americans from the countryside and immigrants from Europe to the nation's rapidly growing cities. As the map shows, the nation at this time found new uses for natural resources but also clashed with Native Americans over land.

In this unit, you will read how western expansion led to the settlement of the Great Plains and pushed Native Americans from their land. You will learn how new inventions and industrial growth led to a movement to protect workers' rights. Finally, you will learn how the United States grew as a world power.

Unit 8 Chapters

Chapter 18   Reshaping the West
Chapter 19   An Industrial Society

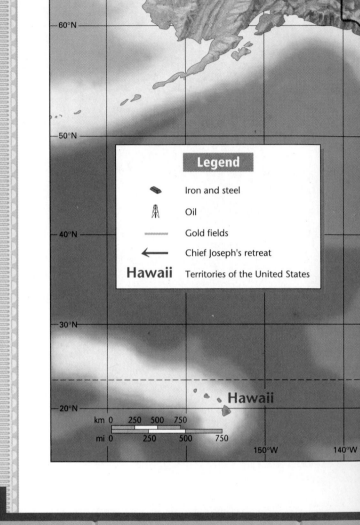

Legend

- Iron and steel
- Oil
- Gold fields
- ← Chief Joseph's retreat
- **Hawaii** Territories of the United States

km 0   250   500   750
mi 0   250   500   750

Unit Timeline

| 1860 | 1870 | 1880 |

Nat Love

This man's nickname was Deadwood Dick. Find out why. *Chapter 18, Lesson 2*

The Homestead Act   1862

Free land on the Great Plains! Would you have moved there? *Chapter 18, Lesson 3*

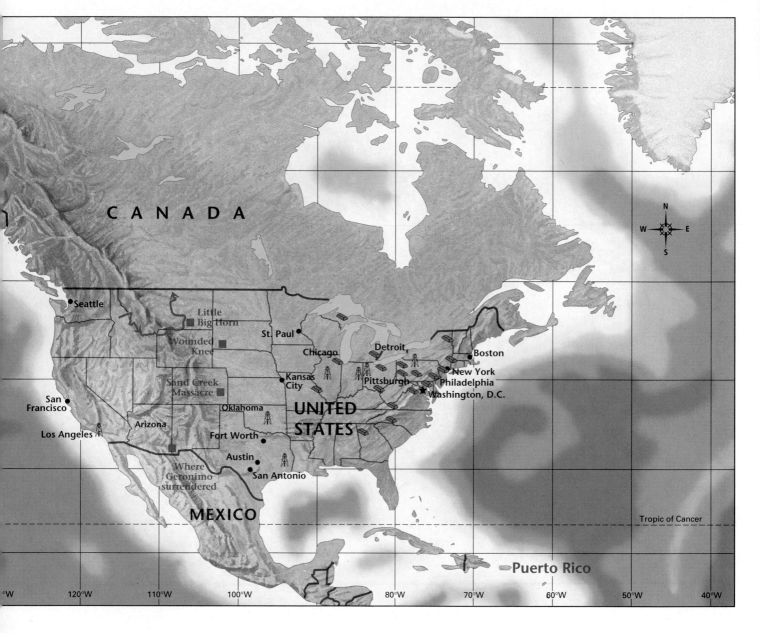

CANADA

Seattle

Little
Big Horn

St. Paul

Wounded
Knee

Chicago

Detroit

Boston

Kansas
City

New York
Pittsburgh

Philadelphia
Washington, D.C.

San
Francisco

Sand Creek
Massacre

Oklahoma

UNITED
STATES

Arizona

Los Angeles

Fort Worth

Austin

Where
Geronimo
surrendered

San Antonio

MEXICO

UNITED
STATES

Tropic of Cancer

Puerto Rico

120°W   110°W   100°W   80°W   70°W   60°W   50°W   40°W

1890   1900   1910

The Typewriter

What inventions changed the way
Americans did business?
Chapter 19, Lesson 1

Immigrants in New York City

Why did so many people want to
come to the United States in the late
1800s? *Chapter 19, Lesson 2*

The Spanish-Amercan War 1898

Which country does the eagle represent? Why is he standing on the
world? *Chapter 19, Lesson 4*

Chapter Preview: *People, Places, and Events*

The Pony Express 1860

Find out why riders raced across the West to deliver mail. *Lesson 1, Page 481*

Railroads Move West 1869

How did the railroad become the most important means of transportation? *Lesson 1, Page 483*

A Cowhand's Spur

Why did ranchers drive cattle herds for miles? *Lesson 2, Page 485*

Linking the East and West

Main Idea Improvements in communication and travel helped to connect the East and West.

Key Vocabulary

pony express
telegraph
transcontinental railroad

Key Events

1860 First pony express

1861 First transcontinental telegraph

1869 First transcontinental railroad

Many 10-day relay races from Missouri to California took place from April 1860 to October 1861. The races weren't run on foot, but on horseback. Eighty riders, most of them teenagers, each traveled about 75 miles on each shift. It was hard work where people could easily be hurt. Unlike ordinary relay racers, the riders didn't pass batons. They passed knapsacks, stuffed with letters. These riders were the mail carriers of their day. The race wasn't really a competition. It was the **pony express,** an important link between western pioneers and their families back East. For almost two years, this mail service kept people across the United States in touch with each other and informed about national events.

◀ This shirt is Cheyenne and was made of animal skin, wool, and hair in about 1860.

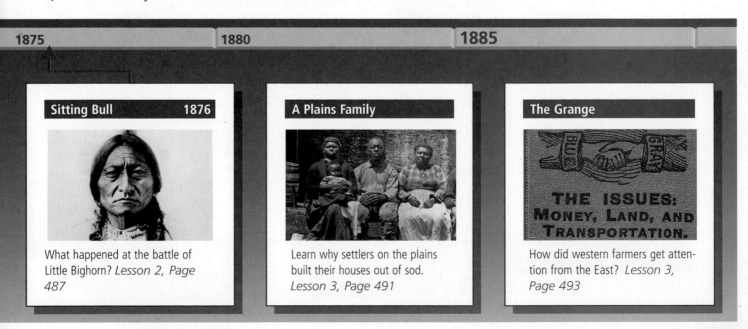

1875   1880   1885

Sitting Bull   **1876**

What happened at the battle of Little Bighorn? *Lesson 2, Page 487*

A Plains Family

Learn why settlers on the plains built their houses out of sod. *Lesson 3, Page 491*

The Grange

THE ISSUES: MONEY, LAND, AND TRANSPORTATION.

How did western farmers get attention from the East? *Lesson 3, Page 493*

481

Original Morse Code

A	·—	N	—·
B	—···	O	· ·
C	·· ·	P	·····
D	—··	Q	··—·
E	·	R	· ··
F	·—·	S	···
G	——·	T	—
H	····	U	··—
I	··	V	···—
J	—··—	W	·——
K	—·—	X	·—··
L	——	Y	·· ··
M	——	Z	··· ·

Question mark	—··—·

Decode the message in the ribbon above using the Morse code translation. **Technology:** *Can you think of reasons why Morse code and not the alphabet might have been used to send messages by telegraph?*

The Telegraph

Focus *How did the telegraph help Americans to communicate?*

The pony express was exciting, but it did not last long as a form of communication. Other, more efficient ways of sending information soon developed.

In 1844, an American named Samuel Morse invented the telegraph. A **telegraph** uses electrical energy to send signals over wires. Companies like American Union, Atlantic and Pacific, and Western Union all saw the chance to make money in telegraph communications. These companies hired workers to string telegraph wires all across the country. By October 1861, the telegraph reached as far as the Pacific Ocean. With this new technology, Americans could now communicate from coast to coast in just a few minutes.

· Tell Me More ·

Communicating by Telegraph

Telegraph stations were built so that people could send their messages out across the country. The man in this picture is preparing his message while the woman is sending one out. The message will be received at another station and translated from Morse code. How do we send messages quickly today?

1 Morse code is tapped in here.

2 Morse code travels across telegraph wires at nearly the speed of light (about 186,282 miles per second).

3 The telegraph receiver presses a groove of dots and dashes into a moving paper strip on the machine.

The Transcontinental Railroad

Focus *How did the transcontinental railroad link East and West?*

During the Civil War, Congress realized that a **transcontinental railroad**, one that ran across the continent, would cut travel time across the United States. It would also quickly move raw materials from the West to factories and markets in the East.

In 1862, Congress funded two companies, the Union Pacific and the Central Pacific, to build a transcontinental railroad. The Union Pacific hired mainly Irish immigrants and Civil War veterans to lay track westward from Omaha, Nebraska. The Central Pacific mainly hired Chinese immigrants to lay track eastward, starting from Sacramento, California. It took these workers seven years to complete their hard and dangerous job. In addition to laying track, workers handled explosives for drilling tunnels through the mountains. The Central Pacific employees even worked through the hard winter of 1866. Accidents buried many of the workers in tunnels under deep snow, but the project continued.

The grueling job ended on May 10, 1869, when the Union Pacific and Central Pacific lines met at Promontory Point, Utah. Cannons boomed and church bells clanged to mark the occasion. Through snowstorms or blazing heat, the railroad could now move people and goods across the continent.

Curious Facts

The two groups working on the transcontinental railroad were racing to lay the most track. The more track that workers laid, the more profits and valuable government land grants their company earned. When they first saw one another, neither side wanted to join up. Each side kept preparing to lay more track. Congress forced them to stop by setting the meeting point at Promontory Point.

Lesson Review

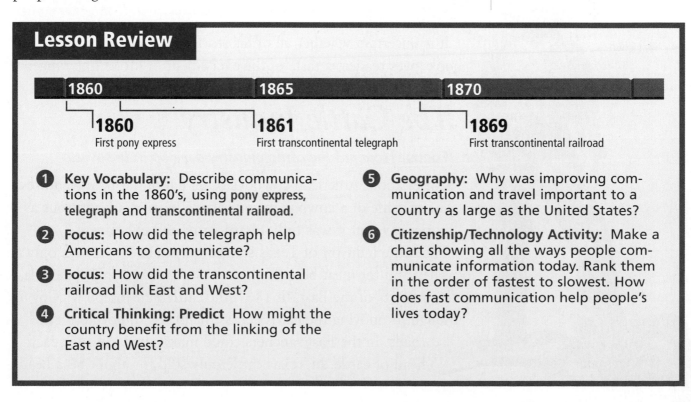

1860	1865	1870
1860 First pony express	**1861** First transcontinental telegraph	**1869** First transcontinental railroad

① **Key Vocabulary:** Describe communications in the 1860's, using **pony express**, **telegraph** and **transcontinental railroad**.

② **Focus:** How did the telegraph help Americans to communicate?

③ **Focus:** How did the transcontinental railroad link East and West?

④ **Critical Thinking: Predict** How might the country benefit from the linking of the East and West?

⑤ **Geography:** Why was improving communication and travel important to a country as large as the United States?

⑥ **Citizenship/Technology Activity:** Make a chart showing all the ways people communicate information today. Rank them in the order of fastest to slowest. How does fast communication help people's lives today?

Life on the Plains

Main Idea Railroads moved settlers west, creating conflict between settlers and Native Americans for the land.

Key Vocabulary

cattle trail
reservation

Key Events

1876 Little Bighorn
1886 Geronimo surrenders
1890 Wounded Knee

Twenty-two-year-old Nat Love waited his turn. Carefully, he lined up the sight on his rifle. Gently, he squeezed the trigger, and in a flash he had hit the target dead center. It was July 4, 1876, and Love had just won the marksmanship competition in Deadwood, South Dakota. There, he earned the nickname Deadwood Dick.

Nat Love was a cowboy who was born in Tennessee in 1854. When he was 15, he headed west to Dodge City, Kansas, to work on a cattle drive. In 1907, Love published his life story. He explained why he had moved west as a young man:

> **"T**he wild cowboy, prancing horses . . . and wild life generally, all had their attractions for me. **"**

Nat Love

It is uncertain whether all of his stories are true, but Love's book gives readers a taste of the excitement of life on the range.

The Cattle Industry

Focus *How did the cattle industry develop in the West?*

Stories about American cowboys often tell of daring adventures. The true life of a cowboy may not have been as adventurous as stories say, but it was full of hard work and excitement.

The cattle industry of Texas started out small. There was only a local demand for meat because there was no way to ship the cattle to the markets of the East. In 1867, the cattleman Joseph McCoy thought of moving the herds across the plains to northern railroads. In the East ranchers could make about $40 for each head of cattle. In Texas cattle only sold for about $6 a head.

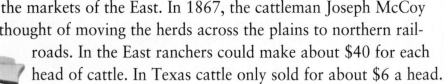

For about 20 years, cattle drives made large profits for the cattle owners. Cowboys drove the herds to the cattle towns, where northern railroads stopped. Cowboys followed **cattle trails**, routes north from Texas across the plains. Then the cattle were loaded on trains and shipped east. (*See map below.*)

The herds, fattened on the grasses of the prairies of Texas, were moved with great care. About 12 cowboys would drive a herd of up to 3,000 head of cattle. Cowboys spent between 10 and 14 hours a day on horseback. They had to be expert riders in order to manage the herd. They protected the cattle from storms, droughts, wild animals, and anything that might spook the herd into a stampede. If the herd did stampede, the cowboys had to round up all of the frantic animals before they could continue along the trail. At the end of the trail, the cowboys were exhausted. Once they reached the cattle towns, the cowboys could finally relax.

Cowhands wore spurs when they were on horseback. The metal end was used to "spur" the horse forward.

Cowhands followed several well-worn trails, from the grazing grounds in the Southwest to the railroads in the North. **Map Skill:** *Which states did each of the cattle trails pass through?*

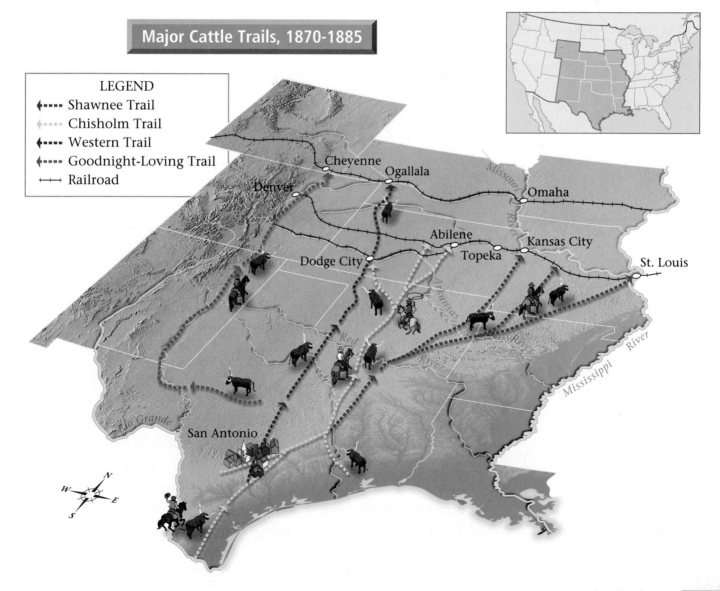

Major Cattle Trails, 1870-1885

LEGEND
- ←---- Shawnee Trail
- ←---- Chisholm Trail
- ←---- Western Trail
- ←---- Goodnight-Loving Trail
- ⊢——⊣ Railroad

Cheyenne
Ogallala
Denver
Omaha
Abilene
Kansas City
Dodge City
Topeka
St. Louis
Missouri River
Arkansas
Red River
Mississippi River
Rio Grande
San Antonio

Many different groups of Native Americans inhabited the plains states when settlers and cattle ranchers began to move west. **Map Skill:** *In which states are the two largest reservations located?*

The buffalo, once plentiful in North America, was important to Native Americans on the plains. **History:** *Why did the settlers hunt the buffalo to near extinction?*

Native Americans on the Plains

LEGEND
- Native American reservations, 1890
- Range of the Buffalo by 1850
- Range of the Buffalo by 1875
- ✕ Battle

Plains Indians

Focus *How did Native Americans respond to the government's reservation policy?*

The growth of ranching was a disaster for Native Americans living on the Great Plains. Cattle took over grazing land from the buffalo. Before the arrival of settlers, millions of buffalo had roamed the Great Plains. Native Americans depended on buffalo for food, clothing, and shelter. They used the entire animal, eating the meat, and making tepee covers and clothing from the hide. They also made bridles from the hair, and tools from the bones.

Many settlers saw the buffalo and Native Americans as obstacles to development in the West. By killing buffalo, settlers believed, they would weaken Native Americans. Settlers hunted buffalo for food, killing thousands to feed the workers building the railroads. They also killed buffalo for sport. Trips were organized for hunters to shoot them from slow-moving trains. Wearing buffalo coats became a fad in the early 1870s, increasing the demand for skins. By 1885, fewer than 1,000 buffalo remained in the United States.

A young Sioux girl sits atop a horse outside the family tepee.

This Sioux child's toy tepee is made of buffalo hide, as are the stuffed dolls and toy horse.

In the 1860s, the U.S. government forced the Plains Indians onto **reservations**, land set aside for Native Americans. The government believed that once they were moved to reservations, Native Americans would give up their old way of life. They would no longer be free to follow the buffalo. Some Native Americans agreed to move to reservations when they signed treaties. Many others protested this policy and fought to hold on to their land and their freedom.

Sitting Bull and Crazy Horse

In the harsh winter of 1876, Sioux (Soo) leaders Crazy Horse and Sitting Bull refused to follow a government order to move their people to a reservation. The government sent Colonel George Custer of the United States 7th Cavalry to enforce the order and move the Sioux people to the reservation. Custer led hundreds of soldiers in an attack on thousands of Sioux camped along the Little Bighorn River, in present-day Montana. The Sioux surrounded the soldiers and shot at them from every side. Finally, the shooting ended. Not one of Custer's soldiers had survived the Battle of Little Bighorn.

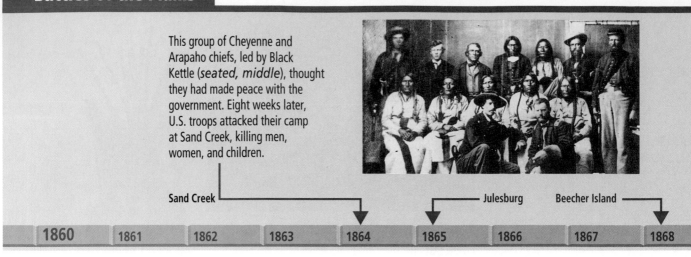

This group of Cheyenne and Arapaho chiefs, led by Black Kettle (*seated, middle*), thought they had made peace with the government. Eight weeks later, U.S. troops attacked their camp at Sand Creek, killing men, women, and children.

Sand Creek					Julesburg		Beecher Island	
1860	1861	1862	1863	1864	1865	1866	1867	1868

Geronimo

Geronimo, a leader of the Apache (uh PACH ee), held out the longest against the government. In 1881, Geronimo fled a reservation in Arizona for the mountains of the Sierra Madre (see EH ruh MAH-dray) in Mexico. Determined to free his people, Geronimo returned to Arizona in 1882. Several powerful chiefs and warriors left the reservation with him and traveled back to Mexico.

In the Sierra Madres, Geronimo was caught between the Mexican government, which wanted to kill him, and the U.S. government, which wanted to imprison him. In 1886, Geronimo surrendered to U. S. soldiers. Geronimo was taken prisoner, and never returned to his life in Arizona.

The Ghost Dance

By 1890, most Native Americans lived on reservations. Although the Sioux had lost their hunting grounds, they held on to their culture. A Paiute (PY yoot) named Wovoka had a vision that inspired them. Wovoka saw the Great Spirit bring to life all Native Americans who were killed by settlers, along with "game of every kind." Wovoka said that if Native Americans danced the Dance of the Ghosts, his vision would come true.

In the fall of 1890, the Ghost Dance spread across reservations in the Dakota Territory. Native Americans believed that the Ghost Dance would bring their dead warriors back to life.

On December 15, 1890, the Sioux leader Sitting Bull was shot and killed on his reservation. Hundreds of Ghost Dancers, frightened that they too would be killed, fled the reservation. A group of soldiers caught up with the Ghost Dancers at Wounded Knee, South Dakota. No one knows for certain who fired the first shot, but it is likely that the soldiers were far better armed than

A traditional dress worn during the Ghost Dance.

Sitting Bull spoke about life on the reservation after the Battle of Little Bighorn, saying "I see my people starving. We want cattle to butcher. That is the way you live, and we want to live the same way."

In 1877 in Montana, a group of Nez Perce were surrounded for five days by U.S. soldiers. Many people were killed. With the survivors suffering from cold and hunger, Chief Joseph surrendered with these words, "I will fight no more forever."

	Adobe Walls		Little Bighorn			Bear Paws		Mill Creek
1871	1872	1873	1874	1875	1876	1877	1878	1879

the Sioux. The soldiers fired at the Sioux with guns and cannons. One Sioux woman recalled the event,

"**W**e tried to run, but they shot us like we were a buffalo."

About 300 Native Americans, including women and children, died in the massacre. About 25 U.S. soldiers also died. The new 7th Cavalry of the United States, whose earlier members were defeated at Little Bighorn, participated in the attack at Wounded Knee.

One result of these clashes was that Native American land was taken and sold or given to settlers moving west to start a new life.

Lesson Review

1870	1880	1890	

1876
Little Bighorn

1886
Geronimo surrenders

1890
Wounded Knee

1 Key Vocabulary: Use each of these words in a sentence: cattle trail and reservation.

2 Focus: How did the cattle industry develop in the West?

3 Focus: How did Native Americans respond to the government's reservation policy?

4 Critical Thinking: Problem Solving Could settlers and Native Americans have lived peacefully on the plains? Why or why not?

5 Theme: Coping with Change Why was the killing off of the buffalo such a hardship for Plains Indians?

6 Geography/Music Activity: Write a song about the cattle drive. Include descriptions about what you might see, the dangers on the trail, and how you feel. Set your song to the tune of a song you know.

Settlers on the Plains

In her novel *My Ántonia*, Willa Cather captures a young boy's sense of awe at seeing a vast, empty land for the first time.

> **"C**autiously I slipped from under the buffalo hide, got up on my knees and peered over the side of the wagon. There seemed to be nothing to see; no fences, no creeks or trees, no hills. . . . There was nothing but land.**"**

Early travelers to the Great Plains were often filled with wonder by what looked like an endless ocean of prairie grass.

The Sodbusters

Focus *What was life like for farmers on the plains?*

In 1862 Congress passed the Homestead Act, offering 160 acres of free land in the West to anyone who would farm it for five years. A

The woman on the right is kneading dough and the couple on the far right sit in their kitchen by a pan of rising dough. On the plains, all cooking was done by hand and from scratch.
Economics: *Why was women's work economically important to life on the plains?*

homestead is land claimed by a settler. Within the first year, settlers had claimed 224,500 acres in Kansas and Nebraska. The real rush to the plains did not begin until after the Civil War.

Between 1862 and 1900, people packed their belongings and headed to the Great Plains. These settlers from other parts of the United States and from Europe were nicknamed **sodbusters** because they had to "bust," or break through, thick sod to prepare the land for farming. Sod is soil that is held together by thick roots of grass. Because wood was scarce on the treeless plains, settlers often built their houses from blocks of sod. For most settlers, plowing sod and building houses were only the first of many hard tasks.

Problems of Farming

Winters on the Great Plains were long and bitterly cold. Summers were unbearably hot. Drought and prairie fires frequently threatened crops. Settlers often used dried manure of buffalo and cattle for fuel. To make matters worse, swarms of grasshoppers swept through the prairies in the 1870s, gobbling up a year's crops in a few hours. As one newspaper editor wrote:

> "They came in untold millions, in clouds upon clouds, until their fluttering wings looked like a sweeping snowstorm in the heavens, until their dark bodies covered everything green upon the earth."

Men, women, and children worked together to bring in the hay. After working in the fields, the women were responsible for preparing food for everyone.

Technology on the Plains

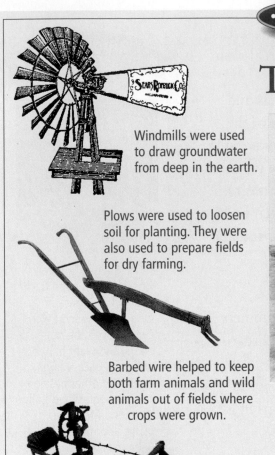

Windmills were used to draw groundwater from deep in the earth.

Plows were used to loosen soil for planting. They were also used to prepare fields for dry farming.

Barbed wire helped to keep both farm animals and wild animals out of fields where crops were grown.

Running a farm on the plains was very difficult work. Successful families were proud of overcoming the harsh weather conditions, insects, and loneliness. They wanted to show off all of their achievements. The family above was photographed in front of their sod house, their farm animals, and much of their farm equipment. Everyone in the family, even the children, had to work hard to make this farm a success.

When the sodbusters were not battling grasshoppers, they were fighting loneliness. Most settlers lived far away from each other and miles from the nearest town. Women, whose household chores kept them at home, often felt terribly isolated. "If I had married at home in West Virginia," one new bride reflected, "I should at least have had kindly neighbor women to turn to for advice . . . ."

Despite many difficulties, some settlers met the challenges of farming the plains. The most serious problem was the lack of rain. On the western plains, farmers could not count on enough rain each year. To cope with the lack of rainfall, they built windmills to pump water to their fields from deep within the ground. They also used a technique called **dry farming** in which they left a field unplanted for a season. Left alone, the field could store moisture in the soil and have enough water to grow a crop in the next planting season. Farmers also loosened the soil of the field and left straw from the previous crop on top of it to help to seal in water.

Grangers and Populists

Focus *How did the Grange and populism help farmers?*

More and more wheat was produced by farmers as the plains became more settled. When a product is plentiful, its price falls because people can buy it whenever and wherever they choose. Sellers have to keep lowering their prices to attract buyers and compete with other sellers. As the price of wheat dropped, farmers could not make enough money.

In 1867, Oliver H. Kelley founded the **Grange,** an organization of farmers who banded together to save money on equipment and supplies. Many Grangers also joined a new political party called the **Populist Party.** The word *Populist* comes from the Latin word for people. In 1896, the Populists tried to elect William Jennings Bryan as President of the United States because he supported farmers. Bryan lost to William McKinley, but he helped farmers gain attention and win a strong voice in national politics.

Although the Grange and the Populists improved conditions for some farmers, the hardships of life on the plains discouraged many settlers. Some farmers moved on to the West Coast. Others went back to the East or returned to Europe. In the late 1800s, an increasing number of people sought new opportunities in the industrial cities of the Midwest.

Ask Yourself

Farmers on the plains worked together to get the things that they needed. When is cooperation important for getting a job done?

? ? ? ? ? ? ? ? ? ? ? ? ? ?

Lesson Review

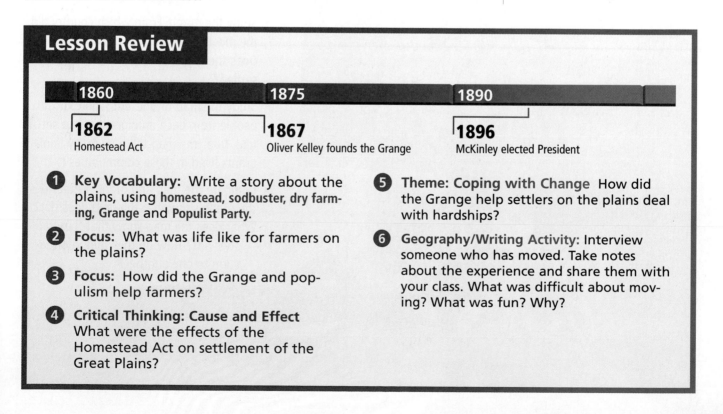

1860	1875	1890
1862	**1867**	**1896**
Homestead Act	Oliver Kelley founds the Grange	McKinley elected President

1 **Key Vocabulary:** Write a story about the plains, using **homestead, sodbuster, dry farming, Grange** and **Populist Party.**

2 **Focus:** What was life like for farmers on the plains?

3 **Focus:** How did the Grange and populism help farmers?

4 **Critical Thinking: Cause and Effect** What were the effects of the Homestead Act on settlement of the Great Plains?

5 **Theme: Coping with Change** How did the Grange help settlers on the plains deal with hardships?

6 **Geography/Writing Activity:** Interview someone who has moved. Take notes about the experience and share them with your class. What was difficult about moving? What was fun? Why?

Comparing Maps and Graphs

A Quilt of Many Peoples

If you had traveled through the Great Plains in 1880, you would have met people from many countries. Although immigrants lived all over the United States, they often settled in communities near others from their home countries. Maps and graphs can help you learn about these communities. Find out about the kinds of information maps and graphs can provide.

❶ Here's How

The map and graph on the next page show information about immigrants who settled in the Dakota Territory in 1880.

- Read the titles on the graph and map. What is the purpose of each one?

- Study the graph. From which country did the most immigrants come? The fewest? Does the graph tell where these groups settled?

- Study the map to find out where most people from each immigrant group settled. Does the map tell how many immigrants lived in these communities?

- Compare the map and graph. What does the graph show that the map does not? What does the map show that the graph does not? How do they add information to one another?

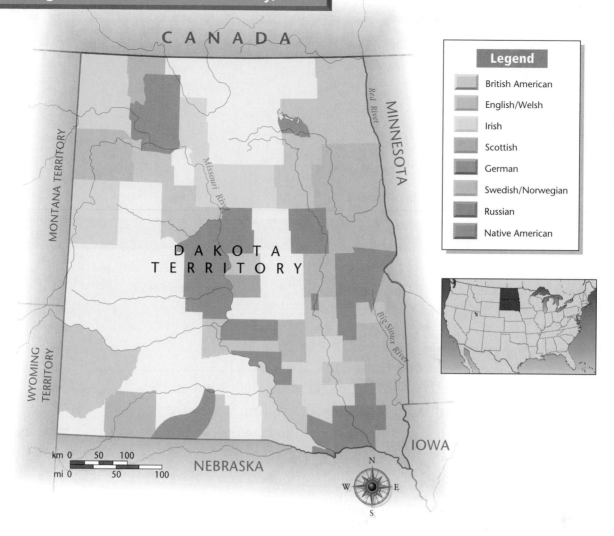

Immigration to the Dakota Territory, 1880

CANADA

MONTANA TERRITORY

Red River

MINNESOTA

Missouri River

DAKOTA
TERRITORY

WYOMING TERRITORY

Big Sioux River

IOWA

km 0   50   100
mi 0   50   100

NEBRASKA

N
W   E
S

Legend

- British American
- English/Welsh
- Irish
- Scottish
- German
- Swedish/Norwegian
- Russian
- Native American

Immigration to the Dakota Territory

9%
21%
5%
8%
12%
32%
11%
2%

- Russian
- Swedish/Norwegian
- German
- Scottish
- Irish
- English/Welsh
- British-American
- Other

② Think It Through

If you saw only the map, what would you know about immigrants to the Dakota Territory? What would you learn if you saw only the graph?

③ Use It

1. Write a paragraph about the information in the graph. Identify the main idea of the graph. Then describe what you learn from each section of the graph.

2. Write a paragraph about the map. Include a statement about each colored area and tell where it is located on the map. Be sure to state the main idea of the map.

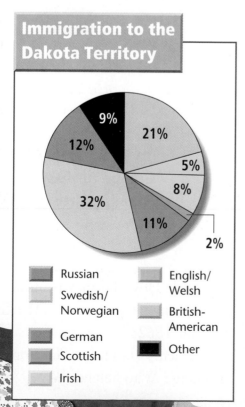

Chapter Review

Chapter Review Timeline

1869
First transcontinental railroad

| 1860 | 1868 | 1876 | 1884 | 1892 | 1900 |

1862
Homestead
Act

1867
Oliver Kelly
founds the Grange

1876
Little Bighorn

1890
Wounded Knee

Summarizing the Main Idea

1 Create a web for each of the following topics: communication and travel, Plains Indians, settlers on the Plains. Brainstorm words and terms and display them in a web such as the following one.

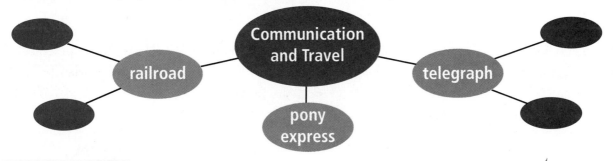

Vocabulary

2 Using at least nine of the following terms, write a postcard to a friend in the East describing life on the Great Plains.

pony express (p. 481)
telegraph (p. 482)
transcontinental railroad
(p. 483)

cattle trail (p. 485)
reservation (p. 487)
homestead (p. 491)
sodbusters (p. 491)

dry farming (p. 492)
Grange (p. 493)
Populist Party (p. 493)

Reviewing the Facts

3 Why did Congress want to build a transcontinental railroad?

4 Why were cattle herded across the plains?

5 What dangers did cowboys face?

6 Why were Native Americans forced onto reservations? How did they protest?

7 Why did many people move to the Great Plains after 1862?

8 What problems did farmers face on the Great Plains? Who helped them?

9 Look at the map and graph on page 495. Design your own map and graph of your class. Show where the boys sit and where the girls sit, and show how many members of your class are girls and how many are boys.

Geography Skills

10 Look at the map of the Cattle Drive trails on page 485. Compare the different trails. Think about the areas they cover. Which trail do you think might be the most difficult to travel? Which might be the easiest?

11 Illustrate a cover for a book about the Great Plains. Include examples of how geography and climate affected the people who lived there.

Critical Thinking

12 Predict How might Americans gain from better communication and transportation?

13 Cause and Effect How did the cattle industry affect how Native Americans and Americans reacted to each other?

14 Interpret Create "a day in the life" of a typical plains family. How might they spend their time? What roles and responsibilities might each family member have?

Writing: Citizenship and Culture

15 Citizenship How are people, crops, and other goods transported around the United States today? Write a brochure describing different types of transportation.

16 Culture What character traits would you need to be a successful cowboy? Write a help wanted ad for a position as a cowboy.

Activities

National Heritage/Music Activity
Work in a group of four or five. Pick a theme such as cattle driving, moving to a reservation, or farming on the plains. Create a sound symphony that reflects your theme. Use classroom objects for instruments or use your voices or hands and feet. Give your composition a title and share it with your classmates.

Internet Option

Check the **Internet Social Studies Center** for ideas on how to extend your theme project beyond your classroom.

THEME PROJECT CHECK-IN

The information you have read about the changes that took place in America during the 1800s will help you begin your project. Ask yourself these questions:
• How did new ways of communication cause changes for people?
• How were the lives of Native Americans affected by the changes of this century?
• How did people join together to cope with some of the changes they faced?

Chapter Preview: *People, Places, and Events*

1850	1860	1870

The Light Bulb   1878

How did the light bulb change life in the city? *Lesson 1, Page 501*

Sears Catalog

Find out why people wanted to shop from a catalog. *Lesson 1, Page 502*

Immigration

Why was school so important to immigrant children? *Lesson 2, Page 510*

Inventions Shape Industry

Main Idea New inventions helped expand industry and create a new age of entrepreneurs.

The huge machines made a tremendous noise. Amid the heat, flying sparks, and hissing steam, workers melted the iron in a blast furnace and then poured it into a huge, pear-shaped converter. When they shot air into the converter, the iron became steel. The workers then poured the new liquid steel into molds.

This was the Bessemer (BEHS uh mur) process, invented in the mid-1800s by the British scientist Henry Bessemer. (At almost the same time, William Kelley developed the process in the United States.) The Bessemer process was one of the most important inventions of its time. Now it became cheap enough to mass produce steel. It could be made in large quantities at a low cost, creating a revolution in construction, manufacturing, and transportation.

◀ These criss-crossed conveyors depict the Ford Motor Company in Michigan in 1927.

Key Vocabulary

urban

rural

entrepreneur

monopoly

Key Events

1872 Andrew Carnegie founds a steel company

1876 Alexander Graham Bell makes the first telephone call

1878 The first successful light bulb is invented

1880   1890   1900

Samuel Gompers   1886

Find out how Samuel Gompers worked to change the labor laws. *Lesson 3, Page 515*

Queen Liliuokalani

How did the queen of Hawaii lose power? *Lesson 4, Page 522*

Yellow Journalism   1898

What were newspapers competing for in the 1890s? *Lesson 4, Page 524*

Inventions Change American Industry

Focus *How did inventions change the way Americans worked and lived?*

Before 1770, most goods were made by hand. Between 1770 and the mid-1800s, however, inventions changed the way people made and shipped goods.

It took time, but with the inventions of the Industrial Revolution, many new American industries were created. Before the

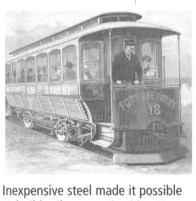

Inexpensive steel made it possible to build rail systems in cities. You can see a cable car like the one above in the advertisement below. **Economics:** *Why would merchants want cable cars to run right by their stores?*

The invention of the elevator made life in growing cities easier. As buildings grew taller, people could ride instead of walk to the top floors.

Tall buildings led to the development of department stores, where one company sold a variety of goods in one place. This change made shopping easier.

"A BUSY BEE-HIVE."
SECTIONAL VIEW OF THE ENORMOUS ESTABLISHMENT OF
MONTGOMERY WARD & CO.
MICHIGAN AVENUE, MADISON AND WASHINGTON STREETS, CHICAGO.

Civil War, most Americans lived in the countryside. Many people worked on farms. From the end of the Civil War to the late 1800s, that pattern began to change. More and more people left the countryside and moved into the cities in search of work in the growing number of factories.

The Rise of Steel

After the development of the Bessemer process, the steel industry grew rapidly. Steel helped to push the nation into a period of tremendous industrial growth. People found endless uses for steel, from bridges, skyscrapers, and ships, to household goods like stoves, hammers, and nails.

Perhaps the most important use of steel was in building the railroad. The first rails were made from iron. Steel rails were stronger and lasted longer than iron ones. Now the railroad companies could build bigger trains. Railroad construction boomed and increased the volume of people and goods that could be transported.

Electricity Lights Up America

The light bulb lit up homes, factories, and offices across the nation. The first successful light bulb was invented in 1878 by a man named Joseph Swan. Thomas Edison was the first person to develop an entire electrical system for a city. It included dynamos (generators) to produce electricity, and wires and fuses to carry the electricity. Edison used the light bulb as part of his total electrical system. Edison supervised the installation of the first power system, which was built in a section of New York City in 1882.

Inventions in the Home and Office

Inventions in communications were also made. In 1876, Alexander Graham Bell made the first telephone call. His assistant remembered that Bell yelled,

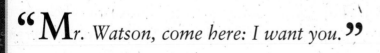

> **"M**r. *Watson, come here: I want you.* **"**

Bell and Watson had been working a long time to develop the telephone. Both men were quite surprised when Watson heard Bell shouting at him through the telephone.

Sometimes new inventions helped to create other inventions. The invention of the elevator and the development of the Bessemer

The light bulb was part of an electrical system that lit up cities across the nation.

The telephone became an important tool for communicating, both in large buildings and across the country.

The typewriter made office work faster and neater.

The sewing machine was used both in factories and in homes, speeding up the production of clothing.

The advertisement above shows women washing at home.

This photograph shows women working in a hat factory.

Inventions like the washing machine *(above)* and the sewing machine changed the way women worked. **Arts:** *Compare the advertisement and the photograph at the top of this page. What different information can be gathered from each picture?*

process for making steel allowed builders to construct much taller office buildings, called skyscrapers. As businesses and industries grew, people wanted better and faster ways to handle their office work. The typewriter soon became the most important machine in the office.

As the production of goods increased, business people found new ways to sell their products. In **urban** areas, or cities, people began to shop in department stores, where they could choose from a variety of goods — all under one roof. People living in **rural** areas, or the countryside, were not left out, however. Both A. Montgomery Ward and Richard W. Sears established mail-order houses. Now people living in rural America could order goods through a catalog.

Big Business Emerges

Focus *How did the nation's entrepreneurs achieve their wealth?*

Much of the credit for the industrialization of America belongs to the nation's entrepreneurs (ahn truh pruh NURZ). An **entrepreneur** is someone who starts a business, hoping to make a profit — an amount of money above and beyond what is needed to run the business. As industries developed, entrepreneurs looked for more profitable ways to run their businesses. Some became extremely wealthy. They made their money in several industries: oil, steel, railroads, and shipping. Some businesses even became **monopolies**, which means they controlled all aspects of a particular industry.

Andrew Carnegie

Several men, like John D. Rockefeller, J. P. Morgan, and Andrew Carnegie, became great entrepreneurs in the late 1800s. Andrew Carnegie was born in Scotland and moved to America when he was 13 years old. His family was very poor, so Carnegie got a job in a factory, working 12 hours a day for 10 cents an hour. He later worked as a telegraph operator and a railroad superintendent.

On a trip to England, he saw the Bessemer converter. He returned to Pittsburgh, declaring:

> **"T**he day of Iron has passed — Steel is King!**"**

In 1872 he founded the company that would become Carnegie Steel. Carnegie himself became one of the richest men in the world. Carnegie provided the funding to build many public libraries, gave money to universities, and set up foundations. When he died in 1919, Carnegie had given away about 90 percent of his money.

The Industrial Revolution changed America. It made some people's lives easier and contributed to the rise of big business and big profits. It also created the promise of jobs, inviting people from all over the world to seek a new life in America.

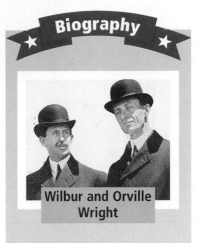

Biography

Wilbur and Orville Wright

The Wright brothers became interested in flying because of a toy helicopter they had as children. In 1900 they traveled to Kitty Hawk, North Carolina, and flew a manned glider. By 1903 they had developed a motor to power their machine. On December 17, 1903, in Kitty Hawk, Orville made the first engine-powered flight. He traveled a distance of 120 feet.

Lesson Review

1870	1875	1880

1872
Andrew Carnegie founds a steel company

1876
Alexander Graham Bell makes the first telephone call

1878
The first successful light bulb is invented

1 **Key Vocabulary:** Describe business in the late 1800s, using **entrepreneur** and **monopoly**.

2 **Focus:** How did inventions change the way Americans worked and lived?

3 **Focus:** How did the nation's entrepreneurs achieve their wealth?

4 **Critical Thinking: Generalize** Does new technology always improve people's lives? Why or why not?

5 **Theme: Coping with Change** How did Andrew Carnegie use the changes in industrial America to his advantage?

6 **Citizenship/Science Activity:** Think of a tool or a machine that you would like to invent to improve people's lives. Make a drawing to explain to others how your invention would work.

Human Systems

How Did Geography Help Pittsburgh Grow?

Did you ever wonder how the town or city where you live came to be there? Cities do not spring up in a particular place without a reason. Geography often plays a big role in their growth.

Pittsburgh is a good example. It grew very quickly into a city. Geography helped in three ways. First, Pittsburgh is located where three major rivers come together. Second, the surrounding region contains mountains full of limestone and coal. Finally, the Great Lakes are close by, making it easy to bring in iron ore from sites around those lakes.

The combination of good transportation and nearby natural resources has made Pittsburgh a major center of industry. Its nickname is "Steel City."

Science Connection

Iron comes from iron ore mined from the earth. To produce steel, iron must be refined, or purified, then mixed with other metals. Iron and steel are cheap, strong, and long-lasting. What products can you think of that are made of steel?

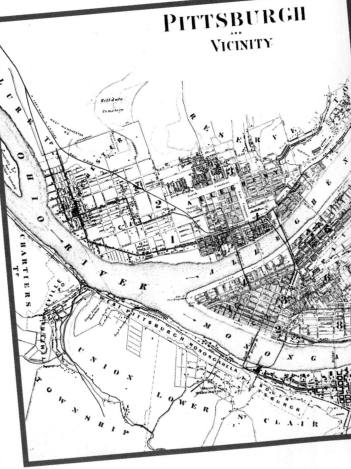

This map of Pittsburgh from the mid-1800s shows its location where three rivers come together. *What other cities have grown along major rivers?*

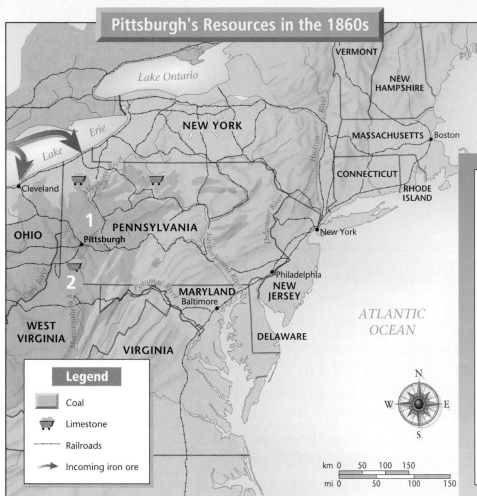

Pittsburgh's Resources in the 1860s

VERMONT

Lake Ontario

NEW HAMPSHIRE

NEW YORK

MASSACHUSETTS • Boston

Lake Erie

Cleveland •

CONNECTICUT

RHODE ISLAND

OHIO

1 PENNSYLVANIA

• Pittsburgh

• New York

2

Philadelphia •

MARYLAND

Baltimore •

NEW JERSEY

ATLANTIC OCEAN

WEST VIRGINIA

DELAWARE

VIRGINIA

Legend

Coal

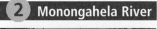 Limestone

Railroads

Incoming iron ore

km 0   50   100   150

mi 0   50   100   150

When railroads came to Pittsburgh in 1851, transportation to the city became even easier. In addition, the railroads needed Pittsburgh's steel for rails. **Map Skill:** *What states on the map besides Pennsylvania have coal?*

1 Pennsylvania Hills

Coal and Limestone
The nearby hills of western Pennsylvania, rich in coal and limestone, helped make Pittsburgh a steel center. Coal heated the furnaces that refined the iron ore and made it into steel. Limestone was mixed with the ore to help melt out impurities.

This photograph from 1907 shows how the rapid growth of industry caused air pollution in Pittsburgh. *What other problems can rapid growth cause?*

2 Monongahela River

Coal Barges
Pittsburgh is located where the Allegheny River joins with the Monongahela to form the Ohio River. These rivers helped make Pittsburgh an industrial center. Raw materials, like iron ore and coal, could be brought in, and finished products, like steel, could be taken out.

Research Activity

Think about the town or city where you live, or a town or city near you.

1 Find out how geography may have influenced its settlement and growth. Why was it originally settled? How did it grow?

2 Draw a map showing the geography of the town or city. Then share what you learned with your class.

I Wonder Who

by Gail Hennessey
illustrated by George M. Ulrich

Have you ever wondered who invented things like the eggbeater, clothes dryer, lawn sprinkler, or pencil sharpener? African Americans had a hand in inventing or improving many practical items that are still part of everyday life.

These pictures show the modern equivalents of interesting inventions by African Americans. Many of the inventions have been improved over time; others have not changed. Nevertheless, every step in an item's development is itself an invention.

Bottle cap
Inventors: Jones and Long
Patent: 610,715
Date: September 13, 1898

Eggbeater
Inventor: W. Johnson
Patent: 292,821. Date: February 5, 1884

Mop
Inventor: Thomas W. Stewart
Patent: 499,402
Date: June 13, 1893

Collapsible ironing board
Inventor: Sarah Boone
Patent: 473,653. Date: April 26, 1892

Invented . . .

Lock
Inventor: W.A. Martin
Patent: 407,738
Date: July 23, 1889

Fountain pen
Inventor: W.B. Purvis
Patent: 419,065
Date: January 7, 1890

Wooden golf tee
Inventor: George F. Grant
Patent: 638,920
Date: December 12, 1899

Metal dustpan
Inventor: L.P. Ray
Patent: 587,607. Date: August 3, 1897

Additional Inventions by African Americans

Blood plasma and blood banks
Inventor: Charles Richard Drew

Handlebar basket for bicycle
Inventor: J.M. Certain
Patent: 639,708
Date: December 26, 1899

Motorized clothes dryer
Inventor: G.T. Sampson
Patent: 476,416
Date: June 7, 1892

Pencil sharpener
Inventor: J.L. Love
Patent: 594,114
Date: November 23, 1897

Refrigerator
Inventor: J. Standard
Patent: 455,891
Date: July 4, 1891

Swivel lawn sprinkler
Inventor: J.W. Smith
Patent: 581,785
Date: May 4, 1897

Traffic signal
Inventor: Garrett A. Morgan
Patent: 1,475,024
Date: November 20, 1923

Truck refrigeration unit
Inventor: Frederick M. Jones
Patent: 2,475,841
Date: July 12, 1949

Response Activities

1. **Classify** Divide the inventions pictured here into categories. For example, one category might be "Things Used in the Home." Make a chart including as many of the inventions as possible.

2. **Descriptive: Write a Letter** A patent gives an inventor the right to make, use, and sell an invention for a certain period of time. Write a letter to the U.S. Patent Office, describing an invention you would like to patent.

3. **National Heritage: Research an Inventor** Research the work of an inventor. Design a pamphlet advertising several of his or her inventions. Include biographical information too.

Immigration and Growing Cities

Main Idea Immigration to America increased in the late 1800s and early 1900s, causing the populations of major cities to grow.

Key Vocabulary

pogrom

ethnic neighbor-
hood

settlement house

Key Events

1886 Statue of
Liberty erected

1892 First immi-
grant passes
through Ellis Island

1910 First immi-
grant passes
through Angel
Island

ary Antin was 12 years old when she came from Russia to America in 1894. The voyage took 16 days. Immigration was a new and sometimes frightening experience. Mary wrote:

> "The captain and his officers ate their dinners, smoked their pipes and slept soundly . . . while we frightened emigrants turned our faces to the wall and awaited our watery graves."

The journey was not all frightening. Mary also wrote about "happy hours on deck, with . . . sunshine . . . dancing and fun."

Antin was one of 14 million immigrants who came to the United States between 1860 and 1900. They were searching for opportunities and better lives.

A New Home

Focus *What was life like for immigrants coming to the United States?*

Most immigrants came from Europe, but others came from Mexico and Asia. Even within the United States, many people moved from the country to the cities. Many African Americans left the rural South for new homes in the North and West.

In the late 1800s, many factors convinced people to leave their homelands. In Europe, a potato famine pushed people off their land. A lack of jobs, unfair laws, and mistreatment encouraged others to leave. Jewish people living in Russia, like Mary Antin, were terribly mistreated. They faced unfair laws and pogroms. A **pogrom** is an organized attack on a group of people.

There were also strong factors pulling immigrants to America. Immigrants were attracted to America's many freedoms and democratic form of government. Also, as industry expanded, many new jobs were created. Immigrants came to find work.

The *Mauretania* was a luxury cruise ship, but it also carried immigrants to the United States. They did not ride in the beautiful cabins, but instead traveled in the lowest deck, called steerage. **Economics:** *Why might most immigrants have traveled in steerage?*

A family arrives at Ellis Island in this photograph *(left)*. On their way they would have passed by the Statue of Liberty which was erected in 1886 in New York Harbor *(below)*.

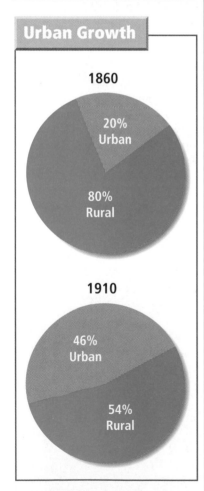

Urban Growth

1860

20% Urban

80% Rural

1910

46% Urban

54% Rural

Chart Skill: By what percent did the urban population grow from 1860 to 1910?

Most European immigrants settled on the East Coast of the United States. Most of them arrived in New York City, where they passed through an immigration station at Castle Garden. Beginning January 1, 1892, immigrants passed through the station on Ellis Island. There, they were examined by doctors and questioned about their health, skills, education, and finances. If immigrants were sick or had no job skills, they could be sent back to Europe.

Immigrants from Asia arrived on the West Coast starting in the middle of the 1800s. Beginning in 1910, they passed through a station on Angel Island in San Francisco Bay. Most people stayed there a few weeks, but some were forced to stay up to two years.

Once immigrants arrived in the United States, they had to adapt to a different way of life. Public schools were especially important to many immigrant children. In school, children learned to speak English and to understand American customs. Mary Antin wrote:

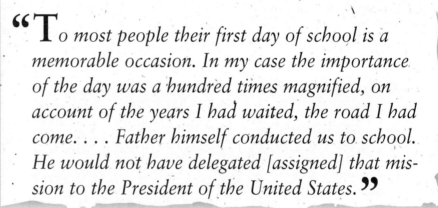

"To most people their first day of school is a memorable occasion. In my case the importance of the day was a hundred times magnified, on account of the years I had waited, the road I had come. . . . Father himself conducted us to school. He would not have delegated [assigned] that mission to the President of the United States."

The Growth of Cities

Focus *Why did cities become crowded in the late 1800s?*

After 1860, more immigrants came to the United States in search of opportunities like the ones Mary Antin found. Many settled in cities. In 1860, fewer than one in every five Americans lived in the city. Fifty years later, twice as many Americans were city dwellers. *(See the pie chart on the left.)* Thousands of new low-paying jobs were created in the cities as industry and business expanded. The growth of the steel industry brought new workers to cities like Pittsburgh, Pennsylvania, and Birmingham, Alabama. The rise of the Chicago meatpacking industry created new jobs there as well.

The Story of Immigration in Four Cities

Immigrants arriving in the United States spread out across the country in search of new homes. **Map Skill:** *About how many miles would an immigrant arriving at Ellis Island in New York have to travel to reach San Antonio?*

San Francisco: A Chinese butcher shop. Immigrants often set up businesses in ethnic neighborhoods to provide goods to their community.

Chicago: Women from a Greek neighborhood wait for the bank to open.

San Antonio: A chili stand run by Mexican Americans. **Cultures:** *Why might serving traditional foods have been important to immigrants living in the United States?*

New York: A fruit stand in New York City. Fresh produce was an important addition to immigrants' diets.

An Industrial Society **511**

Jane Addams

Jane Addams opened Hull House in Chicago in 1889. Hull House was one of the nation's first settlement houses. These places provided services for poor residents of a city.

Hull House offered free medical care and classes in everything from cooking to literature. Soon settlement houses developed in cities throughout the United States. Jane Addams is known as one of the nation's first social workers.

By 1880, four out of five New Yorkers were immigrants or the children of immigrants. Often they lived in **ethnic neighborhoods**, residential areas in a city where people share the same background and culture. Ethnic neighborhoods gave immigrants a place to adjust to their new lives in America. Newspapers and shop signs were printed in the language of the residents. There, the newcomers could speak in their own language and hold onto some of the customs of the "old country."

Ethnic neighborhoods also had problems. Many immigrants lived in tenement houses, terribly overcrowded apartment buildings. In New York City it was common to find 15 or more people living in the same small apartment. Property owners often did not care about keeping their buildings safe and in good repair. They only wanted to collect the rent.

To fight against some of the difficult conditions of city life, people began to create services to provide for the urban poor. **Settlement houses,** where residents could receive medical care, take classes, and where children could play safely, began to spring up in the late 1880s. Though life was often hard for immigrants, they continued to come to the cities in search of new opportunities. City residents, both long-time city dwellers and more recent arrivals, continued to look for new ways to adjust to the growing urban population.

Lesson Review

1880	1900	1920

1886
Statue of Liberty erected

1892
First immigrant passes through Ellis Island

1910
First immigrant passes through Angel Island

1 **Key Vocabulary:** Describe cities in the early 1800s, using **ethnic neighborhood** and **settlement house.**

2 **Focus:** What was life like for immigrants coming to the United States?

3 **Focus:** Why did cities become crowded in the late 1800s?

4 **Critical Thinking: Interpret** What are some of the contributions that immi-grants have made to American society?

5 **Citizenship:** What are some factors that may have helped immigrants feel like new citizens of the United States?

6 **Geography/Research Activity:** Research one of these cities: Chicago, New York, San Antonio, or San Francisco. Write a paragraph telling what immigrants to that city might find there today.

Workers Organize

LESSON
3

Main Idea During the late 1800s, workers formed unions and fought for better working conditions.

In 1889, the South Fork Dam broke. A great wall of water rushed down on the poor section of the city of Johnstown, Pennsylvania, destroying everything in its path. More than 2,200 people were killed. The lake and dam were owned by the South Fork Fishing and Hunting Club. The wealthy club members had failed to keep the dam in good repair.

Some people felt that the flood symbolized what was wrong with America: the great difference between the rich and the poor. Even though the entire town tried to prevent the flood when the rains came, in the end it was the poor community that was destroyed while the wealthy did not suffer much loss.

Key Vocabulary
mechanization
labor union
strike

Key Events
1877 The Great Uprising
1886 The American Federation of Labor formed
1892 The Homestead Strike

A Hard Life for Workers

Focus *How did industrialization change the lives of workers?*

Many workers spent 10-hour days in factories. Others worked underground, mining coal to run those factories. The people who worked in coal mines rarely saw daylight. They went to work before sunrise and arrived home after dark.

Jobs paid so little that many people didn't earn enough money to support their families. Children had to work too. At about the age of 10, children began shining shoes or selling newspapers or cigars. Some children worked at home sewing clothes, while others worked in factories or mines. Children earned even less pay than adults.

Many children, like the boy in this photograph, worked in the coal mines. They carried lamps like the one above.

The Bobbin Machine

The boy above is working at a factory bobbin machine, changing a bobbin. The bobbin machine wound separate strands of thread into one thicker strand.

Jobs changed because of **mechanization,** in which machines performed the jobs that people once did. Workers who had made and sold an entire product were now paid poorly to do simple, boring tasks. The factories and mines were also very dangerous places. Most employers did not provide safe working conditions for their employees. Many factory workers were injured or killed by machines, and mine workers experienced lung problems.

Workers Fight for Change

Focus *Why did workers form unions in the late 1800s?*

In the mid-1800s, there were few rules requiring companies to run their businesses fairly and safely. An individual worker felt powerless to go before a big company to complain or ask for changes. So workers decided to join together, finding strength in numbers. They established **labor unions,** in which groups of workers bargained with company owners over wages and working conditions.

Workers' desire to organize became even stronger in 1877. Many railroads were losing money, so the managers decided to cut wages. In West Virginia, railroad workers went on **strike,** refusing to work. Railroad strikes spread to every major industrial city in the country. In some cities, the state militia and federal troops battled angry mobs. These strikes became known as the Great Uprising. After the Great Uprising, workers used strikes more often to fight for their rights.

Strikes often led to violence and bloodshed. In 1892, a strike took place at the Carnegie Steel plant in Homestead, Pennsylvania. Workers were fighting to keep their union. The Carnegie company fought against them and eventually won the battle. Sometimes the people who went on strike for unions created positive changes in the American workplace, like better pay, safer working conditions, and an eight-hour workday. One of the

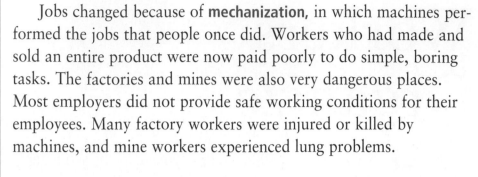

Children were hired to work the bobbin machine *(left)* because their small hands fit between the spools of thread *(right)*. Many fingers were injured in the fast-moving machines.

Yiddish   English   Lithuanian   Italian

Strikes brought people of different ethnic groups together to fight for a common cause. The picture to the left shows strikers with signs in four languages. The strike poster above is in both English and Yiddish. **History:** *Why might strikers have advertised their strikes in different languages?*

leaders of the union movement was Samuel Gompers. Gompers came to the United States from Great Britain in 1863, when he was 13 years old. He worked making cigars and joined the Cigarmakers' Union. In 1886 Gompers was one of the founders and the first president of the American Federation of Labor, or AFL. The AFL was made up of workers from many skilled trades who banded together to improve the lives of workers. The AFL later joined with another union and still exists today.

Lesson Review

1870	1880	1890	

1877
The Great Uprising

1886
The American Federation of Labor formed

1892
The Homestead Strike

1. **Key Vocabulary:** Write a paragraph about work in the late 1800s, using **mechanization, labor union,** and **strike.**

2. **Focus:** How did industrialization change the lives of workers?

3. **Focus:** Why did workers form unions in the late 1800s?

4. **Critical Thinking: Interpret** Why did companies fight against labor unions?

5. **Citizenship:** How did unions help to create better working conditions in industrial America?

6. **Geography/Science Activity:** Research the Carnegie Steel plant. What natural resources from the area were used to make steel? Choose one of these resources and find out how it was used in the Carnegie Steel plant.

Historical Fiction

This bear was brought through Ellis Island by an immigrant child.

The Cat Who Escaped from Steerage

by Evelyn Wilde Mayerson

It was not a happy voyage across the ocean to the United States. The cat that nine-year-old Chanah had smuggled onto the ship had gotten loose. Chanah and her cousin Yaacov had left the steerage area to search for the cat. They found it, but it got away again, and then they found something else — big trouble. Two ship's officers caught them, which would have been bad enough. Then the men discovered that Yaacov was deaf, and they reported this to the inspectors at Ellis Island. Now, just a few miles from America, Yaacov's mother Raizel fears the worst. Chanah and her brother Benjamin and her father Yonkel are at Ellis Island with Raizel and Yaacov to hear the news.

Then things took a serious turn. The officials conferred. One stepped behind Yaacov and clapped his hands behind Yaacov's head. Chanah, who saw this coming, pointed from the fence and Yaacov turned.

"He seems to hear all right," said the interpreter.

"I'm not so sure," said the inspector. "He was slow in turning. Whisper your name, boy. Even with a sore throat, you can whisper."

"He wants your name," said the interpreter.

Yaacov drew an imaginary line down the center of his body, turned in one direction, then the other. Then he fell to the ground, rolling and threshing on the floor.

"What is he doing?" asked the inspector. "Is he having some kind of fit? If that's what he's doing, the interview is over."

Chanah broke from her family, ducked beneath the iron pipe, and ran to the high bench. "I know what he's doing. He's showing you Yaacov, in the Bible. That's his name. That's what he's saying."

"Yaacov is Jacob," explained the interpreter.

The inspector leaned over his desk to peer at Chanah. "Who are you to him?" he asked.

"He's my cousin."

"How do you know that was what he said?"

"Yaacov in the Bible was a twin. That's why he divided himself in half. And when he fell to the ground, that was Yaacov wrestling with the angel. He can talk," insisted Chanah. "He just talks with his hands. Tell him something else," she said to Yaacov.

Immigrants were usually examined by city health officials when they first arrived in the United States.

Yaacov pointed to the inspector's pocket watch, made rippling hand motions, then a pinch of his thumb and forefinger.

"He's saying you have a drop of water inside your watchcase."

The inspector looked. Sure enough, there was a tiny drop of water under the case.

"At least we know his eyesight is good," he said.

Yonkel decided it was time to join the protest. "A different language," he shouted through the mesh. "Like all the different languages here. You need an interpreter, that's all."

Then the inspector lost his temper. "Get that little girl out of here!" he shouted. "Things are getting out of hand. Tell them to be quiet or we'll send them all back."

The inspector appeared to be troubled. He seemed to be thinking, You let in someone who's deaf, then you let in someone else who's blind. Where's it all going to end?

When the inspector shook his head, no one needed an interpreter to figure out that Yaacov would not be permitted to enter.

A great scream went up from Raizel, the kind that rattles from the throat and makes all within hearing feel their scalps crawl. Rifke began to wail, Yonkel to shout.

This postcard shows the main building at Ellis Island as it looked in 1900.

dilemma

a situation that requires a person to choose between actions that are equally difficult

The interpreter, used to such scenes, explained, "The boy has to return. The mother and the other boy can stay, but this one has to go back to Poland."

Raizel began to shriek and tear at her dress, while every other mother and father in the waiting room pressed forward with their hands at their hearts, their throats, knowing that at any time, this could happen to them.

Yaacov's mother was in a painful dilemma. What to do? Her choice was simple, yet terrible: to return with Yaacov, and perhaps never see her husband, Shimson, again; worse, to let Yaacov return alone to live with distant relatives, perhaps never to see him again.

Chanah broke free from Benjamin's clutch, ducked beneath the railing, and again approached the inspector's bench. This time one of her black stockings had fallen to her high-topped shoes, but she made no move to pick it up. "He knows everything," she said. "He can tell you what you had for breakfast this morning and what you had for lunch. Ask him."

"The boy is entitled to an appeal," said the interpreter to the inspector. "You and I both know that can include the testimony of either relatives or lawyers."

"We can't afford a lawyer," shouted Yonkel.

Suddenly weary, the inspector's shoulders sagged. "All right," he said. "Tell him to tell me what I had to eat today."

Chanah asked Yaacov. Yaacov in turn made hand motions that Chanah interpreted.

"He said you had sausage and bread for lunch with coffee to drink, and eggs for breakfast."

"I'll be," said the inspector. "How did he do that?"

Chanah conferred with Yaacov. "He smells the sausage on your breath, and sees the coffee on your teeth, the bread crumbs on your beard, and the eggs on your mustache."

The inspector cocked an eye. He reminded Chanah of a rooster that used to strut in a neighbor's yard. "How does he know that I didn't have the eggs for lunch?"

"Because the egg on your mustache is dry. If you had had it for lunch, the pieces would still be damp."

The two men looked at each other while everyone held their breath. Then the inspector winked at the interpreter. "I say we let in a kid with a sore throat." No translation was needed. The smiles told it all.

translation
the act or process of expressing in a different language

Meet the Author

Evelyn Wilde Mayerson has written many different things — poetry, plays, novels for adults, and children's stories. She calls this book "a grandmother's tale. There are stories like it in every family."

Additional Books to Read

Lyddie
by Katherine Paterson
Read about life as a "mill girl."

If Your Name Was Changed at Ellis Island
by Ellen Levine
Find out what it was like to be an immigrant.

Response Activities

1. **Compare Literature and History** How does the story of Chanah and Yaacov help you understand the experience of immigration?

2. **Expressive: Write a Poem** Have you ever gone somewhere new or done something that you never did before? Write a poem about it. Describe what you did and saw and how you felt.

3. **National Heritage: Economics** Select a country like Mexico, Ireland, or Hungary. Research immigration from that country to the United States. Was there a period when many people immigrated? What reasons did they have for immigrating?

★ CITIZENSHIP ★

Participating

Who Builds a Community?

Suppose you and your classmates had to come up with ideas for improving your community. Could you think of anything? Most neighborhoods and communities in this country are always trying to improve themselves. The case study below shows how reformers 100 years ago tackled some of the same problems we have today.

Case Study

Hull House

American cities in the late 1800s had some of the same problems that cities have today. The reformer Jane Addams, pictured at left, wanted to solve those problems.

In 1889, she and Ellen Gates Starr co-founded Hull House, one of the nation's first settlement houses, in Chicago. A settlement house was like a community center. Trained workers lived there and provided services to the people of the neighborhood. The services could include kindergartens, health clinics, music and art classes, adult education, and daycare.

Hull House was torn down in 1963, but an association named after it still provides many services.

Take Action

Today, some services that used to be offered by settlement houses have been taken over by other organizations. Kindergarten, for example, is part of public school. Health clinics are run by cities and hospitals. But Addams' goal — to improve neighborhood life as a whole — is still a good one. How could you improve your community? Try this:

1 Create a list of 10 services that would improve your community. Think about the needs of people of all different ages.

2 Decide which of the services is most important, which is the second most important, and so on. Rewrite your list in that order.

3 Write your list on the board.

4 Compare the lists. Did everyone come up with the same ideas? Are there any ideas that you could put into practice?

Tips for Participating

- Find out how you can contribute to ongoing projects. Do you have extra time? A special skill? Good ideas?
- Be willing to volunteer. (That means you won't get paid!)
- Once you make a commitment, try to stick with it.

Research Activity

Find out what social services are already available in your community. Talk to teachers, church leaders, and others. Read the local newspaper. Who provides these services and how much money is spent on them each year? Present your data in chart form.

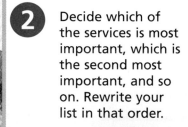

Becoming a World Power

Main Idea American interests expanded throughout the world.

Hawaii's Queen Liliuokalani (lih LEE oh kuh LAH nee) was determined to fight to rule her country. In the 1890s, she fought against the sugar and pineapple planters of Hawaii.

Queen Liliuokalani believed that the planters had taken too much control, and she tried to take back power from them. The planters, who were descendants of Americans, turned to the United States for help. A small group of United States Marines landed in Honolulu, on the island of Oahu in the Hawaiian Islands, in January 1893. They helped the planters to overthrow the queen. In 1895, there was one last attempt to take back power from the planters. This attempt failed. Queen Liliuokalani was taken prisoner and forced to give up her throne. In 1898, the United States annexed Hawaii.

Queen Liliuokalani

Hawaii's sugar and pineapple planters wanted to take control of the government. **Map Skill:** *Where were most of the plantations located in the Hawaiian Islands?*

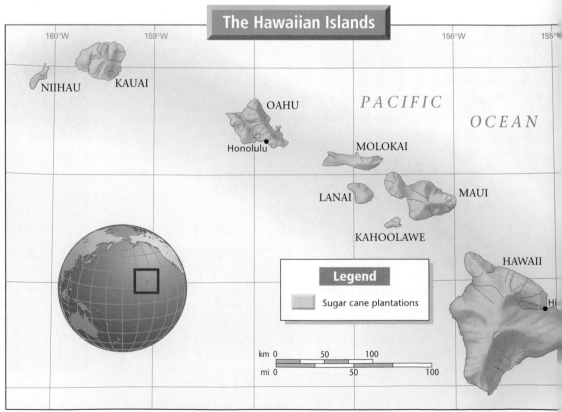

The Hawaiian Islands

NIIHAU
KAUAI
OAHU
Honolulu
PACIFIC OCEAN
MOLOKAI
LANAI
MAUI
KAHOOLAWE
HAWAII

Legend
Sugar cane plantations

km 0   50   100
mi 0   50   100

America Expands

Focus *How did America expand its territory in the late 1800s?*

Hawaii became the 50th state in 1959. A few months before, Alaska had become the 49th state. It was 47 years earlier, however, that Alaska was made a United States territory.

In the 1850s, Russia was defeated in a war against Britain and its allies. Needing money, the Russians offered to sell Alaska to the United States. Secretary of State William H. Seward thought it was a good deal. Seward bargained with the Russians and struggled with Congress, who had to approve the purchase. He succeeded, and in 1867 the United States bought Alaska — an area more than twice the size of Texas — for less than two cents an acre.

Many Americans thought that Alaska was a worthless piece of frozen land and nicknamed it "Seward's Icebox." Then, in 1896, gold was discovered near Alaska, in the Klondike in Canada *(see map below)*. Later, gold was found in Alaska itself. Almost 100,000 gold hunters rushed to Alaska. The unsettled Alaskan wilderness with its harsh weather conditions was a dangerous place, but the gold hunters were willing to take the risk. A few people did find gold. More importantly, they discovered the richness of Alaska and opened up this valuable piece of land to the rest of the nation.

Then & Now

Today, one of the most important resources in Alaska isn't gold, but oil. In 1977, the 800-mile-long Alaska pipeline was completed. It stretches from the Prudhoe Bay oil field on the shores of the Arctic Ocean to Valdez on the southern coast. Prudhoe Bay is the largest oil field in the United States, with estimated reserves of about three and one-half billion barrels.

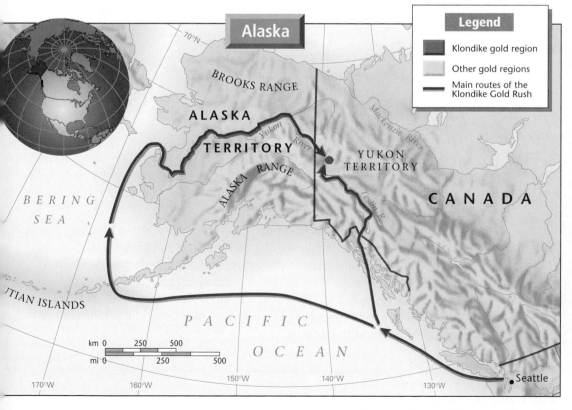

Alaska

Legend
- Klondike gold region
- Other gold regions
- Main routes of the Klondike Gold Rush

BROOKS RANGE

ALASKA TERRITORY

ALASKA RANGE

Yukon River

Mackenzie River

YUKON TERRITORY

CANADA

BERING SEA

ALEUTIAN ISLANDS

PACIFIC OCEAN

Seattle

km 0   250   500
mi 0   250   500

170°W   160°W   150°W   140°W   130°W   70°N

People thought that the Alaska Purchase was a mistake — until gold was discovered in the nearby Klondike. **Map Skill:** *What method of transportation must gold seekers have used to reach the Klondike from Alaska?*

The Spanish-American War

Focus *How did the Spanish-American War help the United States to become a world power?*

The Caribbean islands of Cuba and Puerto Rico were part of the Spanish Empire. For many years, Cubans tried to overthrow the Spanish. Spain imprisoned Cuban rebels and burned their villages.

In 1898, U. S. President William McKinley sent the battleship *Maine* to Havana Harbor in Cuba. The *Maine* blew up, and 266 sailors died. An accident on the ship may have caused the explosion. At the time, however, American newspapers said the Spanish blew it up. They reported the event with huge headlines and drawings of the explosion. This kind of reporting was called **yellow journalism.** *(You can read more about yellow journalism below.)*

· Tell Me More ·

Yellow Journalism

Dramatic pictures like this one helped to convince the people of the United States that Spain had attacked and blown up the battleship *Maine* in Havana Harbor.

The term *yellow journalism* came from two big papers, the *Journal* and the *World*, that competed with one another by both running a popular cartoon called "Yellow Kid." When important stories were reported, both papers would print big headlines and make their stories as exciting as possible to sell more papers. People began to call this kind of reporting "yellow journalism" after the "Yellow Kid" cartoon. Today, yellow journalism means reporting stories in an exaggerated or untruthful manner.

Fighting the War

In April, the United States declared war on Spain. It was a very short war because Spain was not a very strong enemy. Its navy was old and its army was weak. Future President Theodore Roosevelt, who was then the Assistant Secretary of the Navy, put his own regiment together. They were called "Rough Riders," but officially they were the First United States Cavalry Volunteers. Its members came from the cattle ranges, mining camps, and law enforcement agencies of the Southwest. With the help of the Ninth Regiment, a unit made up of African American soldiers, they won the Battle of San Juan Hill in Cuba. Soon, Cuba and Puerto Rico were captured by United States forces.

The image above shows America's expanding interests. The American eagle is holding the U. S. flag in its mouth and stands over Cuba, Panama, and the Philippines.

The other great Spanish colony was the islands of the Philippines in the Pacific Ocean. Admiral George Dewey sailed the U. S. Navy's Pacific fleet into Manila Harbor in the Philippines and destroyed the Spanish fleet.

Four months after the war started, Spain surrendered to the United States forces. From this war, the United States gained three new territories. Those territories were the Philippines, Guam, and Puerto Rico. In just over a hundred years, the United States had gone from being a colony of Great Britain to being a world power with overseas territories of its own.

Lesson Review

1860	1880	1900

1867
Alaska Purchase

1896
Klondike Gold Discovery

1898
The Spanish-American War

1 Key Vocabulary: Describe the 1890s, using **yellow journalism**.

2 Focus: How did America expand its territory in the late 1800s?

3 Focus: How did the Spanish-American War help the United States to become a world power?

4 Critical Thinking: Conclude Most Hawaiians did not want to become part of the United States. Why did it happen?

5 Theme: Coping with Change How did the growth of American industry help America to become a world power?

6 Geography/Math Activity: Using a world map, locate the places discussed in the lesson. Using the scale, find the distance from the United States to Cuba, Puerto Rico, and the Philippines.

Interpreting Political Cartoons

Humor with a Point

Political cartoons are drawings that show points of view about public issues. They often appear in magazines and newspapers. Their point is to make you think about important topics in the news. They usually try to bring a smile to your face as well. Political cartoons rarely give background information, so to understand them you need to know about the issues the artists are commenting on.

The cartoon on the next page makes fun of the conflict over building the Panama Canal in the early 1900s. It shows U.S. President Theodore Roosevelt as a giant, digging the canal himself. A brief history of the Panama Canal will help you understand this cartoonist's viewpoint.

Building the Panama Canal

In the early 1900s, President Roosevelt wanted to build a canal to connect the Atlantic and Pacific oceans. The country of Colombia controlled the best spot for this canal, the Isthmus of Panama. (An isthmus is a narrow strip of land that connects two larger pieces of land.)

After Colombia refused to give the United States control over the isthmus, Roosevelt approved an uprising by Colombians who supported the canal. Once Panama became an independent country, its leaders gave the United States rights to a 10-mile strip of land to build the canal.

The canal was completed in 1914. Some Americans supported Roosevelt's actions, thinking the canal would increase trade and be used by the U.S. Navy. Others thought Roosevelt had interfered too much in Colombia's affairs.

The Panama Canal cuts through the Isthmus of Panama and is 50.72 miles long. When it was completed, a ship's voyage from New York City to San Francisco became much shorter. A trip of more than 13,000 miles became less than 5,200 miles long!

① Here's How

What viewpoint do you think the cartoonist is trying to show? Follow these steps to find out:

- Think about the cartoon's title, "The News Reaches Bogota." (Bogotá is the capital of Colombia.) What do you think this title means?

- Find other clues, such as symbols, pictures, or words, that tell about the issue.

- Look closely at the people the artist has drawn, such as Roosevelt. Examine their size, features, expressions, clothing, and actions. Explain what you think is happening in the cartoon.

- Think about the artist's point of view. What is the artist's opinion about the people in the cartoon?

- If you are not familiar with the subject of the cartoon, find out more about it by reading other resources.

② Think It Through

If the artist were trying to show the opposite viewpoint on the Panama Canal issue, how would the cartoon and the drawing of Roosevelt be different?

③ Use It

1. Find another political cartoon about a current issue in a newspaper or magazine. Write a paragraph about the cartoon, explaining the cartoonist's point of view.

2. Draw your own political cartoon on the same subject or another subject that you choose.

THE NEWS REACHES BOGOTA.

Chapter Review

Chapter Review Timeline

1876
Alexander Graham Bell makes first telephone call

1892
First immigrant passes through Ellis Island

| 1865 | 1872 | 1879 | 1886 | 1893 | 1900 |

1867
Alaska purchase

1886
The American Federation of Labor formed

1898
The Spanish-American War

Summarizing the Main Idea

1 Copy and complete the chart below, indicating a main idea for each lesson and several examples that support it.

	Main Idea	Examples
Lesson 1		
Lesson 2		
Lesson 3		
Lesson 4		

Vocabulary

2 Using at least eight of the following terms, write a paragraph describing your impressions of the United States as a new immigrant.

urban (p. 502)
rural (p. 502)
entrepreneur (p. 502)
monopoly (p. 502)

pogrom (p. 509)
ethnic neighborhood (p. 512)
settlement house (p. 512)

mechanization (p. 514)
labor union (p. 514)
strike (p. 514)
yellow journalism (p. 524)

Reviewing the Facts

3 How did the invention of the Bessemer process affect American industry?

4 What other inventions changed America?

5 How did entrepreneurs influence industry?

6 What were some of the reasons immigrants moved to the United States?

7 What was the purpose of labor unions?

8 Who opposed labor unions?

9 How did America acquire Alaska and Hawaii?

10 What did America gain from the Spanish-American War?

Interpreting Political Cartoons

11 Find an example of a political cartoon in a newspaper or magazine. What symbols do you see? How do they help you understand what the artist is trying to say? Are there other clues in the cartoon? What can they tell you? Write a few sentences explaining the cartoon.

Geography Skills

12 Look at the map of the United States on page 511. What are some of the reasons immigrants settled in the cities shown? If an immigrant family were moving today, where would you suggest they go?

13 Find out about Alaska or Hawaii. What natural resources do they have to offer? What other resources do they have? Do you think the United States has benefited by incorporating them into the country?

Critical Thinking

14 Decision Making If you were a wealthy entrepreneur like Andrew Carnegie, how might you donate some of your money? What causes would you support?

15 Problem Solving The mayor of New York has just given you the job of improving conditions for immigrants. What might you do?

Writing: Citizenship and History

16 Citizenship Find out more about an ethnic group that immigrated to the United States. Write a series of short journal entries. Describe why a person decided to leave, the ocean voyage, and his or her first impressions of life in a new country.

17 History Look at the inventions of the 1800s on page 501. Which one do you think had the most impact on society today? Write an advertisement for that invention.

Activities

Cultures/Music Activity
One of the things many ethnic groups held onto when they arrived in America was music. Find lyrics to a song that was popular for a particular ethnic group. Why do you think the song had meaning for that group?

Geography/Math Activity
Immigrants still arrive in the United States today. Find out where most immigrants have come from in the past 25 years. Create a chart showing where they have come from and the number of immigrants from each group.

Internet Option

Check the **Internet Social Studies Center** for ideas on how to extend your theme project beyond your classroom.

THEME PROJECT CHECK-IN

As you complete your theme project, use the information in this chapter to help you. These questions will prompt you:
- How did industry change people's everyday lives?
- What drew immigrants to America? How did they affect the character of the country?
- How was the country changed by the additional land it acquired?

The United States in the 20th Century

"*For it isn't enough to talk about peace. One must believe in it. And it isn't enough to believe in it. One must work at it.*"

Eleanor Roosevelt

· THEME ·

Responsibility and Freedom

"Freedom, to me, means the right to speak out and tell what I feel. It means the right to different beliefs. I'm glad I live in a free country."

Deshonna Fincher, Fifth Grade
Savannah, GA

As they get older, people gain more freedom and responsibilities. Like people, nations also have responsibilities. During this century, the United States has fought for freedom all over the world. At home, too, our government has taken on more responsibilities, giving help to people who need it and making new laws to protect the rights of all citizens. Today, the United States must work with its neighbors to meet new challenges.

 Theme Project

The 20th Century

You are having a fair to celebrate the 20th century. Represent each decade with a booth. Choose a decade and use these activities to prepare your booth:

- Illustrate your sign with key objects, dates, and faces.
- Make a chart of important events from the decade.
- Play music from the decade.
- Make flyers about important events and people.

RESEARCH: Talk to family members or neighbors. Ask what they remember about major 20th-century events.

◀ Space Shuttle *Challenger* above Baja California in 1984

WHEN & WHERE

ATLAS

Americans began the 20th century with a sense of strength and confidence that would be tested in the coming century. Abroad, the nation was drawn into several wars. At home, it experienced an economic depression and a painful fight for civil rights. Americans struggled to balance freedom with responsibility and to keep the democracy strong.

In this unit, you will learn about the reform movement of the early 1900s. You will read how wars and social movements affected Americans. Finally, you will learn about the Cold War, (shown on the map) and America's efforts to establish strong connections in the Western Hemisphere.

Unit 9 Chapters

Chapter 20 A New World
            Power
Chapter 21 Into the 21st
            Century
Chapter 22 A Hemisphere of
            Neighbors

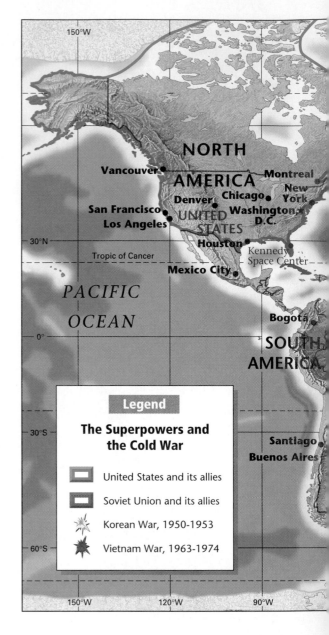

Legend

The Superpowers and the Cold War

United States and its allies

Soviet Union and its allies

Korean War, 1950-1953

Vietnam War, 1963-1974

Unit Timeline

1900	1920	1940

World War I   1917

America helped win this war for the Allies. *Chapter 20, Lesson 2*

The Roaring Twenties

Which decade had flappers, radio, and the first solo flight across the Atlantic? *Chapter 20, Lesson 3*

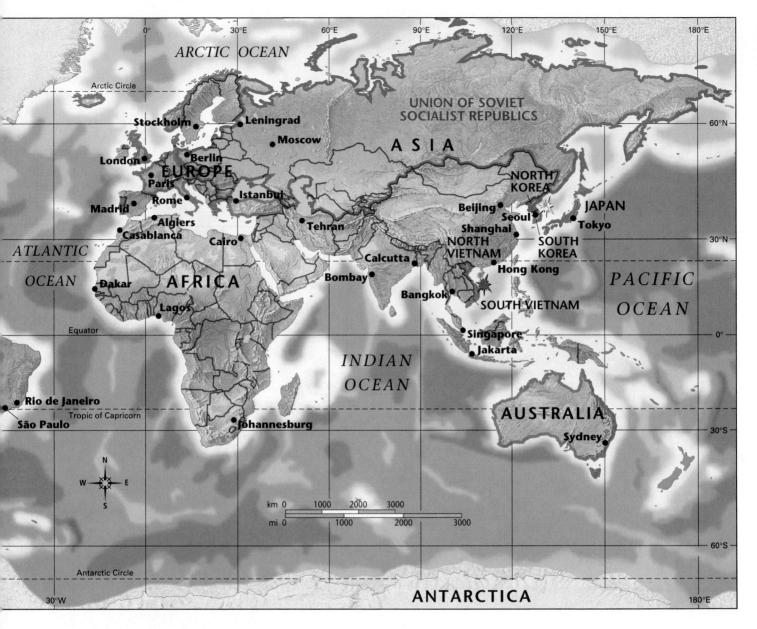

ARCTIC OCEAN

UNION OF SOVIET SOCIALIST REPUBLICS

ASIA

EUROPE

Stockholm
Leningrad
Moscow
London
Berlin
Paris
Rome
Madrid
Istanbul
Algiers
Casablanca
Cairo
Tehran

NORTH KOREA
Beijing
Seoul
JAPAN
Shanghai
Tokyo
NORTH VIETNAM
SOUTH KOREA
Calcutta
Hong Kong

ATLANTIC OCEAN

Dakar
AFRICA
Lagos

Bombay
Bangkok
SOUTH VIETNAM

PACIFIC OCEAN

Equator

INDIAN OCEAN

Singapore
Jakarta

AUSTRALIA

Rio de Janeiro
Tropic of Capricorn
São Paulo
Johannesburg

Sydney

N
W E
S

km 0 1000 2000 3000
mi 0 1000 2000 3000

Antarctic Circle

ANTARCTICA

1960   1980   2000

Franklin Roosevelt

This President promised the country a New Deal. *Chapter 20, Lesson 3*

March on Washington 1963

Who spoke the words "I have a dream . . . ." at this march? *Chapter 21, Lesson 2*

Mexico City Stock Exchange

Mexico City is a business center and one of the largest cities in the world. *Chapter 22, Lesson 2*

Chapter Preview: *People, Places, and Events*

1900   1910   1920

The Progressives

Why is this man smiling?
Lesson 1, Page 535

The Suffragists   1920

Find out how women got the right
to vote. *Lesson 1, Page 538*

World War I   1917

I WANT YOU

America entered World War I and
helped win the war. *Lesson 2,
Page 540*

The Progressives

Main Idea The Progressives worked to reform business and government and to improve American society.

One morning at breakfast, President Theodore Roosevelt was reading a new bestseller called *The Jungle*, by Upton Sinclair.

> "There would come . . . from Europe old sausage that had been rejected, and that was moldy and white — it would be . . . made over for home consumption . . . There would be meat stored in great piles in rooms; and the water from leaky roofs would drip over it, and thousands of rats would race about on it."

Sinclair's description of conditions in Chicago's meat-packing plants was shocking. President Roosevelt was so disgusted he threw his sausages, still warm, out a White House window! *The Jungle* dramatized just one problem reformers wanted to tackle.

◀ This poster is titled "Soldiers Without Guns."

Key Vocabulary

Progressives
muckraker

Key Events

1906 Pure Food and Drug Act

1909 NAACP formed

1911 Triangle Shirtwaist Company fire

1920 19th Amendment

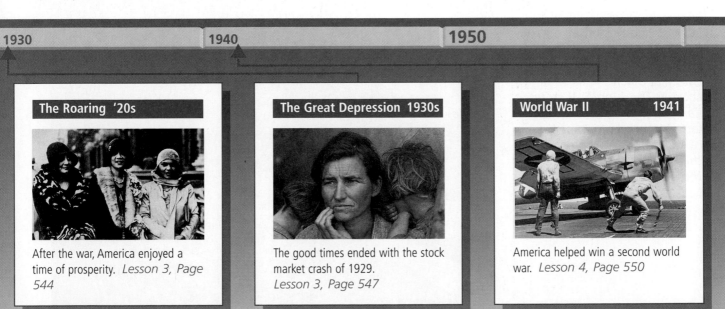

1930   1940   1950

The Roaring '20s

After the war, America enjoyed a time of prosperity. *Lesson 3, Page 544*

The Great Depression 1930s

The good times ended with the stock market crash of 1929. *Lesson 3, Page 547*

World War II   1941

America helped win a second world war. *Lesson 4, Page 550*

Upton Sinclair's important novel *The Jungle* described conditions in meat-packing plants in Chicago in the early 1900s.

Improving People's Lives

Focus *What problems did the Progressives want to solve?*

Conditions at meat-packing plants were terrible. But the nation had other problems as well. By the 1890s, so many people had poured into American cities — from the countryside and from Europe — that there weren't enough jobs to go around. Many people lived in terrible poverty. Many who had jobs worked seven days a week in factories that were unsanitary and unsafe. Some of the people who worked the hardest were children.

On March 25, 1911, a fire broke out at the Triangle Shirtwaist Company, a clothing factory in New York City. Most of the workers there were immigrant women and girls. When they tried to escape, they found themselves trapped. The factory owners had locked the doors to keep workers from taking breaks. In desperation, workers jumped out of windows and down elevator shafts. In half an hour, 146 people died in the fire or by jumping. This terrible tragedy made people pay more attention to working conditions in factories.

Many Americans had been demanding change. In the early 1900s, these reformers were called **Progressives**. They were from all over the country and wanted to reform business and government. Progressives didn't agree about everything, but they all thought that the nation should make progress toward a more just society. Progressive writers like Upton Sinclair were accused of raking up dirt, or muck. So they were called **muckrakers** — people who search for and expose corruption.

In this political cartoon, President Roosevelt is investigating the "muck" in meat packing, the issue that Upton Sinclair wrote about in *The Jungle*. **History:** *Can you figure out what the letters at the bottom of the cartoon say? Why do you think the cartoonist wrote those letters?*

President Roosevelt was a Progressive in many ways. He worked with Congress to pass the Meat Inspection Act in 1906. This law required that meat be packed under sanitary conditions. On the same day, Congress approved the Pure Food and Drug Act, which banned falsely labeled or impure foods and drugs.

The photo above shows what factories like the Triangle Shirtwaist Company looked like.

Women and children *(above)* worked long hours in factories similar to the one shown below.

Crowded factories

People worked in factories like the one below in the early 1900s. After the Triangle Shirtwaist Company fire, New York State passed strict building codes to make workplaces safer.

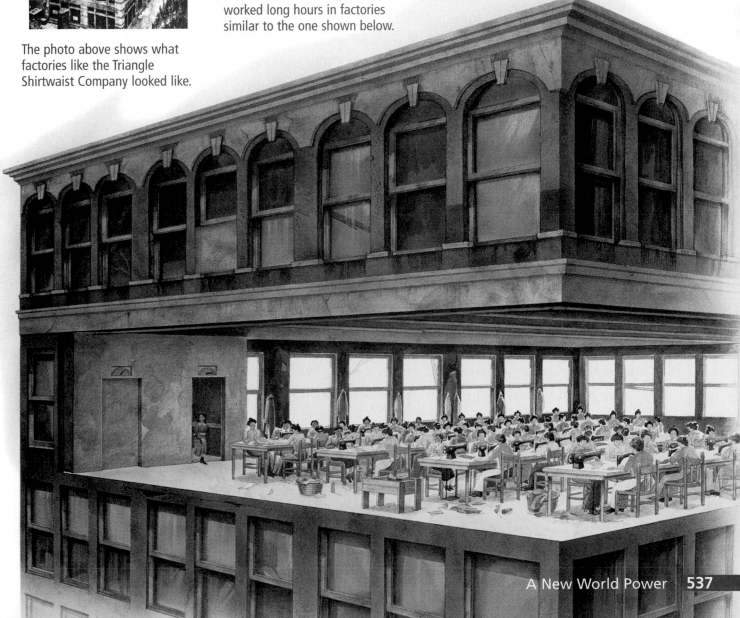

W.E.B. Du Bois

W.E.B. Du Bois was born in 1868, five years after the Emancipation Proclamation. Du Bois was the great-great-grandson of an African American who was freed after fighting in the Revolutionary War. Du Bois was the first African American to receive a doctorate from Harvard. He wrote *The Souls of Black Folk,* which had a great influence on Americans' thinking.

Fighting for Equality

Focus *What did women and African Americans accomplish during the Progressive Era?*

The Progressive Era gave new hope to American women and to African Americans. Women had been fighting for the right to vote since before the Civil War. They formed the National American Woman Suffrage Association. By 1919, the NAWSA had two million members nationwide. Suffragists paraded in New York City and demonstrated in front of the White House in Washington. Finally, in 1920, the 19th Amendment to the Constitution became the law of the land. It gave women the right to vote in all elections.

Although African American men had gained the vote after the Civil War, most southern states had laws that kept them from voting. In addition, African Americans were denied other rights that whites enjoyed. W.E.B. Du Bois, a well-known author, led the fight for equal rights for African Americans. In 1909, Du Bois and others, both black and white, established the National Association for the Advancement of Colored People. The NAACP became a leading force in the struggle for equal rights.

The Progressive Era helped women and African Americans. By 1914, however, Americans' attention shifted from events at home to a war almost 4,000 miles away.

Lesson Review

1905	1910	1915	1920

1906
Pure Food and Drug Act

1909
NAACP formed

1911
Triangle Shirtwaist Company fire

1920
19th Amendment

1 **Key Vocabulary:** Use **muckraker** in a sentence about the Progressive Era.

2 **Focus:** What problems did the Progressives want to solve?

3 **Focus:** What did women and African Americans accomplish during the Progressive Era?

4 **Critical Thinking: Compare** Do you think it's possible for a book to cause change today, the way *The Jungle* did? What about a movie or television program?

5 **Theme: Responsibility and Freedom** How do the government's safety regulations affect your life? Give an example.

6 **Citizenship/Art Activity:** Create a poster supporting the goals of the NAWSA or the early NAACP.

World War I

Main Idea The entrance of the United States into World War I helped end the war.

Two shots rang out. The crowd lining the road on that June day in 1914 were stunned. A young man from Serbia, in Eastern Europe, had assassinated Archduke Francis Ferdinand, a member of the Austrian royal family, as he rode by in his open car. By August, France, Britain, Belgium, and Russia (the **Allies**) were at war against Germany and Austria-Hungary (the **Central Powers**). How could one assassination bring about a world war?

Between 1700 and 1900, the nations of Europe had grown steadily. The needs of these growing populations led to rivalry among the nations. Germany was jealous of the wealth that Britain, France, and Belgium drew from their colonies all over the world. The colonial nations, in turn, were suspicious of Germany's power-ful military. Like dried grass, Europe needed only a small spark to catch fire. The 1914 assassination was the spark that ignited the flames of war.

The War in Europe

Focus *What brought the United States into the war?*

> **"T**he United States must be neutral in fact as well as in name . . . we must be impartial in thought as well as in action.**"**

President Woodrow Wilson spoke those words in 1914. The President believed that America could help settle the conflict only by staying neutral — that is, by not taking sides. For more than two years, the United States did stay out of the war.

Why did the President change his mind about entering the war? One reason was American outrage when, in 1915, Germany

Key Vocabulary

Allies
Central Powers
trench warfare
armistice

Key Events

1914 World War I begins

1915 Germans sink the *Lusitania*

1917 America enters World War I

1918 Armistice signed

Woodrow Wilson

torpedoed the *Lusitania*, a British passenger ship that was also carrying war supplies. Almost 1,200 people died, including more than 100 Americans. As the war went on, Germany continued its attacks on ships carrying civilians, including American ships. Tension between the United States and Germany built. In April of 1917, Wilson persuaded Congress to declare war on Germany.

Help from America

Focus *How did American troops contribute to the Allied victory?*

World War I is remembered for horribly bloody trench warfare. In **trench warfare,** opposing armies seek safety in underground ditches, or trenches, coming out only to surprise the enemy with an attack. After four years of fighting in Europe, neither the Central Powers nor the Allies had gained much ground. Many lives were lost on both sides. American troops arrived in June of 1917, encouraging the Allies and giving them a military advantage. On November 11, 1918, Germany agreed to an **armistice,** a halt in the fighting.

President Wilson went to France to help write the peace treaty. Wilson wanted to create a League of Nations, an international organization to prevent future wars. Though

Soldiers lived in trenches for most of the war. *(See below.)* Each side pounded the other with heavy shelling. The men did everything in the trenches, including writing letters home. **History:** *What would be some of the hardships of living in the trenches?*

In the trenches, soldiers used shaving kits like the one above. Each soldier was given one pair of boots *(right)* to last through his term of service.

Europe after World War I

NORWAY • SWEDEN • FINLAND • ESTONIA • LATVIA • LITHUANIA • EAST PRUSSIA (GERMANY) • U.S.S.R (RUSSIA) • DENMARK • POLAND • IRELAND • GREAT BRITAIN • NETHERLANDS • GERMANY • CZECHOSLOVAKIA • BELGIUM • LUXEMBOURG • FRANCE • SWITZERLAND • AUSTRIA • HUNGARY • ROMANIA • ITALY • YUGOSLAVIA • BULGARIA • TURKEY • PORTUGAL • SPAIN • ALBANIA • GREECE

NORTH SEA • BALTIC SEA • ATLANTIC OCEAN • BLACK SEA • MEDITERRANEAN SEA

Legend

Territory lost by:

- Austria-Hungary
- Germany
- Bulgaria
- Russia
- —— Boundaries of new nations

he thought the Allies' treaty punished Germany too harshly, the President agreed to it — to win the support of France and Britain for the League. Returning home, Wilson couldn't persuade the U.S. Senate to agree to the treaty. America signed a separate treaty with Germany and never joined the League of Nations.

Map Skill: *Look at a current map of Europe, and name a country that no longer exists.*

Lesson Review

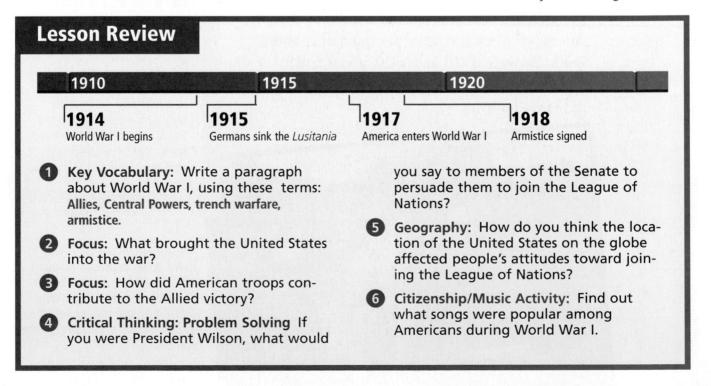

1910	1915	1920	
1914 World War I begins	**1915** Germans sink the *Lusitania*	**1917** America enters World War I	**1918** Armistice signed

1. **Key Vocabulary:** Write a paragraph about World War I, using these terms: **Allies, Central Powers, trench warfare, armistice.**

2. **Focus:** What brought the United States into the war?

3. **Focus:** How did American troops contribute to the Allied victory?

4. **Critical Thinking: Problem Solving** If you were President Wilson, what would you say to members of the Senate to persuade them to join the League of Nations?

5. **Geography:** How do you think the location of the United States on the globe affected people's attitudes toward joining the League of Nations?

6. **Citizenship/Music Activity:** Find out what songs were popular among Americans during World War I.

Human Systems

Why Did African Americans Move North?

About 10 percent of African Americans lived outside the South in 1910. By 1920, that number had risen to more than 25 percent. Geographers call this time of rapid movement by African Americans the Great Migration. The reasons that it occurred explain an important part of the social geography of the United States today.

African Americans had many reasons to leave the South in the early 1900s. The rise of segregation, the loss of voting rights, and low wages made life in the South very difficult for African Americans during this period.

The North held out the hope of a better life. The growth of war-related industries had created new jobs in northern factories. African Americans also hoped to escape racial discrimination in the South. Between 1910 and 1920, about half a million African Americans packed their belongings and moved north.

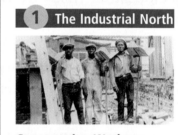

1 The Industrial North

Construction Workers
Most African Americans who moved north went to large industrial cities in the Northeast and Midwest. Their new jobs paid much better wages than farm labor in the South. They worked in railroad yards, coal mines, steel mills, packinghouses, and shipyards.

African Americans continued to move north in smaller numbers until the 1970s. This family left Florida during the 1940s. *Why might it be difficult to adjust to northern cities after living in the rural South?*

Jacob Lawrence was one of many African American writers, artists, and composers working in Harlem in the 1930s.

Art Connection

African American artist Jacob Lawrence used simple, powerful images to tell the story of the Great Migration. Look at the Lawrence painting at left. Why do you think the people are gathered? What is the painting's mood?

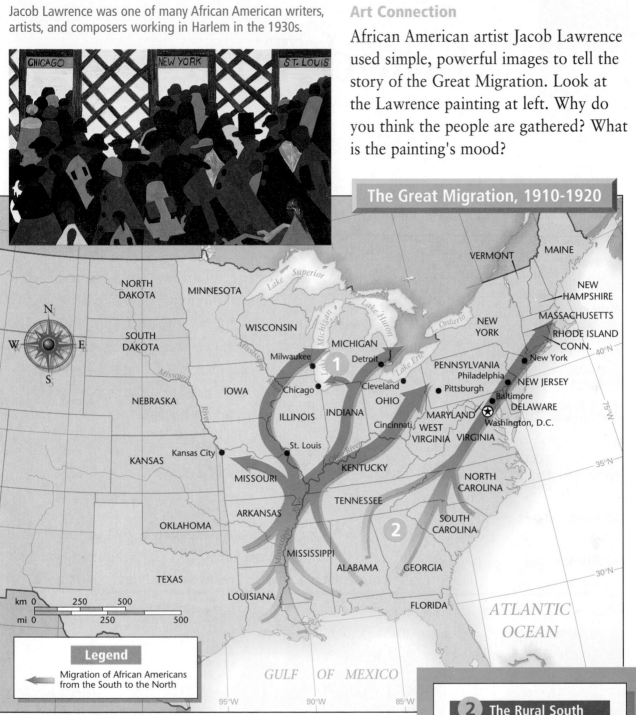

The Great Migration, 1910-1920

Legend

→ Migration of African Americans from the South to the North

A steady stream of African Americans began to move from the rural South to northern cities in 1910. America's entrance into World War I turned that stream into a flood. **Map Skill:** *What region did most people from states along the Mississippi River move to?*

Research Activity

1. Interview several people who moved from one place to another. Find out why they moved.
2. Make a chart showing their different reasons. Share it with the class.

2 The Rural South

Agricultural Laborers
In the rural South, most work was low-paying agricultural labor. During WWI, when northern factory owners advertised for workers, many Southern agricultural laborers responded.

Good Times, Bad Times

Main Idea A period of prosperity after World War I was followed by the worst depression in the nation's history.

Key Vocabulary

stock market
assembly line
depression
Social Security

Key Events

1927 First coast-to-coast radio broadcast of a football game

1929 Stock market crash

1932 FDR elected

1935 Social Security

During World War I, only the military was allowed to broadcast over the radio. The ban against nonmilitary broadcasting was lifted after the war, and the radio industry took off. On January 1, 1927, Americans tuned in to the first coast-to-coast broadcast of a football game — the Rose Bowl from the West Coast. Like television today, radio provided information and entertainment for the whole family. The radio was only part of the fun.

The Roaring Twenties

Focus *How did the United States change in the 1920s?*

Radio brought voices and music into American homes in the 1920s. Movies in those days were silent. In 1927, filmmakers in Hollywood added sound to create the "talkies."

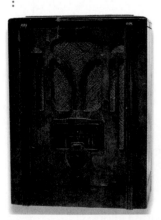

During the 1920s, millions of Americans bought radios. **Culture:** *How did the radio bring Americans together?*

Many women wore short hair and short skirts like the flapper on the cover of this old *Life* magazine *(right)*.

Saxophone

As the 1920s began, women, who had recently gained the vote, joined the work force in larger numbers. Most worked as secretaries and clerks. Some became doctors, lawyers, and business leaders. Many young women, calling themselves flappers, cut their hair short, put on makeup, and wore short skirts.

American culture gained a worldwide audience. Writers and artists expressed the energy of the decade. Among these writers was a group of African Americans living in Harlem, in New York City. Harlem was also a center for a kind of music called jazz. Jazz became popular throughout the country and all over the world. African Americans' creative achievement during this period is often called the Harlem Renaissance.

The spirit of the age could be seen in an airplane pilot named Charles Lindbergh. He was the first person to fly alone, nonstop, across the Atlantic, from New York to Paris. "Lucky Lindy," as he was called, was a great hero to the American people. He reminded them that even in the "machine age," individuals could accomplish great things.

Government and the Economy

From 1921 to 1933, three pro-business Presidents, Warren G. Harding, Calvin Coolidge, and Herbert Hoover led the United States. They believed, as President Coolidge said, "the chief business of the American people is business." The nation prospered. Business leaders built new factories and made large fortunes. They sold shares of their companies, called stock, to people who wanted to profit from the success of business.

Many Americans invested in the **stock market,** a place where people buy and sell shares. If a business does well, the price of its shares goes up. During the 1920s, stock prices rose quickly.

The 1920s brought widespread economic change. In factories workers began to make products on the **assembly line,** where a

These New York City flappers *(top)* might have worn dresses like the one above in the "Roaring Twenties."

product is made by a line of people, each adding, changing, or inspecting a part. Products can be made quickly, cheaply, and in large quantities. Products from the assembly line transformed American life. Cars, for example, gave people more freedom. The boom in business did not last. Soon, more goods were pouring from factories than workers could afford to buy.

• Tell Me More •

Putting the Country on Wheels

Henry Ford *(left)* began his career in 1879, working on machines in Detroit, Michigan. He constructed a gasoline motor in 1893 and built his first car several years later. In 1903, he organized the Ford Motor Company. Ford wanted to build a car that most people could afford. In 1908, he created the Model T. The car was sturdy enough for the country's rough roads and inexpensive enough for many people to buy.

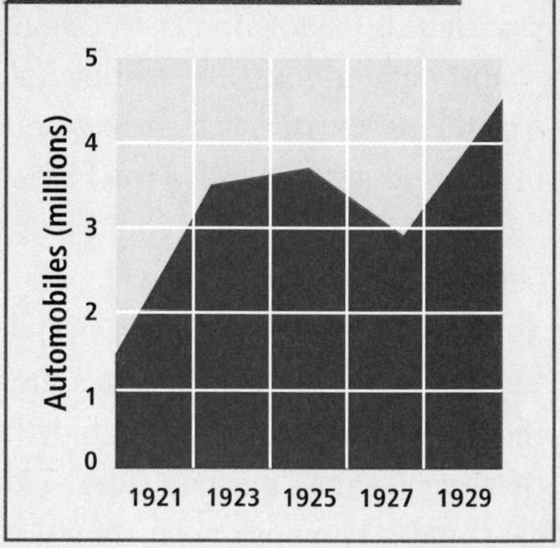

The Assembly Line

The assembly line is a system in which a product moves along a conveyor belt and different workers add to or change parts of it. Here's how it works:

Auto Sales in the 1920s

Automobiles (millions)

5

4

3

2

1

0

1921 1923 1925 1927 1929

1 The body of the car is placed on the conveyor belt. The engine drops in.

2 The seats are attached and stuffed. Frames for the roof and sides are attached.

3 The roof is placed. The sides and roof are secured. Detail work is done on the interior.

4 The car is complete.

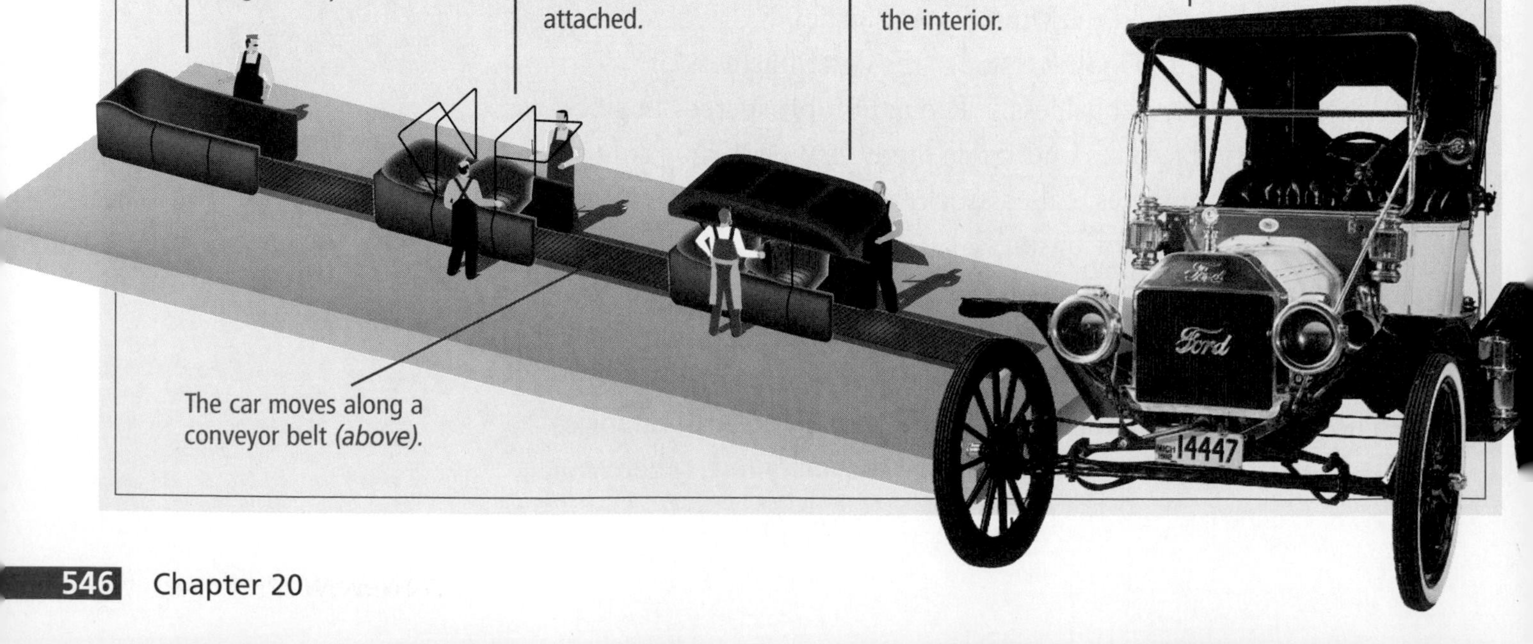

The car moves along a conveyor belt *(above)*.

Ford

14447

The Great Depression

Focus *How did the Great Depression affect American life?*

Thanks to the prosperity of the 1920s, many people invested in the stock market. In 1929, stock prices went down. People panicked. Fearful that the stocks might soon be worthless, people sold their shares at whatever price they could get.

The panic reached its peak on "Black Tuesday" — October 29, 1929. Stock prices fell so fast that day that people called it "a crash." Many banks that had invested heavily in stocks went out of business. Businesses cut back on production and laid off millions of workers. The crash caused a **depression,** a severe business slow-down. There had been depressions before, but none like this.

By 1933, one out of four Americans were out of work. Eleven thousand banks had failed. People demanded action. Franklin Delano Roosevelt became President in 1933. FDR, as Roosevelt was often called, promised a New Deal for the nation.

Trying to restore people's confidence, Roosevelt told people,

> **"T**he only thing we have to fear is fear itself.**"**

The President believed government should take an active role in helping people and in getting them back to work. Roosevelt sent money to the states to help the needy. He set up the Works Progress

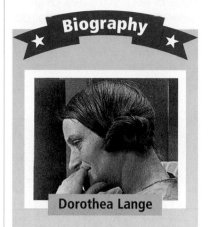

Biography

Dorothea Lange

Dorothea Lange was a well-known photographer. In 1916, she opened a photography studio for wealthy clients in San Francisco. After the stock market crash in 1929, Lange used her camera to show the problems of poor and homeless people. The California Emergency Relief hired her to photograph people who had migrated to California to look for work. Her pictures, like the one below, told the story of the Depression.

This photograph, taken by Dorothea Lange, shows the poverty and despair of people during the Depression. **Economics:** *How does your community help people in need?*

The chart on the right shows some of Roosevelt's New Deal programs. **Chart Skill:** *What do the three programs listed have in common?*

Major Programs of the New Deal, 1933 - 1935

WPA (Works Progress Administration)	Established to give jobs to unemployed people. Roads, buildings, bridges, and airports were built or repaired.
CCC (Civilian Conservation Corps)	Established to employ young men for public projects. More than two million workers planted trees, built dams, and fought forest fires.
Social Security Act	Provided retirement plan for workers. Amendments include disability benefits and health insurance.

FDR had polio, which affected his ability to walk. Seated in his wheelchair, he is pictured at his Hyde Park home, Hilltop Cottage. The child in the photograph is Ruthie Bie, the granddaughter of the cottage's caretaker. Fala, Roosevelt's dog, is on his lap.

Administration (WPA) to give jobs to the unemployed. People in the WPA built roads, bridges, and public buildings. Young people who joined Roosevelt's Civilian Conservation Corps planted trees and maintained parks.

An important part of the New Deal was the Social Security Act of 1935. **Social Security** provided insurance for the unemployed, and money for senior citizens to live on. This program still exists today.

The New Deal helped Americans survive the Great Depression. But it did not bring back the good times of the 1920s. In 1940, one out of seven people was still out of work. The Depression ended in 1942 only because a new war had started in Europe. Soon, factory workers were on the job day and night, building weapons to fight World War II.

Lesson Review

1925	1930	1935

1927
First coast-to-coast radio broadcast of a football game

1929
Stock market crash

1932
FDR elected

1935
Social Security

1. **Key Vocabulary:** Define these terms: **assembly line, stock market, depression, Social Security.**

2. **Focus:** How did the United States change in the 1920s?

3. **Focus:** How did the Great Depression affect American life?

4. **Critical Thinking: Interpret** How did Roosevelt's policies show his belief in the power of government to help people?

5. **Theme: Responsibility and Freedom** Roosevelt's Civilian Conservation Corps put young people to work beautifying the nation. Make a list of things young people can do today to improve their communities.

6. **Geography/Research Activity:** Cars gave people more choice on where to live. Draw a map of the neighborhoods in your city and the roads leading to them.

WORK-IS-WHAT-I
WANT-AND-NOT-CHARITY
WHO-WILL-HELP-ME-
GET-A-JOB-7 YEARS-
IN-DETROIT. NO MONEY
SENT AWAY FURNISH.
BEST-OF-REFERENCES
PHONE RANDOLPH 8381 Room
#59.

Predicting Outcomes Using Graphs

Predicting the Future

The Great Depression caused terrible unemployment. **Unemployment** refers to the number of people who cannot find jobs. During this time, even people who had jobs made less money. You can see how employment and income are related by comparing two graphs. Graphs show **trends,** or patterns over time. Once you recognize a trend, you can **predict** what might happen next.

1 Here's How

- Read the titles of these graphs and think about the information each one shows.

- Read the labels and note that both graphs show data for 1928 to 1935.

- Study the line on each graph. What does its shape tell you?

- Compare the trends on the graphs. During this period, how were unemployment and income related?

- Since you know the trend of each graph, you can predict what might have happened shortly after the last date. Of course, no prediction can be completely accurate.

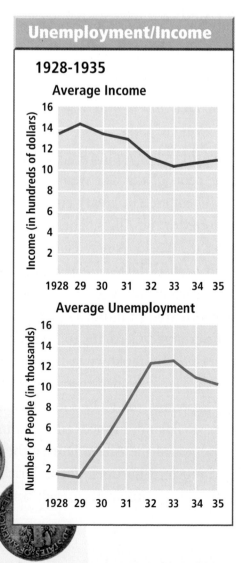

Unemployment/Income

1928-1935

Average Income

Income (in hundreds of dollars)

1928 29 30 31 32 33 34 35

Average Unemployment

Number of People (in thousands)

1928 29 30 31 32 33 34 35

2 Think It Through

What can you learn by looking at two related graphs? How is looking at two graphs different from looking at only one?

3 Use It

1. On a sheet of paper, write down the number of unemployed people and the average income for each date on the graphs.

2. Write a sentence describing the changes in employment and income from 1928 to 1935. Explain how each line helps show this.

World War II

Main Idea Following Japan's attack on Pearl Harbor, the United States entered World War II and helped defeat Germany and Japan.

I t was a beautiful fall morning in Hawaii. Stephen Young was a 19-year-old sailor aboard the *Oklahoma,* a U.S. Navy ship there. He was waiting to go off duty when a bugle blared over the ship's public-address system. It was the call for the crew to man their anti-aircraft guns. "What . . . was this?" Stephen wondered. "Drills on Sunday? They knew we were all waiting to go ashore."

This was no drill. It was December 7, 1941. Three hundred and sixty Japanese planes had launched a surprise attack on the naval base at Pearl Harbor. In that one attack, which lasted about two hours, the Japanese destroyed or damaged 18 ships and 347 planes. More than 2,400 Americans died, and more than 1,000 were wounded.

Mobilizing for War

Focus *How did World War II begin, and why did the United States join the Allies?*

The Pearl Harbor attack led the United States into World War II, but the roots of the war went back to World War I. Defeat had left Germans bitter. The treaty ending the war had forced Germany to pay money to the Allies. Then the Depression hit, affecting nations all over the world. A new German leader, Adolf Hitler, led a political party called the **Nazi Party.** The Nazis blamed Germany's economic problems on those World War I payments. The Nazis also preached hatred of minority groups, especially Jews.

Hitler urged Germans to "settle the score" from the last war by conquering new territory in Europe. In 1936 he formed an alliance with Italy. Japan joined them in 1940. They were the **Axis Powers.**

In September of 1939, Germany went to war against the **Allied Powers** — Poland, France, and Britain. Later, the Soviet Union (Russia) joined the Allies. During the next two years, the Axis conquered much of Europe, North Africa, and Asia.

President Franklin Roosevelt wanted the United States to join

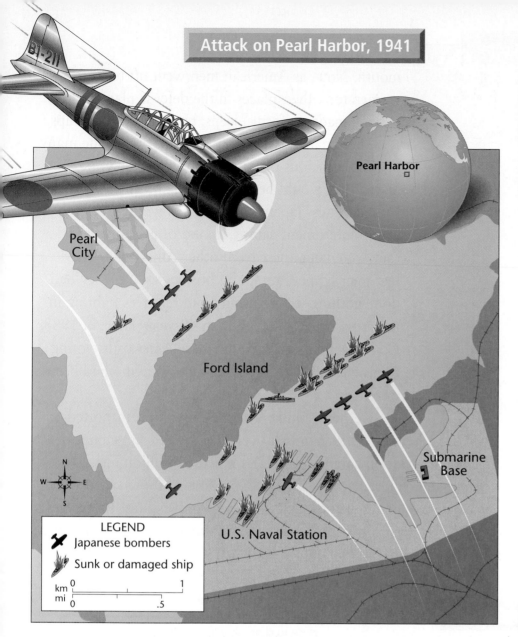

Attack on Pearl Harbor, 1941

Pearl Harbor

Pearl City

Ford Island

Submarine Base

U.S. Naval Station

N
W E
S

LEGEND
Japanese bombers
Sunk or damaged ship

km 0 ———— 1
mi 0 ———— .5

Time: 6:00 A.M.

Japanese planes take off from their carrier in the Pacific Ocean and head for Pearl Harbor.

Time: 7:55 A.M.

The Japanese planes reach Pearl Harbor and begin their attack.

Time: 10:00 A.M.

The attack is completed. The U.S. Pacific Fleet is destroyed.

Map Skill: *Where does the map (above, left) show most of the damage to U.S. ships taking place?*

the Allies. He told Congress that America should support Britain to defend the Four Freedoms: freedom of speech, freedom of religion, freedom from want, and freedom from fear. Congress agreed to send arms and other war goods to the Allies, but many Americans still wanted to stay out of the fighting.

The Japanese attack on Pearl Harbor changed everything. The day afterwards, Roosevelt went to Congress. As millions of Americans listened on their radios, Roosevelt called December 7, 1941, "a date which will live in infamy." With all but one member agreeing, Congress voted to declare war on Japan. When Germany and Italy declared war on the United States on December 11, America became a full-fledged member of the Allied forces.

Americans had been preparing for war. The nation's factories were turning out more weapons than Germany and Japan combined. More than 2,000 aircraft rolled off the country's assembly lines each

Nazi Occupation of Europe

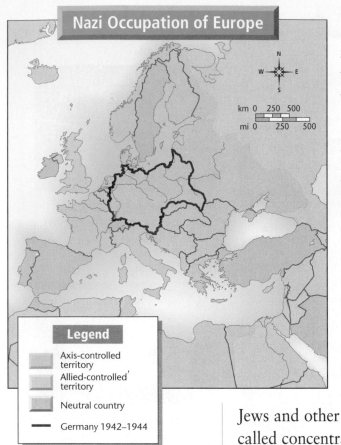

Legend

- Axis-controlled territory
- Allied-controlled territory
- Neutral country
- — Germany 1942–1944

This map shows Europe during World War II. **Map Skill:** *Using an atlas, name three countries that stayed neutral during the war.*

month. Now, as American men went off to war, women took their places in the defense plants. These women made uniforms, jeeps, tanks, and battleships.

The Japanese attack on Pearl Harbor made many people suspicious of Japanese Americans. Some feared they would be loyal to Japan instead of to the United States. Japanese Americans were forced to live in internment camps, a kind of prison where they were kept apart from other Americans. They lost their homes, land, and businesses. Yet they had done nothing wrong. Many had relatives fighting in the army or navy. More than 40 years later, in 1988, Congress apologized to Japanese Americans, voting to give $20,000 to each living person who had been interned.

German soldiers rounded up and transported Jews and other minorities from all over Europe to death camps called concentration camps. The Nazis killed 11 million men, women, and children at the camps. Six million of those killed were Jews. The remaining victims included Gypsies, Russians, Poles, and others. This mass murder is known as the **Holocaust,** which means total destruction.

The Invasion of Normandy, 1944

This small, efficient ship could quickly take up to 36 Allied soldiers close to shore. It was called a LCVP (landing craft, vehicle, personnel).

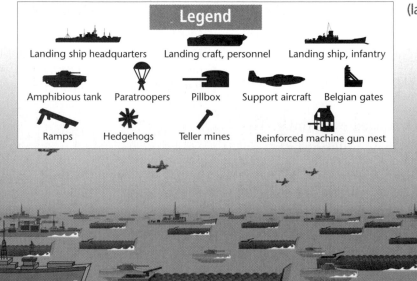

Legend

Landing ship headquarters   Landing craft, personnel   Landing ship, infantry

Amphibious tank   Paratroopers   Pillbox   Support aircraft   Belgian gates

Ramps   Hedgehogs   Teller mines   Reinforced machine gun nest

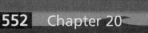

Halting Enemy Power

Focus *What events led to the defeat of the Axis Powers?*

About 5 million Americans served in the armed forces in World War I. World War II was much bigger. About 70 million people from the Allied and Axis nations were involved in the fighting. Of these, more than 16 million were Americans.

World War II was the first war that was fought largely from the air. Allied and Axis airplanes bombed cities throughout Europe and Asia. This air war caused new problems. As in World War I, this war killed more ordinary people — civilians — than soldiers.

When the United States entered the war in 1941, Axis armies held most of Europe. The Allies waged a fierce air war against them, but it was 1943 before they could challenge the Axis on the ground. It took almost two years of bitter fighting before the Axis armies were defeated on land.

On a June morning, Allied troops prepared to cross the English Channel from Britain. Their mission was to land on the beaches of Normandy, France. The Allies planned to free France and the rest of Western Europe from the German army. The invasion of Normandy took place on June 6, 1944 — **D-Day.** (*D* stands for the secret day or date of a planned military operation.) General Dwight

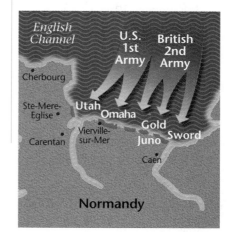

Normandy

The Germans placed antilanding obstacles on the beach to slow down the Allies and their landing craft.

Soldiers on the beach were protected by a tall seawall. Once past the wall, they climbed the cliffs. The Germans mounted many guns in the cliff walls to fire on the Allied soldiers as they tried to reach the top.

Eisenhower talks to the troops before the invasion of Normandy. **History:** *How do you think Eisenhower's presence encouraged the troops?*

D. Eisenhower, supreme commander of the Allied forces, spoke to the troops before the invasion:

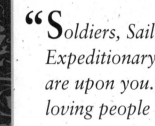

> **"S**oldiers, Sailors and Airmen of the Allied Expeditionary Force! . . . The eyes of the world are upon you. The hopes and prayers of liberty-loving people everywhere march with you. . . .**"**

The invasion of Normandy was conducted with the largest seaborne force in history. It was also the beginning of the end for Germany. During the next several months, the Allies began pushing the Germans out of the countries they had conquered. On May 7, 1945, Germany finally surrendered to the Allies.

Fighting was just as intense in the Pacific. For three-and-a-half years, the war there was fought on land, on sea, and in the air. Even after the Axis Powers in Europe surrendered, Japan fought on.

In April of 1945, President Roosevelt died, and Vice President Harry Truman became President. He decided to use a new weapon against Japan — the atomic bomb. An **atomic bomb** uses nuclear energy to create an enormous explosion. On the morning of August 6, 1945, a U.S. bomber plane dropped an atomic bomb on the city of Hiroshima, Japan. Three days later, a bomb was dropped on Nagasaki, another Japanese city. Together, the two bombs killed about 120,000 people. On September 2, Japan surrendered. For Americans, World War II was over. (The war officially ended on September 9, when Japan surrendered to China.)

The human cost of the war was staggering. About 17 million soldiers and sailors died. Many millions of civilians died. No other

The watch, below, stopped at the exact time the atomic bomb was dropped on Hiroshima.

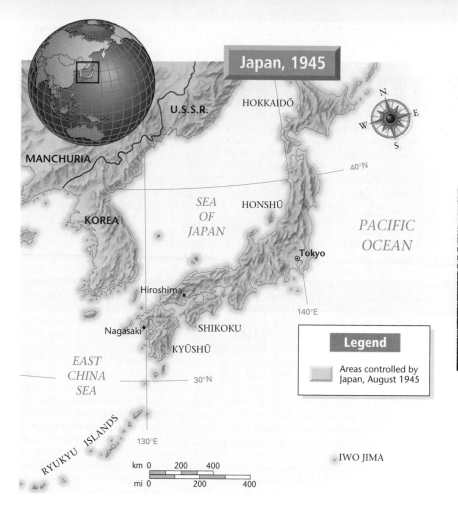

Japan, 1945

HOKKAIDŌ

U.S.S.R.

MANCHURIA

KOREA

SEA
OF
JAPAN

HONSHŪ

40°N

PACIFIC
OCEAN

Tokyo

Hiroshima

140°E

Nagasaki

SHIKOKU

KYŪSHŪ

EAST
CHINA
SEA

30°N

Legend

Areas controlled by
Japan, August 1945

RYUKYU ISLANDS

130°E

IWO JIMA

km 0   200   400
mi 0   200   400

This map of Japan shows the island nation's four major islands and the cities of Hiroshima, Nagasaki, and Tokyo. **Map Skill:** *Which island is Tokyo, the capital of Japan, located on?*

Hiroshima was rebuilt after the atomic bomb destroyed most of the city. The memorial *(lower right)* stands as a reminder of the devastation.

event in human history had caused so much destruction. And those who survived found themselves living in fear of how the atomic bomb might be used in the future.

Lesson Review

1935	1940	1945

1939
World War II begins

1941
Pearl Harbor

1944
D-Day

1945
Germany and Japan surrender

1. **Key Vocabulary:** Write a paragraph about World War II, using these terms: Nazi Party, Holocaust, atomic bomb.

2. **Focus:** How did World War II begin, and why did the United States join the Allies?

3. **Focus:** What events led to the defeat of the Axis Powers?

4. **Critical Thinking: Cause and Effect** How do you think the war affected women's

attitudes about working outside their homes?

5. **Geography:** How did the location of the American base at Pearl Harbor affect the amount of damage done in the attack?

6. **Citizenship/Research Activity:** Find out how the internment camps changed the lives of Japanese Americans.

Chapter Review

Chapter Review Timeline

	1929 Stock market crash	**1945** Germany and Japan surrender

1910 1920 1930 **1940** **1950**

1911 Triangle Shirtwaist Company fire

1917 America enters World War I

1941 Pearl Harbor

Summarizing the Main Idea

1 Copy and complete the chart below. Write the name of a President (or Presidents), and list some of his (or their) key actions.

	President	Actions
Lesson 1	*Theodore Roosevelt*	*Helped pass Meat Inspection Act*
Lesson 2		
Lesson 3		
Lesson 4		

Vocabulary

2 Using at least ten of the following terms, write an opening paragraph for a news report about life in America during the 1900s.

Progressives (p. 536)
muckraker (p. 536)
Allies (p. 539)
Central Powers (p. 539)
trench warfare (p. 540)
armistice (p. 540)

stock market (p. 545)
assembly line (p. 545)
depression (p. 547)
Social Security (p. 548)
Nazi Party (p. 550)
Axis Powers (p. 550)

Holocaust (p. 553)
D-Day (p. 553)
atomic bomb (p. 554)
Allied Powers (p. 550)

Reviewing the Facts

3 How did President Franklin Roosevelt help Americans during the Great Depression?

4 How did the treaty ending World War I contribute to the start of World War II?

5 What two major events led to the end of World War II?

Skill Review: Predicting Outcomes Using Graphs

6 Look at the Skills Workshop on page 549. Between 1928 and 1935, do you think the number of cars, appliances, and other goods people bought went up or down?

7 Based on the predictions you made about what happened after 1935, how do you think people's spending habits changed after that date?

Geography Skills

8 During World War I, trench warfare occurred along the Western Front. Looking at a map of Europe, name two nations that were located along the front.

9 Why do you think the U.S. chose the English coast as the base from which to launch the Invasion of Normandy?

Critical Thinking

10 Compare If the Progressives existed today, what issues in American society would concern them?

11 Cause and Effect What was the connection between the Great Depression and Roosevelt's New Deal?

12 Decision Making Why do you think only one member of the U.S. Congress voted against entering World War II?

Writing: Citizenship and History

13 Citizenship You are a neighbor of a Japanese American family that was sent to an internment camp during World War II. Write a letter to President Franklin Roosevelt explaining why you think the internment camps are unjust.

14 History Write an advertisement for the classified (help wanted) section of a newspaper. Try to persuade readers to join the Progressives.

Activities

Economics/Research Activity
Learn about the stock market. Find out what a typical day is like for *stockbrokers,* people who buy and sell stocks on Wall Street. Do you think you'd like to work on Wall Street someday?

National Heritage/Language Arts Activity
Work in groups to put together a short group speech about the Harlem Renaissance. Share the works of famous artists, writers, or musicians.

Internet Option

Check the **Internet Social Studies Center** for ideas on how to extend your theme project beyond your classroom.

THEME PROJECT CHECK-IN

Use the information about the beginning of the century to begin your project. Think about these questions as you decide which decade you will represent:
• Which important objects, events, or people should be shown on your sign?
• What problems were people concerned about? How did they solve them?
• What political events were important? What new inventions made a difference?
• What were some of the important places of the early century?

Chapter Preview: *People, Places, and Events*

Life in the 1950s

Americans fell in love with television in the 1950s. *Lesson 1, Page 562*

Civil Rights   1963

I HAVE A DREAM
LET FREEDOM RING
JAN. 15, 1929   APRIL 4, 1968
REV. MARTIN LUTHER KING
A GREAT AMERICAN

Martin Luther King, Jr., inspired followers at the March on Washington. *Lesson 2, Page 566*

John F. Kennedy

Jack, Caroline, and Jackie Kennedy: JFK had a short but memorable presidency. *Lesson 3, Page 572*

Life in the 1950s

Main Idea After World War II, relations between the United States and the Soviet Union grew tense.

The day Marnee Myerson began kindergarten in September 1949, the United States was the only nation on earth that could build an atomic bomb. Before the month ended, however, the Soviet Union had tested its own atomic bomb. By the time Marnee entered fourth grade, in 1953, both nations had built far more powerful weapons called hydrogen bombs. "That's when we began having nuclear-attack drills," Marnee remembers. "The bell would ring, and we'd crouch under our desks with our hands over our heads."

Today Marnee, who grew up in Brooklyn, New York, smiles at the memories of hiding under her desk. It was no laughing matter at the time. Some American families bought backyard bomb shelters, which they stocked with food and other supplies. What was the reason for the school drills and the bomb shelters? The Soviet Union and the United States were determined to beat each other in a race to develop powerful bombs — even at the risk of nuclear war.

◀ Crew members board the space shuttle *Endeavor*.

Key Vocabulary

communism
capitalism
Iron Curtain
Cold War
arms race
suburb

Key Events

1947 Cold War begins

1952 U.S. explodes hydrogen bomb

1953 War ends in Korea

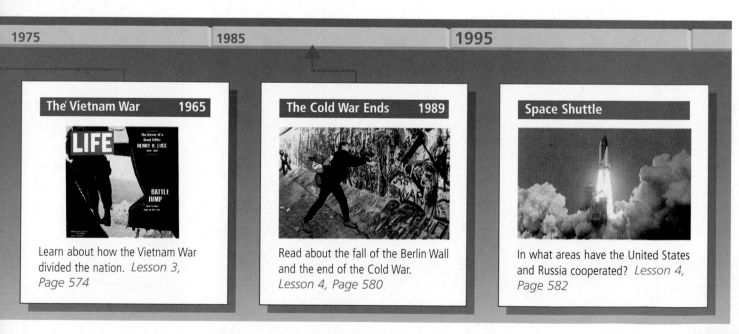

| 1975 | 1985 | 1995 |

The Vietnam War   1965

Learn about how the Vietnam War divided the nation. *Lesson 3, Page 574*

The Cold War Ends   1989

Read about the fall of the Berlin Wall and the end of the Cold War. *Lesson 4, Page 580*

Space Shuttle

In what areas have the United States and Russia cooperated? *Lesson 4, Page 582*

The Cold War

Focus *What were the main events of the Cold War?*

After World War II, the Soviet Union and the United States were the most powerful countries in the world. The two powers had been allies in the war, but after the war, the differences between them became very important. The political and economic system in the Soviet Union was communism. Under **communism,** the government owns and runs most businesses and often decides where people can live and work. In a Communist country, people can vote only for the government's candidates. In the United States, on the other hand, the political system is a representative democracy, which means people can choose their leaders in free elections. The economic system is capitalism. **Capitalism,** or free enterprise, allows individuals, not the government, to choose their work and to own farms, factories, and other businesses.

The Soviets set up Communist governments in the eastern half of Germany and in the nations of Eastern Europe. Great Britain's leader, Winston Churchill, called the line that divided Europe the **Iron Curtain.** It wasn't an actual curtain, but it described the division between the democratic countries of Western Europe and the

The map below shows the way the Iron Curtain divided Europe after World War II. **Map Skill:** *Which country is divided into eastern and western parts?*

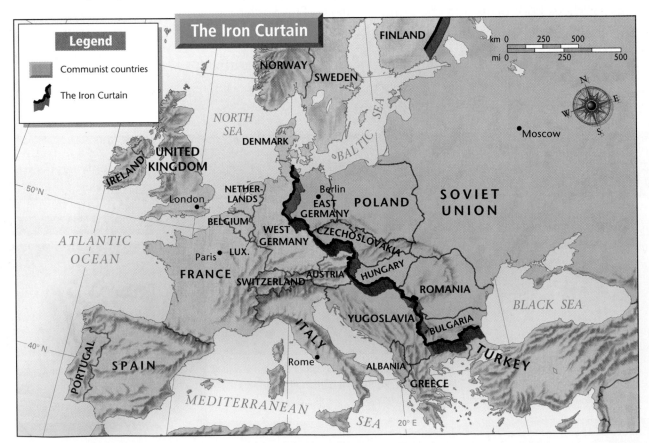

The Iron Curtain

Korea is in eastern Asia. The two photos at left show American troops in Korea during the war there. **History:** *Why did the United States send troops to fight in South Korea?*

Communist countries of Eastern Europe. (*See the map below, left.*)

The Soviet Union wanted to spread communism to the rest of the world, and the United States wanted to stop that spread. By 1947, the two nations were fighting, but with words, not bullets. Their conflict was called the **Cold War** because no weapons were used. The Cold War was very serious because of the threat that the two nations might use their military power against each other.

The Soviets and the Americans fought the Cold War through an **arms race** — a race to build bigger, stronger weapons. The Soviets tested their first atomic bomb in 1949. In 1952 the United States exploded its first hydrogen bomb — a "superbomb," fueled by hydrogen. The Soviets exploded theirs just nine months later. People feared that if the superpowers ever used these powerful bombs against each other, they might destroy the whole world.

In Asia, the Cold War turned white hot in June of 1950, when soldiers from North Korea, a Communist nation, invaded South Korea, which was not Communist. The United Nations (UN) sent troops to aid South Korea. (The UN had been set up near the end of World War II as an international organization to prevent war and to protect human rights.) Most of the troops were American. When the war ended in 1953, Communists still controlled North Korea, but not South Korea. The Korean War ended, but the Cold War between the United States and the Soviet Union continued.

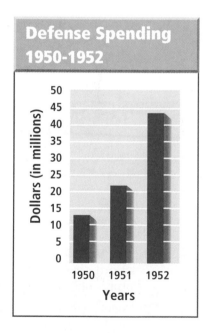

Defense Spending 1950-1952

The chart above shows what the United States spent on national defense from 1950 to 1952. **Chart Skill:** *How much more was spent on defense in 1952 than in 1950? Why do you think defense spending increased?*

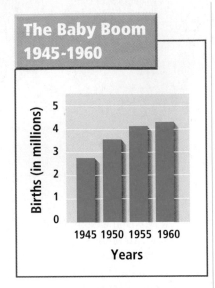

Births (in millions)

5
4
3
2
1
0

1945 1950 1955 1960
Years

The chart above shows the "baby boom" in the United States from 1945 to 1960. **Chart Skill:** *How many more babies were born in 1960 than in 1945?*

Life in the Suburbs

Focus *What was life like for families that moved to the suburbs in the 1950s?*

The American economy boomed in the 1950s. With more money in their paychecks, many young families began moving to the **suburbs,** areas outside of cities designed just for homes. People flocked to the suburbs in search of the "good life." In part, that meant simply a healthy place to raise children. It also meant buying things — everything from stoves and sweaters to cars and cribs.

Those cribs were needed. During the "baby boom" of the 1950s, more than 30 million babies came into the world. In 1957, a peak year, a baby was born every seven seconds.

Nothing Americans bought during the 1950s changed family life as much as television. In 1949, Americans owned only about one million sets. By 1952, 19 million homes had televisions.

In many ways, television expressed the prosperity and optimism of the 1950s. Many popular programs, such as *Father Knows Best* and *Leave It to Beaver,* were about middle-class suburban families. Millions of Americans loved to watch the hilarious antics of the comedienne Lucille Ball, and her husband, actor and musician Desi Arnaz, in their highly rated comedy show, *I Love Lucy.*

Lesson Review

1945	1950	1955	

1947
Cold War begins

1952
U.S. explodes hydrogen bomb

1953
War ends in Korea

1. **Key Vocabulary:** Write a paragraph about the 1950s, using the terms **communism, Cold War,** and **Iron Curtain.**

2. **Focus:** What were the main events of the Cold War?

3. **Focus:** What was life like for families that moved to the suburbs in the 1950s?

4. **Critical Thinking: Cause and Effect** What kinds of American industries do you think were affected by the arms race?

5. **Theme: Responsibility and Freedom** It is often said that living in a democracy is more difficult for citizens than living in an undemocratic country. Why do you think this might be so?

6. **Geography/Research Activity:** Look at a map in an atlas that was published before 1991. Make a list of all the countries that bordered the Soviet Union and China, the two largest Communist countries.

Civil Rights Movement

Main Idea African Americans continued to struggle for racial equality in the 1950s and 1960s.

osa Parks boarded a bus in Montgomery, Alabama, on December 1, 1955. On the crowded ride home, the driver told Mrs. Parks, an African American, to stand up and give her seat to a white man. Mrs. Parks refused. The driver called the police, and Parks was arrested.

A young minister wanted to help ensure Parks's and all African Americans' right to be treated equally. He was the Reverend Martin Luther King, Jr. What he and Mrs. Parks did strengthened the struggle for **civil rights** — that is, for fair and equal treatment under the Constitution.

Segregation

Focus *How did segregation affect African Americans?*

The Constitution of the United States and its amendments say that laws must treat all citizens the same. However, in the 1950s and 1960s, African Americans still couldn't go everywhere white people went. As you will remember from studying Reconstruction, this policy of keeping people of different races apart is called segregation. In 17 states, laws required African American and white children to go to different schools. Laws barred African Americans from "whites only" restaurants, hotels, restrooms, and even drinking fountains. Laws forced them to sit in the back of buses and in some places even kept them from voting.

Despite these laws, many African Americans did become well-educated and successful. Thousands became ministers, doctors, lawyers, teachers, and business owners. Most African Americans, however, were not able to get the kind of education that led to good jobs and a secure future.

Key Vocabulary
- civil rights
- nonviolent protest
- Freedom Rider

Key Events
- **1955** Montgomery bus boycott
- **1960** Lunch counter sit-ins
- **1961** Freedom rides
- **1963** March on Washington
- **1964** Civil Rights Act

Rosa Parks rode the bus in Montgomery, Alabama, after buses there were desegregated.

In 1954, in the case of *Brown v. the Board of Education of Topeka,* the Supreme Court outlawed schools segregated by race. The Chief Justice of the Supreme Court, Earl Warren, wrote,

> "**W**e conclude that in the field of public education the doctrine of 'separate but equal' has no place. Separate educational facilities are inherently unequal. "

Slowly, society began to change. This change began at the nation's grassroots — one neighborhood, one town at a time. Progress was made whenever African Americans joined together to insist on fair treatment. Young people throughout the nation, both black and white, became deeply involved in this effort.

Protest

Focus *How did African Americans gain rights for themselves?*

Rosa Parks wasn't the first African American to be arrested for taking a whites-only seat on a bus in Montgomery, Alabama. Yet her arrest was the first that her community decided to do something about. Their leader, Martin Luther King, Jr., believed in **nonviolent protest**. This meant that people could try to change unfair laws without using violence. Instead, they peacefully refused to obey the laws.

In Montgomery, nonviolent protest took the form of a boycott. A few days after Rosa Parks was arrested, a leaflet was handed out asking African Americans not to ride the buses in Montgomery. For nearly a year, the city's African Americans stayed off the buses. They rode bicycles and walked. Churches helped people share cars. In November 1956, the Supreme Court ruled that it was illegal to have separate bus seats for African Americans and whites. Rosa Parks and her community had won that battle. The fight for civil rights, however, had just begun.

On February 1, 1960, four African American college students showed the world another kind of nonviolent protest. Dressed in jackets and ties, they entered a

CORE, the Congress of Racial Equality, was active during the civil rights movement. Members of CORE became Freedom Riders. The picture below is of a CORE recruitment poster.

LET'S DO THE JOB

WE WANT FREEDOM NOW

TOGETHER!
...IN THE SCHOOLS
...IN HOUSING
...IN EMPLOYMENT
...IN THE COMMUNITY

JOIN CORE
CONGRESS OF RACIAL EQUALITY

Woolworth's store in Greensboro, North Carolina. They sat down at the store's whites-only lunch counter and ordered coffee and doughnuts. "I'm sorry," the white waitress said. "We don't serve you here."

The students didn't budge. They stayed seated until the store closed. The next day they came back with friends. They all stayed calm and polite, even though white customers tried to force them to leave.

Over the next two months, "sit-ins" at whites-only lunch counters were held in 54 cities in nine states. Rather than close down, stores gave in. The Woolworth's in Greensboro held out for six months before agreeing to serve food to African American customers.

In May of 1961, thirteen young blacks and whites headed south by bus from Washington, D.C., using whites-only restrooms and waiting rooms in all the bus stations they visited. These protesters called themselves **Freedom Riders.**

When police jailed riders in Mississippi, the first freedom ride ended. But the U.S. government ordered an end to whites-only sections in airports and in bus and train stations.

In April of 1963, Martin Luther King, Jr., led protests against segregation in Birmingham, Alabama. More than 1,000 African

Freedom Riders wore buttons like this one. **Citizenship:** *Do you think going to jail made the Freedom Riders regret their actions?*

Protesters in Birmingham, Alabama, were met with police dogs and fire hoses. Americans were shocked, and city leaders in Birmingham were forced to end segregation in stores, restaurants, and workplaces there.

Many marchers wore buttons, like the one shown below, at the historic March on Washington, August 1963. **Economics:** *What is the connection between jobs and freedom?*

American young people, some as young as six years old, followed him. Police met the protesters with snarling dogs and fire hoses that delivered painful blasts of water. Pictures of marchers getting bitten by dogs and knocked down by water shocked many Americans. They demanded that the government take action. In May, Birmingham's white leaders agreed to end segregation in the city's stores, restaurants, and workplaces.

Churches throughout the South and the North helped organize protests like those in Birmingham. News of their accomplishments spurred more protest marches. Soon, millions of Americans supported the civil rights movement.

The March on Washington

In August of 1963, more than 250,000 people came to Washington, D.C., to hold an all-day meeting — a rally for civil rights. The crowd was greatly inspired by Martin Luther King, Jr., who spoke about his dream for the future.

> **"I** *have a dream that my four little children will one day live in a nation where they will not be judged by the color of their skin but by the content of their character. . . ."*

The rally sent the nation a clear message. The movement for civil rights was too big and too important to be stopped. In

Martin Luther King, Jr., delivered a memorable speech at the March on Washington, in August 1963. King would be assassinated in 1968.

November of 1963, President Lyndon Johnson spoke to Congress. He said, "We have talked long enough in this country about equal rights. . . . It is time now to write the next chapter — and to write it in the books of law." In 1964, Congress passed the Civil Rights Act, which made segregation illegal in all 50 states. The struggle was far from over, however. In the decades to come, many people would continue working to defend and build on the gains made during the 1950s and 1960s.

Lesson Review

1955	1958	1961	1964	1967

1955
Montgomery bus boycott

1960
Lunch counter sit-ins

1961
Freedom rides

1963
March on Washington

1964
Civil Rights Act

1 **Key Vocabulary:** Write a paragraph about the civil rights movement, using the terms **nonviolent protest** and **Freedom Riders**.

2 **Focus:** How did segregation affect African Americans?

3 **Focus:** How did African Americans gain rights for themselves?

4 **Critical Thinking: Interpret** In his speech at the March on Washington, what did Martin Luther King, Jr., mean by "the content of their character"?

5 **Geography:** Why did the civil rights movement begin in the southern region of the United States?

6 **Citizenship/Art Activity:** Design the kind of banner, poster, or pin you might have taken to the March on Washington.

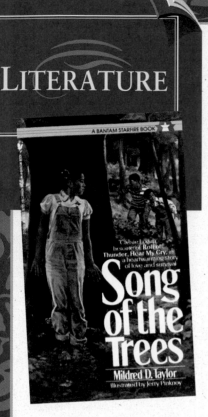

Song of the Trees

by Mildred D. Taylor

It's the 1930s in Mississippi farm country. Cassie Logan's family owns over 200 acres, some of it ancient forest. Mr. Anderson, a neighbor, knows that Cassie's father is miles away, working on a railroad job to earn some money. Mr. Anderson came to visit Big Ma, Cassie's grandmother, and made her an offer she couldn't refuse. He paid her 65 dollars, and he's going to cut down and haul away grand old trees. Even though they need money to buy medicine, no one — not Cassie, her brothers, her mother, or Big Ma — wants to sell the trees. But they have no choice. Cassie is telling the story, and it is the night after the first trees have been chopped down.

That night I was awakened by soft sounds outside my window. I reached for Big Ma, but she wasn't there. Hurrying to the window, I saw Mama and Big Ma standing in the yard in their night clothes and Stacey, fully dressed, sitting atop Lady, our golden mare. By the time I got outside, Stacey was gone.

"Mama, where's Stacey?" I cried.

"Be quiet, Cassie. You'll wake Christopher-John and Little Man."

"But where's he going?"

"He's going to get Papa," Mama said. "Now be quiet."

"Go on Stacey, boy," I whispered. "Ride for me, too."

As the dust billowed after him, Mama said, "I should've gone myself. He's so young."

Big Ma put her arm around Mama. "Now, Mary, you know you couldn't 've gone. Mr. Anderson would miss you if he come by and see you ain't here. You done right, now. Don't worry, that boy'll be just fine."

Three days passed, hot and windless.

Mama forbade any of us to go into the forest, so Christopher-John, Little Man and I spent the slow, restless days hovering as close to the dusty road as we dared, listening to the foreign sounds of steel against the trees and the thunderous roar of those ancient loved ones as they crashed upon the earth. Sometimes Mama would scold us and tell us to come back to the house, but even she could not ignore the continuous pounding of the axes against the trees. Or the sight of the loaded lumber wagons rolling out of the forest. In the middle of washing or ironing or hoeing, she would look up sorrowfully and listen, then turn toward the road, searching for some sign of Papa and Stacey.

On the fourth day, before the sun had risen bringing its cloak of miserable heat, I saw her walking alone toward the woods. I ran after her.

She did not send me back.

"Mama," I said, "How sick are you?"

Mama took my hand. "Remember when you had the flu and felt so sick?"

"Yes'm."

"And when I gave you some medicine, you got well soon afterward?"

billow
to swell or cause to swell out

"Yes'm."

"Well, that's how sick I am. As soon as I get my medicine, I'll be all well again. And that'll be soon now that Papa's coming home," she said, giving my hand a gentle little squeeze.

The quiet surrounded us as we entered the forest. Mama clicked on the flashlight and we walked silently along the cow path to the pond. There, just beyond the pond, pockets of open space loomed before us.

"Mama!"

"I know, baby, I know."

On the ground lay countless trees. Trees that had once been such strong, tall things. So strong that I could fling my arms partially around one of them and feel safe and secure. So tall and leafy green that their boughs had formed a forest temple.

And old.

So old that Indians had once built fires at their feet and had sung happy songs of happy days. So old, they had hidden fleeing black men in the night and listened to their sad tales of a foreign land.

In the cold of winter when the ground lay frozen, they had sung their frosty ballads of years gone by. Or on a muggy, sweat-drenched day, their leaves had rippled softly, lazily, like restless green fingers strumming a guitar, echoing their epic tales.

But now they would sing no more. They lay forever silent upon the ground.

Those trees that remained standing were like defeated warriors mourning their fallen dead. But soon they, too, would fall, for the white *X*'s had been placed on nearly every one.

"Oh, dear, dear trees," I cried as the gray light of the rising sun fell in ghostly shadows over the land. The tears rolled hot down my cheeks. Mama held me close, and when I felt her body tremble, I knew she was crying too.

Meet the Author

Song of the Trees is Mildred D. Taylor's first book about the Logan family. The second book in the series, *Roll of Thunder, Hear My Cry*, won the Newbury Medal in 1977.

Additional Books to Read

A Jar of Dreams
by Yoshiko Uchida
Read about a Japanese American family during the Depression.

Colin Powell: Straight to the Top
by Rose Blue and Corinne J. Naden
This book describes the life of a modern leader.

Response Activities

1. **Predict** Describe what you think will happen when Papa comes home. Why do you think that?

2. **Narrative: Write a Dialogue** Write a dialogue between Cassie and Mr. Anderson. What might she say to him? How might he respond?

3. **Geography: Arts** Choose a natural resource from your region. Create a poster to advertise why this resource is important to your area.

The War in Vietnam

Main Idea In the 1960s, the nation was divided over the war in Vietnam.

Washington, D.C., was icy cold on January 20, 1961, when John F. Kennedy was inaugurated — sworn in as President of the United States. Full of hope, he spoke of commitment to the country:

> "**A**sk not what your country can do for you. . . . Ask what you can do for your country."

Kennedy was the youngest man ever elected President. Charming and confident, he inspired Americans to do great things. He urged the nation to send astronauts to the moon, and he created the Peace Corps. **Peace Corps** volunteers help people in developing nations in such areas as education, agriculture, and small business. In **developing nations,** where about three-fourths of the people in the world live, people don't have enough food, resources, or money.

In November of 1963, less than three years after he became President, Kennedy's body was carried past the place where he had taken the oath of office. He had been assassinated. This tragic event shocked Americans. Yet it was only the first of the decade's many tragedies. Two other important public figures were assassinated during the 1960s — Martin Luther King, Jr., and President Kennedy's brother, Robert Kennedy. The assassinations were signs of the conflicts of these decades.

John F. Kennedy ("JFK") was elected President in 1960. His supporters wore campaign buttons like the one below. **History:** *Why do you think people were willing to volunteer for Kennedy's Peace Corps?*

FOR PRESIDENT
JOHN F. KENNEDY

The Vietnam Conflict

Focus *What effect did the Vietnam War have on Americans?*

One conflict stemmed from American involvement in Vietnam, a country in Southeast Asia. Since 1954, Vietnam had been ripped apart by a civil war between the north and the south. Like North Korea, North Vietnam was largely Communist. South Vietnam, like South Korea, opposed communism.

One of America's goals in its Cold War with the Soviet Union was to keep communism from spreading. The United States backed the government of South Vietnam. President Dwight D. Eisenhower had sent military advisors to South Vietnam as early as the 1950s. Soon the United States became involved in the actual fighting.

Vietnam

Huey in Vietnam

One type of helicopter used by American troops in Vietnam was the "Huey." Compare the illustration, below, with the photo of a Huey in action (left).

A large, powerful engine allowed the Huey to carry heavy cargo.

This is where the pilots sat. Large windows allowed them to see their surroundings.

The large compartment was used to carry troops and supplies as well as to evacuate the injured.

Different kinds of weapons could be mounted on the sides.

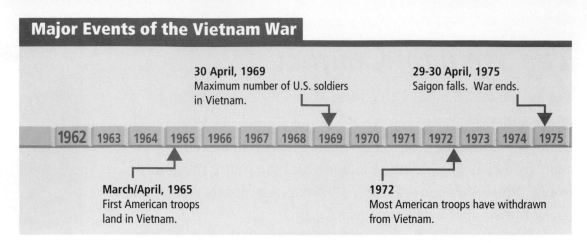

Major Events of the Vietnam War

30 April, 1969
Maximum number of U.S. soldiers in Vietnam.

29-30 April, 1975
Saigon falls. War ends.

| 1962 | 1963 | 1964 | 1965 | 1966 | 1967 | 1968 | 1969 | 1970 | 1971 | 1972 | 1973 | 1974 | 1975 |

March/April, 1965
First American troops land in Vietnam.

1972
Most American troops have withdrawn from Vietnam.

The timeline above shows some of the events of the war in Vietnam. **Timeline Skill:** *When did Saigon, the capital of South Vietnam, fall under the control of the North Vietnamese?*

Life Magazine covered the war in Vietnam.

In 1965, President Lyndon Johnson sent more than 180,000 troops to South Vietnam to help fight against the North Vietnamese. American forces won most major battles of the war, but the Communists wouldn't give in. At the end of 1967, nearly 500,000 Americans were fighting in Vietnam.

A Living Room War

By the 1960s, most Americans owned television sets. That had not been true for any previous wars. Television brought the Vietnam War into the nation's living rooms. Not only did people see vivid pictures of the war in newspapers and magazines, but nearly every night on television they saw Americans killing or being killed thousands of miles away.

These pictures forced Americans to take sides. Those in favor of the war wanted the United States to send more troops to Vietnam in order to win the war quickly. Those against the war said the United States should not be fighting in another country's civil war. They wanted to bring the troops home.

Many people who were against the war staged protests in colleges and elsewhere all over the country. At the UN in New York, 250,000 anti-war protesters gathered in 1967. In Washington, D.C., 55,000 more protesters assembled. Many young men refused to be drafted into the army.

In 1968, Richard Nixon was elected President. He promised to bring about a peaceful solution to the war in Vietnam. He started bringing troops home soon after his election. He sent troops into Vietnam's neighboring country, Cambodia, to fight against the North Vietnamese there. The presence of American troops in Cambodia set off more protests, especially at American colleges.

Eventually, in 1972, the United States did bring its troops home from Southeast Asia. It was the end of the longest war the country had ever fought. The following year, the United States, South Vietnam, and North Vietnam signed a peace treaty. The war wasn't over for the Vietnamese people until 1975. North Vietnam defeated South Vietnam and the entire country came under Communist rule.

The war in Vietnam made many young people think that America had lost its way. They blamed the war and many of the nation's social problems on America's culture, its way of life.

It wasn't only young Americans who wanted the country to change. Many groups were demanding changes that would bring them more freedom and equality.

Ask Yourself

Seeing the Vietnam War on television gave people very strong opinions about whether American troops should be fighting in Vietnam or not. Have you ever seen a television program, such as a news report or a documentary, that made you have a very strong opinion about an issue? What was the issue, and what was your reaction? Did the television program change your mind about it?

? ? ? ? ? ? ? ? ? ? ? ? ? ? ?

Lesson Review

1960	1965	1970	

1963
President Kennedy assassinated

1965
U.S. increases number of troops in Vietnam

1967
Major anti-war protests

1 **Key Vocabulary:** Write a paragraph about President Kennedy, using the terms **developing nation** and **Peace Corps**.

2 **Focus:** What effect did the Vietnam War have on Americans?

3 **Critical Thinking: Compare** How would helicopters be helpful during a war? When would planes be more useful?

4 **Theme: Responsibility and Freedom** Do you think it was wrong for television stations to include upsetting scenes from the Vietnam War on their news programs?

5 **Citizenship/Writing Activity:** Find out more about the Peace Corps. Then write a short essay explaining why Peace Corps volunteers might be needed by some groups or countries.

★ CITIZENSHIP ★

Making Decisions

What Goals Are Best?

Suppose someone gave you $100 for your birthday. What would you do with it? You could buy several little things. You could get one big present. You could put it all in the bank.

How you spend money says something about you. The same is true of nations. The case study below shows how one U.S. President chose to spend national resources. Do you agree with his choice?

Case Study

The Apollo Project

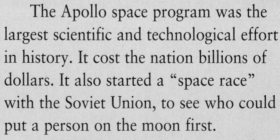

On May 25, 1961, President Kennedy announced that "this nation should commit itself to achieving the goal, before this decade is out, of landing a man on the moon and returning him safely to earth." Almost a year earlier, the Apollo program had begun planning for a manned circling of the moon (not a landing yet).

The Apollo space program was the largest scientific and technological effort in history. It cost the nation billions of dollars. It also started a "space race" with the Soviet Union, to see who could put a person on the moon first.

In 1969, the United States won the race. Neil Armstrong walked on the moon, saying: "That's one small step for man, one giant leap for mankind." Kennedy's vision became a reality.

Take Action

President Kennedy believed that a strong space program was worth spending money on. He thought it would give Americans pride and send the world the message that Americans are an energetic, "can do" people. If you were President, how would you spend national resources? Try this:

1 Spend five to 10 minutes thinking about what the nation needs to do in the next 10 years and why. If you could choose one big project to spend money on, what would it be?

2 Write down your idea and what you think it will accomplish. Include any negative effects your project might cause.

3 Take turns presenting your ideas. List the ideas on the chalkboard, keeping track of how many students had the same idea.

4 As a class, talk about the choices you made. Does the class have a shared vision of the future?

Tips for Making Decisions

- Decide what your choices are.
- Write down the advantages and disadvantages of each choice.
- Compare the advantages and disadvantages to see which list offers the strongest reasons to choose a certain idea.

Research Activity

In the 1960s, the Apollo missions had Americans glued to their television sets. How important is the space program to Americans today? Interview friends and neighbors to find out. Share your findings with the class.

A World of Change

Main Idea In the late 1900s, Americans have created changes because of political, social, and economic concerns.

Key Vocabulary

migrant worker

docked

cosmonaut

Key Events

1965 California grape boycott begins

1975 Indian Self-Determination Act

1989 Berlin Wall comes down

1991 Soviet Union breaks up

1995 *Atlantis-Mir* docking

In Kristen Gresalfi's world, every inch counts. Three of every 100 Americans use a wheelchair. Kristen, a sixth grader from Boyds, Maryland, is one of them. Her wheelchair is 29 inches wide. For most doorways, that's a tight squeeze. In her old home, in fact, she couldn't wheel through her bathroom or bedroom doors.

Kristen's father fixed that. He designed a house that's wheelchair-friendly. It even has a drive-in shower.

Thanks to a federal law, the world outside Kristen's house has gotten friendlier, too. In 1990, Congress passed a law called the Americans with Disabilities Act (ADA). The ADA protects the rights of disabled people to enter schools and other buildings. It requires buildings to have ramps, wide doors, and roomy bathrooms. The ADA has improved life for Kristen — and for the other 49 million disabled Americans.

A group of Boy Scouts raises the American flag together. The boys were attending Boy Scout camp in Rhode Island.

Struggle for Equality

Focus *What rights have Mexican Americans, Native Americans, and women gained in the past three decades?*

Disabled Americans are just one group in the United States that has worked for equal rights. Another group is Mexican Americans.

Nearly two-thirds of all Spanish-speaking people in the United States are Mexican Americans. Most of them live in the West and Southwest of the country. During the 1960s, many Mexican Americans worked as **migrant workers** on farms, which means that they moved from place to place looking for farm work. They worked long hours at back-breaking jobs, but were paid very little money.

In 1965, grape pickers in California went on strike for better pay. Cesar Chávez, a Mexican American whose family members had also been migrant workers, led their struggle. He persuaded millions of Americans to boycott grapes grown in California. The boycott worked. In 1970, the growers signed a contract with the United Farm Workers (UFW), the group Chávez headed. The growers agreed to increase the farm workers' pay and to treat them more fairly.

Cesar Chávez, above, headed the United Farm Workers, who went on strike for better wages and improved working conditions.
Economics: *How can strikes and boycotts help workers?*

Native Americans' Rights

In 1968, the American Indian Movement (AIM) was established to fight for Native Americans' civil rights. AIM wanted to make the Bureau of Indian Affairs, which ran Native American reservations, protect Native Americans against crime and discrimination.

Two hundred members of AIM took over the village of Wounded Knee, South Dakota, in 1973. (In Chapter 18 you read about what happened at Wounded Knee in 1890.) The AIM members said they wouldn't leave until the U.S. Senate looked into the government's treatment of Native Americans. After they had been at Wounded Knee for 71 days, the government promised to consider Native Americans' demands.

Patsy Takemoto Mink

Patsy Takemoto Mink was born in 1927 in Maui, Hawaii. A member of Hawaii's House of Representatives and Senate in the late 1950s, Mink worked on education and women's issues. She was also active in Hawaii's statehood movement. Mink was first elected to the U.S. Congress in 1964, where she continued to work on education and women's issues. She believes women should get "equal pay for equal work."

Government policy gradually began to change. Through the 1970s, the United States returned land to many tribes. More government money now goes to Native American programs in health, education, and housing. The Indian Self-Determination Act of 1975 allows Native American governments to run these programs.

Improving Women's Lives

Women also began to insist on fairer treatment. In 1966, a group of women founded the National Organization for Women (NOW). One of the organization's goals was to help women get good jobs. NOW also wanted to help women get the same pay as men doing the same jobs.

Usually, however, women couldn't get the same jobs as men. Most high-level jobs in business, for example, were out of reach for women. In medicine, only about nine of every 100 doctors were female in 1970.

Still, women pushed for change and made great gains. Between 1970 and 1975, the number of women in medical schools doubled. Even more women began attending law school. Many women became airline pilots, construction workers, firefighters, and cab drivers. They were doing jobs that were once held only by men.

Women became more involved in politics, too. From 1975 to 1989, the number of women in state legislatures doubled. In 1992, four new women were elected to the U.S. Senate. Two women, Sandra Day O'Connor and Ruth Bader Ginsburg, have become Supreme Court justices.

Moving Ahead

Focus *What did the end of the Cold War mean for Americans?*

A major world event of the late 1980s was the gradual breakup of the Soviet Union. Since 1985, Mikhail Gorbachev (Mih KAYL GAWR buh chauf), president of the Soviet Union, had tried to reform the Soviet system. With American Presidents Reagan and Bush urging him on, Gorbachev opened his country to democracy. He allowed the nations of Eastern Europe to turn away from communism, too. In Berlin, Germany, a wall had separated Communist and non-Communist sections of the city since 1961. In 1989, when Germans knocked down the Berlin Wall, no Communist troops interfered. In 1990, both Berlin and Germany were reunited.

Legend

Formerly a communist country or region

Formerly a republic of the Soviet Union

Formerly East Germany

The 15 republics of the Soviet Union split apart on December 25, 1991. After 74 years, the Russian people were able to free themselves from the burden of communism. Gorbachev had tried to keep the republics of the union together. One by one they chose to become separate nations. Gorbachev resigned as president. He gave control of the Soviet army and its nuclear weapons to Boris Yeltsin. Yeltsin was the president of Russia, the largest of the independent republics.

Although Gorbachev was forced to give up his power, his reforms helped bring about the end of Communist rule in Russia. He paved the way for a new spirit of cooperation between his country and the United States.

Between 1991 and 1995, the United States spent about $1.3 billion to help the former Soviet Union take apart nuclear weapons. Several countries — including the United States, Russia, Britain, France, and China — still have nuclear weapons. In May of 1995, most of the world's nations renewed a treaty they had signed earlier. In that treaty, the nations agreed not to develop nuclear weapons. Their goal was a world free of nuclear weapons.

The map above shows Europe after the Cold War. **Map Skill:** *Compare this map to the one on page 560. What new countries have been created out of the Soviet Union?*

Mikhail Gorbachev was *Time Magazine's* Man of the Year for 1987 for helping bring down the Iron Curtain.

TIME

MAN OF THE YEAR

THE EDUCATION OF MIKHAIL SERGEYEVICH GORBACHEV

Colin Powell

The son of Jamaican immigrants, Colin Powell was born in New York City in 1937. He joined the U.S. Army in 1958, and later served in Vietnam. In 1987, Powell was appointed President Ronald Reagan's national security adviser and about two years later became the chairman of the Joint Chiefs. He led the United States and its allies to victory in the 1991 Persian Gulf War.

Issues for the Future: Working Together

"Houston, Atlantis, we have capture." That's what Space Shuttle Commander Robert Gibson announced when the U.S. shuttle *Atlantis* **docked,** or connected, with the Russian space station, *Mir,* in June of 1995. (The first international docking in history occurred when the two nations joined forces in July of 1975: the American spacecraft *Apollo* docked with the Soviet's *Soyuz.*)

In June of 1992, Boris Yeltsin and President Bush agreed that American astronauts and Russian **cosmonauts** — as astronauts are called in Russia — could have joint space missions. Now, the United States and Russia, along with other nations, are working on an international space station program. What's next? Maybe the United States and Russia will work together for another exciting breakthrough — a manned mission to Mars!

The future holds challenges and opportunities. Two things are certain about the world you face today and in the years to come: History will shape you, and you will shape history. You'll shape it most if you get involved in your community, state, and nation. President Kennedy urged, "Ask not what your country can do for you. . . . Ask what you can do for your country." That was good advice in 1961. And it's good advice today — especially for people moving forward to create the history of the 21st century.

Lesson Review

| 1965 | 1972 | 1979 | 1986 | 1993 | |

1965
California grape boy-cott begins

1975
Indian Self-Determination Act

1989
Berlin Wall comes down

1991
Soviet Union breaks up

1995
Atlantis-Mir docking

1 Key Vocabulary: Write three sentences about the lesson, using the terms **migrant worker, docked,** and **cosmonaut.**

2 Focus: What rights have Mexican Americans, Native Americans, and women gained in the past three decades?

3 Focus: What did the end of the Cold War mean for Americans?

4 Critical Thinking: Predict Between 1950 and 1990, the number of women in the workforce went from over 30 percent to almost 60 percent. Do you think the pecentage will continue to go up?

5 Citizenship: How have the actions of Mexican Americans, Native Americans, and women helped them gain rights in the past 30 years?

6 Theme:Responsibility and Freedom/Research Activity: Find out how Americans responded when the Berlin Wall came down in 1989.

Producing Oral Histories

Talking History

You've probably heard older people describing memories of events in their lives. These stories, once they are recorded, become **oral history** — the spoken stories of individuals. Oral histories are an important source of information about the past.

With a tape recorder, a carefully-chosen person to interview, and some research, you too can become an oral historian. Listen carefully, ask good questions, and add to the history of your community.

1 Here's How

Prepare for the Interview

- Pick a topic for your interview, for example, civil rights. You must know about the topic before you begin. Review this book and other sources for information.

- Find the best person to interview. A relative or neighbor might have a good memory of your topic. You can also find people through your local museum or historical society.

- Jot down questions to ask.

- Check your tape recorder. Be sure you have blank tapes.

- Choose a quiet spot for the interview and plan plenty of time.

Conduct the Interview

- Avoid asking questions that require "yes" or "no" answers.

- Encourage your interviewee to expand on answers to questions. Say "Tell me more," or "Can you explain that?"

- Pick up on interesting ideas your interviewee mentions that you didn't plan to ask about.

- Don't interrupt. Talk as little as possible. Take careful notes.

Follow it up

- Review your tape and notes right away to refresh your memory.

- Write about the interview. Try to capture the interviewee's feelings.

- Write a thank-you note to the interviewee.

2 Think It Through

How does the information in an oral history compare with information in a biography?

3 Use It

1. Choose a person to interview and a subject to ask about. Explain why you have chosen this person.

2. Write down the questions you will ask.

3. Conduct your interview and write an oral history report.

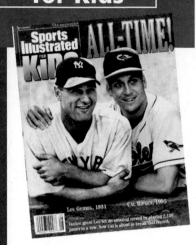

He Keeps Going and Going...

by John Rolfe

Baseball is often called the national pastime. It has been popular since the mid-1800s. Games were even played by soldiers during the Civil War, and by 1876 the National League was already arranging games between professional teams.

Baseball is a game with a long history, and the accomplishments of the great heroes like Babe Ruth, Cy Young, Roberto Clemente, Jackie Robinson, Luis Aparicio, and Hank Aaron are all an important part of that history. Many players have earned their places in the record books and in the Baseball Hall of Fame.

One of the records no one thought would ever be broken was set by New York Yankee Lou Gehrig in 1939. He played 2,130 games in a row. Lou, meet Cal Ripken.

During his streak, Cal has taken his lumps — but not a day off.

Shortstop Cal Ripken, Junior, has played in every Baltimore Oriole game for the past 13 years.

Think about that. Every game for 13 years. That's like never missing a day of school from the time you start kindergarten . . . to the time you finish high school.

Were you born after May 30, 1982, the day Cal began his streak? If so, then his streak is older than you are.

Reaching 2,130

As of June 21, [1995] Cal the Iron Man had played in 2,059 regular season games in a row. If he plays in every game through September 6, he will break Lou Gehrig's major league record of 2,130 games in a row.

Hard Work

Cal's dad became an Oriole coach in 1976. After that, Cal sometimes took batting practice just before the Oriole players took the field. He asked the players questions about fielding and strategy. "I still use their answers," Cal says.

Cal, Senior taught his son two lessons: Have fun and practice hard.

"I didn't make Cal a good player," says his dad. "He worked to make himself a good player."

Cal still works hard. He trains all winter in a gym he built by the side of his house. It has a full basketball court and a batting cage.

Close Calls

"My approach to baseball has really come from my father," Cal says. "Baseball is a team sport, and it's important to be in the line-up every day to [give your team] a chance to win."

So what is it like to be baseball's Iron Man? Go to school every day for 13 years, and you'll begin to know.

On September 6, 1995, Cal Ripken broke Lou Gehrig's record.

Cal has been an All-Star 12 times (through 1994.) In 1992, he was voted the American League's smartest player.

Response Activities

1. **Identify Main Idea** Whose record did Cal Ripken break, and what was so remarkable about his achievement?

2. **Narrative: Write an Article** Interview a friend for an article about "streaks." How many days in a row has he/she gone to school? Write the results of your interview in a magazine article, using direct quotations from your friend.

3. **National Heritage: Research the Hall of Fame** Find out about the Baseball Hall of Fame in Cooperstown, New York. How many players are honored there? Are any of them your favorites? What kinds of things have players accomplished to get into the Hall of Fame?

Chapter Review

Chapter Review Timeline

| 1945 | 1955 | 1965 | 1975 | 1985 | 1995 |

1964 Civil Rights Act

1991 Soviet Union breaks up

1947 Cold War begins

1953 War ends in Korea

1965 United States increases number of troops in Vietnam

Summarizing the Main Idea

1 Copy and complete the following chart, indicating key events that occurred in each decade.

Decade	Key Events
1950s	*hydrogen bombs, Cold War, Korean War, suburbs, "baby boom"*
1960s	
1970s	
1980s	
1990s	

Vocabulary

2 Using at least six of the following terms, write a news summary describing the second half of the 20th century.

communism (p. 560)
capitalism (p. 560)
Iron Curtain (p. 560)
Cold War (p. 561)
arms race (p. 561)

suburb (p. 562)
civil rights (p. 563)
nonviolent protest (p. 564)
Freedom Rider (p. 565)
Peace Corps (p. 572)

developing nation (p. 572)
migrant worker (p. 579)
docked (p. 582)
cosmonaut (p. 582)

Reviewing the Facts

3 What is the difference between a communist and a democratic government?

4 How did life improve for many Americans in the 1950s?

5 What nonviolent protests took place in the 1950s and 1960s?

6 What were the main differences between the Vietnam War and other U.S. wars?

7 How has life changed for women, disabled Americans, Mexican Americans, and Native Americans in the 20th century?

8 What did Gorbachev accomplish?

Producing Oral Histories

9 Choose someone you have read about in this chapter. What if you could interview that person? Prepare some questions you might ask.

10 Write down a story about yourself or your family that might be interesting to tell in an oral history. If a tape recorder is available, read the story into the tape recorder.

Geography Skills

11 Find Korea in an atlas, and trace an outline of the country. Find and label the 38th parallel — the latitude that divides North and South Korea. What is significant about the countries that border North Korea?

12 The case that outlawed segregated schools was called *Brown v. the Board of Education of Topeka.* Find Topeka on a map. What does its location tell you about the extent of segregation in the 1950s?

Critical Thinking

13 Generalize How did the attitude of the United States toward communism affect the nation's involvement in both the Korean and Vietnam wars?

14 Comparing Then and Now How has the civil rights movement changed the lives of

African Americans since the 1950s?

15 Cause and Effect How do you think continued cooperation between the United States and Russia in space can help the cause of peace in the world?

Writing: Citizenship and History

16 Citizenship Write an editorial defending the tactics of people participating in lunch counter sit-ins and "freedom rides."

17 History If you lived in Germany, how would you have felt when the Berlin Wall came down? Write a letter to relatives in another country expressing your thoughts.

Activities

History/Arts Activity
Research how young people in the 1950s spent their time. What kind of music did they listen to? How did they dress? How did they travel? What did they eat? Create a fifties collage using old magazines or your own illustrations.

National Heritage/Research Activity
Write a biography of Martin Luther King, Jr., or of John F. Kennedy. What did they accomplish in their lifetimes? What lasting influence have they had on their country and its citizens?

Internet Option

Check the **Internet Social Studies Center** for ideas on how to extend your theme project beyond your classroom.

THEME PROJECT CHECK-IN

Use the information that you have learned about the late 1900s to complete your project. These questions will help you:
• What new technologies caused changes in America?
• What important issues were Americans concerned about?
• How did events in the rest of the world affect Americans?

A Hemisphere
of Neighbors

Chapter Preview: *People, Places, and Events*

Lake of the Woods

What different kinds of land do Canadians have? *Lesson 1, Page 590*

Quebec City

How have French traditions and language shaped Canada? *Lesson 1, Page 592*

Sierra Madre Occidental

Mexico is a country with many mountain ranges. *Lesson 2, Page 595*

Canada

Main Idea   Canada's many peoples have used the resources of the land to build a prosperous nation.

How do you picture Canada, our neighbor to the north? If you drove all the way across it, what do you think you would see?

Follow the Trans-Canada Highway across southern Canada, and you will find a land much like the United States. You might start driving in Newfoundland, where you can still see, hear, and smell the Atlantic Ocean. As you drive west, you travel first through forests and then over rolling farmland. The Great Lakes appear outside your car window. Next, the road enters prairies much like those of the Great Plains in the United States. Finally, days after you began, you drive through passes in the Rocky Mountains and the Pacific Ranges. After a ride on a ferry, you are on Vancouver Island, and there lies the Pacific Ocean.

Like people in the United States, Canadians are proud that their country stretches "from sea to sea." Also like the United States, Canada is a land of different peoples learning to live together.

Key Vocabulary

Canadian Shield

province

bilingual

French-Canadian

separatist

Key Places

Newfoundland

Vancouver Island

Ontario

Quebec

Montreal

◀ The Angel Monument in Mexico City — a monument to Mexican independence.

| 1980 | 2000 | 2020 |

Mexico City

What is modern Mexico like?
Lesson 2, Page 594

Open-Air Market

What kinds of food do Mexican farmers grow? *Lesson 2, Page 596*

Voting in Mexico

How is democracy growing stronger in the Western Hemisphere?
Lesson 3, Page 603

A Nation Rich in Resources

Focus *How have Canadians used their resources?*

When French explorer Jacques Cartier first sighted Canada in 1534, he declared that he could not see "a cartload of dirt." All he could make out was rock. Cartier stood on a boat, floating in the Atlantic Ocean, and the rocks he described were part of the Canadian Shield. *(See map of Canada's physical regions.)* The **Canadian Shield** is a rock formation that covers much of eastern Canada. What Cartier could not see was that the Shield contains many valuable kinds of minerals — copper, gold, silver, and zinc.

Cartier landed briefly but did not travel very far inland, so he never had a chance to see the rest of the country's riches. *(See chart of natural resources below.)* Canada contains three resources that are in short supply in the world today: trees, petroleum, and good farmland. Many of these are located in the vast areas of western Canada. Canadians take lumber, oil, and crops from this region and process them in the factories of the southeast.

The majority of Canada's 28 million people live in the southeast, in the provinces of Ontario and Quebec. A **province** is an area with its own government, much like a U.S. state. Using resources from the nation's west, the factories of the southeast provinces make steel, cars, paper, fuel, and food products. Canada's manufactured goods make up over 40 percent of the goods it exports to other nations.

Many of these products leave Canada through the St. Lawrence Seaway, a 2,340-mile waterway that connects the Great Lakes to the Atlantic Ocean. The St. Lawrence gives inland Canada a water route to markets in the United States and around the world. Today, Canada trades more with the United States than with any other nation.

In 1993, Canada produced over 27 million metric tons of wheat, 6 million metric tons of corn, and nearly 12 million cattle. In 1992, it produced 186 million cubic meters of lumber. **Chart Skill:** *Which of the resources in the chart do you think is the most valuable?*

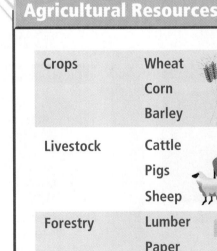

Agricultural Resources

Crops	Wheat Corn Barley
Livestock	Cattle Pigs Sheep
Forestry	Lumber Paper

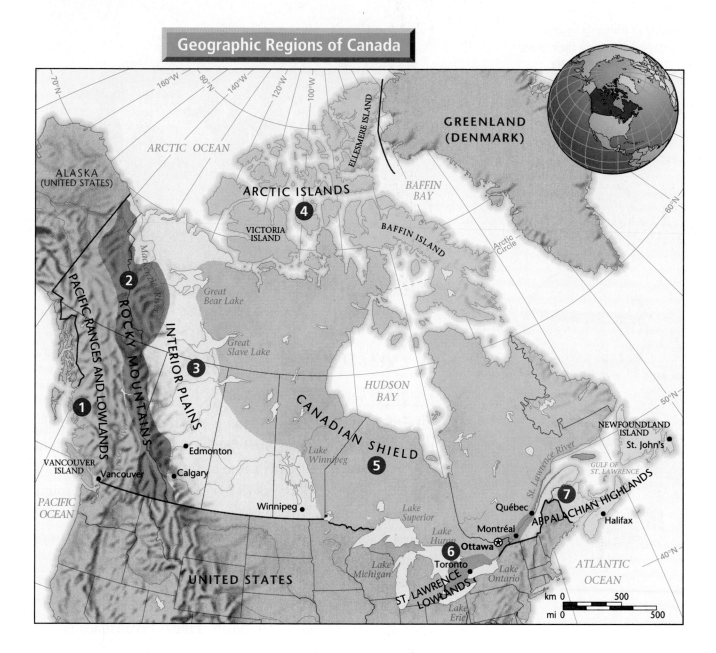

Geographic Regions of Canada

GREENLAND (DENMARK)

ARCTIC OCEAN

ALASKA (UNITED STATES)

ARCTIC ISLANDS **4**

ELLESMERE ISLAND

BAFFIN BAY

VICTORIA ISLAND

BAFFIN ISLAND

Arctic Circle

PACIFIC RANGES AND LOWLANDS

2 ROCKY MOUNTAINS

Mackenzie River

Great Bear Lake

INTERIOR PLAINS

Great Slave Lake

3

HUDSON BAY

CANADIAN SHIELD **5**

1

VANCOUVER ISLAND

Edmonton

Lake Winnipeg

NEWFOUNDLAND ISLAND

St. John's

Vancouver

Calgary

St. Lawrence River

GULF OF ST. LAWRENCE

PACIFIC OCEAN

Winnipeg

Lake Superior

Québec

7 APPALACHIAN HIGHLANDS

Montréal

Halifax

Lake Huron

6 Ottawa

UNITED STATES

Lake Michigan

Toronto

Lake Ontario

ATLANTIC OCEAN

ST. LAWRENCE LOWLANDS

Lake Erie

km 0   500
mi 0   500

1 Pacific Ranges and Lowlands These include the highest mountain in Canada — Mount Logan in the Yukon Territory, which rises 19,850 feet high.

2 Rocky Mountains This mountain range begins in New Mexico. It extends north across western Canada, across Alaska, and into the Arctic Circle.

3 Interior Plains This low, flat region runs south into the great plains of the United States. When glaciers covered Canada, this area was the site of a huge lake.

4 Arctic Islands These are largely covered by ice caps and glaciers. Here, mountains rise nearly 8,000 feet high.

5 Canadian Shield A rock formation that covers close to half of Canada, the Shield was once high mountains. Erosion has worn it almost flat.

6 St. Lawrence Lowlands A heavily populated area, this region contains the Great Lakes, the St. Lawrence Seaway, and cities such as Toronto and Montreal.

7 Appalachian Highlands These are the northern end of a mountain range that begins in Alabama. The Appalachians are the oldest mountains in North America, formed nearly 250 million years ago.

Map Skill: *Which regions are best for farming? Which might attract the most tourists?*

A family of Romanian settlers *(right)* poses outside their home in Saskatchewan. A poster *(below)* encourages immigrants to settle in western Canada. **Geography:** *Why do you think the Canadian government gave away land in the West?*

A Nation of Many Peoples

Focus *What kind of society have Canadians built?*

Like the United States, Canada is mostly a nation of immigrants. Germans started arriving in the 17th century. Chinese and Japanese immigrants came at the turn of the 20th century. During the 1960s and 1970s, a number of blacks immigrated from the Caribbean. Canada is sometimes called a mosaic society — one in which each people keeps part of its own identity while sharing in a common culture.

A visitor driving in the city of Montreal (mohn tree AWL) might be surprised to see a sign with two words on it: *Arrêt* and *Stop*. The sign is in French and English. This is because Canada is a **bilingual** nation, meaning it has two official languages. Together, these two languages symbolize the nation's French and English heritage. It is this dual heritage that has most shaped the country.

Canada has strong British roots. About four out of 10 Canadians have British ancestors. Britain ruled Canada directly until 1867, when it granted Canadians the right to govern themselves. Canada has modeled its government on the way the British make their laws. The Canadian parliament, or legislature, is one example of how their government is similar to Britain's.

French, however, is the first language of one quarter of Canada's people. Most French-speaking Canadians live in the province of Quebec, founded by French settlers. Quebec's version of

The population of Montreal *(left) is over three million. This makes it the second-largest French-speaking city in the world. Only Paris is larger.*

Many signs in Canada are written in both French and English. The sign *(above)* in the Rocky Mountains identifies the Continental Divide in both languages.

MTV features singers from both Quebec and France. Some Québecois (kay beh KWAH) — the French name for those who live in Quebec — would like their province to become an independent nation. These people are known as **French-Canadian separatists.** Others want Quebec to remain part of Canada. This has been a subject of heated debate throughout the country. In 1995, Prime Minister Jean Chrétien (kray TYEHN) expressed the sorrow many feel about these divisions: "Canada with Quebec forms a country. No one knows what would be left without Quebec."

In the end, Québecois and other Canadians will decide whether to keep the country united. Since Britain gave Canada independence, however, the many peoples of Canada have worked together. Using their resources wisely, they have built a prosperous society.

Lesson Review: Geography

1 **Key Vocabulary:** Describe the people of Canada today using these terms: **province, bilingual, French-Canadian separatist.**

2 **Focus:** How have Canadians used their resources?

3 **Focus:** What kind of society have Canadians built?

4 **Critical Thinking: Classify** How are the United States and Canada alike? How are the two nations different? Discuss both the people and the geography of these two countries.

5 **Geography:** How does the St. Lawrence Seaway help Canada trade with other nations?

6 **Citizenship/Writing Activity:** With the help of the Canadian embassy in Washington, D.C., write a class letter to a fifth-grade class in Canada. Tell them what you are studying, and ask them to tell you about themselves.

Mexico

> *Main Idea* Mexico is a growing, urban nation.

Key Vocabulary

petrodollar

infrastructure

standard of living

Key Places

Mexico City

Gulf of Mexico

What if someone took you up in a helicopter and flew over Mexico City? What would you see? A city that stretches out for miles. You would also see mountains towering in the distance. The city lies surrounded by them, in a valley 7,349 feet above sea level.

If the helicopter flew down among the buildings, just over their roofs, you would see that the streets are crowded with people. The population of Mexico City and the area around it is 20 million. You would also see thousands of buses, taxis, and cars.

After the helicopter landed, what would you think? Was this how you pictured Mexico? Mexico is an urban country: Almost 70 percent of Mexicans live in cities. Over one-fifth of all Mexicans now live in the city you just saw.

A Varied Land

Focus *How have Mexico's resources affected its economy?*

Mexico has many different kinds of land. *(See map.)* There are deserts in the north and tropical rain forests in the southeast. Mexico also has over 6,000 miles of coasts. Two long, high mountain ranges run for hundreds of miles from north to south.

Over half the industries in the country are located in Mexico City. This city is also where Mexicans do over 70 percent of their banking business.
Economics: *How does the economy of Mexico City help the rest of Mexico?*

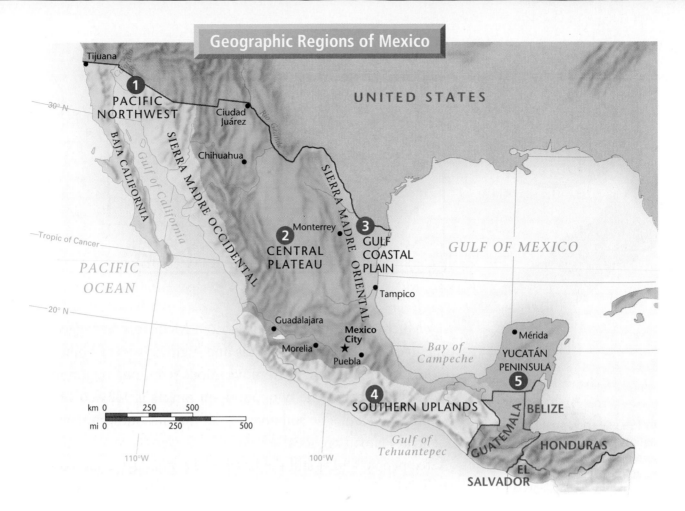

Geographic Regions of Mexico

1 Pacific Northwest On the peninsula of Baja California, mountains rise as high as 10,000 feet. Elevations in the Sierra Madre Occidental, across the Gulf of California, are even higher.

2 Central Plateau This is the largest physical region in Mexico. It is a flat area, bordered on the east by the Sierra Madre Oriental, where mountains can be as high as 13,000 feet.

3 Gulf Coastal Plain This low-lying area contains many rivers, including the Rio Grande, as well as beaches and lagoons. During the 1970s, large reserves of oil were discovered here.

4 Southern Uplands High mountains with steep, narrow valleys characterize this region. Plateaus at high elevations, often called *tablelands,* are farmed by Native American groups.

5 Yucatán Peninsula Rain forests grow in the south of this peninsula. The area also contains many limestone pits, formed naturally by erosion. The Mayas considered these pits sacred.

Map Skill: *Do you think it is difficult to build highways and railroads across Mexico? Why or why not?*

Mineral Resources

Precious Metals	Gold Silver	
Non-precious Metals	Iron Ore	Copper Lead Zinc
Fuel	Coal Petroleum Natural Gas	

In 1993, Mexico produced almost 6 million metric tons of iron ore and over 300,000 metric tons of zinc. In 1992 the country produced almost a billion barrels of petroleum and over 6 million metric tons of coal. **Chart Skill:** *Which of these resources can do the most to help the Mexican economy grow?*

Much of the mountainous land in Mexico is so rugged that no one lives there. Before railroads and highways were built, these mountains made it hard to move goods from one region to another.

Lying between the two mountain ranges is Mexico's huge Central Plateau. The soil and rainfall in the southern part of the Central Plateau are ideal for corn. This was the main crop of the Aztec people and is still the basis of the Mexican diet. Today, however, Mexican farmers grow a wide variety of crops: avocados and cotton, potatoes and sugar cane, mangoes and wheat. Mexican ranches also produce millions of cattle.

The land has other riches, too. *(See resources chart above.)* Both the Aztecs and the Spanish mined silver, and this is still mined there, making Mexico a leading source of silver. The nation's forests produce valuable woods, including mahogany and walnut. In the 20th century, oil has also brought wealth to this country. Mexico sells oil to the United States, Japan, and Europe.

Mexico Today

Focus *How are Mexicans shaping their future?*

Most Mexicans are descended from both Spanish colonists and Native Americans. A blend of these two cultures makes the culture of modern Mexico. You can find this blend in the languages Mexicans speak. Spanish is the official language, but some people still speak Native American languages. You can also see the blend in Mexican art. Artists such as Diego Rivera learned European methods but used shapes and colors from the art of Aztecs and Mayas. Mexico today holds on to its heritage as it develops a modern economy.

Economic Growth

In the 1970s, new oil fields were discovered in the Gulf Coastal Plain and in the Gulf of Mexico. Mexico, it turned out, had far more oil to sell to the world than anyone had known. Between 1976 and 1980, daily production of oil in Mexico nearly tripled. In 1981, Mexico was the fourth-largest producer of oil in the world.

The money earned from selling oil, called **petrodollars,** changed the Mexican economy. The government used this money, as well as foreign loans, to improve the country's highways, railroads, ports, and communications. This system of transportation and communication forms what is called the **infrastructure** of a country. It is part of what an economy needs to grow.

Petrodollars were also invested in building more factories and new industries. Today, Mexican factories make steel, cars, chemicals, and food products. Every year, Mexico exports billions of dollars worth of goods to countries throughout the world.

What country buys more of these goods than any other? The United States is Mexico's biggest customer. Mexico sells many products to its northern neighbor. In the early 1990s, these included over $88 million worth of clothes, $68 million of toys and sporting goods, and over $3 billion of cars and trucks.

Because of increased trade, Mexico and the United States have formed a closer friendship. They have cooperated on many economic and political issues. Individual Mexicans and Americans are also talking more. Some estimate that Mexicans

Vendors arrange their goods in an open-air market *(below).* Traders *(left)* work on the floor of the stock exchange in Mexico City.

Oil tankers and an oil-loading dock in Veracruz. Between 1976 and 1980, the amount of money Mexico earned each year from selling oil increased 12 times — from $500 million to $6 billion. **Economics:** *How did money from selling oil change the Mexican economy?*

spend billions of dollars a year on long-distance phone calls to the United States alone.

Trade and manufacturing have brought new jobs and more money to many Mexicans. This has raised their **standard of living** — the amount of money they spend on themselves and their families. When the standard of living rises, people can have comfortable homes and eat nutritious meals. They can buy cars, stereos, and televisions.

One problem facing modern Mexico, however, is creating enough jobs for everyone. The number of jobs has been growing fast, but the number of people looking for jobs has grown even faster. As a result, many people cannot earn enough money to support themselves and their families. In recent years, population growth has slowed. Even so, almost half the people in Mexico are under 15 years old. Someday, they will all need jobs.

Most experts believe that the Mexican economy will keep growing. One thing modern industries need is educated workers, and the government has been improving its schools for many years. In 1959, there were about five million students in school. By 1980, there were almost 20 million. In 1990, 87 percent of Mexican adults could read and write. As Mexico enters the 21st century, it is working to provide jobs and a better way of life for all its people.

Lesson Review: Geography

1. **Key Vocabulary:** Use the following words to discuss the economy of Mexico: **petrodollar, infrastructure, standard of living.**

2. **Focus:** How have Mexico's resources affected its economy?

3. **Focus:** How are Mexicans shaping their future?

4. **Critical Thinking: Predict** Do you think Mexico and the United States will form a closer friendship in the years to come?

How does trade bring them together?

5. **Citizenship:** Why is education so important to the Mexican economy? Will it help the economy grow? How can it help people find jobs?

6. **Geography/Science Activity:** Research the discovery of new oil fields in Mexico during the 1970s. Find out about the geology of the Gulf Coastal Plain and the Gulf of Mexico. Why did people find oil there?

Nations Working Together

Main Idea People of the Western Hemisphere share common goals.

From the Space Shuttle, astronauts can see the entire Western Hemisphere. They can see North and South America stretching from the top of the world nearly to the bottom — from the white mass of ice at the North Pole to the tip of Argentina. They can see the green of plains and forests, the brown of mountains and deserts, and the blue of the ocean surrounding them. The Great Lakes are visible, and so are the Mississippi and the Amazon rivers. Astronauts can even see some cities. What they can't see is the borders between countries.

"You just get a marvelous view of the world from space," recalls Colonel Frederick Gregory, a Space Shuttle pilot.

Key Vocabulary
- trading partner
- tariff
- NAFTA
- grassroots

> **"Y**ou could see Houston, and then you'd see how really close Houston was to Mexico City, and how close Mexico City was to South America. . . . But the great thing about it was that, unlike. . . maps, there were no state boundaries. You kind of wondered from above. . . how there could be any problems at all down there, because everybody was everybody's neighbor.**"**

Partners in Trade

Focus How has increased trade affected the nations of the Americas?

The Americas extend far beyond the United States, Canada, and Mexico. *(See map.)* There are 20 nations south of Mexico, beginning with Belize and Guatemala and ending with Argentina and Chile. There are also more than 20 island nations in the Caribbean, including Barbados and Cuba.

Many nations of the Americas have been trading partners for centuries. **Trading partners** are countries that buy and sell many goods to each other. Today, there is more trade among these nations than ever before. *(See chart below.)* At your local shopping mall, you can probably find apple juice from Argentina, coffee from Costa Rica, and blue jeans from El Salvador. South American and Caribbean countries are also the fastest-growing market for U.S. exports. In 1993, the United States sold them $80 billion worth of goods, more than double what it sold to them in 1986.

Tariffs and Trade Agreements

Countries in the Western Hemisphere have not always wanted to trade with each other. Sometimes, governments want to encourage people to buy goods manufactured or grown in their own country. To do this, they charge a **tariff,** an extra tax on goods brought into the country. Tariffs make these imports cost more, and this makes people buy lower-priced goods manufactured or grown at home. For many years, the United States placed a tariff on Mexican farm products. That helped American farmers sell more of their crops.

This chart shows the value of goods traded between the countries that signed NAFTA. These figures are from 1993, the year before the agreement went into effect. **Chart Skill:** *Which country exports the most to the others?*

Exports Between Canada, the U.S., and Mexico

	To Canada	To U.S.	To Mexico	Commodities
Canada		$116,783,855,000	$633,685,000	newsprint, wood pulp, timber, crude petroleum. machinery, natural gas, aluminum, motor vehicles and parts, telecommunications equipment
U.S.	$91,864,527,000		$40,253,790,000	capital goods, automobiles, industrial supplies and raw materials, consumer goods, agricultural products, telecommunications equipment
Mexico	$1,557,668,000	$42,838,073,000		crude oil, oil products, coffee, silver, engines, motor vehicles, cotton, consumer electronics

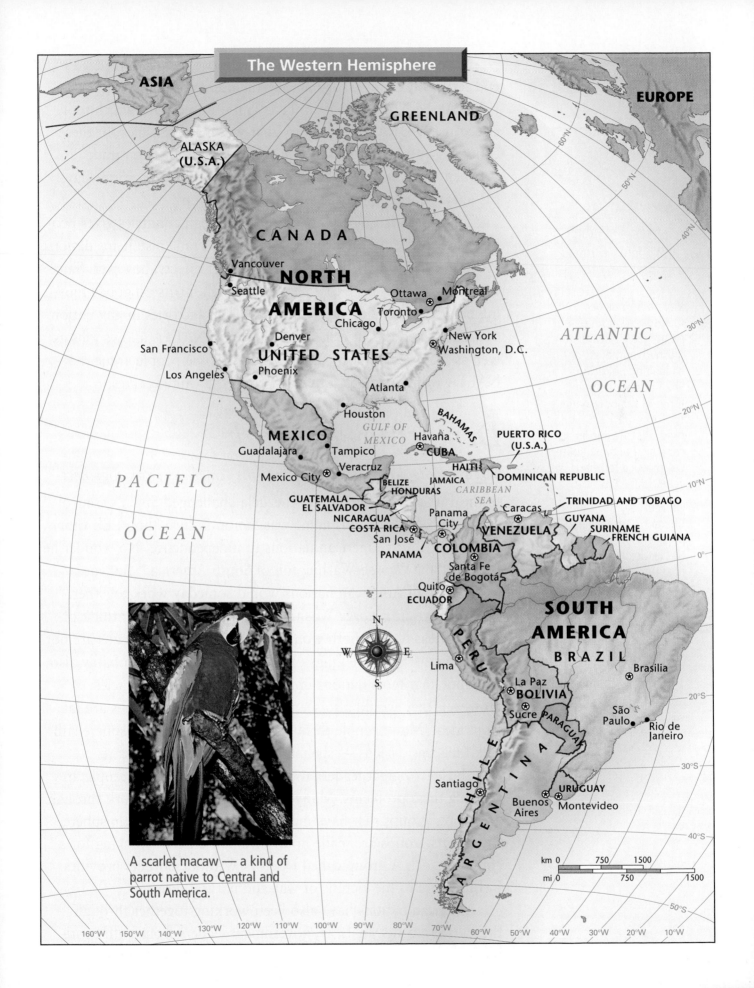

The Western Hemisphere

ASIA

GREENLAND

EUROPE

ALASKA
(U.S.A.)

CANADA

NORTH

Vancouver

Seattle

AMERICA

Ottawa   Montreal
Toronto

Chicago

ATLANTIC

San Francisco

Denver

UNITED STATES

New York
Washington, D.C.

Los Angeles

Phoenix

OCEAN

Atlanta

Houston

BAHAMAS

20°N

MEXICO

GULF OF
MEXICO

Havana

PUERTO RICO
(U.S.A.)

Guadalajara

Tampico

CUBA

HAITI

PACIFIC

Veracruz

JAMAICA

DOMINICAN REPUBLIC

Mexico City

BELIZE

CARIBBEAN
SEA

TRINIDAD AND TOBAGO

GUATEMALA

HONDURAS

EL SALVADOR

NICARAGUA

Caracas

GUYANA

OCEAN

Panama
City

VENEZUELA

SURINAME

COSTA RICA

FRENCH GUIANA

San José

COLOMBIA

PANAMA

Santa Fe
de Bogotá

Quito

SOUTH

ECUADOR

AMERICA

P
E
R
U

B R A Z I L

Lima

Brasilia

La Paz

BOLIVIA

São
Paulo

Sucre

P
A
R
A
G
U
A
Y

Rio de
Janeiro

C
H
I
L
E

A
R
G
E
N
T
I
N
A

Santiago

URUGUAY

Buenos
Aires

Montevideo

N
W   E
S

km 0   750   1500
mi 0   750   1500

A scarlet macaw — a kind of
parrot native to Central and
South America.

160°W 150°W 140°W 130°W 120°W 110°W 100°W 90°W 80°W 70°W 60°W 50°W 40°W 30°W 20°W 10°W

A Hemisphere of Neighbors   **601**

Violeta Barrios de Chamorro

Violeta Barrios de Chamorro is both one of Nicaragua's most distinguished journalists and its leading politician. She became the publisher of the newspaper *La Prensa* in 1978. She used this position to campaign against political injustice for many years.

On February 25, 1990, Chamorro was elected president of Nicaragua. Her leadership helped heal the divisions caused by a civil war that lasted eight years.

Now, the United States, Canada, and Mexico have pledged to end tariffs on goods traded among themselves. The first step was NAFTA, the North American Free Trade Agreement, which took effect in 1994. **NAFTA** is a treaty that will make it easier for these countries to trade with each other. It will end tariffs on trade between the three neighbors over a period of 15 years. Someday, the agreement might cover all American nations.

Trade between North and South American countries gives people more choices in the products they buy. Trade also helps nations grow and develop. NAFTA may have other effects, however. Since companies do not have to worry about high tariffs on goods moving between countries, they can locate their factories in any nation that has signed the agreement. In this way, NAFTA allows jobs as well as factories to move across borders. Some people argue that NAFTA will take many jobs away from the United States.

Democracy at Work

Focus *How do people throughout the Americas work together?*

In the 1800s, a soldier from Venezuela challenged Spain's control over South America. His name was Simón Bolívar (boh LEE vahr), and he led South American nations to independence. No wonder he is called "the George Washington of South America." Bolívar hoped that all American nations would someday work together.

What would George Washington and Simón Bolívar think of the Americas today? Both would be pleased that Americans are not taking orders from the kings of Europe. They would probably also be happy that most nations in the Americas are democracies. However, they would also see that American democracies are far from ideal. Many people throughout the Western Hemisphere still lack life's basic needs — shelter, education, and health care.

Those two great leaders would be encouraged that people are tackling these problems. Many individual Americans work through grassroots groups that have members throughout the hemisphere. **Grassroots** groups are made up of ordinary citizens working for a common goal. A group called Doctors Without Borders provides medical care to the victims of war and natural disasters.

American nations have also been working together through their governments. In 1994, government leaders from both continents and the Caribbean gathered in Miami, Florida. They were all part of a group called the Organization of American States (OAS), and their meeting was called the Summit of the Americas. The OAS is committed to protecting the environment and increasing trade between American nations. Its goals include strengthening democracy and improving health and education.

Discussing the Summit of the Americas in 1994, U.S. Vice President Al Gore declared:

A woman in Guatemala casts her vote in a presidential election.
Citizenship: *How do stronger democracies improve the lives of people throughout the Western Hemisphere?*

> "**N**ever before in history have Latin America, the Caribbean, Canada, and the United States been in such close agreement on all the fundamental [basic] economic, political, and social values that are important to free people. . . . Never have we been more genuinely neighbors . . . . "

The last two centuries have brought many changes to this hemisphere. Bolívar's wish that American nations could work together did not happen in his lifetime, but it is happening in ours.

Lesson Review: Geography

1. **Key Vocabulary:** Write a paragraph about how trade is increasing in the Western Hemisphere. Use these words: **trading partners, tariff, NAFTA.**

2. **Focus:** How has increased trade affected the nations of the Americas?

3. **Focus:** How do people throughout the Americas work together?

4. **Critical Thinking: Cause and Effect** How are countries helped by trading with other nations? How are they hurt? How do tariffs restrict this kind of trade?

5. **Theme: Responsibility and Freedom** What responsibilities do you think the United States has to other nations in the Western Hemisphere? Should we help them politically, economically, or both? Give reasons for your answers.

6. **Geography/Music: Activity:** Listen to recordings of songs from two different South American countries. Describe the similarities and differences between them.

Interpreting Map Perspectives

Turn the World Around

Many people think of their own country as the center of the world. If you live in the United States, then Canada is "up north." Mexico is "down south." We think this way because most maps place north at the top. But Canada is not above our heads. Mexico is not below our feet. We are all on the surface of the earth. Suppose we stand at the North Pole and look south. The world would look completely different. Maps can help us turn the world around and see things from a different perspective.

① Here's How

These maps show two different views of North America. One may look familiar, the other may not.

- Study both maps. How are they different? In the map on the left, north is at the top. South is at the bottom. What country is above the United States on this map? What country is below?

- The map on the right shows south at the top. Which direction is at the bottom? What countries are above and below the United States?

- Now compare the sizes of Canada and the United States on both maps. Which country looks bigger on each map?

- Compare the maps to find features that look the same and different.

② Think It Through

If you put east at the top, where would the countries be? If you put west at the top, where would the countries be?

③ Use It

1. Find each feature below on the two maps. Tell whether it looks the same or different. Explain your answers.
   a) Hudson Bay b) Gulf of Mexico c) Texas d) Montreal e) Florida

2. Use the atlas at the back of this book. Trace a map. Then make another map of the same place from another perspective.

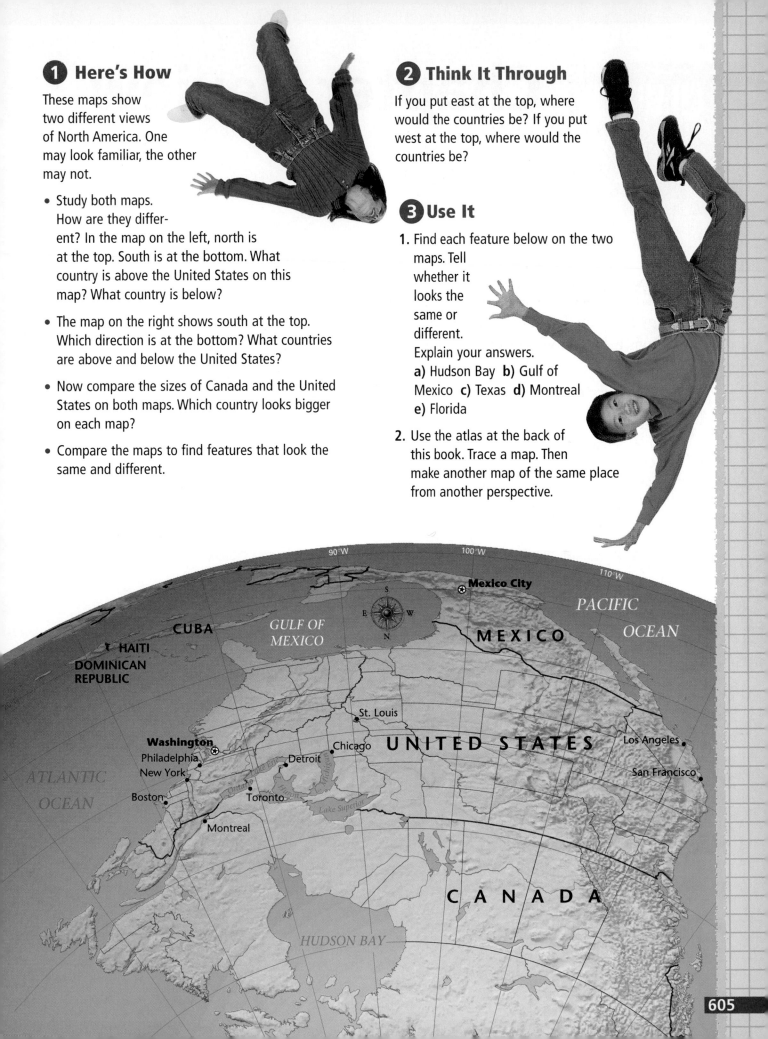

Chapter Review

Summarizing the Main Idea

1 Copy and complete the charts below, showing which geographic regions belong in which country. Use the maps on pp. 591 and 595.

Landforms	Country
Central Plateau	
Rocky Mountains	
Gulf Coastal Plains	
Interior Plains	
Southern Uplands	

Vocabulary

2 Write a newspaper article about trade in the Western Hemisphere using at least 7 of the words below.

Canadian Shield (p. 590)   infrastructure (p. 597)   NAFTA (p. 602)
province (p. 590)   standard of living (p. 598)   grassroots (p. 602)
bilingual (p. 592)   trading partner (p. 600)
petrodollar (p. 597)   tariff (p. 600)

Reviewing the Facts

3 What are Canada's official languages?

4 What is the St. Lawrence Seaway?

5 What do French-Canadian separatists believe should happen in Canada?

6 What groups make up the blend of cultures in modern Mexico?

7 What natural resource brought the most

wealth into Mexico during recent years?

8 How can education help solve the employment problem in Mexico?

9 How has trade between countries in the Western Hemisphere changed?

10 Why do governments place tariffs on imported goods?

11 Look at the map of South America on page 601. What if south were at the top of the map? What would the order of the countries be from top to bottom?

12 If you were looking at the Western Hemisphere from the Space Shuttle, how would you tell the difference between north and south? What geographical features would you look for?

Geography Skills

13 Compare the map of Canada on page 591 with the map of Mexico on page 595. What landforms does each have that the other does not?

14 Use a road map to plan a car trip from Mexico City to Montreal. What roads would you take? How far would you travel each day? Where would you stop?

Critical Thinking

15 **Decision Making** If you were a French-Canadian, would you want Quebec to be a separate nation? Why or why not?

16 **Compare** Compare the mix of cultures in Canada with that in Mexico. How are their blends of cultures similar? Different?

17 **Predict** Will NAFTA one day cover all American nations? Why or why not?

Writing: Citizenship and Economics

18 **Citizenship** What if George Washington and Simón Bolívar did come back to the Western Hemisphere? What would they say? Write a dialogue between them about cooperation in the Americas.

19 **Economics** Write a speech for the Summit of the Americas about education and economic growth. How important is education for a modern economy?

Activities

National Heritage/Art Activity
How is the United States a blend of cultures, as Mexico is? Choose one ethnic group and find out how their culture has influenced modern U.S. culture. Make a poster illustrating their contribution.

Economics/Research Activity
Find out about the products your family buys. Are they made in this country or another country? Make a chart showing all the products your family bought in a week and where they came from.

Internet Option

Check the **Internet Social Studies Center** for ideas on how to extend your theme project beyond your classroom.

THEME PROJECT CHECK-IN

To complete your project, use the information you have about our hemisphere to answer these questions:
• What are some important places in neighboring countries?
• How have the countries in our hemisphere worked together?
• What effect do other American countries have on people in the United States?

Reference Databank

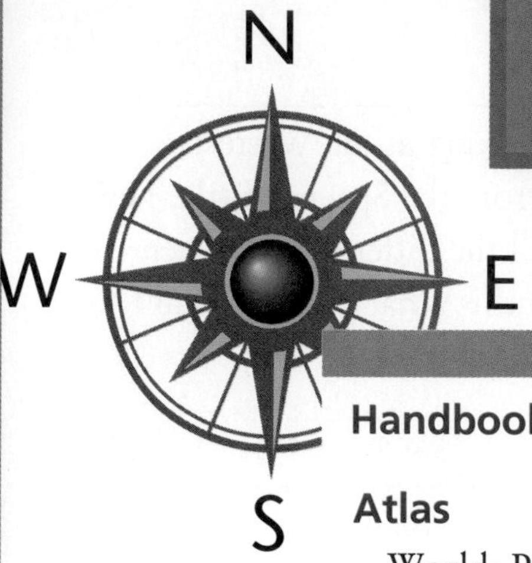

N

W   E

S

Pacific
Ocean

North
America

IN CONGRE
anonimous Declaration

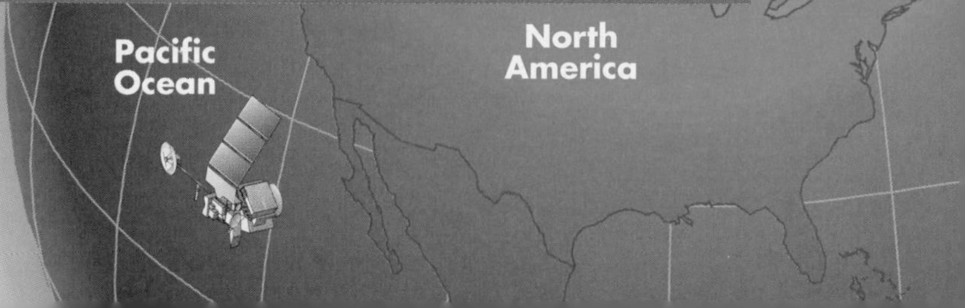

Handbook for Learners

Handbook for Learners

You may have noticed that this book is full of maps, charts, graphs, and photographs. You can learn about the resources of the United States from a map. A chart shows populations of different cities. As you travel through the world of Social Studies, these pictures and their information will be very useful. Knowing how to use and understand them is an important set of skills. You can use this handbook to practice skills you know, or learn new ones.

Contents

Reviewing Map and Globe Skills

Reading Maps

A map is a good place to begin any journey. Where in the world is our nation's capital, the District of Columbia? On what street is the White House? What is the distance between the Lincoln and Jefferson Memorials? Maps can help you answer all these questions.

A map is a special kind of picture of a place — a view from above. Mapmakers use many tools to make accurate maps.

This is a **satellite photograph** of the earth. With satellite photographs, mapmakers locate landforms and bodies of water. Other aerial photographs help mapmakers position streets and buildings correctly.

Use It

If you were making a map from the satellite photo on this page, you'd want to know what you were looking at. Make a list of the landforms and bodies of water you can see in the photograph.

Washington, D. C.

In this photograph you can see parts of the Lincoln Memorial, the Washington Monument, and the Capitol.

Going Further

Make a simple map of your town that includes a title, legend, compass rose, and scale. Make an inset showing the area around your school.

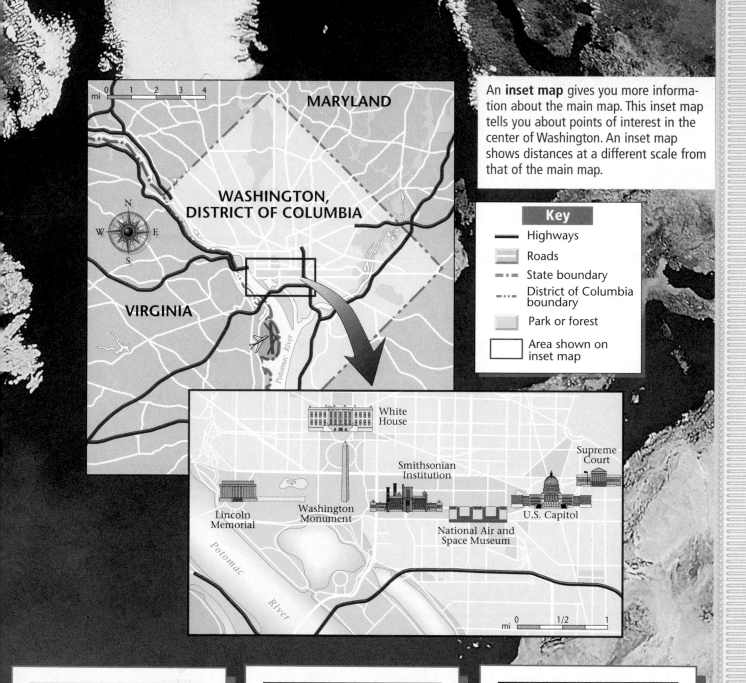

An **inset map** gives you more information about the main map. This inset map tells you about points of interest in the center of Washington. An inset map shows distances at a different scale from that of the main map.

Key
— Highways
Roads
State boundary
District of Columbia boundary
Park or forest
Area shown on inset map

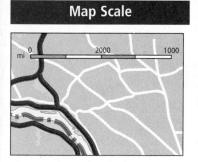

Map Scale

The **map scale** shows the scale of distance on the map. You can use it to measure areas the map covers.

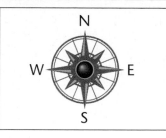

Compass Rose

Compass roses label the cardinal directions — north, south, east, and west. Some compass roses also identify intermediate directions.

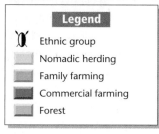

Legend

Legend
Ethnic group
Nomadic herding
Family farming
Commercial farming
Forest

The **legend** or **key** identifies and explains the map symbols. Symbols can include shapes, pictures, and lines. Color may also be used as a symbol.

Dividing Up the Globe

Geographers identify and locate places on the earth by using landforms, bodies of water, and other features. There's another system geographers use to find a global address. It's the system of latitude and longitude. The equator and prime meridian, the bases for finding latitude and longitude, also divide the earth into hemispheres. Hemisphere maps show half the globe at once.

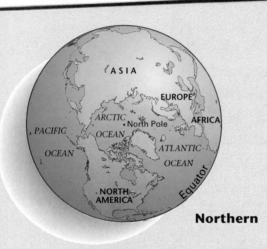

Northern

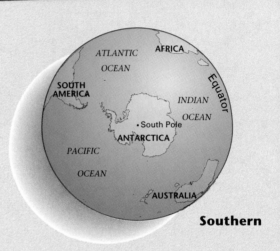

Southern

The equator divides the earth into the **Northern** and **Southern Hemispheres.**

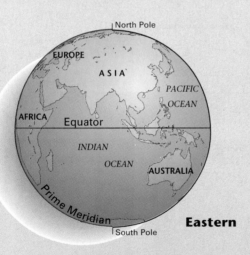

Eastern

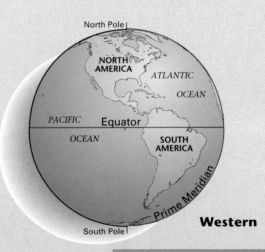

Western

The prime meridian divides the earth into the **Eastern** and **Western Hemispheres.**

Use It

Using the hemisphere maps, make a list of the seven continents — Africa, Antarctica, Asia, Australia, Europe, North America, South America — and list what hemispheres they are found in.

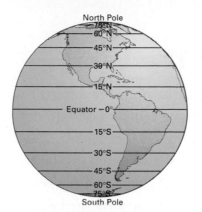

Latitude

Lines of latitude, or parallels, circle the globe in an east-west direction. The equator is at 0° latitude. Geographers number lines of latitude in degrees north or south of the equator.

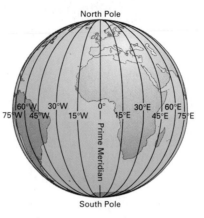

Longitude

Lines of longitude, or meridians, which run from pole to pole, get closer together as they near the poles. The prime meridian is at 0° longitude. Geographers number lines of longitude in degrees east or west of the prime meridian.

This man is using a tool which helps him find his exact latitude.

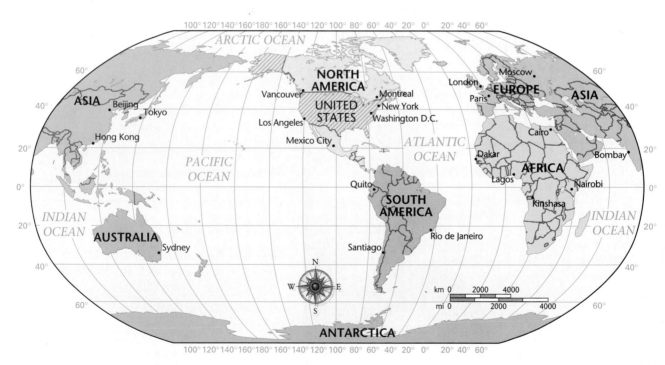

Going Further

Using an atlas or globe, find the coordinates of latitude and longitude of your community, your state capital, and Washington, D.C.

The numbers of latitude and longitude that identify a place's location are its **coordinates.** For example, the coordinates of Tokyo, Japan are 35° N, 139° E.

Reviewing Map and Globe Skills   **613**

Maps of The Land

You can see that there are many different ways to show a part of the world on a map. Each kind of map has a special purpose, with particular information to give the map reader. The four maps on these pages are called physical maps. **Physical maps** give you information about physical features of the land.

A map's title and legend are the key to reading any map. These four maps show resources, landforms, elevation, or climate. Each map uses different symbols to show its information.

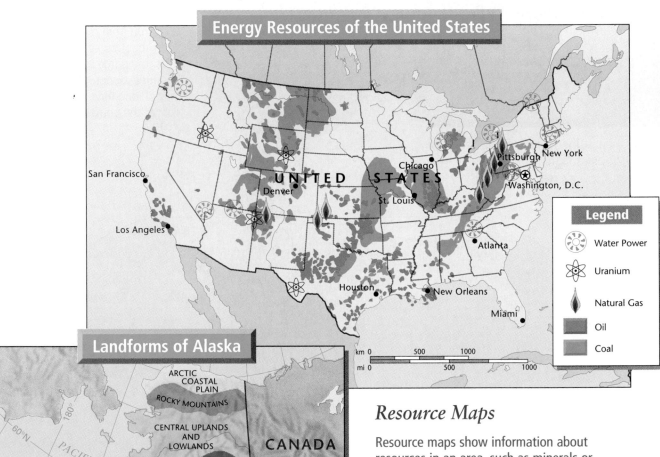

Energy Resources of the United States

Legend

⊙ Water Power

⊛ Uranium

◆ Natural Gas

▬ Oil

▬ Coal

Landforms of Alaska

ARCTIC COASTAL PLAIN
ROCKY MOUNTAINS
CENTRAL UPLANDS AND LOWLANDS
PACIFIC RANGES AND VALLEYS
CANADA
PACIFIC OCEAN

Resource Maps

Resource maps show information about resources in an area, such as minerals or crops. Resource maps can help you understand how people earn a living in a certain region.

Landform Maps

Landform maps show the different types of natural features in an area. This map does not have a legend. Instead, the different landforms are labeled in their general location.

Use It

Look at the map of United States energy resources. What kinds of energy resources do you have in your state? What other states have the same kinds of energy resources?

Western United States

Olympia
Mt. Rainier ▲
(14,410 ft.)
WASHINGTON
Salem ★
CASCADE RANGE
Columbia River
PACIFIC OCEAN
40°N
OREGON
Snake River
IDAHO
Boise ★
COAST RANGES
CENTRAL VALLEY
SIERRA NEVADA
CALIFORNIA
Sacramento ★
Carson City ★
NEVADA
Great Salt Lake
Mt. Whitney (14,495 ft.) ▲
Mt. Elbert (14,433 ft.) ▲
COAST RANGES
▼ Death Valley (−282 ft.)
MOJAVE DESERT
Colorado River
ARIZONA
Phoenix ★
CANADA
100°W
Missouri River
MONTANA
Helena ★
NORTH DAKOTA
SOUTH DAKOTA
WYOMING
ROCKY MOUNTAINS
CONTINENTAL DIVIDE
Cheyenne ★
NEBRASKA
Salt Lake City ★
UTAH
Denver ★
COLORADO
KANSAS
Santa Fe ★
OKLAHOMA
NEW MEXICO
TEXAS
Rio Grande
MEXICO

km 0   250   500
mi 0   250   500

Elevation Maps

Elevation maps show just how much above or below sea level the land is. Elevation maps are color coded so that each color represents a different range of feet or meters.

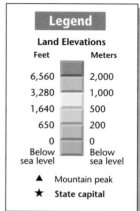

Legend

Land Elevations

Feet	Meters
6,560	2,000
3,280	1,000
1,640	500
650	200
0	0
Below sea level	Below sea level

▲ Mountain peak
★ State capital

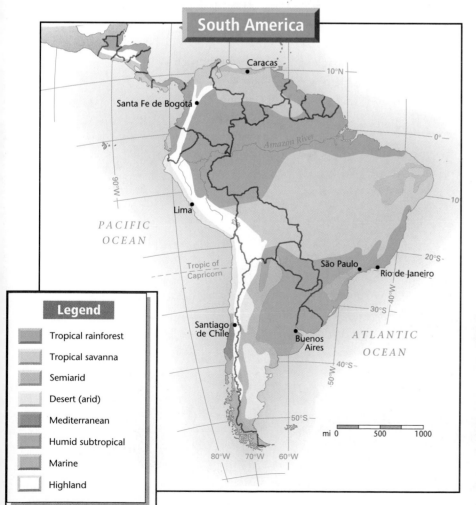

South America

Caracas
10°N
Santa Fe de Bogotá
Amazon River
0°
90°W
Lima
PACIFIC OCEAN
Tropic of Capricorn
10
São Paulo
Rio de Janeiro
20°S
30°S
40°W
Santiago de Chile
Buenos Aires
ATLANTIC OCEAN
40°S
50°W
50°S
80°W 70°W 60°W

mi 0   500   1000

Climate Maps

Climate maps give you information about the average weather at a place over a period of years. Some climate maps show specific information about temperature or precipitation. Others use special names to describe types of climate.

Legend

■ Tropical rainforest
■ Tropical savanna
■ Semiarid
■ Desert (arid)
■ Mediterranean
■ Humid subtropical
■ Marine
□ Highland

Going Further

Think about the area around your community. Make map legends you would use to create landform, elevation, climate, and resource maps for your community.

Maps About People

Geography is about more than the shape of the land. So are maps! Maps can show almost anything you can imagine about what people do on the earth, even where they live and what they eat. These three maps help you understand more about life in different parts of the United States.

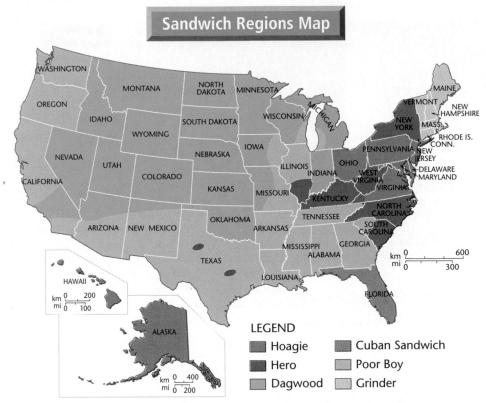

Sandwich Regions Map

LEGEND
- Hoagie
- Hero
- Dagwood
- Cuban Sandwich
- Poor Boy
- Grinder

Culture Maps

Language is an important part of culture. Americans use many different words for the same kind of sandwich. A culture map shows that kind of information.

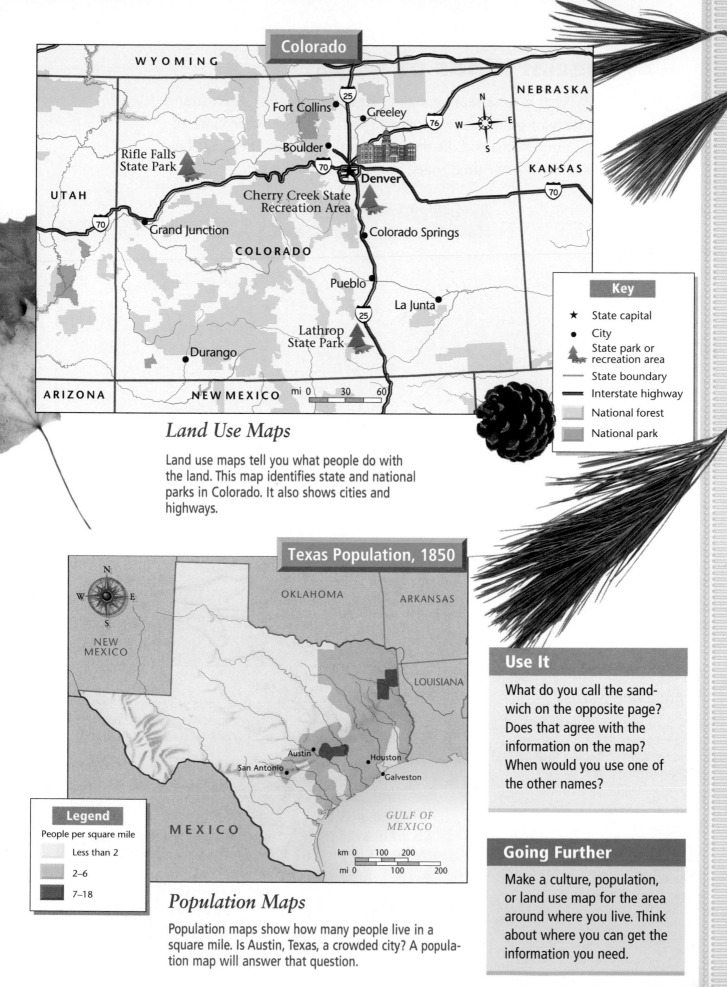

Land Use Maps

Land use maps tell you what people do with the land. This map identifies state and national parks in Colorado. It also shows cities and highways.

Key
- ★ State capital
- ● City
- 🌲 State park or recreation area
- State boundary
- Interstate highway
- National forest
- National park

Population Maps

Population maps show how many people live in a square mile. Is Austin, Texas, a crowded city? A population map will answer that question.

Legend
People per square mile
- Less than 2
- 2–6
- 7–18

Use It

What do you call the sandwich on the opposite page? Does that agree with the information on the map? When would you use one of the other names?

Going Further

Make a culture, population, or land use map for the area around where you live. Think about where you can get the information you need.

Special Kinds of Maps

You've seen maps about land and maps about people. There are still plenty of other kinds of maps to see! There are other kinds of special purpose maps. Like the maps on these pages, they can show roads and towns or time zones; they can even tell a story.

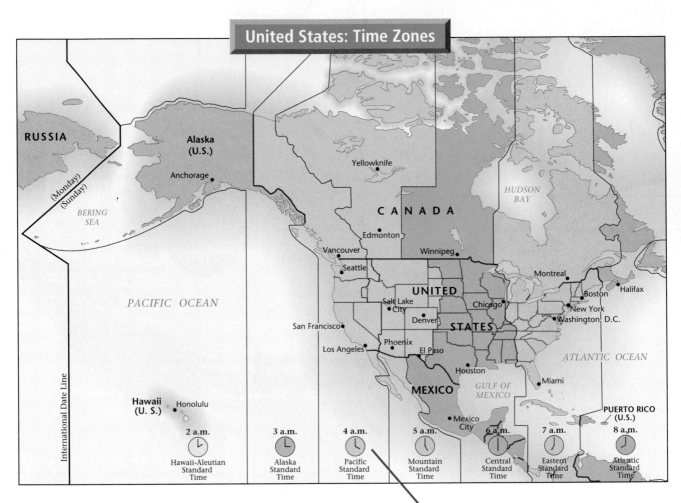

United States: Time Zones

RUSSIA

Alaska (U.S.)

Yellowknife

Anchorage

BERING SEA

(Monday) (Sunday)

HUDSON BAY

CANADA

Edmonton

PACIFIC OCEAN

Vancouver

Winnipeg

Seattle

Montreal

UNITED

Boston   Halifax

Salt Lake City

Chicago

New York

San Francisco

Denver   STATES

Washington, D.C.

Los Angeles

Phoenix

El Paso

ATLANTIC OCEAN

Houston

MEXICO

GULF OF MEXICO

Miami

International Date Line

Hawaii (U. S.)   Honolulu

Mexico City

PUERTO RICO (U.S.)

2 a.m.   3 a.m.   4 a.m.   5 a.m.   6 a.m.   7 a.m.   8 a.m.

Hawaii-Aleutian Standard Time   Alaska Standard Time   Pacific Standard Time   Mountain Standard Time   Central Standard Time   Eastern Standard Time   Atlantic Standard Time

Time Zone Maps

Time zone maps show what time it is in different places. Most U.S. time zone maps use lines and colors to show the nation's different time zones.

These clocks help you compare the time in the time zones. As you move from east to west, it is one hour earlier in each zone.

Use It

It can be hard to tell what time it is in Chicago if you're in Los Angeles. A map makes it easier. What time is it in New York, New York, if it's 9 a.m. in Seattle, Washington? What time is it in Houston, Texas?

Going Further

On a road map of your state, find out how far it is from your community to the state capital. Write down how you would get there.

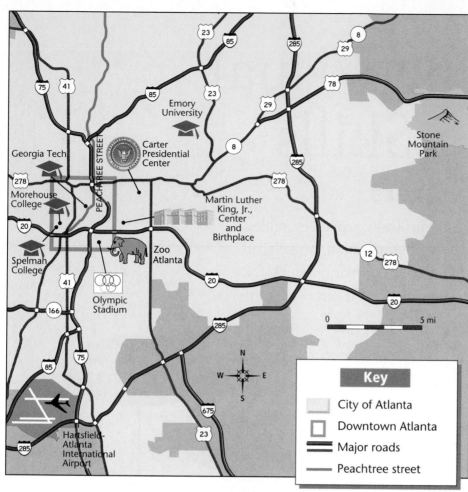

Road Maps

Road maps show the routes that connect cities and towns. Road maps use symbols to identify different kinds of roads and points of interest.

Key

- City of Atlanta
- Downtown Atlanta
- Major roads
- Peachtree street

Story Maps

Story maps use words and pictures to tell a story on a map. This map tells you some of the story of Captain John Smith. Story maps often use numbered captions to show events in order.

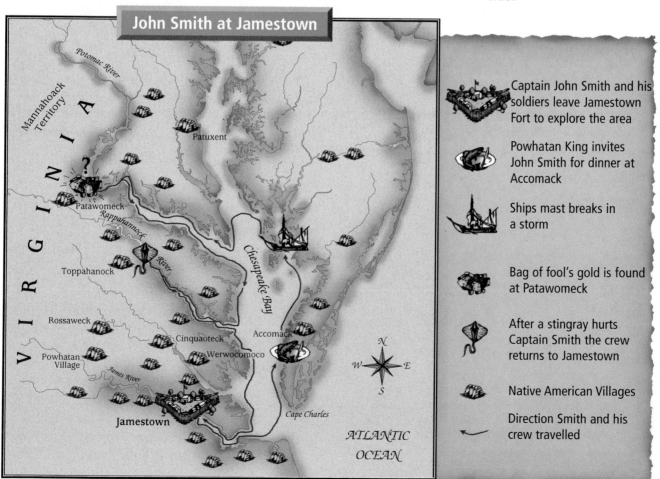

John Smith at Jamestown

Captain John Smith and his soldiers leave Jamestown Fort to explore the area

Powhatan King invites John Smith for dinner at Accomack

Ships mast breaks in a storm

Bag of fool's gold is found at Patawomeck

After a stingray hurts Captain Smith the crew returns to Jamestown

Native American Villages

Direction Smith and his crew travelled

Reviewing Visual Learning Skills

Graphic Organizers

Graphic organizers, such as word webs, schedules, tables, and graphs, can help to organize information. These visual tools let you understand a lot of information quickly. They help you see relationships among the pieces of information.

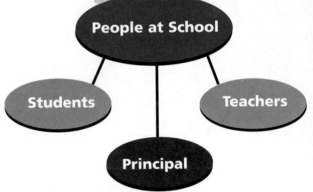

Trains from Boston to New York

Boston	5:00 a.m.	6:40 a.m.	9:20 a.m.	12:15 p.m.
Providence	5:40 a.m.	7:10 a.m.	10:10 a.m.	1:20 p.m.
New Haven	7:50 a.m.	9:30 a.m.	12:00 a.m.	3:25 p.m.
New York	9:30 a.m.	10:50 a.m.	1:40 a.m.	4:30 p.m.

Schedules

A schedule gives information about time — arrival and departure times, or hours of operation, for example. A schedule is a kind of table, with rows and columns.

Word Webs

Word webs show related words or ideas. Word webs can help you think of questions for reports or answer questions about other topics.

Population Table

	1989	1990	1991	1992	1993
Colorado	3,276,000	3,294,000	3,370,000	3,456,000	3,586,000
Arkansas	2,346,000	2,351,000	2,371,000	2,394,000	2,424,000

Tables

Tables organize information into rows and columns. Tables have rows that go across and columns that run down the page. Rows contain information about one subject. Columns have a subject or topic heading.

Use It

You can choose your schedule by looking at a schedule. If you leave Boston on the 12:15 train, when will you arrive in New York? If you have to be in New York before noon, when do you have to leave Boston?

Graphs

Graphs are diagrams of statistics, or number data, about a topic. They can provide data for specific years, showing us how the data has changed over time.

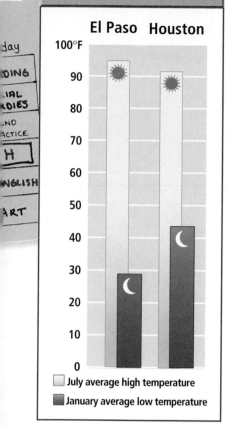

Bar Graphs

A bar graph uses bars to represent data. You can compare information quickly using a bar graph.

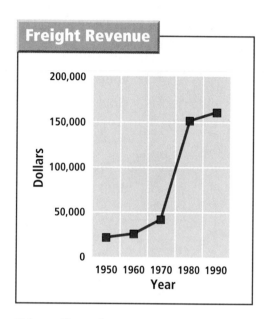

Line Graphs

A line graph is made up of connected points, instead of symbols or bars. Each point is the intersection of information from the horizontal and vertical axes.

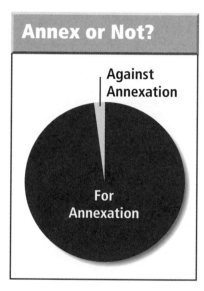

Circle Graphs

A circle or pie graph shows data as parts or percentages of a whole. You can compare "pieces of the pie" to see how they relate to the whole.

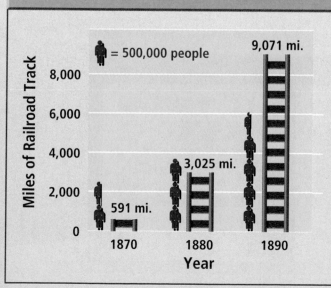

Railroad and Population Growth in Texas

Picture Graphs

A picture graph uses symbols to present information. Each symbol stands for a certain number of objects or an amount. Parts of numbers can be shown by using a fraction of a symbol.

Going Further

Make a circle graph that shows the percentage of age groups in your class. Make a bar graph of the same information. Write about what is different about the graphs.

Sequencing

Sometimes you need to show a process or change in a diagram. Timelines and flow charts are two useful ways to show sequence.

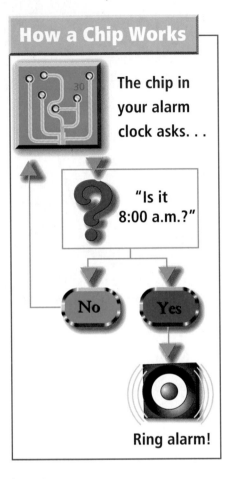

How a Chip Works

The chip in your alarm clock asks. . .

"Is it 8:00 a.m.?"

No   Yes

Ring alarm!

Flow Charts

A flow chart shows the steps of a process, such as the ringing of an alarm clock. Arrows show the "flow" from one stage or event to another.

Timelines

A timeline puts events in chronological order along a vertical or horizontal line. Chronological order is the order in which events occurred.

Chapter Preview: *People, Places, and Events*

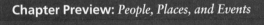

1400   1450   1500

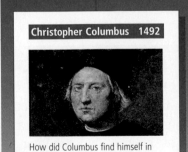

Christopher Columbus 1492

How did Columbus find himself in the Americas? *Lesson 1, Page 93*

Bartolomé de las Casas 1511

Las Casas was upset with the Spanish settlers in the Americas. Find out why. *Lesson 2, Page 109*

Montezuma

What empire did Montezuma rule over? *Lesson 2, Page 102*

Illustrations

A Chinese proverb says, "One picture is worth more than a thousand words." Photographs, paintings, diagrams, cartoons — all of these illustrate people, places, and events in ways that words cannot.

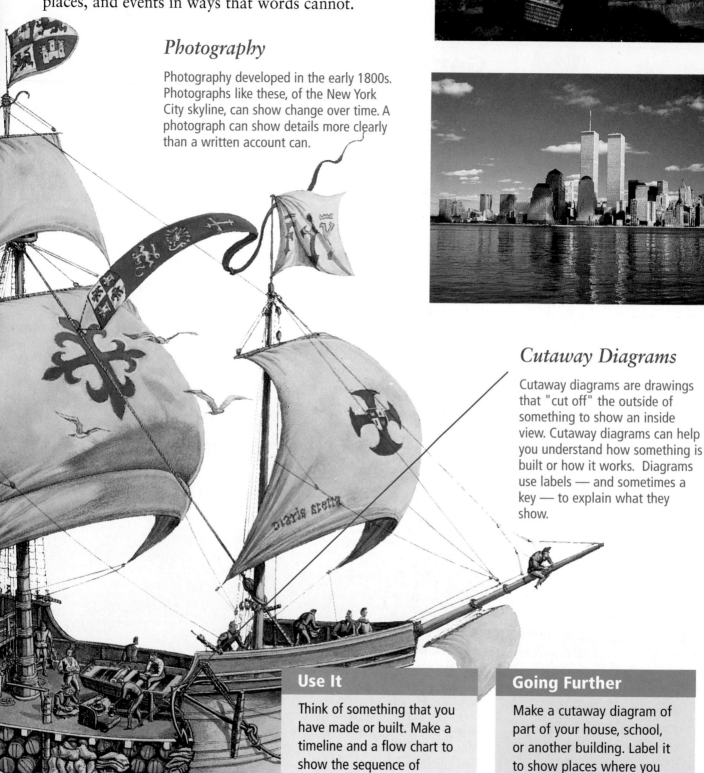

Photography

Photography developed in the early 1800s. Photographs like these, of the New York City skyline, can show change over time. A photograph can show details more clearly than a written account can.

Cutaway Diagrams

Cutaway diagrams are drawings that "cut off" the outside of something to show an inside view. Cutaway diagrams can help you understand how something is built or how it works. Diagrams use labels — and sometimes a key — to explain what they show.

Use It

Think of something that you have made or built. Make a timeline and a flow chart to show the sequence of events.

Going Further

Make a cutaway diagram of part of your house, school, or another building. Label it to show places where you do different things.

Reviewing Social Studies Skills

Korea
by Sylvia McNair
Children's Press, 1986
Call no: DS 902.M35 19

The Koreans: Contempo
and Society
by Donald S. Macdonal
Westview, 1990
Call no: DS 907.6

Gathering Information

Suppose your class is planning a trip to Washington, D.C. You'll need a lot of information before you go. Research — finding information — can give you answers to your questions. The research tools you use for planning your trip are important tools for gathering information on many subjects.

Did you know that people are valuable resources? You probably know a lot about some things. By sharing that information, you can help other people in their research. So, in planning your trip to Washington you might start by talking to people who have been there.

Interviews

Interviews give you in-depth information from one person. For a successful interview, you need to plan in advance. Decide what you want to find out and write down your questions. It helps to organize your questions into categories or groups.

During the interview, write down the answers you are given. When the interview is over, don't forget to say thank you!

Use It

Make a list of questions you'd like to ask people about Washington. Use a survey or interviews to ask several people your questions.

Surveys

Surveys offer people a choice of answers: Have you been to Washington — yes or no? How many days did you stay — 1–2, more than 3, more than 5? When you complete the survey and add up the answers, you can see what the majority of people think or do.

Using the Library

One of the best places to find information on any subject is a library. There you'll find books, encyclopedias, atlases, newspapers, magazines, films — resources of every kind. One of the best resources to help you is the librarian.

To find resources to plan your trip to Washington, begin with the catalogue. Today, library catalogues come in many forms. Some list books and other sources on cards. Other catalogues are in books or on computers.

Use as many different sources as you can. You'll find different kinds of information in a guidebook, an atlas, an encyclopedia, and a history book.

Going Further

Go to the library and find three different sources of information about Washington. Write down the title of each source and describe what you learned from it.

Your librarian can show you where books are. So can the library catalogue. Books you find in the catalogue are filed on the shelves by their **call numbers.** These are listed on the bottom of the spine of the book, as they are here.

KF
5051
.c6
1994

E
276
.c5
1991

PE
1068
.B37
1986

Writing Reports

Whether or not you take a trip to Washington, you can share information about the capital by researching and writing a report. You can include in your report what you learned from surveys and interviews as well as what you learned from your library research. And if you're lucky, you can include what you learned on your own trip to Washington!

You'll find both primary and secondary sources when you do research about Washington. To identify whether or not written material is a primary source, look for clues such as the use of words like *I, me,* or *we.*

"We have indeed come into a new country. You must keep all this to yourself, and when asked how I like it, say that I write you the situation is beautiful, which is true . . . . The house is made habitable, but there is not a single apartment finished, and all withinside except the plastering has been done since Briesler [a servant] came . . . . The great unfinished Audience room [today it is the East Room] I make a drying room to hang up the clothes in."

Primary Sources

Primary sources are first-hand accounts of events that have occurred. If you write a letter or article about your own trip, this description is a primary source. This primary source was written by Abigail Adams when she lived in the White House.

Secondary Sources

Secondary sources are accounts of events written by someone who was not there. A description of your trip written by someone else, who was not there, is a secondary source. This secondary source comes from a book about Washington, D.C.

It made no sense to her that they should be surrounded by forests, and yet not be able to get enough wood to burn in their fireplaces. The Brieslers had not been able to find anyone to cut wood, or to cart it to the house... Everyone in the city was so cold that at last the public officers had sent to Philadelphia for woodcutters and Pennsylvania wagons to carry the wood

Writing a good report requires organization. First, you need to take careful notes about what you read. Then, you need to make a good outline before writing. And you need to write your report in a clear and interesting way.

1 To organize your research, make a **list** of the questions you want your report to answer. Then write each question at the top of a **note card**.

2 Write down the information you find to answer each question. Carefully note the title, author, and pages of the books you use.

3 When you have the information you need, organize your note cards into groups by topic. Then you can begin an **outline** like this one. Use Roman numerals for the main ideas. Use capital letters for the supporting details.

4 Use your outline to write the report. A good **report** includes an introduction, a main body of the report, and a conclusion. In the introduction, tell the reader the main ideas of your report. Present details about each idea in the body of the report. Summarize those ideas in the conclusion.

He made the builders start the main stairway to the

He moved the front door to the north side of the building and turned the old entrance area into the Blue Room. (p. 64)

The White House in the Early 180

I. John and Abigail Adams were the first occupants of the White House.
   A. The White House was not finish
   B. There was no laundry room, so c they moved in in November 1800.
   C. There was a shortage of firewood. T were hung up to dry in a reception house was very cold.

Thomas Jefferson changed the White House by makin it more livable.
   A. He had the   main stairway to the second floor built.
   B. He moved the front door to a better location.
   C. He installed indoor toilets.
   D. He brought a French chef and entertained t dinner.

Use It

Make a list of the differences you see between the primary source from Abigail Adams and the secondary source from the book.

Going Further

Choose a historical building that interests you, such as the Empire State Building. Make a list of questions you'd like to answer about it. If possible, do the research and write a report about the building.

Atlas

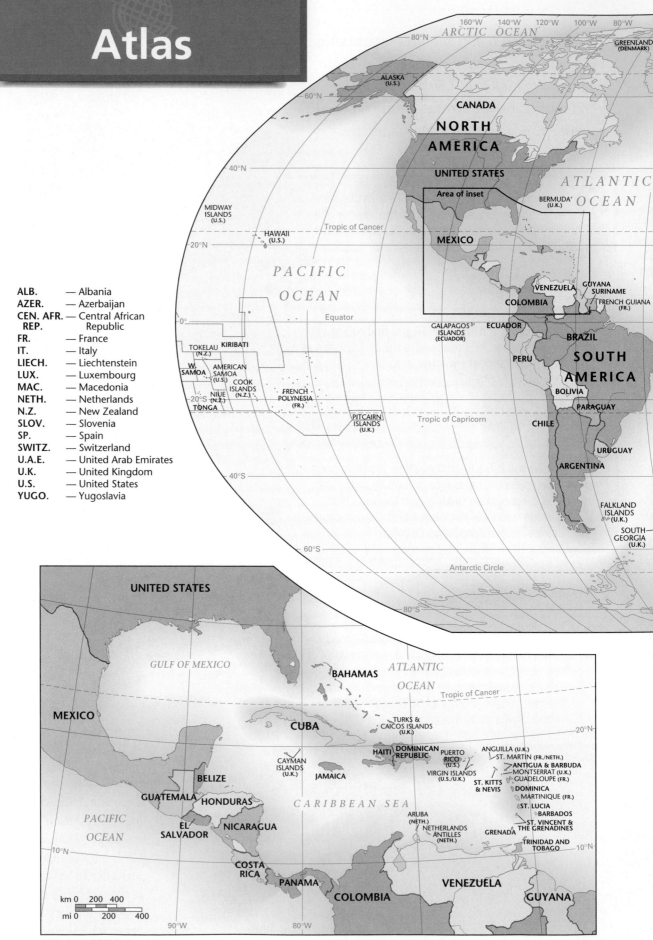

ALB. — Albania
AZER. — Azerbaijan
CEN. AFR. — Central African
REP. — Republic
FR. — France
IT. — Italy
LIECH. — Liechtenstein
LUX. — Luxembourg
MAC. — Macedonia
NETH. — Netherlands
N.Z. — New Zealand
SLOV. — Slovenia
SP. — Spain
SWITZ. — Switzerland
U.A.E. — United Arab Emirates
U.K. — United Kingdom
U.S. — United States
YUGO. — Yugoslavia

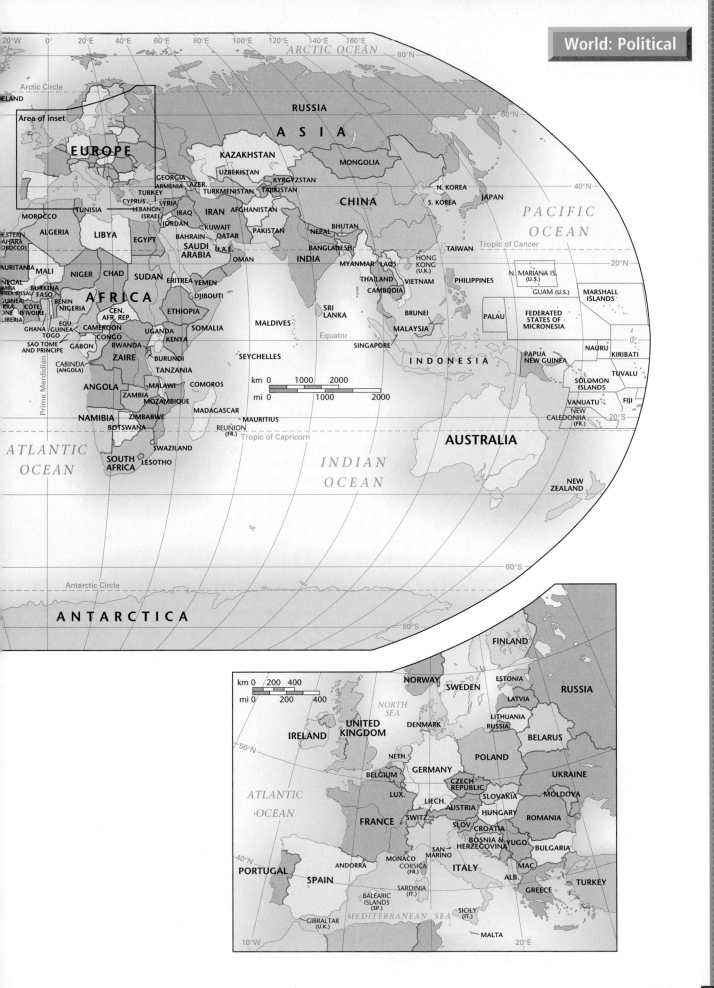

20°W   0°   20°E   40°E   60°E   80°E   100°E   120°E   140°E   160°E

ARCTIC OCEAN   80°N

Arctic Circle

ELAND

Area of inset

RUSSIA   60°N

EUROPE

A   S   I   A

KAZAKHSTAN   MONGOLIA

UZBEKISTAN   KYRGYZSTAN   N. KOREA   40°N
GEORGIA
ARMENIA   AZER.   TURKMENISTAN   TAJIKISTAN   S. KOREA   JAPAN
TURKEY   CHINA
CYPRUS   SYRIA   AFGHANISTAN
LEBANON   IRAQ   IRAN   PAKISTAN   NEPAL   BHUTAN   PACIFIC
ISRAEL   JORDAN   OCEAN
TUNISIA   BAHRAIN   KUWAIT   BANGLADESH   TAIWAN
MOROCCO   QATAR   SAUDI   Tropic of Cancer
ALGERIA   LIBYA   EGYPT   U.A.E.   ARABIA   INDIA   MYANMAR   LAOS   HONG   20°N
WESTERN   KONG
AHARA   OMAN   MYANMAR   (U.K.)   N. MARIANA IS.
ROCCO)   THAILAND   VIETNAM   (U.S.)   MARSHALL
URITANIA   MALI   NIGER   CHAD   SUDAN   ERITREA   YEMEN   CAMBODIA   PHILIPPINES   GUAM (U.S.)   ISLANDS
NEGAL   DJIBOUTI   SRI   BRUNEI   PALAU   FEDERATED
MBIA   BURKINA   AFRICA   LANKA   MALDIVES   MALAYSIA   STATES OF
GUINEA-BISSAU   FASO   NIGERIA   CEN.   ETHIOPIA   Equator   SINGAPORE   MICRONESIA
RRA   GUINEA   AFR. REP.   NAURU
ONE   D'IVOIRE   BENIN   CAMEROON   UGANDA   SOMALIA   SEYCHELLES   INDONESIA   PAPUA   KIRIBATI
LIBERIA   GHANA   EQU.   CONGO   RWANDA   KENYA   NEW GUINEA   TUVALU
TOGO   GUINEA   ZAIRE   BURUNDI   SOLOMON
SAO TOME   GABON   TANZANIA   ISLANDS
AND PRINCIPE   CABINDA   VANUATU   FIJI
(ANGOLA)   ANGOLA   MALAWI   COMOROS   km 0   1000   2000   NEW   20°S
ZAMBIA   MOZAMBIQUE   mi 0   1000   2000   CALEDONIIA
NAMIBIA   ZIMBABWE   MADAGASCAR   (FR.)
BOTSWANA   MAURITIUS   AUSTRALIA
ATLANTIC   SWAZILAND   REUNION
OCEAN   SOUTH   LESOTHO   (FR.)   Tropic of Capricorn   INDIAN
AFRICA   OCEAN   NEW
                                                   ZEALAND

                                                   60°S

Antarctic Circle   80°S

A N T A R C T I C A

km 0   200   400
mi 0   200   400   FINLAND

                         NORWAY   ESTONIA
                    SWEDEN   RUSSIA
                    NORTH   LATVIA
IRELAND   UNITED   SEA   DENMARK   LITHUANIA
        KINGDOM   RUSSIA   BELARUS
                NETH.   POLAND
        BELGIUM   GERMANY   UKRAINE
ATLANTIC   LUX.   CZECH   SLOVAKIA   MOLDOVA
OCEAN   LIECH.   REPUBLIC   HUNGARY   ROMANIA
                FRANCE   SWITZ.   AUSTRIA
                         SLOV.   CROATIA   YUGO.   BULGARIA
                MONACO   SAN   BOSNIA &   MAC.
PORTUGAL   ANDORRA   CORSICA   MARINO   HERZEGOVINA   ALB.
        SPAIN   (FR.)   ITALY   GREECE   TURKEY
                BALEARIC
                ISLANDS
                (SP.)   SARDINIA   SICILY
GIBRALTAR   (IT.)   (IT.)
(U.K.)   MEDITERRANEAN SEA   MALTA

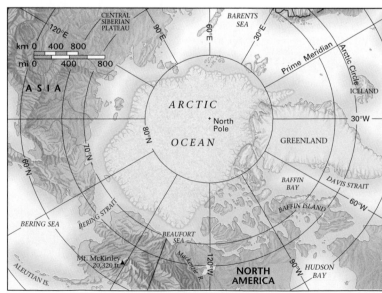
80°N
ARCTIC OCEAN
BEAUFORT
SEA
160°W 140°W 120°W 100°W

BAFFIN
BAY

GREENLAND

Bering Strait

Mt. McKinley
20,320 ft

Mackenzie R.

HUDSON
BAY

NORTH
AMERICA

Lake
Winnipeg

60°N

BERING
SEA

GULF OF
ALASKA

ROCKY MOUNTAINS

Great Lakes

VANCOUVER
ISLAND

GREAT
PLAINS

Missouri R.

40°N

APPALACHIAN MTS.

CAPE HATTERAS

SAN
FRANCISCO
BAY

Mt. Whitney
14,495 ft.

Mississippi R.

ATLANTIC
OCEAN

Tropic of Cancer

GULF OF
MEXICO

WEST INDIES

20°N

YUCATAN
PENINSULA

GREATER
ANTILLES

CARIBBEAN SEA

LESSER ANTILLES

HAWAIIAN IS.

PACIFIC OCEAN

ISTHMUS OF
PANAMA

P O L Y N E S I A

AMAZON
BASIN

Amazon R.

SOUTH
AMERICA

0°   Equator

km 0   1000   2000

mi 0   1000   2000

BRAZILIAN
HIGHLANDS

ANDES MOUNTAINS

Paraná R.

20°S   Tropic of Capricorn

Mt. Aconcagua
22,831 ft.

PAMPAS

40°S

High mountains
Low mountains
Desert
Interior
plains
Coastal
plains

Ice cap

STRAIT OF
MAGELLAN

CAPE HORN

60°S

Antarctic Circle

80°S

© 1996 GEOSYSTEMS GLOBAL CORP.

CENTRAL
SIBERIAN
PLATEAU

120°E

90°E

60°E

30°E

BARENTS
SEA

km 0   400   800

mi 0   400   800

Prime Meridian

Arctic Circle

ASIA

ARCTIC

ICELAND

30°W

80°N

North
Pole

OCEAN

GREENLAND

70°N

60°N

BAFFIN
BAY

DAVIS STRAIT

60°W

BERING SEA

BERING STRAIT

BAFFIN ISLAND

BEAUFORT
SEA

Mackenzie R.

120°W

90°W

HUDSON
BAY

ALEUTIAN IS.

Mt. McKinley
20,320 ft.

NORTH
AMERICA

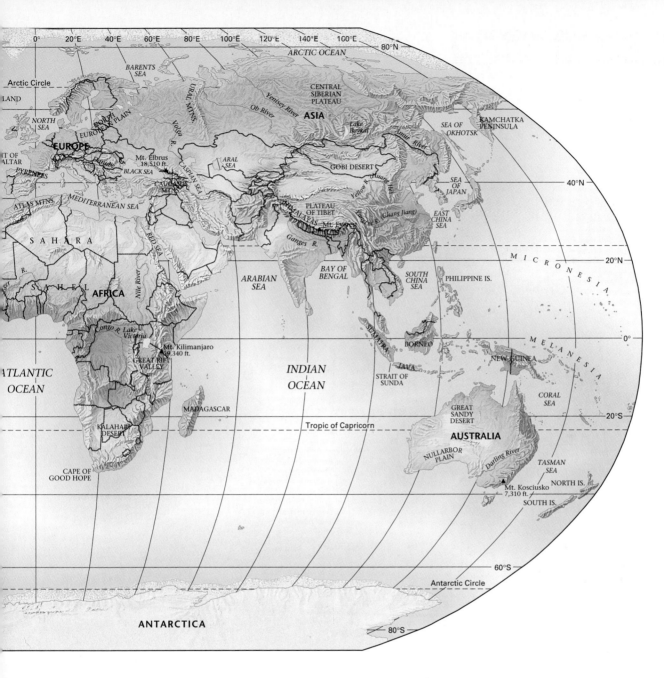

ARCTIC OCEAN

Arctic Circle

LAND

BARENTS
SEA

CENTRAL
SIBERIAN
PLATEAU

URAL MTNS.

Yenisey River

Ob River

ASIA

Lake
Baikal

Amur
River

SEA OF
OKHOTSK

KAMCHATKA
PENINSULA

NORTH
SEA

EUROPEAN PLAIN

EUROPE

Mt. Elbrus
18,510 ft.

Volga R.

CASPIAN SEA

ARAL
SEA

GOBI DESERT

Huang He

Yellow R.

SEA
OF
JAPAN

40°N

T OF
ALTAR

PYRENEES

Danube

BLACK SEA

CAUCASUS
MTNS.

PLATEAU
OF TIBET

HIMALAYAS

Mt. Everest

Yangtze R. (Chang Jiang)

EAST
CHINA
SEA

ATLAS MTNS.

MEDITERRANEAN SEA

RED SEA

Ganges R.

ARABIAN
SEA

BAY OF
BENGAL

SOUTH
CHINA
SEA

PHILIPPINE IS.

M I C R O N E S I A

20°N

SAHARA

r R.

SAHEL

AFRICA

Nile River

Congo R.

Lake
Victoria

Mt. Kilimanjaro
19,340 ft.

GREAT RIFT
VALLEY

SUMATRA

BORNEO

JAVA

STRAIT OF
SUNDA

M E L A N E S I A

NEW GUINEA

0°

ATLANTIC
OCEAN

INDIAN
OCEAN

MADAGASCAR

CORAL
SEA

GREAT
SANDY
DESERT

20°S

KALAHARI
DESERT

Tropic of Capricorn

AUSTRALIA

NULLARBOR
PLAIN

Darling River

TASMAN
SEA

CAPE OF
GOOD HOPE

Mt. Kosciusko
7,310 ft.

NORTH IS.

SOUTH IS.

60°S

Antarctic Circle

ANTARCTICA

80°S

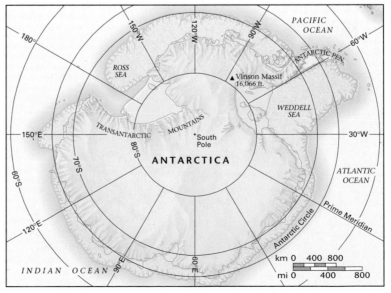

PACIFIC
OCEAN

180

150°W

120°W

90°W

60°W

ROSS
SEA

ANTARCTIC PEN.

Vinson Massif
16,066 ft.

WEDDELL
SEA

150°E

TRANSANTARCTIC MOUNTAINS

South
Pole

ANTARCTICA

30°W

120°E

80°S

70°S

60°E

ATLANTIC
OCEAN

60°S

90°E

60°E

Arctic Circle

Prime Meridian

INDIAN OCEAN

km 0   400   800

mi 0   400   800

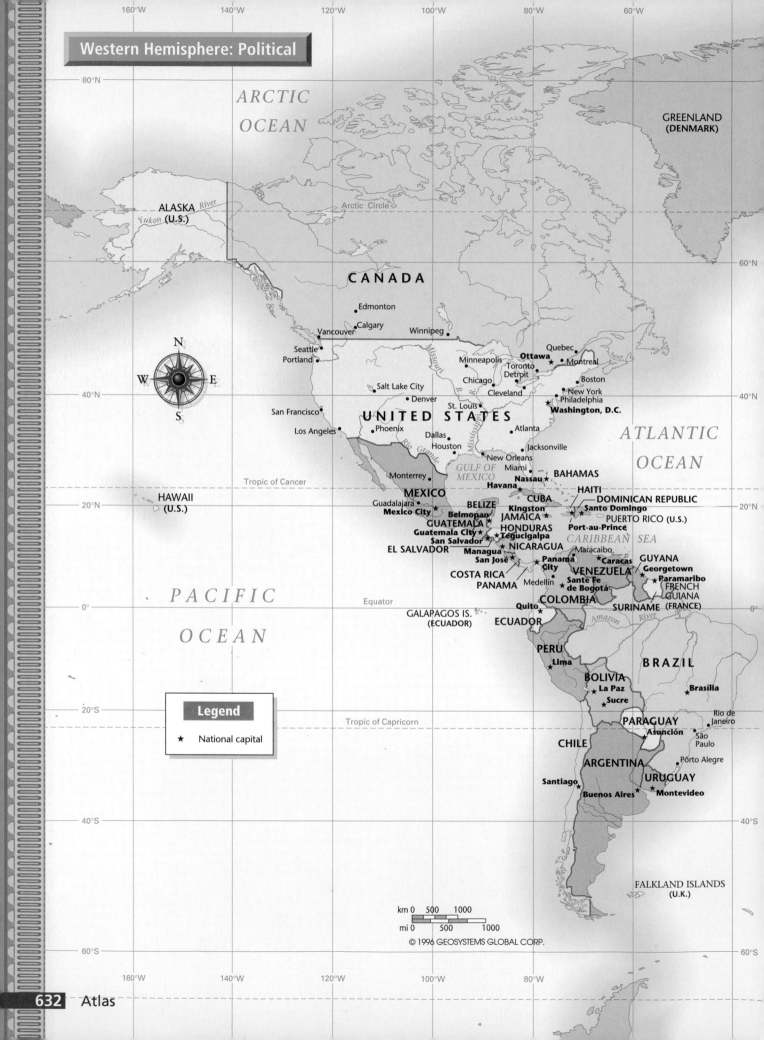

ARCTIC
OCEAN

GREENLAND
(DENMARK)

ALASKA
(U.S.)

Yukon River

Arctic Circle

CANADA

Edmonton
Calgary
Vancouver
Winnipeg
Seattle
Portland
Minneapolis
Quebec
Ottawa ★ Montreal
Toronto
Detroit
Boston
Chicago
Cleveland
New York
Salt Lake City
Denver
St. Louis
Philadelphia
Washington, D.C.
San Francisco
UNITED STATES
Atlanta
ATLANTIC
OCEAN
Los Angeles
Phoenix
Dallas
Houston
Jacksonville
New Orleans
Miami
Monterrey
GULF OF
MEXICO
BAHAMAS
Nassau ★
Havana
HAITI
MEXICO
Guadalajara
CUBA
DOMINICAN REPUBLIC
Mexico City ★
BELIZE
Kingston
Santo Domingo
Belmopan
JAMAICA
PUERTO RICO (U.S.)
GUATEMALA
HONDURAS
Port-au-Prince
Guatemala City ★
Tegucigalpa
CARIBBEAN SEA
San Salvador
NICARAGUA
EL SALVADOR
Managua
Maracaibo
GUYANA
San José
Panama
Caracas
Georgetown
COSTA RICA
City
VENEZUELA
Paramaribo
PANAMA
Medellín
Sante Fe
FRENCH
de Bogotá
GUIANA
SURINAME (FRANCE)
COLOMBIA
Quito
GALAPAGOS IS.
★
(ECUADOR)
ECUADOR
Amazon River

PACIFIC

OCEAN

Equator

PERU
Lima
BRAZIL
BOLIVIA
La Paz
Brasília
Sucre
Rio de
Janeiro
PARAGUAY
Tropic of Capricorn
Asunción
São
Paulo
CHILE
Pôrto Alegre
ARGENTINA
URUGUAY
Santiago
Montevideo
Buenos Aires

FALKLAND ISLANDS
(U.K.)

Tropic of Cancer

HAWAII
(U.S.)

km 0   500   1000
mi 0   500   1000

© 1996 GEOSYSTEMS GLOBAL CORP.

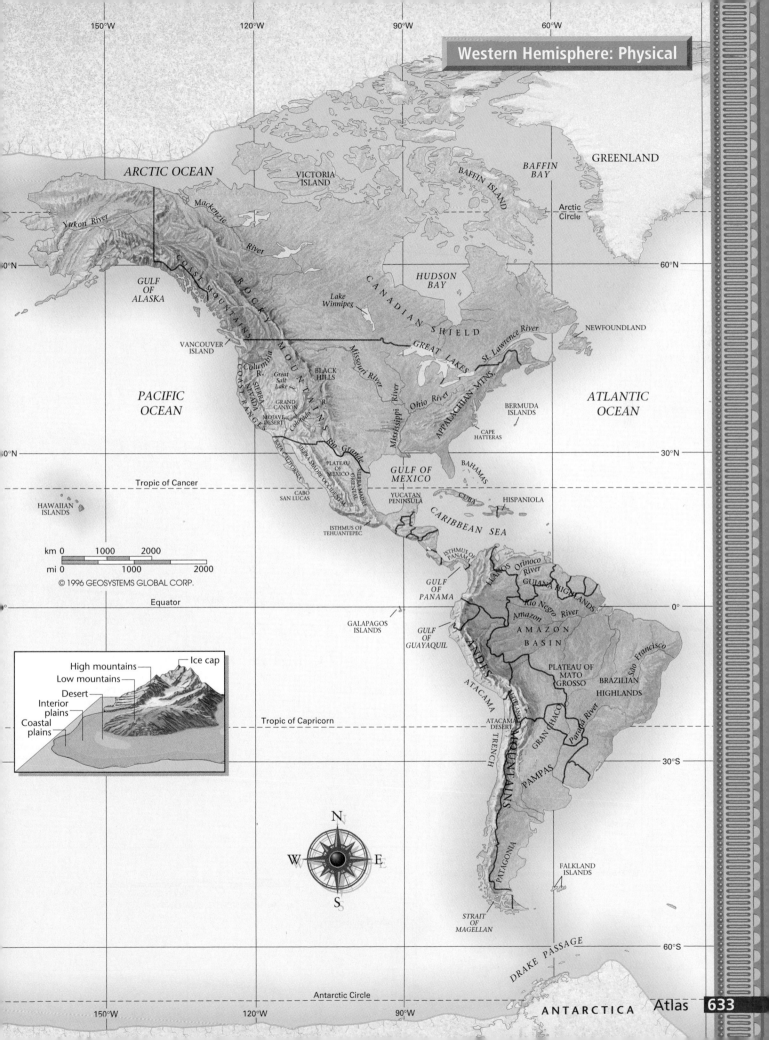

150°W 120°W 90°W 60°W

ARCTIC OCEAN

VICTORIA
ISLAND

BAFFIN
ISLAND

BAFFIN
BAY

GREENLAND

Mackenzie

River

Yukon River

Arctic
Circle

60°N

60°N

GULF
OF
ALASKA

C O A S T M O U N T A I N S

R O C K Y

HUDSON
BAY

C A N A D I A N   S H I E L D

Lake
Winnipeg

NEWFOUNDLAND

VANCOUVER
ISLAND

GREAT
LAKES

St. Lawrence River

PACIFIC
OCEAN

Columbia
R.

Great
Salt
Lake

M O U N T A I N S

BLACK
HILLS

Missouri River

Mississippi River

Ohio River

APPALACHIAN MTNS.

BERMUDA
ISLANDS

ATLANTIC
OCEAN

SIERRA
NEVADA

COAST
RANGES

GRAND
CANYON

MOJAVE
DESERT

Colorado

R.

Rio Grande

CAPE
HATTERAS

30°N

30°N

BAJA CALIFORNIA

SIERRA MADRE OCCIDENTAL

PLATEAU
OF
MEXICO

SIERRA MADRE ORIENTAL

GULF
OF
MEXICO

BAHAMAS

Tropic of Cancer

HAWAIIAN
ISLANDS

CABO
SAN LUCAS

YUCATAN
PENINSULA

CUBA

HISPANIOLA

CARIBBEAN SEA

km 0   1000   2000

mi 0   1000   2000

© 1996 GEOSYSTEMS GLOBAL CORP.

ISTHMUS OF
TEHUANTEPEC

ISTHMUS OF
PANAMA

LLANOS

Orinoco
River

GUIANA HIGHLANDS

GULF
OF
PANAMA

GULF
OF
GUAYAQUIL

Rio Negro River

Amazon

A M A Z O N

B A S I N

São Francisco

Equator

0°

0°

GALAPAGOS
ISLANDS

A N D E S

PLATEAU OF
MATO
GROSSO

BRAZILIAN
HIGHLANDS

ATACAMA

ALTIPLANO

GRAN
CHACO

Paraná River

Ice cap

High mountains

Low mountains

Desert

Interior
plains

Coastal
plains

ATACAMA
DESERT

Tropic of Capricorn

M O U N T A I N S

PAMPAS

30°S

30°S

N

W   E

S

PATAGONIA

FALKLAND
ISLANDS

60°S

60°S

STRAIT
OF
MAGELLAN

DRAKE PASSAGE

Antarctic Circle

ANTARCTICA

150°W 120°W 90°W

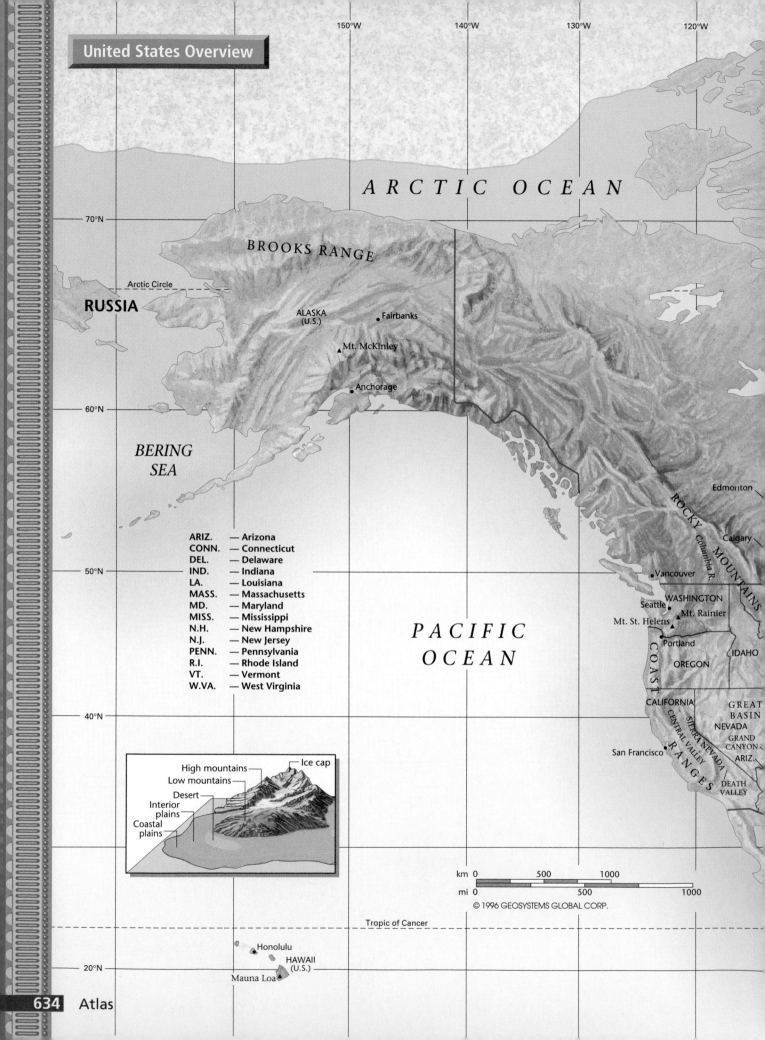

150°W 140°W 130°W 120°W

A R C T I C   O C E A N

70°N

BROOKS RANGE

Arctic Circle

RUSSIA

ALASKA
(U.S.)

• Fairbanks

▲ Mt. McKinley

• Anchorage

60°N

*BERING
SEA*

ROCKY MOUNTAINS

Columbia R.

Edmonton

Calgary

50°N

Vancouver •

WASHINGTON

Seattle •   ▲ Mt. Rainier

Mt. St. Helens ▲

• Portland   IDAHO

OREGON

COAST

CALIFORNIA

GREAT
BASIN

NEVADA

GRAND
CANYON
ARIZ.

San Francisco •

SIERRA NEVADA

CENTRAL VALLEY

R A N G E S

DEATH
VALLEY

ARIZ.	— Arizona
CONN.	— Connecticut
DEL.	— Delaware
IND.	— Indiana
LA.	— Louisiana
MASS.	— Massachusetts
MD.	— Maryland
MISS.	— Mississippi
N.H.	— New Hampshire
N.J.	— New Jersey
PENN.	— Pennsylvania
R.I.	— Rhode Island
VT.	— Vermont
W.VA.	— West Virginia

*PACIFIC
OCEAN*

40°N

Ice cap
High mountains
Low mountains
Desert
Interior
plains
Coastal
plains

km 0   500   1000
mi 0   500   1000

© 1996 GEOSYSTEMS GLOBAL CORP.

Tropic of Cancer

• Honolulu

HAWAII
(U.S.)

Mauna Loa ▲

20°N

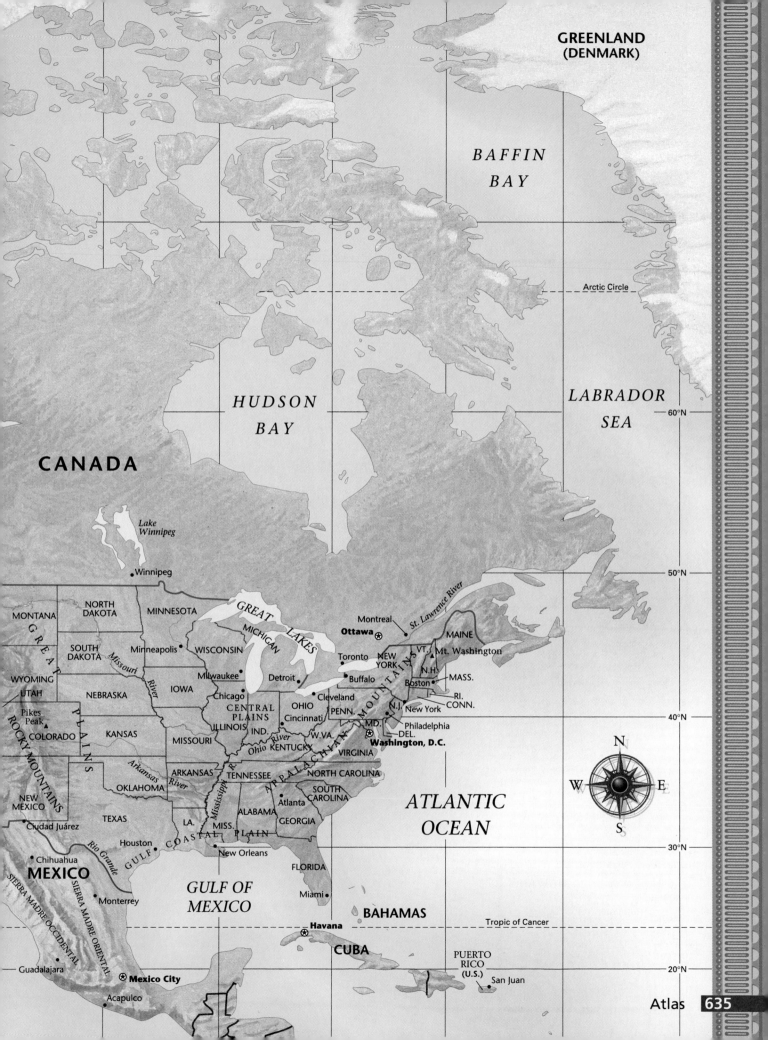

GREENLAND
(DENMARK)

*BAFFIN
BAY*

Arctic Circle

*HUDSON
BAY*

*LABRADOR
SEA*

60°N

CANADA

*Lake
Winnipeg*

• Winnipeg

50°N

MONTANA

NORTH
DAKOTA

MINNESOTA

GREAT LAKES

St. Lawrence River

Montreal •

Ottawa ⊛

MAINE

G R E A T

SOUTH
DAKOTA

Minneapolis •

WISCONSIN

MICHIGAN

Toronto •

NEW
YORK

VT.
N.H.

▲ Mt. Washington

WYOMING

Missouri
River

IOWA

Milwaukee •

Detroit •

Buffalo •

APPALACHIAN MOUNTAINS

Boston •

MASS.

UTAH

NEBRASKA

Chicago •

CENTRAL
PLAINS

OHIO

Cleveland •

PENN.

N.J.

RI.
CONN.

Pikes
Peak ▲

P L A I N S

ILLINOIS

IND.

Cincinnati •

New York •

40°N

COLORADO

KANSAS

MISSOURI

W.VA.

MD.

Philadelphia •
DEL.

ROCKY MOUNTAINS

Ohio River

KENTUCKY

Washington, D.C. ⊛

Arkansas
River

ARKANSAS

TENNESSEE

VIRGINIA

NEW
MEXICO

OKLAHOMA

Mississippi R.

NORTH CAROLINA

N
W   E
S

• Ciudad Juárez

TEXAS

LA.

MISS.

ALABAMA

SOUTH
CAROLINA

**ATLANTIC
OCEAN**

Rio Grande

Houston •

GULF COASTAL PLAIN

Atlanta •

GEORGIA

• Chihuahua

MEXICO

New Orleans •

30°N

SIERRA MADRE OCCIDENTAL

SIERRA MADRE ORIENTAL

Monterrey •

**GULF OF
MEXICO**

FLORIDA

Miami •

BAHAMAS

Tropic of Cancer

Havana ⊛

• Guadalajara

⊛ **Mexico City**

CUBA

PUERTO
RICO
(U.S.)

San Juan •

20°N

• Acapulco

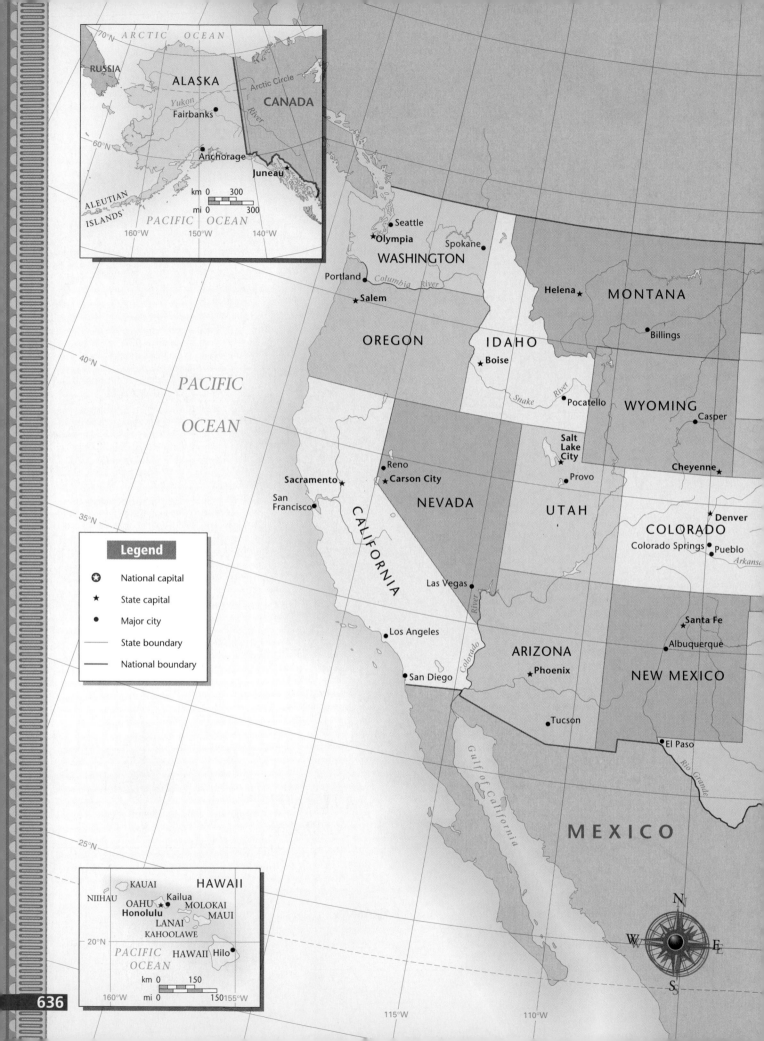

Inset: Alaska

ARCTIC OCEAN

70°N

RUSSIA

ALASKA

CANADA

Arctic Circle

Yukon River

60°N

• Fairbanks

• Anchorage

★ **Juneau**

km 0   300

mi 0   300

ALEUTIAN ISLANDS

PACIFIC OCEAN

160°W   150°W   140°W

Main Map

• Seattle

★ **Olympia**

Spokane •

WASHINGTON

Portland • _Columbia River_

★ Salem

Helena ★   **MONTANA**

• Billings

OREGON

IDAHO

★ **Boise**

Snake River

• Pocatello   **WYOMING**

40°N

PACIFIC

OCEAN

Salt Lake City ★

• Casper

Reno •

★ Sacramento   ★ **Carson City**

San Francisco •

35°N

CALIFORNIA

NEVADA

• Provo

UTAH

Cheyenne ★

★ Denver

COLORADO

Colorado Springs •   • Pueblo

Arkansas

Legend

⊛ National capital

★ State capital

• Major city

— State boundary

— National boundary

Las Vegas •

Colorado River

• Los Angeles

ARIZONA

★ Phoenix

Santa Fe ★

• Albuquerque

NEW MEXICO

• San Diego

• Tucson

• El Paso

Rio Grande

Gulf of California

MEXICO

25°N

Inset: Hawaii

KAUAI

NIIHAU

HAWAII

OAHU ★ • Kailua

Honolulu   MOLOKAI

LANAI   MAUI

KAHOOLAWE

PACIFIC OCEAN

HAWAII • Hilo

20°N

km 0   150

mi 0   150

160°W   155°W

N
W E
S

115°W   110°W

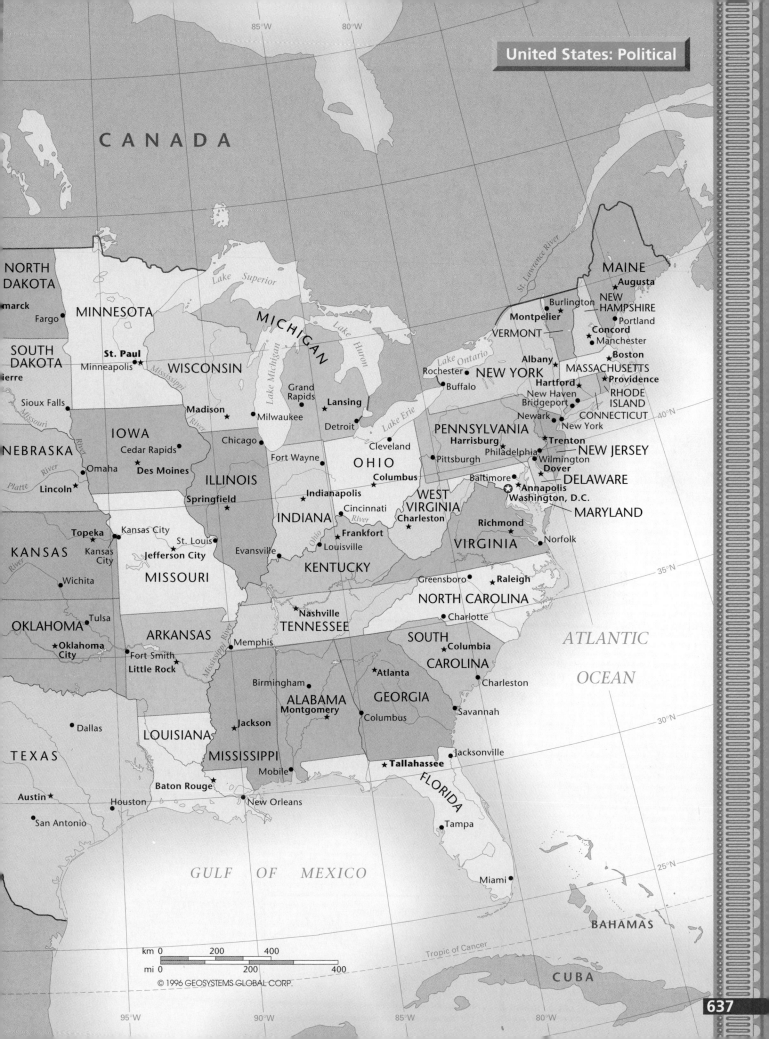

CANADA

NORTH DAKEOTA

marck

Fargo

MINNESOTA

SOUTH DAKOTA

ierre

St. Paul

Minneapolis

Sioux Falls

Lake Superior

Mississippi River

WISCONSIN

MICHIGAN

Lake Huron

Lake Michigan

MAINE

Augusta

Burlington

Montpelier

VERMONT

NEW HAMPSHIRE

Portland

Concord

Manchester

Boston

Lake Ontario

Albany

MASSACHUSETTS

Rochester

NEW YORK

Hartford

Providence

Buffalo

New Haven

RHODE ISLAND

Bridgeport

CONNECTICUT

NEBRASKA

IOWA

Cedar Rapids

Des Moines

Omaha

Lincoln

Platte River

Missouri River

Madison

Milwaukee

Grand Rapids

Lansing

Detroit

Chicago

Fort Wayne

Cleveland

Lake Erie

OHIO

Columbus

PENNSYLVANIA

Harrisburg

Pittsburgh

Newark

New York

Trenton

NEW JERSEY

Philadelphia

Wilmington

Dover

DELAWARE

40°N

ILLINOIS

Springfield

Indianapolis

INDIANA

Cincinnati

Ohio River

Frankfort

Louisville

Baltimore

Annapolis

Washington, D.C.

MARYLAND

WEST VIRGINIA

Charleston

Richmond

Norfolk

VIRGINIA

Topeka

Kansas City

St. Louis

KANSAS

Kansas City

Jefferson City

Evansville

Kansas River

Wichita

MISSOURI

KENTUCKY

35°N

Greensboro

Raleigh

NORTH CAROLINA

OKLAHOMA

Tulsa

Oklahoma City

ARKANSAS

Fort Smith

Little Rock

Memphis

Mississippi River

Nashville

TENNESSEE

Charlotte

SOUTH CAROLINA

Columbia

Charleston

ATLANTIC

OCEAN

Birmingham

Atlanta

GEORGIA

Savannah

Dallas

TEXAS

LOUISIANA

MISSISSIPPI

ALABAMA

Montgomery

Columbus

Jackson

30°N

Austin

Houston

San Antonio

Baton Rouge

Mobile

New Orleans

Tallahassee

Jacksonville

FLORIDA

GULF OF MEXICO

Tampa

25°N

Miami

BAHAMAS

km 0   200   400

mi 0   200   400

Tropic of Cancer

CUBA

95°W   90°W   85°W   80°W

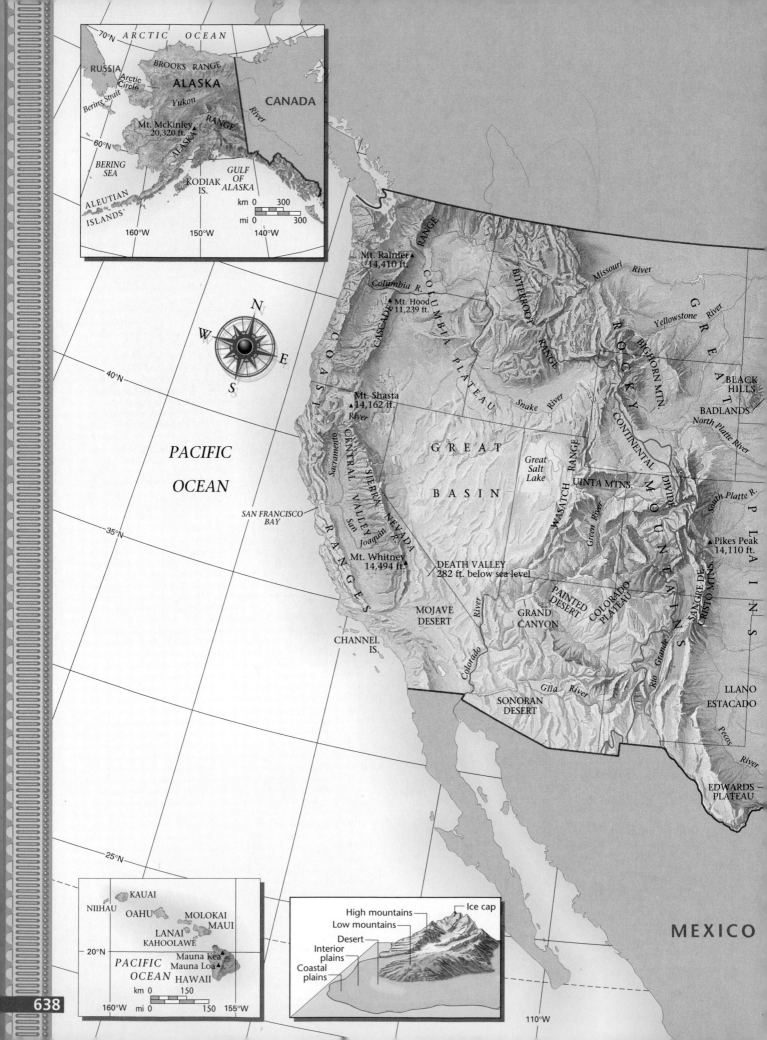

ARCTIC OCEAN

RUSSIA

BROOKS RANGE

ALASKA

Arctic Circle

Yukon

Bering Strait

Mt. McKinley
20,320 ft.

RANGE

ALASKA

CANADA

BERING SEA

GULF OF ALASKA

KODIAK IS.

ALEUTIAN ISLANDS

km 0 — 300
mi 0 — 300

70°N
60°N
160°W   150°W   140°W

N
W · E
S

PACIFIC OCEAN

40°N

35°N

SAN FRANCISCO BAY

25°N

CASCADE RANGE

Mt. Rainier
14,410 ft.

Columbia R.

Mt. Hood
11,239 ft.

Mt. Shasta
14,162 ft.

River

Sacramento

CENTRAL VALLEY

SIERRA NEVADA

San Joaquin R.

Mt. Whitney
14,494 ft.

COAST   RANGES

MOJAVE DESERT

CHANNEL IS.

COLUMBIA PLATEAU

BITTERROOT RANGE

Missouri River

Yellowstone River

Snake River

GREAT BASIN

Great Salt Lake

WASATCH RANGE

UINTA MTNS.

Green River

DEATH VALLEY
282 ft. below sea level

River

GRAND CANYON

Colorado

PAINTED DESERT

COLORADO PLATEAU

Gila River

SONORAN DESERT

ROCKY

BIGHORN MTN.

CONTINENTAL DIVIDE

North Platte River

MOUNTAINS

SANGRE DE CRISTO MTNS.

Rio Grande

GREAT

BLACK HILLS

BADLANDS

South Platte R.

Pikes Peak
14,110 ft.

PLAINS

LLANO ESTACADO

Pecos River

EDWARDS PLATEAU

MEXICO

110°W

KAUAI
NIIHAU
OAHU
MOLOKAI
MAUI
LANAI
KAHOOLAWE
Mauna Kea
Mauna Loa
HAWAII

PACIFIC OCEAN

km 0 — 150
mi 0 — 150

20°N
160°W   155°W

High mountains
Low mountains
Desert
Interior plains
Coastal plains
Ice cap

CANADA

MESABI RANGE

Lake Superior

Lake Michigan

Lake Huron

Lake Erie

Lake Ontario

St. Lawrence River

ADIRONDACK MTNS.

Hudson River

Connecticut R.

WHITE MTNS.

Mt. Washington 6,288 ft.

CATSKILL MTNS.

NANTUCKET
MARTHA'S
VINEYARD
LONG ISLAND

40°N

Mississippi

Missouri

SAND HILLS

Des Moines River

River

CENTRAL
PLAINS

Susquehanna R.

ALLEGHENY PLATEAU

Delaware River

DELAWARE BAY

Platte River

Wabash R.

Ohio River

River

CHESAPEAKE BAY

35°N

Arkansas River

OZARK PLATEAU

A P P A L A C H I A N   M O U N T A I N S

CUMBERLAND PLATEAU

BLUE RIDGE MOUNTAINS

Mt. Mitchell 6,684 ft.

FALL LINE

ATLANTIC COASTAL PLAIN

ATLANTIC
OCEAN

30°N

OUACHITA
MOUNTAINS

Mississippi River

Tennessee River

Chattahoochee R.

Savannah River

Brazos River

Tombigbee R.

Alabama R.

Altamaha River

Sabine River

Pearl River

G U L F   C O A S T A L   P L A I N

Colorado River

PENSACOLA BAY

MOBILE BAY

TAMPA BAY

EVERGLADES

25°N

BAHAMAS

GALVESTON BAY

GULF   OF   MEXICO

Rio Grande

km 0   200   400

mi 0   200   400

© 1996 GEOSYSTEMS GLOBAL CORP.

FLORIDA KEYS

Tropic of Cancer

CUBA

Gazetteer

PLACE	LAT.	LONG.	PAGE
China (country in East Asia)	37°N	93°E	**81**
Colorado (38th state; capital: Denver)	40°N	107°W	**636–637**
Columbia River (Lewis and Clark found mouth of river in 1805)	46°N	120°W	**638–639**
Concord (site in Massachusetts of early Revolutionary War battle)	42°N	71°W	**263**
Connecticut (5th state; capital: Hartford)	42°N	73°W	**160**
Cuba (island nation in Caribbean Sea, south of Florida)	22°N	79°W	**94**
Cumberland Gap (pass through the Appalachian Mountains)	36°N	83°W	**337**
D **Delaware** (1st state; capital: Dover)	39°N	76°W	**186**
Delaware River (flows from New York to Delaware Bay)	42°N	75°W	**187**
Denver (capital of Colorado)	40°N	105°W	**636–637**
E **El Paso** (city in west Texas, on Rio Grande)	32°N	106°W	**636–637**
Ellis Island (island in New York Harbor where immigrants to United States arrived)	41°N	74°W	**511**
England (country in western Europe; part of the United Kingdom)	52°N	2°W	**84**
Europe (6th largest continent)	50°N	15°E	**84**
F **Florence** (city in Italy)	44°N	11°E	**84**
Florida (27th state; capital: Tallahassee)	31°N	85°W	**636–637**

PLACE	LAT.	LONG.	PAGE
France (country in western Europe)	47°N	1°E	**84**
G **Gary** (city in Indiana)	42°N	87°W	**20**
Georgia (4th state; capital: Atlanta)	33°N	84°W	**226**
Germany (country in western Europe)	51°N	10°E	**541**
Gettysburg (site in Pennsylvania of Civil War battle)	40°N	77°W	**436**
Grand Canyon (in Arizona, deep gorge formed by the Colorado River)	36°N	112°W	**638–639**
Grand Teton Mountain (in Teton Range)	44°N	111°W	**14–15**
Great Britain (England, Scotland, and Wales)	57°N	2°W	**177**
Great Lakes (five freshwater lakes between the United States and Canada)	45°N	83°W	**142**
Great Plains (in central North America, high grassland region)	45°N	104°W	**14–15**
Greensboro (city in North Carolina)	36°N	80°W	**636–637**
Guatemala (country in Central America)	16°N	92°W	**601**
Gulf of Mexico (body of water along southern United States and Mexico)	25°N	94°W	**595**
H **Havana** (capital of Cuba)	23°N	82°W	**601**
Hawaii (50th state; capital: Honolulu)	20°N	158°W	**522**
Hiroshima (city in Japan; destroyed by atomic bomb in 1945)	34°N	132°E	**555**
Hispaniola (island in the West Indies)	18°N	73°W	**94**
Honolulu (capital of Hawaii)	21°N	158°W	**522**

PLACE	LAT.	LONG.	PAGE
Houston (city in Texas)	30°N	95°W	**636–637**
Hudson River (in New York; named for explorer Henry Hudson)	43°N	74°W	**144**
Idaho (43rd state; capital: Boise**)**	44°N	115°W	**636–637**
Illinois (21st state; capital: Springfield)	40°N	91°W	**636–637**
Independence (town in Missouri at the start of the Oregon Trail)	39°N	94°W	**408**
India (country in south Asia)	23°N	78°E	**91**
Indiana (19th state; capital: Indianapolis)	40°N	87°W	**19**
Italy (country in southern Europe)	44°N	11°E	**84**
Japan (island country off east coast of Asia)	37°N	134°E	**555**
Kansas (34th state; capital: Topeka)	39°N	100°W	**636–637**
Kentucky (15th state; capital: Frankfort)	38°N	88°W	**435**
Lexington (site in Massachusetts of lst shots fired in Revolutionary War)	42°N	71°W	**263**
Lima (capital of Peru, in South America)	12°S	77°W	**601**
London (capital of United Kingdom)	52°N	0°W	**628–629**
Los Angeles (city in California)	34°N	118°W	**636–637**
Louisiana (18th state; capital: Baton Rouge)	31°N	93°W	**289**
Maine (23rd state; capital: Augusta)	45°N	70°W	**636–637**

PLACE	LAT.	LONG.	PAGE
Mali (country in West Africa)	16°N	0°W	**77**
Maryland (7th state; capital: Annapolis)	39°N	76°W	**212**
Massachusetts (6th state; capital: Boston)	42°N	73°W	**160**
Mexico (country bordering the United States to the south)	24°N	104°W	**595**
Mexico City (capital of Mexico)	19°N	99°W	**595**
Miami (city in Florida)	26°N	80°W	**636–637**
Michigan (26th state; capital: Lansing)	46°N	87°W	**636–637**
Milwaukee (city in Wisconsin)	43°N	88°W	**636–637**
Mississippi (20th state; capital: Jackson)	33°N	90°W	**368**
Mississippi River (principal river of United States and North America)	32°N	92°W	**638–639**
Missouri (24th state; capital: Jefferson City)	38°N	94°W	**426–427**
Missouri River (a major river in United States)	41°N	96°W	**638–639**
Montana (41st state; capital: Helena)	47°N	112°W	**636–637**
Montgomery (city in Alabama)	32°N	86°W	**636–637**
Montreal (city in Quebec, Canada)	46°N	74°W	**601**
Nagasaki (city in Japan; severely damaged by atomic bomb in 1945)	33°N	130°E	**555**
Natchez (city in Mississippi)	32°N	91°W	**289**
Nebraska (37th state; capital: Lincoln)	42°N	102°W	**636–637**
Netherlands (country in northwestern Europe; also called Holland)	52°N	6°E	**628–629**
Nevada (36th state; capital: Carson City)	40°N	117°W	**636–637**

PLACE	LAT.	LONG.	PAGE
Newfoundland (eastern province of Canada)	48°N	57°W	**591**
New Hampshire (9th state; capital: Concord)	44°N	72°W	**160**
New Jersey (3rd state; capital: Trenton)	41°N	75°W	**186**
New Mexico (47th state; capital: Santa Fe)	35°N	107°W	**636–637**
New Netherland (Dutch colony in North America)	41°N	74°W	**144**
New Orleans (city in Louisiana)	30°N	90°W	**636–637**
New York (11th state; capital: Albany)	43°N	78°W	**186**
New York City (large city in New York State)	41°N	74°W	**177**
North America (northern continent of Western Hemisphere)	45°N	100°W	**601**
North Carolina (12th state; capital: Raleigh)	36°N	82°W	**212**
Northwest Territory (land extending from Ohio and Mississippi rivers to Great Lakes)	41°N	85°W	**307**

O **Ohio** (17th state; capital: Columbus) — 41°N — 83°W — **636–637**

PLACE	LAT.	LONG.	PAGE
Ohio River (flows from Pennsylvania to the Mississippi River)	37°N	88°W	**289**
Ohio River Valley (farming region west of the Appalachian Mountains)	37°N	88°W	**235**
Oklahoma (46th state; capital: Oklahoma City)	36°N	98°W	**636–637**
Omaha (large city in Nebraska)	41°N	96°W	**636–637**
Ontario (Canadian province; capital: Toronto)	51°N	89°W	**590**
Oregon (33rd state; capital: Salem)	44°N	122°W	**636–637**
Oregon Territory (area from Rocky Mountains to Pacific Ocean)	45°N	120°W	**406**

PLACE	LAT.	LONG.	PAGE
P **Pacific Ocean** (largest ocean; west of the United States)	0°	170°W	**630–631**
Panama (country in Central America)	9°N	80°W	**601**
Pearl Harbor (United States naval base; attacked by Japan)	21°N	158°W	**551**
Pennsylvania (2nd state; capital: Harrisburg)	41°N	78°W	**186**
Peru (country on the Pacific coast of South America)	10°S	75°W	**601**
Philippines (island country southeast of Asia)	14°N	125°E	**628–629**
Philadelphia (large port city in Pennsylvania)	40°N	75°W	**177**
Pittsburgh (manufacturing city in Pennsylvania)	40°N	80°W	**636–637**
Plymouth (in Massachusetts; site of first Pilgrim settlement)	42°N	71°W	**135**
Portugal (country in western Europe; capital: Lisbon)	38°N	8°W	**91**
Potomac River (runs from western Maryland past Washington, D.C.)	38°N	77°W	**325**
Promontory Point (the place in Utah where the two halves of the Transcontinental Railroad met in 1869)	41°N	112°W	**483**
Puerto Rico (a U.S. territory in the Caribbean; capital: San Juan)	18°N	67°W	**601**

Q **Quebec** (province of Canada; capital: Quebec City) — 47°N — 71°W — **591**

R **Rhode Island** (13th state; capital: Providence) — 42°N — 72°W — **307**

PLACE	LAT.	LONG.	PAGE
Richmond (capital city of Virginia; also was Confederate capital)	38°N	78°W	**212**
Rio Grande (river forming part of the Texas–Mexico border)	26°N	97°W	**638–639**
Roanoke Island (island off the coast of North Carolina; site of first English colony in the Americas)	37°N	80°W	**146**
Rocky Mountains (mountain range in the western United States)	50°N	114°W	**638–639**
Russia (formerly part of the Soviet Union; capital: Moscow)	61°N	60°E	**628–629**

S St. Lawrence River (links the Great Lakes to the Atlantic Ocean)

PLACE	LAT.	LONG.	PAGE
St. Lawrence River (links the Great Lakes to the Atlantic Ocean)	49°N	67°W	**591**
St. Louis (city in Missouri; on Mississippi River)	39°N	90°W	**408**
Sacramento (capital of California)	39°N	122°W	**636–637**
Salem (an early English settlement in Massachusetts)	43°N	71°W	**146**
San Francisco (a major port city in California)	38°N	122°W	**14**
Saratoga (New York site of an important American victory against the British in 1777)	43°N	75°W	**285**
Savannah (oldest city in Georgia)	32°N	81°W	**289,457**
Scandinavia (includes the countries of Norway, Sweden, and Denmark)	62°N	14°E	**74**
Seattle (large city in Washington State)	48°N	122°W	**636–637**
Shenandoah Valley (farming region in Virginia)	39°N	78°W	**15**

PLACE	LAT.	LONG.	PAGE
Sierra Nevada (mountain range mainly in eastern California)	39°N	120°W	**638–639**
Sierra Madre (a system of mountain ranges in Mexico)	27°N	104°W	**595**
South Carolina (8th state; capital: Columbia)	34°N	81°W	**636–637**
Soviet Union (large Communist country that split into separate republics in 1991; capital city: Moscow)	61°N	64°E	**581**
Spain (country in Western Europe; capital: Madrid)	40°N	5°W	**91**

T Tenochtitlán (Aztec city; present-day Mexico City)

PLACE	LAT.	LONG.	PAGE
Tenochtitlán (Aztec city; present-day Mexico City)	19°N	99°W	**104**
Tennessee (16th state; capital: Nashville)	36°N	88°W	**368**
Texas (28th state; capital: Austin)	31°N	101°W	**402**
Tikal (ruins of Mayan city in Guatemala)	17°N	89°W	**41**
Timbuktu (city in Mali, W. Africa)	17°N	3°W	**77**
Trenton (capital of New Jersey)	40°N	75°W	**636–637**
Tucson (city in Arizona)	32°N	111°W	**636–637**

U United States (country in central and northwest North America)

PLACE	LAT.	LONG.	PAGE
United States (country in central and northwest North America)	38°N	110°W	**636–637**

V Valley Forge (George Washington's winter camp in 1777; near Philadelphia)

PLACE	LAT.	LONG.	PAGE
Valley Forge (George Washington's winter camp in 1777; near Philadelphia)	40°N	75°W	**286**
Venice (city in Italy)	45°N	12°E	**84**
Vicksburg, Mississippi (site of Civil War battle)	32°N	91°W	**435**

PLACE	LAT.	LONG.	PAGE
Vietnam (country in southeast Asia)	18°N	107°E	**628–629**
Virginia (10th state; capital: Richmond)	37°N	81°W	**212**

W **Washington, D.C.** (capital of the U.S.)   39°N   77°W   **14–15**

Washington (42nd state; capital: Olympia)	48°N	121°W	**636–637**
West Indies (islands separating the Caribbean Sea and the Atlantic)	19°N	79°W	**630**
Williamsburg (colonial capital of Virginia)	37°N	77°W	**223**
Wyoming (44th state; capital: Cheyenne)	43°N	109°W	**636–637**

Y **Yorktown** (in Virginia; site of last battle of Revolutionary War)   37°N   77°W   **289**

Geographic Glossary

basin
a bowl-shaped area of land surrounded by higher land

bay
part of a lake or ocean extending into the land

coast
the land next to an ocean

delta
a triangular area of land formed by deposits at the mouth of a river

▼ desert
a dry area where few plants grow

▲ glacier
a large ice mass that moves slowly down a mountain or over land

harbor
a sheltered body of water where ships can safely dock

hill
a raised mass of land, smaller than a mountain

island
a body of land completely surrounded by water

isthmus
a narrow strip of land connecting two larger bodies of land

1 lake
a body of water completely surrounded by land

▲ mesa
a wide flat topped mountain with steep sides, found mostly in dry areas

2 **mountain**

a steeply raised mass of land, much higher than the surrounding country

3 **mountain pass**

a gap between mountains

4 **mountain range**

a row of mountains

ocean or sea

a salty body of water covering a large area of the earth

plain

a large area of flat or nearly flat land

▼ plateau

a large area of flat land higher than the surrounding land

▲ prairie

a large, level area of grassland with few or no trees

river

a large stream that runs into a lake, ocean or another river

sea level

the level of the surface of the ocean

strait

a narrow channel of water connecting two larger bodies of water

5 **tree line**

on a mountain, the area above which no trees grow

tributary

a stream or a river that flows into a larger river

valley

low land between hills or mountains

volcano

an opening in the earth, often raised, through which lava and gasses from the earth's interior escape

States and
Their Flags

Alabama 22nd
Heart of Dixie
population:
4,040,587
area: 52,423
square miles
admitted: December 14, 1819

Alaska 49th
The Last
Frontier
population:
550,043
area: 656,424 square miles
admitted: January 3, 1959

Arizona 48th
Grand Can-
yon State
population:
3,665,228
area: 114,006 square miles
admitted: February 14, 1912

Arkansas 25th
The Natural
State
population:
2,350,725
area: 53,182 square miles
admitted: June 15, 1836

California 31st
Golden
State
population:
29,760,021
area: 163,707 square miles
admitted: September 9, 1850

Colorado 8th
Centennial
State
population:
3,294,394
area: 104,100 square miles
admitted: August 1, 1876

Connecticut 5th
Constitution
State
population:
3,287,116
area: 5,544 square miles
admitted: January 9, 1788

Delaware 1st
First State
population:
666,168
area: 2,489
square miles
admitted: December 7, 1787

Florida 27th
Sunshine
State
population:
12,937,926
area: 65,758 square miles
admitted: March 3, 1845

Georgia 4th
Peach State
population:
6,478,216
area: 59,441
square miles
admitted: January 2, 1788

Hawaii 50th
The Aloha
State
population:
1,108,229
area: 10,932 square miles
admitted: August 21, 1959

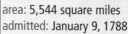

Idaho 43rd
Gem State
population:
1,006,749
area: 83,574
square miles
admitted: July 3, 1890

Illinois 21st
The Prairie
State
population:
11,430,602
area: 57,918 square miles
admitted: December 3, 1818

Indiana 19th
Hoosier
State
population:
5,544,159
area: 36,420 square miles
admitted: December 11, 1816

Iowa 29th
Hawkeye
State
population:
2,776,755
area: 56,276 square miles
admitted: December 28, 1846

Kansas 34th
Sunflower
State
population:
2,477,574
area: 82,282 square miles
admitted: January 29, 1861

Kentucky 15th
Bluegrass
State
population:
3,685,296
area: 40,411 square miles
admitted: June 1, 1792

Louisiana 18th
Pelican State
population:
4,219,973
area: 51,843
square miles
admitted: April 30, 1812

Maine 23rd
Pine Tree
State
population:
1,227,928
area: 35,387 square miles
admitted: March 15, 1820

Maryland 7th
Old Line
State
population:
4,781,468
area: 12,407 square miles
admitted: April 28, 1788

Massachusetts 6th
Bay State
population:
6,016,425
area: 10,555
square miles
admitted: February 6, 1788

Michigan 26th
Great Lakes
State
population:
9,295,297
area: 96,810 square miles
admitted: January 26, 1837

Minnesota 32nd
North Star
State
population:
4,375,099
area: 86,943 square miles
admitted: May 11, 1858

Mississippi 20th
Magnolia
State
population:
2,573,216
area: 48,434 square miles
admitted: December 10, 1817

Missouri 24th
Show Me State
population: 5,117,073
area: 69,709 square miles
admitted: August 10, 1821

Montana 41st
Treasure State
population: 799,065
area: 147,046 square miles
admitted: November 8, 1889

Nebraska 37th
Cornhusker State
population: 1,578,385
area: 77,358 square miles
admitted: March 1, 1867

Nevada 36th
Sagebrush State
population: 1,201,833
area: 110,567 square miles
admitted: October 31, 1864

New Hampshire 9th
Granite State
population: 1,109, 252
area: 9,351 square miles
admitted: June 21, 1788

New Jersey 3rd
Garden State
population: 7,730,188
area: 8,722 square miles
admitted: December 18, 1787

New Mexico 47th
Land of Enchantment
population: 1,515,069
area: 121,598 square miles
admitted: January 6, 1912

New York 11th
Empire State
population: 17,990,455
area: 54,475 square miles
admitted: July 26, 1788

North Carolina 12th
Tarheel State
population: 6,628,637
area: 53,821 square miles
admitted: November 21,1789

North Dakota 39th
Peace Garden State
population: 638,800
area: 70,704 square miles
admitted: November 2, 1889

Ohio 17th
Buckeye State
population: 10,847,115
area: 44,828 square miles
admitted: March 1, 1803

Oklahoma 46th
Sooner State
population: 3,145,585
area: 69,903 square miles
admitted: November 16,1907

Oregon 33rd
Beaver State
population: 2,842,321
area: 98,386 square miles
admitted: February 14, 1859

Pennsylvania 2nd
Keystone State
population: 11,881,643
area: 46,058 square miles
admitted: December 12, 1787

Rhode Island 13th
Ocean State
population: 1,003,464
area: 1,545 square miles
admitted: May 29, 1790

South Carolina 8th
Palmetto State
population: 3,486,703
area: 32,007 square miles
admitted: May 23, 1788

South Dakota 40th
Coyote State
population: 696,004
area: 77,121 square miles
admitted: November 2, 1889

Tennessee 16th
Volunteer State
population: 4,877,185
area: 42,146 square miles
admitted: June 1, 1796

Texas 28th
Lone Star State
population: 16,986,510
area: 261,914 square miles
admitted: December 29, 1845

Utah 45th
Beehive State
population: 1,722,850
area: 84,904 square miles
admitted: January 4, 1896

Vermont 14th
Green Mountain State
population: 562,758
area: 9,615 square miles
admitted: March 4, 1791

Virginia 10th
Old Dominion
population: 6,187,358
area: 42,769 square miles
admitted: June 25, 1788

Washington 42nd
Evergreen State
population: 4,866,692
area: 71,303 square miles
admitted: November 11,1889

West Virginia 35th
Mountain State
population: 1,793,477
area: 24,231 square miles
admitted: June 20, 1863

Wisconsin 30th
Badger State
population: 4,891,769
area: 65,503 square miles
admitted: May 29, 1848
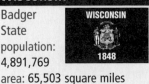

Wyoming 44th
Equality State
population: 453,588
area: 97,818 square miles
admitted: July 10, 1890

District of Columbia
No nickname
population: 606,900
area: 68 square miles
incorporated: 1802

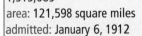
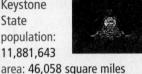

U.S. Presidents

George Washington

(1732–1799)
President from 1789–1797
party: Federalist
home state: Virginia
first lady: Martha Dandridge Custis Washington

John Adams

(1735–1826)
President from 1797–1801
party: Federalist
home state: Massachusetts
first lady: Abigail Smith Adams

Thomas Jefferson

(1743–1826)
President from 1801–1809
party: Democratic–Republican
home state: Virginia
first lady: Martha Jefferson Randolph (daughter)

James Madison

(1751–1836)
President from 1809–1817
party: Democratic–Republican
home state: Virginia
first lady: Dolley Payne Todd Madison

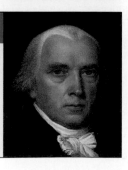

James Monroe

(1758–1831)
President from 1817–1825
party: Democratic–Republican
home state: Virginia
first lady: Elizabeth Kortright Monroe

John Quincy Adams

(1767–1848)
President from 1825–1829
party: Democratic–Republican
home state: Massachusetts
first lady: Louisa Catherine Johnson Adams

Andrew Jackson

(1767–1845)
President from 1829–1837
party: Democratic
home state: Tennessee
first lady: Emily Donelson (late wife's niece)

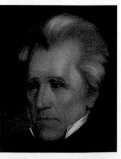

Martin Van Buren

(1782–1862)
President from 1837–1841
party: Democratic
home state: New York
first lady: Angelica Singleton Van Buren (daughter–in–law)

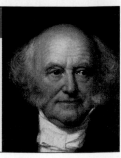

Franklin Pierce
(1804–1869)
President from 1853–1857
party: Democratic
home state: New Hampshire
first lady: Jane Means Appleton
Pierce

William Henry Harrison
(1773–1841)
President 1841
party: Whig
home state: Ohio
first lady: Jane Irwin Harrison
(daughter–in–law)

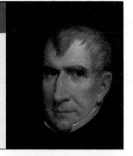

James Buchanan
(1791–1868)
President from 1857–1861
party: Democratic
home state: Pennsylvania
first lady: Harriet Lane (niece)

John Tyler
(1790–1862)
President from 1841–1845
party: Whig
home state: Virginia
first lady: Letitia Christian Tyler

Abraham Lincoln
(1809–1865)
President from 1861–1865
party: Republican
home state: Illinois
first lady: Mary Todd Lincoln

James K. Polk
(1795–1849)
President from 1845–1849
party: Democratic
home state: Tennessee
first lady: Sarah Childress Polk

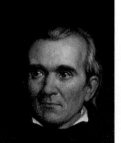

Andrew Johnson
(1808–1875)
President from 1865–1869
party: Democratic
home state: Tennessee
first lady: Eliza McCardle Johnson

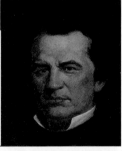

Zachary Taylor
(1784–1850)
President from 1849–1850
party: Whig
home state: Louisiana
first lady: Margaret Mackall Smith
Taylor

Ulysses S. Grant
(1822–1885)
President from 1869–1877
party: Republican
home state: Illinois
first lady: Julia Dent Grant

Millard Fillmore
(1800–1874)
President from 1850–1853
party: Whig
home state: New York
first lady: Abigail Powers Fillmore

Rutherford B. Hayes
(1822–1893)
President from 1877–1881
party: Republican
home state: Ohio
first lady: Lucy Ware Webb Hayes

James A. Garfield

(1831–1881)

President 1881
party: Republican
home state: Ohio
first lady: Lucretia Rudolph
Garfield

Chester A. Arthur

(1830–1886)

President from 1881–1885
party: Republican
home state: New York
first lady: Mary Arthur McElroy
(sister)

William Howard Taft

(1857–1930)

President from 1909–1913
party: Republican
home state: Ohio
first lady: Helen Herron Taft

Grover Cleveland

(1837–1908)

President from 1885–1889 and
1893–1897
party: Democratic
home state: New York
first lady: Frances Folsom Cleveland

Woodrow Wilson

(1856–1924)

President from 1913–1921
party: Democratic
home state: New Jersey
first lady: Edith Bolling Galt Wilson

Benjamin Harrison

(1833–1901)

President from 1889–1893
party: Republican
home state: Indiana
first lady: Caroline Lavina Scott
Harrison

Warren G. Harding

(1865–1923)

President from 1921–1923
party: Republican
home state: Ohio
first lady: Florence Kling Harding

William McKinley

(1843–1901)

President from 1897–1901
party: Republican
home state: Ohio
first lady: Ida Saxton McKinley

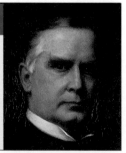

Calvin Coolidge

(1872–1933)

President from 1923–1929
party: Republican
home state: Massachusetts
first lady: Grace Anna Goodhue
Coolidge

Theodore Roosevelt

(1858–1919)

President from 1901–1909
party: Republican
home state: New York
first lady: Edith Kermit Carow
Roosevelt

Herbert Hoover

(1874–1964)

President from 1929–1933
party: Republican
home state: California
first lady: Lou Henry Hoover

Richard M. Nixon

(1913–1994)
President from 1969–1974
party: Republican
home state: New York
first lady: Thelma Catherine (Pat)
  Ryan Nixon

Franklin Delano Roosevelt

(1882–1945)
President from 1933–1945
party: Democratic
home state: New York
first lady: Anna Eleanor Roosevelt
  Roosevelt

Gerald R. Ford

(1913–)
President from 1974–1977
party: Republican
home state: Michigan
first lady: Elizabeth Bloomer Ford

Harry S. Truman

(1884–1972)
President from 1945–1953
party: Democratic
home state: Missouri
first lady: Elizabeth Virginia Wallace
  Truman

Jimmy Carter

(1924–)
President from 1977–1981
party: Democratic
home state: Georgia
first lady: Rosalynn Smith Carter

Dwight D. Eisenhower

(1890–1969)
President from 1953–1961
party: Republican
home state: New York
first lady: Mamie Geneva Doud
  Eisenhower

Ronald Reagan

(1911–)
President from 1981–1989
party: Republican
home state: California
first lady: Nancy Davis Reagan

John F. Kennedy

(1917–1963)
President from 1961–1963
party: Democratic
home state: Massachusetts
first lady: Jacqueline Lee Bouvier
  Kennedy

George Bush

(1924–)
President from 1989–1993
party: Republican
home state: Texas
first lady: Barbara Pierce Bush

Lyndon Baines Johnson

(1908–1973)
President from 1963–1969
party: Democratic
home state: Texas
first lady: Claudia Alta (Lady Bird)
  Taylor Johnson

William Clinton

(1946–)
President from 1993–
party: Democratic
home state: Arkansas
first lady: Hillary Rodham Clinton

In the Declaration of Independence, the colonists explained why they were breaking away from Britain. They believed they had the right to form their own country.

Members of the Continental Congress are shown signing the Declaration of Independence.

The opening part of the Declaration is very famous. It says that all people are created equal. Everyone has certain basic rights that are "unalienable." That means that these rights cannot be taken away. Governments are formed to protect these basic rights. If a government does not do this, then the people have a right to begin a new one.

Forming a new government meant ending the colonial ties to the king. The writers of the Declaration listed the wrongs of King George III to prove the need for their actions.

Colonists said the king had not let the colonies make their own laws. He had limited the people's representation in their assemblies.

The Declaration of Independence

In Congress, July 4, 1776

The unanimous declaration of the thirteen united States of America

INTRODUCTION *

WHEN, *in the course of human events, it becomes necessary for one people to dissolve the political bonds which have connected them with another, and to assume, among the powers of the earth, the separate and equal station to which the laws of nature and of nature's God entitle them, a decent respect to the opinions of mankind requires that they should declare the causes which impel them to the separation.*

BASIC RIGHTS

WE hold these truths to be self-evident: That all men are created equal, that they are endowed by their Creator with certain unalienable rights; that among these are life, liberty, and the pursuit of happiness; that, to secure these rights, governments are instituted among men, deriving their just powers from the consent of the governed; that whenever any form of government becomes destructive of these ends, it is the right of the people to alter or to abolish it, and to institute new government, laying its foundation on such principles, and organizing its powers in such form, as to them shall seem most likely to effect their safety and happiness. Prudence, indeed, will dictate that governments long established should not be changed for light and transient causes; and accordingly all experience hath shown that mankind are more disposed to suffer, while evils are sufferable, than to right themselves by abolishing the forms to which they are accustomed. But when a long train of abuses and usurpations, pursuing invariably the same object, evinces a design to reduce them under absolute despotism, it is their right, it is their duty, to throw off such government, and to provide new guards for their future security. Such has been the patient sufferance of these colonies; and such is now the necessity which constrains them to alter their former systems of government. The history of the present King of Great Britain is a history of repeated injuries and usurpations, all having in direct object the establishment of an absolute tyranny over these states. To prove this, let facts be submitted to a candid world.

CHARGES AGAINST THE KING

HE has refused his assent to laws, the most wholesome and necessary for the public good.

HE has forbidden his governors to pass laws of immediate and pressing importance, unless suspended in their operation till his assent should be obtained; and, when so suspended, he has utterly neglected to attend to them.

HE has refused to pass other laws for the accommodation of large districts of people, unless those people would relinquish the right of representation in the legislature, a right inestimable to them, and formidable to tyrants only.

*Titles have been added to the Declaration to make it easier to read. These titles are not in the original document.

HE has called together legislative bodies at places unusual, uncomfortable, and distant from the depository of their public records, for the sole purpose of fatiguing them into compliance with his measures.

HE has dissolved representative houses repeatedly, for opposing, with manly firmness his invasions on the rights of the people.

HE has refused for a long time, after such dissolutions, to cause others to be elected; whereby the legislative powers, incapable of annihilation, have returned to the people at large for their exercise; the state remaining in the mean time, exposed to all the dangers of invasions from without and convulsions within.

HE has endeavored to prevent the population of these states; for that purpose obstructing the laws for the naturalization of foreigners; refusing to pass others to encourage their migration hither, and raising the conditions of new appropriations of lands.

HE has obstructed the administration of justice, by refusing his assent to laws for establishing judiciary powers.

HE has made judges dependent on his will alone, for the tenure of their offices, and the amount of payment of their salaries.

HE has erected a multitude of new offices, and sent hither swarms of officers to harass our people and eat out their substance.

HE has kept among us, in times of peace, standing armies, without the consent of our legislatures.

HE has affected to render the military independent of, and superior to, the civil power.

HE has combined with others to subject us to a Jurisdiction foreign to our constitution and unacknowledged by our laws, giving his assent to their acts of pretended legislation:

FOR quartering large bodies of armed troops among us;

FOR protecting them, by a mock trial, from punishment for any murders which they should commit on the inhabitants of these states;

FOR cutting off our trade with all parts of the world;

FOR imposing taxes on us without our consent;

FOR depriving us, in many cases, of the benefits of trial by jury;

FOR transporting us beyond seas, to be tried for pretended offenses;

FOR abolishing the free system of English laws in a neighboring province, establishing therein an arbitrary government, and enlarging its boundaries, so as to render it at once an example and fit instrument for introducing the same absolute rule into these colonies;

FOR taking away our charters, abolishing our most valuable laws, and altering fundamentally the forms of our governments;

FOR suspending our own legislatures, and declaring themselves invested with power to legislate for us in all cases whatsoever.

HE has abdicated Government here, by declaring us out of his protection and waging war against us.

HE has plundered our seas, ravaged our coasts, burned our towns, and destroyed the lives of our people.

HE is at this time transporting large armies of foreign mercenaries to complete the works of death, desolation, and tyranny, already begun with circumstances of cruelty and perfidy scarcely paralleled in the most barbarous ages, and totally unworthy the head of a civilized nation.

The king had made colonial assemblies meet at unusual times and places. This made going to assembly meetings hard for colonial representatives.

In some cases the king stopped the assembly from meeting at all.

The king tried to stop people from moving to the colonies and into new western lands.

The king prevented the colonies from choosing their own judges. Instead, he sent over judges who depended on him for their jobs and pay.

The king kept British soldiers in the colonies, even though the colonists had not asked for them.

King George III

The king and Parliament had taxed the colonists without their consent. This was one of the most important reasons the colonists were angry at Britain.

The colonists felt that the king had waged war on them.

The king had hired German soldiers and sent them to the colonies to keep order.

British soldiers became a symbol of British misrule to many colonists.

The colonists said that they had asked the king to change his policies, but he had not listened to them.

HE has constrained our fellow-citizens, taken captive on the high seas, to bear arms against their country, to become the executioners of their friends and brethren, or to fall themselves by their hands.

HE has excited domestic insurrections amongst us, and has endeavored to bring on the inhabitants of our frontiers, the merciless Indian savages, whose known rule of warfare is an undistinguished destruction of all ages, sexes, and conditions.

RESPONSE TO THE KING

IN every stage of these oppressions we have petitioned for redress in the most humble terms; Our repeated petitions have been answered only by repeated injury. A prince, whose character is thus marked by every act which may define a tyrant, is unfit to be the ruler of a free people.

NOR have we been wanting in our attentions to our British brethren. We have warned them from time to time, of attempts by their legislature to extend an unwarrantable jurisdiction over us. We have reminded them of the circumstances of our emigration and settlement here. We have appealed to their native justice and magnanimity; and we have conjured them, by the ties of our common kindred, to disavow these usurpations, which, would inevitably interrupt our connections and correspondence. They, too, have been deaf to the voice of justice and of consanguinity. We must, therefore, acquiesce in the necessity which denounces our separation, and hold them, as we hold the rest of mankind, enemies in war, in peace, friends.

INDEPENDENCE

The writers declared that the colonies were free and independent states, equal to the world's other states. They had the powers to make war and peace and to trade with other countries.

WE, therefore, the representatives of the United States of America, in General Congress Assembled, appealing to the Supreme Judge of the world for the rectitude of our intentions, do, in the name and by authority of the good people of these colonies, solemnly publish and declare, that these United Colonies are, and of right ought to be, FREE AND INDEPENDENT STATES; that they are absolved from all allegiance to the British crown, and that all political connection between them and the state of Great Britain is, and ought to be, totally dissolved; and that, as free and independent states, they have full power to levy war, conclude peace, contract alliances, establish commerce, and do all other acts and things which independent states may of right do. And for the support of this declaration, with a firm reliance on the protection of Divine Providence, we mutually pledge to each other our lives, our fortunes, and our sacred honor.

The signers pledged their lives to the support of this Declaration. The Continental Congress ordered copies of the Declaration of Independence to be sent to all the states and to the army.

NEW HAMPSHIRE
Josiah Bartlett
William Whipple
Matthew Thornton

MASSACHUSETTS
John Hancock
John Adams
Samuel Adams
Robert Treat Paine
Elbridge Gerry

NEW YORK
William Floyd
Philip Livingston
Francis Lewis
Lewis Morris

RHODE ISLAND
Stephen Hopkins
William Ellery

NEW JERSEY
Richard Stockton
John Witherspoon
Francis Hopkinson
John Hart
Abraham Clark

PENNSYLVANIA
Robert Morris
Benjamin Rush
Benjamin Franklin
John Morton
George Clymer
James Smith
George Taylor
James Wilson
George Ross

DELAWARE
Caesar Rodney
George Read
Thomas McKean

MARYLAND
Samuel Chase
William Paca
Thomas Stone
Charles Carroll
of Carrollton

NORTH CAROLINA
Willam Hooper
Joseph Hewes
John Penn

VIRGINIA
George Wythe
Richard Henry Lee
Thomas Jefferson
Benjamin Harrison
Thomas Nelson, Jr.
Francis Lightfoot Lee
Carter Braxton

SOUTH CAROLINA
Edward Rutledge
Thomas Heyward, Jr.
Thomas Lynch, Jr.
Arthur Middleton

CONNECTICUT
Roger Sherman
Samuel Huntington
William Williams
Oliver Wolcott

GEORGIA
Button Gwinnett
Lyman Hall
George Walton

The Constitution of the United States

PREAMBLE*

We the people of the United States, in order to form a more perfect Union, establish justice, insure domestic tranquility, provide for the common defense, promote the general welfare, and secure the blessings of liberty to ourselves and our posterity, do ordain and establish this Constitution for the United States of America.

ARTICLE I
LEGISLATIVE BRANCH

SECTION 1. CONGRESS

All legislative powers herein granted shall be vested in a Congress of the United States, which shall consist of a Senate and House of Representatives.

SECTION 2. HOUSE OF REPRESENTATIVES

1. Election and Term of Members *The House of Representatives shall be composed of members chosen every second year by the people of the several States, and the electors in each State shall have the qualifications requisite for electors of the most numerous branch of the State Legislature.*

2. Qualifications *No person shall be a representative who shall not have attained to the age of twenty-five years, and been seven years a citizen of the United States, and who shall not, when elected, be an inhabitant of that State in which he shall be chosen.*

3. Number of Representatives per State *Representatives ~~and direct taxes~~** shall be apportioned among the several States which may be included within this Union, according to their respective numbers, ~~which shall be determined by adding to the whole number of free persons, including those bound to service for a term of years, and excluding Indians not taxed, three-fifths of all other persons.~~ The actual enumeration shall be made within three years after the first meeting of the Congress of the United States, and within every subsequent term of ten years, in such manner as they shall by law direct. The number of representatives shall not exceed one for every thirty thousand, but each State shall have at least one representative; ~~and until such enumeration shall be made, the State of New Hampshire shall be entitled to choose three, Massachusetts eight, Rhode Island and Providence Plantations one, Connecticut five, New York six, New Jersey four, Pennsylvania eight, Delaware one, Maryland six, Virginia ten, North Carolina five, South Carolina five, and Georgia three.~~*

*The titles of the Preamble, and of each article, section, clause, and amendment have been added to make the Constitution easier to read. These titles are not in the original document.

**Parts of the Constitution have been crossed out to show that they are not in force any more. They have been changed by amendments or they no longer apply.

Preamble The Preamble, or introduction, states the purposes of the Constitution. The writers wanted to strengthen the national government and give the nation a more solid foundation. The Preamble makes it clear that it is the people of the United States who have the power to establish or change a government.

Congress Section 1 gives Congress the power to make laws. Congress has two parts, the House of Representatives and the Senate.

Election and Term of Members Citizens elect the members of the House of Representatives every two years.

Qualifications Representatives must be at least 25 years old. They must have been United States citizens for at least seven years. They also must live in the state they represent.

Number of Representatives per State The number of representatives each state has is based on its population. The biggest states have the most representatives. Each state must have at least one representative. An enumeration, or census, must be taken every 10 years to find out a state's population. The number of representatives in the House is now fixed at 435.

George Washington watches delegates sign the Constitution.

Today Americans often use voting machines on election day.

Number, Term, and Selection of Members In each state, citizens elect two members of the Senate. This gives all states, whether big or small, equal power in the Senate. Senators serve six year terms. Originally, state legislatures chose the senators for their states. Today, however, people elect their senators directly. The Seventeenth Amendment made this change in 1913.

Qualifications Senators must be at least 30 years old and United States citizens for at least nine years. Like representatives, they must live in the state they represent.

President of the Senate The Vice President of the United States acts as the President, or chief officer, of the Senate. The Vice President votes only in cases of a tie.

Impeachment Trials If the House of Representatives impeaches, or charges, an official with a crime, the Senate holds a trial. If two-thirds of the senators find the official guilty, then the person is removed from office. The only President ever impeached was Andrew Johnson in 1868. He was found not guilty.

Election of Congress Each state decides where and when to hold elections. Today congressional elections are held in even-numbered years, on the Tuesday after the first Monday in November.

Annual Sessions The Constitution requires Congress to meet at least once a year. In 1933, the 20th Amendment made January 3rd the day for beginning a regular session of Congress.

---

4. *Vacancies* When vacancies happen in the representation from any State, the executive authority thereof shall issue writs of election to fill such vacancies.

5. *Special Powers* The House of Representatives shall choose their speaker and other officers; and shall have the sole power of impeachment.

SECTION 3. SENATE

1. *Number, Term, and Selection of Members* The Senate of the United States shall be composed of two senators from each State, ~~chosen by the Legislature thereof,~~ for six years; and each Senator shall have one vote.

2. *Overlapping Terms and Filling Vacancies* Immediately after they shall be assembled in consequence of the first election, they shall be divided as equally as may be into three classes. ~~The seats of the senators of the first class shall be vacated at the expiration of the second year, of the second class at the expiration of the fourth year, and of the third class at the expiration of the sixth year, so~~ that one-third may be chosen every second year; ~~and if vacancies happen by resignation, or otherwise, during the recess of the legislature of any State, the executive thereof may make temporary appointments until the next meeting of the legislature, which shall then fill such vacancies.~~

3. *Qualifications* No person shall be a senator who shall not have attained to the age of thirty years, and been nine years a citizen of the United States, and who shall not, when elected, be an inhabitant of that State for which he shall be chosen.

4. *President of the Senate* The Vice President of the United States shall be President of the Senate, but shall have no vote, unless they be equally divided.

5. *Other Officers* The Senate shall choose their other officers, and also a President pro tempore, in the absence of the Vice President, or when he shall exercise the office of the President of the United States.

6. *Impeachment Trials* The Senate shall have the sole power to try all impeachments. When sitting for that purpose, they shall be on oath or affirmation. When the President of the United States is tried, the Chief Justice shall preside: and no person shall be convicted without the concurrence of two-thirds of the members present.

7. *Penalties* Judgment in cases of impeachment shall not extend further than to removal from office, and disqualification to hold and enjoy any office of honor, trust, or profit under the United States: but the party convicted shall nevertheless be liable and subject to indictment, trial, judgement and punishment, according to law.

SECTION 4. ELECTIONS AND MEETINGS

1. *Election of Congress* The times, places and manner of holding elections for senators and representatives, shall be prescribed in each State by the legislature thereof; but the Congress may at any time by law make or alter such regulations, except as to the places of choosing Senators.

2. *Annual Sessions* The Congress shall assemble at least once in every year, ~~and such meeting shall be on the first Monday in December,~~ unless they shall by law appoint a different day.

SECTION 5. RULES OF PROCEDURE

1. *Organization* Each house shall be the judge of the elections, returns and qualifications of its own members, and a majority of each shall constitute a quorum to do business; but a smaller number may adjourn from day to day, and may be authorized to compel the attendance of absent members, in such manner, and under such penalties as each house may provide.

2. *Rules* Each house may determine the rules of its proceedings, punish its members for disorderly behavior, and, with the concurrence of two-thirds, expel a member.

3. *Journal* Each house shall keep a journal of its proceedings, and from time to time publish the same, excepting such parts as may in their judgement require secrecy; and the yeas and nays of the members of either house on any question shall, at the desire of one-fifth of those present, be entered on the journal.

4. *Adjournment* Neither house, during the session of Congress, shall, without the consent of the other, adjourn for more than three days, nor to any other place than that in which the two houses shall be sitting.

SECTION 6. PRIVILEGES AND RESTRICTIONS

1. *Pay and Protection* The senators and representatives shall receive a compensation for their services, to be ascertained by law, and paid out of the treasury of the United States. They shall in all cases, except treason, felony and breach of the peace, be privileged from arrest during their attendance at the session of their respective houses, and in going to and returning from the same; and for any speech or debate in either house, they shall not be questioned in any other place.

2. *Restrictions* No senator or representative shall, during the time for which he was elected, be appointed to any civil office under the authority of the United States, which shall have been created, or the emoluments whereof shall have been increased during such time; and no person holding any office under the United States, shall be a member of either house during his continuance in office.

SECTION 7. MAKING LAWS

1. *Tax Bills* All bills for raising revenue shall originate in the House of Representatives; but the Senate may propose or concur with amendments as on other bills.

2. *Passing a Law* Every bill which shall have passed the House of Representatives and the Senate, shall, before it became a law, be presented to the President of the United States; if he approve, he shall sign it, but if not, he shall return it, with his objections, to that house in which it shall have originated, who shall enter the objections at large on their journal, and proceed to reconsider it. If after such reconsideration two-thirds of that house shall agree to pass the bill, it shall be sent, together with the objections, to the other house, by which it shall likewise be reconsidered, and if approved by two-thirds of that house, it shall become a law. But in all such cases the votes of both houses shall be determined by yeas and nays, and the names of the persons voting for and against the bill shall be entered on the journal of each house respectively. If any bill shall not be returned by the president within ten days (Sundays excepted) after it shall have been presented to him, the same shall be a law, in like manner as if he had signed it, unless the Congress by their adjournment prevent its return, in which case it shall not be a law.

Organization A quorum is the smallest number of members that must be present for an organization to hold a meeting. For each house of Congress, this number is the majority, or more than one-half, of its members.

Rules Each house can make rules for its members and expel a member by a two-thirds vote.

Journal The Constitution requires each house to keep a record of its proceedings. *The Congressional Record* is published every day. It includes parts of speeches made in each house and allows any person to look up the votes of his or her representative.

Pay and Protection Congress sets the salaries of its members, and they are paid by the federal government. No member can be arrested for anything he or she says while in office. This protection allows members to speak freely in Congress.

Restrictions Members of Congress cannot hold other federal offices during their terms. This rule strengthens the separation of powers and protects the checks and balances system set up by the Constitution.

Tax Bills A bill is a proposed law. Only the House of Representatives can introduce bills that tax the people.

Passing a Law A bill must be passed by the majority of members in each house of Congress. Then it is sent to the President. If the President signs it, the bill becomes a law. If the President refuses to sign a bill, and Congress is in session, the bill becomes law ten days after the President receives it.

The President can also veto, or reject, a bill. However, if each house of Congress repasses the bill by a two-thirds vote, it becomes a law. Passing a law after the President vetoed it is called overriding a veto. This process is an important part of the checks and balances system set up by the Constitution.

Orders and Resolutions Congress can also pass resolutions that have the same power as laws. Such acts are also subject to the President's veto.

Taxation Only Congress has the power to collect taxes. Federal taxes must be the same in all parts of the country.

Commerce Congress controls both trade with foreign countries and trade among states.

Naturalization and Bankruptcy Naturalization is the process by which a person from another country becomes a United States citizen. Congress decides the requirements for this procedure.

Coins and Measures Congress has the power to coin money and set its value.

Copyrights and Patents Copyrights protect authors. Patents allow inventors to profit from their work by keeping control over it for a certain number of years. Congress grants patents to encourage scientific research.

Declaring War Only Congress can declare war on another country.

Militia Today the Militia is called the National Guard. The National Guard often helps people after floods, tornadoes, and other disasters.

3. *Orders and Resolutions Every order, resolution, or vote to which the concurrence of the Senate and House of Representatives may be necessary (except on a question of adjournment) shall be presented to the President of the United States; and before the same shall take effect, shall be approved by him, or, being disapproved by him, shall be repassed by two-thirds of the Senate and House of Representatives, according to the rules and limitations prescribed in the case of a bill.*

SECTION 8. POWERS DELEGATED TO CONGRESS

1. *Taxation The Congress shall have the power to lay and collect taxes, duties, imposts, and excises, to pay the debts and provide for the common defense and general welfare of the United States; but all duties, imposts and excises shall be uniform throughout the United States;*

2. *Borrowing To borrow money on the credit of the United States;*

3. *Commerce To regulate commerce with foreign nations, and among the several States, and with the Indian tribes;*

4. *Naturalization and Bankruptcy To establish an uniform rule of naturalization, and uniform laws on the subject of bankruptcies throughout the United States;*

5. *Coins and Measures To coin money, regulate the value thereof, and of foreign coin, and fix the standard of weights and measures;*

6. *Counterfeiting To provide for the punishment of counterfeiting the securities and current coin of the United States;*

7. *Post Offices To establish post offices and post roads;*

8. *Copyrights and Patents To promote the progress of science and useful arts by securing for limited times to authors and inventors the exclusive right to their respective writings and discoveries;*

9. *Courts To constitute tribunals inferior to the Supreme Court;*

10. *Piracy To define and punish piracies and felonies committed on the high seas, and offenses against the law of nations;*

11. *Declaring War To declare war, ~~grant letters of marque and reprisal,~~ and make rules concerning captures on land and water;*

12. *Army To raise and support armies, but no appropriation of money to that use shall be for a longer term than two years;*

13. *Navy To provide and maintain a navy;*

14. *Military Regulations To make rules for the government and regulation of the land and naval forces;*

15. *Militia To provide for calling forth the militia to execute the laws of the Union, suppress insurrections and repel invasions;*

16. *Militia Regulations To provide for organizing, arming and disciplining the militia, and for governing such part of them as may be employed in the service of the United States, reserving to the States respectively the appointment of the officers, and the authority of training the militia according to the discipline prescribed by Congress;*

17. *National Capital* To exercise exclusive legislation in all cases whatsoever, over such district (not exceeding ten miles square) as may, by cession of particular states, and the acceptance of Congress, become the seat of the government of the United States, and to exercise like authority over all places purchased by the consent of the legislature of the State in which the same shall be, for the erection of forts, magazines, arsenals, dock-yards, and other needful buildings;—and

18. *Necessary Laws* To make all laws which shall be necessary and proper for carrying into execution the foregoing powers, and all other powers vested by this Constitution in the government of the United States, or in any department or officer thereof.

SECTION 9 POWERS DENIED TO CONGRESS

1. *Slave Trade* ~~The migration or importation of such persons as any of the States now existing shall think proper to admit, shall not be prohibited by the Congress prior to the year 1808, but a tax or duty may be imposed on such importation, not exceeding ten dollars for each person.~~

2. *Habeas Corpus* The privilege of the writ of habeas corpus shall not be suspended, unless when in cases of rebellion or invasion the public safety may require it.

3. *Special Laws* No bill of attainder or ex post facto law shall be passed.

4. *Direct Taxes* ~~No capitation or other direct tax shall be laid, unless in proportion to the census or enumeration herein before directed to be taken.~~

5. *Export Taxes* No tax or duty shall be laid on articles exported from any State.

6. *Ports* No preference shall be given by any regulation of commerce or revenue to the ports of one State over those of another; nor shall vessels bound to, or from, one State, be obliged to enter, clear, or pay duties in another.

7. *Regulations on Spending* No money shall be drawn from the treasury, but in consequence of appropriations made by law; and a regular statement and account of the receipts and expenditures of all public money shall be published from time to time.

8. *Titles of Nobility and Gifts* No title of nobility shall be granted by the United States: and no person holding any office or profit or trust under them, shall, without the consent of the Congress, accept of any present, emolument, office, or title, of any kind whatever, from any king, prince, or foreign state.

SECTION 10. POWERS DENIED TO THE STATES

1. *Complete Restrictions* No State shall enter into any treaty, alliance, or confederation; grant letters of marque and reprisal; coin money; emit bills of credit; make anything but gold and silver coin a tender in payment of debts; pass any bill of attainder, ex post facto law, or law impairing the obligation of contracts, or grant any title of nobility.

2. *Partial Restrictions* No State shall, without the consent of the Congress, lay any imposts or duties on imports or exports, except what may be absolutely necessary for executing its inspection laws; and the net produce of all duties and imposts, laid by any State on imports or exports, shall be for the use of the treasury of the United States; and all such laws shall be subject to the revision and control of the Congress.

National Capital Congress makes the laws for the District of Columbia, the area where the nation's capital is located.

Necessary Laws This clause allows Congress to make laws on issues, such as television and radio, that are not mentioned in the Constitution.

Slave Trade This clause was another compromise between the North and the South. It prevented Congress from regulating the slave trade for 20 years. Congress outlawed the slave trade in 1808.

Habeas Corpus A writ of habeas corpus requires the government either to charge a person in jail with a particular crime or let the person go free. Except in emergencies, Congress cannot deny the right of a person to a writ.

Ports When regulating trade, Congress must treat all states equally. Also, states cannot tax goods traveling between states.

Regulations on Spending Congress controls the spending of public money. This clause checks the President's power.

Complete Restrictions The Constitution prevents the states from acting like individual countries. States cannot make treaties with foreign nations. They cannot issue their own money.

Partial Restrictions States cannot tax imports and exports without approval from Congress.

Other Restrictions States cannot declare war. They cannot keep their own armies.

Term of Office The President has the power to carry out the laws passed by Congress. The President and the Vice President serve four-year terms.

Electoral College A group of people called the Electoral College actually elects the President. The number of electors each state receives equals the total number of its representatives and senators.

Election Process Originally, electors voted for two people. The candidate who received the majority of votes became President. The runner-up became Vice President. Problems with this system led to the 12th Amendment, which changed the electoral college system.

Today electors almost always vote for the candidate who won the popular vote in their states. In other words, the candidate who wins the popular vote in a state also wins its electoral votes.

Time of Elections Today we elect our President on the Tuesday after the first Monday in November.

Qualifications A President must be at least 35 years old, a United States citizen by birth, and a resident of the United States for at least 14 years.

3. *Other Restrictions* No State shall, without the consent of Congress, lay any duty of tonnage, keep troops, or ships of war in time of peace, enter into any agreement or compact with another State, or with a foreign power, or engage in war, unless actually invaded, or in such imminent danger as will not admit of delay.

ARTICLE II
EXECUTIVE BRANCH

SECTION 1. PRESIDENT AND VICE PRESIDENT

1. *Term of Office* The executive power shall be vested in a President of the United States of America. He shall hold his office during the term of four years, and together with the Vice President, chosen for the same term, be elected as follows:

2. *Electoral College* Each State shall appoint, in such manner as the legislature thereof may direct, a number of electors, equal to the whole number of senators and representatives to which the State may be entitled in the Congress; but no senator or representative, or person holding an office of trust or profit under the United States, shall be appointed an elector.

3. *Election Process* ~~The electors shall meet in their respective States, and vote by ballot for two persons, of whom one at least shall not be an inhabitant of the same State with themselves. And they shall make a list of all the persons voted for, and of the number of votes for each; which list they shall sign and certify, and transmit sealed to the seat of the government of the United States, directed to the President of the Senate. The President of the Senate shall, in the presence of the Senate and House of Representatives, open all the certificates, and the votes shall then be counted. The person having the greatest number of votes shall be the President, if such number be a majority of the whole number of electors appointed, and if there be more than one who have such majority, and have an equal number of votes, then the House of Representatives shall immediately choose by ballot one of them for President; and if no person have a majority, then from the five highest on the list the said house shall in like manner choose the President. But in choosing the President, the votes shall be taken by States, the representation from each State having one vote; a quorum for this purpose shall consist of a member or members from two-thirds of the States, and a majority of all the States shall be necessary to a choice. In every case, after the choice of the President, the person having the greatest number of votes of the electors shall be the Vice President. But if there should remain two or more who have equal votes, the Senate shall choose from them by ballot the Vice President.~~

4. *Time of Elections* The Congress may determine the time of choosing the electors, and the day on which they shall give their votes; which day shall be the same throughout the United States.

5. *Qualifications* No person except a natural-born citizen, ~~or a citizen of the United States at the time of the adoption of this Constitution,~~ shall be eligible to the office of President; neither shall any person be eligible to that office who shall not have attained to the age of thirty-five years, and been fourteen years a resident within the United States.

6. *Vacancies* ~~In case of the removal of the President from office, or of his death,~~ ~~resignation, or inability to discharge the powers and duties of the said office, the~~ ~~same shall devolve on the Vice President, and the Congress may by law provide~~ ~~for the case of removal, death, resignation, or inability, both of the President and~~ ~~Vice President, declaring what officer shall then act as President, and such officer~~ ~~shall act accordingly, until the disability be removed, or a President shall be elect-~~ ~~ed.~~

7. *Salary* The President shall, at stated times, receive for his services a compensation, which shall neither be increased nor diminished during the period for which he shall have been elected, and he shall not receive within that period any other emolument from the United States, or any of them.

8. *Oath of Office* Before he enter on the execution of his office, he shall take the following oath or affirmation:—"I do solemnly swear (or affirm) that I will faithfully execute the office of President of the United States, and will to the best of my ability, preserve, protect and defend the Constitution of the United States."

SECTION 2. POWERS OF THE PRESIDENT

1. *Military Powers* The President shall be commander in chief of the army and navy of the United States, and of the militia of the several States, when called into the actual service of the United States; he may require the opinion, in writing, of the principal officer in each of the executive departments, upon any subject relating to the duties of their respective offices, and he shall have power to grant reprieves and pardons for offenses against the United States, except in cases of impeachment.

2. *Treaties and Appointments* He shall have power, by and with the advice and consent of the Senate, to make treaties, provided two-thirds of the Senators present concur; and he shall nominate, and by and with the advice and consent of the Senate, shall appoint ambassadors, other public ministers and consuls, judges of the Supreme Court, and all other officers of the United States, whose appointments are not herein otherwise provided for, and which shall be established by law: but the Congress may by law vest the appointment of such inferior officers, as they think proper, in the President alone, in the courts of law, or in the heads of departments.

3. *Temporary Appointments* The President shall have power to fill up all vacancies that may happen during the recess of the Senate, by granting commissions which shall expire at the end of their next session.

SECTION 3. DUTIES

He shall from time to time give to the Congress information of the State of the Union, and recommend to their consideration such measures as he shall judge necessary and expedient; he may on extraordinary occasions, convene both houses, or either of them, and in case of disagreement between them with respect to the time of adjournment, he may adjourn them to such time as he shall think proper; he shall receive ambassadors and other public ministers; he shall take care that the laws be faithfully executed, and shall commission all the officers of the United States.

Vacancies If the President resigns, dies, or is impeached and found guilty, the Vice President becomes President. The 25th Amendment replaced this clause in 1967.

Salary The President receives a yearly salary that cannot be increased or decreased during his or her term. The President cannot hold any other paid government positions while in office.

Oath of Office Every President must promise to uphold the Constitution. The Chief Justice of the Supreme Court usually administers this oath.

Military Powers The President is the leader of the country's military forces.

Treaties and Appointments The President can make treaties with other nations. However, treaties must be approved by a two-thirds vote of the Senate. The President also appoints Supreme Court Justices and ambassadors to foreign countries. The Senate must approve these appointments.

Duties The President must report to Congress at least once a year and make recommendations for laws. This report is known as the State of the Union address. The President delivers it each January.

The President delivers the State of the Union address each year.

Impeachment The President and other officials can be forced out of office only if found guilty of particular crimes. This clause protects government officials from being impeached for unimportant reasons.

Federal Courts The Supreme Court is the highest court in the nation. It makes the final decisions in all of the cases it hears. Congress decides the size of the Supreme Court. Today it contains nine judges. Congress also has the power to set up a system of lower federal courts. All federal judges may hold their offices for as long as they live.

General Jurisdiction Jurisdiction means the right of a court to hear a case. Federal courts have jurisdiction over such cases as those involving the Constitution, federal laws, treaties, and disagreements between states.

The Supreme Court One of the Supreme Court's most important jobs is to decide whether laws that pass are constitutional. This power is another example of the checks and balances system in the federal government.

Trial by Jury The Constitution guarantees everyone the right to a trial by jury. The only exception is in impeachment cases, which are tried in the Senate.

Definition People cannot be convicted of treason in the United States for what they think or say. To be guilty of treason, a person must rebel against the government by using violence or helping enemies of the country.

Every American has a right to a trial by jury. Jurors' chairs are shown below.

SECTION 4. IMPEACHMENT

The President, Vice President, and all civil officers of the United States, shall be removed from office on impeachment for, and conviction of, treason, bribery, or other high crimes and misdemeanors.

ARTICLE III
JUDICIAL BRANCH

SECTION 1. FEDERAL COURTS

The judicial power of the United States shall be vested in one Supreme Court, and in such inferior courts as the Congress may from time to time ordain and establish. The judges, both of the Supreme and inferior courts, shall hold their offices during good behaviour, and shall, at stated times, receive for their services, a compensation, which shall not be diminished during their continuance in office.

SECTION 2. AUTHORITY OF THE FEDERAL COURTS

*1. **General Jurisdiction** The judicial power shall extend to all cases, in law and equity, arising under this Constitution, the laws of the United States, and treaties made, or which shall be made, under their authority; to all cases affecting ambassadors, other public ministers and consuls; to all cases of admiralty and maritime jurisdiction; to controversies to which the United States shall be a party; to controversies between two or more States;* ~~between a State and citizens of another State;~~ *between citizens of different States; between citizens of the same State claiming lands under grants of different States, and between a State, or the citizens thereof, and foreign states, citizens or subjects.*

*2. **The Supreme Court** In all cases affecting ambassadors, other public ministers and consuls, and those in which a State shall be party, the Supreme Court shall have original jurisdiction. In all the other cases before mentioned, the Supreme Court shall have appellate jurisdiction, both as to law and fact, with such exceptions, and under such regulations as the Congress shall make.*

*3. **Trial by Jury** The trial of all crimes, except in cases of impeachment, shall be by jury; and such trial shall be held in the State where the said crimes shall have been committed; but when not committed within any state, the trial shall be at such place or places as the Congress may by law have directed.*

SECTION 3. TREASON

*1. **Definition** Treason against the United States shall consist only in levying war against them, or in adhering to their enemies, giving them aid and comfort. No person shall be convicted of treason unless on the testimony of two witnesses to the same overt act, or on confession in open court.*

*2. **Punishment** The Congress shall have power to declare the punishment of treason, but no attainder of treason shall work corruption of blood, or forfeiture except during the life of the person attainted.*

ARTICLE IV
RELATIONS AMONG THE STATES

SECTION 1. OFFICIAL RECORDS

Full faith and credit shall be given in each state to the public acts, records and judicial proceedings of every other State. And the Congress may by general laws prescribe the manner in which such acts, records, and proceedings shall be proved, and the effect thereof.

Official Records Each state must accept the laws, acts, and legal decisions made by other states.

SECTION 2. PRIVILEGES OF THE CITIZENS

1. **Privileges** *The citizens of each State shall be entitled to all privileges and immunities of citizens in the several states.*

2. **Return of a Person Accused of a Crime** *A person charged in any State with treason, felony, or other crime, who shall flee from justice, and be found in another State, shall on demand of the executive authority of the State from which he fled, be delivered up, to be removed to the State having jurisdiction of the crime.*

3. **Return of Fugitive Slaves** No person held to service or labor in one State, under the laws thereof, escaping into another, shall, in consequence of any law or regulation therein, be discharged from such service or labor, but shall be delivered up on claim of the party to whom such service or labor may be due.

Privileges States must give the same rights to citizens of other states that they give to ther own citizens.

Return of a Person Accused of a Crime If a person charged with a crime escapes to another state, he or she must be returned to the original state to go on trial. This act of returning someone from one state to another is called extradition.

SECTION 3. NEW STATES AND TERRITORIES

1. **New States** *New states may be admitted by the Congress into this Union; but no new State shall be formed or erected within the jurisdiction of any other State, nor any State be formed by the junction of two or more States, or parts of States, without the consent of the legislatures of the States concerned, as well as of the Congress.*

2. **Federal Lands** *The Congress shall have power to dispose of and make all needful rules and regulations respecting the territory or other property belonging to the United States; and nothing in this Constitution shall be so construed as to prejudice any claims of the United States, or of any particular State.*

New States Congress has the power to create new states out of the nation's territories. All new states have the same rights as the old states. This clause made it clear that the United States would not make colonies out of its new lands.

SECTION 4. GUARANTEES TO THE STATES

The United States shall guarantee to every State in this Union a republican form of government, and shall protect each of them against invasion; and on application of the legislature, or of the executive (when the legislature cannot be convened) against domestic violence.

Guarantees to the States The federal government must defend the states from rebellions and from attacks by other countries.

ARTICLE V
AMENDING THE CONSTITUTION

The Congress, whenever two-thirds of both houses shall deem it necessary, shall propose amendments to this Constitution, or, on the application of the legislatures of two-thirds of the several States, shall call a convention for proposing amendments, which, in either case, shall be valid to all intents and purposes, as part of this Constitution, when ratified by the legislatures of three-fourths of the several States, or by conventions in three-fourths thereof, as the one or the other mode of ratification may be proposed by the Congress; provided, that no amendment which may be made prior to the year 1808, shall in any manner affect the first and fourth clauses in the ninth section of the first article; and that no State, without its consent, shall be deprived of its equal suffrage in the Senate.

Amending the Constitution An amendment to the Constitution may be proposed either by a two-thirds vote of each house of Congress or by a national convention called by Congress at the request of two-thirds of the state legislatures. To be ratified, or approved, an amendment must be supported by three-fourths of the state legislatures or by three-fourths of special conventions held in each state.

Once an amendment is ratified, it becomes part of the Constitution. Only a new amendment can change it. Amendments have allowed people to change the Constitution to meet the changing needs of the nation.

ARTICLE VI
GENERAL PROVISIONS

*1. **Public Debt** All debts contracted and engagements entered into, before the adoption of this Constitution, shall be as valid against the United States under this Constitution, as under the Confederation.*

*2. **Federal Supremacy** This Constitution, and the laws of the United States which shall be made in pursuance thereof; and all treaties made, or which shall be made, under the authority of the United States, shall be the supreme law of the land; and the judges in every State shall be bound thereby, anything in the Constitution or laws of any State to the contrary notwithstanding.*

*3. **Oaths of Office** The senators and representatives before mentioned, and the members of the several State legislatures, and all executive and judicial officers, both of the United States, and of the several States, shall be bound by oath or affirmation to support this Constitution; but no religious test shall ever be required as a qualification to any office or public trust under the United States.*

ARTICLE VII
RATIFICATION

The ratification of the conventions of nine States shall be sufficient for the establishment of this Constitution between the States so ratifying the same.

Done in Convention by the unanimous consent of the States present the seventeenth day of September in the year of our Lord one thousand seven hundred and eighty-seven and of the independence of the United States of America the twelfth. In witness whereof we have hereunto subscribed our names.

George Washington, President and deputy from Virginia

DELAWARE
George Read
Gunning Bedford, Junior
John Dickinson
Richard Bassett
Jacob Broom

MARYLAND
James McHenry
Daniel of St. Thomas Jenifer
Daniel Carroll

VIRGINIA
John Blair
James Madison, Junior

NORTH CAROLINA
William Blount
Richard Dobbs Spaight
Hugh Williamson

SOUTH CAROLINA
John Rutledge
Charles Cotesworth Pinckney
Charles Pinckney
Pierce Butler

GEORGIA
William Few
Abraham Baldwin

NEW HAMPSHIRE
John Langdon
Nicholas Gilman

MASSACHUSETTS
Nathaniel Gorham
Rufus King

CONNECTICUT
William Samuel Johnson
Roger Sherman

NEW YORK
Alexander Hamilton

NEW JERSEY
William Livingston
David Brearley
William Paterson
Jonathan Dayton

PENNSYLVANIA
Benjamin Franklin
Thomas Mifflin
Robert Morris
George Clymer
Thomas FitzSimons
Jared Ingersoll
James Wilson
Gouverneur Morris

Delegates wait for their turn to sign the new Constitution.

AMENDMENTS TO THE CONSTITUTION

AMENDMENT I (1791)*
BASIC FREEDOMS

Congress shall make no law respecting an establishment of religion, or prohibiting the free exercise thereof; or abridging the freedom of speech, or of the press; or the right of the people peaceably to assemble, and to petition the government for a redress of grievances.

AMENDMENT II (1791)
WEAPONS AND THE MILITIA

A well-regulated militia, being necessary to the security of a free State, the right of the people to keep and bear arms, shall not be infringed.

AMENDMENT III (1791)
HOUSING SOLDIERS

No soldier shall, in time of peace, be quartered in any house, without the consent of the owner, nor in time of war, but in a manner to be prescribed by law.

AMENDMENT IV (1791)
SEARCH AND SEIZURE

The right of the people to be secure in their persons, houses, papers, and effects, against unreasonable searches and seizures, shall not be violated, and no warrants shall issue, but upon probable cause, supported by oath or affirmation, and particularly describing the place to be searched, and the persons or things to be seized.

AMENDMENT V (1791)
RIGHTS OF THE ACCUSED

No person shall be held to answer for a capital, or otherwise infamous crime, unless on a presentment or indictment of a grand jury, except in cases arising in the land or naval forces, or in the militia, when in actual service in time of war or public danger; nor shall any person be subject for the same offense to be twice put in jeopardy of life or limb; nor shall be compelled in any criminal case to be a witness against himself, nor be deprived of life, liberty, or property, without due process of law; nor shall private property be taken for public use without just compensation.

AMENDMENT VI (1791)
RIGHT TO A FAIR TRIAL

In all criminal prosecutions, the accused shall enjoy the right to a speedy and public trial, by an impartial jury of the State and district wherein the crime shall have been committed, which district shall have been previously ascertained by law, and to be informed of the nature and cause of the accusation; to be confronted with the witnesses against him; to have compulsory process for obtaining witnesses in his favor, and to have the assistance of counsel for his defense.

Amendments to the Constitution

Basic Freedoms The government cannot pass laws that favor one religion over another. Nor can it stop people from saying or writing whatever they want. The people have the right to gather openly and discuss problems they have with the government.

Weapons and the Militia This amendment was included to prevent the federal government from taking away guns used by members of state militias.

Housing Soldiers The army cannot use people's homes to house soldiers unless it is approved by law. Before the American Revolution, the British housed soldiers in private homes without permission of the owners.

Search and Seizure This amendment protects people's privacy in their homes. The government cannot search or seize anyone's property without a warrant, or a written order, from a court. A warrant must list the people and the property to be searched and give reasons for the search.

Rights of the Accused A person accused of a crime has the right to a fair trial. A person cannot be tried twice for the same crime. This amendment also protects a person from self-incrimination, or having to testify against himself or herself.

Right to a Fair Trial Anyone accused of a crime is entitled to a quick and fair trial by jury. This right protects people from being kept in jail without being convicted of a crime. Also, the government must provide a lawyer for anyone accused of a crime who cannot afford to hire a lawyer.

---

*The date beside each amendment indicates the year the amendment was ratified.

AMENDMENT VII (1791)
JURY TRIAL IN CIVIL CASES

In suits at common law, where the value in controversy shall exceed twenty dollars, the right of trial by jury shall be preserved, and no fact tried by a jury shall be otherwise reexamined in any court of the United States, than according to the rules of the common law.

AMENDMENT VIII (1791)
BAIL AND PUNISHMENT

Excessive bail shall not be required, nor excessive fines imposed, nor cruel and unusual punishments inflicted.

AMENDMENT IX (1791)
POWERS RESERVED TO THE PEOPLE

The enumeration in the Constitution, of certain rights, shall not be construed to deny or disparage others retained by the people.

AMENDMENT X (1791)
POWERS RESERVED TO THE STATES

The powers not delegated to the United States by the Constitution, nor prohibited by it to the States, are reserved to the States respectively, or to the people.

AMENDMENT XI (1795)
SUITS AGAINST STATES

The judicial power of the United States shall not be construed to extend to any suit in law or equity, commenced or prosecuted against one of the United States by citizens of another State, or by citizens or subjects of any foreign State.

AMENDMENT XII (1804)
ELECTION OF THE PRESIDENT AND VICE PRESIDENT

The electors shall meet in their respective States and vote by ballot for President and Vice President, one of whom, at least, shall not be an inhabitant of the same State with themselves; they shall name in their ballots the person voted for as President, and in distinct ballots the person voted for as Vice President, and they shall make distinct lists of all persons voted for as President, and of all persons voted for as Vice President, and of the number of votes for each, which lists they shall sign and certify, and transmit sealed to the seat of the government of the United States, directed to the President of the Senate; the President of the Senate shall, in the presence of the Senate and House of Representatives, open all the certificates and the votes shall then be counted; the person having the greatest number of votes for President, shall be the President, if such number be a majority of the whole number of electors appointed; and if no person have such majority, then from the persons having the highest numbers not exceeding three on the list of those voted for as President, the House of Representatives shall choose immediately, by ballot, the President. But in choosing the President, the votes shall be taken by States, the representation from each State having one vote; a quorum for this purpose shall consist of a member or members from two-thirds of the States, and a majority of all the States shall be necessary to a choice. And if the House of Representatives shall not choose a President whenever the right of choice shall devolve upon them, before the fourth day of March next following,

Jury Trial in Civil Cases Civil cases usually involve two or more people suing each other over money, property, or personal injury. A jury trial is guaranteed in large lawsuits.

Bail and Punishment Courts cannot treat people accused of crimes in ways that are unusually harsh.

Powers Reserved to the People The people keep all rights not listed in the Constitution.

Powers Reserved to the States Any rights not clearly given to the federal government by the Constitution belong to the states or the people.

Suits Against States A citizen from one state cannot sue the government of another state in a federal court. Such cases are decided in state courts.

Election of the President and Vice President Under the original Constitution, each member of the Electoral College voted for two candidates for President. The candidate with the most votes became President. The one with the second highest total became Vice President.

The 12th Amendment changed this system. Members of the electoral college distinguish between their votes for the President and Vice President. This change was an important step in the development of the two party system. It allows each party to nominate its own team of candidates.

then the Vice President shall act as President, as in case of the death or other constitutional disability of the President. The person having the greatest number of votes as Vice President, shall be the Vice President, if such number be a majority of the whole number of electors appointed, and if no person have a majority, then from the two highest numbers on the list, the Senate shall choose the Vice President; a quorum for the purpose shall consist of two-thirds of the whole number of senators, and a majority of the whole number shall be necessary to a choice. But no person constitutionally ineligible to the office of President shall be eligible to that of Vice President of the United States.

AMENDMENT XIII (1865)
END OF SLAVERY

SECTION 1. ABOLITION

Neither slavery nor involuntary servitude, except as a punishment for crime whereof the party shall have been duly convicted, shall exist within the United States, or any place subject to their jurisdiction.

SECTION 2. ENFORCEMENT

Congress shall have power to enforce this article by appropriate legislation.

AMENDMENT XIV (1868)
RIGHTS OF CITIZENS

SECTION 1. CITIZENSHIP

All persons born or naturalized in the United States, and subject to the jurisdiction thereof, are citizens of the United States and of the State wherein they reside. No State shall make or enforce any law which shall abridge the privileges or immunities of citizens of the United States; nor shall any State deprive any person of life, liberty, or property, without due process of law; nor deny to any person within its jurisdiction the equal protection of the laws.

SECTION 2. NUMBER OF REPRESENTATIVES

Representatives shall be apportioned among the several States according to their respective numbers, counting the whole number of persons in each State, excluding Indians not taxed. But when the right to vote at any election for the choice of electors for President and Vice President of the United States, representatives in Congress, the executive and judicial officers of a State, or the members of the legislature thereof, is denied to any of the male inhabitants of such State, being twenty-one years of age, and citizens of the United States, or in any way abridged, except for participation in rebellion, or other crime, the basis of representation therein shall be reduced in the proportion which the number of such male citizens shall bear to the whole number of male citizens twenty-one years of age in such State.

The Twelfth Amendment allowed parties to nominate teams of candidates, as this campaign poster shows.

Abolition This amendment ended slavery in the United States. It was ratified after the Civil War.

Citizenship This amendment defined citizenship in the United States. "Due process of law" means that no state can deny its citizens the rights and privileges they enjoy as United States citizens. The goal of this amendment was to protect the rights of the recently freed African Americans.

Number of Representatives This clause replaced the Three-Fifths Clause in Article 1. Each state's representation is based on its total population. Any state denying its male citizens over the age of 21 the right to vote will have its representation in Congress decreased.

This etching shows a group of enslaved persons celebrating their emancipation.

Penalty for Rebellion Officials who fought against the Union in the Civil War could not hold public office in the United States. This clause tried to keep Confederate leaders out of power. In 1872, Congress removed this limit.

SECTION 3. PENALTY FOR REBELLION

No person shall be a senator or representative in Congress, or elector of President and Vice President, or hold any office, civil or military, under the United States, or under any State, who, having previously taken an oath, as a member of Congress, or as an officer of the United States, or as a member of any State legislature, or as an executive or judicial officer of any State, to support the Constitution of the United States, shall have engaged in insurrection or rebellion against the same, or given aid or comfort to the enemies thereof. But Congress may by a vote of two-thirds of each house, remove such disability.

Government Debt The United States paid all of the Union's debts from the Civil War. However, it did not pay any of the Confederacy's debts. This clause prevented the southern states from using public money to pay for the rebellion or from compensating citizens who lost their enslaved persons.

SECTION 4. GOVERNMENT DEBT

The validity of the public debt of the United States, authorized by law, including debts incurred for payment of pensions and bounties for services in suppressing insurrection or rebellion, shall not be questioned. But neither the United States nor any State shall assume or pay any debt or obligation incurred in aid of insurrection or rebellion against the United States, or any claim for the loss or emancipation of any slave; but all such debts, obligations and claims shall be held illegal and void.

SECTION 5. ENFORCEMENT

The Congress shall have power to enforce, by appropriate legislation, the provisions of this article.

AMENDMENT XV (1870)
VOTING RIGHTS

Right to Vote No state can deny its citizens the right to vote because of their race. This amendment was designed to protect the voting rights of African Americans.

SECTION 1. RIGHT TO VOTE

The right of citizens of the United States to vote shall not be denied or abridged by the United States or by any State on account of race, color, or previous condition of servitude.

SECTION 2. ENFORCEMENT

The Congress shall have power to enforce this article by appropriate legislation.

AMENDMENT XVI (1913)
INCOME TAX

Income Tax Congress has the power to tax personal incomes.

The Congress shall have power to lay and collect taxes on incomes, from whatever sources derived, without apportionment among the several States, and without regard to any census or enumeration.

AMENDMENT XVII (1913)
DIRECT ELECTION OF SENATORS

Direct Election of Senators In the original Constitution, the state legislatures elected senators. This amendment gave citizens the power to elect their senators directly. It made senators more responsible to the people they represented.

SECTION 1. METHOD OF ELECTION

The Senate of the United States shall be composed of two senators from each State, elected by the people thereof, for six years; and each senator shall have one vote. The electors in each State shall have the qualifications requisite for electors of the most numerous branch of the State legislatures.

SECTION 2. VACANCIES

When vacancies happen in the representation of any State in the Senate, the executive authority of such State shall issue writs of election to fill such vacancies: Provided, that the legislature of any State may empower the executive thereof to make temporary appointments until the people fill the vacancies by election as the legislature may direct.

SECTION 3. EXCEPTION

This amendment shall not be so construed as to affect the election or term of any Senator chosen before it becomes valid as part of the Constitution.

AMENDMENT XVIII (1919)
BAN ON ALCOHOLIC DRINKS

SECTION 1. PROHIBITION

After one year from the ratification of this article the manufacture, sale, or transportation of intoxicating liquors within, the importation thereof into, or the exportation thereof from the United States and all territory subject to the jurisdiction thereof for beverage purposes is hereby prohibited.

SECTION 2. ENFORCEMENT

The Congress and the several States shall have concurrent power to enforce this article by appropriate legislation.

SECTION 3. RATIFICATION

This article shall be inoperative unless it shall have been ratified as an amendment to the Constitution by the legislatures of the several States, as provided in the Constitution, within seven years from the date of the submission hereof to the States by Congress.

AMENDMENT XIX (1920)
WOMEN'S SUFFRAGE

SECTION 1. RIGHT TO VOTE

The right of citizens of the United States to vote shall not be denied or abridged by the United States or by any State on account of sex.

SECTION 2. ENFORCEMENT

The Congress shall have power to enforce this article by appropriate legislation.

AMENDMENT XX (1933)
TERMS OF OFFICE

SECTION 1. BEGINNING OF TERMS

The terms of the President and Vice-President shall end at noon on the 20th day of January, and the terms of senators and representatives at noon on the 3rd day of January, of the years in which such terms would have ended if this article had not been ratified; and the terms of their successors shall then begin.

The Prohibition movement used posters like this to reach the public.

Prohibition This amendment made it against the law to make or sell alcoholic beverages in the United States. This law was called prohibition. Fourteen years later, the 21st Amendment ended Prohibition.

Ratification The amendment for Prohibition was the first one to include a time limit for ratification. To go into effect, the amendment had to be approved by three-fourths of the states within seven years.

Women's Suffrage This amendment gave the right to vote to all women 21 years of age and older.

This 1915 banner pushed the cause of women's suffrage.

Beginning of Terms The President and Vice President's terms begin on January 20th of the year after their election. The terms for senators and representatives begin on January 3rd. Before this amendment, an official defeated in November stayed in office until March.

SECTION 2. SESSIONS OF CONGRESS

The Congress shall assemble at least once in every year, and such meeting shall begin at noon on the 3rd day of January, unless they shall by law appoint a different day.

SECTION 3. PRESIDENTIAL SUCCESSION

If, at the time fixed for the beginning of the term of the President, the President-elect shall have died, the Vice President-elect shall become President. If a President shall not have been chosen before the time fixed for the beginning of his term, or if the President-elect shall have failed to qualify, then the Vice President-elect shall act as President until a President shall have qualified; and the Congress may by law provide for the case wherein neither a President-elect nor a Vice President-elect shall have qualified, declaring who shall then act as President, or the manner in which one who is to act shall be selected, and such person shall act accordingly until a President or Vice President shall have qualified.

SECTION 4. ELECTIONS DECIDED BY CONGRESS

The Congress may by law provide for the case of the death of any of the persons from whom the House of Representatives may choose a President whenever the right of choice shall have devolved upon them, and for the case of the death of any of the persons from whom the Senate may choose a Vice President whenever the right of choice shall have devolved upon them.

SECTION 5. EFFECTIVE DATE

Sections 1 and 2 shall take effect on the 15th day of October following the ratification of this article.

SECTION 6. RATIFICATION

This article shall be inoperative unless it shall have been ratified as an amendment to the Constitution by the legislatures of three-fourths of the several States within seven years from the date of its submission.

AMENDMENT XXI (1933)
END OF PROHIBITION

SECTION 1. REPEAL OF EIGHTEENTH AMENDMENT

The eighteenth article of amendment to the Constitution of the United States is hereby repealed.

SECTION 2. STATE LAWS

The transportation or importation into any State, territory, or possession of the United States for delivery or use therein of intoxicating liquors, in violation of the laws thereof, is hereby prohibited.

SECTION 3. RATIFICATION

This article shall be inoperative unless it shall have been ratified as an amendment to the Constitution by conventions in the several States, as provided in the Constitution, within seven years from the date of the submission hereof to the States by the Congress.

Presidential Succession A President who has been elected but has not yet taken office is called the President-elect. If the President-elect dies, then the Vice President-elect becomes President. If neither the President-elect nor the Vice President-elect can take office, then Congress decides who will act as President.

President Kennedy delivers his inaugural address in 1961.

End of Prohibition This amendment repealed, or ended, the 18th Amendment. It made alcoholic beverages legal once again in the United States. However, states can still control or stop the sale of alcohol within their borders.

AMENDMENT XXII (1951)
LIMIT ON PRESIDENTIAL TERMS

SECTION 1. TWO-TERM LIMIT

No person shall be elected to the office of the President more than twice, and no person who has held the office of President, or acted as President, for more that two years of a term to which some other person was elected President shall be elected to the office of the President more than once. ~~But this article shall not apply to any person holding the office of President when this article was proposed by the Congress, and shall not prevent any person who may be holding the office of President, or acting as President, during the term within which this article becomes operative from holding the office of President or acting as President during the remainder of such term.~~

SECTION 2. RATIFICATION

~~This article shall be inoperative unless it shall have been ratified as an amendment to the Constitution by the legislatures of three-fourths of the several States within seven years from the date of its submission to the States by the Congress.~~

AMENDMENT XXIII (1961)
PRESIDENTIAL VOTES FOR WASHINGTON, D.C.

SECTION 1. NUMBER OF ELECTORS

The District constituting the seat of government of the United States shall appoint in such manner as the Congress may direct:

A number of electors of President and Vice President equal to the whole number of senators and representatives in Congress to which the District would be entitled if it were a State, but in no event more than the least populous State; they shall be in addition to those appointed by the States, but they shall be considered, for the purposes of the election of President and Vice President, to be electors appointed by a State; and they shall meet in the District and perform such duties as provided by the twelfth article of amendment.

SECTION 2. ENFORCEMENT

The Congress shall have power to enforce this article by appropriate legislation.

AMENDMENT XXIV (1964)
BAN ON POLL TAXES

SECTION 1. POLL TAXES ILLEGAL

The right of citizens of the United States to vote in any primary or other election for President or Vice President, for electors for President or Vice President, or for senator or representative in Congress, shall not be denied or abridged by the United States or any State by reason of failure to pay any poll tax or other tax.

SECTION 2. ENFORCEMENT

The Congress shall have power to enforce this article by appropriate legislation.

Two-Term Limit George Washington set a precedent that Presidents should not serve more than two terms in office. However, Franklin D. Roosevelt broke the precedent. He was elected President four times between 1932 and 1944. Some people feared that a President holding office for this long could become too powerful. This amendment limits Presidents to two terms in office.

Presidential Votes for Washington, D.C. This amendment gives people who live in the nation's capital a vote for President. The electoral votes in Washington D.C., are based on its population. However, it cannot have more votes than the state with the smallest population. Today, Washington, D.C. has three electoral votes.

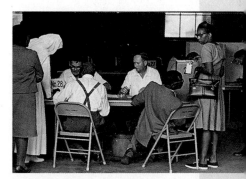

African Americans voting in Selma, Alabama, in 1966.

Ban on Poll Taxes A poll tax requires a person to pay a certain amount of money to register to vote. These taxes were used to stop poor African Americans from voting. This amendment made any such taxes illegal in federal elections.

AMENDMENT XXV (1967)
PRESIDENTIAL SUCCESSION

SECTION 1. VACANCY IN THE PRESIDENCY

In case of the removal of the President from office or of his death or resignation, the Vice President shall become President.

SECTION 2. VACANCY IN THE VICE PRESIDENCY

Whenever there is a vacancy in the office of the Vice President, the President shall nominate a Vice President who shall take office upon confirmation by a majority vote of both houses of Congress.

SECTION 3. DISABILITY OF THE PRESIDENT

Whenever the President transmits to the President pro tempore of the Senate and the Speaker of the House of Representatives his written declaration that he is unable to discharge the powers and duties of his office, and until he transmits to them a written declaration to the contrary, such powers and duties shall be discharged by the Vice President as Acting President.

SECTION 4. DETERMINING PRESIDENTIAL DISABILITY

Whenever the Vice President and a majority of either the principal officers of the executive departments or of such other body as Congress may by law provide, transmit to the President pro tempore of the Senate and the Speaker of the House of Representatives their written declaration that the President is unable to discharge the powers and duties of his office, the Vice President shall immediately assume the powers and duties of the office as Acting President.

Thereafter, when the President transmits to the President pro tempore of the Senate and the Speaker of the House of Representatives his written declaration that no inability exists, he shall resume the powers and duties of his office unless the Vice President and a majority of either the principal officers of the executive departments or of such other body as Congress may by law provide, transmit within four days to the President pro tempore of the Senate and the Speaker of the House of Representatives their written declaration that the President is unable to discharge the powers and duties of his office. Thereupon Congress shall decide the issue, assembling within 48 hours for that purpose if not in session. If the Congress, within 21 days after receipt of the latter written declaration, or, if Congress is not in session, within 21 days after Congress is required to assemble, determines by two-thirds vote of both houses that the President is unable to discharge the powers and duties of his office, the Vice President shall continue to discharge the same as Acting President; otherwise, the President shall resume the powers and duties of his office.

AMENDMENT XXVI (1971)
VOTING AGE

SECTION 1. RIGHT TO VOTE

The right of citizens of the United States, who are 18 years of age or older, to vote shall not be denied or abridged by the United States or by any state on account of age.

Vacancy in the Vice Presidency If the Vice President becomes President, he or she may nominate a new Vice President. This nomination must be approved by both houses of Congress.

Disability of the President This section tells what happens if the President suddenly becomes ill or is seriously injured. The Vice President takes over as Acting President. When the President is ready to take office again, he or she must tell Congress.

The voting age was lowered to 18 in 1971.

Right to Vote This amendment gave the vote to everyone 18 years of age and older.

SECTION 2. ENFORCEMENT

The Congress shall have power to enforce this article by appropriate legislation.

AMENDMENT XXVII (1992)
CONGRESSIONAL PAY

No law, varying the compensation for the services of the senators and representatives, shall take effect, until an election of representatives shall have intervened.

Limits on Pay Raises This amendment prohibits a Congressional pay raise from taking effect during the current term of the Congress that voted for the raise.

from The *Federalist* (No. 10) (1787)

The *Federalist Papers* are a series of 85 letters published by newspapers in 1787 and 1788. Written by Alexander Hamilton, James Madison, and John Jay, it strongly supported ratification of the Constitution. In The *Federalist* (No. 10), James Madison put forth his arguments in support of electing representatives to Congress.

The two great points of difference between a democracy and a republic are: first, the delegation of the government, in the latter, to a small number of citizens selected by the rest; secondly, the greater number of citizens and greater sphere of country, over which the latter may be extended.

The effect of the first difference is, on the one hand, to refine and enlarge the public views, by passing them through the medium of a chosen body of citizens, whose wisdom may best discern the true interest of their country and whose patriotism and love of justice will be least likely to sacrifice it to temporary or partial considerations. . . .

By enlarging too much the number of electors, you render the representative too little acquainted with all their local circumstances and lesser interests; as by reducing it too much, you render him unduly attached to these, and too little fit to comprehend and pursue great and national objects. . . .

Extend the sphere and you take in a greater variety of parties and interests; you make it less probable that a majority of the whole will have a common motive to invade the rights of other citizens.

The Star-Spangled Banner (1814)

Francis Scott Key wrote "The Star-Spangled Banner" in 1814 while aboard ship during the battle of Fort McHenry. The gallantry and courage displayed by his fellow countrymen that night inspired Key to pen the lyrics to the song that officially became our national anthem in 1931.

O say, can you see, by the dawn's early light,
What so proudly we hailed at the twilight's last gleaming,
Whose broad stripes and bright stars, through the perilous fight,
O'er the ramparts we watched were so gallantly streaming?
And the rockets' red glare, the bombs bursting in air,
Gave proof through the night that our flag was still there.
O say, does that Star-Spangled Banner yet wave
O'er the land of the free and the home of the brave?

On the shore, dimly seen through the mists of the deep,
Where the foe's haughty host in dread silence reposes,
What is that which the breeze, o'er the towering steep,
As it fitfully blows, half conceals, half discloses?
Now it catches the gleam of the morning's first beam,
In full glory reflected now shines on the stream;
'Tis the Star-Spangled Banner, O long may it wave
O'er the land of the free and the home of the brave!

O thus be it ever when free men shall stand
Between their loved homes and the war's desolation!
Blest with vict'ry and peace, may the heav'n-rescued land
Praise the Power that hath made and preserved us a nation.
then conquer we must, for our cause it is just,
And this be our motto: 'In God is our trust.'
And the Star-Spangled Banner in triumph shall wave
O'er the land of the free and the home of the brave.

Many students recite "The Pledge of Allegiance" when school begins each day.

The Pledge of Allegiance (1892)

I pledge allegiance to the Flag
of the United States of America,
and to the Republic for which it stands,
one Nation under God, indivisible,
with liberty and justice for all.

from Martin Luther King, Jr.'s "I Have a Dream" Speech (1963)

"I say to you today, my friends, that in spite of the difficulties and frustrations of the moment I still have a dream. It is a dream deeply rooted in the American dream.

I have a dream that one day this nation will rise up and live out the true meaning of its creed: "We hold these truths to be self-evident; that all men are created equal."

I have a dream that one day on the red hills of Georgia the sons of former slaves and the sons of former slaveowners will be able to sit down together at the table of brotherhood....

I have a dream that my four little children will one day live in a nation where they will not be judged by the color of their skin but by the content of their character.

I have a dream today....

... From every mountainside, let freedom ring.

When we let freedom ring, when we let it ring from every village and every hamlet, from every state and every city, we will be able to speed up that day when all of God's children, black men and white men, Jews and Gentiles, Protestants and Catholics, will be able to join hands and sing in the words of the old Negro spiritual, 'Free at last! Free at last! Thank God Almighty, we are free at last!'"

In August 1963, while Congress debated civil rights legislation, Martin Luther King, Jr., led a quarter of a million demonstrators on a March on Washington. On the steps of the Lincoln Memorial he gave a stirring speech in which he told of his dream for America.

Biographical Dictionary

The page number after each entry refers to the place where the person is first mentioned. For more complete references to people, see the Index.

A **Adams, Abigail** 1744–1818, wife of John Adams; noted letter writer (p. 273).

Adams, John 1735–1826, 2nd President of the United States, 1797–1801 (p. 264).

Adams, Samuel 1722–1803, helped inspire the American Revolution (p. 245).

Addams, Jane 1860–1935, social worker who founded Hull House (p. 512).

Allen, Ethan 1738–1789, leader of the Green Mountain Boys (p. 265).

Anthony, Susan B. 1820–1906, reformer who fought for women's rights (p. 387).

Arnold, Benedict 1741–1801, general in Revolution; committed treason (p. 282).

Attucks, Crispus 1723–1770, former slave; killed in the Boston Massacre (p. 249).

Austin, Stephen 1793–1836, settler in Texas; supported Texas statehood (p. 400).

B **Bacon, Nathaniel** 1647–1676, led a rebellion; burned Jamestown (p. 216).

Balboa, Vasco Núñez de 1475–1519, Spanish explorer (p. 94).

Banneker, Benjamin 1731–1806, helped survey Washington, D.C. (p. 325).

Barker, Penelope led a boycott of tea and other British goods, 1774 (p. 252).

Barton, Clara 1821–1912, nurse in Civil War; began American Red Cross (p. 449).

Beecher, Catharine 1800–1878, started teacher-training schools for women (p. 387).

Bell, Alexander Graham 1847–1922, invented the telephone (p. 501).

Berkeley, William 1606–1677, governor of Virginia; policies led to Bacon's Rebellion (p. 215).

Bessemer, Henry 1813–1898, English scientist; invented process to convert iron to steel (p. 499).

Blackwell, Elizabeth 1821–1910, first woman physician in modern times (p. 387).

Bolívar, Simón 1783–1830, helped free several South American countries from Spain (p. 602).

Boone, Daniel 1734–1820, frontiersman who cut trail into Kentucky (p. 336).

Bowie, Jim 1796–1836, colonel in the Texas army who died at the Alamo (p. 40l).

Bradford, William 1590–1657, governor of Plymouth Colony (p. 135).

Brant, Joseph 1742–1807, Mohawk chief who fought for British (p. 291).

Brown, John 1800–1859, abolitionist who led rebellion at Harpers Ferry (p. 428)

Bruce, Blanche K. 1841–1898, African American planter and politician (p. 471).

Bryan, William Jennings 1860–1925, lawyer and populist who ran for President three times (p. 493).

Bush, George 1924–, 41st President of the United States, 1989–1993 (p. 580).

C **Cabeza de Vaca, Álvar Núñez** 1490?– ?1557, Spanish explorer (p. 103).

Cabot, John 1450–1499, Italian explorer; reached Newfoundland (p. 114).

Calhoun, John C. 1782–1850, politician who supported slavery and states' rights (p. 427).

Carnegie, Andrew 1835–1919, entrepreneur; made a fortune in the steel industry; supported many causes (p. 503).

Cartier, Jacques 1491–1557, French explorer; sailed up St. Lawrence River (p. 115).

Chamorro, Violeta Barrios de 1929–, Became president of Nicaragua in 1990 (p. 602).

Chávez, Cesar 1927–1993, Mexican American labor leader; founded the United Farm Workers (p. 579).

Clark, George Rogers 1752–1818, captured three British forts during Revolutionary War (p. 288).

Clark, William 1770–1838, explored Louisiana Purchase with Lewis (p. 338).

Clay, Henry 1777–1852, proposed the Missouri Compromise and the Compromise of 1850 (p. 426).

Columbus, Christopher 1451–1506, Italian navigator; reached America (p. 92).

Cooper, James Fenimore 1789–1851, novelist and historian; wrote stories about the American frontier (p. 358).

Corbin, Margaret 1751–?1800, woman patriot who fought in the Revolutionary War (p. 281).

Cornwallis, Charles 1738–1805, English general in Revolutionary War; surrendered to Americans in 1781 (p. 290).

Coronado, Francisco Vázquez de 1510–1554, Spanish conquistador (p. 103).

Cortés, Hernán 1485–1547, Spanish conquistador (p. 101).

Crazy Horse 1849?–1877, Sioux chief who defeated Custer at Little Bighorn (p. 487).

Crèvecoeur, Michel Guillaume Jean de 1735–1813, French essayist; wrote about life in America (p. 192).

Crockett, Davy 1786–1836, pioneer and member of Congress; died at the Alamo (p. 401).

Custer, George 1839–1876, army officer killed by Sioux at Little Bighorn in battle called Custer's Last Stand (p. 487).

D **Davis, Jefferson** 1808–1889, president of Confederacy during Civil War (p. 429).

Dawes, William 1745–1799, patriot who rode with Paul Revere (p. 263).

de la Cruz, Juana Inés 1651–1695, Mexican nun who was outstanding poet and scholar (p. 121).

de Soto, Hernando 1500?–1542, Spanish explorer (p. 104).

Dias, Bartholomeu 1450?–1500, Portuguese navigator (p. 91).

Dix, Dorothea 1802–1887, reformer who worked to improve care for the mentally ill (p. 389).

Dorantes, Esteban ?–?1539, enslaved African who became explorer (p. 103).

Douglass, Frederick 1817–1895, abolitionist and writer; escaped from slavery (p. 385).

Du Bois, W.E.B. 1868–1963, educator who helped create the NAACP (p. 538).

E **Edison, Thomas A.** 1847–1931, inventor of the light bulb, the moving-picture camera, and the phonograph (p. 501).

Edwards, Jonathan 1703–1758, preached American Puritanism (p. 171).

Eisenhower, Dwight D. 1890–1969, general in U.S. Army; 34th President of the United States, 1953–1961 (p. 573).

Elizabeth I 1533–1603, Queen of England, 1558–1603; supported Walter Raleigh's colonization of Virginia (p. 112).

Equiano, Olaudah 1745–1797 West African taken into slavery; was freed and became abolitionist in England (p. 177).

F **Ford, Henry** 1863–1947, automobile manufacturer; made cars on assembly line (p. 546).

Forten, Charlotte 1837–1914, African American teacher (p. 463).

Forten, James 1766–1842, African American abolitionist and reformer (p. 385).

Franklin, Benjamin 1706–1790, printer, writer, publisher, scientist, and inventor (p. 200).

Freeman, Eilzabeth 1744?–1829, enslaved woman who sued for and won her freedom (p. 296).

Fulton, Robert 1765–1815, civil engineer; built first profitable steamboat (p. 373).

G **Gálvez, Bernardo de** 1746–1786, Spanish colonial administrator (p. 288).

Gama, Vasco da 1460–1524, Portuguese navigator (p. 91).

Garrison, William Lloyd 1805–1879, reformer and abolitionist (p. 384).

George III 1738–1820, King of England, 1760–1820; supported policies that led to American Revolution (p. 242).

Ginsburg, Ruth Bader 1933–, Associate Justice of U.S. Supreme Court (p. 580).

Gompers, Samuel 1850–1924, founder of the AFL (American Federation of Labor) (p. 514).

Gorbachev, Mikhail 1931–, president of the former Soviet Union (p. 580).

Gore, Albert, Jr. 1948–, became Vice-President under Bill Clinton in election of 1992 (p. 603).

Grant, Ulysses S. 1822–1885, 18th President of the United States, 1869–1877; Union general in Civil War (p. 434).

Greene, Nathanael 1742–1786, general in South during Revolutionary War (p. 288).

Grimke, Angelina 1805–1879, abolitionist and supporter of women's rights (p. 384).

Grimke, Sarah 1792–1873, abolitionist and supporter of women's rights (p. 384).

H **Hale, Nathan** 1755–1776, patriot spy during Revolutionary War; hanged by British (p. 282).

Hamilton, Alexander 1755–1804, contributor to *Federalist*; first Secretary of the Treasury (p. 312).

Hancock, John 1737–1793, first signer of Declaration of Independence (p. 262).

Henry, Patrick 1736–1799, Revolutionary leader and orator (p. 243).

Houston, Samuel 1793–1863, first president of Republic of Texas (p. 401).

Hudson, Henry ?–1611, English navigator; gave name to Hudson River (p. 114).

I **Irving, Washington** 1783–1859, writer of humorous tales, history, and biography (p. 358).

Isabella 1451–1504 Queen of Spain, 1474–1504; supported and financed Columbus (p. 93).

J **Jackson, Andrew** 1767–1845, 7th President of the United States, 1829–1837; encouraged Western expansion (p. 367).

Jay, John 1745–1829, contributor to *Federalist*; Chief Justice, U.S. Supreme Court (p. 295).

Jefferson, Thomas 1743–1826, 3rd President of the United States, 1801–1809; wrote Declaration of Independence (p. 270).

Johnson, Andrew 1808–1875, 17th President of the United States, 1865–1869; impeached, then acquitted (p. 468).

Johnson, Lyndon 1908–1973, 36th President of the United States, 1963–1969; took office after Kennedy was assassinated (p. 567).

K **Kalb, Baron de** 1721–1780, soldier in French army; served in American Revolution (p. 287).

Kelley, Oliver H. 1826–1913, one of the original organizers of National Grange (p. 493).

Kennedy, John F. 1917–1963, 35th President of the United States, 1961– 1963; assassinated (p. 572).

Key, Francis Scott 1779–1843, writer of "*Star-Spangled Banner*" (p. 348).

King, Martin Luther, Jr. 1929–1968, civil rights leader; assassinated (p. 563).

Knox, Henry 1750–1806, first U.S. Secretary of War (p. 323).

L **Lange, Dorothea** 1895–1965, documentary photographer (p. 547).

Lafayette, Marquis de 1757–1834, French; fought in American Revolution (p. 287).

las Casas, Bartolomé de 1474–1566, Spanish missionary opposed to slavery (p. 105).

Lee, Richard Henry 1732–1794, delegate to Continental Congress (p. 264).

Lee, Robert E. 1807–1870, commander of Confederacy (p. 433).

Lewis, Meriwether 1774–1809, explored Louisiana Purchase with Clark (p. 338).

Liliuokalani, Queen Lydia Kamekeha 1838–1917, last queen of Hawaii (p. 522).

Lincoln, Abraham 1809–1865, 16th President of the United States; issued Emancipation Proclamation; assassinated (p. 429).

Lindbergh, Charles 1902–1974, first person to fly alone nonstop across Atlantic Ocean (p. 545).

Livingston, Robert R. 1746–1813, first U.S. Secretary of Foreign Affairs (p. 270).

Love, Nat 1854–1921, African American cowboy called "Deadwood Dick" (p. 484).

Lowell, Francis Cabot 1775–1817, built first complete cotton spinning and weaving mill in the United States (p. 375).

Lucas, Eliza 1722–1793, introduced growing of indigo (blue dye) in South (p. 214).

Lyon, Mary 1797–1849, founder of Mount Holyoke, a college for women (p. 387).

M **Madison, Dolley** 1768–1849, wife of James Madison; first lady during War of 1812 (p. 349).

Madison, James 1751–1836, 4th President of the United States (p. 310).

Magellan, Ferdinand 1480?–1521, Portuguese explorer (p. 94).

Malinche Aztec interpreter and guide for Cortez in 1519 (p. 100).

Mann, Horace 1796–1859, educator who reformed public schools (p. 388).

Marion, Francis 1732?–1795, commander in American Revolution (p. 288).

Marquette, Jacques 1637–1675, French explorer; sailed down Mississippi River (p. 116).

Marshall, John 1755–1835, Chief Justice of U.S. Supreme Court (p. 326).

McClellan, George 1826–1885, general in Union Army (p. 456).

McKinley, William 1843–1901, 25th President of the United States (p. 493).

Metacomet ?–1676, Native American leader (p. 173).

Mink, Patsy Takemoto 1927–, member of U.S. Congress; supports women's rights; (p. 580).

Monroe, James 1758–1831, 5th President of the United States, 1817–1825 (p. 337).

Montezuma 1480?–1520, Aztec emperor during Spanish conquest of Mexico (p. 102).

Morgan, J.P. 1837–1913, banker (p. 503).

Morris, Gouverneur 1752–1816, member of Continental Congress (p. 316).

Morse, Samuel 1791–1872, invented telegraph code (called Morse Code) (p. 482).

Mott, Lucretia 1793–1880, directed first women's rights convention at Seneca Falls (p. 387).

N **Narváez, Pánfilo de** 1470?–1528, Spanish explorer (p. 103).

O **O'Connor, Sandra Day** 1930–, first female Supreme Court justice (p. 580).

Oglethorpe, James 1696–1785, founder of Georgia (p. 219).

Oñate, Juan de 1549?–?1624, conquerer and colonizer of New Mexico (p. 124).

Osceola 1800?–1838, Native American leader in Florida (p. 370).

Otis, James 1725–1783, colonial leader in Massachusetts legislature (p. 245).

P **Paine, Thomas** 1737–1809, wrote *Common Sense*, urging a declaration of independence (p. 270).

Parks, Rosa 1913–, African American who refused to obey segregation laws in Alabama (p. 563).

Penn, William 1644–1718, founder of Pennsylvania (p. 190).

Pocahontas 1595?–1617, married colonist John Rolfe; converted to Christianity; Indian name: Matoaka (p. 131).

Ponce de Léon, Juan 1460?–1521, Spanish explorer in Florida (p. 104).

Pontiac ?–1769, Ottawa Indian chief; united Native American nations (p. 238).

Popé Pueblo leader who led a revolt against Spanish settlers in 1680 (p. 125).

Powhatan 1550?–1618, father of Pocahontas, head of Algonquin tribes (p. 130).

R **Randolph, Edmund** 1753–1813, U.S. Attorney General and Secretary of State (p. 311).

Revels, Hiram R. African American Senator during Reconstruction (p. 471).

Revere, Paul 1735–1818, rode from Boston to Lexington to warn Patriots that the British were coming (p. 250).

Rivera, Jacob Rodrigez Spanish Jew who sought religious freedom in Rhode Island in 1748; taught use of whale blubber (p. 179).

Rockefeller, John D. 1839–1937, entrepreneur and creator of Standard Oil Co. (p. 503).

Rolfe, John 1585–1622, English colonist; married Pocahontas (p. 131).

Roosevelt, Franklin D. 1882–1945, 32nd President of the United States, 1933–1945 (p. 547).

Roosevelt, Theodore 1858–1919, 26th President of the United States, 1901–1909 (p. 14).

Rush, Benjamin 1745?–1813, member of Continental Congress (p. 316).

S **Sacagawea** 1787?–1812, Shoshone interpreter for Lewis and Clark (p. 339).

Salem, Peter, patriot who fought at Battle of Bunker Hill in 1775 (p. 266).

Santa Anna, Antonio López de 1795–1876, Mexican general and president during Texas revolution (p. 401).

Scott, Dred 1795?–1858, enslaved African who sued for his freedom (p. 429).

Sequoyah 1770?–1843, Native American scholar; studied Cherokee (p. 371).

Seward, William Henry 1801–1872, U.S. Secretary of State responsible for Alaska purchase (p. 523).

Shays, Daniel 1747?–1825, led a rebellion of Massachusetts farmers (p. 308).

Sheridan, Philip 1831–1888, Union general in Civil War (p. 456).

Sherman, Roger 1721–1793, member of Continental Congress (p. 270).

Sherman, William Tecumseh 1820–1891, Union general in Civil War (p. 457).

Sitting Bull 1834?–1890, Sioux chief; fought at Battle of Little Bighorn (p. 487).

Slater, Samuel 1768–1835, set up cotton mill in Rhode Island (p. 374).

Smith, John 1580–1631, leader of Jamestown colony (p. 130).

Stanton, Elizabeth Cady 1815–1902, organized first women's rights conference in Seneca Falls (p. 387).

Steuben, Baron Friedrich von 1730–1794, Prussian soldier; trained American soldiers for Revolution (p. 287).

Stevens, Thaddeus 1792–1868, U.S. Congressman; leader during Reconstruction (p. 468).

Stowe, Harriet Beecher 1811–1896, author of *Uncle Tom's Cabin* (p. 387).

Sutter, John 1803–1880, California colonist; gold found on his property (p. 414).

T **Tecumseh** 1768?–1813, Shawnee chief; killed fighting for the British in War of 1812 (p. 347).

Townshend, Charles 1725–1767, sponsored the Townshend Acts on American colonies (p. 244).

Truman, Harry S. 1884–1972, 33rd President of the United States, 1945–1953 (p. 554).

Truth, Sojourner 1797?–1883, abolitionist and supporter of women's rights (p. 387).

Tubman, Harriet 1821?–1913, helped enslaved Africans to freedom (p. 386).

Turner, Nat 1800–1831, led rebellion of enslaved people; was captured and hanged (p. 379).

W **Warren, Earl** 1891–1974, Chief Justice of U.S. Supreme Court (p. 564).

Warren, Mercy Otis 1728–1814, author of political works (p. 245).

Washington, George 1732–1799, commanded Continental armies during Revolution; first President of the United States, 1789–1797 (p. 235).

Webster, Daniel 1782–1852, senator from Massachusetts; U.S. Secretary of State (p. 368).

Webster, Noah 1758–1843, wrote first American dictionary (p. 352).

Wheatley, Phillis 1753?–1784, African American poet (p. 267).

Whitefield, George 1714–1770, popular Great Awakening minister (p. 171).

Whitman, Marcus 1802–1847, missionary and pioneer in Oregon territory (p. 407).

Whitney, Eli 1765–1825, inventor of the cotton gin (p. 376).

Wilson, Woodrow 1856–1924, 28th President of the United States, 1913–1921 (p. 539).

Wright, Orville 1871–1948, made first successful flight in motorized plane (p. 503).

Wright, Wilbur 1867–1912, made first successful flight in motorized plane (p. 503).

Y **Yeltsin, Boris** 1931–, president of Russia (p. 581).

Young, Brigham 1801–1877, Mormon leader; settled in Utah (p. 409).

Z **Zavala, Lorenzo de** 1788–1836. Mexican leader who supported Texan independence (p. 401).

Zenger, John Peter 1697–1746, was acquitted in landmark freedom-of-the-press trial in 1734 (p. 206).

Glossary

The Glossary defines key vocabulary as it is used in this book. Remember that many words have more than one meaning. The definitions given here are the ones that will be most helpful in reading this book. The page number in parentheses refers to the page on which each word or phrase is introduced.

A **abolitionist** (ab uh LISH uhn ist) a person who believed slavery was wrong and fought to make it illegal. (p. 384)

address (uh DREHS) an official speech. (p. 456)

agriculture (AG rih kuhl chur) skill in growing plants for food; farming. (p. 39)

Allied Powers (AL yd POW urz) countries that included Britain, France, the Soviet Union, the United States, and Canada during World War II. (p. 550)

Allies (AL yz) countries that included France, Belgium, Britain, Russia, the United States, and Canada during World War I. (p. 539)

ally (AL y) a person or group that has joined with another to accomplish a specific goal. (p. 238)

ambush (AM bush) to attack by surprise from a hiding place. (p. 103)

amendment (uh MEHND muhnt) a change made to the Constitution. (p. 321)

annexation (an ihk SAY shuhn) adding more territory to a country. (p. 402)

apprentice (uh PREHN tihs) someone working for a more experienced person to learn a skill. (p. 204)

Arabic numeral (AR uh bihk NOO mur uhl) one of our symbols for numbers, such as 1,2,3. (p. 84)

archaeologist (ahr kee AHL uh jist) a scientist who learns about people who lived long ago by studying the things they left behind. (p. 36)

armada (ahr MAH duh) a large number of warships acting together like an army; a fleet. (p. 112)

armistice (AHR mih stihs) an agreement between two armies to stop fighting; a truce. (p. 540)

arms race (ahrms rays) a competition between two countries to invent and build more powerful weapons. (p. 561)

assassinate (uh SAS uh nayt) to murder for a political reason. (p. 459)

assembly line (uh SEHM blee lyn) a method of manufacturing goods in which the thing being made moves from worker to worker and everyone does only part of the job. (p. 545)

astrolabe (AS truh layb) an instrument that measures the distance between the sun or stars and the horizon; once used by sailors for navigation. (p. 84)

atomic bomb (uh TAHM ihk bahm) a weapon invented during World War II that uses nuclear energy to create an enormous explosion. (p. 554)

Axis Powers (AK sihs POW ehrz) Germany, Italy, and Japan during World War II. (p. 550)

B **backcountry** (BAK kuhn tree) the frontier area of each colony. (p. 202)

banish (BAN ihsh) to drive someone out of a country or region. (p. 168)

basin (BAY sihn) a low-lying area surrounded by higher land. (p. 16)

battle map (BAT uhl map) a map that uses symbols to show how a battle was fought. (p. 240)

bilingual (by LIHNG gwuhl) having two official languages. (p. 592)

blockade (blah KAYD) an attempt to stop all traffic from entering or leaving an area so goods cannot be shipped or supplies bought. (p. 435)

boomtown (BOOM toun) a town offering many chances to make money and filled with people just arriving. (p. 416)

boundary (BOUN duh ree) a line that separates the territory of one group from that of another. (p. 53)

boycott (BOI kaht) when a group refuses to buy certain products as a way of protesting. (p. 245)

C **cabinet** (KAB uh niht) a group appointed by a President to help govern the country. (p. 322)

Canadian Shield (kuh NAY dee uhn sheeld) a rock formation that covers nearly half of Canada. (p. 590)

canal (kuh NAL) a waterway made by people so boats can transport goods. (p. 374)

candidate (KAN dih dayt) a person trying to get elected to a political office. (p. 368)

capitalism (KAP ih tuhl ihz uhm) an economic system that allows people to choose their work and to own farms, factories, and other businesses. (p. 560)

carpetbagger (KAHR piht bag ur) a word southerners used to describe northerners who came to the South after the Civil War. (p. 471)

cash crop (kash krahp) a crop that a farmer grows only to sell. (p. 213)

casualties (KAZH oo uhl teez) people killed, wounded, or lost in a battle or war. (p. 264)

cattle trail (KAT uhl trayl) a route from the open range to a town with a railroad, where cattle could be shipped east. (p. 485)

cause-and-effect relationship (KAWZ uhnd ih FEHKT rih LAY shuhn shihp) when one event makes another event happen. (p. 205)

Central Powers (SEHN truhl POW urz) the forces of Italy, Germany, and Austria-Hungary during World War I. (p. 539)

century (SEHN chuh ree) 100 years. (p. 47)

charter (CHAHR ter) a written agreement giving someone the right to establish a colony. (p. 130)

checks and balances (chehks uhnd BAHL uhns ehz) a system of separating government so each part keeps the others from taking too much power. (p. 320)

circumnavigate (sur kuhm NAV i gayt) to sail completely around the world. (p. 95)

civil rights (SIHV uhl ryts) the right to fair and equal treatment, guaranteed by the Constitution. (p. 563)

civil war (SIHV uhl wawr) a war fought between two groups or regions of a nation. (p. 432)

civilian (sih VIHL yuhn) a person who is not in the military. (p. 450)

civilization (sihv uh lih ZAY shuhn) a culture with cities, a government, and many different jobs for people to do. (p. 41)

Cold War (kohld wawr) when two countries are almost at war but not actually fighting. (p. 561)

colony (KAHL uh nee) a settlement ruled by a distant country. (p. 122)

Columbian Exchange (kuh LUHM bee uhn ihks CHAYNJ) the transfer of peoples, plants, and animals across the Atlantic Ocean after Columbus's first trip to the Americas. (p. 106)

committees of correspondence (kuh MIHT eez uhv kawr ih SPAHN duhns) a network of groups that shared information about what the British were doing and what actions the colonies should take. (p. 255)

communism (KAHM yuh nihz uhm) a system in which the government owns most businesses and often decides where people can live and work. (p. 560)

compromise (KAHM pruh myz) an agreement in which each side of an argument gives up something it wants in order to stop fighting. (p. 315)

confederacy (kuhn FEHD ur uh see) an organization of groups that band together for a purpose. (p. 54)

Confederate (kuhn FEHD ur iht) having to do with the states that fought against the Union during the Civil War. (p. 429)

congress (KAHNG grihs) a meeting of representatives to discuss plans for the future. (p. 237)

conquistador (kohn keehs tah DOHR) a Spanish soldier in the 16th century who helped conquer the native civilizations of Central and South America. (p. 101)

constitution (kahn stih TOO shuhn) a written plan of how a country's government will work. (p. 306)

Continental Divide (kahn tuh NEHN tuhl dih VYD) a stretch of high land along the Rocky Mountains that separates streams and rivers that flow east from those that flow west. (p. 408)

contour map (KAHN tur map) a map that shows how high land rises above sea level. (p. 410)

contraband (KAHN truh band) property that one army seizes from another during a war. (p. 445)

convention (kuhn VEHN shuhn) a meeting of representatives to accomplish a specific goal. (p. 309)

corps (kawr) an organized group of people who do something together. (p. 338)

cosmonaut (KAHZ muh nawt) the Russian word for "astronaut." (p. 582)

credit (KREHD iht) a way of buying things with borrowed money. (p. 464)

culture (KUHL chur) a way of life shared by a group of people. (p. 21)

D **D-Day** (DEE day) June 6, 1944, the day the Allied Powers began their invasion of France during World War II. (p. 553)

debtor (DEHT ur) someone who owes money to someone else. (p. 219)

declaration (dehk luh RAY shuhn) something a person or a group writes or speaks to make their position clear; a statement. (p. 270)

degree (dih GREE) a unit of measurement that is 1/360 of the surface of the earth. (p. 116)

delegate (DEHL ih giht) one person chosen to speak or act for a number of people. (p. 264)

democracy (dih MAHK ruh see) a government in which the people make political decisions by voting, and the majority rules. (p. 311)

depression (dih PREHSH uhn) a period when many businesses close and it becomes very difficult for most people to earn a living. (p. 547)

desertion (dih ZUR shuhn) when a soldier runs away from the military. (p. 458)

developing nation (dih VEHL uh pihng NAY shuhn) a country without enough food, jobs, and other resources for the people who live there. (p. 572)

diplomat (DIHP luh mat) a person sent by his or her government to talk with other governments. (p. 295)

direct quotation (dih REHKT kwoh TAY shuhn) repeating the exact words someone said or wrote. (p. 359)

dispute (dih SPYOOT) to fight with words; to argue. (p. 403)

dissenter (dih SEHN tur) a person who refuses to go along with what his or her leaders believe. (p. 169)

diverse (dih VURS) coming from many different backgrounds. (p. 21)

docked (dahkd) when two or more craft are connected in space. (p. 582)

draft (draft) a system of choosing people and forcing them to serve in the military. (p. 451)

drought (drout) a long period when almost no rain falls and crops are not able to grow properly. (p. 60)

dry farming (dry FAHR mihng) a method of farming used in dry regions, in which a field is left unplanted for a year so the soil can store water and have enough moisture for a crop to grow the next season. (p. 492)

duty (DOO tee) a tax imposed by a government on goods brought into a country. (p. 244)

E **emancipation** (ih MAN suh pay shuhn) freedom from slavery. (p. 446)

emperor (EHM pur ur) a man who rules different groups of people throughout a large area. (p. 81)

empire (EHM pyr) a variety of territories and groups of people controlled by one government. (p. 43)

enslaved (ehn SLAYVD) when someone has been forced into a system where he or she works for no pay and can be bought and sold as property. (p. 91)

entrepreneur (ahn truh pruh NUR) a person who starts his or her own business rather than working for someone else. (p. 502)

environment (ehn VY ruhn muhnt) the things that surround someone, including water and land. (p. 26)

epidemic (ehp ih DEHM ihk) an outbreak of disease that makes many people sick at once. (p. 107)

ethnic neighborhood (EHTH nihk NAY bur hud) a section of a city where people who share the same culture live. (p. 512)

executive branch (ihg ZEHK yuh tihv branch) the part of the government that carries out the laws and oversees the government; the President. (p. 320)

expedition (ehk spih DIHSH uhn) a journey taken by a group for a definite purpose. (p. 338)

export (ihk SPAWRT) a product shipped to another country to be sold. (p. 213)

F **fall line** (fawl lyn) a line connecting waterfalls up and down the East Coast that marks the place where the height of the land drops. (p. 188)

federal system (FEHD ur uhl SIHS tuhm) a system in which a central government shares power with the governments of separate regions. (p. 315)

fortify (FAWR tuh fy) to make a place difficult to attack by making it more like a fort. (p. 265)

forty-niner (FAWR tee NY nur) a person who went to look for gold in California in 1849. (p. 414)

free state (free stayt) a state that did not allow slavery. (p. 426)

freedmen (FREED mehn) African Americans who had been enslaved before the Civil War. (p. 462)

Freedom Riders (FREE duhm RY durz) black and white people who protested segregation by riding buses in the South and using whites-only areas in the bus stations they visited. (p. 565)

French-Canadian separatist (frehnch kuh NAY dee uhn SEHP ur uh tihst) a French-Canadian who believes the province of Quebec should be an independent nation. (p. 593)

frontier (FRUHN tihr) an area still in a natural state that settlers have just started moving into. (p. 336)

G **geographer** (jee AHG ruh fur) a person who studies the earth and its features. (p. 19)

glacier (GLAY shur) a mass of ice that moves slowly over land. (p. 36)

Grange (graynj) an organization designed to help farmers financially. (p. 493)

grassroots (GRAS roots) a word to describe groups of ordinary citizens working toward a common goal. (p. 602)

H **hacienda** (ah SYEHN dah) a plantation or a large ranch owned by Spanish colonists. (p. 123)

hero (HEER oh) an unusual person who has accomplished something great. (p. 354)

Holocaust (HAHL uh kawst) the mass murder by the Nazis of 11 million people. (p. 552)

holy experiment (HOH lee ihk SPEHR uh muhnt) a phrase William Penn used to describe his colony of Pennsylvania, because it was governed according to Quaker beliefs. (p. 191)

home front (hohm fruhnt) all the people who are not fighting but who live in a country at war. (p. 450)

homestead (HOHM stehd) frontier land claimed by a settler. (p. 491)

House of Burgesses (hous uhv BUR jihs iz) the law-making branch of Virginia's government. (p. 215)

I **immigrant** (IHM ih gruhnt) a person who comes to live in a new country. (p. 21)

immunity (ih MYOO nih tee) the ability to resist getting sick from a disease. (p. 107)

impeach (ihm PEECH) for Congress to accuse a President of being unfit to hold office. (p. 469)

import (IHM pawrt) an item brought into one country from another. (p. 176)

impressment (ihm PREHS muhnt) the act of seizing people and forcing them into military service. (p. 346)

inauguration (ihn AW gyuh ray shuhn) the formal ceremony at which a government official, particularly the President, is sworn into office. (p. 322)

indentured servant (ihn DEHN churd SUR vuhnt) a person who agreed to work for a certain number of years in return for passage to America, food, clothing, and shelter. (p. 131)

Industrial Revolution (ihn DUHS tree uhl rehv uh LOO shuhn) great changes in how people lived and worked that were caused by the invention of new kinds of machinery. (p. 373)

industry (IHN duh stree) a business that makes a product or offers a service that can be sold to other people. (p. 179)

inflation (ihn FLAY shuhn) when items people want to buy cost more and the money they have to buy them is worth less. (p. 451)

infrastructure (IHN fruh struhk chur) a country's system of transportation and communication. (p. 597)

injustice (ihn JUHS tihs) something one person does to another that is wrong. (p. 447)

interchangeable part (ihn tur CHAYN juh buhl pahrt) a part that fits right into each thing being made in a factory, without having to be changed or adjusted. (p. 376)

interpret (ihn TUR priht) to figure out the meaning of something, particularly a document. (p. 274)

intervention (ihn tur VEHN shuhn) when one country involves itself with events inside another. (p. 287)

invasion (ihn VAY zhuhn) the entrance of an armed force into another country in order to conquer it. (p. 112)

invest (ihn VEHST) to put money into a business in the hope of earning a profit. (p. 130)

Iron Curtain (EYE urn KUR tn) the line that divided the democratic countries of Western Europe and the communist countries of Eastern Europe. (p. 560)

irrigation (ihr ih GAY shuhn) a method of moving water in order to grow crops in dry land. (p. 27)

Islam (ihs LAHM) a religion based on the belief that there is only one God and that Muhammad was his most important prophet. (p. 77)

J **judicial branch** (joo DISH uhl branch) the part of government that resolves disputes about the Constitution and decides the meaning of other laws; the Supreme Court. (p. 320)

L **labor union** (LAY bur YOON yuhn) an organization of workers who bargain with company owners over wages and working conditions. (p. 514)

landform (LAND fawrm) a physical feature of the earth's surface, such as a mountain or a valley. (p. 14)

legend (LEHJ uhnd) a story that is told over and over again by many generations of people. (p. 103)

legislative branch (LEHJ ih slay tihv branch) the part of government that makes the laws; the Senate and the House of Representatives. (p. 319)

levee (LEHV ee) a long hill of dirt or stone built to turn back floodwaters. (p. 26)

Loyalist (LOI uh lihst) an American colonist who was loyal to Britain. (p. 254)

M **magistrate** (MAJ ih strayt) a political leader who made the laws in a Puritan village. (p. 168)

Manifest Destiny (MAN uh fehst DEHS tuh nee) the belief that the United States could and should expand across the continent. (p. 403)

mass production (mas pruh DUHK shuhn) the making of goods in large quantities, using interchangeable parts and an assembly line. (p. 376)

massacre (MAS uh kur) the killing of many people, particularly defenseless people. (p. 250)

mechanization (mehk uh nih ZAY shuhn) the use of machines to make products that people once made by hand. (p. 514)

meetinghouse (MEE tihng hous) the building in a Puritan village where people gathered to discuss religion and government. (p. 162)

mercenary (MUR suh nehr ee) a soldier who fights in a foreign army just to earn money. (p. 281)

merchant (MUR chunt) a person who makes money by buying and selling goods. (p. 81)

Mesoamerica (mez oh uh MEHR ih kuh) the southern part of North America, including Central America. (p. 41)

mestizo (mehs TEE zoh) a child or descendant of a Spanish colonist and a Native American. (p. 123)

Middle Passage (MIHD uhl PAHS ihj) the voyage enslaved Africans made, against their will, from Africa across the Atlantic Ocean to the Americas. (p. 177)

migrant worker (MY gruhnt WUR kuhr) a person who moves from place to place looking for work, particularly farm work. (p. 579)

migrate (MY grayt) to move from one area to another area. (p. 36)

militia (muh LIHSH uh) an army made up of ordinary citizens instead of professional soldiers. (p. 262)

mineral (MIHN ur uhl) a substance that can be mined from the earth and sold or traded. (p. 16)

minute (MIHN iht) a unit of measurement that is 1/60 of a degree. (p. 116)

Minuteman (MIHN iht man) a member of the American colonial militia who was prepared to fight at a minute's notice. (p. 262)

mission (MIHSH uhn) a settlement of missionaries. (p. 125)

missionary (MIHSH uh nehr ee) someone who travels to a foreign country to do religious work. (p. 143)

mobilize (MOH buh lyz) for a country to prepare for war. (p. 433)

monopoly (muh NAHP uh lee) the control by one company of all of one kind of business. (p. 502)

mosque (mahsk) a house of worship for people who believe in Islam. (p. 78)

muckraker (MUHK rayk ur) a newspaper reporter who wrote about things that businesses and the government were doing wrong. (p. 536)

N **NAFTA** the North American Free Trade Agreement, which eliminates barriers to trade between the United States, Mexico, and Canada. (p. 602)

natural resource (NACH ur uhl REE sawrs) anything found in nature that people can use, particularly things they can sell. (p. 16)

navigation (nav ih GAY shuhn) the science of planning and controlling the direction of a ship. (p. 99)

Nazi Party (NAHT see PAHR tee) a political party in Germany, headed by Adolf Hitler, that led the country into World War II. (p. 550)

negotiate (nih GOH shee ayt) to talk to someone in order to reach an agreement; to bargain. (p. 295)

neutral (NOO truhl) not supporting either side in a war. (p. 288)

nonviolent protest (nahn VY uh luhnt PROH test) a method of peaceful protest in which people fight unfair laws by simply refusing to obey them. (p. 565)

Northwest Passage (nawrth WEHST PAS ihj) a water route through North America that would allow Europeans to sail west to Asia. (p. 114)

O **oral history** (AWR uhl HIHS tuh ree) an interview about a historical event with a person who actually experienced it. (p. 583)

organizational chart (awr guh nih ZAY shuhn l chart) a chart that shows how a government or a business is run. (p. 317)

overseer (OH vuhr see uhr) the man on plantations in the South who was in charge of enslaved people working in the fields. (p. 379)

P **paraphrase** (PAR uh frayz) to tell what someone said or wrote without repeating their exact words. (p. 359)

Parliament (PAHR luh muhnt) the group of representatives who make laws in Britain. (p. 242)

pass (pas) a break or opening that makes it easier to travel across a mountain range. (p. 406)

Patriot (PAY tree uht) an American colonist who opposed the British. (p. 254)

patroon (puh TROON) a wealthy man who was given land in Dutch colonies in exchange for paying to bring settlers to North America. (p. 145)

Peace Corps (pees kawr) an organization of volunteers who help people in developing nations. (p. 572)

pelt (pehlt) an animal skin with hair or fur still on it. (p. 144)

peninsula (puh NIHN syuh luh) a piece of land that sticks out into the water but remains connected at one end to the mainland. (p. 265)

petition (puh TIHSH uhn) a written request signed by many people and given to their government. (p. 270)

petrodollar (PEHT roh dahl ur) money earned from selling oil to other countries. (p. 597)

Piedmont (PEED mahnt) a region of rolling hills east of the Appalachian Mountains. (p. 188)

Pilgrim (PIHL gruhm) a person who travels to a sacred place; a Puritan who left England to settle in Plymouth Colony. (p. 136)

pilgrimage (PIHL gruh mihj) a journey made by religious people to a place they consider sacred. (p. 78)

pioneer (py uh NEER) one of the first settlers to travel into an unknown territory. (p. 336)

plantation (plan TAY shuhn) a large farm where crops are grown and the people who tend it live on the land. (p. 107)

plateau (pla TOH) a high, flat area that rises above the nearby land, often like a tabletop. (p. 15)

pogrom (puh GRAHM) an organized attack on a group, particularly on Jews in Eastern Europe. (p. 509)

political cartoon (puh LIHT ih kuhl cahr TOON) a drawing that makes a certain statement about a public event. (p. 526)

political party (puh LIHT ih kuhl PAHR tee) a group of people with similar goals who work together to gain power in government. (p. 324)

pony express (POH nee ihk SPREHS) a system for moving mail rapidly that was used across frontier areas in the United States. (p. 481)

population density (pahp yuh LAY shuhn DEHN sih tee) the number of people living in an area. (p. 24)

population map (pahp yuh LAY shuhn map) a map that shows population density. (p. 24)

Populist Party (PAHP yuh list PAHR tee) a political party in the 1890s that tried to help farmers. (p. 493)

post road (pohst rohd) a route used to deliver mail. (p. 222)

precedent (PREHS ih dehnt) a past decision that is used as a model for a later decision. (p. 322)

predict (prih DIHKT) to make a careful guess about the future based on the past. (p. 549)

presidio (prih SEE dee oh) a Spanish fort. (p. 125)

primary source (PRY mehr ee sawrs) an account of a historical event written by someone who actually experienced it. (p. 132)

privateer (pry vuh TEER) **(1)** the captain of an armed, privately owned ship, whom the government has given permission to attack enemy ships. (p. 111) **(2)** any private ship operated by such a person. (p. 279)

proclamation (prahk luh MAY shuhn) an official announcement. (p. 238)

profit (PRAHF iht) what a business earns; the money left over after all the expenses have been paid. (p. 224)

Progressive (pruh GREHS ihv) a political reformer in the early 20th century. (p. 536)

propaganda (prahp uh GAN duh) information chosen in order to change people's thinking. (p. 250)

proprietor (pruh PRY ih tur) the owner of something, particularly land or a business. (p. 189)

province (PRAHV ihns) an area with its own government, much like a U.S. state. (p. 590)

pueblo (PWEH bloh) a community of Native American groups living in the Southwest. (p. 44)

Puritan (PYUR ih tn) a Protestant during the 16th and 17th centuries who wanted to change the Church of England. (p. 135)

R **Radical Republican** (RAD ih kuhl rih PUHB lih kuhn) a congressman who believed that the national government should do everything necessary to protect the rights of African Americans. (p. 468)

ratify (RAT uh fy) for a state to approve the Constitution or an amendment to it. (p. 315)

rebel (rih BEHL) to fight against people in power, particularly a government. (p. 102)

Reconstruction

Reconstruction (ree kuhn STRUHK shuhn) a plan for rebuilding the South after the Civil War. (p. 468)

redistribute (ree dih STRIHB yoot) to divide and sell property. (p. 463)

region (REE jehn) an area with certain characteristics that set it apart from surrounding areas. (p. 19)

religious persecution (rih LIHJ uhs pur sih KYOO shuhn) keeping people from worshipping God the way they think is right. (p. 145)

religious toleration (rih LIHJ uhs tahl uh RAY shuhn) allowing people to worship God the way they think is right. (p. 189)

Renaissance (rehn ih SAHNS) the period between the 14th and 16th centuries when Europeans made many advances in art, literature, and science. (p. 85)

repeal (rih PEEL) to take a law out of effect. (p. 243)

representative (rehp rih ZEHN tuh tihv) a person chosen by a group to speak or act for them. (p. 215)

republic (rih PUHB lihk) a government in which citizens elect leaders to represent them. (p. 311)

reservation (rehz ur VAY shuhn) land set aside for Native Americans. (p. 487)

reservoir (REHZ ur vwahr) a pond or lake where people store water. (p. 28)

revolution (rehv uh LOO shuhn) the overthrow of a government. (p. 281)

rural (ROOR uhl) coming from or belonging in the countryside. (p. 502)

S **saga** (SAH guh) Icelandic legends about events that happened in the past. (p. 74)

scalawag (SKAL uh wag) a name given to white southerners who supported the Union. (p. 470)

secede (sih SEED) for a state to break away from the rest of the country. (p. 429)

secondary source (SEHK uhn dehr ee sawrs) a broad overview or a careful analysis of a historical event, based on primary sources. (p. 132)

segregation (sehg rih GAY shuhn) the practice of separating people by race. (p. 471)

self-sufficient (sehlf suh FIHSH uhnt) when a group or an individual can provide themselves with everything they need; independent. (p. 163)

Separatists (SEHP ur uh tihsts) Puritans who wanted to leave the Church of England. (p. 135)

settlement (SEHT uhl muhnt) a small community of people in a frontier region. (p. 114)

settlement house (SEHT uhl muhnt hous) a place built to help poor people in U.S. cities. (p. 512)

sharecropping (SHAIR krahp ihng) a system in which landowners rented land in return for a portion of the farmer's crop. (p. 464)

shipyard (SHIHP yahrd) a place where ships are built and repaired. (p. 179)

siege (seej) when an army surrounds a city, keeps out supplies, and tries to force the inhabitants to give up. (p. 436)

slave state (slayv stayt) a state that permitted slavery. (p. 426)

slavery (SLAY vuh ree) a system in which people could be bought and sold and forced to work with no pay. (p. 91)

Social Security (SOH shuhl sih KYOOR ih tee) a program that provides money for the unemployed, for those who are too sick to work, and for older people who have retired. (p. 548)

sodbusters (SAHD buhs turz) a name given to the first settlers to farm the Great Plains, because they had to break through the tough tangle of roots in the dirt, called "sod." (p. 491)

standard of living (STAN durd uhv LIHV ihng) the money people have to spend on themselves and their families. (p. 598)

stock (stahk) a share or part of a company. (p. 130)

stock market (stahk MAHR kiht) a place where people buy and sell shares in companies. (p. 545)

strategy (STRAT uh jee) a plan of action for fighting a war. (p. 282)

strike (stryk) an organized refusal to work by people trying to win higher wages and better working conditions from their employer. (p. 514)

subsistence (suhb SIHS tuhns) a word used to describe farmers who raised just enough to feed themselves and their families. (p. 202)

suburb (SUHB urb) an area between the city and the countryside designed mainly for homes. (p. 562)

suffrage (SUHF rihj) the right to vote. (p. 368)

surplus (SUHR pluhs) an extra amount of anything, but particularly of something people need. (p. 40)

surrender (suh REHN dur) for one side in a battle or war to give up. (p. 290)

symbol (SIHM buhl) something that stands for something else. (p. 355)

T **tariff** (TAR ihf) a tax charged on goods brought into a country. (p. 600)

tax (taks) money people give their government to help pay for the services it provides them. (p. 242)

telegraph (TEHL ih graf) a way of communicating that sends electrical signals over wires. (p. 482)

temperance (TEHM pur uhns) the decision to drink little alcohol or none at all. (p. 388)

tenement (TEHN uh muhnt) a rundown apartment building located in a city, usually rented mostly to poor people. (p. 382)

territory (TEHR ih tawr ee) an area of land that is ruled by government; a frontier region before it became a U.S. state. (p. 307)

tidewater (TYD waw tur) a coastal area of the South with rivers that rise and fall with the tides. (p. 212)

total war (TOHT l wawr) a strategy in which an army destroys factories, railroads, farms, and cities to keep the enemy from getting the supplies it needs and to make civilians tired of the war. (p. 457)

trading partner (TRAYD ihng PAHRT nur) a nation that frequently trades goods with another. (p. 600)

transcontinental railroad (trans kahn tuh NEHN tuhl RAYL rohd) a railroad that runs across a continent. (p. 483)

treason (TREE zuhn) a revolt against one's own government. (p. 272)

trench warfare (trehnch WAWR fair) a war fought from ditches dug in the ground. (p. 540)

trend (trehnd) a pattern over time. (p. 549)

triangular trade (try ANG gyuh lur trayd) trade between Africa, Europe, and North America. (p. 176)

trustee (truh STEE) a person who is responsible for individuals, organizations, or money. (p. 219)

U **Underground Railroad** (UHN dur ground RAYL rohd) a secret network of men and women who led enslaved African Americans to freedom before the Civil War. (p. 385)

unemployment (uhn ehm PLOI muhnt) the condition of not having a job. (p. 549)

Union (YOON yuhn) another word for the United States; the states that remained united under the Constitution during the Civil War. (p. 426)

urban (UR buhn) coming from or belonging to a city. (p. 502)

V **viceroy** (VYS roi) a person sent by the king to rule a colony. (p. 122)

virtue (VUR choo) a good point about someone; a characteristic others feel they should imitate. (p. 354)

volunteer (vahl uhn TIHR) a person who chooses to join the military. (p. 433)

W **wampum** (WAHM puhm) a form of money made from polished shells. (p. 172)

wilderness (WIHL dur nihs) a large area of land left in its natural condition. (p. 161)

woodland (WUD luhnd) an area that is largely covered by trees. (p. 52)

Y **yellow journalism** (YEHL oh JUR nuh lihz uhm) newspaper reporting that tells stories in an exaggerated or untruthful manner. (p. 524)

yeoman (YOH muhn) a farmer who owns enough land to provide his family's basic needs. (p. 200)

Index

Page numbers with *m* before them refer to maps. Page numbers with *p* refer to pictures. Page numbers with *c* refer to charts.

Credits

Acknowledgments: American Voices

p. 3 Robert Frost; The Gift Outright, by Robert Frost, Henry Holt, 1961. p. 4 Maya Lin; "First She Looks Inward," by Jonathan Coleman, in Time magazine, November 6, 1989. p. 6 Thomas Jefferson; Declaration of Independence, July 4, 1776, found in Familiar Quotations, by John Bartlett, Little, Brown and Company, 1980.

Unit Opener Quotes

Unit 1 Blackfoot Chief; Touch the Earth: A Self-Portrait of Indian Existence, by T.C. McLuhan, Outerbridge & Dienstfrey, 1971. Unit 2 Christopher Columbus; Famous Phrases from History, by Charles F. Hemphill, Jr., Jefferson & London: McFarland, 1982. Unit 3 Anne Bradstreet; The Works of Anne Bradstreet, Jeannine Hensley, ed., The Belknap Press of Harvard University Press, 1967. Unit 4 George Washington; in a letter to John Banister, Valley Forge, April 21, 1778, in The Harper Book of American Quotations, by Gorton Carruth and Eugene Ehrlich, Harper & Row, 1988. Unit 5 Roger Wilkins; The Washington Post magazine, June 28, 1987. Unit 6 Elizabeth Cady Stanton; The New Encyclopedia Britannica, vol. 11, Encyclopedia Britannica, Inc., 1991. Unit 7 Abraham Lincoln; Speech to Republican State Convention, Springfield, Illinois, June 16, 1858, in The Harper Book of American Quotations, Gorton Carruth and Eugene Ehrlich, eds., HarperCollins, 1988. Unit 8 Frederick Douglas; Speech in Canandaigua, New York, August 3, 1857, in The Harper Book of American Quotations, Gorton Carruth and Eugene Ehrlich, eds., HarperCollins, 1988. Unit 9 Eleanor Roosevelt; The Harper Book of American Quotations, Gorton Carruth and Eugene Ehrlich, eds., HarperCollins, 1988.

Permissioned Material

"As I Walk This Road," by Ricardo Rojas, from Rising Voices: Writings of Young Native Americans, selected by Arlene B. Hirschfelder and Beverly R. Singer. Copyright © 1992 by Arlene B. Hirschfelder and Beverly R. Singer. Reprinted by permission of Ricardo Rojas. Selection from Benjamin Franklin, by Ingri and Edgar Parin d'Aulaire. Copyright © 1950 by Doubleday. Reprinted by permission of Bantam Doubleday Dell Books for Young Readers, a division of Bantam Doubleday Dell Publishing Group, Inc., New York, New York. All rights reserved. Selection from The Cat Who Escaped from Steerage, by Evelyn Wilde Mayerson. Copyright © 1990 by Evelyn Wilde Mayerson. Reprinted by permission of Cantrell-Colas, Inc., Literary Agency on behalf of the author. Selection from Charlie Skedaddle, by Patricia Beatty. Copyright © 1987 by Patricia Beatty. Reprinted by permission of William Morrow and Company, Inc. "Colonists in Bondage: Indentured Servants in America," from Early American Life magazine, October 1979. Copyright © 1979 by The Early American Society, Inc. Reprinted by permission. "The Fur Trade," by Jack Rudolph, from Cobblestone magazine: The North American Beaver Trade, June 1982. Copyright © 1982 by Cobblestone Publishing, Inc., 7 School Street, Peterborough, NH 03458. Reprinted by permission of the publisher. Illustration from The Gettysburg Address, by Abraham Lincoln, illustrated by Michael McCurdy. Illustrations copyright © 1995 Michael McCurdy. Reprinted by permission of Houghton Mifflin Company. All rights reserved. Selection from Harriet Tubman: Antislavery Activist, by M.W. Taylor. Copyright © 1991 by Chelsea House Publishers, a division of Main Line Book Company, 1-(800)-362-9786. Reprinted by permission. "He Keeps Going and Going and Going . . . " by John Rolfe, from Sports Illustrated for Kids magazine, August 1995. Copyright © 1995 by Time, Inc. Reprinted by permission of Sports Illustrated for Kids. All rights reserved. Selection from the "I Have a Dream Speech," by Martin Luther King, Jr. Copyright © 1963 by Martin Luther King, Jr. Copyright © renewed 1991 by Coretta Scott King. Reprinted by permission of The Heirs to the Estate of Martin Luther King, Jr., c/o Writers House, Inc., agents for the Estate. "I Wonder Who Invented . . . , " by Gail Hennessey, from Cobblestone magazine: African American Inventors, February 1992. Copyright © 1992 by Cobblestone Publishing, 7 School Street, Peterborough, NH 03458. Reprinted by permission of the publisher. Selection from Pedro's Journal, by Pam Conrad, illustrated by Peter Koeppen. Text copyright © 1991 by Pam Conrad. Illustrations copyright © 1991 by Peter Koeppen. Reprinted by permission of Boyds Mills Press, Inc. Selection from Phillis Wheatley: Poet, by Victoria Sperrow, Junior World Biography Series. Copyright © 1992 by Chelsea House Publishers, a division of Main Line Book Company, 1-(800)-362-9786. Reprinted by permission. All rights reserved. "Resurrecting Patriots, and Their Park," by Douglas Martin, from The New York Times, September 23, 1995. Copyright © 1995 by The New York Times Company. Reprinted by permission. Selection from The Sad Night: The Story of an Aztec Victory and a Spanish Loss, written and illustrated by Sally Schofer Mathews. Text and illustrations copyright © 1994 by Sally Schofer Mathews. Reprinted by permission of Clarion Books, a division of Houghton Mifflin Company. All rights reserved. Selection from Song of the Trees, by Mildred D. Taylor, illustrated by Jerry Pinkney. Text copyright © 1975 by Mildred Taylor. Illustrations copyright © 1975 by Jerry Pinkney. Cover illustration copyright © 1984 by Max Ginsburg. Reprinted by permission of Dial Books for Young Readers, a division of Penguin Books USA, Inc. Selection from The Story of Sacajawea, Guide to Lewis and Clark,

by Della Rowland. Copyright © 1989 by Parachute Press, Inc. Reprinted by permission of Bantam Doubleday Dell Books for Young Readers, a division of Bantam Doubleday Dell Publishing Group, Inc., New York, New York. All rights reserved."The Story of the Star Spangled Banner," by Lester David, from Boys' Life magazine, July 1995. Text copyright © 1995 by Lester David. Reprinted by permission of the author. Cover reprinted by permission of Boys' Life and the Boy Scouts of America. "We Are the Many," by Ingrid Putesoy, from Rising Voices: Writings of Young Native Americans, selected by Arlene B. Hirschfelder and Beverly R. Singer. Copyright © 1992 by Arlene B. Hirschfelder and Beverly R. Singer. Reprinted by permission of the Havasupai Tribe."We Turn Sap to Syrup," by Peter Martin as told to Carolyn Duckworth, from Ranger Rick magazine, February 1988. Copyright © 1988 by the National Wildlife Federation. Reprinted by permission. Selection from Where Was Patrick Henry on the 29th of May?, by Jean Fritz, illustrated by Margot Tomes. Text copyright © 1975 by Jean Fritz. Illustrations copyright © 1975 by Margot Tomes. Reprinted by permission of Coward, McCann and Geoghegan, Inc., a division of The Putnam Publishing Group.

Fair Use Quotes

p. 14 Theodore Roosevelt; National Geographic magazine, October 1994. National Geographic Society. p. 52 Lorraine Canoe; The New York Times, January 3, 1995. p. 63 Navajo song; World of American Indians, Princeton University Press, 1973. p. 75 To See a World, by Armento et al., Houghton Mifflin Company, 1994. p. 78 North America from Earliest Discovery to First Settlements, by David B. Quinny, Harper & Row, 1975. p. 125 Don Juan de Oñate; The Patriotic Chiefs, by Alvin M. Josephy, Penguin Books USA, 1961. p. 134 William Bradford; Of Plymouth Plantation 1620-1647, by William Branford, Alfred A. Knopf, 1975. p. 139 John Winthrop; The Puritan Dilemma: The Story of John Winthrop, by Edmund S. Morgan, Little, Brown and Company. p. 142 Father Paul Le Jeune; The Jesuit Relations and Allied Documents: Travels and Explorations of The Jesuit Missionaries in New France 1610-1791, Rueben Gold Thqaites, ed., The Burrows Brothers Company, 1897. p. 173 Narragansett Chief; America: Pathway to the Present, Prentice Hall. p. 174 Child Life in Colonial Days, by Alice Morse Earle, Macmillan, 1929. p. 177 Olaudah Equiano; Equiano's Travels: His Autobiography, Heineman, 1967. p. 192 Michel Guillaume Jean de Crèvecoeur; Letters from an American Farmer, 1782. p. 200 Benjamin Franklin; The Autobiography and Other Writings, by Benjamin Franklin, Pantheon, 1989. p. 211 London play; Everyday Life in Early America, by Louis Wright, 1965. p. 214 Eliza Lucas; Eliza Pinckney, by Harriet Horny Ravenel, Charles Scribners' Sons, 1896. p. 218 Red, White and Black, by Gary Nash, Prentice Hall, 1992. p. 222 Home Life in Early Colonial Days, by Alice Morse Earle, Macmillan, 1926. p. 244 The Perfect Crisis: The Beginning of the Revolutionary War, by Neil R. Stout, New York University Press, 1976. p. 250 The Boston Massacre, by Hiller Zobel, W.W. Norton, 1970. p. 267 Annals of America, Encyclopedia Britannica, 1976. p. 271 John Adams; The Story of the Declaration of Independence, by Dumas Malone, Oxford University Press, 1954. p. 272 Benjamin Franklin; Signers of the Declaration of Independence, National Park Service, 1995. p. 273 Abigail Adams; Notable American Women, Harvard University Press, 1973. p. 281 King George; Portrait of America, by Stephen B. Oates. p. 282 Captain Nathan Hale; The Fire of Liberty, by Edmond Wright, St. Martin's Press, 1983. p. 286 Redcoats and Rebels: The American Revolution Through British Eyes, by Christopher Hibbert, W.W. Norton & Company, 1990. p. 287 Baron von Steuben; The Glorious Cause, by Robert Middlekauff, Oxford University Press, 1982. p. 290 General Nathanael Greene; Redcoats and Rebels: The American Revolution Through British Eyes, by Christopher Hibbert, W.W. Norton & Company, 1990. p. 294 George Washington; George Washington, by James Thomas Flexner, Little, Brown and Company, 1967. p. 308 A People's History of the United States, by Howard Zinn, HarperCollins, 1980. p. 309 George Washington; This Is America My Country, Donald H. Sheehan, ed., 1952. p. 316 Mercy Otis Warren; We the People: Voices and Images of the New Nation, edited by Alfred F. Young et al., Temple University Press, 1993. p. 316 Benjamin Rush; Ibid. p. 318 James Madison; The Living U.S. Constitution, by Saul K. Padover, Meridian, 1995. p. 322 George Washington; George Washington and the New Nation (1783-1793), by James Thomas Flexner, Little, Brown and Company, 1970. p. 324 Thomas Jefferson; A New Dictionary of Quotations, by H.L. Menkin, Alfred A. Knopf, 1966. p. 324 Alexander Hamilton; Ibid. p. 335 Thomas Jefferson; The Annals of America, vol. 4, 1797-1820, Encyclopedia Britannica, 1968. p. 346 George Washington; Documents of American History, Henry Steele Comanger ed., Appleton-Century Crofts, 1968. p. 355 Encyclopedia Americana, Grolier, 1991. p. 369 Daniel Webster; A History of the United States, by Daniel J. Boorstein and Brooks Mather Kelley, Prentice Hall, 1981. p. 371 Creek woman; "Legend of the Trail of Tears," by Elizabeth Sullivan, from Indian Legends of the Trail of Tears, 1974. p. 375 Mary Paul; Farm to Factory: Women's Letters 1830-1860, edited by Thomas Dublin, Columbia University Press, 1993. p. 377 Eli Whitney; The World of Eli Whitney, by Jeanette Mirsky and Allan Nevis, Macmillan, 1952. p. 378 Solomon Northrup; Voices of the Old South: Eyewitness Accounts 1829-1861, by Allan Gallay, University of Georgia Press, 1994. p. 385 Frederick Douglas; My Bondage and My Freedom, by Frederick

Douglass, Miller, Orton & Mulligan, 1855. p. 387 Sojourner Truth; *Ar'n't I a Woman?*, by Deborah Gray White, W.W. Norton & Company, 1985. p. 389 Dorothea Dix; "Plea for the Humane Treatment of the Insane," by Dorothea Dix, in *The Annals of America*, vol. 7, 1971. p. 403 John O'Sullivan; *Oxford Companion to American History*, by Thomas H. Johnson, Oxford University Press, 1966. p. 407 *The Far Western Frontier 1830-1860*, by Ray Allen Billington, Harper & Row, 1962. p. 408 Amelia Stewart Knight; *The Oregon Diary of Amelia Stewart Knight*, edited by Harold R. Carpenter, from *Clark County History*, Volume 6, 1965. p. 409 Curly Chief; *Native American Testimony: A Chronicle of Indian-White Relations from Prophesy to Present 1492-1992*, Viking Penguin, 1991. p. 409 Brigham Young; *The Far Western Frontier 1830-1860*, by Ray Allen Billington, Harper & Row, 1962. p. 414 *California: An Interpretive History*, by James J. Rawls and Walton Bean, McGraw Hill, 1993. p. 415 Louise Clappe; Ibid. p. 427 Daniel Webster; *Encyclopedia of American History* 6th ed, Richard Morris, ed., HarperCollins, 1982. p. 433 Robert E. Lee; *Battle Cry of Freedom*, by James McPherson, Oxford University Press, 1988. p. 444 Frederick Douglas; *Negro's Civil War*, by James McPherson, Pantheon, 1965. p. 446 Emancipation Proclamation; *Documents of American History*, edited by Henry Steele Commager, Appleton-Century-Crofts, 1973. p. 446 London newspaper; *A History of the United States*, by Daniel J. Boorstin, Prentice Hall, 1989. p.448 Carrie Berry; *Tara Revisited*, by Catherine Clinton, Abbeville Publishers, 1995. p. 449 *Voices From the Civil War*, by Milton Meltzer, HarperCollins 1989. p. 449 Belle Boyd; *Women in the Civil War*, Phyllis Emert, ed., Discovery Enterprises, 1995. p. 449 *War, Terrible War*, by Joy Hakim, Oxford University Press, 1994. p. 455 Abraham Lincoln; *Abraham Lincoln Complete Works*, by John G. Nicolay and John Hay, The Century Company, 1894. p. 456 Abraham Lincoln; *Battle Cry of Freedom: The Civil War Era*, by James M. McPherson, Oxford University Press, 1988. p. 457 General William T. Sherman; *Battle Cry of Freedom: The Civil War Era*, by James M. McPherson, Oxford University Press, 1988. p. 462 Mary Brody; *Been in the Storm So Long: The Aftermath*, by Leon F. Litwack, Alfred A. Knopf, 1979. p. 462 *Reconstruction: Opposing Viewpoints*, Brenda Stalrup ed., Greenhaven Press, 1995. p.463 *Reconstruction and Reform*, by Joy Hakim, Oxford University Press, 1994. p. 465 Millie Freedman; *War, Terrible War*, by Joy Hakim, Oxford University Press, 1994. p. 468 Thaddeus Stevens; *Reconstruction: Opposing Viewpoints*, Brenda Stalrup ed., Greenhaven Press, 1995. p. 471 Millie Freedman; *War, Terrible War*, by Joy Hakim, Oxford University Press, 1994. p. 489 *Bury My Heart at Wounded Knee*, by Oll Brown, Henry Holt & Company. p. 490 Willa Cather; *My Ántonia*, by Willa Cather, Houghton Mifflin Company. p. 491 *The Pioneers*, Time-Life Books, 1974. p. 492 *The Women*, by Joan Swallow Reiter, Time-Life Books. p. 501 Alexander Graham Bell; *The People in Chronology*, Holt, Rinehart & Winston, 1979. p. 503 Andrew Carnegie; *The Robber Barron*, by Matthew Josephson, Harcourt Brace, 1962. p. 508 Mary Antin; *The Promised Land*, by Mary Antin, Houghton Mifflin Company, 1969. p. 510 Ibid. p. 535 Upton Sinclair; *The Jungle*, by Upton Sinclair, Cambridge: Robert Bentley. p. 539 Woodrow Wilson; *Quotations in History*, by Alan Palmer, Harper & Row, 1976. p. 547 Frankin Delano Roosevelt; *Quotations in History*, by Alan Palmer, Harper & Row, 1976. p. 554 General Dwight D. Eisenhower; *Time* magazine, June 6, 1994. p. 564 Earl Warren; *Documents of American History* vol. II, edited by Henry Steele Commager and Milton Cantor, Prentice Hall. p. 566 Martin Luther King, Jr.; Reference Library of Black America, Gale Research, Detroit, 1994. p. 572 John F. Kennedy; *Let the Words Go Forth: The Speeches, Statements, and Writings of John F. Kennedy*, by Theodore Sorensen, Delacorte, 1988. p. 599 Colonel Frederick Gregory; *Black Stars in Orbit*, by Khephra Burns and William Miles, Harcourt Brace, 1995. p. 603 Vice President Gore; U.S. Department of State Dispatch, November 28, 1994, vol. 5, No. 48.

Photo Credits

Cover (inset) © David Young Wolff/PhotoEdit; (bk) Donovan Reese/Tony Stone Images **Back Cover** (m) The Granger Collection; (br) Earth Imaging/Tony Stone Images **i** David Young Wolff/PhotoEdit **ii–iii** (inset) Fred J. Maroon; (bk) Donovan Reese/Tony Stone Images; (br) Earth Imaging/Tony Stone Images **vi** Richard Alexander Cooke **vii** Courtesy of the Haffenreffer Museum of Anthropology, Brown University. Photo: Cathy Carver **viii** Courtesy, American Antiquarian Society **ix** National Museum of American History/Smithsonian Institution **x** Smithsonian Institution, Washington, D.C. **xi** © Theo Westenberger 1994 **xiii** Independence National Historic Park **2** Bob Daemmrich **3** David Muench **4** (bl) Alan Smith/Tony Stone Images **4–5** © 1986 James Balog/Collins Publishers **6** Grant Faint/The Image Bank **6–7** (bk) Donovan Reese/Tony Stone Images; (m) Stephen Wilkes/Image Bank **7** Stephen Wilkes/The Image Bank **8–9** Randy Wells/Tony Stone Images, Inc. **12** (t) © David Muench 1995; (bl) Gary Yeowell/Tony Stone Images; (br) Tony Stone Images, Inc.; (bc) Mike Abrahams/Tony Stone Images, Inc. **13** (t) National Geographic Image Collection; (bc) © Jim Richardson/Westlight; (br) Peter Lamberti/Tony Stone Images, Inc.; (bl) Robert Brenner/PhotoEdit **14** © David Muench 1995 **15** (bl) Courtesy Grand Teton Natural History Association; (bc) © David Muench 1995; (br) Courtesy National Park Service; (t) Courtesy National Park Service **17** (tr) John Coletti/The Picture Cube; (b) Mike Abrahams/Tony Stone Images, Inc.; (l) Ken Graham/Tony Stone Images, Inc. **18** Comstock **21** Bob Daemmrich **22** Doug Plummer **23** Richard Pasley 1983/Stock Boston **24** Denver Public Library, Western History Division **25** Alan Becker/Image Bank **26** (bl) © Jim Richardson/Westlight; (br) © Jim Richardson/Westlight **27** © Frank P. Rossotto/The Stock Market **28** (t) Peter Lamberti/Tony Stone Images, Inc.; (b) Superstock **29** © David Harp 1995 **30** Michael Heron/Woodfin Camp **31** Courtesy South Florida Water Management District **34** (bc) Museum of the American Indian; (bl) Comstock; (t) © David Muench 1995 **35** (bl) Comstock; (br) Museum of the American Indian. Photo: David Heald; (t) Lynn Johnson; (bc) Peabody Museum, Harvard University. Photo: Hillel Burger **36** UPI/Bettmann Archives **37** Al Grillo/Alaska Stock Images **38** Dr. Dennis Stanford/Smithsonian Institution, Washington, D.C. **40** Tony Stone Images, Inc. **41** (b) Michel Zabé; (t) Odyssey/Robert Frerck **42** (l) © Richard Alexander Cooke III; (r) Michel Zabé **43** (b) © Richard Alexander Cooke III; (t) Michel Zabé **44** (r) © Richard Alexander Cooke III; (l) NASA: John C. Stennis Space Center **45** (br) Courtesy National Park Service; (l) (tr) Jerry Jacka **46** (r) The Saint Louis Art Museum. Eliza McMillan Fund; (l) Georgia Dept. of Natural Resources. Photo: David Kamenski **47** Odyssey/Robert Frerck **48** British Library **49** The Bodleian Library, folio 47 r. **50** (l) Erich Lessing/Art Resource, N.Y.; (r) Museo del Templo Major **52** Suzanne DeChillo/NYT Pictures **55** Richard Pasley/Stock Boston **56** Cranbrook Institute **56–57** Jeff Hunter/The Image Bank **58** (r) © Richard Alexander Cooke III; (b) Lynn Johnson; (t) Peabody Museum, Harvard University. Photo: Hillel Burger **60** (tr) Eugene and Clare Thaw Collection, Fenimore House Museum, Cooperstown, NY. Photo: John Bigelow Taylor; (b) Courtesy Department of Library Services, American Museum of Natural History, #3181 (2); (c) Alaska State Library, Alaska Historical Collection, #PCA 87–23; **61** Terry E. Eiler/Mugwump **62** Jerry Jacka **63** © David Muench 1995 **64** (r) Courtesy Morning Star Gallery, Santa Fe, N.M. Photo: Addison Doty; (l) Terry Eiler/Mugwump **65** Skjold Photographs **68–69** Peter Christopher **72** (t) Bibliotheque National/Sonia Halliday Photographs; (br) Giraudon/Art Resource, NY; (bl) Universitetets Oldsaksamling; (bc) Comstock **73** (t) C. M. Dixon; (bl) Dallas & John Heaton/Stock Boston; (br) Scala/Art Resource, N.Y. Biblioteca Nazionale Central, Florence; (bc) Wan-go Weng **74** Universitetets Oldsaksamling **77** Comstock **80** The Bodleian Library, Oxford **81** National Palace Museum, Taipei, Taiwan. Photo: Wan-go Weng **82** (bl) Statens Historiska Museum (ATA); (bc) Smithsonian Institution, Washington, D.C.; (tc) Chinese and Japanese Special Fund, Courtesy of Museum of Fine Arts, Boston; (tl) (l) Cary Wolinsky/Stock Boston; (tr) Mark Sexton/Peabody & Essex Museum **83** (br) Art Resource; (bc) Giraudon/Art Resource, NY **84** (b) Researcher, Eric Lessing/Art Resource; (t) Shaun Egan/Tony Stone Images, Inc. **85** Sacla/Art Resource, NY **88** (bc) Sevilla. Biblioteca Colombina/MAS; (br) Scala/Art Rource, NY; (t) Capitol Historical Society/National Geographic Society Image Collection; (bl) Scala/Art Resource, NY **89** (br) © Musée de L'Homme. Photo: M. Delaplanche; (t) National Maritime Museum; (bl) Ten Views in the Island of Antiqua, 1832, Plate IV by Willian Clark. By permission of the British Library; (bc) Tim Lynch/Stock Boston **90** (bl) (cl) (br) (cr) National Maritime Museum, London **91** Werner Forman/Art Resource, NY **92** Scala/Art Resource, NY **93** Photographic Services, The Royal Collection © Her Majesty Queen Elizabeth II **94** Marc Bernheim/Woodfin Camp & Associates **97** (r) Botany Library, Harvard University; (l) Cosmo Condina/Tony Stone Images, Inc. **98** (r) The American Numismatic Society; (l) Miguel Rojas Mix, Paris **100–101** Ned M. Seidler © National Geographic Society **101** (br) (bc) Higgins Armory Museum, Worcester, Massachusetts. Photo: Don Eaton **102** (l) Laurie Platt Winfrey, Inc.; (r) LIENZO DE TLAXCALA, 1560. American Museum of Natural History; (c) LIENZO DE TLAXCALA, 1560. By permission of Tozzer Library, Harvard University **103** Granger Collection **104** (c) (l) (r) Library of Congress **105** Dr. William C. Stone/U.S. Deep Caving Team **106** Ten Views in the Island of Antiqua, 1832, Plate IV by Willian Clark. By permission of the British Library **107** Notices of Brazil in 1828 and 1829, London: 1830 by Robert Walsh. By permission of the British Library **111** By kind permission of the Marquess of Tavistock and Trustees of the Bedford Estates **112** Launch of Fireships Against the Spanish Armada unknown artist. National Maritime Museum, London **113** Bridgeman/Art Resource, NY **114** (lc) Courtesy Massachusetts Fish & Wildlife Commission. Photo: Mark Sexton of the Peabody and Essex Museum, Salem; (b) Courtesy of Mackinac State Historic Parks **114–115** Vallard Atlas map 9, NE coast of N.A. circa 1547. Huntington Library **120** (br) Virginia State Library; (bl) University of Mexico City; (bc) Jerry Jacka; (t) Public Relations, Plimoth Plantation/Ted Curtin **121** (bc) Albany Institute of History and Art; (br) Coordinator of Rights & Reproductions, New York Historical Society; (bl) Courtesy Vose Galleries of Boston, Inc. **123** Museo Nacional de Ethnologia, Madrid **124** Jerry Jacka **126** Laurence Parent **127** (b) © 1992 Donovan Reese; (t) © David Muench 1995 **128** Trustees of the British Museum **129** Trustees of the British Museum **130** Colonial Williamsburg Foundation **131** National Portrait Gallery, Smithsonian Institution/Art Resource, NY **134** Courtesy Vose Galleries of Boston, Inc. **135** Library of Congress; (t) Steve Dunwell/The Image Bank **137** (b) (t) Pilgrim Society **138** (t) Collection of the New York Historical Society; (b) Pilgrim Society **139** Courtesy American Antiquarian Society **140** Pilgrim Society **140–141** Jeff Hunter/The Image Bank **144–145** Museum of the City of New York, The J. Clarence Davies Collection **145** (r) The Henry Francis duPont Wintherthur Museum **154–155** Peter Vitale/*Historic Charleston: Great American Homes*, published by Oxmoor House, Inc., courtesy of Rebus, Inc., New York, NY, 1988 **158** (t) Old Sturbridge Village; (bl) Comstock; (bc) Phil D. Swanson; (br) Wadsworth Atheneum, Hartford. Museum Purchase **159** (t) Thomas Russell/The Picture Cube; (bl) Detail, The Fine Arts Museums of San Francisco, Gift of Mr. & Mrs. John D. Rockefeller 3rd, 1979.7.3; (bc) Yale University Art Gallery, Bequest of Eugene Phelps Edwards; (br) Royal Albert Memorial Museum, Exeter, England **160** Courtesy of the Haffenreffer Museum of Anthropology, Brown University. Photo: Cathy Carver **168** Kindra Clineff/The Picture Cube **169** Wadsworth Atheneum, Hartford. Museum Purchase **170–171** David Hiser/Photographers Aspen **171** National Portrait Gallery **172** (t) Courtesy American Antiquarian Society; (b) Courtesy of the Fruitlands Museums, Harvard, Massachusetts **173** Tom Herde/The Boston Globe **175** (c) © Addison Gallery of American Art, Phillips Academy, Andover, MA. All rights reserved.; (tl) (tc) (tr) (bl) (br) (bc) Amanda Merullo/Historic Deerfield **177** Royal Albert Memorial Museum, Exeter, England **178** (b) Peabody & Essex Museum. Photo: Mark Sexton; (tr) Peabody & Essex Museum; (tc) Peabody Essex Museum. Photo: Mark Sexton **179** Redwood Library and Athenaeum, Newport, Rhode Island. Gift of Emma Rodman and Anna L. Snelling. **180** Steve Dunwell **181** Courtesy of The Bostonian

Museum **415** (t) History Department, The Oakland Museum; (b) Denver Public Library, Western History Dept.; (c) History Department, The Oakland Museum; (l) California State Library **416** Levi Strauss & Company **417** Montana Historical Society **420–421** CLB Publishing, Godalming **424** (br) Smithsonian Institution, Washington, D.C.; (bl) Metropolitan Museum of Art; (bc) Collection of Edith Hariton/Antique Textile Resource/Picture Research Consultants, Inc.; (t) Library of Congress **425** (t) Schlesinger Library, Radcliffe College; (bl) (bc) (br) Library of Congress **427** Library of Congress **428** (b) The Fine Arts Museums of San Francisco, Gift of Mr. & Mrs. John D. Rockefeller 3rd, 1979.7.60; (t) Collection of Edith Hariton/Antique Textile Resource/Picture Research Consultants, Inc. **429** Missouri Historical Society **430** (bl) The Gibbes Museum of Art, Carolina Art Association; (tr) Collection of Janice L. and David J. Frent; (br) The Corcoran Gallery of Art, Mary E. Maxwell Fund **431** (t) (b) Collection of Janice L. and David J. Frent **432** (l) (c) C. Paul Loane from *Echoes of Glory: Arms and Equipment of the Union.* Photo: Larry Sherer © 1991 Time-Life Books Inc.; (br) Private Collection **433** (br) Confederate Memorial Hall from *Echoes of Glory: Arms and Equipment of the Confederacy.* Photo: Larry Sherer © 1991 Time-Life Books Inc.; (bc) Museum of the Confederacy; (bl) Private Collection **434** (b) Mark Sexton; (t) High Impact Photography, Inc. **437** Dave Bartruff/Stock Boston **438** Fredericksburg National Military Park from *The Civil War: Rebels Resurgent.* Photo: Larry Sherer © 1985 Time-Life Books Inc. **439** (b) Library of Congress; (t) Reproductions George Eastman House **441** Private Collection **442** (t) Mead Art Gallery, Amherst College Museum Purchase 1946.129; (l) Stamatelos Brothers from *Echoes of Glory: Arms and Equipment of the Union.* Photo: Larry Sherer © 1991 Time-Life Books Inc. **444** Library of Congress **445** (t) Massachusetts Historical Society; (b) William Gladstone **446** High Impact Photography, Inc. **447** West Point Museum, United States Military Academy, West Point, NY **448** Atlanta History Center **449** (tr) Courtesy American Antiquarian Society; (br) Division of Political History, Smithsonian Institution, Washington, D.C.; (bl) U.S. Army Military History Institute **450** (bl) (br) (tl) Division of Political History, Smithsonian Institution, Washington, D.C.; (tc) Library of Congress **454** (bl) Library of Congress; (br) Division of Political History, Smithsonian Institution, Washington, D.C.; (bc) The New York Historical Society; (t) Tom Till **455** (t) (br) Library of Congress; (bc) Collection of Janice L. and David J. Frent; (bl) Valentine Museum, Cook Collection **456** (b) National Archives; (t) Library of Congress **458** Museum of the Confederacy **459** Illinois State Historical Society **462** Cook Collection, Valentine Museum **463** (b) William Gladstone; (t) Moorland-Spingarn Research Center **464** Division of Political History, Smithsonian Institution, Washington, D.C. **465** Valentine Museum, Cook Collection **466** Library of Congress **468** (bl) Library of Congress **469** (bl) Library of Congress; (br) Courtesy, American Antiquarian Society **470** (b) Library of Congress; (t) Nancy Gewitz/Antique Textile Resource/Picture Research Consultants, Inc. **472** Culver Pictures, Inc. **476–477** Library of Congress 480 (t) © 1996 The Detroit Institute of Arts, Founders Society. Purchased with funds from Flint Ink Corporation **480** (bl) Wells Fargo History Department; (bc) Library of Congress; (br) History Department, Oakland Museum **481** (br) Collection of Janice L. and David J. Frent; (bc) Nebraska State Historical Society; (t) Wells Fargo History Department; (bl) Denver Public Library, Western History Division **482** (bl) Charles Phillips; (bc) Library of Congress; (br) Division of Political History, Smithsonian Institution, Washington, D.C.; (bc) New York Historical Society **484** Library of Congress **485** (tr) History Department, Oakland Museum **486** Yva Momatiuk/Stock Boston **487** (tl) Library of Congress; (tr) © Theo Westenberger 1994 **488** (b) National Museum of American Indian, Smithsonian Institution; (t) Denver Public Library, Western History Division **489** (l) Denver Public Library, Western History Division; (r) National Anthropological Archives, Smithsonian Institution, Washington, D.C. **490** (bl) (br) Montana Historical Society **491** (br) (tr) (bl) Montana Historical Society **492** (r) Library of Congress; (cl) Deere & Company; (bl) Charles Phillips/Ellwood House Museum **494** (t) The Vesterheim Norwegian-American Museum; State Historical Society of North Dakota **498** (br) Courtesy of the Ellis Island Immigration Museum; (bc) Sears Roebuck and Company; (bl) U.S. Department of the Interior, National Park Service, Edison National Historic Site; (t) Henry Ford Museum and Greenfield Village **499** (t) UPI/Bettmann Archives; (bl) George Meany Memorial Archives; (bc) Courtesy of Bishop Museum; (br) Library of Congress **500** (b) Chicago Historical Society; (r) Otis Elevator Company Historic Archives; (l) Culver Pictures, Inc. **501** (t) U.S. Department of the Interior, National Park Service, Edison National Historic Site; (bc) Brooks Walker/National Geographic Society Image Collection; (tc) Division of Political History, Smithsonian Institution, Washington, D.C.; (b) Slater Mill Historic Site **502** (l) Pictorial Collections, Hagley Museum & Library; (c) Collection of Sharon & Daniel Kleitman, Photo courtesy Sally Fox; (r) Brown Brothers **503** UPI/Bettmann Archives **504** Rare Books Division, Free Library of Philadelphia **505** (c) Library of Congress; (bl) Michaud Grapes/Photo Researchers **508–509** Tony Stone Images, Inc. **509** (t) Chermayeff & Geismar/Metaform. Photo: Karne Yamauchi; (c) Brown Brothers **511** (tr) Chicago Historical Society; (tl) Bancroft Library; (br) Library of Congress; (bl) Institute of Texas Cultures, San Antonio, Texas. Courtesy Estate of Robert Moss Ayers **512** Chicago Historical Society **513** (l) Library of Congress; (r) Pennsylvania Historical and Museum Commission, Bureau of Historic Sites and Museums **514** (br) Picture Research Consultants & Archves; (tl) Library of Congress **515** (r) Urban Archives, Temple University, Phildelphia, PA; (l) Brown Brothers **516** Chermayeff & Geismar/Metaform. Photo: Karne Yamauchi **517** UPI/Bettmann Archives **518** Chermayeff & Geismar/Metaform. Photo: Karne Yamauchi **520** Chicago Historical Society **522** Courtesy of Bishop Museum **523** Brown Brothers **524** (l) New York Historical Society; (r) Library of Congress **525** Granger **527** Theodore Roosevelt Collection, Harvard College Library **530–531** Scene from the IMAX® film "The Dream Is Alive," © 1985 Smithsonian Institution/Lockheed Corporation **534** (br) National Archives; (bc) Library of Congress; (t) National Archives; (bl) Brown Brothers **535** (bc) Library of Congress; (t) Courtesy of the Decorative & Industrial Arts Department of the Chicago Historical Society; (br) National Archives; (bl) Schomburg Center for Research in Black Culture, New York Public Library **536** (t) Courtesy Houghton Library, Harvard University; (b) Culver Pictures, Inc. **537** (tl) ILGWU Archives, Labor Management Documentation Center, Cornell University; (r) Brown Brothers **538** Brown Brothers **539** The Bettmann Archive **540** (l) (r) Collection of Colonel Stuart S. Corning, Jr.; (c) Imperial War Museum **542** (b) Library of Congress; (t) Temple University Libraries **543** (br) Picture Research Consultants & Archives; (t) Detail, The Phillips Collection, Washington, D.C. **544** (l) Division of Political History, Smithsonian Institution, Washington, D.C.; (c) Library of Congress; (r) Division of Political History, Smithsonian Institution, Washington, D.C. **545** (t) Schomburg Center for Research in Black Culture, New York Public Library; (b) Division of Political History, Smithsonian Institution, Washington, D.C. **546** (t) Henry Ford Museum and Greenfield Village; (b) Courtesy Ford Motor Company **547** (t) History Department, The Oakland Museum; (b) Library of Congress **548** Franklin D. Roosevelt Library **549** © 1930 Detroit News **551** (c) (b) (t) National Archives **554** (t) National Archives; (b) John Launois/Black Star **555** Schomburg Center for Research in Black Culture, New York Public Library **558** (bl) Publishing Division, SuperStock; (br) © The Mark Shaw Collection/Photo Researchers; (bc) Private Collection; (t) NASA/Johnson Space Center **559** (t) UPI/Bettmann Archives; (bl) Co Rentmeester, LIFE Magazine; (bc) UPI/Bettmann Archives; (br) NASA/Johnson Space Center **561** (tl) (tr) UPI/Bettmann Archives **563** UPI/Bettmann Archives **564** Private Collection **565** (t) Bruce Roberts/Photo Researchers; (b) Private Collection **566** (t) Charles Moore/Black Star; (b) Private Collection **567** (r) (l) James P. Blair/National Geographic Society Image Collection **572** Collection of Janice L. and David J. Frent **573** Philip Jones Griffith/Magnum Photos **576** (t) (b) NASA **578** Rick Friedman/Black Star **579** (t) (b) Bob Fitch/Black Star **580** Dennis Brack/Black Star **581** © 1988 TIME Inc. Reprinted by permission **588** (br) Kal Muller/Woodfin Camp; (bl) Malak Photographs, Ltd.; (t) Cliff Hollenbeck; (bc) Saskatchewan Archives Board **589** (br) NASA; (t) Tony Stone Images, Inc.; (bc) Michael Ma Po Shun/Tony Stone Images, Inc.; (bl) © 94 Viviane Moos/The Stock Market; (br) © Richard Alexander Cooke III **592** (r) Saskatchewan Archives Board; (l) National Archives of Canada **593** (l) Tony Stone Images, Inc.; (r) Phil & Karen Smith/Tony Stone Images, Inc. **594** (bl) © 94 Viviane Moos/The Stock Market **594–595** Tony Stone Images, Inc. **597** (r) © Richard Alexander Cooke III; (b) Poulides/Thatcher/Tony Stone Images, Inc. **598** (tl) (cl) Terrence Moore/Woodfin Camp **599** NASA/Johnson Space Center **601** Tony Stone Images, Inc. **602** UPI/Bettmann Archives **603** UPI/Bettmann Archives **609** Earth Imaging/Tony Stone Images, Inc. **610** (bc) George Chan/Photo Researchers, Inc. **610–611** Earth Imaging/Tony Stone Images **613** David Parker/Science Photo Library/Photo Researchers **623** (t) Library of Congress **646** (ml) © Robert Frerck/Woodfin Camp & Associates, Inc.; (t) Harald Sund/The Image Bank; (mr) © Gerard Champlong/The Image Bank **647** (ml) © Linde Waidhofer 1993/Liaison International; (tr) © John Eastcott/Yva Momatiuk/Woodfin Camp & Associates, Inc. **646–647** Ken Graham/Bruce Coleman, Inc. **650–653** (all) White House Historical Association **654** Yale University Art Gallery, Trumbull Collection **655** Royal Academy of Arts, London (detail) **656** Anne S. K. Brown Military Collection **657** Independence National Historic Park **658** © Benn Mitchell/The Image Bank **663** Dennis Brack/Black Star **664** Steve Dunwell/The Image Bank **666** Independence National Historic Park **669** (t) Collection of Janice L. and David J. Frent; (b) Hulton Deutsch Collection **671** (t) Picture Research Consultants & Archives; (b) Museum of American Political Life **672** John F. Kennedy Library **673** Black Star **674** Bob Daemmrich/Stock Boston **676** (t) Maryland Historical Society; (b) Bob Daemmrich **677** Flip Schulke/Black Star

Assignment Photo Credits

Ralph J. Brunke: 408; Dave Desroches: 141, 207, 257, 330 (l), 395, 468, 521, 577, 625 (r); John MacLachlan: 309 (tr); Ilene Perlman: 248 (bl); Tony Scarpetta: 40 (bl), 57, 132–133, 193 (tr), 215 (br), 265 (br), 416 (br), 494 (b), 506–507, 574 (b); Mark Sexton: 82 (tr); Dorey Sparre: 604–605; Tracey Wheeler: 57 (insets), 141 (inset), 207 (inset), 257 (insets), 395 (inset), 468 (inset), 521 (insets), 577 (inset), 624 (tl)

Illustrations

Francis Back: 92–93, 201, 622–623; William Brinkley: 412; Pat Rossi Calkin: 307; David Fuller: 320; Glasgow & Associates: 116; 161; 308; 546, 573; Nenad Jakesevic: 54–55, 76–77, 126–127, 178, 212–213; Matthew Pippin: 162, 214, 356–357; Robert Pratt: 14–15; Jared Schneidman: 42–43; Steve Stankiewicz: 372–373, 514; Rob Wood/Wood Ronsaville Harlin, Inc.; Wood Ronsaville Harlin, Inc.: 38, 62–63, 122–123, 136, 236–237, 280, 312–313, 407, 537

Maps

David Mackay Ballard: 263, 269; Brian Callanan: 142–143; Susan Carlson: 53, 59, 251, 294; DLF Group: 20, 160, 186, 212, 240–241, 289, 370, 436, 485, 486, 551, 616; © 1996 GeoSystems Global Corp.: 10–11, 70–71, 156–157, 232–233, 302–303, 364–365, 422–423, 478–479, 532–533, 628–639; GeoSystems Corp.: 17, 19, 24–25, 30–31, 37, 77, 81, 84, 93–95, 104, 113, 117, 135, 144, 146, 177, 181, 220, 226, 239, 285, 307, 337, 348, 368, 386, 402, 405, 408, 411, 426, 430, 435, 457, 495, 505, 511, 522–523, 541, 543, 552 top, 555, 560, 581, 591, 595, 601, 604–605, 611–615, 617–618, 619 top; Glasgow and Associates: 22–23; Nenad Jakesevic: 108–109, 127, 130, 223; Ellen J. Kuzdro: 41, 236; A.L. Lorenz: 187, 406; Ortelius Design: 74–75, 619; Bob Pratt: 14–15; Mike Reagan: 91, 340–341; Rob Schuster: 552–553